AFRICAN-AMERICAN TRADITIONS IN SONG, SERMON, TALE, AND DANCE, 1600s–1920

Recent Titles in
The Greenwood Encyclopedia of Black Music

Bibliography of Black Music Volume 1: Reference Materials
Dominique-René de Lerma

Bibliography of Black Music Volume 2: Afro-American Idioms
Dominique-René de Lerma

Bibliography of Black Music Volume 3: Geographical Studies
Dominique-René de Lerma

Bibliography of Black Music Volume 4: Theory, Education, and Related Studies
Dominique-René de Lerma

Biographical Dictionary of Afro-American and African Musicians
Eileen Southern

THE GREENWOOD ENCYCLOPEDIA OF BLACK MUSIC

AFRICAN-AMERICAN TRADITIONS IN SONG, SERMON, TALE, AND DANCE, 1600s–1920

An Annotated Bibliography of Literature, Collections, and Artworks

Compiled by
EILEEN SOUTHERN *and* JOSEPHINE WRIGHT

Greenwood Press
New York • Westport, Connecticut • London

Library of Congress Cataloging-in-Publication Data

Southern, Eileen.
African-American traditions in song, sermon, tale, and dance, 1600s-1920 : an annotated bibliography of literature, collections, and artworks / compiled by Eileen Southern and Josephine Wright.
p. cm.—(The Greenwood encyclopedia of Black music, ISSN 0272-0264)
ISBN 0-313-24918-0 (alk. paper)
1. Afro-American arts—Bibliography. 2. Afro-Americans—Music—Bibliography. I. Wright, Josephine R. B. II. Title.
III. Series.
Z5956.A47S68 1990
[NX512.2.A35]
016.7'0089'96073—dc20 90-34101

British Library Cataloguing in Publication Data is available.

Library of Congress Catalog Card Number: 90-34101
ISBN: 0-313-24918-0
ISSN: 0272-0264

First published in 1990

Greenwood Press, 88 Post Road West, Westport, CT 06881
An imprint of Greenwood Publishing Group, Inc.

Printed in the United States of America

The paper used in this book complies with the Permanent Paper Standard issued by the National Information Standards Organization (Z39.48-1984).

10 9 8 7 6 5 4 3 2 1

For Joseph Southern

CONTENTS

PREFACE

This work had its genesis in the summer of 1976, when the present authors joined forces to compile a bibliography for a new course we planned to introduce into the General Education curriculum, Humanities area, at Harvard University. In the course, "Humanities 7: The Afro-American Folk Arts and Religion," we proposed to take an unconventional approach to the study of African-American traditions in the song, dance, tale, and sermon, which would focus on the integration of these arts in social and historical context rather than on their distinctiveness. Further, we would concentrate attention on the folk arts of the nineteenth century inasmuch as we felt these arts to be the roots of such twentieth-century genres as jazz, blues, gospel, "intoned sermons," and "rapping," among others. A Course-development Grant given us by the President's Office enabled us to move forward with little delay.

Early on, it became obvious that there was no easily accessible work to which one could turn for an overview of the literature available on the subject. Despite a number of fine bibliographies in print (see the Selected Bibliography for the present work), as a whole they presented serious shortcomings, leaving too many gaps in the bibliographical literature. Some were too limited in scope for our purposes in that they concentrated on one folk genre to the neglect of the others. Some focused on a relatively short time-span; others covered a longer period but gave short shrift to primary materials. Some were superficial in their coverage, and some covered too wide a geographical area to give a well-balanced overview of the subject. Then finally, almost all the publications slighted the contributions of African-Americans to the literature. It became self-evident that priority had to be given to bibliographical research in planning for the new course.

This Bibliography is an outgrowth of the reading list we compiled for the Humanities 7 course (or Hum 7, as students nick-named it). Our research suggested that an enormous wealth of information about black folklore lay untapped in the literature for any number of reasons: it may be uncatalogued, or poorly indexed, or widely scattered, or perhaps as yet undiscovered. What researchers needed was a comprehensive, systematically organized, annotated guide to the primary materials of the field, which could then contribute to the establishing of a solid, empirical base for the literature and the developing of a sophisticated, disciplined methodology for handling it.

Once the traditional primary record has been brought under bibliographical control, the scholar is freed to proceed with his main activities---examining the sources, determining their reliability, and selecting those which fit his needs. It should no longer be necessary for those writing about black-American culture to reach general conclusions based on relatively meager evidence, as has happened too frequently in previously published work on the subject.

In recognition of this need, the Bibliography attempts to provide a broad survey of the primary materials that inform us of the folk-arts traditions of African-Americans in the United States over a period of almost 300 years, from the 1630s to 1920 (see further in the Introduction). Gathered together for the first time are significant materials relating to all four of the principal folk arts---the songs, sermons, tales, and dance---during the time-span as stated above. We arrived at the final lists after scanning thousands of widely varied sources: travel books, local histories, personal writings, fiction, nonfiction, slave narratives, court and civil records, and similar publications.

Our exploration of periodical literature, which included examination of full runs wherever available, took us not only to such popular magazines as the ATLANTIC MONTHLY, CENTURY MAGAZINE, and LIPPINCOTT'S, but also to children's magazines like the RIVERSIDE and ST. NICHOLAS; to abolitionist publications like the ANTI-SLAVERY RECORD and LIBERATOR; to such professional journals as the FOLIO and NEW YORK MUSICAL GAZETTE; to agricultural journals like DE BOW'S REVIEW; and to such religious serials as the OUTLOOK, ZION'S HERALD, and the black-published AME CHURCH REVIEW.

In addition to its importance as a resource book for factual information, the Bibliography is valuable for its citation of sources that include texts of sermons, folk tales, and folksongs, not only as found in anthologies but also those in the collections published in periodicals and books, and those tucked away in travel books and personal writings. In many instances, these texts are placed in social context: the collector who wrote down the texts offers comment on the occasion, performance practice, spectator participation, and similar matters.

Perhaps the most novel feature of the Bibliography is its inclusion of iconographical materials. Our research activities included combing through art books and periodicals, museum catalogs, the illustrated periodical press, and books of all types in search of pictures that depict aspects of black-American folk culture. To our surprise, we found the pictorial record of black-American folk culture to be extraordinarily rich and extensive. The pictures fall largely into four categories---portraits, genre or story-telling scenes, depictions of events, and cartoons---representing a wide range of types, from oil paintings and water colors to engravings, woodcuts, and photographs (the last-named beginning in the late nineteenth century). In many ways the pictorial annotations are more informative than those for the literary sources, for the materials clearly indicate, to use a hackneyed expression, that "a picture is worth a thousand words."

As might be expected, the iconographical entries often complement the literary ones, and some themes run thoughout the book. Name and subject indexes are provided to assist users in tracing connections among the literary entries or between literary and pictorial entries, and an index of the first lines of songs facilitates searching out concordances.

It is our hope that this work will meet the needs of scholars engaged in researching Afro-American folk expression, irrespective of their disciplines; that as it documents the history of the folk traditions, it will at the same time offer tools for shattering myths and obliterating the degrading stereotypes of the black folk artist that have developed over the years. And finally, we believe that the Bibliography offers means to gaining insight into the incredible richness of African-American folk culture and better understanding of the people who produced the culture.

Future plans include the publishing of a companion volume to the present work, which will offer a pictorial record of Afro-American traditions in the sermon, song, tale, and dance during the time-span 1630s-1920.

Josephine R. B. Wright

ACKNOWLEDGMENTS

The preparation of this bibliography has been supported in part by a grant from the National Endowment for the Humanities, an independent federal agency, supplemented by funds for research assistance from Harvard University, where the project was housed. We are grateful to to Harvard for this support and for the research leaves given us during the four-year period of the grant, 1979-83. We also are grateful to the College of Wooster for the research grants given to Josephine Wright through its Faculty Development Fund and the Henry Luce Distinguished Scholarship Award.

Like most bibliographers, we are indebted to previously published bibliographies, though none has the same focus and scope as ours. Some indication of the useful resources available to us at the beginning of our project is found in the bibliography for the present work. The models provided by RILM Abstracts (INTERNATIONAL REPERTORY OF MUSIC LITERATURE), of which Barry Brook is editor-in-chief, and RIdIM Abstracts (INTERNATIONAL REPERTORY OF MUSICAL ICONOGRAPHY) inspired us to adapt the format of their entries to our purposes. Our iconographical procedures reflect the influence of Howard Brown's and Joan Lascelle's Index of Musical Iconography, described in MUSICAL ICONOGRAPHY (1972).

During the many years of work on the project, we have accumulated more debts to colleagues at universities across the nation than can be fully recognized here. Whether or not named below, all have our deepest gratitude.

From the outset our Advisory Committee was generous with support and encouragement---David Driskell, the late Lorenzo Greene, Dominique-Rene de Lerma, Albert Lord, Sterling Stuckey, and Joseph Washington---and never failed to respond to requests for assistance over the years.

Because the Bibliography gathers together a wide variety of source materials, its compiling frequently took us outside our fields of expertise. We are deeply indebted to those scholars in other disciplines who read parts of this work and shared with us their helpful suggestions and criticisms: among them, Howard Mayer Brown (iconography of music), art historians Alford L. Eiseman and Lynn Moody Igoe, black-literature specialists Henry L. Gates and John Terrence Reilly, and black-dance historian Lynne Fauley Emery. Our thanks go also to Samuel A. Floyd of the Center for Black Music Research, who read parts of this work.

Other colleagues who were helpful in various ways include archivist Daniel Williams, American-music historians Anne Dhu Shapiro and Adrienne Fried Block, and black-music historians D. Antoinette Handy, Doris E. McGinty, and Jon Michael Spencer. Additionally, we are indebted to computer-scientist Robert Weidmann, who assisted us in forcing a personal computer (vintage of 1979) to accomodate to the demands of a project that really called for a large, main-frame computer, and coped with our often desperate calls for technical help. The expertise he put at our disposal from the beginning made possible a successful completion of the project. Finally, we wish to express our deep appreciation to program-analyst April Southern Reilly, who devised computer programs to fit our special needs and cheerfully rescued us when we fell in over our heads.

The greater part of the research was conducted in the Harvard University libraries, at the Library of Congress, and in London at the British Museum Library.

We are indebted to the librarians and staffs of these libraries for cheerful assistance and many kindnesses, especially of the Theatre Collection, Widener Memorial Library, Houghton Library, Fogg Art Museum, Music Library, and Interlibrary Loan Office at Harvard; the Prints and Music Divisions at the Library of Congress; and the Research and Music Divisions at the British Museum.

We also gratefuly acknowledge the many courtesies extended to us by librarians and staffs at other libraries, some of which are named below (in alphabetical order by city): Albany (New York)---New York State Library; Ann Arbor---William L. Clements Library at the University of Michigan; Boston---Boston Public Library, Boston Athenaeum, Boston Museum of Fine Arts, Massachusetts Historical Society; Chicago---Newberry Library; Cleveland---John G. White Collection of the Cleveland Public Library; Detroit---E. Azalia Hackley Memorial Collection of the Detroit Public Library; Durham---Southern Historical Collection at the University of North Carolina; Hampton---Hampton University Art Museum.

Also Nashville (Tennessee)---Special Collections of Fisk University Library; New York City---New York Public Library, especially the Americana Division of the Music Research Library at Lincoln Center, Prints Division, Art and Architecture Division, and Schomburg Center for Research in Black Culture; New York University libraries; Queensborough Public Library; New York Historical Society library; Union Theological Seminary.

Also Oberlin (Ohio)---Oberlin College libraries; Philadelphia---library of the Pennsylvania Historical Society, and the Library Company of Philadelphia; Pittsburgh---Stephen Foster Memorial at University of Pittsburgh; Providence (Rhode Island)---John Hay Library at Brown University; Tuskegee (Alabama)---Tuskegee Institute; Washington, D.C.---Moorland-Spingarn Research Center, Howard University; Wooster (Ohio)---Andrews Library at The College of Wooster; and Worcester (Massachusetts)---American Antiquarian Society.

The fine work and cooperative spirit of research assistants associated with the project are greatly appreciated: Lewis Porter (in the early stages of the project), Christopher Johnson (1979-81), and the Harvard students who worked with us from time to time.

We gratefully acknowledge the enthusiastic assistance and dedication of Mary K. Donaldson, who joined the project in its first year as a secretary, but early transcended that role to become a collaborator in view of her definitive contributions to the work, particularly in her area of expertise, American art history. Our indebtedness to her can hardly be repaid.

We also express appreciation to James Sabin of Greenwood Press for his initial encouragement of our work and for later helpful suggestions, and to Greenwood staff members for their contributions to the production of the book.

For my husband Joseph, we have a very special, deeply felt gratitude for his steadfast support and continual encouragement. No task was too small or too large for him to take on: inputing data, research, devising computer programs to fit our special needs, preparing copy for production, proof-reading, and more. This book is as much his as ours.

GUIDE TO THE USE OF THE BIBLIOGRAPHY

This annotated, classified, comprehensive bibliography covers a time-span of almost 300 years---from the early seventeenth century through the second decade of the twentieth century---in the cultural history of African-Americans in the United States. The materials of the Bibliography fall into three general categories: literary publications, ephemeral printed matter, and manuscripts; iconographical records, such as paintings, engraved illustrations, and photographs; and collections of songs, tales, and sermon texts. Though the Bibliography's 2,328 items represent a large variety of informative materials, they do not exhaust the vast, untapped wealth of primary resources available to researchers in the field of black folk culture. With this in mind, the Bibliography may be perceived as functioning on two levels, on the one hand offering a compendium of the sources essential to the study and understanding of African-American culture, and on the other hand constituting a foundation for future research into the subject.

Like most bibliographies, this one is both selective and incomplete. From the outset, it was decided to limit selections to: (1) works published in the English language or works translated into English; (2) works published or produced during the time-span 1630s-1920, though in a few instances publications that appeared after 1920 are included for historical or sociological reasons; and (3) works reporting on the emergence and development of African-American oral traditions within the continental United States, thus excluding works about black folk culture in the Caribbean, Central America, and South America.

The starting and terminal dates for the Bibliography reflect historical circumstances associated with the subject. It was in 1638 that one of the earliest references to black culture, if not the very first, appeared in print (see no. 62). For the next 250-plus years black culture was in the process of developing, of "becoming" a distinctive culture. By the early twentieth century the folk traditions had been established and the foundations laid for the emergence of a unique, modern black culture. With the 1920s came the beginning of a new era in the history of African-American culture, the so-called Negro Renaissance, and this provides an appropriate cut-off date for the Bibliography.

Finally, the focus of the Bibliography is wholly on folk culture, as indicated by its title; reference to the fine arts or cultivated arts is limited to the extent these arts relate to the oral traditions of black folk.

Working within these guidelines, we systematically scanned several thousand sources, selecting works for their usefulness in illuminating one or more aspects of the black cultural traditions in specific ways, such as providing eyewitness accounts of black cultural activities or texts of the folk, creative literature.

The Criteria for Selecting the Works.

1. Choices were limited to primary materials and secondary sources containing primary particulars. Attempts were made to establish the author's credibility, reliability, and sensitivity of perception.

2. The historical importance of the author and the publication affected the selecting process. Efforts were made to find works by men and women known for their explication and interpretation of American culture, especially black-American culture. Similarly, priority was given to the "firsts" in various areas---the first collection of slave songs, the first compilation of Brer Rabbit tales, the first description of a black-church religious service.

3. Efforts also were made to insure that a wide variety of "voices" be included in the Bibliography. Consequently, the social circumstances and the viewpoint of potential informants were taken into consideration in order to secure representatation from both black and white authors, male and female, free black and enslaved black, American and European, participant and spectator, the anonymous and the well-known.

Any work was eligible for inclusion, no matter how brief or extensive, if it met the criteria. The literary sources, for example, range in size from single-sheet broadsides, programs, playbills, and short periodical articles to multivolume works. Some collections have as few as a half-dozen items, others have as many as 150 or more songs or tales. The artworks rank in size and importance from the minuscule---anonymous line engravings, for example, that were fitted into the width of a magazine column to illustrate a point made in the text---to the large, famous paintings of prominent artists of the time, which had been exhibited in major galleries and museums.

Generally excluded from the Bibliography are manuscripts, archival sources, unpublished scholarly papers, and newspaper articles, although exceptions were made for notable materials.

EDITORIAL PROCEDURES

The overall plan of the Bibliography is essentially chronological. Its four major sections are entitled: "The Colonial-Federalist Era, 1630s-1800"; "The Antebellum Era, 1801-1862"; "The Post-Emancipation Era, 1863-1899"; and "The Early Twentieth Century, 1900-1920." A fifth section, "The WPA Slave Narrative Collection," represents an exception to the chronological ordering. Though its materials focus on the narratives of ex-slaves and, consequently, belong to the Post-Emancipation Era, these narratives were not collected until the 1930s, and publication came much later (see below under "The WPA Slave Narrative Collection"). Despite the fact of its publication after the Bibliography's terminal date, the Collection is included because of its essentiality for any serious discussion of American slavery.

Within the subsections of the Bibliography the ordering of materials is by classification as literature, artworks, and collections. The literature and artworks subsections are further classified by subject under the following headings: (1) "Social Activities," (2) "The Religious Experience," (3) "The Song," and (4) "The Tale."

LITERATURE

Under "Social Activities" are listed works that include discussion of social customs, holiday and harvest festivals, processions, and wedding receptions. The "Religious Experience" entries refer to sermons and exhortations, the religious dance (particularly the shout), various kinds of religious services, and such ceremonies as baptism, wedding, funeral, and burial. Entries in "The Song" categories contain comment on: folksong types, such as spirituals, worksongs, and blues; performance practice; and the basic elements of the vocal music. Entries listed under "The Tale" include discussion of story-telling traditions. It may be assumed that all folk artists discussed in the annotations are black unless otherwise denoted. Generally, the context makes clear the racial identity of persons other than the folk artists.

Predictably, there is some overlapping among the entries. In many instances a work fits into more than one category---such as the article, for example, that contains extensive discussion of several aspects of black folk culture. On the other hand, a source that contains only a folksong text or tale finds its place easily in one section. The Subject Index may be used as a guide to related information in the Bibliography, and as well for cross-reference leads.

Entries are arranged alphabetically by author name (or editor) and by title of anonymous works. Where several works are attributed to a single author, the listing is chronological by date of publication, except that original works appear before edited ones. Wherever possible first names and middle initials have been given for authors who are identified only by surnames or initials in the sources. Similarly, names have been supplied, if possible, for those represented only by pseudonyms.

Each entry consists of two parts, the first containing bibliographical data, and the second, the annotation and lists of texts (songs, tales, sermons) included in the source. In the cases where an edition other than the original has been used, the facts of publication are given for both if known. Author names and titles are spelled as given on the title pages, the punctuation of the long, old-style titles is retained, and ellipsis dots are used to indicate omissions in the titles. In the interest of clarity, no efforts have been made to include the various kinds of accents used with some of the names and titles.

Since many of the sources that were consulted are no longer in print, or are available only in special collections, every effort has been made to locate at least one reprint in order to make the Bibliography materials more accessible to researchers. It was not until the late 1960s that reprints of nineteenth-century books related to black culture first began to appear in significant numbers, released by such publishers as the Negro Universities Press, Books for Libraries Press, and Arno Press. Microform reprints, which in recent years have increasingly become available, are identified in the Bibliography either by indication of the format (microfiche or microfilm) or by the publisher's name (such as University Microfilms).

Example:

Andrews, Ethan Allen. SLAVERY AND THE DOMESTIC SLAVE-TRADE IN THE UNITED STATES. IN A SERIES OF LETTERS ADDRESSED TO THE EXECUTIVE COMMITTEE OF THE AFRICAN UNION FOR THE RELIEF AND IMPROVEMENT OF THE COLORED RACE. Boston: Light & Stearns, 1836. 201 pp. Reprint. Washington, DC: Microcard Editions, 1970.

Discussion of slavery in Maryland and the District of Columbia by a New Englander includes description of a worship service in a black church on Sharp Street (Baltimore), with special reference to the sermon and congregational responses (88-89). Also comment on the musical quality of "the African voices" (93).

Text of 1 sermon: Philip's going down to Samaria (88).

Since few of the sources have indexes, page numbers (set off in parentheses) have been inserted in the annotation to facilitate access to the relevant discussion in the text, except in the case of short articles. For page references in multi-volume works, the number of the volume is given first, followed by a colon and the page number---for example, 2:59, which denotes page 59 in volume 2 of the work. Although the main purpose of the annotation is to identify passages in the source that offer comment on, or description of, black cultural traditions, the annotation frequently provides a context for understanding an event by explaining its circumstances or pointing up the relationship between the event and its narrator-informant.

Example:

Schoolcraft, Mary Howard. THE BLACK GAUNTLET: A TALE OF PLANTATION LIFE IN THE SOUTH. Philadelphia: J. B. Lippincott & Company, 1860. 569 pp. Reprint. Freeport, NY: Books for Libraries Press, 1971.

Sketches of plantation life in South Carolina include references to slave musicians providing music for their masters (22), to songs of the boatmen (27), to prayer-meetings and singing-meetings (151). Description of a funeral contains references to exhorting by the preacher and to congregational singing (161-62).

Where sources include song, tale, or sermon texts, a list of the texts is appended to the annotation. Sermons and tales generally are listed by their titles, and songs are listed by the first lines of their verses. Only those songs with a minimum of four lines of text are included in the appended lists, although the annotation may contain references to songs with fewer than four lines. In the interest of clarity, quotation marks for the titles and first lines are omitted, but the method used for the listing clearly sets off these items.

Example:

Robinson, William H. FROM LOG CABIN TO PULPIT; OR, FIFTEEN YEARS IN SLAVERY. Eau Claire, WI: The Author, 1903. 123 pp. Rev. ed. Eau Clare, WI: James H. Tifft, 1913. 200 pp. Page references below are to the 1903 ed.

Autobiography of the ex-slave preacher (b. 1848) from Wilmington, North Carolina, includes references to a slave ball, where the music was provided by tambourine, banjo, and bones (70). Also discussion of the use of kettles and other cooking utensils by the slaves to muffle the sound of singing and prayers during worship services.

Texts of 3 songs: 1. He delivered Daniel from the lion's den (53). 2. Get you ready, there's a meeting here tonight (71). 3. Free at last (114).

THE ARTWORKS

The criteria used for the iconographical entries of the Bibliography are essentially the same as used for the literary works, although the resources are considerably limited in comparison. Except in the few instances where inferior painters made copies of well-known paintings, the artworks discussed in the Bibliography are primary sources. Artists and illustrators of important historical position are represented side by side with folk and amateur artists. The caricature, a vital part of the American national heritage, frequently is represented in the Bibliography. Though some of the caricatures depict black Americans in a demeaning manner, it is nevertheless essential to include them in any survey of the resources available to researchers in the history of black culture.

Like the entries for the "Literature" sections, the iconographical entries are organized by subject matter, and employ the same headings. Entries under "Social

Activities" focus primarily on communal social gatherings, such as harvest festivals, processions, and wedding receptions. Additionally, a number of these illustrations offer depictions of the dance and the musical instruments used to accompany dancing. Entries within the "Religious Experience" section offer pictorial comment on religious services, choral groups, worshipers dancing the holy dance called the shout, domestic religious scenes, and preachers and exhorters.

The "Song" entries refer to the various kinds of workers, especially street criers, who sing as they work. Also included are domestic scenes showing mothers singing lullabies to babies. Within the subsection of "The Tale" the entries focus on images of the black storyteller, who most often is a male telling stories to white children, but also occasionally is a female. To locate illustrations of specific subjects and to correlate literary and iconographical themes, the reader is advised to use the Artworks Subject Index.

Within the four subdivisions of the "Artworks" the arrangement is alphabetical by artist name or by title of anonymous artworks. Where several works are attributed to a single artist, the listing is chronological by date of completion, or by date of publication in the case of prints. Wherever possible first names and middle initials are given for authors who are identified by only surnames or initials in the sources. Similarly, original names are supplied, if possible, for authors represented by pseudonyms in the sources.

Entries in the iconographical listings present nine points of information, as follows: (1) name of the artist or illustrator, (2) title of the artwork, (3) its date, (4) the medium, (5) name of the engraver, (6) present geographical location, (7) bibliographical facts for the book or periodical in which the artwork first was published or reproduced, (8) modern reprints, and (9) the annotation.

1. Where the name of the artist, illustrator, or photographer was not entered on the artwork, we consulted contemporaneous books and articles, catalogs, and modern reference books for clues to his or her identity. In some cases, initials were entered at the bottom of the picture on either the left or right side.

   Occasionally, it was assumed that the author of a book was responsible also for its illustrations, particularly if he was known to be a professional artist. The same assumption applies to the identity of photographers, both professional and amateur. If there were doubts about the person responsible for the artwork, a question mark follows the name.

2. If the artist illustrator could not be identified, the entry begins with the title of the artwork, similar to the way anonymous books are listed in the Bibliography. This anonymity is not uncommon: whereas the artist occasionally was given credit for his prints, and, less frequently, the engraver was identified, most prints of the nineteenth century are as anonymous as photographic illustrations have been in modern times until recently.

   The title keeps its original spelling and punctuation. Where an illustration was identified by a caption rather than a title, a shortened form of the caption is used in lieu of a title, and the full caption is given in the annotation. For those artworks with identification of neither the artist nor title, a provisional title based on the matter of the picture is used, so indicated by the word "untitled" in brackets following the substitute title.

3. The date of the artwork is given as entered on the work or found in catalogs. The dates of prints proved to be practically impossible to pin down precisely, as was true also regarding certain kinds of artifacts. Therefore, efforts were made to identify the earliest source(s) in which the print was published (that is, book or periodical), and to distinguish among those sources and reprints. We cannot be sure, of course, that the illustrator made his print expressly for the source in which it was published, or that our research has uncovered the earliest sources. The approximate dates that have been assigned to such prints are enclosed in brackets in the entry.

4. For the medium of paintings and other works in the fine-arts category, the descriptions entered in catalogs and art literature were accepted. In the case of prints, however, it was not always possible to determine which process was used; indeed, even art specialists sometimes disagree about the process used in making a specific illustration. Whereas it was fairly easy to identify woodcuts, line engravings, pen-and-ink drawings, and photographs, some of the illustrations resisted analysis. In such instances the question mark following the medium represents an educated guess. For many of the prints, particularly those published in the late nineteenth century, the term "mixed media" as used in the Bibliography is quite appropriate.

5. Conventionally, the engraver added the letters _Sc._ (abbreviation for the Latin _sculpsit_) to his name in order

to differentiate it from the name of the original artist, whose name was indicated by del. (for delineavit). But names rarely were entered for engravers, though they sometimes were identified on title pages or in the text of the article or book containing the print.

6. The geographic location of paintings is given as follows: city; museum, gallery or other institution; and name of the collection (if relevant). Then follow the bibliographical facts for an early publication in which the artwork has been reproduced, which in most cases was an exhibition catalog or book-length study of an individual artist. In most instances, the quality of the color reproduction was the deciding factor in our selecting one publication in preference to another for listing in the Bibliography.

Example:

Clonney, James Goodwyn. "Militia Training." 1841. Oil on canvas. Philadelphia, Pennsylvania Academy of Fine Arts. Reproduced in THE U.S.A.: A HISTORY IN ART, by Bradley Smith, 154. New York: Thomas Y. Crowell Company, 1975.

7. For the print or photograph, as distinguished from the painting, the term "published" is used (rather than "reproduced") to apply to its inclusion in the primary literary source. The bibliographical data are entered as follows: title, author, page number (or catalogue number), facts of publication.

Example:

Sheppard, William Ludlow, and J. Wells Champney. "The Carnival--White and Black Join in Its Masquerading." [1875]. Wood engraving by F. Juengling. Published in THE GREAT SOUTH, by Edward King, 38. Hartford, CT: American Publishing Company, 1875.

8. The term "reprint" is used to refer to publication of the illustration in later sources. It was not uncommon for nineteenth-century authors (and publishers?) to lift illustrations from each other's books, apparently without permission. Sometimes the "borrowed" print carried a different title. The month and year of publication, but not page numbers, are given for illustrations published in the popular periodical press.

Example:

[Benjamin Samuel Green Wheeler?]. "The Juvenile Band, Fernandina." [1878]. Pen-and-ink. Published in "The Sea Islands," by Samuel Green Wheeler Benjamin. HARPER'S NEW MONTHLY MAGAZINE 57 (November 1878). Reprint. THE SOCIAL IMPLICATIONS OF EARLY NEGRO MUSIC IN THE UNITED STATES, edited by Bernard Katz, 68. New York: Arno Press and the New York Times, 1969.

9. The annotation provides detailed description of the activities shown in the picture and occasional comment on other matters that help to place the activities in social context. In the interest of clarity, arabic numbers are used when referring to folk artists except at the the beginning of a sentence, where numbers are spelled out.

For each entry there is discussion of the nature of the activity represented, the persons involved, the setting, and other relevant information. Included among the activities are music-making, preaching, dancing, story-telling, and teaching; which may take place in settings that are formal or informal, indoors or outdoors, with or without background; on such occasions as religious services, dances, work festivals, and ritual ceremonies such as weddings and funerals.

Music-makers are identified as soloists or members of ensembles; singers, as performing with or without accompaniment; dancers, as soloists or couples, performing with or without musical accompaniment. The spoken-arts practitioners, the preachers and story-tellers, are placed in social context---in the church, in the fields, in the home.

Where the artwork depicts instrumental performance, the instruments are listed and note made of the social position of the players (if relevant), which most frequently is indicated by their attire. There is considerable confusion among specialists in regard to instrument terminology, particularly in the case of folk instruments. In the interest of simplification, instruments are identified by general type---such as fiddle, drum, horn, trumpet, banjo, guitar, cello, and mandolin. Other details are added as necessary.

Several illustrations, for example, show an instrument that belongs to the trumpet family but does not have fingerholes or the "folded shape" of the modern trumpet. Therefore it is described as a "straight trumpet" and the conventional instrument, simply as "trumpet." Other instrument types with variable features include the banjo, which may have four or five strings (the extra string is the "short fifth string"); the fiddle, which may have three or four strings; and folk-crafted instruments, which may have been made from gourds, wooden boxes, logs, bones of an animal, kitchen utensils, and the like.

In describing musical activity, we have given special attention to the position of the performer and how he uses his instrument: Is he indoors or outdoors, is he sitting or standing on a raised platform or on the ground, is he standing on a podium or the floor? Does he hold his fiddle in the traditional folk position or tuck it under his chin? Does he pluck or bow his cello? These questions and related ones are addressed in the annotation.

The annotation concludes with an indication of the general purpose of the activity, for which the term "occasion" has been adopted. The term "domestic" is used to apply to informal music making where the performers obviously are singing, playing, or dancing for their own gratification, and onlookers are not included in the picture. When performers are making music for the enjoyment of others, no matter how informal the situation or how few the participants, the term "entertainment" is used.

COLLECTIONS

Texts for oral literature were published in two types of collections. Most frequently the compiler gathered a number of songs (or tales) between the covers of a book, provided the collection with an introduction, and published it as an anthology. Sometimes, however, the compiler published his collection in a popular magazine or journal, or as part of a book. In the interest of consistency, we made the arbitrary decision to treat a gathering of eight or more songs (or tales) as a collection, irrespective of its published format. If an article or book contains eight or more songs or tales, it is listed under "Collections."

A source may be listed twice: first in a "Literature" section if it contains discussion of cultural traditions, and a second time under "Collections" if it also includes a number of texts. The Subject Index can be used to facilitate searching out and tracing relationships among entries listed in more than one place.

The entries under "Collections" include the basic bibliographical data for the source and indication of the number of items it contains. Then follows an alphabetical listing of the items---by title for tales, and by first lines (hereafter firstlines) of the verses and choruses for songs. Serious consideration was given to the idea of listing songs by their titles, then rejected because titles rarely are used in the literature to refer to Negro folksongs, even today. Moreover, the titles vary from source to source and consequently are unreliable indicators.

THE WPA SLAVE NARRATIVE COLLECTION

The ex-slave narratives in this forty-one-volume collection of oral-histories were collected during the years 1936-38 by interviewers employed in the Federal Writer's Project of the WPA (Works Progress Administration; also known as Work Projects Administration). Taken down from more than 3,500 ex-slaves, the narratives were published under the editorship of George P. Rawick during the years 1972-79. (See nos. 1786-1856 of the Bibliography.) The full title of the series, THE AMERICAN SLAVE: A COMPOSITE AUTOBIOGRAPHY, indicates its substance, as does also the title of the first volume, FROM SUNDOWN TO SUNUP: THE MAKING OF THE BLACK COMMUNITY.

Most of the typescript interviews were deposited in the Library of Congress, the remainder held in state archives. In 1972 Rawick began to publish the narratives (Greenwood Press) with the goal of making them widely available so that it would be "possible to gain a perspective on the slave experience in North America from those who had been slaves." The oral histories came out in four series: (1) Series 1 (7 vols.); (2) Series 2 (12 vols.); (3) Supplement, Series 1 (12 vols.); and (4) Supplement, Series 2 (10 vols.). Researchers should observe that the Texas Narratives, which constitute volumes 2-10 of the final series, have an awkward pagination, which runs from page 1 through the seven volumes to the final-page 4377.

The Slave Narrative Collection is here treated as an independent entity, consequently is represented in none of the Bibliography's indexes, largely because of the impracticality of merging so huge an index with the present ones. Undoubtedly, it would have demanded the addition of a second volume to our work. More important, however, is the fact that the ex-slave narrators were interviewed late in life, when their memories of the past had dimmed. Therefore, they did not, or could not, differentiate between the genuine folksongs they sang and the other songs they remembered, such as the hymns, minstrel songs, and popular songs of their time. Because of this, many of the songs discussed in the narratives do not meet the criteria we established.

In 1981 Donald M. Jacobs, assisted by Steven Fershleiser, published the INDEX TO THE AMERICAN SLAVE (Greenwood Press), which includes name and subject indexes for the Collection, but misses many references to slave culture.

In the Bibliography, the ex-slave narratives are handled in the same way as other entries. Arabic numbers enclosed in parentheses are used to indicate the pages where there is discussion of cultural matters, and lists of the songs, tales, and sermons for which there are texts are appended to the annotations. Where a volume holds eight or more texts, it is given a separate listing, with its songs alphabetically arranged, under the heading RAWICK SONG COLLECTIONS.

INDEXES

The Bibliography contains four kinds

of indexes: name, subject, illustration, and song. The name index comprises two lists: one of authors, editors, and collectors, and a second of artists, illustrators, and photographers. The subject indexes include one for literature and one for the artworks. The song indexes, too, are subdivided into lists of verse firstlines and chorus firstlines.

1. The name indexes include contemporary editors and ghost writers, but not modern editors. Slave narratives are indicated in the author-name index by use of an asterisk following the entry number.

2. The subject index is general, including all subjects discussed under the "Literature" sections, and, as well, proper names not listed in the name indexes.

3. The index of artworks also is a general index, which provides leads to themes treated in the pictorial works.

4. With a few exceptions, the songs listed in the annotations and collections are entered in the Index of Songs. For songs that have only texts in the sources, the sign (T) follows the text incipit in the index. Songs that include music are listed separately from those with texts only. Chorus firstlines are listed separately from verse firstlines, though the sources do not always distinguish between choruses and verses. The chorus of a song in one collection may appear as the first stanza in another source; similarly, the first stanza in one collection may be the second, third, or any other stanza in another source.

Excluded from the song indexes are the following types: play-party songs, ring-game songs, field hollers, street cries, and choruses consisting of nonsense syllables. Additionally, the songs of the WPA Slave Narrative Collection have been excluded, as stated above.

The firstlines of songs are presented with the spellings intact, but with such changes in punctuation as necessary to clarify the meaning and preserve consistency in style. Distinctions have been made between the vocative <u>O</u> and the exclamatory <u>Oh</u>, (which do not always appear in the sources), and the comma is used to set off exclamations and transitional adverbs from the remainder of the text incipit; for example, as in:

"Oh, whah you running, sinner"
or
"Well, I heard a mighty rumblin'"

The song indexes can be used in two ways: (1) to identify the source in which a given song might be published and (2) to track down the different versions of a song as published in several sources. In either case it is necessary to consider the fact that the alphabetization of the indexes is affected by the dialectal forms of the texts as presented in the sources.

One of the common procedures used by the nineteenth-century transcribers was to represent the sound "th" by the letter "d" and the sound of "I" by "ah" or "e," as in the following examples:

1. "Den [=then] chain dat [=that] lion daown"
2. "Ah [=I] got shoes, you got shoes"
3. "Ef [=if] religion were a thing"

Sometimes the initial letter of a word is omitted, as in:

1. " 'Raslin' [=Wrestlin'] Jacob, let me go"
2. " 'Rived [=arrived] in the goodly land"

Most common of all is the practice of inserting or omitting a word at the beginning of the text. The two examples below represent identical versions of the same songs.

1. "I couldn't hear nobody pray"
   "And I couldn't hear nobody pray"
   "Couldn't hear nobody pray"

2. "I ain't gonna study war no' mo'"
   "Ain't gonna study war no' mo'"
   "Well, I ain't gonna study war no' mo"

In summary, a search for the several versions of a song should include, after the simple-statement type of incipit has been located, a check through firstlines beginning with the following words: And, But, Den (=Then), For, Oh, Well, and Yes.

When songs survive in identical versions (or almost identical), the text's firstline appears once in the index, followed by the relevant entry numbers. For this kind of listing, if one of the sources contains a standard-English version, that version is chosen for the index listing.

Where texts differ in regard to one or more words, each text is listed independently in the index. The following first lines represent different songs, despite similarities among the three texts:

1. "Nobody knows the trouble I see"
2. "Nobody knows the trouble I've seen"
3. "Nobody knows the trouble I've had"

Finally, we offer a comment on terms and definitions. The several terms that have been used over the centuries to refer to Africans enslaved in the New World (and their descendents) are used interchangeably in this Bibliography:

African-American, African, Afro-American, black, black-American, colored, and Negro. Particularly in the colonial and antebellum eras were blacks referred to as Africans, though they might have been third- or fourth-generation American. Some confusion exists in the sources regarding the terms "slave" and "servant" as applied to the enslaved blacks, the slaveholders preferring the latter in order to avoid using "slave." In the Bibliography terms are used as given in the source materials, which vary in their usage from one to the other.

Regarding some oral-traditions forms, the word "song" is used in the Bibliography to refer to both the musical unit with melody and text and the text independent of melody. No efforts are made to distinguish between the spiritual and the secular song, except as such distinctions appear in the sources.

"Pattin' juba" was an accompaniment for social dancing that involved striking various parts of the body, an action that produced percussive sounds so organized rhythmically as to provide an acceptable substitute for instrumental accompaniment.

The holy dance, called the "shout," was a ritual circle dance, which was accompanied by the singing of religious songs. Generally, it took place on Sundays in the praise cabin after the formal worship service or at the mid-week prayer meeting, but occasionally it was performed also as recreation, especially by children. The sources do not clearly differentiate between the sermon and the exhortation, except the latter typically was associated with the illiterate religious leader as distinguished from the ordained minister, and we have made no effort to do so in the annotations.

INTRODUCTION

The African peoples who were forcibly brought to the New World during the fifteenth to the nineteenth centuries and sold into slavery were cut off from their political, cultural, and social institutions, and thrust into an alien, harsh environment that demanded immediate accommodation to the ways and values of the European colonists. In their desperate struggles for physical and psychical survival, the slaves trusted in ancient tribal traditions to provide them with the strength and stamina to "endure and preserve their humanity in the face of insuperable odds" (Stuckey 1968, 437). Although they came from a variety of nations, in particular those inhabiting Africa's west coast, they nevertheless could communicate with each other because of cultural values they shared in common.

At the heart of their culture were their religions, which, encompassing the song, drum, and dance along with prayer, proverbs, and ceremonies, pervaded just about every phase of their lives, from birth to the grave. Through music and dance the African could build a bridge to the supernatural, where he could communicate with the ancestral spirits, the lesser deities, and the Supreme Being. To be sure, secular musical traditions also played an important role in the lives of the Africans---the work-songs, dance and festival musics, cante-fables, and other recreational forms. When the Ibo native Olaudah Equiano declared his people to be "almost a nation of dancers, musicians, and poets," he spoke as well for other nations of West Africa.

The aim of this historical survey is to trace the development of an African-American folk-culture complex in the United States from the time of its emergence in colonial times to the state of its arts at the beginning of the Negro (or Harlem) Renaissance in the 1920s---based on evidence provided by the materials of the Bibliography.*

THE COLONIAL-FEDERALIST ERA, 1630s-1800

Ever since early colonial times the black man's culture has held a special fascination for visitors to the American shores, who, in the books they published after returning home, rarely failed to comment on its exotic customs and folkways. Initially indifferent, the Americans in time developed an understanding of, and appreciation for, the cultural gifts of the black man that have contributed so largely to American culture in particular, and world culture in general. Eventually, they too began to publish accounts of their experiences with the African-American culture that flourished in their midst.

Of sixty-four works issued during the colonial period that include discussion of some aspect of Afro-American culture, almost half were written by Britishers, including a woman. Frenchmen account for six publications, Africans for two, and a German and a Swede for one each. Primarily merchants and army officers, the European authors also counted among their numbers "gentlemen authors," clergymen, a professional musician, a naturalist, a white indentured servant, and a farmer. About a dozen accounts are the product of American writers, of whom the

*The Name and Subject Indexes can be consulted to locate entries in the Bibliography that relate to the present discussion.

majority were clergymen, and the others statesmen, local historians, a young male tutor, an artist-naturalist, and an ex-slave.

The writings of Francis Asbury, Samuel Davis, Nicholas Cresswell, Alexander Hewatt, John Leland, and Le Page du Pratz ---to name a few---not only offer information about slave culture in the colonial period, but also attest to the strength of African survivals among the slaves at a time when they were being assimilated into a new religious and social environment.

These early writers employed a variety of formats for their publications, most frequently the travelogue, but also diaries, journals, letters, regional and national histories, sermons, and political tracts. Additionally, runaway-slave advertisements, broadsides, and other kinds of ephemeral publications provide sources of information about black culture.

Early Glimmers of the Folk Culture. However cut off from the mainstream of society, the slaves were vitally affected by the nation's institutions and sociopolitical-cultural events and processes, and their culture evolved and developed within the framework of American culture in general. The early exposure of some slaves to Christianity, for example, produced a leadership class that later would play an important part in the development of a distinctive black church that syncretized African elements and rituals with Christian beliefs and ceremonies.

Writing in 1680, Morgan Godwyn was one of the first clergymen to observe that despite the religious instruction given them, some slaves clung to their "idolatrous dances and revels." Others noted that slaves conducted their own meetings away from their masters (and often in secrecy). Throughout the eighteenth century and into the nineteenth, missionaries to the slaves would echo Godwyn's complaint: Christianity confronted by African cultism frequently resulted in an Afro-Christianity that was difficult to keep under control.

The evidence indicates that black preachers early began to appear on the scene: some of them were trained by the white missionaries, others were self-taught. Runaway-slave advertisements of the time are replete with references to black preachers: an advertisement in 1746, for example, identifies the runaway as "Preaching Dick"; another, dating from 1767, states that runaway Hannah "pretends much to the religion the Negroes of late have practiced." Some whites, writing about their attendance at religious services of the slaves, found them to be "noisy," "wild," "almost raving," and the worshipers to be "more subject to bodily exercises" [a euphemism for dancing?] than the whites. It is evident that by the eighteenth century, African-Americans were beginning to develop their own distinctive religious practices in apparent disregard for the models held up to them by white missionaries.

With the emergence of religious societies among the slaves, there naturally developed a black religious leadership. The African priest and African shaman of the Motherland, who became the slave preacher or exhorter and the slave conjurer on this side of the Atlantic, had become so common by the mid-eighteenth century as not to excite special attention.

Some members of the clergy, however, had misgivings about the quality of leadership offered by black preachers. New England minister Charles Chauncey, for example, evinced concern in 1743 over the "rise of uneducated exhorters," particularly among the blacks. Balancing this point of view were the observations of churchmen like Francis Asbury, Thomas Coke, and Freeborn Garrettson, who contended that the black illiterate exhorters often displayed great gifts for conducting religious exercises. Several of these men won widespread celebrity for their exhorting skills, particularly "Black Harry" Hosier, Andrew Marshall, and Richard Allen.

For almost nineteen percent of the black population in the United States, the post-Revolutionary War period was a time of transition from slavery to freedom. Some slaves obtained their freedom as a consequence of their fighting in the war; others were emancipated, beginning in 1777, as one northern state after another passed legislation that provided either for the gradual abolition of slavery within its borders or for slavery's immediate termination.

With the gaining of freedom, the ex-slaves began to organize various kinds of fraternal groups and benevolent societies, which inevitably took responsibility for the religious and educational activities of their people. The freedmen also began to associate themselves with the established Protestant denominations about them, particularly the Methodists and Baptists.

The self-governing black congregations first appeared in the South among the Baptists in the South. Founded in 1788, the First African Church at Savannah, Georgia, is credited with being the earliest permanent black congregation. In the decade of the 1790s, independent black congregations began to spring up in the North, at first among Methodists and Episcopalians, then later, during the first decade of the nineteenth century, among Baptists and Presbyterians. Three of the Methodist groups later severed their ties with the white parent churches and obtained charters giving them independent denominational status ---first, the Union African Methodist

Episcopal Church in 1813, then the African Methodist Episcopal Church in 1816, followed by the African Methodist Episcopal Zion Church in 1821.

It was not only the African-American's distinctive religious practices that engaged the attention of European writers; it was also observed that the slaves had their own characteristic social songs, dances, musical instruments, and performance practice. British merchant John Josselyn, traveling in New England during the years 1638-39, was one of the first to comment on the special quality of the African voice: in 1639 he wrote in his journal, "The Second of October about 9 of the clock in the morning, Mr. Maverick's Negro woman came to my chamber window, and in her own Countrey language and tune sang very loud and shrill." In other colonial sources, too, can be found comment on the peculiar quality of the black singer's voice as compared to that of whites, using such terms as "plaintive," "loud," "melodious," and "a torrent of sacred harmony."

Other aspects of slave music also were noted. William Bartram observed in 1776 that he heard black workers singing songs "of their own composition"; Cresswell, Du Pratz, and others described colonial slave dances, such as the jig and calinda; still others, among them John Harrower, John Smyth, and Moreau de Saint Mery, described the instruments found among the slaves, such as the banza or banjer (banjo types), barrafou (a xylophone type), fiddle, fife, flute, and various kinds of drums. Contemporary sources also include comment on unusual performance practice---in a runaway-slave advertisement, for example, the slaveholder points out that his slave whistler produced sounds "in a peculiar manner with his tongue."

By the end of the eighteenth century, black Americans had laid the foundation for a folk culture that was peculiarly an amalgamation of African and Euro-American elements, overlaid with a predominantly African tone. Some of the Africanisms were clear and visible; some were fragmentary or submerged; all contributed to the thriving of an African culture on the nation's plantations.

THE ANTEBELLUM ERA, 1801-1862

Judged by any standards, the antebellum era was the most momentous period in the history of the United States, a time of extraordinary events. While the westward expansion movement carried the borders of the United States to the Pacific Ocean, there was concomitantly an enormous increase in the population, primarily because of immigration, which brought more than 9,000,000 Europeans to the nation over a period of sixty years.

Soon after the War for Independence, European visitors began coming in large numbers to the young republic, and after the War of 1812, their numbers increased dramatically. Throughout the century tourists poured into the new nation by the hundreds of thousands, traveling about the country in all directions, their travels made easier than in earlier times because of the improvements in transportation that had taken place with the coming of the steamboat and, later, the train.

The published records of their adventures were eagerly read by their compatriots and frequently denounced by the Americans, who resented the often severe criticism of the Europeans, particularly of the institution of slavery. Sometimes the visitors remained in the United States to become citizens, and they too published accounts of their experiences. As for the Americans, they left home in sizable numbers to travel in the South and the West for the first time and published books about their adventures after returning home.

American literature and the arts made impressive beginnings during the early nineteenth century, owing to the emergence of professional writers and the founding of "American schools" in literature and painting. Over the nation, scholars and amateurs organized historical societies, from which came both local histories and the first general histories of the nation. And there was a veritable explosion of book and media publishing---general-interest magazines, newspapers, scholarly journals, and specialized journals of various kinds.

Over all loomed the question of slavery and the inevitable conflict it presaged between the North and the South. Perhaps no single segment of American society received more attention in the press during the late antebellum and the war years than did the black man, particularly the slave. Hundreds of thousands of publications poured from the presses in the United States and in Europe in the format of books, pamphlets, articles in newspapers and magazines, and ephemeral matter. While there are no statistics on the precise number of publications that dealt with some aspect of slavery, it is probable that they numbered in the thousands and, predictably, they centered on political, economic, social, and moral issues to a general neglect of cultural matters. Despite this, the Bibliography contains more than 500 entries that include commentary on some feature of Afro-American folk culture.

Who were the authors of these publications? For the most part they were travelers, European and American, who were coming in close contact with slavery for the first time. They came from all walks of life and represented a wide diversity of viewpoints. As during the colonial period, a large majority were merchants and other businessmen, clergymen, and army and naval officers. Then there were politicians, lawyers, historians, tutors, teachers, scientists, lecturers, sportsmen, and above all, journalists. The arts and the belle lettres were represented by novelists, poets, musicians, actors, and artists. And the turbulent times produced three new classes of writers: abolitionists, apologists for slavery, and the fugitive slaves who published their autobiographies as slave narratives.

More than four-fifths of the antebellum entries in this Bibliography were published during the last two decades before the Civil War, which reflects the nation's tremendous growth of interest by the mid-century years in the question of slavery. The works generally fall into ten categories: travelogues, various kinds of histories (local, regional, institutional), biographical writings, church and court reports, hymnals, journals and diaries, anthologies, political and sociological writings, fiction, and periodical literature (covering the same kinds of subject matter as the books).

A fresh approach to publication-format was devised by the professional journalist, who, traveling as a correspondent for his newspaper or magazine, published a series of articles about his observations, then later gathered them together for publication in book format. Most important of these journalists was Frederick Law Olmsted (of the NEW-YORK DAILY TIMES and NEW-YORK DAILY TRIBUNE), whose incisive commentary on slavery in the decade of the 1850s through the early '60s provided a model for later writers because of his acute observations, careful interviews, and keen eye for detail. Other influential journalists of the antebellum period who published in book format were James Redpath (NEW-YORK TRIBUNE) and the British correspondent William Howard Russell (LONDON TIMES).

With the mid-century years came more publishing houses, newspapers, and magazines. Before the 1850s, articles about slave culture were published chiefly, though not exclusively, in six magazines or newspapers: the LIBERATOR, DE BOW'S REVIEW, CHRISTIAN-WATCHMAN & REFLECTOR, NATIONAL ANTI-SLAVERY STANDARD, SOUTHERN CHRISTIAN ADVOCATE, and ZION'S HERALD & WESLEYAN JOURNAL. Now the field was widened with the entry of several important new serials, among them, HARPER'S NEW MONTHLY MAGAZINE (1850), FRANK LESLIE'S ILLUSTRATED NEWSPAPER (1855), and HARPER'S WEEKLY (1857).

These periodicals made available to writers a larger market than had existed in previous decades, and encouraged them to expand their reaches to wider audiences. Concomitantly, the new literature exerted a powerful influence on how the black man was perceived by the way it created images and stereotypes.

In addition to the new journalism, the mid-century period is distinctive for the growing popularity of a relatively new literary genre, the novel (and its kindred magazine serial) based on plantation life, often called the "plantation romance." A related type is the novel that includes discussion of African-style festivals, such as James Fenimore Cooper's SATANSTOE (1845), with its detailed description of a Pinkster festival, and George Troop's BERTIE; OR, LIFE IN THE OLD FIELD (1851), with its extensive comment on a John Kooner celebration. Although a few novels drawing on the plantation theme had appeared earlier---among them, George Tucker's THE VALLEY OF SHENANDOAH (1824) and John Pendleton Kennedy's SWALLOW BARN (1832) ---it was not until the 1850s that they began to compete with the travelogue as a source of information about black culture.

Harriet Beecher Stowe's UNCLE TOM'S CABIN (1852) was of course a watershed: few plantation novels published thereafter escaped its influence. Indeed, some were specifically intended as counterstatements, such as Robert Criswell's UNCLE TOM'S CABIN CONTRASTED WITH BUCKINGHAM HALL, THE PLANTER'S HOUSE (1852) or William Smith's LIFE AT THE SOUTH; OR, UNCLE TOM'S CABIN LIKE IT IS (1852). And Stowe, herself, feeling it necessary to defend the authenticity of her novel, published a rejoinder, A KEY TO UNCLE TOM'S CABIN (1853).

In the fiction and the nonfiction, the book and the periodical literature that poured from the presses, writers generally brought under closer scrutiny than in the past the African-style folkways ---the burial rites, the "praise cabin" and "brush-arbor" worship services, the corn-shuckings and other social activities of the slaves, and, above all, the singing asssociated with plantation life. Writers seemed to take extra care in presenting their "scenes," "visits," "pictures," and "sketches" of slavery to the public, emphasizing the fact that their scenes were "drawn from real life" or were "a record of facts, not fiction." Moreso than in previous years they relied heavily on quotation to give the desirable touches of realism and authenticity, and incorporated dialogue and texts of songs and sermons whenever possible.

Writings about Slave Festivals. Since the late-eighteenth century the nation had been growing more aware of the special quality of the black man's cultural traditions, if not through personal experiences with his music and dancing, then certainly through contemporaneous publications, which provided images, both positive and negative, of the black folk artist in action.

In New England, for example, it was the festival called "Lection Day," which took place in the spring (generally May or June), lasting from one day to as long as a full week, when gatherings of slaves and freedmen elected their own black governors and celebrated the event with parades, music, and games. Of the several entries in the Bibliography that refer to this festival, including one written by a black woman whose brother served as a " 'lected governor," earliest is a local history dating from 1827, Joseph Felt's ANNALS OF SALEM FROM ITS FIRST SETTLEMENT.

In the mid-Atlantic states, it was Pinkster Day (the name adapted from Pentecost Sunday) that attracted white audiences to an outdoor, African-style celebration, which lasted from two or three days to a week in the spring. The earliest account of the festival, published in 1803 by Andrew Adgate, takes the form of a lengthy ode of some forty-five stanzas, A PINKSTER ODE FOR THE YEAR 1803. Therein the particulars of Pinkster Day are recounted in detail, with special attention given to the dance leader, King Charley of Guinea. This festival seems to have been especially fascinating for writers; from time to time throughout the nineteenth century reports were published on the festival.

A southern festival, called the John Canoe, which seems to have flourished primarily on the coasts of southern Virginia and North Carolina, shows strong similarities to a Caribbean festival and indirect ties to Africa. No fewer than four reports about it were published in the antebellum period, the first anonymously in 1837, "Scenes in North Carolina," in the LIBERATOR.

In the deep South, it was the slave dancing in New Orleans's Congo Square that engaged the attention of whites, who described the festival in dozens of books and articles. English-born Henry Latrobe left the most precise account, though not the earliest, after watching it during his stay in New Orleans in the years 1818-20. All the reports published about slave festivals in the antebellum period emphasize the overpowering African tone of the singing, dancing, and choice of musical instruments.

The Antebellum Black Church. For many visitors, and Americans as well, the most remarkable feature of black culture was the worship service of the black church. It was there that narrative, song, dance, and drama melded often into profound and moving spectacle, over which towered the African priest-turned-preacher.

In writing about the black church, whites of all classes---clergymen, travelers, teachers, journalists, historians, and others---grappled with the inadequacies of the English language to explain the extraordinary, and often incredible, happenings in the worship service. Over and over again they tried to describe the preacher's style of oratory, the fervor of congregational response to his emotional outpourings of preachment and prayer, his magnetic hold on the worshipers, the sheer artistry of the performance as a whole.

For many questions that arose there seemed to be no rational answers: for example, how could the black illiterate exhorters gain such secure control over the Bible and its teachings? To be sure, not all black folk preachers were illiterate; some ordained ministers made a deliberate decision to serve their congregations as "spiritual" rather than "learned" preachers. Richard Allen may have been the first one to recognize the dichotomy in print when, in his autobiography, he observed, "Sure am I that reading sermons will never prove so beneficial to the colored people as spiritual or extempore preaching" (Allen [1833] 1887, 30).

It is not surprising that white writers, in trying to describe the fiery sermons to which they listened, usually resorted to summarizing them or taking down the texts verbatim, in addition to identifying the Biblical text, when possible, on which the sermons were based. The first appearance of the summarized sermon in the historical record is an anonymous article entitled "Religious Intelligence: An Account of the Baptism of Nine Negroes in Boston, May 26, 1805."

The observer describes in great detail the ceremony led by the black Baptist minister Thomas Paul and his brother Benjamin: the congregation gathering at 8 o'clock in the morning at a house near the waterside; the ritual march, two by two, to the waterside; the sermon (based on Rom. 6:4 and Col. 2:12), prayers, and singing; and the return, two by two, to the house---all this watched by a "large number of people who came to see something new."

Although possibly the first of its kind, this report would not be unique. No fewer than thirty-two sermons and prayers are cited in antebellum literature, about two-thirds of them summarized or transcribed, and the remainder indicated by title or Biblical text. Other early examples are found in Abigail Mott, BIOGRAPHICAL SKETCHES... (1837): two short sermons of Solomon Bayley (based on Rom. 8:9 and Gal. 5:14) and an excerpt from a sermon by the celebrated folk preacher known only as Uncle Jack. In the early nineteenth century the summarized sermon was most common; later, writers more frequently attempted to record the sermon as delivered, quoting the sermon in its entirety or a part of it, and after the Civil War the use of dialect in quotation was pervasive.

Congregational singing in the black church contributed enormously to the exoticism of the worship service for white visitors. Typically, the black worshipers sang both the traditional Protestant hymns and their own "improvised hymns" during the course of the service. A New Englander (identified in the literature only as Leonard), when visiting a plantation service in Florida in 1858, observed that the slaves used the term "spiritual himes" for their own improvised songs to distinguish their songs from the hymns of Watts and Wesley. This suggests how the practice might have developed of calling the slaves' improvised religious songs "Negro spirituals," a practice that became common in later years.

Another exotic feature of worship practices for white visitors was a religious dance associated with informal religious activities, which generally took place after the formal services. What seems obvious from the vantage point of the present is that the African-style dance described in colonial literature reappeared in the antebellum era as a "holy dance," and became an integral part of the religious ceremonies of black folk congregations.

The exact point in time when this amalgamation began to take place cannot be pinned down. As early as 1801 Methodist clergyman William Colbert observed, after visiting a black church, that "the Lord was praised in the song, in the shout, and in the dance"; in 1810 Christian Schultz described religious dancing he saw in New Orleans; and John Fanning Watson, writing in 1819, complained that in the "black's quarter" of the Methodist camp meetings in the Philadelphia area,

> the coloured people get together, and sing for hours together...in the merry chorus manner of the southern harvest field, or husking-frolic method, of the slave blacks; and also very greatly like the Indian dances. With every word so sung, they have a sinking of one or other leg of the body alternately; producing an audible sound of the feet at every step, and as manifest as the steps of actual negro dancing in Virginia (Watson [1819] 1983, 63).

This graphic description of the black Christian's holy dance seems to omit no detail of its performance, although the term shout is not used. The dance was by no means limited to the Eastern Seaboard or the South; for example, James Dixon, visiting an African church in Pittsburgh in 1849, noted in METHODISM IN AMERICA... (1849) that "the people danced to their own melody" after the sermon.

By the 1840s writers were using the term "ring dance" for the holy dance, as in Charles Lyell, A SECOND VISIT TO THE UNITED STATES (1849), and by the 1860s they were identifying it as the "shout" or the "glory shout." The first use of the term and description of the dance in print apparently was in an anonymous article entitled "An Englishman in South Carolina, December 1860 and July, 1862" (Epstein 1977, 233). The most concise and thorough descriptions, however, would come after Emancipation in the late 1860s.

Throughout the nineteenth century the shout was controversial. White observers, while admitting its entrancement, generally believed it to be barbaric, even lascivious. Unaware of the African traditions represented in the shout, the whites could not appreciate the importance of the dance for black Americans. For black folk, the shout was a form of worship, along with music and prayer, and the highest level of spiritual involvement was reached when the Holy Spirit took possession of their souls. More than any other of the slave's traditions, the shout, with its fusing of ritual dancing and spirit possession, symbolized the clash between African and European cultures.

From the very beginning, the church fathers, white and black, tried to wipe out such "heathenish" practices as the shout. Writing in the 1840s, black clergyman Daniel Payne noted that his efforts had been unsuccessful:

> About this time I attended a "bush meeting," where I went to please the pastor whose circuit I was visiting. After the sermon they formed a ring, and with coats off sung, clapped their hands and stamped their feet in a most ridiculous and heathenish way.... I then went, and taking the leader by the arm, requested him to desist and to sit down and sing in a rational manner.... He replied: "The Spirit of God works upon people in different ways...there must be a ring here, a ring there, a ring over yonder, or sinners will not get converted..." (1888, 255).

The shout is not to be confused with secular dancing, despite similarities between the performance styles of the two genres, nor with the voodoo dance, which had its own rituals.

Social Activities of the Slaves. Secular dances of black folk were called ring dances, jigs, shuffles, and breakdowns. Specially gifted dancers displayed their skills in shake-downs, double-shuffles, cross-cut steps, backsteps, the pigeon-wing, and a variety of dances associated with places, such as the Virginny hoe-down, Georgia rattle-snake, and Alabamy kick-up.

To accompany the dancing, the slaves relied primarily on the fiddle, banjo, and home-crafted instruments made from horse and cow jawbones, gourds, and whatever else was convenient. Depending upon availability and the importance of the occasion, the number and kind of instruments used to accompany the dancing varied: sometimes only a "juba patter" or a whistler was at hand; for holiday dances or a festival such as Pinkster or John Canoe, there might be added to the fiddle-banjo ensemble African percussion and European instruments (cello, horn, tambourine, triangle).

One singular practice associated with slave dancing, "pattin' juba," was described again and again in the literature. The performer, or "patter," struck alternately various parts of the body---slapping the thighs, striking the elbows (and sometimes shoulders), clapping the hands, and tapping the feet---all in such precise rhythm as to produce sounds adequate for accompanying the dance. In one of the early descriptions of pattin', James Hungerford noted that the patter also recited verses "in a monotonous tone of voice" as he patted (a practice that seems to foreshadow the "rapping" of the 1980s).

By the late 1830s the term "pattin' juba" had become so common that writers no longer bother to explain its meaning. Nevertheless, some of the descriptions that appeared in publications of the 1850s---such as those of Lewis Paine, Solomon Northup, and Frederick Douglass ---are useful for the additional information they provide about the many different ways of pattin'.

Surprisingly, there is very little in antebellum literature about the folktale, one of the most important of the African traditions. Here and there are references to slaves telling African tales to their fellows, or to the planter's children. To be sure, Joseph Cobb, in his MISSISSIPPI SCENES (1851), identifies some of the tale types found among the slaves, and a few sources include tale texts. But as a genre, the antebellum folktale received little attention in comparison to that given to the slave's sermon, song, and dance.

Songs of the Antebellum Era. Many of the hymns that the African-Americans sang in their worship services served as musical tinder for the so-called Negro spirituals, which would be published in large numbers after the Civil War. Black folk composers pulled various phrases, couplets, refrains, and even full stanzas from their favorite hymns; added to the texts the fragments of other phrases, interlines, and refrains to compose new texts; and then invented tunes for the new texts---or used familiar tunes. The Bible also served as a source of inspiration for the folk composers, who used its verses as creatively as they did the hymn texts.

Although no spirituals have come down to us from the early nineteenth century, references to these religious songs and how they were composed appear in a number of sources, such as John F. Watson, METHODIST ERROR...(1819) and William Faux, MEMORABLE DAYS IN AMERICA (1823).

However, there are secular-song texts dating from the early antebellum years. Street cries, for example, are found in a publication of 1809, STREET CRIES OF NEW YORK, which includes texts of cries sung by three black peddlers. And two worksongs come from the South: John Lambert, touring in Georgia during the years 1806-8, was struck by the songs of slave boatmen and included in his book, TRAVELS THROUGH CANADA AND THE UNITED STATES (1816), not only description of the singing but also a song text, "We are going to Georgia, boys." A decade or so later, another traveler in Georgia, James Kirke Paulding, wrote down the text of a song he heard during the summer of 1816, "Going away to Georgia," in his book LETTERS FROM THE SOUTH (1817).

By the 1830s slave-song texts were appearing regularly in books and periodical literature; in many instances two or three texts were recorded, and occasionally as many as five or six. In commenting on the slave songs, writers carefully stressed the difference between "genuine negro songs" and the Ethiopian minstrel songs, generally to the disparagement of the latter in terms of creativity. All together, about 175 slave-song texts are extant in antebellum publications (including variants of songs that were published in more than one source), and approximately twice that number are referred to by title, first line, or refrain of a song. The repertory comprises both religious and secular songs in roughly even numbers.

It appears that most writers recorded the texts of the slave songs they heard with little regard for any social or historical significance of the songs. An exception must be made, however, in the case of a missionary of the Methodist Episcopal Church (identified in the literature only as "C."). He seems to have perceived that the songs he heard while working among the slaves on South Carolina's Sea Islands were not merely individual bursts of musical improvisation, but perhaps part of a traditional repertory of religious slave songs.

The series of three articles he published in 1843, all entitled "Missionary Sketches" (nos. 199-201), contains the texts (mostly spirituals) of eight songs and two choruses, and refers to others by quoting their opening couplets---the whole constituting a small collection of slave songs of the Sea Islands. This set may well be the earliest publication in history of a slave-song collection, and as such, it serves as a precursor of the collections that would proliferate after the Civil War.

The sound of the slave music held unending fascination for white listeners: again and again they tried to describe the vocal quality of the voice and the incessant inventing and improvising of song materials. Inevitably, this led some persons to experiment with writing the slave melodies on a musical staff, and indeed, publications began to appear during the 1850s that include both music and text for the songs.

First, apparently, was George Washington Clark's THE HARP OF FREEDOM (1856), an anti-slavery song collection, which contains a melody for the slave song "Oh, whar is de spot what we were born on." James Hungerford's THE OLD PLANTATION, published in 1859, includes two songs with music and text that the transcriber heard on a Maryland plantation in 1832, "Sold off to Georgy" and "Roun' de corn, Sally." Finally, in 1861, appeared music and text for the spiritual that would become celebrated the world over, "Go down, Moses," published by Thomas Baker.

Other kinds of melodies represented in mid-century publications are the street cries of four black peddlers in CITY CRIES (1850) by William Croome; a dance tune in Solomon Northup's autobiography, TWELVE YEARS A SLAVE (1853); and the melody of a chanted prayer notated by composer George Frederick Root in his article, "Congregational Singing among Negroes" (1855).

George Root was in the vanguard of the professional musicians who commented in print on some aspect of slave music, a practice that increasingly would involve larger numbers of musicians and scholars over the years, black and white. And with the founding of such music journals as the CHORAL ADVOCATE (later entitled the NEW YORK MUSICAL REVIEW) in 1850 and DWIGHT'S JOURNAL OF MUSIC in 1852, musicians were provided additional platforms for expressing their opinions.

The Slave Narrative. As a genre the so-called slave narrative had its genesis in such publications as A NARRATIVE OF THE SUFFERINGS AND SURPRIZING DELIVERANCE OF BRITON HAMMON, A NEGRO MAN... (1760). Three narratives published in the eighteenth century and a number that appeared in the early nineteenth century offer comment on some aspect of slave culture. But it was during the years 1840s-60s that slave-narrative publishing reached its zenith. By the end of the nineteenth century thousands of narratives had been published in the format of books, pamphlets, magazine and newspaper articles, broadsides, and other kinds of records (Starling 1981, xvii, 225).

No fewer than forty-three of the antebellum narratives represented in this Bibliography contain cogent comment on black culture. Aaron's THE LIGHT OF TRUTH AND SLAVERY...(1827) heads the list. Seven narratives were published in the next decade, the works of rebel Nat Turner (1831), church father Richard Allen (1833), and escaped slaves Charles Ball (1836), Moses Roper (1837), and James Williams (1838). Then came the slave narrative's heyday, bringing celebrity to such authors as Frederick Douglass, William Wells Brown, and Linda Jacobs, among many others.

Whatever the pressures that may have been imposed on the slave narrator by white sponsors, editors, and amanuenses to shape his story to the purposes of abolitionists and the eradication of slavery, he seems to have been free to discuss matters regarded as inconsequential by the whites, such as plantation folkways. The black narrator, like the white narrator, reported on religious rituals, recreational activities, and other features of plantation daily life, but seen from his perspective, these matters take on a different character.

A master communicator like Frederick Douglass, for example, could explain not only the "what" of slave life but also the "why":

> The remark is not unfrequently made, that slaves are the most contented and happy laborers in the world. They dance and sing, and make all manner of joyful noises---so they do; but it is a great mistake to suppose them happy because they sing. The songs of the slave represent the sorrows, rather than the joys, of his heart; and he is relieved by them, only as an aching heart is relieved by its tears (Douglass 1845, 36).

Support for the publishing of slave narratives came from both individuals and antislavery organizations, including one that hardly was a typical institution---the Underground Railroad. A clandestine operation developed over the years to assist slaves in escaping to freedom, the movement had its own agents or conductors, escape routes, and stations. The agents slipped into the South, acquainted the waiting slaves with the escape plans, and made arrangements for the flight. Generally, conductors and slaves traveled at night, guided by the North Star, and rested during the day at designated stations---their goals, the terminals set up at points along the Ohio River and in southern Pennsylvania and New Jersey.

Stories about the slaves' experiences and breath-taking escapes were widely published and eagerly received by the public. Some of the conductors, too, were immortalized in the literature, such as ex-slaves Harriet Tubman and Sojourner Truth and the white Quaker Levi Coffin, whose activity earned him the title "President of the Underground Railroad."

Iconography of Antebellum Folk Culture. For the cultural historian, pictorial sources can be extremely helpful in illuminating the function of creative expression in the black community and, as well, in American society in general (Donaldson 1986). Moreover, the examination of art works from the iconographical perspective often brings to light specific information that may be illusive or unavailable in literary sources (Brown 1980, 11). Take, for example, the matter of instrumental music on the plantation: pictorial sources report on the instruments played, on who played them, and how they were played. Genre scenes can set the folk artist in social context---the preacher in his pulpit or presiding over a burial, the dancers jumping about during a holiday celebration, the story tellers gathered around a camp fire, and the like.

The two paintings represented in the Bibliography that date from colonial-federalist times indicate the image of slave culture prevalent during that period and predict future stereotypes. Both "The Old Plantation" (anonymous) and Samuel Jennings's "Liberty Displaying the Arts and Sciences" show dancers and banjoists in action, and African influences are obvious in the movements of the dancers and the choice of accompanying instruments.

Of the seventy-seven antebellum artworks listed in the Bibliography, about two dozen are magazine illustrations; a dozen, illustrations for books; and two or three, broadsheet advertisements and a sheet-music cover. The remainder of the antebellum artworks are oil paintings or watercolors. The illustrations date no earlier than the 1850s, reflecting the fact that the popularity of the engraved pictorial representation was closely interlinked with the establishment and growth of the illustrated press in the United States (a point to which I shall return).

Generally, the illustration, as distinguished from the painting, represents a specific theme, person, or scene discussed in the narrative, and ordinarily all persons depicted are black. It is of interest that ex-slave Henry Bibb's narrative of 1850 includes a plantation-scene illustration; since no artist attribution is given, it may be that Bibb, himself, made the original sketch. If so, Bibb is the only ex-slave represented in African-American cultural history by both narrative and drawing.

Genre scenes may be found among both illustrations and paintings. A style that became very popular, genre painting initially appeared in the United States in the second decade of the nineteenth century (Hills 1974, 2). With the aim of portraying real-life activity, the genre scene depicts people from various levels of society going about their daily tasks.

The paintings discussed in the Bibliography typically present a naturalistic approach to the subject matter, showing black folk as real persons (though sometimes idealized) and gatherings of the folk as real events, for whom models obviously were used. The illustrations, on the other hand, frequently focus on the "typical" gathering---say, typical slaves singing typical worksongs lustily at a typical corn-shucking festival.

Of the early antebellum painters, John Lewis Krimmel makes the largest contribution to an understanding of black folk-life in his time. His topographical scenes of Philadelphia citizens celebrating the Fourth of July (c.1812, 1819) show canvases crowded with people of all ages, black and white, conversing with one another and generally enjoying the holiday, against a background of the city's buildings---this in a period when black folk rarely were included in such scenes. His ubiquitous black fiddlers are set in social context, viewed as a natural and integral part of the American scene, not as the outsider (as in paintings by some artists) or as an exotic figure to be patronized.

Krimmel's influence on the public's perception of the black fiddler was considerable, for his works were well exhibited, widely collected, and made accessible to the general public through engravings and lithographs (Hills 1974, 5). The works also were copied for many years after his death in 1821.

Russian diplomat Pavel Svin'in, who visited black churches in Philadelphia during the years 1812-13, is less sympathetic in his approach, but his watercolors nevertheless reveal much about black religious folkways of the time. Equally informative, but for the social scene, is Christian Mayr's depiction of a slave formal dance, "Kitchen Ball at White Sulphur Springs" (1838).

Most of the bibliography's antebellum paintings date from the 1850s and sixties; they include portraits such as William Sidney Mount's celebrated portrayals of black musicians, and genre paintings such as Eastman Johnson's "Negro Life at the South" (1859, popularly dubbed "My Old Kentucky Home") and John Antrobus's "A Plantation Burial" (c.1860).

In the early 1850s---when men of letters were discovering that, because of the proliferation of newspapers and magazines, careers in journalism offered promise of rich rewards---the painters, illustrators, and engravers began to discover that a new profession awaited them as well, that of the pictorial journalist.

Before the 1850s illustrations rarely were to be found in books and magazines, except for art journals; after the first illustrated weeklies appeared in 1851, engraved illustrations became so popular that one contemporary observer protested the "illustration mania" that had overcome American publishers (Preston and White 1979, 91). Chief among the magazines that published illustrations of black folk were HARPER'S NEW MONTHLY MAGAZINE and FRANK LESLIE'S ILLUSTRATED NEWSPAPER.

The demand for the engraving increased enormously over the years, not only for illustrating magazines but as well for enhancing the pages of the book. In response to the public's seemingly insatiable curiosity about black folk, the artist-reporter produced pictorial portrayals of slave life that paralleled the verbal descriptions of the journalists---depicting views of corn-shuckings, holiday dances, worship services, burial rituals, and other kinds of plantation activity. Illustration titles tended to be specific and informative, such as "Winter Holydays in the Southern States," "Plantation Frolic on Christmas Eve," "Reading the Bible to the Slaves," or "Slavery as It Exists in America" (all anonymous).

In some instances, the authenticity of the illustrations is questionable, for the artist-engraver may not have visited the places he depicted but rather relied on the sketches of others or on photographs. For this reason, and others, some of the portrayals are not truly representative of the scenes they purport to depict, being overly sentimentalized or stereotypical or caricatural.

During the early 1860s many of the nation's artists, like its writers, became involved with chronicling the activities of the Civil War, often to the neglect of their pre-war interests. Some enlisted in the army; others signed up as artist-correspondents for newspapers and magazines; and some obtained permission to follow the troops as freelance artists-reporters. The sketches they made while out in the field were sent back to the press, where they were quickly engraved and published in the weekly and monthly periodicals. Later the same engravings might appear in books.

THE LATE ANTEBELLUM ERA

The last few years before the Civil War brought deeply felt and widespread apprehension to Americans as they became increasingly preoccupied with the issue of slavery and its apparently unsolvable problems. The Compromise of 1850 and other political events of the fifties did little to lessen the strain, and the publishing of UNCLE TOM'S CABIN in 1852 served only to increase the tension between antislavery and proslavery protagonists.

In October 1859 matters were brought to a violent climax by the fiery abolitionist John Brown of Kansas. Setting out to strike a decisive blow for the freedom of the slaves, and aided by a small band of followers, black and white, he seized the federal arsenal at Harpers Ferry, Virginia, hoping thereby to obtain enough ammunition to wage full-scale battles. Brown's mission failed, and he was hanged, but his brave stand made him a martyred hero for many, particularly the slaves. Throughout the war the rallying cry of black troops would be the "John Brown Song":

John Brown's body lies a mouldering in the grave
John Brown's body lies a mouldering in the grave
John Brown's body lies a mouldering in the grave
But his soul goes marching on.

The next year, 1860, brought even more momentous events with the election of the Republican Abraham Lincoln to the presidency in November, and the secession of South Carolina from the Union in December. The new president's avowed goal to save the Union, no matter the cost, and the secession of more southern states made war inevitable.

On 12 April 1861, Confederate troops fired the first gun of the war on Union forces garrisoned at Fort Sumter, South Carolina. As the fighting got under way, almost immediately fugitive slaves began to seek refuge behind Union Army lines, and as the Army moved deeper into Confederate country, additional thousands of slaves came under its jurisdiction when the slaveholders fled their plantations. Since the federal government had not developed a policy for this undoubtedly unexpected happening, there was great confusion until a Union officer, Benjamin Butler, moved into the vacuum, declaring the fugitive slaves to be "contraband of war," and therefore not to be returned to their masters.

The federal government moved so slowly with its policy-making that private persons (white and black) began organizing relief societies to ease the suffering of the contraband. First to make a concrete move was the American Missionary Association (founded in 1846), which in September 1861 sent Lewis C. Lockwood as a missionary to Fort Monroe (Virginia) to start a program there. Within a short time he had set up Sabbath Day schools in several places.

About the same time, on 17 September, black teacher Mary S. Peake opened the first "day school" for freedmen. This marked the beginning of a long odyssey of northerners, particularly from New England, into the South to teach the ex-slaves and, later, the second and third generations of freedmen.

By late 1861 the Union Army had seized the Sea Islands off the coasts of South Carolina and Georgia, and the government moved to set up a program there that would organize the contraband into labor units and provide them with schools---in effect, that would assist them in making the difficult transition from slavery to freedom. In December, the government selected Port Royal as the site for the first undertaking, with the lieutenant colonel William Reynolds as superviser.

The so-called Port Royal experiment offers the most compelling example of the close interaction between the New Englander and the contraband (that is, white and black) that existed any place in the nation. Because of its primary role in the transcription and publication of slave songs and tales, Port Royal would leave an indelible mark on the history of American folklore (see below under "Folksong Collecting"). The federal program included also the communities of Beaufort, St. Helena Island, Paris Island, and Hilton Head Island.

Throughout the North abolitionists organized relief societies in a major philanthropic effort to assist the federal government with the Sea Islands program, sending down teachers and supplies of all kinds. The first contingent of volunteers arrived in February 1862; some stayed only the time as called for in their contracts, but others remained for as long as twenty or more years. Ultimately, the government established operations similar to those at Port Royal in other places of the South that were taken over by the Union Army, but Port Royal remained the model as the first and most successful.

From the beginning of the war, black men clamored to join in the fight, but the federal government was firmly set against arming ex-slaves, indeed, even arming free blacks. After much agitation, the factions that were supporting the rights of black men to fight for their country won out over their adversaries. In July 1862 two acts of great importance to black folk became effective: the Confiscation Act, which authorized the President to use persons of "African descent" in any way necessary to futher the cause of the war, and the Enlistment Act, which authorized the employment of black troops.

By the end of 1862, three black regiments, composed of contraband, ex-slaves, and freedmen, had been mustered into the Union Army: the Louisiana Native Guards, the First South Carolina (Colored) Volunteers, and the First Kansas (Colored) Volunteers. Many others would follow. Initially the Army discriminated against black soldiers in regard to wages, giving them only seven dollars a month, plus three for the care of their uniforms, in contrast to the ten dollars plus three given to the white soldiers. Black soldiers strongly protested the discrimination---one regiment refused to accept any wages at all---and added a new song to their increasing repertory of war folksongs: "Ten dollar a month, tree ob dat for clothin'." It was not until 1864 that the matter was satisfactorily adjusted.

From the beginning, the war inspired both professionals and amateurs to publish accounts of their wartime experiences. Journalists sent south by their newspapers and magazines to cover the war added human-interest stories to their reports on the contraband's religious and social activities and the black soldier's army-camp lifestyle. Additionally, missionaries, teachers, and travelers flooded the nation with their published diaries, letters, reports, social commentary, and travelogues---all testifying to the strange environment in which they found themselves and the alien black folk among whom they worked and lived. Over time, intimate personal relations developed between white and black---the army officer and "his men", the teacher and her pupils---and this, too, was reflected in the materials that came off the presses.

Predictably, the largest number of articles about slave culture published during this period came from persons visiting or residing in South Carolina. No fewer than thirty-eight of the antebellum titles in the Bibliography represent discussion of some aspect of black cultural activity in that state, twenty-five of them specifically about happenings in Port Royal, and the remainder about Hilton Head, Beaufort, and St. Helena Island. Writers residing in Fort Monroe, Virginia, or nearby contributed seven articles to the literature, and a few came from writers living in Washington, D.C., where thousands of contraband had settled during the first year of the war.

Writers commented on the same kind of activities as had earlier writers, except they replaced the word "slave" with the word "contraband." Even the slave narrative was updated: William Davis, for example, entitled his narrative "The Story of a Contraband" (1862).

A number of the song texts quoted in these late-antebellum articles reflect the contraband's sense of his new freedom, although emancipation was still in the future. He exulted in the planter's dilemma---"De Northmen dey's got massa now"; he prayed to God for reassurance ---"Jesus'll git us out of dis"; and he anticipated some of the gifts of freedom---"No more driver call for me." Most widely sung of all the contraband songs was "Go down, Moses."

Through the year 1862 President Lincoln moved slowly but inexorably toward his goal with his plans for emancipating the slaves. In June he abolished slavery in the District of Columbia and in the territories, and in July he proposed a plan to his cabinet for freeing slaves in the states that had seceded from the Union. Follow through on his plan had to be delayed for important reasons, but a Union victory in September at the Battle of Antietam gave the president the opportunity for which he had been waiting: On 22 September 1862 he issued a Preliminary Emancipation Proclamation, declaring that on 1 January 1863 "all persons held as slaves within any State, or designated part of the State, the people whereof shall be in rebellion against the United States, shall be then, thenceforward, and forever free."

THE POST-EMANCIPATION ERA, 1863-1899

On New Year's Eve 1862, black people all over the nation gathered together to sing and pray as they waited for the hour of midnight to bring into law the Emancipation Proclamation. Possibly no documents in history are so poignant and moving as those that report on the first hours of emancipation for millions of slaves in the United States. Observers in black churches and white churches, in contraband camps and army camps, in such large secular temples as Boston's Tremont Temple and New York's Cooper Institute, and on the street---all tried to convey in words totally inadequate for the purpose the awesome tone of the celebrations.

Ex-slave William Wells Brown wrote about the service that was held in the "Contraband Camp" of the District of Columbia, where "great preparation" had been made:

> The fore part of the night was spent in singing and prayer, the following being sung several times--
>
> Oh, go down, Moses,
> Way down in Egypt's land:
> Tell King Pharaoh
> To let my people go.
>
> Oh, Pharaoh said he would go cross
> Let my people go.
> But Pharaoh and his host was lost,
> Let my people go.
> Chorus---Oh, go down, Moses, &c.
>
> .... After this an old man struck up, in a clear and powerful voice, "I am a free man now: Jesus Christ has made me free!" the company gradually joining in; and before the close, the whole assemblage was singing in chorus (Brown 1867, 111).

After the extemporaneous speeches came more singing, then prayers, exhortations, more singing, and more extemporaneous speaking.

> Just before midnight, Dr. Nichols requested all present to kneel, and to silently invoke the blessing of the Almighty. The silence was almost deadly when the clock announced the new year; and Dr. Nichols said, "Men and women (for you are this day to be declared free, and I can address you as men and women), I wish you a happy new year!" An eloquent prayer was then offered by an aged negro; after which, all rose, and joined in singing their version of "Glory! glory! hallelujah!" shaking each other by the hand and indulging in joyous demonstrations... (Brown 1867, 117).

It was not until 31 January 1865, however, when Congress passed the Thirteenth Amendment, that slavery was abolished throughout the United States. That year was notable also for the establishment in March of the Freedmen's Bureau of the War Department, which was intended to assist the slave in making the difficult adjustment to freedom. But the Bureau made only limited efforts, and they met with minimal success.

The next year, in 1866, the American Missionary Association and other denominational groups, assisted by private philanthropy, began to establish secondary and collegiate institutions, of which the best known to the general public would be Fisk University (1866), Hampton Institute (1868), and Tuskegee Institute (1881). Discussion of the tragic results of the Reconstruction Acts of 1867 is beyond the scope of the present discussion. It should be noted, however, that the Reconstruction period ended in 1877 when President Rutherford withdrew federal troops from the South, and thereafter white supremacy became the law of the land in the South, as indeed it was de facto in most other places of the nation.

Post-Emancipation Literature. After the Civil War, writings about the black man, now freedman, became more numerous than ever before, and embraced more categories of authors than previously. The "new" authors included university scholars, public school teachers, politicians, librarians, folklorists, social scientists, and professional musicians. Women are represented in the literature in ever increasing numbers: some of them were southern belles and housewives who published autobiographical works reflecting their experiences during and after the War; some of them, wives of army officers; and many of them, teachers.

Black male writers greatly multiplied their numbers and the fields they represented, coming from the ranks of novelists, editors, poets, school teachers, university scholars and administrators, folklorists, biographers, politicians, and Ethiopian minstrels. Black women, too, contributed to the literature in sizable numbers with autobiographical works and religious tracts.

As in the past, the publications took a variety of forms: in addition to the standard fiction and nonfiction publications, there are more editorials and letters to the editor; reviews of books and concerts; and, for the first time, anthologies of songs, tales, and poetry. Of the thousands of works published in the post-emancipation years, 908 can be identified that include description of, or references to, some aspect of black culture.

The Collecting of Folksong. We have alluded to the warm relations that develloped between the white teachers and missionaries of the North and the contraband and slaves in the South, particularly in the Sea Islands of South Carolina. Many of the whites had known each other before joining the crusade to the South, especially those from New England and the middle states, and newcomers were warmly accepted into the missionary-teacher ranks of the Sea Islands communities.

New England was well represented also in army camps on the Sea Islands, particularly in the person of Thomas Wentworth Higginson, colonel of the Union Army's first black regiment, the First South Carolina Volunteers. It was a strange and exotic world for both blacks and whites, the latter finding the culture they encountered to be particularly challenging. They recorded their experiences in diaries and journals, wrote letters home to friends and family, and later published their personal writings in periodicals or in book format.

Most frequently discussed in the publications were the religious rituals and songs of the slaves. Many of the Sea Islands company, like most Americans, scarcely knew the difference between Ethiopian minstrel songs and genuine slave songs before arriving at Port Royal. Once there, however, their circumstances inspired them to folkloristic activities: collecting songs and tales and describing rituals and folkways.

By early 1862 the first wave of northerners had settled on the Islands, and folklorism had made its first conquests; most active among them were Elizabeth Botume, Laura Towne, Charles Nordhoff, Charles Picard Ware, Harriet Ware Pearson, Thomas Higginson, and Charlotte Forten, one of the few black teachers at Port Royal. In 1864 the anonymous author of "The Original Negro Minstrelsy of the War" observed:

> The war has brought into publicity a new and quaint species of literature, heretofore almost wholly unknown. We now have a curious collection of genuine negro songs, composed, set to music, and sung by the negro himself.

This collector published thirteen song texts, of which eleven are spirituals. One of them, "Roll, Jordan, roll," had been published previously in the 1843 collection discussed earlier (see above under "Songs of the Antebellum").

Curiosity was not the only motivation to action for the amateur folklorists: some feared that the songs would disappear with the eradication of slavery, noting that the young freedmen, once educated, became ashamed of the slave songs. And more than one collector saw a parallel between European folklorism, then in its heyday, and the burgeoning folklore movement in the United States. Higginson noted:

> The war brought to some of us, besides its direct experiences, many a strange fulfilment of dreams of other days. For instance, the present writer had been a faithful student of the Scottish ballads, and had always envied Sir Walter [Scott] the delight of tracing them out amid their own heather, and of writing them down piecemeal from the lips of aged crones. It was a strange enjoyment, therefore, to be suddenly brought into the midst of a kindred world of unwritten songs, as simple and indigenous as the Border Minstrelsy, more uniformly plaintive, almost always more quaint, and often as essentially poetic (1870, 197).

It was against this background that four young enthusiasts set about the task of collecting and transcribing a large gathering of slave songs with a view to publication. Compilers William Francis Allen, Charles Ware, and Lucy McKim Garrison, aided by her husband (Wendell Garrison) solicited contributions from all those known to have small (or large) collections, and in 1867 presented to the public their magnus opum, SLAVE SONGS OF THE UNITED STATES.

The work comprises 136 songs, an additional nineteen variants, and a thirty-six page introduction, written by Allen, that sets the songs in historical, sociological, and musicological context. Consisting primarily of religious songs, the repertory also includes fourteen secular songs, of which three are work-songs and seven are items belonging to the creole-song repertory of Louisiana.

SLAVE SONGS OF THE UNITED STATES contains at least three items that offer links to antebellum sources: the choruses of no. 35 ("O, my King Emanuel") and no. 92 ("O shout, O shout away") were cited by John Watson in 1819, and no. 1 ("Roll, Jordan, roll") was published in 1843. By the time SLAVE SONGS finally left the presses in 1867, no fewer than twenty-two of its texts had been previously published in periodicals, most of them by Forten during the years 1862-64. Surprisingly, one of the war's most popular songs, "Go down, Moses," was not included in SLAVE SONGS.

The publishing of SLAVE SONGS was a milestone in the history of slave culture. The collection inspired emulation by other folklorists and set high standards for those who would publish anthologies in the future. Another milestone was erected in 1871, when in October of that year, student singers of Fisk University set out on a concert tour, singing Negro spirituals, to raise money for their impoverished institution. After some initial rebuffs, they met with enormous success, which inspired other student groups to tour and raise money to aid their struggling institutions. Within a few years professional black choral groups, calling themselves Jubilee Singers, began to concertize.

All these groups published collections of the songs they sang on their concerts; some collections ran into several editions and dozens of printings. Allen had set a precedent with his introduction to SLAVE SONGS: most of the compilers and transcribers who came after him included introductions to their anthologies, which placed the songs in historical, sociological, and cultural context, and commented on performance practice.

Most important of Allen's successors were: (1) T. W. Higginson, informant on, collector of, black-soldier songs; (2) J. B. T. Marsh, Gustavus D. Pike, Frederick Loudin, and Theodore F. Seward, all of whom reported on the songs of the Fisk Jubilee Singers as editors, collectors, or transcribers (editions published from 1872 to 1903); and (3) Thomas P. Fenner, Mary Ford Armstrong, Helen W. Ludlow, Frederic C. Rathbun, and Bessie Cleaveland, collector-transcribers and editors of the song collections of the Hampton Student Singers (published from 1874 to 1916).

Undoubtedly inspired by Fisk and Hampton, other college groups also published collections representing their repertories, among them, the South Carolina Singers in 1872, the New Orleans University Singers in 1881, and Helen W. Ludlow for the Tuskegee Singers in 1884. The professional groups who published collections include Slayton's Jubilee Singers (1882), Coleman's Jubilee Singers (1883), and Jacob Sawyer's Original Nashville Students (1884). Finally, there are the large collections compiled by individuals like Marshall W. Taylor and William Eleazer Barton, and the numerous small collections that were published in both periodicals and books.

The JOURNAL OF AMERICAN FOLK-LORE and Hampton Institute's SOUTHERN WORKMAN published folksongs regularly, sometimes accompanied by extensive comment, sometimes with no comment at all.

It is worthy of note that the song collector-transcribers all avowed they "took down" the songs "directly from the lips of the ex-slave singers"; that the songs were being "recorded for the first time, from memory, by student ex-slave singers"; that the songs had "not been before reduced to music." They commented on the difficulties involved in trying to capture on a musical staff the complicated rhythms and illusive pitches of the slave songs, and how the songs were never performed twice in the same way.

Collectors of song texts met with similar difficulties in trying to pin down exactly the words they heard from the singers' lips and to decipher the dialectal forms. In the absence of evidence to the contrary, we may assume that the songs gathered during the years 1860s-1880s represent the initial attempts to preserve the slave-song repertory, and that the songs were transcribed from the lips of the ex-slaves. In later years writers would turn to published collections for their musical examples rather than attempting to obtain them directly from ex-slave informants.

Collectively, what these publications did was to establish African-American folksong as a distinctive repertory with its own special features, making it possible to put the body of songs in historical and socio-cultural context, to discuss its performance practice, and analyze it musically in the same way as other repertories are treated. The folkloristic activities of the compilers not only preserved for posterity a repertory that was in danger of disappearing, they gave it a dignity, a respectability that lifted it from its original level of a trivial, even nonsensical, folk expression (as many regarded it) to the level of a unique American folk music.

For researchers, the importance of gaining access to nineteenth-century texts of the slave songs, tales, and sermons cannot be overemphasized. The Bibliography makes the process easier by providing indexes to the collections and listing page references for texts in the annotations. Along with the published slave narratives, the oral creative expression of the slaves offers incredible riches as primary material for the examination of slave life and thought.

The Collecting of Folk Tales. Amateur folklorists of the 1860s extended their cultural explorations into fields other than song; at the same time as some collectors were gathering the "quaint, genuine negro songs," others were turning up examples of the folk tales slaves had been sharing around their campfires for generations. During the years 1868-70 a series of anonymous articles, all entitled "Negro Fables," appeared without comment in the RIVERSIDE MAGAZINE FOR YOUNG PEOPLE. The ten tales, which were gathered on the South Carolina Sea Islands, are about Brer Rabbit and his friends, and may well represent the earliest publication in history of Brer Rabbit tales. Again the Sea Islands emerge as a place of historical importance---the locale for a pioneering venture in the gathering of slave folktales as well as the slave folksongs.

Within the decade, other rabbit tales began to appear: in 1870 Thaddeus Norris included two such tales in an article about Negro superstition, one of them, the classic "Brer Rabbit and the Tar Baby"; during the year 1875-76 Abigail Holmes Christensen published four tales starring the rabbit and his cohorts; in 1877 came an article about Negro folklore by William Owens, which included seven tales about Buh Rabbit and company; and in 1878 Anna Porter published five tales, among them, another version of "Brer Rabbit and the Tar Baby". The same year saw the first publication of an Uncle Remus sketch by Joel Chandler Harris, an editor at the ATLANTA CONSTITUTION. In addition to rabbit tales, the periodical literature of the 1870s includes Negro tales about men, conjuring, and ghosts.

The year 1880 brought a landmark in the history of Afro-American folklore with the publication in book format of UNCLE REMUS, HIS SONGS AND SAYINGS by Harris. At the same time, it marked the beginning of a new epoch: thereafter, Brer Rabbit and friend Uncle Remus would be permanently associated with Harris, despite evidence that Brer Rabbit had flourished long before coming to the attention of Harris. According to some scholars, Harris was influenced by earlier collectors, particularly William Owens.

In a review of the Harris book, William Francis Allen observes that its dialect, representing the area of Atlanta, Georgia (Harris's home ground) differed from the dialect used by Brer Rabbit in the Sea Island collections. Although Atlanta became the natural habitat of Harris's Brer Rabbit, the canny rabbit did not easily part company with the Sea Islands: during the 1880s-90s two major collections gathered on the Islands appeared in print, NEGRO MYTHS FROM THE GEORGIA COAST (1888) by Charles C. Jones and AFRO-AMERICAN FOLKLORE, TOLD ROUND CABIN FIRES ON THE SEA ISLANDS OF SOUTH CAROLINA (1892) by Abigail Christensen. Other important collectors of the time were Alcee Fortier, who contributed a new genre to the literature with his creole songs and tales, and Mary Alicia Owen, a specialist who collected voodoo tales.

Through the 1890s, Brer Rabbit tales appeared from time to time in periodical literature, some of Sea Islands origin, others collected in Virginia, Louisiana, and of course Georgia. Additionally, the repertory was enlarged by other Negro tale types: about preachers, witches, ghosts, the creation, men and animals, men and women, the slave John and his master, and any number of "why" and "how" tales; for example, "Why some men are black," "Why the rabbit has a short tale," "How the Negro got the name of coon."

Professional and amateur folklorists became increasingly curious about the origin of the slave tales as more of the tales were published, and they presented their views on the platforms of national and international folklore congresses, as well as in the press. Most frequently, the issue debated was whether the tales should be traced to Africa or Europe, and if both traditions were involved, which had exerted the stronger influence.

In the racist climate of the time, some scholars were reluctant to concede that slaves could have produced such an impressive body of literature, and found it important to prove that the slaves had learned the tales from their white masters. It should be observed that a few collectors were interested in investigating the similarities of themes found in Indian and Afro-American tales.

Unlike the slave-music collectors, folktale enthusiasts had no recourse to a large number of professional journals for publishing their findings. But the JOURNAL OF AMERICAN FOLK-LORE and the SOUTHERN WORKMAN could be relied upon to publish tales regularly, and the general interest monthlies published tales from time to time.

All in all, more than 400 Negro tales were published and discussed in print during the last third of the nineteenth century, excluding those of Joel Chandler Harris. This number of course seems paltry when compared to the hundreds of folksongs that were published, but the tale collections nevertheless provided a solid base for building a distinctive, Negro folktale repertory in the future.

The Negro Theme in Literature. The publication of Negro folktales had a significant and lasting impact on southern literature: in the 1880s, for example, white southerners began to use Negro themes in their writings, particularly the poetry and short stories. In the vanguard were John Alfred Macon, author of UNCLE GABE TUCKER; OR, REFLECTION, SONG, AND SENTIMENT IN THE QUARTERS (1883); Irwin Russell, author of the long narrative poem "Christmas Night in the Quarters"(1888); and Thomas Nelson Page and Armistead Gordon, authors of BEFO' DE WAR. ECHOES IN NEGRO DIALECT (1891). As suggested by these titles, writers used Negro dialect as the chosen language for the genre, employed imagery that reflected plantation traditions, and quoted liberally from slave songs, tales, and sermons. These practices established a vogue for what might be labeled the "plantation-school style" that lasted for many decades.

During the 1890s the movement broadened to include black poets, among them, James Edwin Campbell, ECHOES FROM THE CABIN (1895); Daniel Webster Davis, WEH DOWN SOUF AND OTHER POEMS (1897), and Paul Laurence Dunbar, most of whose published work belongs to the twentieth century. Ultimately, Dunbar of course would become the uncrowned poet laureate of the genre.

The Post-Emancipation Black Church. Few post-Civil War writings that commented on black folk culture failed to take notice of its religious rituals. Writers attempted to give realistic portrayals of the eloquent, charismatic preacher, half-speaking and half-chanting his sermons, astounding listeners with his thorough knowledge of the Scriptures despite his inability to read the Bible. One intrepid commentator, poet Sidney Lanier, even ventured to record on the musical staff a few phrases of a "typical negro sermon," with its characteristic, gradual transition from speech to "speech-song."

Observers discussed the congregational antiphonal responses to the preacher: the moans, groans, and hearty cries of "Amen," "Oh, glory," and "Yes, Lord." They remarked the torrential outbursts of song, which were accompanied by foot-tapping, hand-clapping, and a swaying of the body, all in time to the music. They discussed the congregation's singing of "improvised hymns" called spirituals in addition to the standard hymns of Watts, the Wesleys, and their contemporaries. And they wrote endlessly about the ever-lasting shout.

As in antebellum times, writers fell back on the use of quotation to make their accounts both credible and entertaining, relying especially on dialectal language. More than 100 sermons and exhortations are summarized or excerpted in post-emancipation literature, and, additionally, a considerable number are referred to by title or function (that is, funeral, baptism, wedding). Some sources cite the Biblical texts on which the sermons were based.

When the published antebellum-sermon repertory is joined to that of the post-Emancipation period, there results a corpus that offers extraordinary insight into the theology of black folk preaching. The sources report on the aspirations of the preacher in delivering God's messages to his congregation; of the themes returned to again and again; of his choice of biblical narrative, imagery, and language; and of the structure of his sermon.

Early in its history, the black church had begun to distinguish between the manuscript or "book" sermon and the improvised "spiritual" sermon (see above under The Antebellum Black Church). The deciding factor was not the educational preparation of the preacher---a good illiterate preacher would have memorized the Bible---but rather the deliberate choice of the minister and his congregation.

By mid-century, there had developed a widespread tradition for the "spiritual" sermon, and a number of them were passed from preacher to preacher in the same way as other oral forms were disseminated. Using traditional themes and structural outlines, the sermons allowed for the preacher's spontaneous improvisation on subject matter and format even as he addressed the congregation.

The best known sermons of the 1880s-90s were: (1) Adam and Eve in the Garden of Eden, (2) The barren fig tree, (3) Dry bones in de valley, (4) Daniel in the lion's den, (5) The eagle stirreth her nest, (6) Horse a pawin' in de valley, (7) The prodigal son, and (8) The resurrection of Christ. Some of these sermons were still circulating in the 1920s and '30s (Oliver 1984, 140-68).

Possibly the earliest reference to a spiritual sermon is the one that appears in an eighteenth-century document. Issac P. Cook, in an article about the celebrated exhorter "Black Harry" Hosier, identifies the sermon delivered by Harry at a Baltimore Methodist Conference in April 1781 as "The barren fig tree." Several decades later, in 1846, we find another reference to a traditional sermon: the Englishman Charles Lyell, after visiting the Baptist Church at Savannah (Georgia), describes the sermon of the minister, Andrew Marshall, as delivered "without notes, in good style" and indicates it was based on the theme of "an eagle teaching her newly fledged offspring to fly" in quite an unorthodox manner. Known in the oral tradition as "The eagle stirreth her nest," this sermon may well have originated with Marshall, one of the most celebrated black preachers of his time.

The northern clergyman George Washington Smalley seems to have been the first to give tacit recognition to the concept of traditional sermons when, in 1867, he published an article entitled "Negro Sermons." The practice of collecting and publishing traditional or "spiritual" sermons, however, became common only much later.

Typically, sermon collections of the nineteenth century include the output of only the compiler: for example, Lucius Holsey's gathering includes fifteen of his sermons and thirteen addresses, and John Jasper's biography contains summaries of many of his sermons. Most frequently, sermons are quoted in articles that treat some aspect of ex-slave religious rites, and occasionally an author will quote from as many as three or four sermons.

Of the several preachers who became widely known for their preaching skills, none was more celebrated than John Jasper, ex-slave minister of the African Baptist Church in Richmond, Virginia, particularly for his famous sermon "De Sun Do Move." Others were Henry Evans, Ralph Freeman, and the Lucius Holsey mentioned above. Frequently, writers identify the celebrated preachers only by first name, prefixed by the title "Uncle."

The literature of the post-Emancipation period reflects ever so gently a growing dissension in the institutional black church after Emancipation. As the century unfolded, it became evident that two distinct approaches to worship were evolving in the church: On the one hand, there was the folk church, direct heir to the plantation praise-cabin and brush arbor traditions, which gloried in its old-time ways, self-educated preachers, and emotionalism in worship. On the other hand there was slowly developing a church for the newly educated, which aspired to modernize its services, educate its pastorate, and discard the old-time ways.

In retrospect, it seems clear that underlying the tension was the issue of whether the Africanisms that had infused antebellum religious practices should be retained or rejected after Emancipation. The literature includes more articles than ever before on voodoo cermonies; African-style burial rites; foot-washing and baptism ceremonies; and the shout, with its many variants---"marching out of Egypt," "marchin' round Jericho," the "dead march," and "rockin' Daniel."

S. A. Martson reports on instances where rural preachers refused to share their pulpits with preachers who "used books" (that is, Bibles and hymnals) in preparing their sermons, so great was the animosity of the former against the latter. At the same time, there were reports on churches whose members had abandoned the shouting and other religious excesses, and on places where the old plantation spirituals no longer were sung, being replaced with gospel hymns.

Post-Emancipation Social Activities. Although an enormous amount of attention was given in the literature to the religious concerns of the emancipated slaves, it does not follow that all ex-slaves gave up secular song and dance. On the contrary, secular activities remained very much alive in ex-slave communities. Novelists, historians, travelers, journalists, and autobiographers---caught up in the huge waves of nostalgia that engulfed many in the post-Civil War period, particularly the Southerners---describe with vivid detail the cornshuckings, juba pattin', and jig and shuffle dancing that had taken place on antebellum plantations, and continued to thrive after the war.

There also were writers who looked back to the eighteenth century, recalling in print the colorful, African-style Pinkster, John Canoe, and Congo Plaza festivals that had flourished in by-gone days.

Fortunately, at least a few writers of the time had a sharp eye for the changes that came with the freedom of blacks, and it is from them that we learn the names of the new dances and the kinds of instruments that were added to the ubiquitous fiddle-banjo-bones combination to provide dance music on the plantation.

Most stylish of the new dances was the cakewalk, which was destined to become one of the western world's most popular society dances by the turn of the century. In December 1870, the date of our earliest reference, it was described as a "festival peculiar to the colored race," which took place annually during the Christmas holidays at Richmond, Virginia. Later reports, which come primarily from the periodical press, indicate that the cakewalk was not confined to Virginia but was widespread throughout the South.

Francis Frederick, author of a slave narrative published in 1869, offers an intriguing description of an antebellum plantation dance he saw in the 1850s that has the earmarks of the cakewalk, but is not so identified by name. The participants "promenaded in couples, putting on remarkable and grotesque airs." The only missing element here is the awarding of a cake to the winning couple as a prize.

Other new dance types frequently mentioned in post-war writings include the breakdown, hoedown, pigeon-wing, ragging dance, and variants of the shuffle. The new instruments added to the plantation dance-music combination include the harmonica, accordion, quills, and jews harp. The tambourine and triangle become more common, and while the fiddle remains the leading dance instrument, the guitar and mandolin begin to compete with the banjo as accompanying instruments. And, as in antebellum times, the folk musicians who could not afford to buy instruments crafted their own.

Emancipation brought a new kind of black folk musician to the attention of the public: free to wander wherever he chose, he did so in such large numbers as to compose a new class---the street musician. Traveling alone, or in groups as small as a couple and as large as ten or more, these itinerant music vendors roamed the nation from north to south, and east to west, responding to requests to play the popular music of the day, while at the same time transferring their plantation music repertory and traditions to the nation's streets. Consequently, the public gradually came to know a greater variety of plantation music than had ever been known in the past.

The phenomenon occasioned some lively combinations: a banjoist accompanied by a harmonica player, a single man playing a harmonica and triangle simultaneously, bottle and jug bands composed wholly of boys, and adult string and brass bands. One unusual practice resulted in "chin" music, wherein the music-makers produced vocal sounds by manipulating the larnx and cheeks, all the while tapping the feet to provide a rhythm accompaniment. Street soloists included both the whistler and the singer, who sang a capella or to the accompaniment of his banjo or guitar.

Controversies over Black Folk Music. With all the attention given by the press to the music of the newly emergent freedmen, it is not surprising that among the cognocenti disagreements would arise from time to time about some aspect of the ex-slave music or its musical practices. During the year 1883-84 it was the "Banjo Controversy" over which instrument, the banjo or fiddle, was the premier plantation instrument. It began in December 1883 when Joel Chandler Harris published an article, "Plantation Music and the Banjo," in which he stated that slaves did not play banjoes and bones on antebellum plantations in Georgia, but rather fiddles, fifes, and quills. Almost immediately a southern novelist challenged Harris's statement in a letter to the editor. His response provoked another, which in turn provoked others. Finally, no fewer than six letters to the editor had been published over the next few months, each writer staking out a claim for the fiddle or the banjo to be the supreme instrument on the plantations in his area of the country.

Ten years later a weightier controversy filled the pages of the newspaper and periodical presses, one that had serious repercussions. In May 1893, Czech composer Antonin Dvorak, at that time musical director of the National Conservatory of Music in New York City, gave a response that evoked considerable concern among professional musicians when he was questioned about the possibility of founding a "national school of composition" in the United States. Saying he had given the matter much thought, he stated that he was

> satisfied...that the future music of this country must be founded upon what are called the negro melodies. This must be the real foundation of any serious and original school of composition to be developed in the United States.

The nation's music establishment generally was incensed over the idea that a national school of music should be based on a Negro slave music, and reacted immediately, indignantly, and vociferously. The MUSICAL RECORD (Boston) published responses from nine eminent composers within the next three months---of which all attacked Dvorak's posture. Music historians, critics, composers and concert artists made known their stance, and the debate lasted in the press, both popular and serious, for many years, stimulated by even more provocative pronouncements from Dvorak in 1895.

Generally, the arguments narrowed down to two points of view: First, Negro folksong could not serve as a basis for a national school of American music because it was an inferior music and not truly American; white folk music was the only genuine folk expression of the United States. Second, Negro folksong was unacceptable because it was not the slaves original music, but merely a copy of the white man's song.

Ironically, only a few decades earlier the press had been filled with praise for the originality and the expressive power of the slave songs. Unlike the slave-song collectors of the 1860s, the late-nineteenth-century authorities on slave music did not go among black folk to record the old slave songs, but rather based their discussion on analysis of the music available in such collections as those of the Fisk Jubilee Singers and Hampton Institute Students.

Post-Emancipation Iconography of Black Culture. No fewer than 238 artworks produced in the post-Emancipation period portray some aspect of black-American culture. More than a third of the artworks deal with religious matters; the remainder depict recreational and work activities, and various kinds of social portraiture. As in the antebellum period, the artists and illustrators favored genre painting as the best way to show the circumstances of everyday life for the ex-slaves.

The works fall into three categories: (1) the engraved illustration used to illuminate texts of books and magazine articles; (2) the engraved illustration produced independently of a text; and (3) the painting. The function of the second type of illustration was to tell a story, like the painting, but it was commissioned by a publisher and issued in the popular magazines.

Particularly informative are the pictorial essays of this period, which present a sequence of pictures related to a single theme as, for example, the five-scene "Georgia---The Cultivation of Rice---Work in the Field and Mill." The fourth scene of this essay, Georgiana Davis's "Courtyard of a Rice Mill. The Noon Hour" (1883), shows men and women dancing during their lunch-break.

During the early 1860s, the war engaged the primary attention of artists and illustrators. The Bibliography contains entries for about twenty paintings and engraved illustrations of war scenes that bring to notice some view of black culture. Both sides are represented: the Confederacy in such works as "The South as Secession Found It and as It Leaves It (1863, anonymous) and "Night Amusements in the Confederate Camp" (1863, Frank Vizetelly); the Union forces in works like "A Bivouac Fire on the Potomac" (1861, Winslow Homer), "Yanks Expedition---Extempore Musical and Terpsichorean Entertainment at the U.S. Arsenal..." (1862, Francis Schell), and "War in Louisiana" (1864, anonymous). Contrabands are pictured in both sportive scenes, as in the anonymous "Work's Over---Scenes among the Beaufort Contrabands" (1861), and religious scenes, as William Sheppard's "Prayer Meeting in a Contraband Camp---Washington, 1862."

Generally these Civil War works belong to the "picturesque" tradition in that they depict the ex-slaves in sentimentalized or stereotypical scenes. There are exceptions, however; to cite instances, Homer's painting, "Defiance: Inviting a Shot before Petersburg, Virginia," with its heroic black banjoist (1864), and Thomas Nast's two versions of a military event involving music, "Entrance of the Fifty-Fifth Massachusetts (Colored) Regiment into Charleston, S. C., February 21, 1865."

Even before the war had ended, artists began to turn their attention to other themes. A painting by William Carlton, entitled "Watch Meeting, December 31, 1862," captures the poignancy of a small group of men and women gathered together for a worship service on the eve of Emancipation. Nast's celebrated illustration, "Family Worship on a Plantation in South Carolina" (1863), gives no hint that not too far away a war was tearing the nation apart. Other artists, too, looked more closely at a South that would disappear with the emancipation of the slaves, among them, John Ehninger in "Old Kentucky Home" (1863), and John Pettie in "Kalampin, the Negro" (1863).

After the war, publishers sent their artist-reporters south, along with the journalists, to report on the status of the freedmen, and the drawings they made were engraved not only for publication in the popular magazines, but also in the nostalgic fictional and biographical writing that poured from the presses during the 1870s-90s. Particularly were they called on to illustrate books about the old slave festivals of colonial days ---New England's 'Lections, New York's Pinkster Days, North Carolina's John Canoe events, Congo Square dancing in New Orleans and, above all, plantation life in the South "befo' de war." Outdoor or indoor plantation scenes are represented in the Bibliography by some thirty or more artworks.

Wood engravings account for the large majority of the post-Emancipation illustrations discussed in the Bibliography. Other processes represented include the lithograph, pen-and-ink, wash, crayon, and mixed media. In the 1890s, photographs began to replace engravings in publications, and the Bibliography lists several, along with two stereographs.

Judging from the pictorial evidence (which the literary evidence confirms), Emancipation brought few changes in the social habits of black folk: dancing remained their favorite pastime, not only because it was one of the few outlets available to them but also because they genuinely enjoyed the dance. They also enjoyed making music, telling tales around the campfire, hunting, and celebrating at harvest time with such activities as corn-shucking and log-rolling festivals.

Artworks of the period also reflect the new occupational pursuits of the ex-slaves, which took them away from the plantation to urban areas and frontiers, where they worked in factories, on the wharves and riverboats, on the streets as peddlers, in the logging camps, and in oyster-fishing grounds. As discussed above, street musicians wandered widely over the land after Emancipation, entertaining on street corners, in hotels and bars, at train stops, and even on the trains.

Preeminent among the illustrators in terms of both quantity and quality of output was Edward Windsor Kemble, with William Ludlow Sheppard running a close second. Like most of the illustrators mentioned in the bibliography, these men had been well trained in the fine arts before entering the commercial art field. A few painters also won success during this period as freelance illustrators, among them, Winslow Homer and Alfred R. Waud.

After the war, painters and illustrators renewed the interest that they had initiated in the 1850s in depicting cultural activities of the blacks. Apparently they preferred to paint portraits ---of dancers, banjoists, guitarists, fiddlers, and preachers---and domestic genre scenes involving a few figures. The few large-group genre paintings on record most frequently depict religious services.

During the last quarter of the nineteenth century, certain themes became popular with both painters and illustrators, foremost among them, the representation of children, particularly small boys. The boys are pictured dancing with each other; dancing with girls; dancing with adults; taking dancing lessons; teaching each other to dance; playing fiddle, banjo, guitar, triple-coil horn, and mandolin; playing in boy bands; singing, whistling, and producing "chin music"; interacting with adolescent boys; interacting with adults; interacting with white adults and children; and participating in work activities. Additionally, they appear in scenes where the main focus is on adults and children have secondary roles, as, for example, in forming "second liners" in parades.

Another theme popular with artists and illustrators, and obviously the public as well, was the dance, particularly as the scene focused on the specialist dancer. The dance illustrations feature a wide variety of types, from the formal ball to the lone individual who dances for self-amusement, without musical accompaniment, in a deserted field.

In some pictures, couples and/or singles display their special skills in front of other dancers; in other pictures, they dance before spectators, as for example, in Arthur Frost's "The Cakewalk" (1892). In all instances, the artists seem to have taken painstaking care to depict the correct poses and movements of the breakdown, hoedown, pigeon-wing, bamboula, juba, and other dances of the time. Rarely are women shown as solo dancers, but occasionally a dancing couple is composed of two women.

Few, if any, of the artworks of this period reflect the turmoil and bitterness of the Reconstruction Era and the hostility met by the ex-slaves in a society reluctant to accept them as American citizens. Except in a few instances, white and black meet on the canvas and magazine page in the same roles they had been given before Emancipation---black folk are entertainers and whites are appreciative spectators. It is noteworthy, however, that when the ex-slaves are shown in segregated activities, such as religious services or dances and holiday celebrations, they are more likely to be caricatured than was true in the antebellum era.

From the vantage point of the present, it can be seen that the years 1850s-70s represent the heyday of the fine arts movement to record pictorial details of black cultural life in the United States ---if it can be called a movement. Certainly, for some thirty years or more, artists of all schools were caught up in the national maelstrom of controversy over the black folk whose condition of slavery was the root cause of the Civil War.

The artists' curiosity led many of them into the South, where they visited plantations, went into army camps, and walked city streets in search of the exotic people discussed so heatedly in the popular and serious literature of the time. A number had come from abroad: Englishmen John Antrobus, James Clooney, and Eyre Crowe; Irish Thomas Hovenden; and the Swiss Franz Buchser. Others were born in the North and traveled south for the first time during this period, among them, George Fuller, Winslow Homer, and John Ehninger.

The interests of painters in depicting black culture had developed slowly over the years. To summarize: three paintings are extant from the eighteenth century, of which two are anonymous; six are extant from the early nineteenth century, the works of Heriot, Krimmel, and Svin'in; and seven have come down to us from the decades of the thirties and forties, representing the output of Clonney, Mayr, and Mount. Then came a big outbreak of intense activity. Beginning in 1850 and continuing through the next three decades, no fewer than fifteen painters contributed to the nation's store of paintings depicting aspects of black culture, some of them with two or more works. Thereafter the number of painters involved drops dramatically: only three painters of black culture can be identified for the 1880s; for the 1890s there are only four.

By the turn of the century, paintings of American life (that is, white American life) no longer included black folk, and paintings depicting black folk exclusively had become increasingly rare. "In the early nineteenth century," art historian Patricia Hills has observed, "one or two blacks often appeared in paintings of the daily life of white people to denote the scene as specifically American" (1974, 58). And, as the Bibliography indicates, paintings and illustrations of the nineteenth century that focused on the black folk artist frequently show whites in the background ---slaveholders, travelers, rural neighbors, people on city streets, soldiers ---forming appreciative and generally admiring onlookers.

But with the changes brought about by Emancipation, Americans felt compelled to reexamine the position of black folk in mainstream society and to work out ways to keep them in their "rightful places." Hills points out:

> In terms of images, white painters had difficulties incorporating the "freed" blacks into integrated scenes of "respectable" gentility, except where they functioned as servants. The artists did not escape the hypocrisy and prejudices of their time.... It is not surprising that in the paintings of middle-class, urban life, which appeared in the 1870s and 1880s, blacks virtually disappeared (1974, 72).

It is worthy of mention that the artworks of the nineteenth century represent, for the most part, the black cultural experience as interpreted by white males---unlike the situation as regards literature, where the contributions of black writers and white women make up a significant part of the whole. Only two illustrators represented in the Bibliography can be identified as women with certainty (of course some of the anonymous work may have been produced by women), and only one black artist, Henry Ossawa Tanner, is represented in the Bibliography. One can speculate that a different kind of picture might have been drawn had more minorities participated in the making of it.

This is not to say that the white male did not record the cultural-social circumstances of the slaves and freedmen as he perceived them. But some illustrators and painters, their eyes blinded by racism, were harsh in their delineations, particularly in their reliance on negative stereotypes. On the other hand, some artists were able to depict blacks with a warmth, sympathy, and noble simplicity that gave them dignity despite their lowly status. Both approaches, positive and negative, contribute to a better understanding of black folk life in the nineteenth century.

THE EARLY TWENTIETH CENTURY, 1900-1920

The closing years of the nineteenth century brought a sharp drop of public interest in the folklore of the black man as compared to previous periods. White America had other, more important, concerns: the new immigrants pouring into the country, the growing strength of the feminist movement, the social and economic dislocations caused by increasingly complex technological developments, and the transforming of the nation from an agrarian to an urban society.

Moreover, the popular press seemed to be focusing on new kinds of black cultural expression---several times removed from the slavery-time folk expression--- which were commercially successful and gave promise of appealing to mainstream society. Such terms as coon song, ragged time or ragtime, blues, vaudeville, and, later, jazz were used to describe the new styles and forms.

The Literature. The Bibliography contains 348 items published in the early twentieth century that comment upon some aspect of black folk culture. Relatively few of the works represent the views of amateurs or generalists, as in previous eras, but rather are the product of such specialists as historians, sociologists, folklorists, and professional musicians. As in earlier times, some historians kept alive memories of the old slave festivals, particularly Pinkster and 'Lection Day, in their local and regional histories. Noticeably reduced in numbers are the travel accounts that occupied such a prominent place in nineteenth-century literature.

It is noteworthy that by this time black historians had begun to contribute to the literature their own accounts of their people's history. They wrote histories of the Negro (Benjamin Brawley, W. E. B. DuBois, Booker T. Washington); of the black church (DuBois, Carter G. Woodson); and of black denominations, such as the A.M.E. Church (Levi Coppin, Charles Smith) and black Baptists (William Hicks). In 1915 Woodson joined with four scholars to found the Association for the Study of Negro Life and History, and served as the first editor of its JOURNAL OF NEGRO HISTORY, which began circulation in 1916.

The white memorists of this period, and there are more than two dozen, seem caught in a web of nostalgia for the antebellum days: they write of plantation festivals, Christmas celebrations, slave weddings, funerals, and colorful religious services. Mostly these chroniclers were ex-slaveholders, and their numbers included quite a few women, who were either slaveholders themselves or daughters of slaveholders. Black men, too, turned to the past in their slave narratives, of which about fifteen were published during this period, giving considerable attention to plantation life "befo' de war," especially as regards religious matters.

The nonfiction pieces and short stories generally employ the same themes as the books, those dealing with the antebellum life being most numerous. For the most part, the novelists and poets also seemed to prefer reliving the past rather than concerning themselves with contemporary developments. Significantly, writers no longer had to go into the field to secure the examples of folklore that brought credibility to their writings; they simply consulted one of the many collections available in print.

By the turn of the twentieth century Afro-American folklore had been accepted by the academic establishment as a legitimate subject for scholarly inquiry, and its historiography was beginning to take shape. Within a few years it would have its own canon, its own methodology, its distinctive repertories, and its inner circles of research specialists. The day of the cultivated amateur, whose folklore-collecting in the nineteenth century contributed to its survival, was coming to an end---his place taken by the professionals, particularly the anthropologists, sociologists, musicologists, and folklorists.

The Collecting of Folklore. The vogue for song collecting that had begun after the Civil War gained momentum in the early twentieth century. Almost three-dozen collections are listed in the Bibliography, and because several of the collections were very large, the total count of songs represents a considerable increase over the number published in the post-Emancipation period. The collections come from a variety of sources: institutions, both educational and religious; touring concert companies; professional musicians, music critics, and composers; university and independent scholars and folklorists; and amateur enthusiasts.

Hampton Institute continued to publish new, enlarged editions of its original collections, and additionally commissioned folklorist Natalie Curtis Burlin to gather more songs from the Hampton students and to make cylinder recordings of the songs. New printings of the revised and enlarged edition of the FISK JUBILEE SONGS (1892) continued to appear, but the major work of collecting new songs in the Nashville (Tennessee) area was taken over by members of the Work family---Frederick Jerome Work and John Wesley Work II, the latter a faculty member at Fisk University---who produced three large collections.

For the first time, a secondary school, the Calhoun Colored School in Alabama, joined the ranks of institutional collectors, with Emily Hallowell as the compiler-transcriber. Also for the first time, the black church entered the arena: the National Baptist Publishing Board released a collection of 160 songs "obtained from the various rice, cane, and cotton plantations of the South" by K. D. Reddick and Phil Lindsley in order "to save the old slave songs for posterity."

Concert companies continued to publish their repertories; among them, the N. Clark Smith choral groups, William Carter's Canadian Jubilee Singers, and the [Charles] Williams' Jubilee Singers. Independent scholar-collectors published songs in both article and book format; and even amateurs had little difficulty in finding publishers for their gatherings.

The new element in all this song collecting was it was engaging the attention of scholars and professionals for the first time. In their writings John Avery Lomax, Howard Odum, E. C. Perrow, and John Wesley Work, among others, help to place Negro song in socio-cultural context, discuss basic elements of the folksong and its types, and describe performance practice. The Reverend Henry Hugh Proctor and others develop theories about the theology of the songs and the spiritual meaning. Twentieth-century collectors often made special efforts to search out secular songs as well as the traditional spirituals, and as a consequence discovered new types of worksongs and field hollers, and a new form called the blues.

In the field of music, newly founded professional journals, such as the MUSICIAN, MUSICAL QUARTERLY, MUSICAL AMERICA, MUSICAL OBSERVER, and the ETUDE, provided a forum for scholars who approached the discussion of Negro folksong from a musicological viewpoint, under such topics as "American Folksong" (Louis C. Elson), "Folk Song and American Music" (Daniel Gregory Mason), and "Capturing the Spirit of Real Negro Music" (John Tasker Howard).

Literary journals, like the LITERARY DIGEST and NEW REPUBLIC, welcomed serious discussion of Negro folklore, as did also the new educational magazines, historical quarterlies, and folklore journals. Scholars contributed articles on black folksong to the giant reference books, GROVE'S DICTIONARY OF MUSIC AND MUSICIANS and HISTORY OF AMERICAN MUSIC, and some gave space to discussion of Negro folksong in their one-volume music histories (Elson). The popular magazines continued to offer a platform for less serious discussion of Negro folkways.

Some of the debates that had been conducted through the media in the late nineteenth century carried over into the twentieth: Did Negro folksong have African origins or was it simply an imitation of white folksong? Was Negro folksong worthy to serve as the basis for an American school of music? Was there danger of "spiritual corruption" when composers made concert harmonizations of Negro spirituals? Should trained composers use Negro themes in their compositions?

Writers also posed new questions and advanced new arguments in editorials, letters to the editor, the articles they published in journals, and the papers they read at scholarly conferences: What was this new music called ragtime? How did it relate to Negro folksong and to American music in general? What changes in the black man's lifestyle accounted for the emergence of the blues?

In 1914, music critic Henry Krehbiel published a book, AFRO-AMERICAN FOLK SONG, which brought together the several strands of folk-music research underway at that time, and suggested the direction in which future scholarly inquiry might move. His critical study includes: the collection of data and its interpretation; musical analysis; statistical classification; evaluation of the historical, cultural, and societal contexts in which the songs developed; and a set of representative examples. The book is a landmark in the historiography of Afro-American folksong, and presents a model for future investigation.

A different kind of musical analysis is offered by black sociologist W. E. B. DuBois in THE SOULS OF BLACK FOLK (1903), which is no less a landmark in its own way than the Krehbiel study. In Chapter 14, "Of the Sorrow Songs," DuBois poses a question and answers it:

> What are these songs, and what do they mean? I know little of music and can say nothing in technical phrase, but I know something of men, and knowing them, I know that these songs are the articulate message of the slave to the world ([1903] 1965, 380).

He observes that despite the protestations of modern scholars that "life was joyous to the black slave," the songs bear "heart-touching witness" to a different reality:

> They are the music of an unhappy people, of the children of disappointment; they tell of death and suffering and unvoiced longing toward a truer world, of misty wanderings and hidden ways ([1903] 1965, 380).

DuBois offers searching insight into the history of the slave songs and discusses the various types and their musical and textual features, giving particular attention to a group he identifies as "ten master songs."

Although the collecting of Negro tales lagged behind song collecting, the relatively few folklorists who went into the field to gather tales compensated for their small numbers by their industry and enthusiasm. In addition to such professional folklorists as Alcee Fortier and Elsie Clems Parsons, several black classroom teachers and university professors became involved. They collected tales from their students and from ex-slaves in the community, and encouraged their students to collect from friends and family.

Two major collections resulted from the revived interest in collecting Negro tales: Thomas Talley's NEGRO FOLK RHYMES and William John Faulkner's THE DAYS THE ANIMALS TALKED, which, although published after our terminal date, are included in the Bibliography because of their historical importance. Both collectors were faculty members of Fisk University, which was noted as a center for its folkloristic activity as well in the field of music.

Contributions representing the black perspective on the tales also are to be found in the works of poets Junius Mord Allen and Joseph Cotter, of Charles Chesnutt the novelist, and of course the renowned Paul Laurence Dunbar. Finally, it should be noted that the nation's ex-slave population offered a particularly rich source of folklore. Gathered from all parts of the South, Negro folktales were published mostly in the JOURNAL OF AMERICAN FOLKLORE, but a scattering also appeared in the SOUTHERN WORKMAN and in such black magazines as the CRISIS, COLORED AMERICAN MAGAZINE, and ALEXANDER'S MAGAZINE. Additionally, a half-dozen or so collections were published in book format.

The New Black Church. The subject of the contemporary Negro's religion seemed to possess a strange fascination for writers of this period, and it received more attention in print than any other single subject. Scholars, white and black, comment on the nature of the black man's religion, its distinctive features, how the old-time religion compares to the present-day religion, and the influence of African traditions on contemporary religious rituals. Sociologists especially evince concern for the "spiritual world" in which the black man lived at the beginning of the twentieth century (W. E. B. DuBois, Robert Park).

The ever-articulate DuBois discusses at great length the characteristics of Negro religious life in his THE SOULS OF BLACK FOLK---this, in addition to his other major publications on the black church. "Three things," he points out, "characterized this religion of the slave---the Preacher, the Music, and the Frenzy." Most important of these elements was the Frenzy or "Shouting," which occurred when the "Spirit of the Lord" seized the devotee, and made him "mad with supernatural joy." Believers knew that "without this visible manifestation of the God there could be no true communion with the Invisible" ([1903] 1965, 338-39).

In the numerous discussions of black religion published during this period there are indications that the old-time slave religion still retained its power over the masses. Some churchmen protest the "excessive emotionalism" in the worship service; the popularity of the shout and its variants such as "Rockin' Daniel; the "mystic preachers" and their "apocalyptic sermons"; and the prevalence of voodoo rites. There is ongoing concern about the lack of educational opportunities for black religious leaders and the shortage of trained preachers.

Other writers find positive elements in the folk church---the power of the "chanted" sermons and prayers, the distinctive quality of the improvised songs of preacher and congregation, the African survivals in religious practices.

Several sources include reports on the traditional sermons in oral circulation among black preachers. Phoebe Estes's biography of legendary Peter Vinegar, for example, contains fragments of four sermons he preached and refers to sixteen additional ones delivered either by him or by contemporaries. At least two of the sermons were known to nineteenth-century preachers, "The eagle stirreth her nest" and "Dry bones in de valley," and further research undoubtedly would uncover more.

Iconography of Black Culture in the Early Twentieth Century. By 1900 it was evident that the worlds of the fine arts and the illustrated press had lost interest in the black man's culture. Seventy-eight artworks made during the years 1900-20 can be identified as picturizing some aspect of African-American oral traditions. This number of course contrasts greatly with the much larger number of black-culture-related artworks produced during the previous era. Photographs account for about half the total; eight are paintings; three, artifacts; and the remainder, illustrations that employ mixed-media techniques, pen-and-ink, and the like.

The number of popular magazines that regularly published items relating to black culture had dwindled to a very few by this period, and at the same time, fewer writers were commissioning artists to illustrate books about black folklore. Authors largely dictated the subject matter of early twentieth-century illustrations and, as we have seen, they consistently turned to the antebellum past, evoking nostalgic memories of the "good ol' times" had by all, white and black, in the old South.

Consequently, the artists and illustrators offer scenes peopled with the old plantation types---banjoists, fiddlers, preachers, and singers---but, significantly, rarely including whites except in Uncle Remus pictures. Some books, along with the SOUTHERN WORKMAN, published photographs which show contemporary, all-black scenes of children at play and in school, of World War I soldiers, street vendors, and community figures. These proved to be predictive of future directions for pictorial portrayals of black life and culture.

With the second decade of the century, however, came a high point---indeed, a milestone---in the iconography of black music. The "milestone," comprising a group of paintings, had its genesis in the International Exhibition of Modern Art, better known as the Armory Show, held in 1913 at the Armory in New York City. For the first time, the American public was exposed to the avant-garde paintings and sculpture of modern European artists, and the show had a lasting impact on the development of American art.

Also for the first time, some of the artists who had come to New York to exhibit their works were exposed to Afro-American culture. Captivated by its exoticism, two of the painters from Paris,

Albert Gleizes and Francis Picabia, recorded their impressions in watercolor and oil paintings. According to available evidence, these are the earliest paintings in history of the new music called jazz.

But it was the American Charles Demuth who should be regarded as the father of pictorial jazz. During the years 1915-17 he made four watercolors of the jazzmen and singers who entertained at the Marshall's cafe in New York's Black Bohemia district. His paintings not only were the first to depict jazz combos, they also broke the taboo against showing blacks and whites together: the patrons in his nightclub scenes are integrated.

The Negro Renaissance and Beyond. With the 1920s came a watershed in the history of African-American culture: called the Negro Renaissance (also known as the Harlem Renaissance and New Negro Movement), it brought forth an extraordinary outpouring of Negro creativity in the literary and fine arts, and in music and the theatre arts. The New Negro, whose creative activities made New York City's Harlem the intellectual and cultural capital of the black world, felt himself charged with a mission to redefine the identity of his people and to assert the legitimacy of his culture (Locke [1925] 1977, 3-16).

In his rediscovered race-consciousness, the black artist acknowledged his indebtedness to the past and gave priority to exploring his history and cultural traditions. Though the most obvious manifestation of the Harlem Renaissance artist's interest in folklore was his use of Negro themes in his poetry, fiction, and music, he was well aware of the importance of scientifically collecting and analyzing the folklore. In the field of music, for example, some of the same composers who made concert arrangements of the old plantation songs in their efforts to "elevate" the folk forms to a higher level, could be found out in the field searching for new folksongs.

Apart from the Negro Renaissance movement, there was a surge of interest in Negro folklore in the 1920s, especially among academicians, and it is probable that more collections were published in that single decade than in the previous twenty years. The Bibliography's terminal date of 1920 precludes discussion of the publications, but it should be noted that the nation's first collection of blues (with both music and texts), W. C. Handy's BLUES; AN ANTHOLOGY (1926), came out during the decade.

The case of twentieth-century slave interviews is a special one, and we have bent the rules to include them in the Bibliography. Throughout the nineteenth century there are of course records of white writers interviewing slaves; some of the interviews were used as bases for slave narratives, and others were published as articles in the popular press. It was not until the years 1929-34, however, that the conducting of ex-slave interviews on a large scale got under way---initiated by four black professors: John B. Cade at Southern University in Louisiana, Charles S. Johnson at Fisk in Tennessee, J. Ralph Jones in Georgia, and Lawrence Reddick at Kentucky State College. Graduate students and in-service, public-school teachers provided a ready source of interviewing and research assistance, and the interviews generally were taken from ex-slaves who lived in areas surrounding the institutions.

In 1936 the federal government inaugurated a comprehensive, nation-wide program of collecting interviews from surviving ex-slaves under the auspices of the Federal Writer's Project of the WPA (Works Progress Administration), and appointed the folklorist John A. Lomax as director. The two-year program generated thousands of typescript-pages of interviews, which were deposited at the Library of Congress under the title The Slave Narrative Collection, and there made available to researchers for study. Over the years 1972-79 George P. Rawick published the Collection, adding to it typescript interviews he had found in state archives and similar places.

Because of the Bibliography's concentration on the slave experience, it was impossible to leave out so important a source of information about slave creative expression. There are problems, however, in regard to interpreting the data provided by the oral histories because of the long lapse of time between the ex-slave's actual experiences and the conducting of the interview when memory was beginning to fade (Blassingame, 1972, xliii). Perhaps even more significant for the present discourse is that the interviews present pieces of folklore that have been removed from their original social situation and consequently lack reliability.

We have stated elsewhere our hope that the Bibliography will sum up present knowledge of the primary-material resources available for research in the Afro-American traditions of song, tale, sermon, and dance and, at the same time, serve as a basis for continuing study of the subject. Much has been written about the black man's creative folk expression, and much of what has been written is controversial. The importance of applying careful historical method to the study of Afro-American culture cannot be overstressed. If the data collected is critically examined and evaluated, the results will be rewarding, leading to a deeper understanding of the roots of black culture and a fuller appreciation of the historical dimensions of its contemporary forms.

Writing about black folk is arduous at best. As historian Page Smith reminds us, "The tragic nature of their collective experience is so profound and the strategies they have devised for living in white America so subtle and so intricate that it is only perhaps in music and in the arts generally that one begins to fathom the excruciating reality" (1982, xvi).

Eileen Southern

Reference List

Allen, Richard. [1833] 1887. THE LIFE EXPERIENCE AND GOSPEL LABORS OF THE RT. REV. RICHARD ALLEN.... Philadelphia: A.M.E. Publishing House.

Blassingame, John W. 1972. THE SLAVE COMMUNITY. PLANTATION LIFE IN THE ANTEBELLUM SOUTH. New York: Oxford University.

Brown, Howard. 1980. "Iconography of Music." THE NEW GROVE DICTIONARY OF MUSIC AND MUSICIANS. Edited by Stanley Sadie. s.v. "Iconography." London, Macmillan Company.

Brown, William Wells. 1867. THE NEGRO IN THE AMERICAN REBELLION. Boston: Lee & Shepard.

Donaldson, Mary K. 1986. "Paintings and Illustrations of Nineteenth-Century Black Folk Culture in the U.S." Typescript.

Douglass, Frederick. [1845] 1982. NARRATIVE OF THE LIFE OF FREDERICK DOUGLASS, AN AMERICAN SLAVE. WRITTEN BY HIMSELF. New York: Penguin Books.

DuBois, W. E. B. [1903] 1965. THE SOULS OF BLACK FOLK. In THREE NEGRO CLASSICS. New York: Avon Books.

Epstein, Dena. 1977. SINFUL TUNES AND SPIRITUALS: BLACK FOLK MUSIC TO THE CIVIL WAR. Urbana: University of Illinois Press.

Higginson, Thomas Wentworth. 1870. ARMY LIFE IN A BLACK REGIMENT. Boston: Fields, Osgood, & Company.

Hills, Patricia. 1974. THE PAINTER'S AMERICA. RURAL AND URBAN LIFE, 1810-1910. New York: Praeger and Whitney Museum of American Art.

Locke, Alain, ed. [1925] 1977. THE NEW NEGRO. New York: Atheneum Books.

Oliver, Paul. 1984. SONGSTER AND SAINTS. VOCAL TRADITIONS ON RACE RECORDS. Cambridge: Cambridge University Press.

Payne, Daniel Alexander. 1888. RECOLLECTIONS OF SEVENTY YEARS. Nashville: Publishing House of the A.M.E. Sunday School.

Preston, Howard S., and Dana F. White. 1979. "Knickerbocher Illustrations of the Old South: John William Orr." In OLMSTEAD SOUTH... Edited by Dana White and Victor A. Kramer. Westport, CT: Greenwood Press.

Smith, Page. 1982. TRIAL BY FIRE. A PEOPLE'S HISTORY OF THE CIVIL WAR AND RECONSTRUCTION. New York: McGraw-Hill Book Company.

Starling, Marion Wilson. 1981. THE SLAVE NARRATIVE: ITS PLACE IN AMERICAN HISTORY. Boston: G. K. Hall.

Stuckey, Sterling. 1968. "Through the Prism of Folklore: The Black Ethos in Slavery." In MASSACHUSETTS REVIEW 9: 417-37.

Watson, John F. 1819. METHODIST ERROR .... Trenton, NJ: D. & E. Fenton.

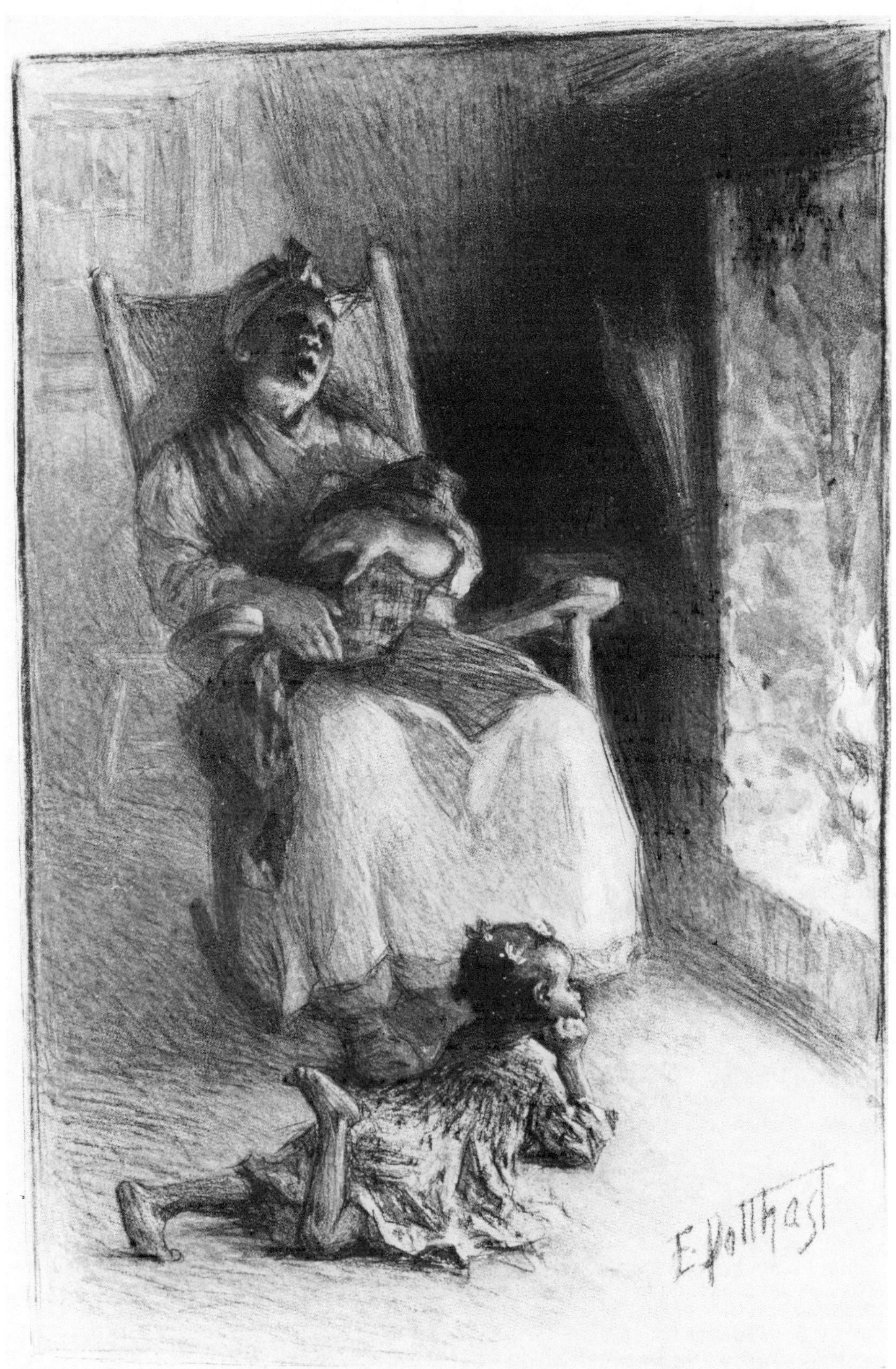

By the Fireplace

The Music for the Dance

The 'Coon Hunt

Evening at the Quarters

A Colored Preacher

A Negro Funeral

AFRICAN-AMERICAN TRADITIONS IN SONG, SERMON, TALE, AND DANCE, 1600s–1920

I

THE COLONIAL-FEDERALIST ERA

LITERATURE: 1600s–1800

SOCIAL ACTIVITIES

1 "Account of the Negroe Insurrection in Southern Carolina." THE COLONIAL RECORDS OF THE STATE OF GEORGIA..., compiled by Allen D. Candler, 22, pt. 2. Atlanta: C. P. Byrd, 1913.

In correspondence sent by James Oglethorpe to Harman Vereist, dated 9 October 1739, Savannah (Georgia), there are references to the dancing, singing, and beating on drums by Negroes participating in the Stono (South Carolina) insurrection (234).

2 Anburey, Thomas. TRAVELS THROUGH THE INTERIOR PARTS OF AMERICA BY THOMAS ANBUREY, LIEUTENANT IN THE ARMY OF GENERAL BURGOYNE. 2 vols. London: William Lane, 1789. Reprint. Boston: Houghton Mifflin Company, 1923.

British officer refers in his diary entry, dated 20 January 1779, Jane's Plantation (near Charlottesville, Virginia), to slaves playing the fiddle to amuse their owner (2:191).

3 Attmore, William. JOURNAL OF A TOUR TO NORTH CAROLINA. Edited by Lida Tunstall Rodman. James Sprunt Historical Publications, published under the direction of the North Carolina Historical Society. Chapel Hill: University of North Carolina Press, 1922. 46 pp.

English merchant, who settled in the American colonies in 1713, traveled to North Carolina in 1787 on business matters. His diary entries for December 13 and 25 refer to slave lifestyles in North and South Carolina, including African burial rites (26-27) and slaves dancing to the music of a banjo (43).

4 Bayard, Ferdinand. TRAVELS OF A FRENCHMAN IN MARYLAND AND VIRGINIA. With a Description of Philadelphia and Baltimore in 1791.... Translated and edited by Ben C. McCary. Williamsburg, VA: Printed for R. C. McCary, 1950. 182 pp.

French visitor to the United States mentions black fiddlers who played near the stage where a play was being produced by strolling Irish players (50). Also observation that blacks sang mournful love songs as they returned home tired from the day's work (84), and sang the Psalms of David in the church galleries on Sunday (87).

5 Bonnefoy, Antoine. "Journal of Antoine Bonnefoy." 1741. Translated by J. Franklin Jameson. Published in TRAVELS IN THE AMERICAN COLONIES, edited by Newton D. Mereness, 237-55. New York: Macmillan Company, 1916.

This account of a prisoner of the Cherokees, a French soldier traveling in Louisiana in 1741, includes reference to a Negro slave belonging to English traders: "a drum beaten by one of their negroes who was a drummer" (150).

6 Burnaby, Andrew. TRAVELS THROUGH THE MIDDLE SETTLEMENTS IN NORTH AMERICA. IN THE YEARS 1759 AND 1760. WITH OBSERVATIONS UPON THE STATE OF THE COLONIES. 2d ed. London: T. Payne, 1775. 198 pp. Reprint. Ithaca: Cornell University Press, 1960.

Detailed description of whites dancing "jiggs," which the author, a British clergyman, states was "a practice originally borrowed, I am informed, from the Negroes" (36). This description is repeated verbatim, without acknowledgement of its source, in A CONCISE HISTORICAL ACCOUNT OF ALL THE BRITISH COLONIES IN NORTH-AMERICA....

7 A CONCISE HISTORICAL ACCOUNT OF ALL THE BRITISH COLONIES IN NORTH-AMERICA, COMPREHENDING THEIR RISE, PROGRESS, AND MODERN STATE....London: Printed for J. Bew, 1775. 196 pp.

Observation that Virginians "are immoderately fond of dancing. Towards the close of an evening when the company are pretty well tired with country-dances, it is usual to dance jigs: a practice originally borrowed, I am informed, from the Negroes" (182-83). Description of the dance given in a footnote (183).

8 Cresswell, Nicholas. THE JOURNAL OF NICHOLAS CRESSWELL, 1774-1777. Introduction by Samuel Thornely, a Descendent. New York: Dial Press, 1924. 287 pp.

English author's comment on the black musicians he encountered during his travels in America during the years 1774-1777 includes description of a "Negro Ball" he watched in Virginia and the observations that on Sundays the blacks danced to the music of a four-string gourd banjo and their songs satirized their treatment in "very droll music" (18-19; 29 May 1774). Also references to blacks playing fiddle and banjo at a barbecue on St. Mary's River (30), to the "Negro" tunes used to accompany the "everlasting jigs" at the annual ball of the whites in Alexandria, Virginia (53), and to the funeral customs of the blacks (39-40).

9 Crevecoeur, Michel Guillaume Jean de. [J. Hector St. John, pseud.]. SKETCHES OF EIGHTEENTH CENTURY AMERICA; "MORE LETTERS FROM AN AMERICAN FARMER." Edited by Henri L. Bourdin, Ralph H. Gabriel, and Stanley T. Williams. New Haven: Yale University Press, 1925. 342 pp.

This French farmer lived during the years c.1759-80 in Orange County, New York; returned to France in 1780; then re-settled in New York after the Revolutionary War. His first publication was LETTERS FROM AN AMERICAN FARMER (London, 1782). In this second book about his experiences in New York, he comments on the "Negro fiddle" (96) and on blacks sharing in the festivities of their masters, although they also held "their own meetings" (148).

10 Equiano, Olaudah. THE INTERESTING NARRATIVE OF THE LIFE OF OLAUDAH EQUIANO, OR GUSTAVUS VASSA, THE AFRICAN. WRITTEN BY HIMSELF. 1789. New York: Printed and sold by W. Durell, 1791. 2 vols. Reprints. THE LIFE OF OLAUDAH EQUIANO....New York: Negro Universities Press, 1969. GREAT SLAVE NARRATIVES.... Edited by Arna Bontemps. Boston: Beacon Press, 1969.

Narrative of the Ibo native (1745?-97) includes comment on the importance of music/dance/poetry to Africans: "We are almost a nation of dancers, musicians, and poets. Thus every great event... is celebrated in public dances which are accompanied with songs and music suited to the occasion" (1:7). Also identification of the three important instrument types: the stickado (=thumb piano), drums, and guitar-types (1:8). While in Charlestown, South Carolina, Equiano observed that the slaves used the Sabbath as a holiday rather than as a day of worship (2:191).

11 Fairfax, Thomas. JOURNEY FROM VIRGINIA TO SALEM, MASSACHUSETTS, 1799. London: Printed for Private Circulation, 1936. 33 pp.

The author---Ninth Baron Fairfax of Cameron, Scotland, and a resident of Belvoir and Vaucluse in Fairfax County, Virginia---refers to a black man who played the "banjoe" for the amusement of "his own colour" in Richmond, Virginia, in 1799 (2).

12 Fithian, Philip Vickers. JOURNAL AND LETTERS OF PHILIP VICKERS FITHIAN, 1773-1774; A PLANTATION TUTOR OF THE OLD DOMINION. Edited by John Rogers Williams for the Princeton Historical Association. Princeton: Princeton University Library, 1900. Reprint. Edited by Hunter D. Farish. Williamsburg, VA: Colonial Williamsburg, Inc., 1943, 1945, 1957. Page reference below is to the 1900 edition.

A graduate in 1772 of the College of New Jersey (later Princeton University), Fithian went in 1773 to Nomini Hall, the plantation of Robert Carter in the Tidewater region of Virginia, to teach Carter's children. His diary entries on slave life include references to slaves playing the fiddle and banjo (62).

13 Franklin, Benjamin. THE WRITINGS OF BENJAMIN FRANKLIN. Collected and edited by Albert Henry Smyth. Vol. 6. New York: Macmillan Company, 1906.

In a letter to the Marquis de Condorcet, dated 20 March 1774, London, Franklin briefly discusses the plight of the free Negro in the United States and concludes with the statement: "They make good Musicians" (221-22).

14 Franklin, James, Esq. THE PHILOSOPHICAL AND POLITICAL HISTORY OF THE THIRTEEN UNITED STATES OF AMERICA.... London: J. Hinton and W. Adams, 1784. 156 pp.

Description of a "jig" danced by white Virginians, which was borrowed from the Negroes (91).

15 Hamilton, Alexander. GENTLEMAN'S PROGRESS. THE ITINERARIUM OF DR. ALEXANDER HAMILTON.

1744. Edited by Carl Bridenbaugh. Published for the Institute of Early American History and Culture at Williamsburg, Virginia. Chapel Hill: University of North Carolina Press, 1948. 267 pp.

Native of Maryland traveling in the Middle Colonies and New England refers to black fiddlers in Philadelphia (28) and on board his ship (85).

16 Harrower, John. THE JOURNAL OF JOHN HARROWER: AN INDENTURED SERVANT IN THE COLONY OF VIRGINIA, 1773-1776. Edited by Edward Miles Riley. Williamsburg, VA: Colonial Williamsburg, Inc., 1963. 202 pp.

English-born bondsman refers to "Negroes learning their Catechism" (48) and describes the "barrafou" (xylophone) played by a slave (89).

17 Hewatt, Alexander. AN HISTORICAL ACCOUNT OF THE RISE AND PROGRESS OF THE COLONIES OF SOUTH CAROLINA AND GEORGIA. London: Printed for Alexander Donaldson, 1779. 2 vols. Reprint. Spartanburg, SC: Reprint Company, [1971].

Discussion of the slave insurrection at Stono, South Carolina, includes references to the drumming, singing, and dancing of the slaves (2:72-73, 2:103). Also references to the fact that most of the slaves were "great strangers to Christianity, and as much under the influence of Pagan darkness, idolatry, and superstition as they were at their first arrival from Africa" (2:100).

18 Jefferson, Thomas. NOTES ON THE STATE OF VIRGINIA....Philadelphia: Prichard & Hall, 1788. 244 pp. Reprint. Published for the Institute of Early American History and Culture. Chapel Hill: University of North Carolina Press, 1954. Page reference below is to the 1788 edition.

Discussion by author (later to become president of the United States) includes description of the "Banjar" as a guitar type brought to America by the slaves: "and which is the origin of the guitar, its chords being precisely the four lower chords of that instrument." Observation that "In music they are more generally gifted than the whites, with accurate ears for tune, and time; and they have been found capable of imagining a small catch" (150).

19 Moreau de Saint-Mery, Mederic Louis Elie. DANCE. Philadelphia: Published by the Author, 1796. An Article Drawn from the Work by M. L. E. Moreau de St. Mery entitled: REPERTORY OF COLONIAL INFORMATION, Compiled Alphabetically (1796). Translated, and With an Introduction by Lily and Baird Hastings. New York: Published by DANCE HORIZONS, 1976. 73 pp.

This article, part of a larger work that was never published but is extant in manuscript format, discusses dance performance practice of the slaves and black freedmen in colonial America (44-73) and describes such dance instruments as the banza (a guitar type) and drums (52-53), and such dances as the Kalenda, Chica, and vaudoux (55-65).

20 RUNAWAY SLAVE ADVERTISEMENTS. A DOCUMENTARY HISTORY FROM THE 1730s TO 1790. 4 vols. Collected by Lathan N. Windley. Vol. 1, VIRGINIA AND NORTH CAROLINA, 468 pp.; Vol. 2, MARYLAND, 437 pp.; Vol. 3, SOUTH CAROLINA, 778 pp.; Vol. 4, GEORGIA, 198 pp. Westport, CT: Greenwood Press, 1983.

Almost 6,000 slave advertisements collected from twenty-one colonial newspapers of five colonies (as indicated above). There is no index, and the author provides no "analysis or interpretation"; states that the advertisements are to be used as "raw materials of history." The most numerous references to slave music makers appear in the VIRGINIA GAZETTE. Page numbers given below are from vol. 1 of the Gazette unless otherwise indicated.

Descriptive phrases used most frequently are: "plays exceedingly well on the violin" (61, 69, 76, 231, 335) or "plays...well on the banjer"; is fond of playing the violin" (237, 244, 251, 260, 313, 329, 343) or is fond...the banjer" (210, 224); "plays on the fife extremely well" (416). Advertisements also refer to preachers (109, 217, 385, 421); singers (219, 339), dancers (392, 393). Some advertisements indicate performance practice, as "he is fond of whistling, which he performs in a peculiar manner with his tongue" (204) and "can play on the violin, and is fond of singing with it" (327). Not all fiddlers are good; some play "tolerably well" (356, 359) or are described as "a sort of a fiddler" (307). Some are multi-talented, as Mark, who "can blow the French horn, play the fiddle, whistles many tunes, well enough to be heard at a surprising distance" (366). A Georgia slave "is a good dancer and proud of it" (4:64). Few references to female singers or dancers: "she has...an uncommon good voice" (364).

21 Schoepf, Johann David. REISE DURCH EINIGE DER MITTLERN UND SUEDLICHEN VEREINIGTEN NORDAMERIKANISCHEN STAATEN (1788). Translated by Alfred J. Morrison as TRAVELS IN THE CONFEDERATION.... New York: Bergman Publishers, 1911. Reprint. 1968. 2 vols.

German physician and chief surgeon of the Ansbach troops in America traveled through New England and the southeastern United States in 1783-1784. His account includes discussion of slaves he observed in Charleston, South Carolina, of slave dancing, and of the city's curfew on such assemblies (2: 221).

22 Sewall, Samuel. DIARY OF SAMUEL SEWALL, 1674-1729. Collections of the Massachusetts Historical Society, Fifth Series, vols. 5-7. Boston: Massachusetts Historical Society, 1878-82.

Puritan Judge Sewall includes references to black servants in his diary, kept over a period of fifty-five years; to Col. Hobbey's Negro, a trumpeter who blew him a levit on 1 January 1704/05; and to Marshall's Negro woman, who was taken into the church on 16 December 1711.

23 Smyth, John F. D. A TOUR IN THE UNITED STATES OF AMERICA. 2 vols. London: Printed for G. Robinson, 1784. Reprint. New York: Arno Press and the New York Times, 1968. Reprint of Chapter 6. "Manner of Living of the Different Ranks of Inhabitants of Virginia." AMERICAN MUSEUM 1 (March 1787): 245-48.

English traveler's discussion of slave life in Chapter 6 includes description of a "negroe dance," where music was furnished by a "banjor (a large hollow instrument with three strings) and the quaqua (somewhat resembling a drum)"; also discussion of dance performance practice.

24 THE SOUTH CAROLINA GAZETTE, 1732-1775. Edited by Hennig Cohen. Columbia: University of South Carolina Press, 1954. 273 pp.

Compilation includes advertisements about slave fiddlers (94, 104-06), other slave musicians, and dancers. See also Cohen, "A Negro 'Folk-Game' in Colonial South Carolina." SOUTHERN FOLKLORE QUARTERLY 16 (September 1952): 183-84, which includes a quotation from an anonymous essay describing a clandestine gathering of slaves on 17 September 1772.

25 VIRGINIA GAZETTE INDEX, 1736-1780. Edited by Lester J. Cappon and Stella F. Duff. Published for the Institute of Early American History and Culture. Williamsburg, VA: Colonial Williamsburg, Inc., 1950. 2 vols.

Index points to fifty-four items about slave musicians (1079), seven items about slave preachers (1079). Also one reference to a slave banjoist (51); twenty-six references to slave fiddlers (389, 1078, some overlapping with slave-musician references); three references to slaves as fiddle makers (389, 1078); and two to dancers (1078). Advertisement of 26 March 1767 is one of the few references to a woman's activities: "Hannah...pretends much to the religion the Negroes of late have practiced."

THE RELIGIOUS EXPERIENCE

26 AN ACCOUNT OF MISSIONARIES SENT TO SOUTH CAROLINA. THE PLACES TO WHICH THEY WERE APPOINTED, THEIR LABOURS AND SUCCESS, &c. IN THAT COLONY. ORIGINALLY PUBLISHED IN THE HISTORY OF THE BRITISH EMPIRE IN AMERICA. London, 1708. Reprints. THE BRITISH EMPIRE IN AMERICA; CONTAINING THE HISTORY OF THE DISCOVERY, SETTLEMENTS.... By John Oldmixon. London, 1721. HISTORICAL COLLECTIONS OF SOUTH CAROLINA.... Edited by B. R. Carroll. Vol. 2. New York: Harper & Brothers, 1836.

History of the missionaries in South Carolina under the auspices of the Church of England, from 1702 to the 1720s, includes references to the religious instruction given to slaves (540) and to baptisms (540-42, 553, 557).

27 Allen, Richard. SPIRITUAL SONG. Originally published as a broadside. Philadelphia: "Printed for and Sold by the Rev. Richard Allen." c.1800. Reprint. EARLY NEGRO WRITING, 1760-1837, edited by Dorothy Porter, 559-61. Boston: Beacon Press, 1971.

Allen (1760-1831), first Bishop of the African Methodist Episcopal Church, discusses the noise and "confusion" in the worship services of black churches in a poem of eleven, eight-line stanzas. Concludes that the Scriptures offer precedence for dancing, shouting, and noise in worshipping God; also desires the "precious soul may be fill'd with the flame."

28 Asbury, Francis. THE JOURNAL AND LETTERS OF FRANCIS ASBURY. New York: N. Bangs & T. Mason, 1821. 3 vols. Reprint. Nashville: Abingdon Press, 1958.

Methodist church father reports on his preaching in black churches in Philadelphia and Baltimore (25 October 1795) and the emotional responses of some blacks to his preaching (24 January 1773, 2 August 1773, 25 February 1775, 7 July 1776). Also on black exhorters who "displayed gifts in public exercises" (28 March 1779), particularly Harry Hosier (13 May 1781, 27 October 1781).

29 [Bacon, Thomas.] TWO SERMONS PREACHED TO A CONGREGATION OF BLACK SLAVES AT THE PARISH CHURCH OF S. P. IN THE PROVINCE OF MARYLAND. BY AN AMERICAN PASTOR. London: Printed by John Oliver, 1749. 79 pp.

Rector of the Parish Church of St. Peter in Talbot County, Maryland, outlines in detail the kind of religious instruction that should be given the slaves. Observes that religious instruction reaches few, that "much the greatest Number...are deprived of a great Part of the Benefit they might otherwise receive." Both sermons based on Ephesians 6:8.

30 _____. FOUR SERMONS UPON THE GREAT AND INDISPENSIBLE DUTY OF ALL CHRISTIAN MASTERS AND MISTRESSES TO BRING UP THEIR NEGRO SLAVES IN THE KNOWLEDGE AND FEAR OF GOD....London: Printed by J. Oliver, 1750. 142 pp.

All four sermons based on Colossians 4:1. Strong admonition to slaveholders about their responsiblities to their slaves and the importance of observing the slave's humanity: "some regard him as belonging to a different species." References to the "noisy riot and drumming, which now seems to be the nightly Employment in most quarters" on the plantations (92), to the fact that the slaves remain heathen when left to themselves (92), that they scoff at religion (75). Suggests that some slaves be given religious instruction so they can teach others (131) and states that he, Bacon, has baptized twenty slaves (124).

31 Bluett, Thomas. SOME MEMOIRS OF THE LIFE OF JOB, THE SON OF SOLOMON THE HIGH PRIEST OF BOONDA IN AFRICA; Who Was a Slave about Two Years in Maryland; and Afterwards Being Brought to England, Was Set Free, and Sent to His Native Land in the Year 1734. London: Printed for Richard Ford, 1734. 63 pp.

Slave narrative includes reference to Job, as a Muslim slave in Maryland, withdrawing into the woods to pray by himself (20).

32 Boucher, Jonathan. REMINISCENCES OF AN AMERICAN LOYALIST, 1738-1789, Being the Autobiography of the Revd. Jonathan Boucher, Rector of Annapolis in Maryland, and afterwards Vicar of Epsom, Surrey, England. Edited by His Grandson Jonathan Bouchier. Boston: Houghton Mifflin Company, 1925. 201 pp.

Englishman, who went to Virginia as a tutor in 1759 and was admitted to holy orders in 1762, refers to his baptism of 115 slaves in November 1765 and 313 slaves in March 1766 at the Saint Mary's Church in Caroline County, Virginia (57). He used "two or three serious and sensible black men" to teach the children on Sundays (59).

33 Chauncy, Charles. SEASONABLE THOUGHTS ON THE STATE OF RELIGION IN NEW ENGLAND.... Boston: Rogers & Fowle, 1743. 424 pp.

New England clergyman observes that there has been an increase in the number of uneducated exhorters, especially among blacks, who have "taken up the practice of preaching" (226).

34 Coke, Thomas. EXTRACTS OF THE JOURNALS OF THE LATE REV. THOMAS COKE'S FIVE VISITS TO AMERICA. London: Printed by G. Paramore, 1793. 195 pp.

Methodist church father, and one of the organizers of the Methodist Church, made five visits to America during the years 1784-1792. Refers to the organizing conference of the Methodist Society in the United States (held on Christmas Eve, 1784, in Baltimore, Maryland) and states that church father Francis Asbury gave to Coke "his black (Harry by name)" [i. e., Asbury's servant] to accompany Coke on his travels (16). Coke discusses Harry in glowing terms, noting that "amazing power attends his preaching, though he cannot read" (18). Discussion of Harry's preaching in St. Eustatius, West Indies (64).

35 Davies, Samuel. THE STATE OF RELIGION AMONG THE PROTESTANT DISSENTERS IN VIRGINIA; IN A LETTER TO THE REV. MR. JOSEPH BELLAMY, OF BETHLEM, IN NEW-ENGLAND: FROM THE REVEREND MR. SAMUEL DAVIES.... Boston: Printed by S. Kneeland, 1751. 44 pp.

Presbyterian clergymen Davies was a missionary in Virginia before he became president of the College of New Jersey (called Nassau Hall; later Princeton University). His letter includes references to the number of Negroes who "attended" his sermons during his three-year stay in Hanover County, Virginia, and to the number of adults he baptized (23-24).

36 _____. LETTERS FROM THE REV. SAMUEL DAVIES AND OTHERS: SHEWING THE STATE OF RELIGION IN VIRGINIA, SOUTH CAROLINA, &c., PARTICULARLY AMONG THE NEGROES.... London: Printed by J. & W. Oliver, 1761. 36 pp.

Letters of Davies discuss the slaves singing psalms, the vocal quality of the singing (14, 16, 17), and slave dancing on the Sabbath (15).

37 "Eighteenth-Century Slaves as Advertised by Their Masters." JOURNAL OF NEGRO HISTORY 1 (1916): 163-216.

Collection of a large number of slave advertisements under the title "Documents" by the editor of the Journal, Carter G. Woodson, reveals much about slave life. References to folk preachers and exhorters (202-05) and to players on the fiddle, fife, drum, flute, and "banjer."

38 Fawcett, Benjamin. A COMPASSIONATE ADDRESS TO THE CHRISTIAN NEGROES IN VIRGINIA, AND OTHER BRITISH COLONIES IN NORTH-AMERICA. With an Appendix Containing Some Account of the Rise and Progress of Christianity among That Poor People. 2d ed. Salop, England: Printed by F. Eddowes and F. Cotton, 1755. 40 pp.

Methodist clergyman, in discussing the singing of the slaves, quotes from a letter written by Samuel Davies about the slaves having "an Ear for Musick, and a kind of extatic [sic] Delight in Psalmody" (37). The address is dated October 31, 1755, Kidderminster [England].

39 Garrettson, Freeborn. THE EXPERIENCE AND TRAVELS OF MR. FREEBORN GARRETTSON, MINISTER OF THE METHODIST-EPISCOPAL CHURCH IN NORTH-AMERICA. Philadelphia: Printed by Parry Hall, 1791. 276 pp.

References to the responses of slaves to his preaching (72, 76) and to a black boy who "exceeded all the youths that ever I saw for a gift and power in prayer." (69)

40 Godwyn, Morgan. THE NEGRO'S & INDIANS ADVOCATE, SUING FOR THEIR ADMISSION INTO THE CHURCH; OR, A PERSUASIVE TO THE

INSTRUCTING AND BAPTIZING OF THE NEGRO'S [sic] AND INDIANS IN OUR PLANTATIONS.... London: Printed for the Author by J. D., 1680. 174 pp.

English clergyman, who served as a minister in a Virginia church in 1665, discusses the state of the slaves, complaining about their "Idolatrous dances and Revels" and "their Worship and Ceremonies of religion" (33). Also objects to their "dance and musick" (105).

41 [Jarratt, Devereux.] A BRIEF NARRATIVE OF THE REVIVAL OF RELIGION IN VIRGINIA IN A LETTER TO A FRIEND....2d ed London: Printed by R. Hawes, 1778. 35 pp.

Rector of Bath, Dinwiddie County, Virginia, includes in his account a letter from Thomas Rankin to the Rev. Mr. Wesley, dated June 24, 1778. Rankin discusses the response of worshippers, black and white, to his sermons on July 7 and 30, noting that the faces of some were "bathed in tears" and others rejoiced "with joy unspeakable" (30-31, 34). Also comments that he had to beg the worshippers to compose themselves when he "preached from Ezekiel's vision of the 'dry bones'" (32).

42 [Jones, Absalom, and Richard Allen.] NARRATIVE OF THE PROCEEDINGS OF THE BLACK PEOPLE, DURING THE LATE AWFUL CALAMITY IN PHILADELPHIA, IN THE YEAR 1793: AND A REFUTATION OF SOME CENSURES, THROWN UPON THEM IN SOME LATE PUBLICATIONS. Philadelphia: Printed for the Authors, 1794. 28 pp. Reprint. Philadelphia: Rhistoric Publications, 1969.

Narrative includes reference to the African Church in Philadelphia in 1794 (5) and concludes with an original hymn of Richard Allen's: Ye ministers, that are called to preaching.

43 Jones, Hugh. THE PRESENT STATE OF VIRGINIA. ... London: Printed for John Clarke, 1724. Edited by Richard Morton. Published for the Virginia Historical Society. Chapel Hill: University of North Carolina Press, 1956. 295 pp.

English-born minister discusses the religious instruction given to slaves in his churches in Virginia and southern Maryland; also baptism, marriage, etc. (23, 229). Also refers to the fact that the "new Negroes...obstinately persist in their own barbarous ways" (99).

44 Kalm, Peter. TRAVELS INTO NORTH AMERICA. ...Translated into English by John Reinhold Forster. 2d ed. London: T. Lowndes, 1772. 2 vols. Reprint. A GENERAL COLLECTION OF THE BEST AND MOST INTERESTING VOYAGES AND TRAVELS.... Edited by John Pinkerton. Vol. 13. London: Hurst, Reese, and Orme, 1808-1814.

Swedish naturalist observes that the colonists pay little attention to the spiritual welfare of their slaves, letting them "live in their pagan darkness" (503). Also references to slave singing and dancing (504).

45 Knox, William. THREE TRACTS RESPECTING THE CONVERSION AND INSTRUCTION OF THE FREE INDIANS AND NEGROE SLAVES IN THE COLONIES. ADDRESSED TO THE VENERABLE SOCIETY FOR THE PROPAGATION OF THE GOSPEL IN FOREIGN PARTS. [London, 1768]. 41 pp. Reprint. Washington, DC: Microcard Editions, 1970.

"The Negroes in general have an ear for musick, and might without much trouble be taught to sing hymns, which would be the pleasantest method of instructing them...." (39)

46 Le Jau, Francis. THE CAROLINA CHRONICLE OF DR. FRANCIS LE JAU, 1706-1717. Edited by Frank J. Klingberg. Berkeley: University of California Press, 1956. 220 pp.

Le Jau was sent to South Carolina by the Society for the Propagation of the Gospel (SPG) to succeed Samuel Thomas, and worked in South Carolina during the years 1706-1717. This collection of his correspondence includes discussion of the religious instruction given to slaves in preparation for their conversion to Christianity (74, 120), references to slave preachers (70), and to the slaves dancing on Sundays (61, 72, 122).

47 Leland, John. THE VIRGINIA CHRONICLE: WITH JUDICIOUS AND CRITICAL REMARKS UNDER XXIV HEADS.... Fredericksburg, VA: Printed by T. Green, 1790. 46 pp.

English clergyman observes the importance of religion to the slaves: "The poor slaves, under all their hardships, discover as great inclination for religion, as the free-born do. When they engage in the service of God, they spare no pains. It is nothing strange for them to walk twenty miles on Sunday morning to meeting, and back again at night. They are remarkable for learning a tune soon, and have very melodious voices" (13). Also discussion of their religious services, noting that they are "more noisy in time of preaching...and more subject to bodily exercise...than are whites."

48 A LETTER TO AN AMERICAN PLANTER, FROM HIS FRIEND IN LONDON. London: H. Reynell, 1781. 24 pp.

Discussion of the religious practices of the slaves in a letter dated 1 October 1770 includes comment on their "strong Attachment to the idolatrous Rites and Practices of their own Country" (5) and to the fact that they spend Sundays in the "ridiculous Recreations usual with them in their own Country" (14). Recommends that "some few...be taught the Principles of our Religion...and then be appointed to convey Instruction to their Fellow-Slaves of lower capacities, in their own Language" (7).

49 Marrant, John. A NARRATIVE OF THE LORD'S WONDERFUL DEALINGS WITH JOHN MARRANT, A BLACK (NOW GOING TO PREACH THE GOSPEL IN NOVA-SCOTIA), BORN IN NEW-YORK, IN NORTH-AMERICA. Edited by Rev. W. Aldridge. 4th ed. London: R. Hawes, 1785. 40 pp. Reprint. New York: Garland Publishers, 1978.

Ex-slave author (1755-91) describes his visit to a plantation outside Charleston, South Carolina, with his brother (32-33). Refers to slaves holding secret prayer meetings in the woods after midnight to avoid persecution from slaveholders.

50 Mather, Cotton. "Rules for the Society of Negroes, 1693." Broadside. Boston: B. Harris, 1693. Reprint. MASSACHUSETTS BROADSIDES, BALLADS...PRINTED IN MASSACHUSETTS, 1693-1800. Vol. 75. Massachusetts Historical Society Collections. Boston: Massachusetts Historical Society, 1922.

The Puritan minister of Boston wrote in his diary in October 1693 that a "company of poor Negroes, of their own accord," had come to him for help in organizing a religious society. He entered into his diary eight of the nine rules that were drawn up, of which the first included reference to opening meetings by singing a psalm.

51 Meacham, James. "A Journal and Travels of James Meacham. Part 1, May 19 to August 31, 1789." HISTORICAL PAPERS. Series 9. Published by the Trinity College Historical Society and the North Carolina Conference Historical Society (1912): 66-95.

Methodist preacher, active in Virginia, discusses the quality of slave singing: "I scarcely ever heard anything to equal it upon earth" (88), and how the slaves shouted when they became happy during worship services (90, 94).

52 Moreau de Saint-Mery, Mederic Louis Elie. MOREAU DE ST. MERY'S AMERICAN JOURNEY (1793-1798). Introduction by Steward L. Mims. Translated and edited by Kenneth and Anna M. Roberts. New York: Doubleday & Company, 1947. 394 pp.

Account of the French traveler includes comment on the slaves worshipping in a white Methodist church at Norfolk, Virginia (48). Also references to their attending church services on Sunday mornings and their dancing on Sunday evenings (60).

53 THE OLD DOMINION IN THE SEVENTEENTH CENTURY. A DOCUMENTARY HISTORY OF VIRGINIA, 1606-1689. Edited by Warren Billings. Published for the Institute of Early American History and Culture. Chapel Hill: University of North Carolina Press, 1975. 324 pp.

Chapter 6, entitled "Bound Labor: Slavery," includes references, dated 1690, to the slaves meeting in great numbers for funerals, solemnities, and feasts (160, 173); also references to slave baptisms (148-74 passim).

54 Priest, William. TRAVELS IN THE UNITED STATES OF AMERICA; COMMENCING IN THE YEAR 1793 AND ENDING IN 1797. WITH THE AUTHOR'S JOURNALS OF HIS TWO VOYAGES ACROSS THE ATLANTIC....Musician, Late of the Theatres in Philadelphia, Baltimore and Boston. London: Printed for J. Johnson, 1802. 214 pp.

In a Letter to "Dear Friend," dated January 1, 1797, the English musician discusses Negro slavery, and refers to the ordination of a black Episcopal priest in Philadelphia [i.e., Absalom Jones] (184). Reprint of passages about the black man's musicality from the writings of Thomas Jefferson (185-95).

55 Prince, Hezekiah. "Twelve Hundred Miles on Horseback One Hundred Years Ago: The Diary of Hezekiah Prince." Edited by George Prince. NEW ENGLAND MAGAZINE n.s. 9 (February 1894): 723-34.

In his travel diary of a journey in 1793 through Massachusetts, Connecticut, Pennsylvania, and Virginia, the author comments on the religious practices of the slaves in Virginia, describing ing their services as "wild, and at times almost raving...." (733)

56 [Schaw, Janet]. JOURNAL OF A LADY OF QUALITY. BEING THE NARRATIVE OF A JOURNEY FROM SCOTLAND TO THE WEST INDIES, NORTH CAROLINA, AND PORTUGAL, IN THE YEARS 1774 TO 1776. Edited by Evangeline Walker Andrews and Charles McLean Andrews. New Haven: Yale University Press, 1921. 341 pp.

The editors have determined the author to be Janet Schaw, a native of Scotland. She discusses blacks in North Carolina participating in funeral rites for their deceased slaveholder: "the Negroes assembled to perform their part of the funeral rites, which they did by running, jumping, crying, and various exercises" (171).

57 Seward, William. JOURNAL OF A VOYAGE FROM SAVANNAH TO PHILADELPHIA, AND FROM PHILADELPHIA TO ENGLAND, MDCCXL. London: J. Oswald and other booksellers, 1740. 87 pp.

"Companion in travel" with the Reverend George Whitefield observes that Negroes who belong to the Society come to Whitefield for "spiritual advice" (6, 7, 11), and that a "Negroe School" is to be established in Philadelphia (11, 18).

58 Stiles, Ezra. THE LITERARY DIARY OF EZRA STILES. Edited by Franklin Bowditch Dexter. New York: Charles Scribner's Sons, 1901. 3 vols.

Diary of the president of Yale College (1778-1795) refers to the religious instruction of blacks (19 February 1770, 11 February 1771, 24 February 1771, 10 July 1772, 9 March 1773, 16 March 1774); to their baptism (24 March 1771, 26 September 1773); and to the training of "Negro ministers" to serve as missionaries to Africa (8 April 1773, 13 April 1773). Observation that "they sang well" (24 February 1772).

59 Whitefield, George. THREE LETTERS FROM THE REVEREND MR. G. WHITEFIELD.... LETTER III. TO THE INHABITANTS OF MARYLAND, VIRGINIA, NORTH AND SOUTH-CAROLINA, CONCERNING THEIR NEGROES. Philadelphia: Printed and Sold by B. Franklin, 1740. 15 pp.

Letter dated January 23, 1739, Savannah [Georgia] includes the complaint that the slaves are "kept ignorant of Christianity...and permitted to openly profane the Lord's Day, by their Dancing, Piping and such like" (14).

THE SONG

60 Bartram, William. TRAVELS THROUGH NORTH AND SOUTH CAROLINA, GEORGIA, EAST AND WEST FLORIDA. Philadelphia: Printed by James & Johnson, 1791. 522 pp.

American artist/naturalist discusses the singing of slaves on a Georgia plantation near Savannah: "The slaves...were mounted on the massive, timber logs; the regular heavy strokes of their gleaming axes re-echoed in the deep forests; at the same time...the sooty sons of Afric...in chorus sung the virtues and beneficence of their master in songs of their own composition" (310). Dated: 22 April 1776.

61 INSTRUCTIONS FOR THE TREATMENT OF NEGROES. London: Printed for Shepperson & Reynolds, 1786. Reprint 1797. 134 pp.

Manual written for a plantation in Barbados, Spring-Head Plantation, was intended to apply generally to African slaves in all the colonies. Discussion includes references to the singing of the slaves: "Many of them have good voices. Most of them have a fine ear. I desire that such of them as are happily possessed of those faculties may be taught to sing psalms" (106-7).

62 Josselyn, John. AN ACCOUNT OF TWO VOYAGES TO NEW-ENGLAND.... London: Printed for Giles Widdows, 1674. 279 pp. Reprints. New York: D. Appleton & Company, 1866. Hanover, NH: University Press of New England, 1988.

Britisher traveled in New England during the years 1638-39 and 1663-71. "The Second of October [1639] about 9 of the clock in the morning Mr. Maverick's Negro woman came to my chamber window, and in her own Countrey language and tune sang very loud and shrill...." (28)

63 Le Page du Pratz, Antoine Simon. THE HISTORY OF LOUISIANA, OR OF THE WESTERN PARTS OF VIRGINIA AND CAROLINA; Containing a Description of the Countries that Lie on Both Sides of the River Mississippi.... Originally published as HISTOIRE DE LA LOUISIANNE (1758). Translated from the French of M. Le Page du Pratz. With Some Notes and Observations Relating to Our Colonies. London: Printed for T. Becket, 1774. 387 pp. Reprint. New Orleans: J. S. W. Harmanson, 1947. Facsimile of 1774 edition. Edited by Joseph G. Tregle, Jr. Baton Rouge: Louisiana State University Press, 1975.

The French planter arrived in Louisiana in August 1718 and remained on a plantation for two years, then moved to Natchez country among the Indians, spending a total of sixteen years in Louisiana. Chapter 4, entitled "Of the Negroes of Louisiana" (357-66), includes references to the slaves singing loudly as they work (364), to their attachment to musical toys called gris gris (358), and to their dancing the Calinda on Sundays in groups as large as three or four hundred (366).

64 Rush, Benjamin. A VINDICATION OF THE ADDRESS, TO THE INHABITANTS OF THE BRITISH SETTLEMENTS, ON THE SLAVERY OF THE NEGROES IN AMERICA, IN ANSWER TO A PAMPHLET ENTITLED, "Slavery not Forbidden by Scripture. ... " Philadelphia: Printed by J. Dunlap, 1773. 54 pp.

Physician/statesman refers to the amusements and songs of Negroes: some of the songs he regarded as "obscene and warlike," others were plaintive and expressed the black man's misery (29-30).

II

THE ANTEBELLUM ERA

LITERATURE: 1801-1862

SOCIAL ACTIVITIES

65 "The African Slave Trade." Review of CAPTAIN CANOT, OR TWENTY YEARS OF AN AFRICAN SLAVER, by Brantz Mayer (1854). DE BOW'S REVIEW 18 (January 1855): 16-20.

Discussion includes reference to the dancing "of native Africans" and their "lineal descendants in Congo-square, New Orleans," to the accompaniment of the "tom-tom beat."

66 Aimwell. Absalom [Andrew Adgate]. A PINKSTER ODE FOR THE YEAR 1803. Most Respectfully Dedicated to Carolus Africanus, Rex: Thus Rendered in English; King Charles, Captain General and Commander in Chief of the Pinkster Boys. Albany, NY: Printed Solely for the Purchasers and Others, 1803. 12 pp. Reprints. Geraldine R. Pleat and Agnes N. Underwood, eds. "A Pinkster Ode, Albany, 1803." NEW YORK FOLKLORE QUARTERLY 8 (Spring 1952): 31-45. Micro-opaque. Worcester, MA: American Antiquarian Society, 1966.

Ode in honor of King Charley (d. 1824), drummer and master of the Pinkster Day celebrations of the slaves in Albany, New York, includes references to the Guinea dance performed by Charley and the gathered slaves to the music of various instruments (fiddle, fife, drum, hollow drum, and banjo) and the singing of the on-lookers. Charley is quoted as saying: "This day our Bosses make us free."

67 "Albany, Fifty Years Ago." HARPER'S NEW MONTHLY MAGAZINE 14 (March 1857): 451-63.

Discussion of "Pinkster Hill" in Albany, New York, and its festivities, includes references to slaves dancing in the African style and to King Charley, native of Angola, as leader of the dancing.

68 [Allen, Samuel.] "Sketches of the West." AMERICAN AGRICULTURIST 2 (1843), 3 (1844). Reprinted as "Sketches of Kentucky." TRAVELS IN THE OLD SOUTH, SELECTED FROM PERIODICALS OF THE TIME. Vol. 2. Edited by Eugene L. Schwaab and Jacqueline Bull, 289-303. Lexington: University Press of Kentucky, 1973. Page reference below is to the Schwaab edition.

Discussion of a slave singing improvised verses to the tune of "Long time ago," a "popular old negro air."

Text of 1 song: Den goin' down to Loudeville (Cho: Long time ago) (291).

69 Ashe, Thomas. TRAVELS IN AMERICA PERFORMED IN 1806, FOR THE PURPOSE OF EXPLORING THE RIVERS ALLEGHANY, MONOGAHELA, OHIO, AND MISSISSIPPI, AND ASCERTAINING THE PRODUCE AND CONDITION OF THEIR BANKS AND VICINITY. London: R. Phillips, 1808. 366 pp. Reprint. Micro-opaque. Louisville, KY: Lost Cause Press, 1956.

This book, using the format of letters written by an English traveller, includes references to slaves playing "bangies" in Wheeling, West Virginia, in April 1806 (88, 100).

70 Ball, Charles. SLAVERY IN THE UNITED

STATES. A NARRATIVE OF THE LIFE AND ADVENTURES OF CHARLES BALL, A BLACK MAN, WHO LIVED FORTY YEARS IN MARYLAND, SOUTH CAROLINA AND GEORGIA AS A SLAVE. Edited by Isaac Fisher. Lewiston, PA: John Shugert, 1836. 400 pp. Reprint. Detroit: Negro History Press, 1969.

Narrative includes discussion of the religious beliefs of slaves (125) and detailed description of a festival that took place after the "laying-by" of corn and cotton (singing, dancing, banjo playing, and the telling of stories from Africa, 154). Also reference to the playing of a black fiddler for white dinner parties (218).

71 Bernard, John. RETROSPECTIONS OF AMERICA, 1797-1811. Edited from the Manuscript by Mrs. Bayle Bernard.... New York: Harper & Brothers, 1887. 380 pp. Reprint. London: Benjamin Blom, 1969.

English actor discusses the centrality of dancing for the slaves, giving detailed description of their vigorous dancing after having walked "5 or 6 miles after a hard day's work" (207).

72 [Berquin-Duvallon]. TRAVELS IN LOUISIANA AND THE FLORIDAS, IN THE YEAR 1802, GIVING A CORRECT PICTURE OF THOSE COUNTRIES. Translated from the French by John Davis. New York: Isaac Riley Company, 1806. 181 pp. Reprint. Ann Arbor, MI: University Microfilms International, 1980.

Discussion of the gypsy and Negro fiddlers who provide music for dancing at the winter carnival in New Orleans (26-27) and of a slave burial (89).

73 Bibb, Henry. NARRATIVE OF THE LIFE AND ADVENTURES OF HENRY BIBB, AN AMERICAN SLAVE. Written by Himself. With an Introduction by Lucius C. Matlack. 1849. 3d ed. New York: The Author, 1850. 204 pp. Reprint. New York: Negro Universities Press, 1969.

Ex-slave (b. 1815), a native of Shelby County, Kentucky, includes references in his autobiography to the Sunday activities of the slaves---dancing, pattin' juber, singing, and playing on the banjo and bones (23).

74 Brown, John. SLAVE LIFE IN GEORGIA; A NARRATIVE OF THE LIFE, SUFFERINGS, AND ESCAPE OF JOHN BROWN, A FUGITIVE SLAVE, NOW IN ENGLAND. Edited by L. A. Chamerovzow. London: Published by the Editor, 1855. 250 pp. Reprint. Savannah, GA: Beehive Press, 1972.

Ex-slave (b. c.1818), who escaped from slavery about 1847, describes slave life (including a chapter on the Underground Railroad), and refers to music in the slave-pen of New Orleans, where the fiddler played jigs to make the slaves dance for exercise each day (113).

75 Campbell, John. NEGRO-MANIA. Philadelphia: Campbell and Powers, 1851. Reprint. Washington, DC: Microcard Editions, 1970.

Anthology compiled by a member of the Philadelphia Social Improvement Society includes detailed discussion of the music of Africans and their musical instruments (171), and quotation of Thomas Jefferson's statements on the slave "banjar" (437).

76 Carleton, George Washington. THE SUPPRESED BOOK ABOUT SLAVERY! PREPARED FOR PUBLICATION IN 1857--NEVER PUBLISHED UNTIL THE PRESENT TIME. New York: Published by the Author, 1864. 432 pp. Reprint. New York: Arno Press and the New York Times, 1968.

Discussion of slave coffles and the use of slave violinists in the coffles to play music for the walking (164-65).

77 Castelnau, Francis de La Porte, Comte de. 1. "Essay on Middle Florida, 1837-1839." 2. "Comte de Castelnau in Middle Florida, 1837-39." Translated by Arthur R. Seymour. FLORIDA HISTORICAL QUARTERLY 26 (January 1948): 199-255; (April 1948): 300-324.

French naturalist, who traveled in North America during the years 1837-41, refers to the black crew of a boat which was "occupied on deck in part with those foolish and ridiculous dances peculiar to Negroes while others raised their voices and sang almost savage melodies" (205). Also references to dancing and dance instruments: a mandolin made of a gourd and a horse's jaw bone, the teeth of which were scraped with a hollow stick (243, 316).

78 Caulkins, Frances. M. HISTORY OF NORWICH, CONNECTICUT. Norwich: Thomas Robinson, 1845. 359 pp. Reprint. Chicago: Library Resources, Inc., 1971.

Local historian discusses the 'Lection Day celebrations and parades of black "governors" in the late-eighteenth century in Norwich, Connecticut (185).

79 Child, David Lee. THE DESPOTISM OF FREEDOM; OR, THE TYRANNY AND CRUELTY OF AMERICAN REPUBLICAN SLAVE-MASTERS, SHOWN TO BE THE WORST IN THE WORLD, IN A SPEECH DELIVERED AT THE FIRST ANNIVERSARY OF THE NEW ENGLAND ANTI-SLAVERY SOCIETY, 1833. Boston: Young Men's Anti-Slavery Association, 1833. 72 pp. Reprint. Freeport, NY: Books for Libraries Press, 1971.

Author refers to Rev. John Rankin's description of a slave coffle processing through Kentucky in 1824 with two musicians at the head of the column. In the midst of the group a slave was hoisting the American flag (13-14).

80 Claiborne, John Francis. "A Trip through

Piney Woods." PUBLICATIONS OF THE MISSISSIPPI HISTORICAL SOCIETY 9 (1906): 487-538. Originally published in NATCHEZ FREE TRADER AND GAZETTE, 1841-42.

Comment on the Negro fiddlers who played for weddings, quilting parties, and house raisings (535). Also reference to a fiddler who played a Virginia jig (537).

81 "Code Noir; or, Black Code of Louisiana." THE COMMERCIAL REVIEW OF THE SOUTH AND WEST 1 (May 1846): 410-11. [Later entitled DE BOW'S REVIEW.]

Discussion of Louisiana's adoption in 1806 of the Code Noir, which permitted the slaves to assemble on Sundays to dance and play games.

82 Coke, Edward Thomas. A SUBALTERN'S FURLOUGH: Descriptive of Scenes in Various Parts of the United States, Upper and Lower Canada, New Brunswick, and Nova Scotia During the Summer and Autumn of 1832. London: Saunders & Otley, 1833.

Discussion refers to a dance band of black musicians in Lebanon Springs, Virginia, composed of two violinists and a bassist (236-37).

83 "The Colored Population of Philadelphia." NATIONAL ANTI-SLAVERY STANDARD 9 (4 January 1849): 126.

Discussion of the amusements of black Philadelphians notes their "strong addiction" to music and dancing and the rich quality of their voices in song. References to the dance halls, such as the "Astor House" and establishments located on Baker, Small, and Mary Streets, which were the popular gathering places on Saturday nights. Also discussion of dance performance practice.

84 Cooper, James Fenimore. SATANSTOE; OR, THE LITTLEPAGE MANUSCRIPTS. A TALE OF THE COLONY. New York: Burgess, Stringer & Company, 1845. 2 vols. Reprint. New York: American Book Company, 1937. Page references below are to the reprint.

This novel is set in colonial New York (when the colony had a Dutch culture) with focus "on a neck of land, called Satanstoe," in Westchester County of New York. The action of the story begins in 1751; included are references to the amusements of blacks (26) and a description of Pinkster, "the great Saturnalia of the New York blacks" (55-60), with its African-style performances.

85 Creecy, James. SCENES IN THE SOUTH, AND OTHER MISCELLANEOUS PIECES. Washington, DC: Thomas McGill, 1860. 294 pp. Reprint. Freeport, NY: Books for Libraries Press, 1972.

This posthumous publication, based on Creecy's manuscript, includes a description of slave dancing in Congo Square of New Orleans, Louisiana, on Sunday afternoons, and lists the instruments used--banjos, tom-toms, violins, jawbones, triangles, and various others (19-23)—as seen by Creecy in 1834. Also references to the chanting of slave street peddlers, male and female (39).

86 Criswell, Robert. "UNCLE TOM'S CABIN" CONTRASTED WITH BUCKINGHAM HALL, THE PLANTER'S HOME; OR, A FAIR VIEW OF BOTH SIDES OF THE SLAVERY QUESTION. New York: D. Fanshaw, 1852. 152 pp. Reprint. New York: AMS Press, 1973.

Novel based on a fictitious plantation near Charleston, South Carolina, includes description of a slave corn-husking festival and references to extemporaneous songs composed by the slaves (69). Also discussion of the slave musicians forming bands (fiddle, banjo, and bones) to provide music for entertainment of the master and his family (113-14) and for slave dances (148).

87 Cuming, Fortescue. SKETCHES OF A TOUR TO THE WESTERN COUNTRY, THROUGH THE STATES OF OHIO AND KENTUCKY; A VOYAGE DOWN THE OHIO AND MISSISSIPPI RIVERS, And a TRIP THROUGH THE MISSISSIPPI TERRITORY AND PART OF WEST FLORIDA. Commenced at Philadelphia in the Winter of 1807 and Concluded in 1809. Pittsburgh, PA: Cramer, Spear & Eichbaum, 1810. Reprint. EARLY WESTERN TRAVELS, 1748-1846. Vol. 4. Edited by Reuben Gold Thwaites. Cleveland, OH: Arthur H. Clark, 1904.

Notes about the voyage of an unidentified "gentleman," which are attached to Cuming's account, include references to slave dancing on the levee of New Orleans on Sunday, March 3, 1799: "vast numbers of negro slaves, men, women, and children, assembled together on the levee, drumming, fifing and dancing, in large rings" (333). And again, "upwards of one hundred negroes of both sexes assembled on the levee, fiddling, dancing, and singing (336).

88 Davis, John. TRAVELS OF FOUR YEARS AND A HALF IN THE UNITED STATES OF AMERICA DURING 1798, 1799, 1800, 1801, AND 1802. Dedicated by Permission to Thomas Jefferson, Esq., President of the United States. Bristol, England: R. Edwards, Printer, 1803. 454 pp. Reprint. New York: Henry Holt & Company, 1909.

English journalist and book-maker traveled about the United States mostly on foot. His discussion of slavery refers to a slave playing the "banjer" (144), to a black fiddler playing a jig (136), and to African survivals in Guinea love songs taught to a slave by his parents, who were natives of Guinea (146).

89 De Voe, Thomas. THE MARKET BOOK, CONTAINING A HISTORICAL ACCOUNT OF THE PUBLIC

MARKETS IN THE CITIES OF NEW YORK, BOSTON, PHILADELPHIA, AND BROOKLYN.... 2 vols. New York: Printed for the Author, 1862. 621 pp. Reprint. New York: A. M. Kelley, 1970.

Discussion of slave dancing in the public markets of New York, especially Bear Market (322) and Catherine Market (344-45), refers to the breakdown, jig, and shake-down, and to three dancers by name. Also discussion of instrumental performance practice, to pattin' parts of the body, and to Pinkster.

90 Dickens, Charles. NOTES ON AMERICA. New York: Harper & Brothers, 1842. 92 pp.

English novelist describes the dancing he saw at Almack's in the Five Points area of New York City, referring to the black dancer Juba [William Henry Lane] in dancing the single shuffle, double shuffle, cut, and cross-cut. Also references to Juba playing the tambourine (36).

91 Drake, Daniel. DR. DANIEL DRAKE'S LETTERS ON SLAVERY TO DR. JOHN C. WARREN, OF BOSTON. REPRINTED FROM THE NATIONAL INTELLIGENCER, WASHINGTON, APR. 3, 5, AND 7, 1851. Reprint. New York: Schuman's, 1940.

Letter on "Amusements and Sleep" includes discussion of how Kentucky slaves spend their leisure time (16). Also referencs to slave marriages (21) and to an itinerant slave preacher of Alabama who preached to both white and black congregations (25).

92 Dresser, Amos. THE NARRATIVE OF AMOS DRESSER, WITH STONE'S LETTERS FROM NATCHEZ. ... New York: American Anti-Slavery Society, 1836. 42 pp. Reprint. Microcard. Louisville, KY: Lost Cause Press, 196-.

Ex-slave's comment on a slave coffle marching to the music of two slave violinists (6-7) and on religious services held on the plantation (28).

93 Duncan, John Morison. TRAVELS THROUGH PART OF THE UNITED STATES AND CANADA IN 1818 AND 1819. Glasgow: University Press, 1823. 2 vols. Reprint. Microfilm. Ann Arbor, MI: University Microfilms International, 1982.

English visitor to the United States describes the annual parade of free blacks in Boston, Massachusetts, in commemoration of the abolition of slavery in Massachusetts. Refers to marching and music-making of several bands (1:59-60).

94 EARLY WESTERN TRAVELS, 1748-1846. Collected and edited by Reuben Gold Thwaites. 30 vols. Cleveland: Arthur Clark Company, 1904-7.

Collection of reprints includes a detailed index in vols. 31 and 32, with numerous references to slave life and culture. Nevertheless, there are some omissions from the index, as follows: the discussion of slave dancing in New Orleans, as reported by Estwick Evans in 1818 (8:336); slave dancing in Arkansas, reported by Thomas Nuttall in 1820 (13:317); and the reports on slave funeral ceremonies at Cape Girardeau, Missouri, in "James's Account of S. H. Long's Expedition" (17:91).

95 Eldridge, Elleanor. MEMOIRS OF ELLEANOR ELDRIDGE. Providence, RI: B. T. Albro, 1842. 128 pp.

Free black writer, b. 1785 in Warwick, Rhode Island, discusses her brother's election as a black governor in Negro 'Lection Day festivities in New England (37) and comments on her own singing and dancing (35).

96 Felt, Joseph Barlow. ANNALS OF SALEM FROM ITS FIRST SETTLEMENT. Salem: W. & S. B. Ives, 1827. 611 pp. Reprint. Microfiche. Louisville, KY: Lost Cause Press, 1972.

Local historian's account of Salem, Massachusetts, includes discussion of the slave festivities that took place in the last week of May, at which time the slaves elected their own Negro "governors" (419) and celebrated their 'Lection Day. Also description of the slaves dancing to music of the fiddle (420).

97 Finch, John. TRAVELS IN THE UNITED STATES OF AMERICA AND CANADA. London: Longman, Rees, Orme, Brown, Green, and Longman, 1833. 455 pp.

English traveler comments on the slaves making musical instruments from gourds and stalks of corn; also on the "Bandjo" and the importance of music in their lives (237-38).

98 Flint, Timothy. RECOLLECTIONS OF THE LAST TEN YEARS, PASSED IN OCCASIONAL RESIDENCES AND JOURNEYINGS IN THE VALLEY OF THE MISSISSIPPI, FROM PITTSBURG, AND THE MISSOURI TO THE GULF OF MEXICO, AND FROM FLORIDA TO THE SPANISH FRONTIER.... Boston: Cummings, Hilliard & Company, 1826. 395 pp. Reprint. RECOLLECTIONS...in a Series of Letters to the Rev. James Flint, of Salem, Massachusetts. New York: Alfred A. Knopf, 1932. Carbondale, IL: Southern Illinois University Press, 1968.

New England minister, who began his travels in 1816, comments on the performance of "the great Congo dance" in New Orleans (140) and on blacks singing and "scraping the fiddle" (345).

99 Fluegel, J. G. "Pages from a Journal of a Voyage down the Mississippi to New Orleans in 1817." Edited by Felix Fluegel. LOUISIANA HISTORICAL QUARTERLY 7 (July 1924): 414-40.

German traveler's entries in his journal, dated

February 16, 1817, and April 11, 1817, include comment on the dancing of blacks in New Orleans and on their richly ornamented attire (427, 432).

100 Foster, George. "Philadelphia in Slices." Series of articles published in the NEW-YORK TRIBUNE, 21 October 1848-15 February 1849. Reprint. PENNSYLVANIA MAGAZINE OF HISTORY AND BIOGRAPHY 93 (January 1969): 23-72. Page references below are to the reprint.

Articles include comment on black fiddlers, and on the folksong "Cooney in de holler" being used as dance music. Also references to the dancing in Philadelphia's Dandy Hall (40-41), to the Virginny breakdown (63) and to the beauty of the black voice (64).

101 _____. NEW YORK BY GAS LIGHT WITH HERE AND THERE A STREAK OF SUNSHINE. New York: Dewitt and Davenport, 1850. 127 pp. Reprint of excerpts in READINGS IN BLACK AMERICAN MUSIC. Edited by Eileen Southern. 1971. 2d ed. New York: W. W. Norton, 1983.

Journalist notes a typical "dance orchestra" in New York City's Five Points area on Saturday nights consists of fiddle, trumpet, and bass drum (73), and gives detailed description of the instrumental performance practice. Also comment on the dancing and observation that the folksong "Cooney in de holler" is used for dance music.

102 "From a Missionary in North Carolina." AMERICAN MISSIONARY NEWSLETTER 8 (December 1853): 11.

Clergyman discussing a slave coffle that he saw in North Carolina observes that two or three slaves played violins as they marched "to keep up the appearance of merriment."

103 Frost, John. "The Militia Training, Or One Good Turn Deserves Another." THE GIFT: A CHRISTMAS AND NEW YEAR'S PRESENT, 195-208. Philadelphia: Carey and Hart, 1842.

Discussion of two black boys dancing "a genuine African reel, or pas de deux," to the music of a fiddle (192).

104 Furman, Gabriel. ANTIQUITIES OF LONG ISLAND. Edited by Frank Moore. New York: J. W. Bouton Company, 1875. 271 pp. Reprint. Port Washington, NY: I. J. Friedman, 1968.

Volume includes transcription of a manuscript compiled by Furman during the years 1824-1838. Discussion of the Pinkster Day festival, originally held on the first Monday in June, includes references to the Toto dance performed on these occasions, with description of its accompaniment, typically the "banjo drum" formed from a hollow log and a parchment skin. Comment on King Charley, eighty-five-year-old Guinea native, who officiated at the dances.

Text of 1 song (Negro Pinckster Music): With hurried step and nodding knee (266).

105 Gilmore, James Robert. AMONG THE PINES; OR, SOUTH IN SECESSION-TIME. 6th ed. New York: J. R. Gilmore, 1862. Also published as LIFE IN DIXIE'S LAND; OR, SOUTH IN SECESSION-TIME. London: Ward & Lock, 1863. 282 pp. Reprint of a chapter: "Among the Pines." CONTINENTAL MONTHLY 1/3 (MARCH 1862): 322-20. Reprints. New York: Haskell House Publishers, 1969. Detroit: Negro History Press, 1970.

Author who visited South Carolina in 1860 states his book to be "a record of facts," not a "work of fiction." Detailed discussion of slavery includes references to singing and improvisation (22-26, 33); singing with banjo accompaniment (42-43); dancing and singing to the accompaniment of bones, fiddle, and/or banjo (145-48, 283). A chapter is devoted to "The Negro Funeral" (196-206), which includes excerpts from the funeral sermon, and description of the second funeral (296-97).

106 Hall, Baynard F. FRANK FREEMAN'S BARBER SHOP: A TALE. New York: Charles Scribner, 1852. 343 pp. Reprint. Microcard. Louisville, KY: Lost Cause Press, 1967.

Novel about plantation life in the South includes discussion of the Christmas celebrations of the slaves, with comment on the plantation dance and its "single, double, compound, complex, implex, wiggle and twist...steps" (103). Also references to the "corn-stalk jigs and banjo dances" of the slaves (22).

Text of 1 boat song (17): Oh, how glad dis niggah are/Oh, he, yo, yo).

107 Head, Franklin H. "The Legends of Jekyl Island." NEW ENGLAND MAGAZINE n.s. 8 (May 1893): 393-99.

Discussion of the early white settlers on Jekyl Island, off the Georgia coast, includes an excerpt from a letter written about 1736 by Lady Oglethorpe, wife of General James Edward Oglethorpe, which refers to visiting aristocrats and the singing of their black servants. Reference to one servant who served as a trumpeter, blowing a conch shell.

108 Hentz, Caroline Lee Whiting. THE PLANTER'S NORTHERN BRIDE. A NOVEL. 2 vols. Philadelphia: A. Hart, 1854. Reprint. Chapel Hill: University of North Carolina Press, 1970. Page references below are to vol. 2.

Written by a New Englander, this "plantation romance" includes comment on the slave preacher and his religious services (55); on a woman's burial services (55) and the funeral service held "several weeks afterwards" (59); on dancing the "Virginia breakdown" and "Georgia rattlesnake" with the accompaniment of violin and banjo (39); and on the dance "jump Georgia motion" (59).

Text of 1 song: Where now is good old Dilsy (Cho: Safely in de promised land) (55).

109 Holmes, Isaac. AN ACCOUNT OF THE UNITED STATES OF AMERICA, DERIVED FROM ACTUAL OBSERVATION, DURING A RESIDENCE OF FOUR YEARS IN THAT REPUBLIC.... London: Caxton Press, 1823. 476 pp. Reprint. New York: Arno Press and the New York Times, 1974.

Englishman's observation that the slaves are "passionately fond of music and dancing" and comment on their worksongs (326) and their Sunday afternoon dances in Louisiana and Mississippi, where they danced a "Congo dance" to the accompaniment of only a folk-crafted drum and the singing of onlookers (332). Also the observation that there are many black Methodists, and they are "very noisy in their meetings" (389).

110 Horn, Charles Edward. "National Melodies of America." SOUTHERN LITERARY MESSENGER 5 (November 1839): 770-73.

Author, in discussing the origin of an Ethiopian song he had written, states it was based on his observation of how the slaves sang and danced to the accompaniment of fiddle and banjo on the several plantations he visited near Natchez, Mississippi, in the spring of 1837. Also discussion of a comic song that he heard sung by a slave boy.

Reference to 1 song: As I was gow'en down Shinbone Alley.

111 Houstoun, M. Charlotte J. F. [Matilda Charlotte J. Fraser]. HESPEROS; OR, TRAVELS IN THE WEST. 2 vols. London: John W. Parker, 1850. Reprint. Micro-opaque. Louisville, KY: Lost Cause Press, 1962.

Detailed discussion of sugar manufacturing on a Louisiana plantation includes references to the slave festivities that take place when all is completed---three or four days of dancing, singing, etc.---and comment on the voice quality of the singing (2:156-57).

112 Ingraham, Joseph Holt [Kate Conyngham, pseud.]. THE SUNNY SOUTH; OR, THE SOUTHERNER AT HOME, EMBRACING FIVE YEARS' EXPERIENCE OF A NORTHERN GOVERNESS IN THE LAND OF SUGAR AND COTTON. Philadelphia: G. Evans, 1860. Reprint. New York: Negro Universities Press, 1968.

Published by a novelist of New England, this book consists of a collection of "Letters from the South," which earlier were published in the SATURDAY COURIER under the author's pen name, Kate Conyngham. There are references to the use of a bell "to call the slaves up" (51), and to the voice quality of the women's singing (67). Detailed discussion of the plantation fiddler, who was also the music and dance teacher, and to one of his "concerts," where the orchestra included fiddle, banjo, an instrument composed of two hollow sticks, and a home-made drum (104-5). Also detailed description of a slave wedding and its orchestra of three fiddles, banjo, and castanets (144-45).

113 Irving, Washington. SALMAGUNDI. New York: G. P. Putnam & Company, 1857. 243 pp. Reprint. New York: AMS Press, 1973.

In Article No. 5 (dated 7 March 1807) there is reference to the inclusion of tambourines in the black band, along with drums, fifes, and trumpets (49, 51).

114 [Irving, Washington.] A HISTORY OF NEW YORK FROM THE BEGINNING OF THE WORLD TO THE END OF THE DUTCH DYNASTY...by Diedrich Knickerbocker. 1809. Revised edition in one volume with an essay on Irving's Life and Work by Charles Dudley Warner. New York: G. P. Putnam's Sons, 1880. 525 pp.

Comic history (published originally in 1809) of colonial New York refers to Dutch Negroes who were "exquisite performers on three-stringed fiddles" and were noted for their talents as whistlers (103-4) and to a band of boys and Negroes who played upon "rattle-bones" and clam shells (261).

115 Jacobs, Harriet Brent [Linda Brent]. INCIDENTS IN THE LIFE OF A SLAVE GIRL. WRITTEN BY HERSELF. Edited by Lydia Maria Child. Boston: Published for the Author, 1861. 306 pp. Reprint. New York: Harcourt Brace Jovanovich, 1973.

In one of the few slave narratives written by a woman, Brent (1815?-97) tells how she escaped from slavery at the age of twenty-seven and remained hidden in an attic for nearly seven years before finally gaining her freedom. She was encouraged to publish her book by Bishop Daniel Payne of the A. M. E. Church and Lydia Child, editor of the NATIONAL ANTI-SLAVERY STANDARD. In her description of the Johnkannaus [=John Canoe] festival at Christmas in North Carolina are comments on how the dancers keep time to the music of triangles, jawbones, and sheepskin gumbo boxes, beaten by a dozen men (121-22).

Texts of 2 songs: 1. Ole Satan's church is here below (73). 2. Poor massa, so dey say (122).

116 "Juba at Vauxhall." ILLUSTRATED LONDON NEWS, 5 August 1848. See also 24 June 1848 and 1 July 1848.

Discussion of performances in London of the black-American minstrel Juba (=William Henry Lane) states "But the Nigger Dance is a reality" and refers to 4 dances: the Virginny breakdown, the Alabama kick-up, the Louisiana toe-and-heel, and the Tennessee double-shuffle. Also discussion of Juba's tambourine performance practice.

117 Kennedy, John Pendleton. SWALLOW BARN: OR, A SOJOURN IN THE OLD DOMINION. 1832. Rev. ed. New York: George P. Putnam, 1851. 506 pp. Reprint. Baton Rouge: Louisiana State University Press, 1986.

Account of a northerner's visit to a plantation on the James River in Virginia, near City Point, in the summer of 1829 includes discussion of the slave Carey playing the "banjoe," and how he "sings the inspirations of his own muse, weaving into song the past or present annals of the family" (101-3). Also detailed description of slaves dancing a jig over "two sticks lying crosswise upon the ground" and slapping their thighs alternately and throwing up their elbows to the time of the music" (160, 454); of young boys entertaining the master, using "an old watering-pot for a drum" (310).

One song text: The rich man comes from down below (Cho: Yo ho, yo ho) (102).

118 Kurz, Rudolph Friedrich. JOURNAL OF RUDOLPH FRIEDRICH KURZ. An Account of His Experiences Among Fur Traders and American Indians on the Mississippi and the Upper Missouri Rivers During the Years 1846 to 1852. Translated by Myrtis Jarrell. Edited by J. N. B. Hewitt. Published for the Smithsonian Institution. Washington, DC: United States Government Printing Office, 1937. 382 pp. Reprint. Lincoln: University of Nebraska Press, 1970.

Swiss artist comments on the slaves' activities during their New Year's holidays (8), on their singing (12), and on a New Year's Eve dance in 1851 at St. Joseph, Missouri (69).

119 Lanman, Charles. HAW-HO-NOO; OR, RECORDS OF A TOURIST. Philadelphia: Lippincott, Grambo and Company, 1850. 266 pp. Reprint. Micro-opaque. Louisville, KY: Lost Cause Press, 1969.

In a chapter entitled "Plantation Customs" (139-45) there is description in great detail of the slaves' celebration of Christmas and of the singing and dancing to music of banjo and fiddles, to the "double-shuffle" and the "pigeon-wing," and to improvisation. Comment on the pathos and harmony in the choral singing. This chapter is reprinted in a later publication, ADVENTURES IN THE WILDS OF THE UNITED STATES (see no. 120).

120 ____. ADVENTURES IN THE WILDS OF THE UNITED STATES AND BRITISH AMERICAN PROVINCES. Philadelphia: John W. Moore, 1856. 2 vols. Reprint. Microfiche. Louisville, KY: Lost Cause Press, 1983.

Vol. 2, Part 1, entitled "A Winter in the South," includes comment on slaves dancing to the music of fiddle and banjo (98, 258), on boatmen singing for passengers a song that was "an incoherent chant, wild and mournful...[with] impromptu words" (149), and on the "loud and plaintive" singing of boatmen when unloading bales of cotton (167). The chapter entitled "Plantation Customs" (273-79) describes in great detail Christmas celebrations of the slaves and the corn-shucking festival (176-79). This chapter is a reprint of material published in the author's publication HAW-HO-NOO (see no. 119).

Text of 1 song: We's up the Chattahoochee (149).

121 Latrobe, Benjamin Henry. THE JOURNAL OF LATROBE, Being the Notes and Sketches of an Architect, Naturalist and Traveler in the United States from 1796 to 1820. With an Introduction by J. H. B. Latrobe. New York: D. Appleton, 1905. Reprints. IMPRESSIONS RESPECTING NEW ORLEANS--BENJAMIN HENRY LATROBE, DIARY AND SKETCHES, 1818-1820. New York: Columbia University Press, 1951. THE JOURNALS OF BENJAMIN HENRY LATROBE, 1799-1820: FROM PHILADELPHIA TO NEW ORLEANS. The Papers of Benjamin Henry Latrobe, Series 1. Edward C. Carter, Editor in chief. Published for the Maryland Historical Society. New Haven: Yale University Press, 1980. Reprint of selected passages in READINGS IN BLACK AMERICAN MUSIC, edited by Eileen Southern. 1971. 2d ed. New York: W. W. Norton & Company, 1983. Page numbers refer to the 1905 edition unless otherwise indicated.

Journal includes description of funeral processions (191-92, 230-32); of a camp meeting where blacks "sang and danced the Methodist turnabout" (250-57); and of the Sunday dances in African style on the Commons in the rear of the city [i.e., Place Congo] (179). Also description of musical instruments used for dancing---cylindrical and square drums, stringed instruments, a woodblock, and a percussion made from a "calabash"---and discussion of performance practice (179-81). The manuscript diary includes a note on a musical staff, representing the "burden" sung by the women "on one single note" in response to the man's song for the dancing "in some African language" (music illustration in PAPERS, p. 204).

122 "Letter from a Teacher at the South." DWIGHT'S JOURNAL OF MUSIC 2 (26 February 1853): 164.

Identified as "A Down East Music Teacher," a former teacher of Georgia discusses musical tastes in that state. Includes reference to the black man singing his own songs accompanied by the banjo.

123 Long, John Dixon. PICTURES OF SLAVERY IN CHURCH AND STATE, INCLUDING PERSONAL REMINISCENCES, BIOGRAPHICAL SKETCHES, ANECDOTES.... Philadelphia: Published by the Author, 1857. 418 pp. Reprint. New York: Negro Universities Press, 1969.

Account of slavery by a Methodist minister---a native of Maryland who settled in Philadelphia in 1856---includes discussion of pattin' juba performance practice, banjo playing (17-18), and tale telling (259). Also discussion of funeral rites, with distinction between "buryings" and funerals (19-20); of Methodist camp meetings, with comment on the voice quality of "a thousand African throats" (157-60); of the meaning of the slave songs (197-98); of folk preaching (312-13); and of "Negro prayer meetings," including the holy dance, and songs the slaves "composed by themselves" (383-84).

Reference to 1 song: The judgement day is rolling around (22). Texts of 3 songs: 1. Juber, Cesar boy, Ash-cake in de fire (Cho: 'Possum up de gum tree) (18). 2. William Rino sold Henry Silvers (Cho: Hilo! Hilo!) (198). 3. Working all day (Cho: When will Jehovah hear our cry) (198). Reference to 1 sermon theme: Moses was an abolitionist (312).

124 Mackay, Alexander. THE WESTERN WORLD; OR, TRAVELS IN THE UNITED STATES IN 1846-1847; EXHIBITING THEM IN THEIR LATEST DEVELOPMENT, SOCIAL, POLITICAL, AND INDUSTRIAL; INCLUDING A CHAPTER ON CALIFORNIA. London: Richard Bentley, 1849. 3 vols. Reprint. New York: Negro Universities Press, 1968.

Discussion of English lawyer and journalist includes references to black preachers and to the sects that attracted blacks: Presbyterian, Baptist, Methodist, and Latter-Day Saints (2:131). Also comment on the slaves' singing and dancing and on the banjo as the "chief" instrument for accompanying the dancing, in which there is "an elaborate use of the heel." Discussion of the "plaintive airs" of the slaves (2:133).

125 "Management of Negroes upon Southern Estates." DE BOW'S REVIEW OF THE SOUTHERN AND WESTERN STATES 10, n.s. 4 (1851): 325-28, 369-79, 621-27. Reprint. THE NEGRO AND HIS FOLKLORE IN NINETEENTH CENTURY PERIODICALS, edited by Bruce Jackson, 341-52. Published for American Folklore Society. Austin: University of Texas Press, 1967.

Anonymous author no. 1 (325-28) refers to slaves singing at work (328). Anonymous author no. 2 (621-27) discusses the dance accompaniment provided by the fiddle, triangle, and patting Juba (625), and religious services on the Sabbath (625). Author signing himself "A Small Farmer" (369-79), states that he has been carrying out his system of managing slaves successfully for twenty years and refers to slaves dancing to the music of fiddles (371); also comment on plantation religious services (370).

126 Maude, John. A VISIT TO THE FALLS OF NIAGARA IN 1800. London: Longmans, Rees, Orme, Brown & Green, 1826. 313 pp.

English traveler in the United States during the years 1793-1803 comments on black fiddlers (3, 16).

127 [McDougall, Frances Harriet.] SHAHMAH IN PURSUIT OF FREEDOM; OR, THE BRANDED HAND. TRANSLATED FROM THE ORIGINAL SHOWMAH, AND EDITED BY AN AMERICAN CITIZEN. New York: Thatcher & Hutchinson, 1858. 599 pp. Reprint. Freeport, NY: Books for Libraries Press, 1971.

The fictional Shahmah Shah of Algiers toured in the United States in 1852 and wrote letters recounting his experiences to his friend Hassan, who remained at home. Detailed discussion of pattin' juber and comparison of its performance practice to that seen "among the negroes of Nubia and the Upper Nile" (275-77); and of the emotional appeal of the slave singing, its quality, and improvisatory character (273-75). Also reference to the Negro woman who was the first person to organize a Sabbath School in New York City (316). Although the author does not give the name of the woman, the reference probably is to Katy Ferguson (see no. 297).

128 Mordecai, Samuel. RICHMOND IN BY-GONE DAYS DAYS; BEING REMINISCENCES OF AN OLD CITIZEN. Richmond: G. M. West, 1856. 321 pp. Reprints. New York: Arno Press and the New York Times, 1975. Selected passages in READINGS IN BLACK AMERICAN MUSIC. Edited by Eileen Southern. 1971. 2d ed. New York: W. W. Norton, 1983.

Discussion of the celebrated slave violinist Sy Gilliat, and flutist London Brigs of Richmond, Virginia (179, 310), and of slaves singing in a tobacco factory in Richmond (296).

129 Munsell, Joel. THE ANNALS OF ALBANY. Albany, New York: J. Munsell, 1850-59. 10 vols. Reprint. Chicago: Library Resources, 1970.

This work consists of reprints of various kinds of articles relating to the history of Albany, New York. Vol. 5 includes references to slave celebrations of the feast of Pentecost, called Pinkster (5:29, 5:232).

130 "Musical Correspondence; Marion Ala., July 20." DWIGHT'S JOURNAL OF MUSIC 13 (14 August 1858): 157-58.

Letter refers to the performance of native, original songs by the plantation slaves, accompanied by the fiddle and banjo.

131 Northup, Solomon. TWELVE YEARS A SLAVE. Narrative of Solomon Northup, A Citizen of New-York, Kidnapped in Washington City in 1841, and Rescued in 1853, From a Cotton Plantation Near the Red River, in Louisiana. Edited by David Wilson. Auburn: Derby and Miller, 1853. 336 pp. Reprint edited by Sue Eakin and Joseph Logsdon. Baton Rouge: Louisiana State University Press, 1968.

Slave narrative of violinist Northup offers an illuminating account of slave lifestyles and the role of the slave musician. Includes references to the dancing of slaves on the auction block (17) and at holiday times (181-82, 213-20), to "pattin'" (219), and to the slave wedding (221).

Texts of 3 dance songs: 1. Harper's creek and roaring ribber (Cho: Up dat oak and down dat ribber) (219). 2. Who's been here since I've been gone? (Cho: Hog Eye, Old Hog Eye, and Hosey, too) (200). 3. Ebo Dick and Jurdan's Joe (Cho: Hop, Jim, along) (220). Music of 1 dance song: "Harper's creek..." (verso of 321).

132 [Olmsted, Frederick]. "A Mississippi Home." NATIONAL ANTI-SLAVERY STANDARD 21 (4 August 1860): [1]. Reprinted from Olmsted's JOURNEY IN THE BACK COUNTRY (see no. 322).

Contains references to slave preachers, and to slaves dancing cotillions and reels to the music of fiddles and banjos.

133 "On Board a Slaver." HARPER'S WEEKLY 4 (2 June 1860): 346-47.

Description of the voyage of the slave ship Flora, from the West Coast of Africa to the Americas, includes discussion of the collection of human cargo, daily routines of the slaves, and amusements organized by the crew. References to the slaves dancing to the music of drums and cymbals.

134 Paine, Lewis W. SIX YEARS IN A GEORGIA PRISON. NARRATIVE OF LEWIS W. PAINE, WHO SUFFERED IMPRISONMENT SIX YEARS IN GEORGIA, FOR THE CRIME OF AIDING THE ESCAPE OF A FELLOWMAN FROM THAT STATE, AFTER HE HAD FLED FROM SLAVERY. WRITTEN BY HIMSELF. New York: Printed for the Author, 1851. 187 pp. Reprints. Microfiche. Louisville, KY: Lost Cause Press, 196-? Chapter entitled "Amusements" reprinted in READINGS IN BLACK AMERICAN MUSIC, edited by Eileen Southern. 2d ed. New York: W. W. Norton, 1983.

White school teacher includes detailed discussion of slave life in his narrative. Refers to the Hotchkiss Codification of the statute law of Georgia that prohibited slaves from beating drums or blowing horns and other loud instruments (140). Also discussion of log-rolling and corn-shucking festivals, pattin' juber and other performance practice, and dancing to the music of fiddles (177-86).

135 Patten, J. Alexander. "Scenes in the Old Dominion. Number Two--A Tobacco Market." Reprinted as "Scenes from Lynchburg." TRAVELS IN THE OLD SOUTH.... Edited by Eugene L. Schwaab and Jacqueline Bull. Lexington: University Press of Kentucky, 1973. Page references below are to TRAVELS, vol. 2.

References to the slave who blows a "long tin" horn to call tobacco buyers to a public auction (2:537) and description of slaves whistling "tunes of the plantations where they were born" on the streets in the evening hours. Also comment on informal contests held among gangs of whistlers (2:541).

136 Paulding, James Kirke. LETTERS FROM THE SOUTH, WRITTEN DURING AN EXCURSION IN THE SUMMER OF 1816 BY THE AUTHOR OF JOHN BULL & BROTHER JONATHAN.... New York: James Eastburn & Company, 1817. 2 vols. Reprint. New York: AMS Press, 1973.

Book consists of a collection of letters written to "Dear Frank." Letter 11, about slavery, includes discussion of musical matters (1:118, 119, 122), with references to the banjo and to blacks who sing as they row boats on the canal at Richmond, Virginia, similarly to the Venetian gondoliers.

Text of 1 song: Going away to Georgia (Cho: Ho, heave, ho) (127).

137 Playfair, Robert. RECOLLECTIONS OF A VISIT TO THE UNITED STATES AND BRITISH PROVINCES OF NORTH AMERICA, IN THE YEARS 1847, 1848, AND 1849. Edinburgh: T. Constable & Company, 1856. 266 pp. Reprint. Micro-opaque. Louisville, KY: Lost Cause Press, 1957.

British traveller comments on a Negro festival (unidentified) that was held annually in the city of New York, and on the marching and accompanying music (136). Also comment on the musical instruments used to play for dancing that he saw in Virginia Springs: violin, tambourine, and a percussion made from bones and a skull (174).

138 Randolph, J. Thornton [Charles Jacobs Peterson]. THE CABIN AND PARLOR; OR, SLAVES AND MASTERS. Philadelphia: T. B. Peterson, 1852. Reprint. Freeport, NY: Books for Libraries Press, 1971. 324 pp.

Novel about life in the antebellum South includes description of a slave holiday and refers to the slaves singing and dancing to the music of fiddles (78-79).

139 Rankin, John. LETTERS ON AMERICAN SLAVERY, ADDRESSED TO MR. THOMAS RANKIN, MERCHANT AT MIDDLEBROOK, AUGUSTA COUNTY, VIRGINIA. Boston: Garrison & Knapp, 1833. 118 pp. Reprint. New York: Negro Universities Press, 1970.

One of the letters written by the Rev. James H. Dickey, dated 30 September 1824, includes comment on a slave coffle he witnessed in Paris, Kentucky, during the summer of 1822. Men and women were chained two abreast and forced to march to accompaniment music produced by two slave violinists (45-46). In the middle of the procession a slave carried the American flag.

140 Roos, Rosalie. TRAVELS IN AMERICA, 1851-

1855. Translated and edited by Carl L. Anderson. Published for the Swedish Pioneer Historical Society. Carbondale: Southern Illinois University Press, 1982. 152 pp.

Swedish teacher, who resided in South Carolina, wrote letters to her family back in Sweden about her experiences, which were published by her granddaughter. Detailed discussion of slave dancing during the Christmas holidays (70-71) and of a funeral procession (126).

141 Russell, William Howard. THE CIVIL WAR IN AMERICA. Boston: Gardner A. Fuller, 1861. 189 pp. Reprint. Microfiche. Louisville, KY: Lost Cause Press, 1985.

British correspondent for the LONDON TIMES, whose book takes the format of letters, discusses a slave dance on a plantation in Natchez, Mississippi, and describes the jig, in a letter dated 14 June 1861 (149, 151).

142 _____. PICTURES OF SOUTHERN LIFE: SOCIAL, POLITICAL, AND MILITARY. New York: James G. Gregory, 1861. 143 pp. Reprint. Microfiche. Louisville, KY: Lost Cause Press, 1985.

Journalist's account includes discussion of a slave dance he witnessed on a plantation in Natchez, Mississippi, on June 14, 1861, and description of couples dancing a kind of Irish jig and the double shuffle to the music of fiddlers (94, 96).

143 "Scenes in North Carolina." THE LIBERATOR 7 (26 May 1837): [85].

One of seven short sketches written by an anonymous woman about slave life in North Carolina, this sketch includes comment on the John Cooner festival celebrated by slaves during the Christmas holidays and description of their masks and costumes. Also discussion of death and funeral rites among the slaves and reference to a slave woman who died singing "a sort of lullaby."

144 Schultz, Christian. TRAVELS ON AN INLAND VOYAGE THROUGH THE STATES OF NEW-YORK, PENNSYLVANIA, VIRGINIA, OHIO, KENTUCKY, AND TENNESSEE, AND THROUGH THE TERRITORIES OF INDIANA, LOUISIANA, MISSISSIPPI, AND NEW ORLEANS; PERFORMED IN THE YEARS 1807 AND 1808, INCLUDING A TOUR OF NEARLY SIX THOUSAND MILES. WITH MAPS AND PLATES. 2 vols. New York: Isaac Riley, 1810. Reprint. Ridgewood, NJ: Gregg, [1968].

Volume 2 contains a description of "religious" dancing among the slaves in New Orleans and description of the band of drums that accompanied the dance (2:195).

145 Sears, Robert. A PICTORIAL DESCRIPTION OF THE UNITED STATES.... ILLUSTRATED WITH NUMEROUS ENGRAVINGS. New York: Published by Robert Sears, 1857. 648 pp. Reprint. Microopaque. Louisville, KY: Lost Cause Press, 1962.

Author provides text and illustrations of important buildings and scenes for every state in the Union at that time (thirty-six). References to black culture include description of the slave funeral, which occurred "several weeks after the burial" (348).

146 "A Secret History of the African Slave Trade." DOUGLASS' MONTHLY 3 (March 1861): 425-26.

Reprint of excerpts from an article in the NEW YORK EVENING POST describes life aboard a slaver, including reference to the slaves on the ship being forced to dance.

147 Smith, Horatio. FESTIVALS, GAMES, AND AMUSEMENTS. ANCIENT AND MODERN. With additions by Samuel Woodworth. New York: J. & J. Harper, 1831. 355 pp. Reprint. Microfilm. New Haven, CT: Research Publications, Inc., 1975.

In the Appendix, Woodworth discusses "American Festivals, Games, and Amusements," including comment on the slaveholders' practice of allowing the slaves to have a "week's recreation, including Christmas and New-Year's," for their carnival celebrations, and on the "ludicrous and extravagant manner" of their plays and the "grotesque style" of their masks and costumes (352). The description suggests this was a John Cooner festival, although that term is not used.

148 Smith, William B. "The Persimmon Tree and the Beer Dance." THE FARMER'S REGISTER 6 (1 April 1838): 58-61. Reprint. THE NEGRO AND HIS FOLKLORE IN NINETEENTH-CENTURY PERIODICALS, edited by Bruce Jackson. Published for the American Folklore Society. Austin: University of Texas Press, 1967.

Description of a "Beer Dance" festival of slaves on a plantation in Prince Edwards County, Virginia, includes discussion of songs, dancing and relevant performance practice, and pattin' juba to the music of the banjo.

Texts of 3 songs: 1. Old black bull come down de hollow (Cho: Who-zen John, who-za). 2. I went from the great house. 3. Juber up and juber down.

149 Smith, William L. LIFE AT THE SOUTH; OR, "UNCLE TOM'S CABIN" AS IT IS. Being Narratives, Scenes, and Incidents in the Real "Life of the Lowly." Buffalo, NY: George H. Derby & Company, 1852. 519 pp. Reprint. Ann Arbor, MI: University Microfilms International, 1968.

Account includes description of slave dances and performance practice, with special reference to a small boy who beat on a large watering-can as if it were a drum (53, 158-61, 164, 290, 293).

150 Steward, Austin. TWENTY-TWO YEARS A SLAVE, AND FORTY YEARS A FREEMAN.... Worcester, MA: William Alling, 1857. 360 pp. Reprint. New York: Negro Universities Press, 1969.

Ex-slave (1793-1860) discusses slave life in Virginia and in central New York, including description of a slave ball held at Easter time (30-31).

151 Stuart, Isaac William [Scaeva, pseud.]. HARTFORD IN THE OLDEN TIME: ITS FIRST THIRTY YEARS. BY SCAEVA. Edited by William B. Hartley. Hartford, CT: F. A. Brown, 1853. 316 pp. Reprint. Selected passages READINGS IN BLACK AMERICAN MUSIC. Edited by Eileen Southern. 2d ed. New York: W. W. Norton, 1983.

New England author discusses the black 'Lection Day festivals in colonial Connecticut, the election of black "governors," the parade through the city streets with the accompaniment of the music of fifes, fiddles, clarionets, and "assorted metal objects." Also references to blacks holding a Friday-night dance following the election (37-39).

152 Sturgis, C. F. MELVILLE LETTERS; OR, THE DUTIES OF MASTERS TO THEIR SERVANTS. Charleston, SC: Southern Baptist Publication Society, 1851. [47], 128 pp. Reprint. See Sturgis in Holland Nimmons McTyeire, DUTIES OF MASTERS TO SERVANTS: THREE PREMIUM ESSAYS.... Charleston: Southern Baptist Publication Company, 1851. Reprint. Freeport, NY: Books for Libraries Press, 1971.

Fictitious correspondence between two "brothers" describing slave festivities after "the crop is laid by" (81-85) includes comment on the dances and instruments---fiddle, banjo, and bones used as castenets---and the dance tunes "Old Viginny" and "Walk Jaw-bone." Also description of a black preacher's "discourses" and of religious singing (100-1).

153 Sullivan, Edward Robert. RAMBLES AND SCRAMBLES IN NORTH AND SOUTH AMERICA. London: Richard Bentley, 1852. 424 pp. Reprint. Microfilm. New Haven, CT: Research Publications, 1975.

English traveller refers to a quadroon ball in New Orleans where a dance resembling the Spanish fandango was performed without castanets (223).

154 Thorpe, Thomas Bangs. "Sugar and the Sugar Region of Louisiana." HARPER'S NEW MONTHLY MAGAZINE 7 (November 1853): 746-67.

Writer-artist of Massachusetts, who lived in Louisiana during the years 1836-1854, in discussing the sugar-growing region near Louisiana's Gulf Coast, includes comment on plantation life, on slave holidays, slave balls, and the plantation fiddler (767).

155 _____. "Cotton and Its Cultivation." HARPER'S NEW MONTHLY MAGAZINE 8 (March 1854): 447-63.

Discussion of cotton cultivation in the United States includes references to Christmas Day celebrations of the slaves, singing and instrumental music, performance practices, and dancing to the music of fiddles. Also discussion of the religious instruction of slaves.

156 _____. "Remembrances of the Mississippi." HARPER'S NEW MONTHLY MAGAZINE 12 (December 1855): 25-41.

Description of scenes viewed by the author while traveling down the Mississippi River includes comment on the singing of black deck-hands and on a man dancing the Virginia hoe-down.

157 _____. "Christmas in the South." FRANK LESLIE'S ILLUSTRATED NEWSPAPER 5 (2 January 1858): 62.

Discussion of Christmas festivities on the plantation includes comment on dance performance practice in regard to the ring dance, the musical instruments used (fiddle, banjo, bones), and on the Juba patters and the double shuffle.

158 Throop, George Higby [Gregory Seaworthy]. BERTIE; OR, LIFE IN THE OLD FIELD. A HUMOROUS NOVEL. Philadelphia: A. Hart, 1851. 242 pp. Reprint. Charlotte, NC: Heritage House, 1958.

Novel about a sea voyage to Norfolk, Virginia, includes discussion of the social customs in that city. Refers to black drivers improvising plaintive, monotonous songs (39) and a black coachman playing the violin to the accompaniment of the banjo (87). Detailed description of the John Kooners festival of the slaves during the Christmas holidays, including references to the masks and costumes of the John Kooner "mummers" (217-19).

Text of 1 song: O, dear maussa, wish ye Merry Christmas (219). References to 3 John Kuner songs: 1. Blow dat horn ag'in (218), 2. By on de row (219), 3. Hoozy! O, John Hoozy (219).

159 Trux, Jacob. J. "Negro Minstrelsy." PUTNAM'S MONTHLY 25 (January 1855): 72-79.

Discussion of Ethiopian minstrel songs of the period includes reference to performance practice associated with genuine slave singing in regard to boat songs (76-77), corn-shucking festivals (77), and improvisation (78).

Texts of 2 songs: 1. Cow boy on middle e' island (Cho: Ho! meleety, ho!): 2. Old Mans William, he gone to legislatur (Cho: Ah! chogaloga, chogaloga, chogalog).

160 Turnbull, Jane, and Marion Turnbull. AMERICAN PHOTOGRAPHS. 2 vols. London: T. C. Newby, 1859. Reprint. Micro-opaque. Louisville, KY: Lost Cause Press, 1963.

Two English sisters touring in the United States, Canada, and Cuba during the years 1852-1857 discuss the black workers they heard singing on the levee in New Orleans (2:43), and a Christmas ball where a shuffle step was danced to the music of two violins and a banjo (2:70-72). Also references to a religious service in Richmond, Virginia (2:216-18).

161 Updike, Wilkens. HISTORY OF THE EPISCOPAL CHURCH IN NARRAGANSETT, RHODE ISLAND. To Which Is Appended AMERICA DISSECTED by Rev. J. Macsparran. New York: Henry M. Onderdonk, 1847. 533 pp.

General historical survey includes discussion of slavery in Rhode Island (168-78) and description of the Election Day celebrations of the "Negro governors," held annually on the third Saturday in June and accompanied by dancing, games, and athletic exercises (177-78).

162 "A Visit to a Negro Cabin in Virginia." FAMILY MAGAZINE (New York) 3 (December 1835): 242-45. Reprints. FAMILY MAGAZINE (Cincinnati) 1 (February 1836): 42-45. FAMILY MAGAZINE (Philadelphia) 3 (1843): 42-45.

Extract from a travel journal includes comment on the singing at a corn-shucking festival, where there were from eighty to 100 participants. One man, chosen for his skill at improvisation, sat on top a pile of corn and "gave out a line in a sort of rapid chant, at the end of which the whole party joined in a chorus."

Text of 1 song: Oh, Jenny gone to New-Town (Cho: Oh, Jenny gone away).

163 Watkins, James. STRUGGLES FOR FREEDOM; OR THE LIFE OF JAMES WATKINS, FORMERLY A SLAVE IN MARYLAND, U.S., IN WHICH IS DETAILED A GRAPHIC ACCOUNT OF HIS EXTRAORDINARY ESCAPE FROM SLAVERY....1852. 19th ed. Manchester, England: Printed for the Author, 1860. 104 pp. Reprint. Washington, DC: Howard University Press, 1975.

Ex-slave author, b. 1823 in Cuckerville County, (near Baltimore) Maryland, discusses how slave children were forced to amuse plantation visitors by "performing various antics," such as imitating animals...with "others beating juba, dancing the forestep, the backstep, and the middle step" (12). Also description of a Methodist Camp Meeting in 1840, where "whites [were] in front of the minister, and the coloured people behind them." (18).

Text of 1 juba song: I went down the sandy point (Cho: And juba this, and juba that/ And juba killed the white-haired cat) (12).

164 Watson, John Fanning. "Olden Time Researches and Reminiscences of New York City." New-York Historical Society. Ms. BV.Sec.W, dated 1828. New York City.

Local historian, discussing the slaves on Long Island, New York, comments on their going "in great crowds" to Brooklyn to hold their "field frolics" on the Dutch holidays (62). Also comment on the slaves dancing in the public markets to the music of tom-toms and horns (63).

165 _____. HISTORIC TALES OF OLDEN TIME: CONCERNING THE EARLY SETTLEMENT AND ADVANCEMENT OF NEW-YORK CITY AND STATE. New York: Collins & Hannay, 1832. 214 pp.

Identification of the present-day center of City Hall in New York (between Wall and Broad Streets) as a gathering place for slave-holiday celebrations before the Revolutionary War (120). Observation made that slaves used to dance in the public markets, where they used "tomtoms, horns, etc., for music" (122).

166 _____. ANNALS AND OCCURRENCES OF NEW YORK CITY AND STATE, IN THE OLDEN TIME: BEING A COLLECTION OF MEMOIRS, ANECDOTES, AND INCIDENTS CONCERNING THE CITY, COUNTRY, AND INHABITANTS FROM THE DAYS OF THE FOUNDERS.... Philadelphia: Henry F. Anners, 1846. 390 pp.

References to slave dancing in the markets of New York to the music of tomtoms and horns and to slaves holding their "field frolics" on Dutch holidays, such as "Pinxter" (204). Also comment on the slave fiddler who played a three-string fiddle for a dancing class (212).

167 _____. ANNALS OF PHILADELPHIA AND PENNSYLVANIA IN THE OLDEN TIME. BEING A COLLECTION OF MEMOIRS, ANECDOTES, AND INCIDENTS OF THE CITY AND ITS INHABITANTS AND OF THE EARLIEST SETTLEMENTS OF THE INLAND PART OF PENNSYLVANIA, FROM THE DAYS OF THE FOUNDERS. Philadelphia: Elijah Thomas, 1857. 2 vols. Reprint. Microfilm. New Haven, CT: Yale University Library, 1987.

Book includes a chapter entitled "Negroes and Slaves," in which there is discussion of how the slaves danced and sang in African style at their jubilees on the last days of the annual fairs held in Philadelphia (2:265).

THE RELIGIOUS EXPERIENCE

168 Abbott, John Stevens Cabot. SOUTH AND

NORTH; OR, IMPRESSIONS RECEIVED DURING A TRIP TO CUBA AND THE SOUTH. New York: Abbey & Abbot, 1860. 352 pp. Reprint. Microfiche. Louisville, KY: Lost Cause Press, 1962.

Historian describes his visit to an African church in New Orleans on 11 December 1859 (75-76), commenting on the sermon preached by the untutored slave and on the "extempore" singing of the congregation.

169 Adams, Nehemiah. A SOUTH-SIDE VIEW OF SLAVERY; OR, THREE MONTHS AT THE SOUTH IN 1854. 2d ed. Boston: T. R. Marvin, 1855. 222 pp. Reprint. Microfiche. Louisville, KY: Lost Cause Press, 196-.

Boston clergyman refers to bands composed of slaves in military dress, playing quick-step tunes (20) and discusses the singing of the choirs in black churches (26-27, 211-12), all in Savannah, Georgia.

170 _____. THE SABLE CLOUD; A SOUTHERN TALE, WITH NORTHERN COMMENTS. Boston: Ticknor and Fields, 1861. 275 pp. Reprint. Westport, CT: Negro Universities Press, 1970.

Discussion of the burial of a baby slave (2-3), of worship services held on Easter Monday in South Carolina (59, 63), of a slave wedding (61-62), and briefly of a Methodist prayer meeting (90-91).

171 "African Barbarians." ZION'S HERALD AND WESLEYAN JOURNAL (=ZION'S HERALD) 22 (19 March 1851): [45].

Discussion of voodoo and its priestess, Betsey Toledano, and of the arrest of black women in New Orleans for participating in a voodoo ceremony. Comment on voodoo as an African religion (with its own rituals and symbols) and how it was brought to America by slaves. References to voodoo songs and a voodoo ceremonial room.

172 "The African Colony." CHRISTIAN WATCHMAN & REFLECTOR (=WATCHMAN-EXAMINER) n.s. 2 (31 March 1821): 63.

Article (dated Norfolk, Virginia, 21 January 1821) describes the repatriation of four slaves back to Africa by the Norfolk Colonization Society. Comment on the black preachers (two from Norfolk and one from Petersburg, Virginia,) who officiated at a ceremony and on a sermon delivered by the Petersburg preacher on board the brig prior to the departure of the slaves.

173 "An African Funeral." CHRISTIAN WATCHMAN & REFLECTOR (=WATCHMAN-EXAMINER) 33 (12 August 1852): 132.

Description of a slave funeral (place and date not indicated) including "mourning" practices---mourners seated in a circle, women wailing to the beating of a drum---and after-burial practices: for example, mourners dancing around a fire at night to ward off the spirit of the deceased.

174 THE AFRICAN METHODIST EPISCOPAL POCKET HYMN BOOK; SELECTED FROM DIFFERENT AUTHORS. Published by Richard Allen for the African Methodist Connection in the United States. Philadelphia: J. H. Cunningham, Printer, 1818. Preface signed by Allen, James Champion, and Daniel Coker. Later editions (titles vary slightly) were published throughout the century, beginning in 1833 (see also nos. 236, 871, 872).

This, the first "official" A. M. E. hymnal, was compiled after the Church received its charter of incorporation in 1816. The hymnal compiled by Richard Allen in 1801 is not cited in histories of the A. M. E. Church (see no. 176). Although this 1818 edition includes no folksongs, it is useful as an indicator of the hymns sung in black churches of the antebellum period. Phrases from the most popular of the hymns were carried over into the repertory of Negro spirituals, which was developing during this period.

175 Alexander, James Edward. TRANSATLANTIC SKETCHES COMPRISING VISITS TO THE MOST INTERESTING SCENES IN NORTH AND SOUTH AMERICA AND THE WEST INDIES. Philadelphia: Key and Biddle, 1833. 2 vols. Reprint. Microfiche. Louisville, KY: Lost Cause Press, 1966.

Discussion of the religious service of a black congregation in Memphis, Tennessee (2:255). Most of the references are to black folk traditions in the West Indies: for example, to the dancing of "Joan Johnny" (2:94) or the musical instrument called the "bamba, a bent bow" (2:212).

176 Allen, Richard, ed. A COLLECTION OF SPIRITUAL SONGS AND HYMNS SELECTED FROM VARIOUS AUTHORS BY RICHARD ALLEN, AFRICAN MINISTER. Philadelphia: John Ormrod, 1801. 54 hymns. 2d ed. A COLLECTION OF HYMNS AND SPIRITUAL SONGS FROM VARIOUS AUTHORS. BY RICHARD ALLEN, MINISTER OF THE AFRICAN METHODIST EPISCOPAL CHURCH. Philadelphia: T. L. Plowman, 1801. 64 hymns. Reprints. Microprint. Worcester, MA: American Antiquarian Society, 1964 (Shaw-Shoemaker, EARLY AMERICAN IMPRINTS, Series no. 2 [1801-20], nos. 38, 39). Reprint of List of Contents in READINGS IN BLACK AMERICAN MUSIC. Edited by Eileen Southern. 2d ed. New York: W. W. Norton, 1983.

Allen (1760-1831), founder and first bishop of the African Methodist Episcopal Church, was the compiler of this first hymnal published expressly for use by black congregations. It includes hymns to which have been attached "wandering refrains" or choruses, a novel practice for that time period.

Texts of 3 wandering choruses: (1) Hallelujah to

the Lamb (hymn nos. 1, 50); (2) Sinners, can you hate that Saviour (no. 45); (3) Hail the gospel jubilee (no. 56 in 2d ed.).

177 -----. THE LIFE EXPERIENCE AND GOSPEL LABORS OF THE RT. REV. RICHARD ALLEN. To Which Is Annexed The Rise and Progress of the African Methodist Episcopal Church in the United States of America....Written by Himself and Published at His Request. Philadelphia: Martin and Boden, 1833. 60 pp. Reprints. Philadelphia: A. M. E. Publishing House, 1887. New York: Abingdon Press, 1960.

Allen discusses in his autobiography his experiences as an itinerant preacher and as the minister of the Bethel Church in Philadelphia, among other topics. He observes that reading sermons is "not as beneficial to the colored people as spiritual or extempore preaching" (30).

178 Allen, William, ed. MEMOIR OF JOHN CODMAN ...WITH REMINISCENCES, BY JOSHUA BATES. Boston: T. R. Marvin and S. K. Whipple & Company, 1853. 408 pp.

New England clergyman's discussion of his visit to the South in 1824 includes references to the old slave Scipio, who served as "priest, physician, and nurse" for the slaves on a plantation near Richmond, Virginia (120), and to worship services in a church near Fairfield, Virginia, where the black members of the congregation withdrew to the woods during intermissions to listen to "one of their own number, whom they call an 'exhorter'" (121).

179 Anderson, Thomas. INTERESTING ACCOUNT OF THOMAS ANDERSON, A SLAVE, TAKEN FROM HIS OWN LIPS BY J. P. CLARK. N. p., c.1854. 12 pp. Reprint. Microfiche. Louisville, KY: Lost Cause Press, 1968.

Antebellum slave preacher (b. 1785) of Virginia discusses his religious conversion, his struggle to learn to read the Bible, and his preaching the Gospel.

180 Andrew, James O. "A Fortnight among the Missions to Blacks: I." SOUTHERN CHRISTIAN ADVOCATE 20 (14 May 1857): 199.

Missionary discusses his work among the slaves on rice plantations near Charleston, South Carolina, and Savannah, Georgia, in a letter dated 29 April 1857. Refers to the singing of hymns by slaves and related performance practice.

181 Andrews, Ethan Allen. SLAVERY AND THE DOMESTIC SLAVE-TRADE IN THE UNITED STATES. IN A SERIES OF LETTERS ADDRESSED TO THE EXECUTIVE COMMITTEE OF THE AFRICAN UNION FOR THE RELIEF AND IMPROVEMENT OF THE COLORED RACE. Boston: Light & Stearns, 1836. 201 pp. Reprint. Washington, DC: Microcard Editions, 1970.

Discussion of slavery in Maryland and the District of Columbia by a New Englander includes description of a worship service in a church on Sharp Street in Baltimore, with special reference to the sermon and congregational responses (88-89). Also comment on the "quality" of "the African voices" (93).

Reference to 1 sermon: Philip's going down to Samaria (88).

182 Arthur, T. S. "Cato and Joe at the Love-Feast." SOUTHERN CHRISTIAN ADVOCATE 10/33 (22 January 1847): 132. Reprint. ZION'S HERALD AND WESLEYAN JOURNAL 18/6 (10 FEBRUARY 1847): 24.

Detailed description of a Negro Love Feast in Baltimore, Maryland, at the Bethel Meeting House on Fish Street. Transcriptions of the texts of 2 exhortations, both based on the theme "forgiveness of sins."

183 ASSOCIATION FOR THE RELIGIOUS INSTRUCTION OF NEGROES. Second Annual REPORT OF THE MISSIONARY TO THE NEGROES IN LIBERTY COUNTY, GEORGIA. Charleston, n. p., 1835. 23 pp. Reprint. Atlanta University Black Culture Collection. Microfilm. Wooster, OH: Bell & Howell, 1974.

Report on the status of the black religious community in Liberty County, Georgia, in 1835, describes the organization of black congregations (8), the administration of the churches by white clergy, and the annual appointments of the slave exhorters as supervisors of black congregations during the absence of the white clergy. Outlines the duties of the exhorter in addition to preaching, such as solemnizing marriages.

184 Atwater, Horace Cowles. INCIDENTS OF A SOUTHERN TOUR; OR, THE SOUTH AS SEEN BY NORTHERN EYES. Boston: J. P. Magee, 1857. 120 pp. Reprint. Microcard. Louisville, KY: Lost Cause Press, 1968.

Northern clergyman describes a plantation religious service and relevant performance practice (91, 93-94).

185 B., B. L. S. "Slave Preaching." LITTELL'S LIVING AGE 65 (5 May 1860): 326-29.

Excerpts from an Englishwoman's memoirs discuss her visits to slave churches in the antebellum South (in Louisville, Kentucky, and New Orleans, Louisiana) and slave preachers. Description of sermons and congregational performance practice.

Text fragment of 1 sermon: 1. If a man desire the office of bishop, he desireth a good work.

186 B., J. "Negro Melody." SOUTHERN CHRISTIAN ADVOCATE 20 (3 July 1856): 17.

Visitor to a plantation in the South comments on

the slaves singing "songs of Zion" in a letter dated 18 June [1856]. Observes that the "sable band" assembled in the evening, formed a line and "approached with measured tread along the garden walk" while serenading their missionary preacher.

187 Bangs, Nathan. THE LIFE OF THE REV. FREEBORN GARRETTSON: COMPILED FROM HIS PRINTED AND MANUSCRIPT JOURNALS, AND OTHER AUTHENTIC DOCUMENTS. New York: Published by G. Lane & C. B. Tippett for the Methodist Episcopal Church, 1845. 294 pp. Reprint. Microfilm. Ann Arbor, MI: University Microfilms International, 1974.

Biography of Methodist clergyman Garrettson includes references to "Black Harry" Hosier, who accompanied Garrettson on his tour of New England in 1790 (186, 190), and to the several occasions on which Hosier's preaching attracted large crowds that were "curious and admiring" (161, 187, 189, 192, 194, 195). Also references to the "extravagant" worship practices of black Methodists (223, 224).

188 "Baptism: The Negroes in and around Beaufort, S. C." INDEPENDENT 14 (14 August 1862): 3.

Description of a public baptism ceremony on Ladies' Island, opposite Beaufort, South Carolina, where thirty-four candidates were baptized.

189 Baylies, H. "Tour of the Southwest." ZION'S HERALD AND WESLEYAN JOURNAL (=ZION'S HERALD) 22 (24 September 1851): [153].

Resident of Edgartown, Massachusetts, writing of his travels through the interior of Alabama, comments on the singing of religious songs by the slaves and describes a quilting bee he saw near Mobile, Alabama.

190 _____. "Tour of the Southwest---2. The Negroes." ZION'S HERALD AND WESLEYAN JOURNAL (=ZION'S HERALD) 22 (29 October 1851): [173].

Discussion of slavery in the South, including description of a religious service, with comment on the oratory style and sermon of the slave preacher, the singing of the congregation, their improvised religious songs, and related performance practice.

Text of 1 song: 1. We'll range Jerusalem around.

191 Bell, Priscilla Wakefield. EXCURSIONS IN NORTH AMERICA. Described in Letters from a Gentleman and His Young Companion to Their Friends in England. 2d ed. London: Darton, Harvey & Darton, 1810. Reprint. Microfilm. New Haven, CT: Research Publications, 1975.

Correspondence of Englishmen Arthur Middleton and Henry Franklin contains several references to blacks, including description of an African church in Philadelphia (9).

192 Bodichon, Barbara Leigh Smith. AN AMERICAN DIARY, 1857-1858. Edited from the Manuscript by Joseph W. Reed, Jr. London: Routledge & Kegan Paul, c.1972. 198 pp.

Englishwoman traveling in America on her wedding trip describes visits to black churches (82, 87-88, 105-8, 119, 125) and observes that slaves in some places continued their African customs of worship (96). Also comment on singing and performance practice (88, 119): how the slaves imitated musical instruments with their voices and added "peculiar" musical sounds at the end of verses.

Text of 1 chorus: I'm going home to glorie (108). Reference to 1 sermon text: History of John.

193 Bremer, Frederika. HOMES OF THE NEW WORLD: IMPRESSIONS OF AMERICA. Translated by Mary Howitt. 2 vols. New York: Harper & Brothers, 1853. Reprints. New York: Negro Universities Press, 1968. Selected passages in READINGS IN BLACK AMERICAN MUSIC. Edited by Eileen Southern. 1971. 2d ed. New York: W. W. Norton, 1983.

Swedish novelist Bremer visited the United States during the years 1849-1850, and after returning to Europe wrote this book, which was so popular that it went through five printings in one month. The format of the book is a series of letters written to friends in Europe, interspersed with entries in her diary. She includes detailed description of her visits to black churches in Charleston, South Carolina (1:392-94), Washington, D. C. (1:490-92), Cincinnati, Ohio (2:157-60), and a class meeting in a Methodist church of New Orleans, Louisiana (2:234-38). She also describes a camp meeting near Charleston, South Carolina (1:306-17). Her discussion of worksongs includes description of firemen on ships singing as they worked (2:174), songs of boatmen (1:385), and slaves singing in the tobacco factories in Richmond, Virginia (2:509-10). Also comment on the slaves improvising and composing their own songs (1:369-71, 393) and making their own musical instruments (1:371). There is a reference to two African songs sung by a slave (1:394).

Text of 1 song: What ship is this that's landed on the shore (Cho: It's the old Ship of Zion, hallelujah) (2:157-60).

194 _____. "Frederika Bremer on Slavery." NATIONAL ANTI-SLAVERY STANDARD 14 (5 November 1853): 94.

Excerpts from the Swedish novelist's book, HOMES OF THE NEW WORLD (see no. 193), include discussion of her visits to black churches. References to blacks singing "their own religious songs" without instrumental accompaniment and comment on the folk preacher, his oratory style, and the communal responses of his congregation.

Text of 1 song: What ship is this that's landed at the shore? (Cho: O, glory halleluiah!). Summary of 1 sermon: Those who come out of great afflictions.

195 _____. AMERICA OF THE FIFTIES: LETTERS OF FREDRIKA BREMER. Selected and edited by Adolph B. Benson. New York: The American-Scandinavian Foundation, 1924. 340 pp. Reprint. Microfiche. Chicago: Library Resources, Inc., 1970.

Discussion of the author's visits to black churches and detailed description of performance practice in Charleston, South Carolina (149-51), Washington, D.C. (190-91), and Savannah, Georgia (132-35). Also description of camp meeting held near Macon, Georgia (114-23), religious service in a slave cabin (104-5), and a class meeting of the AME Church in New Orleans (274-80). Comment on the importance of song to the slave (106-7), the use of the drum to call the slaves to work (97), and the singing of black firemen on the steamer Belle Kay as it sailed down the Mississippi (261-62).

196 Brown, Henry Box. NARRATIVE OF HENRY BOX BROWN, WHO ESCAPED FROM SLAVERY ENCLOSED IN A BOX 3 FEET LONG AND 2 WIDE. Written from a Statement of Facts Made by Himself, with Remarks upon the Remedy for Slavery by Charles Stearns. Boston: Brown & Stearns, 1849. 92 pp. Reprint. Wilmington, DE: Scholarly Resources, Inc., 1970.

Ex-slave, born 1815 in Louisa Country, Virginia (near Richmond), describes a slave baptism conducted at night by an old slave, Uncle John (23-24).

197 Buckingham, James Silk. THE EASTERN AND WESTERN STATES OF AMERICA. 3 vols. London: Fisher, Sons and Company, 1842. Reprint. Microfiche. Louisville, KY: Lost Cause Press, 1973.

Description by an English traveler of a religious service in "one of the principal Methodist meeting-houses of Colored people in Philadelphia" includes quotation of some of the phrases used by the preacher and the call-and-response interchange between preacher and congregation (2:327-29).

198 Burke, Emily P. REMINISCENCES OF GEORGIA. Oberlin: James M. Fitch, 1850. 252 pp. Reprint. Microfiche. Louisville, KY: Lost Cause Press, 1968.

Teacher of New England, who taught in a Georgia female seminary for five months, published this book in the format of thirty letters, which have an extensive discussion of slavery. References to a slave singing in her own African language about her homeland (123) and to slave amusements on Sundays (149). Description of slaves dancing around bonfires in the evening (121-22), of a slave burial at night (232), and of a "colored" camp meeting (244-45).

199 C. "Missionary Sketches: Old Friday." SOUTHERN CHRISTIAN ADVOCATE 7 (7 July 1843): 14.

Methodist missionary describes his pastoral visit to Friday, an African slave who is approximately eighty years old. Observes that Friday still follows the ways of worship that he brought with him from Africa and refers to an Arabic prayer text, "Allah je Allah." Also discussion of the night burial of a slave.

200 _____. "Missionary Sketches: Boating on the River." SOUTHERN CHRISTIAN ADVOCATE 7 (14 July 1843): 18.

Missionary's discussion of his work among the slaves in South Carolina includes references to the religious instruction of children, the singing of slave boatmen, and relevant performance practice.

Texts of 2 songs: 1. I gwine cross tomorrow morning (Cho: De army gone over). 2. O brodder, take care Satan.

201 _____. "Missionary Sketches: Life on a Negro Mission." SOUTHERN CHRISTIAN ADVOCATE 7 (29 December 1843): 114.

Discussion of missionary work among the slaves on the Sea Islands of South Carolina includes comment on their singing both hymns from the hymnals and songs of their own improvisation.

Texts of 6 songs: 1. O weep not, Mary (Cho: Jesus rose from the dead). 2. Free grace and a dying Lamb (Cho: We hear from heaben today). 3. O backslider, you better go pray. 4. Broder Cesar set on the tree of life (Cho: Roll, Jordan, roll). 5. News from heaben de oder day (Cho: Rally all round de promise land). 6. O Lord, what shall I do (Cho: No hidin' place for sinner here). Texts of 2 couplets: 1. Dis berry same Jesus we hear dese people de talk about. 2. Possum fat and hominy. Reference to 1 song: Massa hab de grog bottle.

202 C., E. "Slavery in Tennessee." NATIONAL ANTI-SLAVERY STANDARD 5 (27 March 1845): 169.

Discussion of slave preachers in Tennessee.

203 C., L. M. "Letters from New York.---No. 12." NATIONAL ANTI-SLAVERY STANDARD 2 (2 December 1841): 103.

Discussion of the sermon of a blind, ex-slave preacher at a church on Asbury Street (New York City) includes comment on his oratory style.

Reference to 1 sermon: Paul and Silas in prison.

204 _____. "Letters from New York.---No. 13." NATIONAL ANTI-SLAVERY STANDARD 2 (9 December 1841): 107.

Discussion of the preaching of Julia Pell of Philadelphia, daughter of a fugitive slave, includes comment on her oratory style and on the communal responses of the congregation to her preaching.

205 "The Camp Meeting." LIBERATOR 12 (28 October 1842): 172. Reprint from the Salem OBSERVER.

Description of a camp meeting held at Orne's Point, (Massachusetts ?). Reporter observes that blacks and whites worshipped together, and comments on the black preacher who addressed the congregation, and on the camp-meeting hymns, especially one sung by the black worshipers: You will see your Lord a-coming.

206 Campbell, Israel. BOND AND FREE; OR, YEARNINGS FOR FREEDOM FROM MY GREEN BRIER HOUSE. Being the Story of My Life in Bondage and My Life in Freedom. Philadelphia: Published by the Author, 1861. 320 pp. Reprint. Microfiche. Denver, CO: Information Resources Division, 1977.

Narrative of an ex-slave who escaped from slavery and became a minister includes a detailed description of slave life.

Text of 1 song: Oh, I do believe, I do believe (203). Text of 1 wedding sermon: 1 Peter 2:1-2 (23).

207 Carpenter, Russell. OBSERVATIONS ON AMERICAN SLAVERY AFTER A YEAR'S TOUR IN THE UNITED STATES. London: E. T. Whitfield, 1852. 69 pp.

English traveler's account includes description of a slave prayer meeting he visited in Charleston, South Carolina, in 1851, and comment on the prayers, singing of hymns and other religious songs, and performance practice (35-36).

Reference to 1 song: I go before you to Galilee (Cho: Hallelujah)

208 Cartwright, D. S. "Negro Freedom an Impossibility under Nature's Laws." DE BOW'S REVIEW 30 (May-June 1861): 648-59.

Comment on the blacks' Satanic worship practices through Vandoua [=voodoo], on the cult of the snake, and on voodoo cults in New Orleans.

209 Catto, William T. A SEMI-CENTENARY DISCOURSE, DELIVERED IN THE FIRST AFRICAN PRESBYTERIAN CHURCH, PHILADELPHIA, ON THE FOURTH SABBATH OF MAY, 1857.... 111 pp. Philadelphia, Joseph M. Watson, 1857. Reprint. Freeport, NY: Books for Libraries Press, 1971.

Written by the Church's pastor, this book is virtually a history of black Christianity in Philadelphia during the first half of the nineteenth century. An appendix give sketches of the black churches in the city in 1850. Discussion of the founding of the first black Presbyterian church includes comment on the practice of holding religious services in private homes and on the street under the leadership of ex-slave John Gloucester, later chosen as the Church's first minister (47-48). Also reference to a fiddler (28-29).

210 Caulkins, Nehemiah. "Narrative of Mr. Caulkins." LIBERATOR 9 (24 May 1839): [81]-82. Reprint. ANTI-SLAVERY EXAMINER 4 (1839): 11-17.

Discussion of slavery on plantations in the vicinity of Wilmington, North Carolina, from 1820 to 1835, includes comment on the slaves' songs and ring dances. Also description of a plantation religious service.

Text of 1 song: Hurra for good massa (Cho: Hurra, I'm going to de city).

211 "A Centenarian Coloured Preacher." NATIONAL ANTI-SLAVERY STANDARD 16 (19 January 1856): [1].

Summary of an address by Rev. Krebs about Rev. Andrew Marshall, pastor of the First African Baptist Church of Savannah, Georgia, describes a religious service at the church. Comment on the the preacher's "reading" the hymn which was sung by the congregation.

Summary of 1 sermon: The importance of the death of Christ and the astonishing results.

212 Child, Lydia Maria. "The Black Saxons." LIBERATOR 11 (8 January 1841): [5]-6. Reprint as "The Meeting in the Swamp." THE FREEDMAN'S BOOK. Boston: Ticknor & Fields, 1865.

Short story written by the abolitionist includes description of a prayer meeting of slaves held near Charleston, South Carolina, during the War of 1812, and comment on the slave preacher and on the slaves singing "half-suppressed snatches of songs."

213 Clay, Thomas Savage. DETAIL OF A PLAN FOR THE MORAL IMPROVEMENT OF NEGROES ON PLANTATIONS. Read before the Georgia Presbytery. N.p. Printed at the Request of the Presbytery [of Bryan County, Georgia], 1833. 23 pp. Reprint. Microfiche. Louisville, KY: Lost Cause Press, 1966.

Discussion of the kind of religious instruction that should be given the slaves. Reference to the slave children's "fondness for music" and "correctness of their ear in measuring time." thus making it comparatively easy to teach them hymns (9).

214 Coker, Daniel. JOURNAL OF DANIEL COKER, A DESCENDENT OF AFRICA, FROM THE TIME OF LEAVING NEW YORK ON THE SHIP ELIZABETH.... Baltimore, MD: Edward Coale, 1820. 52 pp. Reprint. New York: Kraus International, 1970.

Text of a sermon delivered by Coker (1780-1846) on shipboard, which was based on Rom. 1:6, and references to the "songs of Zion" sung by the black people below deck (18).

215 Colbert, William. "A Journal of the Travels of William Colbert, 1794-1814." Manuscript. About 2,000 pp. Garrett Theological Seminary, Evanston, IL. Available in microfilm. 2 reels.

Methodist clergyman includes numerous references to black Methodist groups in his day-by-day account of experiences, which included preaching and exhorting to Methodist classes, church congregations, Love Feasts, and camp meetings. Frequent comment on the "liveliness" of black groups, to their "great shouts" or "extravagant shouts...amazing agitation, noisiness...[and] high spirits." On one occasion "the Lord was praised in the song, in the shout, and in the dance" (7 December 1801, p. 1157). Specific discussion of the singing at the Bethel Church, Philadelphia, with the comment that his companions made satirical remarks about the kind of song being performed (27 September 1804), and at the Zoar Church in Philadelphia in regard to "melodious and animating" singing after a church service (6 December 805). Many references to Black Harry Hoshure [Hosier], including praise of his "powerful preaching" (8 June 1803, 12 January 1805, 20 January 1805, 2 September 1805, etc.). Also several references to Richard Allen, minister of Bethel.

216 "Colored Church in Richmond." CHRISTIAN WATCHMAN & REFLECTOR (=WATCHMAN-EXAMINER) 24 (23 June 1843): 99.

Letter from the editor of the BAPTIST RECORD, dated Richmond, 8 June [1843], discusses his attendance at the black Baptist church and comments on singing and relevant performance practice.

217 "Colored Class Meetings." ZION'S HERALD AND WESLEYAN JOURNAL (=ZION'S HERALD) 27 (17 June 1857): 96. Reprinted from LONG'S PICTURES OF SLAVERY [see no. 123].

Discussion of the religious instruction given by the Methodist Episcopal Church to slaves refers to the fact that Protestant hymn books are often the only source of catechism for them. Description of a Sunday morning prayer-meeting.

218 "A Colored Man's Eloquence." ZION'S HERALD AND WESLEYAN JOURNAL (=ZION'S HERALD) 27 (16 January 1856): 10.

Correspondent for the Washington, D. C., MORNING STAR discusses the sermon of a young licensed black preacher, Mr. Collins, whom he heard at the Asbury Chapel in Washington, D. C. Synopsis of the sermon text and discussion of performance practice.

Summary of 1 sermon: Speak unto the Children of Israel that they go forward (Exodus 14:15).

219 "A Colored Preacher." CHRISTIAN WATCHMAN & REFLECTOR (=WATCHMAN-EXAMINER) 43 (14 August 1862): [1].

Discussion of the Rev. Abraham Murchison, a black pastor in Hilton Head, South Carolina, at the examination of candidates for baptism includes comment on his practice of "reading the hymn by heart" and on the prohibition of hand clapping and feet stamping at his services.

220 Commonwealth [pseud.]. "A Day or Two at Beaufort." CHRISTIAN WATCHMAN & REFLECTOR (=WATCHMAN-EXAMINER) 43 (30 January 1862): [1].

Newpaper correspondent's discussion of his visit to Beaufort, South Carolina, includes comment on the efforts of the northern missionaries to instruct the ex-slaves and on the training of black teachers and preachers. Also comment on the fact that the missionaries aimed to educate "head men" on the plantations, who would oversee their "less enlightened brethern."

221 ____. "South Carolina Correspondent." CHRISTIAN WATCHMAN & REFLECTOR (=WATCHMAN-EXAMINER) 43 (14 August 1862): [2].

Discussion of the dedication of a black Baptist church at Hilton Head, South Carolina, in a letter dated 28 July 1862, includes comment on the sermon and on the congregations's spontaneous singing of a spiritual at the conclusion of the service.

Text of 1 song: Blow, Gabriel blow.

222 "Congregational Singing in Richmond, Virginia." DWIGHT'S JOURNAL OF MUSIC 18 (12 January 1861): 333.

Essay about the music of blacks in Richmond refers to the singing of the slaves in the tobacco factories and describes the singing in the black church.

223 "Contraband Camp at Port Royal, South Carolina." AMERICAN MISSIONARY (MAGAZINE) n.s. 6 (January 1862): 17-18.

Observation that contrabands in the army camp at Port Royal held nightly prayer meetings.

224 Cowper, [William]. "Miscellany: Prince Moro." CHRISTIAN WATCHMAN & REFLECTOR 6 (=WATCHMAN-EXAMINER) (September 1825): 168.

Account of a captured African prince of the Mohammedan faith, who was enslaved in Fayetteville, North Carolina, about 1808, refers to the slave's African homeland and his position there as a "pray-God" to his king. Observation that the slave spoke both Arabic and English.

225 Crafts, F. A. "Letter from District of Columbia." ZION'S HERALD AND WESLEYAN JOURNAL (=ZION'S HERALD) 18 (10 February 1847): 22.

Letter dated 19 January [184-], Alexandria, Virginia, includes comment on the religious institutions in Washington, D. C., and on the colored Methodists, who numbered about 400 individuals and worshipped in a segregated church. Also dedescription of a black Love Feast in Washington.

Synopses of 4 exhortations.

226 D'Arusmont, Frances Wright. VIEWS OF SOCIETY AND MANNERS IN AMERICA; IN A SERIES OF SHORT LETTERS FROM THAT COUNTRY TO A FRIEND IN ENGLAND DURING...1818, 1819, AND 1820. New York: E. Bliss and E. White, 1821. 387 pp. Reprint. Microfiche. Denver, CO: Information Resource Division, 1977.

English writer's discussion of slavery in the United States includes references to the dancing of slaves (56) and to African churches and their preachers in northern cities (53).

227 Dalcho, Frederick. AN HISTORICAL ACCOUNT OF THE PROTESTANT EPISCOPAL CHURCH IN SOUTH CAROLINA. Charleston: Published by E. Thayer, 1820. 613 pp. Reprint. New York: Arno Press and the New York Times, 1972.

Account includes discussion of the "Negroe School House" set up in Charleston, South Carolina, by Commissary Alexander Garden, which was operative for twenty-two years, with the slaves Harry and Andrew serving as teachers (148-93).

228 Dalton, William. TRAVELS IN THE UNITED STATES OF AMERICA, AND IN PART OF UPPER CANADA. Appleby, England: R. Bateman, 1821. 256 pp. Reprint. Microfiche. Ottawa: Canadian Institute for Historical Reproductions, 1982.

English traveler describes his visit to a black church in Philadelphia in 1819 (36-37).

Reference to 1 sermon text: Romans 8:19.

229 Davies, Ebenezer. AMERICAN SCENES, AND CHRISTIAN SLAVERY; A RECENT TOUR OF FOUR THOUSAND MILES IN THE UNITED STATES. London: John Snow, 1849. 324 pp. Reprints. New York: Johnson Reprint Company, 1969. New York: Arno Press and the New York Times, 1973.

English minister, who had lived in the West Indies, entered the United States through New Orleans and traveled northward. His discussion of slavery includes references to slave drivers forcing members of a slave coffle to dance to the music of a fiddle in order to prevent them from praying at night or sinking into further melancholy (94); to slave boatmen on the "flat boats" (carrying cargo) who danced to fiddle music (97); and to religious services in a Methodist church of Baltimore (198-99) and in a Congregational church of New Haven, Connecticut (262-63).

Reference to 1 sermon text: Behold, I come quickly (Revelation) (198).

230 De Bow, James Dunwoody B. "Plantation Life ---Duties and Responsibilities." DE BOW'S REVIEW 29 (November 1860): 357-68.

Editorial about Holland N. McTyeire's book, DUTIES OF CHRISTIAN MASTERS (1851), includes description of a plantation barbecue (360), discussion of the church as a "social institution" (364), and of the use of music at work and at worship (366). Observation that a slave singer has been heard giving out the lines to himself when singing a hymn.

231 "Denmark Vesey." ATLANTIC MONTHLY 7 (June 1861): 728-44.

Biographical sketch of the slave-insurrection leader Vesey (1767-1822), based on official reports, includes comments on the texts he used in preaching to the slaves: Zechariah 14: 1-3 and Joshua 6:21 (731). Also references to Gullah Jack of Angola, "a conjurer by profession" (732-33) and to the closing of the African Church in Charleston (735).

232 Dickson, Andrew Flinn. PLANTATION SERMONS; OR, PLAIN AND FAMILIAR DISCOURSES FOR THE INSTRUCTION OF THE UNLEARNED. Philadelphia: Presbyterian Board of Publication, c.1856. 170 pp. Reprint. Microfiche. Chicago: Library Resources, Inc., 1971.

Twelve sermons written by a Presbyterian missionary of South Carolina for the religious instruction of slaves. The eighth sermon, entitled "The New Creature," quotes a couplet from a slave song.

Text of 1 couplet: Free, oh free, my Lord (p. 110).

233 _____. LESSONS ABOUT SALVATION FROM THE LIFE AND WORDS OF THE LORD JESUS. Being a Second Series of Plantation Sermons. Philadelphia: Presbyterian Board of Publication, 1860. 264 pp.

Collection of fifteen sermons intended for the religious instruction of slaves includes discussion of religious practices of the slaves (8-11). Observes that the slaves alter religious songs learned from whites by introducing "vivid" imageries. References to the songs of field hands and to three Protestant hymns popular among slaves.

Text of 1 couplet: Free, oh free, my Lord, Free from every sin! (10).

234 Dix, John R. TRANSATLANTIC TRACINGS AND POPULAR PICTURES FROM AMERICAN SUBJECTS. BY THE AUTHOR of PEN AND INK SKETCHES.... London: W. Tweedie, 1853. 337 pp. Also published as TRANSATLANTIC TRACINGS; OR, SKETCHES OF PERSONS AND SCENES IN AMERICA. ...1853.

English traveler discusses the black experience in three chapters: Chapter 11, "The Camp Meeting---A Western Sketch" (185-209); Chapter 13, "Southern Sketches--Glances at Negro Life" (229-43); and Chapter 15, "Negro Camp Meeting at Flushing, Long Island, State of New York" (280-300). His book includes detailed description of a funeral (233-36) near Richmond, Virginia; of a worship service in Richmond, where the congregation engaged in "ridiculous repetitions of verses of hymns" (242); of a religious service on board a ship en route to a camp meeting on Long Island, and comment on the fiddler who accompanied the singing (286-289); and of the singing and sermons at the camp meeting on Long Island (240-300). Includes the text of a sermon delivered by a black exhorter from Kentucky, the Rev. Julius Caesar H. Hain (201-9).

Text of 1 sermon: The battle between David and Goliath (201-9). Text of 1 song (290):I'm 'listing for de 'oly war (Cho: Will you go 'long wid me?).

235 Dixon, James. METHODISM IN AMERICA: WITH THE PERSONAL NARRATIVE OF THE AUTHOR, DURING A TOUR THROUGH A PART OF THE UNITED STATES AND CANADA. London: Printed for the Author, 1849. 498 pp. Reprint. Microfiche. Ottawa: Canadian Institute for Historical Reproductions, 1981.

Includes description of the English author's visit to the African Asylum (conducted by Methodists) in New York City, where the children sang "some of their sweet and pathetic ditties having relation to their circumstances" for the visitors (28-29), and of the new African Church in Pittsburgh, where the "people sang some of their own peculiarly soft and melancholy airs" after the sermon and "danced to their own melody" (67).

236 THE DOCTRINES AND DISCIPLINE OF THE AFRICAN METHODIST EPISCOPAL CHURCH. Philadelphia: John H. Cunningham, 1817. 192 pp.

Section 22, entitled "Of the Spirit and Truth of Singing," offers insight into the church-music repertory and performance practice of the early A. M. E. Church. The sixteen precepts given include admonitions against singing "too slow," singing "hymns of your own composing," and singing "fuge [sic] tunes...in our public congregations." Preachers are urged to "exhort every person in the congregation to sing."

237 Douglass, Frederick. MY BONDAGE AND MY FREEDOM. With an Introduction by Dr. James McCune Smith. New York and Auburn: Miller, Orton & Mulligan, 1855. 464 pp. Reprint. New York: Arno Press and the New York Times, 1968. Selected passages in READINGS IN BLACK AMERICAN MUSIC. Edited by Eileen Southern. 2d ed. New York: W. W. Norton, 1983. See also nos. 429, 1138.

In this book, the second autobiography published by ex-slave Douglass (1818?-1895), he discusses the meaning of the slave songs (96-101), offering a restatement of the ideas he presented in his NARRATIVE... (1845). Also he describes a camp meeting (192-94); refers to the "raising of a hymn" (217); comments on the double meaning of some slave song texts (278-79); and describes two dances: 1. pattin' Juba. 2. Jubilee beating (252).

Texts of 2 songs: 1. I am going away to the great house (Cho: O yea! O yea!) (98). 2. We raise de wheat (Cho: Walk over!) (252-53).

238 Douglass, William. ANNALS OF THE FIRST AFRICAN CHURCH IN THE UNITED STATES OF AMERICA, NOW STYLED THE AFRICAN EPISCOPAL CHURCH OF ST. THOMAS, PHILADELPHIA.... PARTLY DERIVED FROM THE MINUTES OF A BENEFICIAL SOCIETY, ESTABLISHED BY ABSALOM JONES, RICHARD ALLEN AND OTHERS, IN 1787, AND PARTLY FROM THE MINUTES OF THE AFORESAID CHURCH. Philadelphia: King & Baird, Printers, 1862. 172 pp. Reprint. New York: New York Public Library, 1974.

Detailed account of the founding of the Free African Society in Philadelphia and the St. Thomas Church includes references to the rules for musical procedures in worship services (54).

239 Dow, Lorenzo. HISTORY OF COSMOPOLITE; OR, THE FOUR VOLUMES OF LORENZO'S JOURNAL CONCENTRATED IN ONE; CONTAINING HIS EXPERIENCE & TRAVELS, FROM CHILDHOOD TO 1814 .... New York: Printed and Sold by John C. Totten, 1814. 360 pp. 3d ed., rev. and enl. Philadelphia, 1816. Page references below are to the 1814 edition.

Itinerant Methodist minister refers to black preachers he heard during his travels---Moses in Camelton, near Augusta, Georgia (136), and Andrew in Savannah, Georgia (133). Also discusses a black woman at one of his services who "fell down and lay like a corpse for some time...[then later] came to, and praised God" (139).

240 Drew, Samuel. THE LIFE OF THE REV. THOMAS COKE...CONCLUDING WITH AN ABSTRACT OF HIS WRITINGS AND CHARACTER. London: Printed by Thomas Cordeux, 1817. 391 pp.

Biography of the pioneer Methodist church father gives an account of [Black] Harry Hosier, with comment on how Harry became a Methodist preacher and on his relations with Coke (174-76).

241 Elliott, E. N., ed. COTTON IS KING, AND PRO-SLAVERY ARGUMENTS: COMPRISING WRITINGS OF HAMMOND, HARPER, CHRISTY, STRINGFELLOW, HODGE, BLEDSOE, AND CARTWRIGHT....Augusta, GA: Pritchard, Abbott, and Loomis, 1860. 980 pp.

Dan Christy's publication in this collection, COTTON IS KING: OR, SLAVERY IN THE LIGHT OF POLITICAL ECONOMY, includes discussion of black preachers, who are identified as emigrants from the United States to Canada, where they "assume to themselves the grave character and Holy office of ministers and preachers of the Gospel in all extravagances...."(185) The monograph of J. H. Hammond, SLAVERY IN THE LIGHT OF POLITICAL SCIENCE, reprints a letter, dated 28 January 1845 from Silver Bluff, South Carolina, which states that the majority of the communicants of the Methodist and Baptist churches in the South were colored. Also brief discussion of slave congregations in South Carolina (656).

242 Ellsworth, W. L. "Reminiscences of a Camp-Meeting." LADIES' REPOSITORY 8 (November 1848): 341-48.

Clergyman's discussion of a camp-meeting he attended in the autumn of 1839 (location not given) includes comment on the oratory of the black preacher who addressed the congregation, and an excerpt of the sermon, which was based on the song: "Old Ship of Zion."

Text of 1 sermon: Old Ship of Zion.

243 "An Englishman in South Carolina, December 1860, and July, 1862." Parts 1, 2. CONTINENTAL MONTHLY 2 (July-December 1862): 689-94; 3 (January-June 1863): 110-17. Reprint. TRAVELS IN THE OLD SOUTH.... Edited by Eugene L. Schwaab, 2:560-73. Lexington: University Press of Kentucky, 1973.

Part 1. Observation that slave marriages generally take place on Christmas Day (694).

Part 2. Description of "negro weddings" involving six couples that took place on Christmas Day (115-16) and of the "shout" as a "dance of Negro men and women to the accompaniment of their own voices" (114). Songs and dance were "improvised continuously for about an hour."

244 Ethiop [pseud.] "Afric-American Picture Gallery---Fifth Paper." ANGLO-AFRICAN MAGAZINE 1 (July 1859): 216-17. Reprint. New York: Arno Press and the New York Times, 1968.

Fictitious account of a slave worship service in the South refers to the sermon of a white minister, who tells the slaves to obey their masters. He praises the slaves who exhort their fellowmen to follow the instructions of the minister, and discusses the "skeptical, unruly slaves...from which class was descended Nat Turner."

245 Farkas, Sandor Boloni. JOURNEY IN NORTH AMERICA, 1831. First published as UTAZAS ESZAK-AMERIKABAN, 1834. Translated and edited by Arpad Kadarkay. Santa Barbara, CA: ABC-Clio, Inc., 1978.

Travelogue of the native of Transylvania, Hungary, includes a description of a religious service in a black church of Baltimore (183). Also comment on the fact that Philadelphia had ten Negro churches in 1831 (212).

246 Faux, William. MEMORABLE DAYS IN AMERICA: BEING A JOURNAL OF A TOUR TO THE UNITED STATES BY W. FAUX, AN ENGLISH FARMER. London: Printed for W. Simpkin and R. Marshall, 1823. 2 vols. Reprint as FAUX'S MEMORABLE DAYS IN AMERICA, NOVEMBER 27, 1818-JULY 1820....In EARLY WESTERN TRAVELS 1748-1846, edited by Reuben Gold Thwaites, vols. 11, 12. Cleveland: Arthur H. Clark Company, 1905. Reprint of Thwaites. New York: AMS Press, 1966. Page references are to Thwaites, 1905 ed.

English farmer, who visited the United States during the years 1818-1820, includes comment in his book on a black church service he attended in Georgetown, Virginia (11:119) and description of a service at the African church in Philadelphia (12:84). Also comment on boat songs and performance practice of singers near Charleston, South Carolina (11:95).

References to 2 refrains: 1. Oh, come to Zion, come (12:84), 2. O won't you have my lovely bleeding Jasus [sic] (12:84).

247 Fearon, Henry Bradshaw. SKETCHES OF AMERICA. A NARRATIVE OF A JOURNEY OF FIVE THOUSAND MILES THRU THE EASTERN AND WESTERN STATES OF AMERICA.... London: Printed by Straham & Spottiswoode, 1819. 454 pp. Reprint. Microfiche. Louisville, KY: Lost Cause Press, 1980.

Account of an Englishman traveling in the United States in 1817-1818 includes references to black churches in New York (45), Boston (114), and Philadelphia (161, 167). Also refers to an ordinance of New Orleans in regard to slave dancing on Sundays (276-78).

248 Fee, John G. "Distribution of Bibles to Slaves---The Colored Preacher." AMERICAN MISSIONARY (MAGAZINE) n.s. 3 (November 1859): 256.

Minister comments on the religious services of a Baptist congregation at Frankfort, Kentucky.

Summary of 1 sermon: Repent ye therefore and be converted, that your sins may be blotted out.

249 Ferguson, John. MEMOIR OF THE LIFE AND CHARACTER OF REV. SAMUEL HOPKINS, D.D., FORMERLY PASTOR OF THE FIRST CONGREGATIONAL CHURCH IN NEWPORT, RHODE ISLAND. Boston: Leonard W. Kimball, 1830. 196 pp.

Includes discussion of Newport Gardner, ex-slave singing-school master, and other "pious Africans" of Newport, Rhode Island, who were educated by Rev. Hopkins and sent to Africa as missionaries (87, 90, 184).

250 Finch, Marianne. AN ENGLISHWOMAN'S EXPERIENCE IN AMERICA. London: Richard Bentley, 1853. 385 pp. Reprint. Ann Arbor, MI: University Microfilms International, 1974.

Travel account includes description of a worship service in the African Baptist Church at Richmond, Virginia (297-99). "After the departure of the minister, there was an amateur performance of singing and exhortation...."

251 Finley, James B. SKETCHES OF WESTERN METHODISM: BIOGRAPHICAL, HISTORICAL, AND MISCELLANEOUS. ILLUSTRATIVE OF PIONEER LIFE. Cincinnati: Printed at the Methodist Book Concern for the Author, 1855. 551 pp. Reprint. Ann Arbor, MI: University Microfilms International, 1978.

Account of pioneer Methodist preachers, written by Finley, who was one of them, includes short sketches of two black pioneers---Cuff, a plantation exhorter (379-85), and John Stewart, the first missionary to go to the Wyandott Indians (388-92). Also discussion of the oratory style and the quality of their singing.

252 Foote, William Henry. SKETCHES OF NORTH CAROLINA, HISTORICAL AND BIOGRAPHICAL, ILLUSTRATIVE OF THE PRINCIPLES OF A PORTION OF HER EARLY SETTLERS. New York: Robert Carter, 1846. 593 pp. Reprint. Microfiche. Louisville, KY: Lost Cause Press, 1957.

Presbyterian clergyman, who visited congregations in North Carolina and Virginia in his capacity as Secretary of Foreign Missions, includes letters from various clergymen who worked with congregations. A letter written by Samuel M'Corkle describes the rather violent activities of worshippers in a camp meeting near Lexington, N. C. (8 January 1802), giving special attention to black participants (392). Also discussion of a black woman who became filled with the spirit.

253 Forrest, William S. HISTORICAL AND DESCRIPTIVE SKETCHES OF NORFOLK AND VICINITY.... Philadelphia: Lindsay and Blackston, 1853. 496 pp.

Discussion of the history of Norfolk, Virginia, during the period 1650-1850 includes references to religious practices, singing, and shouting. Also a detailed description of a slave funeral (420-21, 424).

254 French, Austa Malinda Cwinchell. SLAVERY IN SOUTH CAROLINA AND THE EX-SLAVES; OR, THE PORT ROYAL MISSION. New York: Winchell M. French, 1862. Reprint. Atlanta University Black Culture Collection. Microfilm. Wooster, OH: Bell & Howell, 1974.

Discussion of the plantation preacher, his "deep spiritual experience, sound sense, and capacity to state Scripture facts, narratives, and doctrines" despite his inability to read (131-32). Observation that "some of them line hymns from memory with great accuracy...and repeat Scripture most appropriately, and correctly."

255 G. "Condition of the Slaves at the South." LIBERATOR 5 (25 April 1835): 65.

Letter, dated Georgia, 28 March 1835, discusses the condition of the slave in Georgia, observing that few slaves in that state attend religious meetings.

256 G., J. B. "The Contrabands near Washington." NATIONAL ANTI-SLAVERY STANDARD 23 (13 December 1862): [4].

Article, dated Minor's Hill, Virginia, 1 Dec. [1862], includes description of a contraband camp near Washington, D. C., during the Civil War, with comment on the preaching and exhortations of ex-slaves and black soldiers in the Union Army, and on the songs of the slaves.

Text of 1 chorus: The devil's mad and I am glad. Text of 1 song: I'll serve my Jesus.

257 Gilbert, Olive. NARRATIVE OF SOJOURNER TRUTH. A BONDSWOMAN OF OLDEN TIME. 1850. Battle Creek, MI: Published for the Author, 1878. 320 pp. Reprint. New York: Arno Press and the New York Times, 1968.

Sojourner Truth (c.1797-1883), born a slave (Isabella) in Ulster County, New York, was over forty years old when she was freed under a New York Act of 1817. She preached at camp meetings, in homes and churches, and sang "with the strong barbaric accent of the native African" (161).

References to 2 songs: 1. It was early in the morning (117). 2. O glory, glory, glory, Won't you come along with me? (167).

258 Gilman, Caroline Howard. "The Country Visit, Chapter X, Singing Hymns." ROSE BUD, OR YOUTH'S GAZETTE 2 (9 August 1834): 199.

Reference to black children singing hymns for white children.

Text of 1 song: Master Jesus is my Captain (Cho: I'm walking on to Jesus).

259 _____. RECOLLECTIONS OF A SOUTHERN MATRON. New York: Harper & Brothers, 1838. 272 pp.

American author and poet discusses slave life in a series of romanticized essays about the antebellum South, including the singing of boatmen (69-70, 107), a plantation burial (81-83), and slave superstitions.

Text of 1 boat song: Hi de good boat Neely (69-70).

260 Gilmore, James Robert [Edmund Kirke, pseud.]. "A Funeral among Slaves." NATIONAL ANTI-SLAVERY STANDARD 23 (14 June 1862): [4]. Reprint. CHRISTIAN WATCHMAN & REFLECTOR (=WATCHMAN-EXAMINER) 43 (10 July 1862): 4.

Description of a plantation slave funeral in South Carolina and comment on the slave preacher and the funeral oration he delivered.

Text of 1 sermon: De Lord say dat de dust shill return to de earth as it war.

261 Goodrich, John Bartholomew. "Temperance." INDEPENDENT 35 (12 July 1883): 874-76.

Publication of an address given at the [African] Baptist Church in Richmond, Virginia, in 1847 includes the text of a song sung by a black man and an excerpt from a slave exhortation.

Song text: I'ze bound for de land of Canaan.

262 Grandy, Moses. NARRATIVE OF THE LIFE OF MOSES GRANDY, LATE A SLAVE OF THE UNITED STATES OF AMERICA. Edited by George Thompson. London: C. Gilpin, 1843. Boston: Oliver Johnson, 1844. 45 pp. Page references below are to the 1844 edition.

Narrative of ex-slave (b. 1786?) about his life in North Carolina includes references to slaves holding their own religious meetings before the insurrection of 1831, that is, the so-called Nat Turner revolt. After the insurrection, slaves were prohibited from holding religious meetings in their homes under penalty of flogging. Description of prayer meetings that were held in the woods (35-36) and identification of Grandy's brother-in-law Isaac as a preacher.

263 Gurney, Joseph John. A JOURNEY IN NORTH AMERICA, DESCRIBED IN FAMILIAR LETTERS TO AMELIA OPIE. Norwich, England: Printed for Private Circulation by Josiah Fletcher, 1841. 414 pp. Reprint. Microfiche. Louisville, KY: Lost Cause Press, 1973.

Quaker minister comments at length on the slavery he saw during his three-year travels in the United States. Refers to Friends who preached in a black Methodist church in Philadelphia: [they] "received our gospel message with extreme cordiality, and we found no small difficulty in restraining their audible responses" (86).

264 H. "Letter to the Editor: Journey through Upper Canada and the United States, 1820-1821." CHRISTIAN OBSERVER (New York) 22 (1822): 16-23; 475-81; 553-61; 626-32; 688-99; 755-64. Vol. 23 (1823): 18-23; 86-91; 151-56; 218-24; 283-88; 351-59.

Collection of letters written by an Englishman during his travels includes discussion of slavery especially in Virginia (22: 555-57; 23: 155), South Carolina (22: 688-94), the Gulf States (22: 761-64), Tennessee (23: 154), and Baltimore, MD (23: 219-20). Observation that slave holidays in Virginia consisted of one day in April, one day in May, and four days for Christmas; that slaves attended religious services on Sundays and once during the week. Also references to slave preachers in Virginia.

265 H., W. H. "The Liberated Slaves at Beaufort. Letter from One of the Teachers." LIBERATOR 32 (2 May 1862): 72.

Letter from a New England school teacher working among the freedmen in Beaufort, South Carolina, dated March [1862], contains description of a religious service.

266 Hancock, William. AN EMIGRANT'S FIVE YEARS IN THE FREE STATES OF AMERICA. London: T. Cautley Newby, 1860. 321 pp. Reprint. Ann Arbor, MI: University Microfilms International, n.d.

Description of a New Year's Eve midnight service in a black Methodist "chapel" of New York (112).

267 Harlan, Mary B. ELLEN; OR, THE CHAINED MOTHER, AND PICTURES OF SLAVERY IN KENTUCKY. DRAWN FROM REAL LIFE. Cincinnati: Published for the Author by Applegate & Company, 1855. 259 pp. Reprint. Micro-opaque. Louisville, KY: Lost Cause Press, 1984.

Anti-slavery novel refers to the sermons of antebellum slave preachers in the South (58-61) and includes the text of a Negro camp-meeting spiritual.

Text of 1 song: What ship is this that shall take us home? (Cho: O, glory hallelujah!) (43).

268 Henson, [Josiah]. "Slavery: Escape from Bondage." ZION'S HERALD AND WESLEYAN JOURNAL 16 (12 February 1845): 28.

Narrative of the ex-slave preacher (1789-1883) includes discussion of his exhortations and his work among his fellow slaves.

269 _____. THE LIFE OF JOSIAH HENSON, FORMERLY A SLAVE...AS NARRATED BY HIMSELF, With a Preface by T. Biney. 1849. Edited by Samuel A. Elliot. London: Charles Gilpin, 1852. 118 pp.

The ex-slave offers insight into the experience

of a slave becoming an exhorter and developing his preaching skills (14, 28, 66-67).

270 _____. TRUTH STRANGER THAN FICTION. FATHER HENSON'S STORY OF HIS OWN LIFE, WITH AN INTRODUCTION BY MRS. H. B. STOWE. Boston: John P. Jewett & Company, 1858. 212 pp. Reprints. New York: Corinth Books, 1962. Microfiche. Louisville, KY: Lost Cause Press, 1968.

In his narrative the ex-slave discusses black preachers at a prayer meeting in Kentucky (56), refers to his father having played the banjo for plantation dances (6), and describes slave dancing at Christmas time (20).

271 Hodgson, Adam. REMARKS DURING A JOURNEY THROUGH NORTH AMERICA IN THE YEARS 1819, 1820, AND 1821 IN A SERIES OF LETTERS. Collected, arranged, and published by Samuel Whiting. New York: J. Seymour, printer, 1823. 335 pp. Reprint. Westport, CT: Negro Universities Press, 1970.

Collection of twenty letters, originally published in the London CHRISTIAN OBSERVER by this Englishman, who emigrated to the United States in 1820, includes comment on slave life in the South in the 1820s. Description of a funeral service in Georgia (58-59), discussion of slave preachers in Virginia (102), and comment on how the slaves celebrated their holidays in Virginia (100-103).

Reference to 1 sermon: The Lord is a Sun and a Shield (59).

272 Holcombe, William Henry. "Sketches of Plantation Life." KNICKERBOCKER 57 (June 1861): 619-33.

Physician's discussion of plantation life on Lake Concordia, Louisiana, includes comment on the slave wedding (619), the slave preacher and religious services (620); dance performance practice, including the "flaunting of red and yellow handkerchiefs" and plantation fiddlers (626); and song performance practice. Observation that the authentic music of the slaves differs from the music of Ethiopian minstrels.

273 Howe, Henry. "Amelia County." HISTORICAL COLLECTIONS OF VIRGINIA.... Charleston, SC: Babcock & Company, 1845. 544 pp. Reprint. Baltimore: Regional Publishing Company, 1969.

Detailed account of the celebrated slave preacher Uncle Jack (1743?-1843), of Amelia County, Virginia, who was kidnapped in Africa at the age of seven and was sold to a planter on the James River (174-75).

274 Hundley, Daniel Robinson. SOCIAL RELATIONS IN OUR SOUTHERN STATES. New York: Henry B. Price, 1860. 367 pp. Reprint. Baton Rouge: Louisiana State University, 1979.

Discussion of slavery includes description of the singing of boatmen, their "wild and indescribable" songs, and relevant performance practice (344-5). Also references to the religious beliefs of the slaves (349-50) and to "Brudder Jones" telling the story of Zaccheus (89).

275 HYMNS FOR THE USE OF THE AFRICAN METHODIST EPISCOPAL ZION CHURCH. Published by Sam'l M. Giles, Christopher Rush, and Joseph P. Thompson. New York: Printed at the Office of the Zion's Standard and Weekly Review, 1838. Later editions: 1849, 1856, 1869 (titles vary slightly in later editions).

Although this hymnal has no folksongs, it includes hymns from which phrases were taken that served as musical tinder for the composing of the Negro spiritual.

276 [Ingraham, Joseph Holt.] THE SOUTHWEST. BY A YANKEE. New York: Harper & Brothers, 1835. 2 vols. Reprint. Westport, CT: Negro Universities Press, 1968.

Travel narrative of the New England novelist and educator includes comment on black street criers in New Orleans (1:100), on slaves dancing the fandango in the Place Congo, New Orleans (1: 162), and on the prohibition of black preaching in Mississippi (2:265). Description of slaves improvising a sugar-cane worksong in Louisiana and its performance practice (1:241).

277 "An Inside View of Slavery." Unsigned review of AN INSIDE VIEW OF SLAVERY, by Charles Parsons (see no. 331). NATIONAL ANTI-SLAVERY STANDARD 16 (20 January 1856): [4].

Reviewer discusses conditions of slaves in the South, including description of a metal gag that was inserted into the mouth of a slave preacher to prevent him from exciting slaves to religious fever at midnight services. References to the religious piety of slaves and to slave sermons.

278 Jobson, Frederick. AMERICA AND AMERICAN METHODISM. London: James S. Virtue, 1857. 399 pp. Reprint. Ann Arbor, MI: University Microfilms International, n.d.

English Methodist minister's letters to his wife about his experiences in 1856 were published in book format. Detailed description of a black religious service in Baltimore, including discussion of the vocal quality of the choir and congregation singing, of the congregational exclamations, and of the members singing "their own African pieces" at the end of the service.

References to 2 choruses (88): 1. Canaan, bright, Canaan. 2. Praise to the Lord.

279 Jones, Charles Colcock. THE RELIGIOUS

INSTRUCTION OF THE NEGROES, A SERMON DELIVERED BEFORE ASSOCIATIONS OF PLANTERS IN LIBERTY AND M'INTOSH COUNTIES, GEORGIA. Princeton, NJ: D'Hart & Connolly, 1832. 38 pp. Reprint. Washington, DC: Microcard Editions, 1970.

Presbyterian minister Jones spent a large part of his life as a missionary of the Association for the Religious Instruction of Negroes in Georgia. Here he refers to "black preaching as a wide-spreading evil" and condemns the "secrecy and nocturnal meetings in old fields and plantations where no white persons reside" (36).

280 _____. THE RELIGIOUS INSTRUCTION OF THE NEGROES IN THE UNITED STATES. Savannah, GA: Thomas Purse, 1842. 277 pp. Reprint. Westport, CT: Negro Universities Press, 1969.

Jones's discussion of formal religious matters includes references to evening prayer services on the plantation (117) and to the slaves singing "chants, and catches, and hallelujah songs of their own composing" (265-6).

281 _____. SUGGESTIONS ON THE RELIGIOUS INSTRUCTION OF THE NEGROES IN THE SOUTHERN STATES.... Philadelphia: The Presbyterian Board of Publication, 1847. 132 pp.

Discussion of the slaves' fondness for singing places emphasis on the importance of motivating them to sing appropriate psalms and hymns in religious meetings with the hope that such songs "will gradually be substituted for many songs" they are in the habit of singing" (25). Comment that slaves singing hymns outside the religious service often line-out the hymn to themselves (56). Admonition against letting prayer meetings become "scenes of shouting, singing and boisterous excitement" (32). Excerpt from THOUGHTS ON FAMILY WORSHIP by J. W. Alexander includes complaints about the slaves singing hymns that are "full of error, if not of absurd irrelevance" (55-56).

282 Jones, Thomas H. THE EXPERIENCE AND PERSONAL NARRATIVE OF UNCLE TOM JONES.... ALSO THE SURPRISING ADVENTURES OF WILD TOM, OF THE ISLAND RETREAT, A FUGITIVE NEGRO FROM SOUTH CAROLINA. Boston: J. E. Farwell & Company, 1855. 54 pp.

Ex-slave author was a "driver" on the plantation where "Wild Tom" lived, an African of "unmixed blood." Author points out that Tom "had secretly returned to the practice of certain wild rites, which in his early youth, he had learned from his mother, who herself had been kidnapped from the coast of Africa, and who had been, as he often told me, zealously devoted to her country's superstitions" (30).

283 Jones, Thomas H. THE EXPERIENCE OF THOMAS H. JONES, WHO WAS A SLAVE FOR FORTY-THREE YEARS. Written by a Friend as Given to Him by Brother Jones. 1850. Springfield, MA: H. S. Taylor, 1854. 48 pp. Reprint. Philadelphia: Rhistoric Publications, 1969.

Ex-slave narrative includes discussion of the narrator's religious experiences (22-28) and his being "taken into the church," as well as references to a religious meeting held in a cabin (26).

Reference to 1 sermon: On being born again, from the words of Jesus to Nicodemus.

284 Kemble, Frances Anne. JOURNAL OF A RESIDENCE ON A GEORGIAN PLANTATION IN 1838-1839. New York: Harper & Brothers, 1863. 337 pp. Reprints. New York: Alfred A. Knopf, 1961. Athens: University of Georgia Press, 1984.

English actress Kemble married an American slaveholder and spent three-and-a-half months on his plantations on two small islands at the mouth of the Altamaha River on the coast of Georgia. Entries in her diary refer to religious services on the plantation (92, 262), to the singing of the boatmen (163-64, 192, 259-60) including descriptions of voice quality, of the character of the music, and performance practice.

Text of 1 song: Jenny shake her toe at me (Cho: Jenny gone away) (163). Texts of 2 choruses: 1. Fare you well, and good-by (164). 2. Oh my massa told me there's no grass in Georgia (128).

285 _____. RECORDS OF LATER LIFE. 3 vols. London: Richard Bentley & Son, 1882. Reprint. Microfilm. New Haven, CT: Research Publications, 1976.

Collection of letters written by the English actress at various times during the years 1834-1848 (she was married to Pierce Butler, a slaveholder, during those years). Included is discussion of a slave funeral (1:229-230) and comment on the singing of boatmen as they traveled from one plantation to another, including an observation that the "airs...have a strong affinity to Scotch melodies in their general character."

286 [Kingsley, Zephaniah.] A TREATISE ON THE PATRIARCHAL SYSTEM OF SOCIETY, AS IT EXISTS IN SOME GOVERNMENTS AND COLONIES IN AMERICA, AND IN THE UNITED STATES, UNDER THE NAME OF SLAVERY, WITH ITS NECESSITY AND ADVANTAGES. By an Inhabitant of Florida. 4th ed. [N.p.] 1834. 24 pp.

Discussion of plantation life on St. John's River, Florida, includes the observation that the slaves were permitted to dance on Saturday nights and Sunday mornings (23) but religious activities were discouraged. References to "the danger and hurtful tendency of superstition (by some called religion)," to secret societies, the "nightly prayer meetings" held once or twice a week, and the "abundance of preaching and praying" (21-22).

287 Knight, Henry Cogswell [Arthur Singleton, pseud.]. LETTERS FROM THE SOUTH AND WEST, BY ARTHUR SINGLETON. Boston: Richardson and Lord, 1824. 159 pp. Reprint. Microfiche. Chicago: Library Resources, 1970.

A letter written from Virginia, dated 1816, includes references to "Methodist meetings" of the slaves and to those who are "seeking" (75). Also the observation that the blacks sing as they work and description of a funeral (77). A letter written from New Orleans in 1819 comments on the slaves meeting "on the green" on Sabbath eves, where they "rock the city with their Congo dances" (127).

288 [Leavitt, Joshua.] "Our Colored Brethern." LIBERATOR 4 (14 June 1834): 96.

Report on the visit of an abolitionist editor of the NEW YORK EVANGELIST to a religious service of blacks in Philadelphia includes comment on the sermon of the preacher, the Rev. Mr. Corr, which was "full of glowing imagery."

289 [Leonard.] "Prayer Meeting in Uncle Sam's Cabin." SOUTHERN CHRISTIAN ADVOCATE 12 (2 December 1858): 105.

New England visitor, reminiscing about Christmas holidays he spent on a plantation on St. John's River in Florida, describes a prayer meeting of the slaves and their singing of improvised songs, called "spiritual himes" by the slaves.

Texts of 3 songs: 1. I wonder whar my brother gone (Cho: Hallelujah, they roll him). 2. I cannot tarry here, my time's a rollin' round. 3. I have a field a-ripening.

290 Lester, Charles Edwards, ed. CHAINS AND FREEDOM; OR, THE LIFE AND ADVENTURES OF PETER WHEELER, A COLORED MAN YET LIVING. A Slave in Chains, A Sailor on the Deep, and A Sinner at the Cross. Three Volumes in One. By the Author of the MOUNTAIN WILD FLOWER. New York: E. S. Arnold and Company, 1838? 260 pp.

Narrative about slavery in the North, written by a white author, uses partly dialogue format with the slave Peter, born 1789 at Little Egg Harbour, New Jersey. Includes comment on a Methodist camp meeting held in the early-nineteenth century at Auburn, or Plane Hill, near Philadelphia (96-98).

Text of 1 chorus: I can see Jesus Christ (96-98). Reference to 1 chorus: 1. Glory, hallelujah (96-98).

291 Lewis, George. IMPRESSIONS OF AMERICA AND THE AMERICAN CHURCHES. FROM THE JOURNAL OF THE REV. G. LEWIS. Edinburgh, Scotland: W. P. Kennedy, 1845. 432 pp. Reprint. Westport, CT: Negro Universities Press, 1968.

Presbyterian minister of the Free Church of Scotland, who traveled in the United States in 1844, offers detailed discussion of a communion service in the African Methodist Episcopal Church of Mobile, Alabama (167-169), with references to the deacons as "practised singers" (170). Also description of a church service in New Orleans (194) and references to the nightly prayer services held on a plantation in Savannah, Georgia, led by a slave called a "leader" (128). Mention of Andrew Marshall, the "coloured" folk preacher (129).

Reference to 1 sermon text: Who shall forbid water that these be baptized (194).

292 Lewis, John Delaware. ACROSS THE ATLANTIC. BY THE AUTHOR OF "SKETCHES OF CANTABS." London: George Earle, 1851. 274 pp. Reprint. Micro-opaque. Louisville, KY: Lost Cause Press, 1962.

Travel account of an Englishman includes references to "cartloads of negro labourers" who were "chaunting forth songs" (194) and description of a camp meeting (192-208), where a special part of the encampment was set aside for black members (197).

293 Lieber, Francis. LETTERS TO A GENTLEMAN IN GERMANY, BEING WRITTEN AFTER A TRIP FROM PHILADELPHIA TO NIAGARA. Philadelphia: Carey, Lea & Blanchard, 1834. 356 pp. Also published as THE STRANGER IN AMERICA. 1835. Reprint. New York: Johnson Reprint Corporation, 1971.

Detailed discussion by the German scholar of a black Methodist sermon in Philadelphia (327-29) and of a camp meeting held in Westchester, near Philadelphia, which refers to the "considerable number of Negroes...who had no tents and were given a separate place to sit" (303-27).

294 Linton, John J. "A Minister for Sale." NATIONAL ANTI-SLAVERY STANDARD 16 (26 January 1856): [1].

Author draws attention to advertisements in southern newspapers about the sale of licensed slave preachers.

295 Lockwood, Lewis C. "Mission to the Freed 'Contrabands' at Fortress Monroe, Virginia." AMERICAN MISSIONARY (MAGAZINE) n.s. 5, Supplement (1 October 1861): 243-44; 247-50.

Northern clergyman working as a missionary among the freedmen in a contraband camp at Fortress Monroe, Virginia, describes, in a letter dated 4 September 1861, a prayer meeting of ex-slaves. Comment on the sing-song manner of their recitation of prayers and their style of chanting religious songs. A second letter, dated 16 September 1861, refers to a congregation's joyous singing of a chant about Joseph and Moses, which was "introduced about nine years ago" (250).

Text of 1 chorus: Go down to Egypt, Tell Pharoah (243).

296 Long, Stephen Harriman. ACCOUNT OF AN EXPEDITION FROM PITTSBURGH TO THE ROCKY MOUNTAINS. PERFORMED IN THE YEARS 1819, 1820....Philadelphia: H. C.Carey & I. Lea, 1823. 2 vols. Reprint in EARLY WESTERN TRAVELS, 1748-1846, edited by Reuben Gold Thwaites. Vols. 14-17. Cleveland: Arthur H. Clark, 1905. Reprint of Thwaites. Microfiche. Chicago: Library Resources, 1971. Page reference below is to the Thwaites edition.

Army major offers detailed discussion of slave burial ceremonies he witnessed at Cape Girardeau, Missouri, including references to the "second burial" a month later (17:91).

297 Lundie, Mary E. [Mary Lundie Duncan]. AMERICA AS I FOUND IT. By the Author of A MEMOIR OF MARY LUNDIE DUNCAN. London: James Nisbet & Company, 1852. 380 pp. Reprint. Microfilm. New Haven, CT: Research Publications, 1975.

English writer devotes a chapter to black folk, "The Coloured Race" (214-30). Her discussion includes description of their singing and the character of the songs (218-20), and comment on the church service she attended in Washington, D. C. (224-25). Also discussion of Katy Ferguson, the first person to hold Sabbath-School classes in the city of New York, who had weekly prayer meetings in her home for forty years (220-21).

298 Lyell, Charles. TRAVELS IN AMERICA IN THE YEARS 1841-42.... New York: Wiley & Putnam, 1845. 2 vols. Reprint. New York: Arno Press and the New York Times, 1978.

English geologist refers to slaves "singing loudly and joyously in chorus after their day's work was over" (1:144), to a slave wedding (1: 146), and to a funeral in Philadelphia (1:165).

299 Lyell, Charles. A SECOND VISIT TO THE UNITED STATES OF NORTH AMERICA.... London: John Murray, 1849. 2 vols. 753 pp. Reprint. New York: Readex Microprint, 1970.

The geologist visited the United States four times. In this account of his travels he refers to the singing of boatmen (1:244, 1: 327), black Methodists dancing a "ring" dance (1:270), and slave preachers in Georgia, Kentucky, and the South Carolina Sea Islands (2:4-5, 2:283-84, 2: 354).

300 M'Nemar, Richard. THE KENTUCKY REVIVAL, OR, A SHORT HISTORY OF THE LATE EXTRAORDINARY OUT-POURING OF THE SPIRIT OF GOD, IN THE WESTERN STATES OF AMERICA, AGREEABLY TO SCRIPTURE PROMISES, AND PROPHECIES CONCERNING THE LATTER DAY.... Cincinnati: From the Press of John W. Browne, 1807. 144 pp. Reprint. Early American Imprints. Micro-opaque. Worcester, MA: American Antiquarian Society, 1968

Although no direct discussion of black religious activities is included, this account is valuable for its depiction of the very first camp meetings held in the United States, in 1800 in Logan and Christian counties of Kentucky, and for its documentation of the fact that there was no race discrimination or segregation in these meetings (such as later would appear in the camp-meeting movement) (31).

301 Malsby, M. A. "A Prayer-Meeting at a Corn Shucking." SOUTHERN CHRISTIAN ADVOCATE 23 (19 January 1860): [9].

Description of a corn-husking festival that took place on a minister's plantation near Louisville, Kentucky, in which both blacks and whites participated, refers to the antiphonal singing of the slaves and to performance practice associated with their songs. The corn-husking ended quietly with a meal, followed by prayers and the singing of hymns.

302 Marryat, Frederick. A DIARY IN AMERICA WITH REMARKS ON ITS INSTITUTIONS. 3 vols. London: Printed for Longman, Orme, Brown, Green, and Longman, 1839. Reprint. Ann Arbor, MI: University Microfilms International, 1973.

English naval officer, who visited the United States in 1837, discusses slavery, including reference to "coloured people" at a camp meeting near Cincinnati, Ohio (2:180-83), and offers description of a black church he visited in Kentucky (3:155-56).

303 Martineau, Harriet. SOCIETY IN AMERICA. 2 vols. New York: Saunders and Otley, 1837. Reprint. New York: AMS Press, 1966.

Widely published historian and intellectual, Martineau visited the United States during the years 1834-36. Her discussion of slavery and black culture includes comment on the sermon of a slave preacher, and a striking quotation from it: "Come down, O Lord, Come down, on your great white horse a-kicking and snortin'" (1:386).

304 McBride, J. "Underground Railroad--Express Line." LIBERATOR 22 (29 October 1852): 174.

Clergyman describes a black church service that he attended in Ohio on 4 October 1852. Comment on the collection of funds for a fugitive slave from Kentucky and on a "fugitive song" sung by the congregation.

Reference to 1 song: O, come, come away.

305 MEMOIR OF MRS. CHLOE SPEAR, A NATIVE OF

AFRICA, WHO WAS ENSLAVED IN CHILDHOOD.... By a Lady of Boston. Boston: James Loring, 1832. 108 pp. Reprint. Microfiche. Louisville, KY: Lost Cause Press, 1965.

Discussion of ex-slave Chloe (c.1750-1815), who held religious meetings in her home (71).

306 Milburn, William Henry. TEN YEARS OF PREACHER-LIFE; OR, CHAPTERS FROM AN AUTOBIOGRAPHY. New York: Derby & Jackson, 1859. 363 pp. Reprints. (excerpts). "From Milburn's Ten Years of Preacher-Life: South Side View." SOUTHERN CHRISTIAN ADVOCATE 22 (20 October 1859): 292. Micro-opaque. Louisville, KY: Lost Cause Press, 1960.

Methodist preacher, in discussing his travels as an itinerant minister, devotes one chapter to discussion of the slaves (337-52). Detailed description of a camp meeting (62-63).

Texts of 3 songs (341): 1. Jesus, my all, to heaven is gone (Cho: And we shall gain the victory) 2. There's a rest for the weary. 3. What ship is this that will take us home? Text of 1 chorus: Oh, brethern, will you meet me?

307 "Miscellaneous Item." MUSICAL GAZETTE (Boston) v. 1, no.12 (6 July 1846): 91.

Comment on the practice of slaves "lining-out" a hymn even when singing to themselves. Example cited of a slave lining-out as he dug a ditch.

Text of 1 song: Oh, Satan, he came by my heart.

308 "Miscellaneous News Items." DOUGLASS' MONTHLY 2 (July 1859): 112.

Brief item in newspaper published and edited by black abolitionist Frederick Douglass refers to Flora Hawkins of the African Church in Cincinnati, Ohio, who died in the act of shouting at a church service.

309 "More about the Contrabands: Beaufort and Vicinity." NATIONAL ANTI-SLAVERY STANDARD 22 (30 November 1862): [1].

Miscellaneous collection of articles from northern newspapers regarding contrabands on the Sea Islands of South Carolina includes references to slaves holding prayer meetings, singing "wild" melodies, and to performance practice.

310 Mott, Abigail. BIOGRAPHICAL SKETCHES AND INTERESTING ANECDOTES OF PERSONS OF COLOR. 1826. 2d ed. New York: Mahlon Day, 1837. 260 pp. Reprint. New Haven, CT: Research Publications, 1975. Page references below are to the 2d ed.

Excerpts from contemporary books and periodicals include transcripts of two short sermons of the ex-slave Solomon Bayley, who at that time lived in Caldwell, near Monrovia, Africa (45-48); an excerpt from a farewell sermon of Lott Carey, Baptist minister and Virginia native, who became a missionary to Sierra Leone (114); and an excerpt from a sermon delivered by "Jack," a black Methodist preacher. Also inclusion of an article about Clarinda (d. 1832), a native of South Carolina, who was a dance fiddler before she was converted. Afterwards she held religious meetings in her home (41-51).

311 Murat, Achille. AMERICA AND THE AMERICANS BY THE LATE ACHILLE MURAT. Translated from the French by Henry J. Bradfield. New York: William H. Graham, 1849. 260 pp. Reprint. Buffalo: G. H. Derby, 1951.

Detailed description of a camp meeting includes casual references to the blacks in attendance (95-99). Also comment on the slaveholder's feelings about the black preachers "connected with the religious societies of the North," who were "unremitting in their exertions to create discontent among our Negroes" (85).

312 Murray, Charles Augustus. TRAVELS IN NORTH AMERICA DURING THE YEARS 1834, 1835, & 1836.... 2 vols. London: Richard Bentley, 1839. Reprint. Micro-opaque. Louisville, KY: Lost Cause Press, 1960. Page references below are to vol. 1.

British traveler's account includes description of a slave wedding (117-18) and comment on the "religion of the Negroes," indicating it to be "a compound of superstition and absurdity." Observation that the slaves "always prefer their own preachers...to any white minister" (168).

313 "A Negro Baptism Scene." CHRISTIAN WATCHMAN & REFLECTOR (=WATCHMAN-EXAMINER) 36 (9 August 1855): [1].

Description of a baptism ceremony in a slave church in the South includes comment on the members of the congregation singing hymns "in their own peculiarly pleasant style," and on the oratory style of the preacher.

Synopsis of 1 sermon: Christ as a sacrifice for sin.

314 "A Negro Love Feast." LITTELL'S LIVING AGE 29 (28 June 1851): 616-17. Reprint. CHRISTIAN WATCHMAN & REFLECTOR (=WATCHMAN-EXAMINER) 32 (10 July 1851): 112.

Description of a love feast conducted by slaves at a Methodist mission within the South Carolina Conference (place not indicated) includes summaries of exhortations given by seven slaves, of which two were women.

315 "A Negro Preacher in the South." DE BOW'S REVIEW 28 (March 1860): 352-55.

Discussion of a slave preacher named George,

who was literate, and who preached at the court house in Pulaski, Mississippi, on two occasions.

316 "Negro Preaching." CHRISTIAN WATCHMAN & REFLECTOR (=WATCHMAN-EXAMINER) 38 (5 February 1857): [1].

Snopsis of a sermon the writer heard at an African meeting-house (city not indicated) on the topic of the depravity of the human heart includes comment on the "directness" and "pungency" of the preacher's oratory style and on the groans in response from the Amen Corner.

317 "The Negroes at Fortress Monroe." DOUGLASS' MONTHLY 4 (September 1861): 526.

Reprint of an article from the NEW YORK TRIBUNE, dated 7 August 1861, which comments generally on the social conditions and work of contraband slaves at Fortress Monroe, Virginia, during the Civil War, and describes their singing of religious slave songs.

318 "The Nigger Preacher." CHRISTIAN WATCHMAN & REFLECTOR (=WATCHMAN-EXAMINER) 26 (8 August 1845): [125]. Reprinted from the KENTUCKY BANNER AND PIONEER.

Missionary discusses the reluctance of the white clergy to administer to the slaves for fear of ostracism by other whites. Also offers comment on the religious services of the slaves, on the plantation preacher, on their sacred chant, and their religious dancing.

319 O'Neall, John Belton. THE NEGRO LAW OF SOUTH CAROLINA. Collected and Digested by John Belton O'Neall. Columbia, SC: Printed by John G. Bowman, 1848. 56 pp. Reprint. Microfiche. Chicago: Library Resources, 1970.

Writer's discussion of South Carolina legislation he feels should be repealed includes the Act of 1800, which prohibited slaves meeting for religious or educational purposes (24); and the Act of 1740, which prohibited slaves from beating drums, blowing horns, or playing other loud instruments (26).

320 Oliphant, Laurence. PATRIOTS AND FILIBUSTERS; OR, INCIDENTS OF POLITICAL AND EXPLORATORY TRAVEL. London: William Blackwood and Sons, 1860. 242 pp. Reprinted from BLACKWOOD'S MAGAZINE "With Corrections and Additions."

Englishman touring the United States in 1856, comments, after visiting plantations in South Carolina, on the fact that the slaves "had given up dancing, held constant prayer-meetings, and never sang anything but their own sacred compositions" (141-43). Also discussion of performance practice.

Texts of 6 songs: 1. Oh, I takes my text in Matthew (Cho: There's a meeting here tonight). 2. In that morning, true believers. 3. I want to sing as the angels sing. 4. Master Jesus send for me (Cho: Lord, I must go). 5. The heavenly bell is ringing loud. 6. Broders, don't you hear the horn (Cho: Yes, Lord, I hear the horn).

321 Olmsted, Frederick Law. A JOURNEY IN THE SEABOARD SLAVE STATES, WITH REMARKS ON THEIR ECONOMY. New York: Mason Brothers, 1859. 723 pp. Reprint. Westport, CT: Negro Universities Press, 1968. Page references below are to the 1859 edition.

Journalist/landscape architect Olmsted traveled in the South in 1853-54 and published articles about his experiences in the NEW-YORK DAILY TIMES under the byline "Yeoman," and in the NEW-YORK DAILY TRIBUNE as "The Southerner at Home." His account includes descriptions of a funeral (25-27), field hollers (394-5), a slave funeral in Charleston, South Carolina (405), funerals on plantations (449-500), performance practice of singing, and juba dancing (551). Also discussion of such subjects as "The Musical Talent of Negroes" and "Slave High Life."

Texts of 2 songs (608-10): 1. Ye see dem boat way dah ahead (Cho: Oa hoio hieu). 2. John come down in de holler.

322 ____. A JOURNEY IN THE BACK COUNTRY IN THE WINTER OF 1853-54. New York: Mason Brothers, 1860. 492 pp. Reprint. Excerpts published as "Aspects of Southern Society." NATIONAL ANTI-SLAVERY STANDARD 21/1 (11 August 1860): [4]. New York: Schocken Books, 1970.

Based on notes made by Olmsted on his trip into the South, the author regarded this as the "third volume of a work" which included A JOURNEY IN THE SEABOARD STATES (see no. 321) and A JOURNEY THROUGH TEXAS (1857). His description of plantation life includes references to slave preachers and religious exercises (92-93), singing and dancing to music of fiddles and banjos (146), and a religious service in New Orleans, Louisiana (187-96).

Reference to 1 sermon: I have fought the good fight (188).

323 ____. JOURNEYS AND EXPLORATIONS IN THE COTTON KINGDOM: A TRAVELLER'S OBSERVATIONS ON COTTON AND SLAVERY IN THE AMERICAN SLAVE STATES. 2 vols. London: Sampson, Low, Son & Company, 1861. Also published as THE COTTON KINGDOM.... New York: Mason Brothers, 1861. Reprint. New York: Alfred A. Knopf, 1953. 626 pp.

This book, based on earlier publications by the author (see nos. 321, 322), includes discussion of a funeral and "burying" in Richmond, Virginia (1: 43-45), references to field hollers (1:214), and to slave dancing accompanied by fiddles and banjoes (2:73). Description of worship services in a plantation prayer house (1:259-60) and in

New Orleans (1:309-17), and of stevedores singing worksongs (1:347).

Text of 1 song: Ye see dem boat way dah ahead (Cho: Oa hoio hi eu) (1: 347).

324 ____. THE PAPERS OF FREDERICK LAW OLMSTED: Vol. 2, SLAVERY AND THE SOUTH, 1852-1857. Edited by Charles E. Beveridge and Charles Capen McLaughlin. Baltimore, MD: Johns Hopkins University Press, 1981. 503 pp.

Journalist/landscape architect Olmsted traveled in the South for fourteen months and reported on his travels in seventy-five articles, which were published in the New York newspapers. Later the articles were published in book format (see nos. 321-3). This book, which includes "all of Olmsted's significant statements on the South, slavery, and the sectional crisis" that did not appear in his books, includes references to slave funerals (194) and to the religious exercises of the slaves (167).

325 "One Clergyman Selling Another." NATIONAL ANTI-SLAVERY STANDARD 11 (19 December 1850): 117. Reprint from the ANTI-SLAVERY BUGLE.

Comment on a sermon delivered by Tabbs Grosse, a licensed slave preacher of the Methodist Episcopal Church (Mason County, Kentucky), for the benefit of purchasing freedom from his owner, Parson Montgomery. Description of the slave preacher's oratory style and his sermon.

Reference to 1 sermon: Go ye into all the world and preach the Gospel to every creature.

326 "Our Black Population." NATIONAL ANTI-SLAVERY STANDARD 12 (6 November 1851): 93-94. From the Louisville PRESBYTERIAN HERALD.

Discussion of the relationship of the Presbyterian Church to blacks includes the comment that the slaves preferred to attend worship services conducted by one of their own color, and discussion of their preachers and religious teachers.

327 Palmer, Gideon. "Reminiscences of Several Tours in the Southern States, Made with a Design to Introduce the Manufacture of Cotton-Seed Oil, with Observations and Reflections on the State of Society." NATIONAL ANTI-SLAVERY STANDARD 1 (18 February 1841): 145-46.

Businessman of Connecticut, discussing his visit to Petersburg, Virginia, in 1830, comments on the different denominational houses of worship erected for slaves on a tract of land in the vicinity, called "Old Field Plains." References to slave preaching, praying, and singing.

Text of 1 chorus: And we'll praise Him again, when we pass over Jordan.

328 Palmer, John. JOURNAL OF TRAVELS IN THE UNITED STATES OF AMERICA, AND IN LOWER CANADA, PERFORMED IN THE YEAR 1817.... London: Printed for Sherwood, Neely, and Jones, 1818. 456 pp. Reprint. Microfilm. Woodbridge, CT: Research Publications, 1980.

Account of an English tourist includes description of a free Negro's funeral he witnessed in Pittsburgh (52) and of song performance practice in the worship services of four black churches he visited in Philadelphia.

329 Park, Edward A. MEMOIR OF THE LIFE AND CHARACTER OF SAMUEL HOPKINS, D.D. Boston: Published by the Author. 1830. 2d ed. Boston: Doctrinal Tract and Book Society, 1854. 264 pp.

Discussion of two slaves, Salmar Nubia and Newport Gardner, both of Newport, Rhode Island, who were trained to become missionaries to Africa (154-56). They later gained their freedom and were active in the Congregational Church affairs. In 1826 they sailed from Boston for Liberia.

330 Parkinson, Richard. A TOUR IN AMERICA, IN 1798, 1799, AND 1800. EXHIBITING SKETCHES OF SOCIETY AND MANNERS, AND A PARTICULAR ACCOUNT OF THE AMERICAN SYSTEM OF AGRICULTURE, WITH ITS RECENT IMPROVEMENTS. London: Printed for J. Harding and J. Murray, 1805. 2 vols. Reprint. Ann Arbor, MI: University Microfilms International, 1978.

General discussion of slavery (412-56) includes one reference to religious practices: "There are a great many negro priests; but where they preach I cannot tell. The lower class of [white] people, such as worked for me, said, that they had known a black fellow give a better sermon than they ever heard from a white man" (459).

331 Parsons, Charles Grandison. INSIDE VIEW OF SLAVERY; OR, A TOUR AMONG THE PLANTERS. With an Introductory Note by Mrs. H. B. Stowe. Boston: John P. Jewett and Company, 1855. 318 pp. Reprint. New York: Argosy-Antiquarian, 1969.

Northern physician kept a journal during his tour of the southern states in 1852-53 and later published a book based on the journal. His discussion includes references to slave preaching (159-60), to the singing of "colored boys" in Georgia (247), to slave children dancing a ring dance (276), and to the singing of slaves (277).

Text of 1 song: 1. Oh sister, watch that heart (277). References to 3 songs (276): 1. I'm gwine way up yonder 2. See God feeding on the lambs. 3. When I get ober Jordan.

332 Paulding, James Kirke. SLAVERY IN THE UNITED STATES. New York: Harper and Brothers, 1836. 312 pp. Reprint of excerpt.

"Slavery in Virginia." FARMER'S REGISTER 4 (July 1836): 180-83.

Notherner's discussion of the domestic and social relations between master and slave includes references to the favorite pastime activities of slaves (singing, dancing to music of fiddles, telling tales in the cabins); to the plantation preacher (194, 202-4, 208-10); to slave funerals (192-93); and to the practice in Virginia of making the funeral an occasion for rejoicing. Also comment on the decline in banjo playing and the singing of banjo-songs.

333 Peck, John Mason. FORTY YEARS OF PIONEER LIFE. MEMOIR OF JOHN MASON PECK, D.D. Edited from His Journals and Correspondence by Rufus Babcock. Philadelphia: American Baptist Publication Society, c.1864. 360 pp.

Baptist minister's discussion of his missionary experiences in Missouri and Kentucky includes references to his preaching among the Missouri slaves in 1819 and to their baptizings (161). Also comment on his assistance at the ordination of black preacher J. B. Meacham in St. Louis in February 1826 (210), and on slave dancing (90).

334 Pennington, James W. C. THE FUGITIVE BLACKSMITH; OR, EVENTS IN THE HISTORY OF JAMES W. C. PENNINGTON. 2d ed. London: Charles Gilpin, 1849. 87 pp. Reprints. FIVE SLAVE NARRATIVES, edited by William Loren Katz. New York: Arno Press and the New York Times, 1968. Microfilm. New York: International Microfilm Press, 1970.

Ex-slave author (1807-1870) was the first Afro-American to graduate from a European university (D.D., Heidelberg) and the first man to write a textbook history of the black man. His autobiography includes description of an exhorter who preached on Sundays, lined-out "spiritual songs," and presided at slave funeral services (67).

335 Phildoulos [pseud.]. "Slavery; The Negro Character." ZION'S HERALD AND WESLEYAN JOURNAL (=ZION'S HERALD) 14 (8 November 1843): 180. Reprint. "The Negro Character." THE LIBERATOR 13 (24 November 1843): [185].

Extract, dated 11 October 1843, from the tracts of abolitionist William Ellery Channing, refers to Stephen Johnson, a slave preacher in Mississippi, who preached before both black and white congregations.

336 Phillips, W. S. "Home Religious Chronicle: Letter from South Carolina---Revival---Interesting Baptism." CHRISTIAN WATCHMAN & REFLECTOR (=WATCHMAN-EXAMINER) 43 (6 November 1862): [2].

Northern Baptist missionary describes the baptism of ex-slaves in South Carolina.

Text of 1 song: Sister Sarah, do you want to get religion?

337 Pickard, Kate E. R. THE KIDNAPPED AND THE RANSOMED; BEING THE PERSONAL RECOLLECTIONS OF PETER STILL AND HIS WIFE "VINA," AFTER FORTY YEARS OF SLAVERY. Syracuse, NY: William T. Hamilton, 1856. 409 pp. Reprint. New York: Negro Universities Press, 1968.

Slave narrative includes reference to a marriage conducted by a slave preacher and to the songs sung on this occasion (344).

338 Pierce, Edward Lillie. "The Contrabands at Fortress Monroe." ATLANTIC MONTHLY 8 (November 1861): 626-40.

Government agent's discussion of the condition of ex-slaves at Fortress Monroe, Virginia, at the onset of the Civil War includes comments on blacks holding prayer-meetings without the assistance of a preacher. Also discussion of the prayers and exhortations of the slaves (635), and of slaves penning their hopes for freedom upon the Scriptures, which promised the deliverance of Daniel from the lion's den (638).

339 [_____.] "Experiences among the Contraband." NATIONAL ANTI-SLAVERY STANDARD 22 (9 November 1861): [1].

Includes discussion of the religious life of contraband slaves at Port Royal, South Carolina, at the onset of the Civil War.

340 [_____.] "The Refugees of South Carolina: Report of the Government Agent." NATIONAL ANTI-SLAVERY STANDARD 22 (1 March 1862): [1].

Report reprinted from the NEW-YORK TRIBUNE includes comment on the religious practices of the ex-slaves on the Sea Islands off South Carolina, and the "glory shout" that ended their services.

341 _____. THE NEGROES AT PORT ROYAL. Report of E. L. Pierce, Government Agent, to the Hon. Salmon P. Chase, Secretary of the Treasury. Boston: R. F. Wallcutt, 1862. 36 pp. Reprint. New York: Negro Universities Press, 1970.

Discussion of life on the plantations of Port Royal, St. Helena, Hilton Head, and other islands of South Carolina includes references to religious gatherings and description of the "glory shout" (31).

342 "The Pious Slave." NATIONAL ANTI-SLAVERY STANDARD 7 (4 June 1846): 4.

Description of the conversion experience of a slave preacher.

343 Pollard, Edward Alfred. BLACK DIAMONDS GATHERED IN THE DARKEY HOMES OF THE SOUTH. ... New York: Pudney & Russell, 1859. 155 pp. Originally published as THE SOUTHERN SPY; OR, CURIOSITIES OF NEGRO SLAVERY IN THE SOUTH. LETTERS FROM A SOUTHERNER TO A NORTHERN FRIEND (1859). Reprint. New York: Negro Universities Press, 1968.

This collection of letters includes comments on slave religion, superstitions, and devotional songs (23-27) and on black preachers and exhorters (36-37). Also description of the performance practice associated with singing a harvest song (129).

Reference to 1 sermon: Death knocking at heels (37).

Texts of 5 songs: 1. Oh, run, brother, run, Judgement Day is comin' (23). 2. Go back, angels! go back, angels (34). 3. Oh, carry me away, my Lord (36). 4. I am gwine home, children (36). 5. Oh, hallelujah! Glory in my soul (37). Texts of 2 choruses: 1. Oh, heaven, sweet heaven, when shall I see (34). 2. Oh, wheel her boys (129).

344 ____. "A Regathering of 'Black Diamonds' in the Old Dominion." SOUTHERN LITERARY MESSENGER 29 (October 1859): 294-96.

Fictional (?) narrative of a traveler's visit to Virginia during the antebellum era includes discussion of the black preacher and his oratory style (295). Also comment on the slave songs and performance practice.

Text of 1 chorus: Oh, wheel her boys (296).

345 Poole, Caroline B. "A Yankee School Teacher in Louisiana, 1835-1837: The Diary of Caroline B. Poole." Edited by James A. Padgett. LOUISIANA HISTORICAL QUARTERLY 20 (July 1937): 651-79.

Entry for 16 March 1837 refers to blacks mourning their dead, praying and singing through most of the night (677).

346 Postell, J. C. "Campmeeting among the Coloured People in the Fort Valley Mission." SOUTHERN CHRISTIAN ADVOCATE 10 (18 September 1846): 59.

Letter from a Methodist missionary, dated 13 August [1846], describes a camp meeting held near Fort Valley (Georgia). Reference to slave children from the nearby mission singing their "spiritual songs" in a spirited manner.

347 "The Prayers of Slaves." INDEPENDENT 12 (20 June 1861): 4.

Discussion of a pious slave preacher, who was one of the first to take advantage of the Contraband Act, includes an excerpt of his prayer for the deliverance of his people from bondage.

348 R., E. W. "The Liberated Slaves at Beaufort: Letter from One of the Teachers." LIBERATOR 32 (2 May 1862): 72.

Northern schoolteacher, in discussion of her work among the freed slaves on Beaufort Island, South Carolina, describes a worship service at the black Baptist Church on St. Helena Island.

349 Randolph, Peter. SKETCHES OF SLAVE LIFE; OR, ILLUSTRATIONS OF THE "PECULIAR INSTITUTION." BY PETER RANDOLPH, AN EMANCIPATED SLAVE. 2d ed. Boston: Published for the Author, 1855. 82 pp. Reprint. Philadelphia: Rhistoric Publications, 1969.

Ex-slave Randolph (c.1825-1887), a native of Prince George's County, Virginia, includes in his narrative a description of "burying" and funeral services (13-15) and refers to a song sung on the auction block (10), to the slave preacher (26), to slaves dancing to the music of a gourd banjo (30), to religious meetings in the swamps (30), and how slaves improvised songs used in worship services (31).

Texts of 2 songs: 1. O, that I had a bosom friend (Cho: No more rain, no more snow) (31). 2. O, fare you well (Cho: Sisters, fare you well) (10).

350 Ranger [pseud.]. "Letters from the Army." CHRISTIAN WATCHMAN & REFLECTOR (=WATCHMAN-EXAMINER) 43 (15 May 1862): [2].

Newspaper correspondent at Yorktown observes that religious meetings of the black population were held Wednesday evenings and Sunday afternoons and describes a typical prayer meeting of the contraband slaves. Excerpts of prayer texts.

Text of 1 couplet: The Lord said unto Moses, Let my people go.

351 Redpath, James. THE ROVING EDITOR; OR, TALKS WITH SLAVES IN THE SOUTHERN STATES. ... New York: A. B. Burdick, 1850. 349 pp. Review of this book in the ANGLO-AFRICAN MAGAZINE 1 (October 1859): 329-30. Reprint. New York: Negro Universities Press, 1968.

Journalist, who became a correspondent for the New York TRIBUNE beginning in 1852, in discussing social, economic, and political aspects of slavery, includes comment on the slave preacher on the southern plantation and his sermons.

Reference to 1 song: Jordan am a hard road to trabble (4). Excerpt from 1 sermon: The death of John the Baptist (260-261).

352 Reed, Andrew. "Visit to an African Church." CHRISTIAN WATCHMAN & REFLECTOR (=WATCHMAN-EXAMINER) 16 (4 September 1835): [140].

Minister, discussing his visit to the African Church in Lexington, Virginia, notes that slaves were denied permission to hold worship services unless a white person was present.

Synopsis of 1 sermon: The Spirit saith, Come.

353 "Religious Conditions of the Slaves." NATIONAL ANTI-SLAVERY STANDARD 15 (25 November 1854): [2].

Discussion of the slaves worshipping in the segregated galleries of white churches in the South includes the observation that only about one-fifth of the slave population attended such services. Comment on how the slaves sang and swayed back and forth in their pews during the sermon.

354 "The Religious Instruction of Slaves." CHRISTIAN WATCHMAN & REFLECTOR (=WATCHMAN-EXAMINER) 26 (19 December 1845): 202.

Excerpt pertaining to the proceedings of a meeting held in Charleston, South Carolina, about the religious instruction of the slaves includes letters from the missionaries to the slaves. One letter notes the employment of licensed black preachers in Richland District, South Carolina.

355 "Religious Intelligence: An Account of the Baptism of Nine Negroes in Boston, May 26, 1805." CHRISTIAN'S MAGAZINE, REVIEWER, AND RELIGIOUS INTELLIGENCER 1 (1805):66-69.

Description of a baptismal service held at a black church in West Boston, Massachusetts, in May 1805, includes comment on the ritual march to the baptismal pool by members of the congregation and on the singing. Also a summary of the sermon.

Sermon text: Romans 6:4, Col 2:12.

356 Rice, John Holt [Rusticus, pseud.]. "The Pious African." LITERARY AND EVANGELICAL MAGAZINE (=VIRGINIA EVANGELICAL AND LITERARY MAGAZINE) 10 (1827): 22-25.

Editor offers a character sketch of an elderly black Baptist preacher, Jack, a native of Virginia, and of other black preachers who enjoyed great influence over their congregations because of their religious "fanaticism."

357 Richards, Addison. "The Rice Lands of the South." HARPER'S NEW MONTHLY MAGAZINE 19 (November 1859): 721-38.

Description of plantation life in the Carolinas and in Georgia refers to the work activities, religious practices, leisure-time pursuits, and singing performance practice of the slaves. Also comment on the plantation preacher.

Excerpt of 1 sermon: The Story of Zaccheus (734).

358 Roberts, James. THE NARRATIVE OF JAMES ROBERTS: SOLDIER IN THE REVOLUTIONARY WAR AND AT THE BATTLE OF NEW ORLEANS. Chicago: Printed for the Author, 1858. 32 pp. Reprints. Hattiesburg, MS: The Book Farm, 1945. Chicago: Library Resources, 1970.

Ex-slave (b. 1753) describes a prayer meeting in his autobiography (20-21) and refers to two black regimental musicians who played the fife and drum for military maneuvers (16).

359 Rogers, Seth. "Letters of Dr. Seth Rogers, 1862-1863; A Surgeon's War Letters." PROCEEDINGS OF THE MASSACHUSETTS HISTORICAL SOCIETY 43 (February 1910): 337-98.

White surgeon with the First South Carolina Volunteers (Colored), in letters written to his daughter, refers to the religious songs sung by boatmen as they rowed (346), to the nightly praise meetings and chants of the black soldiers (342), and to the fact that Colonel Higginson had transcribed some songs of the blacks (346).

360 Root, George Frederick. "Congregational Singing among Negroes." NEW YORK MUSICAL REVIEW AND CHORAL ADVOCATE 6 (29 March 1855): 107.

American composer's description of a service at the African Church in Richmond, Virginia, includes references to the congregation singing a "quaint" melody in slow tempo and to the chant-like quality of their prayers.

Text and musical incipit of 1 prayer: O Lord, bless our pastor, stand by him and preserve him.

361 Roper, Moses. A NARRATIVE OF THE ADVENTURES AND ESCAPE OF MOSES ROPER FROM AMERICAN SLAVERY; WITH A PREFACE BY THE REV. T. PRICE. 1838. 3d ed. London: Darton, Harvey & Darton, 1839. 193 pp. Reprints. Philadelphia: Rhistoric Publications, 1969. New York: Negro Universities Press, 1970.

Ex-slave, born in Caswell County, North Carolina, discusses how the slaves sang as they worked in the fields, and comments on a slave exhorter who preached on the plantation (61-62).

Text of 1 song: I am happy, Lord, pity poor me.

362 Royall, Anne. SKETCHES OF HISTORY, LIFE AND MANNERS IN THE UNITED STATES BY A TRAVELLER. New Haven, CT: Printed for the Author, 1826. Reprint. New York: Johnson Reprint Company, 1970. 392 pp.

Anne Royall published nine volumes of travels. Despite her extreme hostility to blacks, particularly "free blacks," who were too impudent for her taste, she reveals information in this book about the black church (2, 104, 105, 274). Comment also on the black poet George Horton (156).

363 "Sable Clouds": "Religious Trust among the

Contrabands." NATIONAL ANTI-SLAVERY STANDARD 22 (10 August 1861): [3]

Letter dated from Outposts near Hampton, Virginia, 31 July 1861, includes discussion of a religious song sung by contrabands and of associated performance practice.

Text of 1 song: Jesus'll git us out o' dis (Cho: An' we'll go home to Can'an).

364 Schoolcraft, Mary Howard. THE BLACK GAUNTLET: A TALE OF PLANTATION LIFE IN THE SOUTH. Philadelphia: J. B. Lippincott & Company, 1860. 569 pp. Reprint. Freeport, NY: Books for Libraries Press, 1971.

Sketches of plantation life in South Carolina include references to slave musicians providing music for their masters (22), to songs of Negro boatmen (27), and to slave prayer-meetings and singing-meetings (151). Description of a slave funeral contains references to exhorting by the preacher and to congregational singing (161-62).

365 "Sharper, the Colored Preacher." CHRISTIAN WATCHMAN & REFLECTOR (=WATCHMAN-EXAMINER) 16 (30 May 1835): [85]. Reprinted from the CHARLESTON OBSERVER, entitled "Journal of a Missionary to the Negroes...."

Entry dated 28 May [1835] gives an obituary for the slave preacher Sharper, who preached to black congregations for more than twenty years. Also discussion of his "remarkably apt" references to the Scriptures in his sermons.

366 "Sketches of South-Carolina: Number 2--- The Sea Islands." KNICKERBOCKER 21 (January 1843): 36-42.

Discussion of the author's travels through the South Carolina Sea Islands includes comment on the songs of boatmen and of a plantation preacher. Also description of a slave funeral.

367 "Slavery in Virginia." FARMER'S REGISTER (Petersburg, Virginia) 4 (July 1836): 180-83. Excerpt reprinted from SLAVERY IN THE UNITED STATES.

Virginian slaveholder discusses the plantation funeral and slave preachers, and comments on the "disuse" of the banjo and the lessening importance of banjo songs.

368 "The Southern Press: The Negro Church Nuisance." NATIONAL ANTI-SLAVERY STANDARD 10 (20 September 1849): 65. Reprinted from the COLUMBUS [Georgia] ENQUIRER.

Author draws attention to a city ordinance of Columbus, Georgia, dated 1833, which prohibits the slaves from preaching or exhorting when seven or more persons of color are present, without first obtaining a certificate of good character and other credentials from three, white ordained clergy and written permission from the Justices of the Inferior Court.

369 "A Southern Scene." THE MUSICAL WORLD AND TIMES (New York) 9 (6 July 1854): 113.

Discussion of a visit to a plantation Baptist church in the antebellum South includes comment on the "mourner's" bench, the singing of lined-out hymns and "spiritual songs" at prayer meetings, on the holy dance and performance practice.

370 Spencer, Peter, compiler. THE AFRICAN UNION HYMN BOOK. DESIGNED AS A COMPANION FOR THE PIOUS, AND FRIENDS OF ALL DENOMINATIONS. COLLECTED FROM DIFFERENT AUTHORS. Wilmington, DE: Printed by R. Porter, 1822. 144 pp.

Collection of 132 hymn texts compiled by the minister of the Union African Methodist Episcopal Church in Wilmington, Delaware, (but without references to the appropriate tunes for singing the hymns). Early example of a hymn written by a black author that refers specifically to the black experience, "On Afric's land our fathers roamed" (119).

Wandering (?) refrains of 2 hymns: 1. Nor will I let him go. 2. To Canaan's promis'd land (113).

371 Stevens, Abel. SKETCHES AND INCIDENTS. New York: G. Lane and P. P. Sandford, 1844. 166 pp.

Sketch about "Black Harry" [Hosier] of St. Eustatius, Antigua, refers to this Methodist slave exhorter who preached in both the United States and in the West Indies during the 1790s and the turn of the nineteenth century (94-102).

372 Stevens, Charles Emery. ANTHONY BURNS: A HISTORY. Boston: John P. Jewett & Company ny, 1856. Reprints. Westport, CT: Negro Universities Press, 1969. 295 pp. Williamstown, MA: Corner House Publications, 1973.

Biography of the fugitive slave Burns (1834-1862), who was arrested in Boston on 24 May 1854, includes discussion of the ritual ordination of slave preachers and exhorters (165-66), and distinguishes between the "burial" and the "funeral." Refers to the singing of "wild Negro airs" (167).

373 "The Story of a Fugitive Slave." NATIONAL ANTI-SLAVERY STANDARD 13 (27 May 1852): 4.

Biographical sketch of Thomas Jones, a fugitive slave of North Carolina, informs how he became an exhorter and leader of Sunday Schools. Comment on the singing of "happy songs" after the prayer-meetings held in slave cabins.

374 Stowe, Harriet Beecher. A KEY TO UNCLE TOM'S CABIN: PRESENTING THE ORIGINAL FACTS

AND DOCUMENTS UPON WHICH THE STORY IS FOUNDED.... Cleveland: Jewett, Proctor & Worthington, 1853. Reprint. Port Washington, NY: Kennikat Press, 1968. 262 pp.

Discussion by the author of UNCLE TOM'S CABIN includes references to the relationship between music and slave coffles, i.e., singing, fiddles and banjos (164-65, 210); to a religious service (27); and to funeral customs (9-10).

375 Stuart, Dennar. "A Camp-Meeting in Tennessee." HARPER'S NEW MONTHLY MAGAZINE 26 (December 1862): 97-101. Reprint. CHRISTIAN WATCHMAN & REFLECTOR (=WATCHMAN-EXAMINER) 44 (5 February 1863): 1-2.

Description of a Methodist camp-meeting service in Tennessee during 1816 includes references to religious practices of the slaves.

Text of 1 camp-meeting song: By and by we'll go and meet them (Cho: Safe in the promised land). Text of 1 couplet: O stem the storm. Text of 1 sermon: He that endureth to the end shall receive a crown for life.

376 Stuart, James. THREE YEARS IN NORTH AMERICA. Edinburgh: Robert Cadell, 1833. 2 vols. Reprint. New York: Arno Press and the New York Times, 1974.

English visitor describes a slave prayer-meeting in St. Louis, Missouri (2:343-44), and a camp meeting in Flushing, New York (2:555). Also refers to black preachers and their sermons.

377 "A Sunday at Port Royal: The Negro-Sunday School--The Contraband Regiment." NATIONAL ANTI-SLAVERY STANDARD 23 (26 July 1862): [1].

Article, dated Hilton Head, South Carolina, 7 July 1862, refers to the singing at a contraband Sunday school on the island. Observation made that the songs and dances of Negro recruits have "a spice of the native African in their rhythm and choruses."

378 Sutcliff, Robert. TRAVELS IN SOME PARTS OF NORTH AMERICA IN THE YEARS 1804, 1805, AND 1806. York, England: Printed for W. Alexander, 1811. 293 pp. Reprint. Micro-opaque. Louisville, KY: Lost Cause Press, 1959.

Quaker merchant of Sheffield, England, traveled in the United States, then settled there permanently in 1811. Refers to a Methodist camp meeting where there was a "great number" of black families (107-8) and to a little black boy who told stories to the children of the slaveholding family about his African capture (212).

379 Svin'in, Pavel Petrovich. PICTURESQUE UNITED STATES OF AMERICA, 1811, 1812, 1813, BEING A MEMOIR ON PAUL SVININ, RUSSIAN DIPLOMATIC OFFICER, ARTIST, AND AUTHOR, CONTAINING COPIOUS EXCERPTS FROM HIS ACCOUNT OF HIS TRAVELS IN AMERICA.... Edited and translated by Avrahm Yarmolinsky. New York: W. E. Rudge, 1930. 46 pp.

Russian diplomat describes his visit to a black Methodist church in Philadelphia and the minister's sermon (20). Also comment on the congregational singing of psalms in a "loud, shrill monotone."

Reference to 1 sermon: The destruction of the universe (20).

380 Thompson, John. THE LIFE OF JOHN THOMPSON, A FUGITIVE SLAVE. CONTAINING HIS HISTORY OF 25 YEARS IN BONDAGE, AND HIS PROVIDENTIAL ESCAPE. WRITTEN BY HIMSELF. Worcester, MA: The Author, 1856. 143 pp.

Narrator, b. 1812 in Maryland, gives a detailed account of slave life on the plantation, and comments on the plantation fiddler (19) and religious services (101-2).

381 Tilmon, Levin. A BRIEF MISCELLANEOUS NARRATIVE OF THE MORE EARLY PART OF THE LIFE OF L. TILMON, PASTOR OF A COLORED METHODIST CONGREGATIONAL CHURCH IN THE CITY OF NEW YORK. WRITTEN BY HIMSELF. Jersey City: W. W. & L. A. Pratt, 1853. 97 pp. Reprint. Microfilm. Woodbridge, CT: Research Publications, 1977.

Ex-slave (1807-1863), born in Maryland, discusses a sermon he heard (30), comments on a bush meeting and religious service in August 1845 (42-43), and associates fiddling and dancing with sin (79).

Text of 1 sermon: Corinth 4:17 (30-39).

382 Tower, Philo. SLAVERY UNMASKED; BEING A TRUTHFUL NARRATIVE OF A THREE YEARS' RESIDENCE AND JOURNEYING IN ELEVEN SOUTHERN STATES.... Rochester: E. Barrow & Brothers, 1852. Reprint. Westport, CT: Greenwood Press, 1975. 432 pp.

Northern clergyman, in a discussion of worship services of the slaves, includes excerpts of two slave sermons (198-202, 253-55).

Sermon excerpts: 1. Paul's charge to Timothy (2 Timothy 4:8). 2. Blessed are the dead that die in the Lord (Revelation). Text of 1 song: City-ho, City-ho, whar de ole boss lub-um go (274).

383 Trollope, Frances M. DOMESTIC MANNERS OF THE AMERICANS. London: Whittaker, Treacher, & Company, 1832. 2 vols. Reprint. Micro-opaque. Louisville, KY: Lost Cause Press, 1961.

English novelist includes in her book comment on the sermon of a black preacher at a camp-meeting in Indiana (238-39).

384 Turner, Nat. THE CONFESSIONS OF NAT TURNER, THE LEADER OF THE LATE INSURRECTION IN SOUTHAMPTON, VA., As Fully and Voluntarily Made to Thomas R. Gray.... Baltimore: Thomas R. Gray, 1831. 23 pp. Reprint. NAT TURNER'S SLAVE REBELLION..., by Herbert Aptheker. New York: Grove Press, 1966.

Slave narrator (1800-1831) offers insight into the informal education and philosophy of the slave preacher in the 1830s.

385 Tuttle, J. F. "A Negro Meeting." INDEPENDENT 12 (4 October 1860): 6.

Description of a revival meeting held at a black Methodist church in Baltimore, Maryland, includes comment on the performance of the congregation, on mourners who rolled and writhed in great anguish, on the singing of "Negro hymns," and on the prayers.

References to 3 songs: 1. Will you go to glory with me? 2. Oh, there will be mourning. 3. Passing away.

386 "Uncle Harry; Or, the Tender Sensibilities of a Pious African." LIBERATOR 3 (17 August 1833): 132.

Character sketch of an elderly preacher born in Port Tobacco, Maryland, includes discussion of how he became a preacher.

387 Viator [pseud.]. "The Night Funeral of a Slave." DE BOW'S REVIEW 20 (February 1856): 218-21. Reprinted from the HOME JOURNAL.

Northern traveler in Georgia describes a plantation slave burial he saw, with comment on the black preacher and singing performance practice. Also references to the singing of the slaves on other occasions.

388 "The Virginia Negro Preacher." CHRISTIAN WATCHMAN & REFLECTOR (=WATCHMAN-EXAMINER) 20 (15 February 1839): [25].

Character sketch of an elderly, black Baptist preacher of southeastern Virginia refers to his philosophical discussions about the Bible.

389 W. "A Camp-Meeting Reminiscence: Old Harry's Experience." SOUTHERN CHRISTIAN ADVOCATE 7 (12 January 1844): 122.

Methodist minister describes a devotional service held after-hours by black worshippers at a camp meeting in South Carolina. Refers to hymn singing and relevant performance practice, and transcribes the text of a slave exhortation.

Text of 1 sermon: The consolation of religion.

390 Walker, Susan. JOURNAL OF MISS SUSAN WALKER, MARCH 3RD TO JUNE 6TH, 1862. Edited by Henry Noble Sherwood. QUARTERLY PUBLICATION OF THE HISTORICAL AND PHILOSOPHICAL SOCIETY OF OHIO 7 (January-March 1912): 3-48. Reprints. Cincinnati, OH: Press of Jennings and Grahm, [1912]. Microfiche. Louisville, KY: Lost Cause Press, 1987.

Entry dated 15 March [1862] includes a detailed discussion of the shout, performed by freedmen, that this New England school marm observed in Port Royal, South Carolina (16). Also comment on performance practice, on the singing of religious songs "extempore," and on the songs of boatmen (19).

391 Watson, John Fanning. METHODIST ERROR; OR, FRIENDLY CHRISTIAN ADVICE, TO THOSE METHODISTS WHO INDULGE IN EXTRAVAGANT RELIGIOUS EMOTIONS AND BODILY EXERCISE. By a Wesleyan Methodist. Trenton, NJ: D. & E. Fenton, 1819. 180 pp. Reprints. Micro-opaque. New York: Readex Microprint, 1980. Selected passages in READINGS IN BLACK AMERICAN MUSIC, edited by Eileen Southern. 2d ed. New York: W. W. Norton & Company, 1983.

Local historian and church father condemns the singing of improvised hymns to melodies adapted from old songs by black Methodists of Philadelphia (28). Describes religious dancing and how camp-meeting songs are composed from "short scraps of matter" (29-31).

References to 2 refrains: 1. Touch but one string, 'twill make heaven ring, 2. Go shouting all your days (Cho: Glory, glory, glory).

392 Weld, Charles Richard. A VACATION TOUR IN THE UNITED STATES AND CANADA. London: Longman, Brown, Green & Longmans, 1855. 394 pp. Reprint. Ann Arbor, MI: University Microfilms International, n.d.

English historian's account of his travels in the United States includes discussion of a religious service held in the African Baptist Church of Richmond, Virginia (294-97) and of a baptism ceremony on the banks of the James River (297-98).

393 Whipple, Henry Benjamin. BISHOP WHIPPLE'S SOUTHERN DIARY, 1843-1844. Edited by Lester B. Shippee. Minneapolis: University of Minnesota, 1937. 208 pp. Reprint. New York: Da Capo Press, 1968.

Clergyman, who became Bishop of the Protestant Episcopal Church of Minnesota, travelled in the South during the years 1843-44. His journal entries include detailed description of slave life: workers on the wharves (87), boat rowers (13, 33), the baptism of children (21), the worship service (35), the celebration of Christmas (48), of popular songs among the slaves, and of song performance practice (33). The appendices include a reprint of the "Slave Laws in Georgia" (181).

Texts of 4 songs (33): 1. Dis ole niggar lub a gal. 2. Blow dis niggar off to New Yak. 3. De speckle taters cotch dis niggar. 4. Laugh you niggar, laugh away.

394 White, William Spottswood. THE AFRICAN PREACHER. AN AUTHENTIC NARRATIVE. Philadelphia: Presbyterian Board of Publication [c.1849]. 139 pp. Includes obituary that originally was published in WATCHMAN OF THE SOUTH, 4 May 1843, pp. 100-101. Reprint. Freeport, NY: Books for Libraries Press, 1972.

Biography of a popular slave preacher of Virginia, "Uncle Jack" (c.1747-1843), who was licensed to preach although he could read only the Bible. Includes complaints about "noise and disorder" in the religious services of the slaves (33-34) and description of a night funeral (138-39).

395 Wightman, William May. LIFE OF WILLIAM CAPERS, D.D. 1856. Nashville, TN: Southern Methodist Publishing House, 1858. 516 pp. Reprint. Nashville, TN: Publishing House of the M. E. Church, South, 1902.

Biography includes biographical sketch of Rachel Wells, called "Maum Rachel," the first colored person to join the Methodist Society in Charleston, South Carolina, and the oldest member of the Methodist Church at the time of her death in August 1849 (391-97). Also comments on the first Methodist missions to slaves, which were established in 1829 on plantations bordering the Ashley and Santee Rivers in South Carolina (291).

396 Williams, James. NARRATIVE OF JAMES WILLIAMS, WHO WAS FOR SEVERAL YEARS A DRIVER ON A COTTON PLANTATION IN ALABAMA. Edited by John Greenleaf Whittier. New York: American Anti-Slavery Society, 1838. 108 pp. Reprint. Wilmington, DE: Rhistoric Publications, n.d.

Ex-slave, born 1805 in Maryland, refers in his autobiography to slave preachers (25-27, 70-74), to themes of sermons preached by slaves (26), to singing in the slave quarters (72), and to the use of horns to awaken slave workers (46).

THE SONG

397 Aaron. THE LIGHT AND TRUTH OF SLAVERY; AARON'S HISTORY. Worcester, MA: Printed for Aaron, 1827. 48 pp. Reprint. Microfiche. Louisville, KY: Lost Cause Press, 197-.

Narrative of ex-slave includes references to slaves dancing and singing in order to forget their troubles (15-16).

Text of 1 song: Here I go to be baptised (Cho: Sing glory, sing glory) (21).

398 Abdy, Edward S. JOURNAL OF A RESIDENCE AND TOUR IN THE UNITED STATES OF NORTH AMERICA FROM APRIL, 1833, TO OCTOBER, 1834. London: John Murray, 1835. 3 vols. Reprint. New York: Negro Universities Press, 1969.

Englishman offers penetrating comments on the black experience, for both free and slave.

Text of 1 song: I born in Sout Calina (Cho: And he boun' for Lousy-Anna) (3:104).

399 "African Labor and African Ditties." MUSICAL WORLD AND TIMES (New York) 6 (6 August 1853): 213. Reprinted from BUILDER.

Description of the construction of a country church on the Sea-Island of St. Helena, South Carolina, by approximately 100 African slaves who were liberated from a slaver. References to Africans singing in their native language as they worked, and text of the worksong in African dialect with English translation.

Text of 1 song: Tartar-jimbongo (=Daddy give me money to buy a little pig).

400 Agricola [pseud.] "Management of Negroes." DE BOW'S REVIEW 19 (September 1855): 358-63.

Discussion of the management of slaves includes advice: slaves should be encouraged to sing or whistle lively tunes while at work; "drawling tunes" should not be permitted because they slow the pace of the work activity. Author disapproves of giving the slaves a week's holiday at Christmas, or of permitting them to tell folk tales, or witch and ghost stories, which "excite the young imagination."

401 Alger, William Rounseville. "Speech." LIBERATOR 32 (31 January 1862): 17-18.

Text of a speech delivered by Unitarian minister and author in Boston before the Massachusetts Anti-Slavery Society in January 1862 includes the text of a song sung by the contrabands.

Text of 1 song: Oh, praise an' thanks! De Lord he come to set de people free.

402 Andrew, James O. "A Fortnight among the Missions to Blacks: 3." SOUTHERN CHRISTIAN ADVOCATE 20 (28 May 1857): 207.

Missionary discusses his work among the slaves on rice plantations in the Beaufort and Savannah areas of Georgia. References to the improvised songs of boatmen and relevant performance practice.

Text of 1 couplet: Old Satan, you needn't to pick arter me.

403 Armistead, Wilson. A TRIBUTE FOR THE NEGRO. BEING A VINDICATION OF THE MORAL, INTELLECTUAL, AND RELIGIOUS CAPABILITIES OF THE COLOURED PORTION OF MANKIND; WITH PARTICULAR REFERENCE TO THE AFRICAN RACE. Manchester, England: W. Irwin, 1848. 564 pp. Reprint. Miami, FL: Mnemosyne Publishers, 1969.

Comments on the Africans of the Amistad (ship), who sang their native songs at a public meeting in Boston in 1841 (500).

404 Barker, Joseph, ed. THE LIVES OF LEWIS, MILTON, AND CYRUS CLARKE, THREE CELEBRATED FUGITIVE SLAVES: The Trial of Jonathan Walker, For Helping Slaves to Escape, to together with a Mass of Information Respecting American Slavery. Wortley, England: Printed by Joseph Barker, [1846].

Slave narratives edited by Englishman include discussion of "why" the slaves sang.

Text of 1 song: Hurra for good ole Massa (Cho: Hurra, I'm going to de city) (110).

405 Bibb, Henry. "The Plantation Song." NATIONAL ANTI-SLAVERY STANDARD 5 (8 August 1844): 40.

Text of 1 plantation song, recorded by ex-slave Bibb, which was sung by slaves who were being sent to the deep South to be sold: See these poor souls from Africa (Cho: There is a better day a-coming, go sound the jubilee).

406 "Black Tom, the Sweep." GLEASON'S PICTORIAL DRAWING-ROOM COMPANION 2 (14 February 1852): 112.

Description of a boy chimney sweep in New York, includes reference to 1 street cry: Sweep oh-o-ho.

407 Brougham, John. DRED; OR, THE DISMAL SWAMP, A PLAY IN FIVE ACTS. Dramatized (by Special Permission) from Harriet Beecher Stowe's Novel. New York: Samuel French, ca.1856. 43 pp. Reprint. New York: Readex Microprint, 1966.

Anti-slavery play contains the texts of 2 songs: 1. My way is dark and cloudy (12). 2. If you get there before I do (Cho: I'm bound for the land ob Canaan (13).

408 Brown, David. THE PLANTER; OR, THIRTEEN YEARS IN THE SOUTH. BY A NORTHERN MAN. Philadelphia: H. Hooker, 1853. 275 pp. Reprint. Micro-card. Louisville, Lost Cause Press, 196-.

Discussion of plantation life in the South includes comment on slave boatmen working near St. Augustine, Florida, who sang "extempore songs," keeping time to the music as they rowed (84-88).

409 Brown, William Wells. NARRATIVE OF WILLIAM W. BROWN, A FUGITIVE SLAVE. WRITTEN BY HIMSELF. Boston: published at the Anti-Slavery Office, 1847. 110 pp. Reprint. New York: Johnson Reprint Corporation, 1970.

Autobiography of ex-slave Brown (1814-1884) up to the time he escaped from slavery in Lexington, Kentucky, includes text of a song, of which he states: "I have often heard the slaves sing, when about to be carried to the far south. It is said to have been composed by a slave."

Text of 1 song (51): See those poor souls from Africa (Cho: Go sound the jubilee).

410 _____. THE ANTI-SLAVERY HARP; A COLLECTION OF SONGS FOR ANTI-SLAVERY MEETINGS. Boston: Bela Marsh, 1849. 47 pp. Reprint. Philadelphia: Rhistoric Publications, 1969.

Collection of thirty anti-slavery songs includes the names of the tunes appropriate for the singing of the verses. One song, entitled "Song of the Coffle Gang, is said to be sung by slaves, as they are chained in gangs, when parting from friends for the far-off South."

Text of 1 song: See those poor souls from Africa (Cho: We are stolen and sold to Georgia) (29).

411 Bryant, William Cullen. "A Corn Shucking in South Carolina." NATIONAL ANTI-SLAVERY STANDARD 11 (6 June 1850): 8.

Excerpt from author's LETTERS OF A TRAVELLER; OR, NOTES OF THINGS SEEN IN EUROPE AND AMERICA (1850) describes a corn shucking festival of slaves in South Carolina. Discusses songs and dancing. Refers to a mock military parade as part of the festivities.

Reference to 2 songs: 1. Jenny gone away. 2. The monkey song (Cho: Dan, Dan, who's de dandy?). Texts of 2 songs: 1. Johnny come down de hollow (Cho: O, hollow!), 2. De cooter is de boatman (Cho: John, John Crow).

412 _____. "A Tour in the Old South." PROSE WRITINGS OF WILLIAM CULLEN BRYANT. Vol. 2, TRAVELS, ADDRESSES, AND COMMENTS. Edited by Parke Godwin. New York: D. Appleton & Company, 1884. Reprint. New York: Russell and Russell, 1964.

Description of the American poet's travels through Georgia, Florida, Virginia, and South Carolina during March-April 1843 includes references to slaves singing ballads and playing the banjo. Detailed description of a corn-shucking festival in Barnwell District, South Carolina, including comment on the corn-shucking songs and dancing (29-35). Festival concluded with a "mock military parade."

Texts of 2 songs: 1. Johnny come down de hollow. 2. De cooter is de boatman (Cho: John John crow). Reference to 2 songs: 1. Jenny gone away. 2. Monkey song (Cho: Dan, Dan, who's de dandy).

413 ____. LETTERS OF A TRAVELLER; OR, NOTES OF THINGS SEEN IN EUROPE AND AMERICA. New York: George P. Putnam, 1850. 442 pp. Reprint. Microfilm. New Haven, CT: Research Publications, 1975.

Letter (dated 2 March 1843, Richmond, Virginia) discusses slaves singing psalms in a tobacco factory (73-75). Another letter (dated 29 March 1843, Barnwell District, South Carolina) describes a slave corn-shucking festival (82-89). Discussion of the songs, performance practice, and dancing to music made by a slave whistling and beating two sticks on the floor. Description of a mock military parade as part of the festivities.

Texts of 2 songs (85-86): 1. Johnny come down de hollow (Cho: Oh hollow!). 2. De cooter is de boatman (Cho: John, John Crow). Reference to 2 songs: 1. Jenny gone away. 2. The monkey song (Cho: Dan, Dan, who's de dandy).

414 Carroll, Bartholomew Rivers (?). "An Editorial Voyage to Edisto Island." CHICORA 1 (August 1842): 47, 63. Reprint of passages in "Negro Boatmen's Songs," by Jay B. Hubbell. SOUTHERN FOLKLORE QUARTERLY 18/4 (December 1954): 244-45. Page references below are to Hubbell.

Description of the singing of black oarsmen as they rowed to Edisto Island.

Texts of 3 songs: 1. Now we gwine leab Charlestown city (Cho: Pull boys, pull). 2. Mass Ralph, Mass Ralph, 'e is a good man (Cho: Oh ma Riley). 3. One time upon dis ribber (Cho: Long time ago).

415 Channing, William Ellery. "Facts Showing the Character of Slavery." LIBERATOR 6 (18 June 1836): 99.

In excerpts from his book SLAVERY, abolitionist minister and author of religious books discusses the singing of the slaves and describes the context in which a group of slaves composed one of their songs.

Reference to 1 song: We got no massa.

416 Child, Lydia Maria. "Charity Bowery." THE LIBERTY BELL, BY FRIENDS OF FREEDOM. Edited by Maria W. Chapman, 26-43. Boston: Published for the Massachusetts Anti-Slavery Fair, 1839. Reprint. NORTH STAR 1 (3 March 1848): [4].

Collection of short essays and poems includes one about an old slave, Charity Bowery. Also a song identified as "a specimen of their hymns."

Text of 1 song: A few more beatings of the wind and rain (Cho: There's a better day a-coming).

417 Clark, George Washington. THE LIBERTY MINSTREL. New York: Published by the Author, 1844. 215 pp.

Collection of anti-slavery songs includes one, "Song of the Coffle Gang," of which the text was written by slaves.

Text of 1 song: See those poor souls from Africa (22-23).

418 ____. THE HARP OF FREEDOM. New York: Miller, Orton & Mulligan, 1856. 335 pp.

Large collection of anti-slavery songs includes the music of one slave song, which has been given a parody text by the author, "O when we go back dar" (54). The incipit of the original text of the slave song is given (54).

Music of 1 song and text incipit: O whar is de spot what we were born on (54).

419 Combe, George. NOTES ON THE UNITED STATES OF NORTH AMERICA DURING A PHRENOLOGICAL VISIT IN 1838-1839-1840. Philadelphia: Carey & Hart, 1841. 2 vols. Reprint. New York: Arno Press and the New York Times, 1974.

English traveler refers to a young black chimney sweep of Philadelphia, whose street cries resemble a Tyrolese "yoddle" (1:328).

420 "The Contrabands of South Carolina." NATIONAL ANTI-SLAVERY STANDARD 22 (21 December 1861):[1]. From the [New York] TRIBUNE.

Discussion of the condition of slaves on the Sea Islands of South Carolina includes references to slave songs and two texts.

Texts of 2 songs: 1. De Northmen dey's got massa now (Cho: Glory hallelujah!). 2. O massa a rebel, we row him to prison.

421 "A Corn Shucking." Unsigned review of William Cullen Bryant's LETTERS OF A TRAVELLER.... DE BOW'S REVIEW 9 (September 1850): 326-27.

Description of a corn-shucking festival in the Barnwell District (South Carolina) refers to various types of corn songs, to men dancing to the music of a whistler, who beat two sticks on the floor as he whistled.

Texts of 2 songs: 1. Johnny come down de hollow (Cho: Oh, hollow). 2. De cooter is de boatman (Cho: John, John Crow. References to 2 songs: 1. Jenny gone away. 2. The monkey song.

422 THE CRIES OF NEW-YORK. New York: Printed and Sold by Samuel Wood, 1809. 47 pp. Reprint. New York: Readex Microprint, 1979.

Comment on black street vendors of buttermilk (26) and baked pears (21), and of chimney sweeps (40-41).

Two cries: 1. Butter mil-leck. 2. Bake pears.

423 Croome, William H. CITY CRIES; OR, A PEEP AT SCENES IN TOWN BY AN OBSERVER. Philadelphia: George S. Appleton, 1850. 102 pp.

This collection of "24 designs" of street criers of Philadelphia contains a description and illustration of each. The black criers are: 1. chimney sweep (16-18), 2. white-wash man (28-30), 3. crab-man (60-62), 4. ice-cream man (66), 5. hot-corn woman (68-70), 6. hominy-man (80-82), 7. split-wood man (88-90), 8. pepper-pot woman (96-98).

Texts and music of 4 street cries: 1. Y'ere's the white whitey-wash, brown whitey-wash. 2. Crabs! Crabs alive! Buy any Crabs. 3. Split wood! Split wood: 4. Pepper-pot! All hot.

424 D. "Aunt Hester." ZION'S HERALD AND WESLEYAN JOURNAL (=ZION'S HERALD) 19 (15 November 1848): [181].

Letter dated 14 September 1848 from Attakapas, Louisiana, presents a brief narrative about the slave Hester, who was persecuted because she gave religious instruction to her fellow slaves. Comment on the prayer meetings of the slaves and on their singing.

425 D., C. W. "Contraband Singing." INDEPENDENT 12 (5 September 1861): 7. DWIGHT'S JOURNAL OF MUSIC 19 (7 September 1861): 182. Reprint. THE NEGRO AND HIS FOLKLORE IN NINETEENTH-CENTURY PERIODICALS. Edited by Bruce Jackson. Published for the American Folklore Society. Austin: University of Texas Press, 1967.

Discussion of the singing of extemporaneous songs and lined-out hymns by the ex-slaves in contraband camps at Fortress Monroe, Virginia.

Text of 1 song: Shout along, children (Cho: Hear the dying Lamb).

426 "A Day with the Congaree Missionary." SOUTHERN CHRISTIAN ADVOCATE 14 (30 August 1850): 50.

Description of a slave religious service on a plantation mission in South Carolina includes discussion of the singing of the slaves and relevant performance practice.

427 Delany, Martin Robison. BLAKE; OR, THE HUTS OF AMERICA. 1859. Reprint. Boston: Beacon Press, 1970. 321 pp.

Delany's novel, the first by a black author to be published in the United States, appeared serially, first in the ANGLO-AFRICAN MAGAZINE (January-July 1859), then in the WEEKLY-ANGLO AFRICAN (November 1861-May 1862). Parts of it are autobiographical. Delany's comments include description of dancing and singing (67), of the performance practice of Mississippi boatmen (100), of firemen on boats (124-25), and of a conjurer in North Carolina (112-14).

Texts of 3 songs: 1. See wives and husbands torn apart (32). 2. In eighteen-hundred and twenty-three (91) [both texts are variants of the Song of the Coffle Gang]. 3. We'll honor our Lord and Master (104). Text of 1 chorus: I'm a-going to Texas---O! (82).

428 Denison, C. W. "Will the Contrabands Fight?" DOUGLASS' MONTHLY 4 (March 1862): 618.

U. S. chaplain stationed at Port Royal, South Carolina, discusses the bravery and valor of contraband recruits in the Union Army. Refers to a song about "Moses leading the Israelites from Egypt" that had been sung in Virginia for several years, but was forbidden in certain parts of that state and was never heard south of Virginia.

429 Douglass, Frederick. NARRATIVE OF THE LIFE OF FREDERICK DOUGLASS, AN AMERICAN SLAVE. WRITTEN BY HIMSELF. Boston: Anti-Slavery Office, 1845. 125 pp. Reprints. Cambridge, MA: Belknap Press of Harvard University Press, 1960. New York: Penguin Books, 1982.

This, the first autobiography of ex-slave Douglass, includes discussion of the meaning of the slave songs (36-38) and a description of family devotions, where Douglass had to "raise the hymn" (93). (See also nos. 237, 1138).

Reference to 1 song: I am going away to the great house.

430 Editor's Table: "Oh! Let My People Go---The Song of the Contrabands." CONTINENTAL MONTHLY 2 (July 1862): 112-13.

One of the first spirituals to be published, this song was transcribed by the Rev. Lewis C. Lockwood, at that time chaplain of a contraband camp at Fortress Monroe, Virginia.

Text of 1 song: The Lord, by Moses, to Pharaoh said (Cho: Oh! go down, Moses, away down to Egypt's land).

431 "The Emancipated Slaves at Port Royal." NATIONAL ANTI-SLAVERY STANDARD 22 (1 February 1862): [1].

Description of Christmas celebrations on General Drayton's plantation in 1861 at Hilton Head, South Carolina, includes comment on the singing of religious songs, on slave prayers, and on the shout.

Text of 1 shout song: Say brothers, will you meet me on Canaan's happy shore?

432 [Evangelicana.] "Account of a Black Man." MASSACHUSETTS MISSIONARY MAGAZINE 5 September 1807): 152. Reprint from PHILADELPHIA MAGAZINE.

Account of a woman's visit to a residence in Trenton, New Jersey, where she encountered an unidentified elderly male slave, who sang songs of his own composition for her.

Reference to 1 song: I shall be white, and I shall be happy.

433 "Every-Day Commerce, Nos. IV and V. Steamboats and Steamboating in the Southwest." DOLLAR MAGAZINE 8 (July-October 1851): 4-8, 148-51. Reprinted in TRAVELS IN THE OLD SOUTH.... Edited by Eugene L. Schwaab, vol. 2, 397-406. Lexington: University Press of Kentucky, 1973. Page reference below is to the Schwaab edition.

Discussion of the singing of black firemen on Mississippi River boats and comment on a refrain "invariably sung by negroes when they have anything to do with or about a fire---whether working at a New Orleans fire engine or crowding wood into the furnaces of a steamboat" (398).

Text of 1 chorus: Fire on the quarter deck.

434 Featherstonhaugh, G. W. EXCURSION THROUGH THE SLAVE STATES. New York: Harper & Brothers, 1844. 168 pp. Reprint. Washington, DC: Microcard Editions, 1970.

Englishman, who made a trip through the South in 1834-1835, refers to slave coffles and how slave drivers attempted to keep the slaves cheerful by encouraging them to sing to the music of the banjo. Also comments on the Negro "slave drivers," who amused the slaves by telling lively stories (36-37).

435 Felton, Mrs. LIFE IN AMERICA. A NARRATIVE OF TWO YEARS' CITY AND COUNTRY RESIDENCE IN THE UNITED STATES. Hull, England: John Hutchinson, 1838. 120 pp.

English woman, who traveled in the United States during the years 1836-1837, discusses slavery at great length. Refers to the voice quality of the slaves: "their voices are rich and melodious... at church, their singing is much admired" (63).

436 Foote, William Henry. SKETCHES OF VIRGINIA, HISTORICAL AND BIOGRAPHICAL. 2 vols. Philadelphia: William S. Martien, 1850. Reprints. Richmond, VA: John Knox Press, 1966. Microfilm. Ann Arbor, MI: University Microfilms International, n.d. Page references are to vol. 1 of the 1850 ed.

Extensive discussion of contemporary legislation that marked the movement of Africans from servitude to slavery in the seventeenth century (1: 22-25). Reprint of passages from the letters of Samuel Davies (see no. 35) about the slaves' responses to religious instruction and their fondness of singing (1:286-89). Also quoting of passages from the address of a black exhorter to black communicants in 1788 in Virginia (1:423).

437 Forten, Charlotte. "Letter from St. Helena's Island, Beaufort, S. C." LIBERATOR 32 (12 December 1862): 199.

Afro-American school teacher of Philadelphia discusses her work among the freed slaves in Beaufort, South Carolina. Brief comment on the songs of boatmen.

438 Gay, S. H. "The Hundred Conventions---Conclusion." LIBERATOR 14 (26 January 1844): 15.

Discussion of the activities of northern abolitionists and their network of underground railroads to aid fugitive slaves includes comment on the songs sung by fugitive slaves.

Text of 1 song: Our bondage it shall end, by and by.

439 Gosse, Philip Henry. LETTERS FROM ALABAMA (U. S.): CHIEFLY RELATING TO NATURAL HISTORY. London: Morgan and Chase, 1859. 306 pp. Reprint. Mountain Brook, AL: Overbrook House, 1983.

English naturalist, who resided in Alabama for seven or eight months, revised nineteen Letters, originally published in the HOME FRIEND magazine, for this publication. Discusses the "pleaing and even musical" quality of the "hog calls" of the slaves (62-63) and the "sonorous voices" of the slaves singing during opossum hunts, with reference to a recurring refrain--"big racoon... a sittin' on a rail" (230-31). Also description of the singing of the black stevedores as they stowed bales of cotton.

Text of 1 song: I think I hear the black cock say (Cho: Fire the ringo, fire away) (305-6).

440 Grayson, William John. "The Autobiography of William John Grayson." Edited by Samuel Gaillard Stoney. SOUTH CAROLINA HISTORICAL AND GENEOLOGICAL MAGAZINE 49 (January 1948): 23-40.

South Carolina lawyer and politician comments on the singing of slave boatmen near Charleston, South Carolina, in the 1850s and on performance practice and song improvisation (24).

441 H. "Reminiscences of a Missionary to the Blacks." SOUTHERN CHRISTIAN ADVOCATE 12 (25 August 1848): 45.

Southern missionary discusses his work among the slaves in South Carolina. States that slaves on one plantation in his circuit knew none of the "Songs of Zion" but sang only "harvest songs" of their own improvisation.

442 Hall, Basil. TRAVELS IN NORTH AMERICA IN THE YEARS 1827 AND 1828. 3 vols. Edinburgh: Printed for Cadell & Company, 1829.

A captain in the Royal Navy of England states that black boatmen "accompanied their labor by a wild sort of song...resembling that of the well-known Bunder-boatmen at Bombay" (3:216).

443 Hall, Francis. TRAVELS IN CANADA AND THE UNITED STATES IN 1816 AND 1817. Boston: Printed for the Author, 1818. 332 pp.

English traveler quotes from a book entitled LETTERS FROM VIRGINIA a passage about a slave coffle, with the slaves singing a "little wild hymn of sweet and mournful melody" (216-17).

444 Harris, William Tell. REMARKS MADE DURING A TOUR THROUGH THE UNITED STATES OF AMERICA, IN THE YEARS 1817, 1818, and 1819. By William Tell Harris In a Series of Letters to Friends in England. London: Sherwood, Neely, & Jones, 1821. 196 pp. Reprint. Ann Arbor, MI: University Microfilms, 1974.

Letter no. 7 includes references to songs sung by slaves "while stowing away the cotton" (69).

445 Hinman, C. T. "Correspondence: Two Weeks in Charleston." ZION'S HERALD AND WESLEYAN JOURNAL [=ZION'S HERALD] 16 (26 February 1845): 34.

Description of a religious service at the Southern Methodist Church in Charleston, South Carolina, where some 500 to 600 slaves were crowded into the galleries, includes comment on their congregational responses to the preaching---described as "half-stilted bursts of praise to God" and "the expressive Amen."

446 Holdich, Mrs. L. A. "Hester, the Slave." LADIES' REPOSITORY 21 (December 1861): 740-45. Reprinted in CHRISTIAN WATCHMAN & REFLECTOR (=WATCHMAN-EXAMINER) 43 (23 January 1862): [4].

Northern woman's record of her visit to a southern plantation includes discussion of a slave named Hester.

Text of 1 song: Angels come for Sister Flora (Cho: Over the river).

447 Hungerford, James. THE OLD PLANTATION, AND WHAT I GATHERED THERE IN AN AUTUMN MONTH. New York: Harper & Brothers, 1859. 369 pp. Reprint. Selected passages in READINGS IN BLACK AMERICAN MUSIC. Edited by Eileen Southern. 2d. ed. New York: W. W. Norton & Company, 1983. Microfiche. Louisville, KY: Lost Cause Press, 198-.

Lawyer Hungerford visited a plantation in southern Maryland in 1832. Discussion includes references to improvisations, performance practice, and work songs (corn songs, boat songs: 99-101, 183-92), dancing "juber" and improvising juber rhymes (190-99), and to a "bush-meeting" (311).

Texts and music of 2 songs: 1. Farewell, fellow sarvants! Oho! Oho! (184), 2. Hooray for all de lubly ladies (Cho: Roun' de corn, Sally) (191). Text of 1 dance piece (recited, not sung): Juber lef' un Juber right, Juber dance wid all yo' might (196-98).

448 [Kinnard, J., Jr.] "Who Are Our National Poets?." KNICKERBOCKER 26 (October 1845): 331-41. Reprints. THE NEGRO AND HIS LORE-LORE IN NINETEENTH CENTURY PERIODICALS. Edited by Bruce Jackson. Published for the American FolkLore Society. Austin, University of Texas Press, 1967. Also reprint in BLACK PERSPECTIVE IN MUSIC 3 (Spring 1975): 83-94.

Author credits the slave as a source of material for the songs and dances of Ethiopian minstrels, maintaining that most of America's national poetry originated in the state of Virginia, whose slaves were exported to the other slave states. This explains similarities in songs and dances performed by slaves in the deep South. Discussion of the songs of black boatmen and relevant performance practice; also of songs and dances accompanied by violin, banjo, or jaw-bone lute.

Texts of 3 songs: 1. Massa and missus promised me. 2. Jenny get your hoe-cake done, 3. Oh, my ole massa gwine to Washington (Cho: Zip e duden duden). Reference to 1 song: As I was gwine down Shinbone Alley.

449 Kirke, Richard. "Through the Cotton States." Parts 1-3. KNICKERBOCKER 58 (October 1861): 314-23; (November 1861): 412-23; (December 1861): 508-15.

This account of travel in South Carolina includes discussion of songs sung by slaves. Texts of four songs, which appear to be minstrel songs rather than genuine plantation songs as claimed by the author.

450 Lambert, John. TRAVELS THROUGH CANADA, AND THE UNITED STATES OF NORTH AMERICA, IN THE YEARS 1806, 1807, AND 1808. London: Baldwin, Cradock, and Joy, 1816. 2 vols. Reprint. Microfiche. Ottawa: Canadian Institute for Historical Micro-reproductions, 1985.

English traveler discusses songs of slave boatmen working near Savannah, Georgia. Refers to song performance practice (2:254).

Text of 1 song: We are going down to Georgia boys (Cho: Aye, aye, to see the pretty girls, boys) (2:254).

451 Lea, Lona. "A Year of My Life." SOUTHERN LITERARY MESSENGER 36 (January 1862): 48-52.

Narrative of the author's visit along the Potomac during the antebellum era refers to servants singing on Sabbath evenings. Reference to one song and description of its performance practice.

Reference to 1 song: Way over in Jordan (50).

452 "The Levee at New Orleans." ILLUSTRATED LONDON NEWS 32 (5 June 1858): 552.

Author refers to the singing of hundreds of slaves as they work, loading and unloading bales of cotton from river steam-boats docked at the levee in New Orleans.

453 "Life and Travel in the Southern States." GREAT REPUBLIC MONTHLY 1 (1859): 80-84. Reprint in TRAVELS IN THE OLD SOUTH SELECTED FROM PERIODICALS OF THE TIME. Edited by Eugene L. Schwaab and Jacqueline Bull. Vol. 2. Lexington: University Press of Kentucky, 1973. Page reference below is to the Schwaab edition.

Description of the slaves singing as they picked cotton on plantations of South Carolina includes references to worksongs: "While at work in the cotton fields, the slaves often sing some wild, simple melody, by way of mutual cheer, which usually ends with a chorus..." (491).

454 Lockwood, Lewis, collector. "The Song of the Contrabands."--"O Let my People Go"... arranged by Thomas Baker. Boston: Oliver Ditson & Company, 1861. Reprint. SINFUL TUNES AND SPIRITUALS, by Dena Epstein, 366-71. Urbana: University of Illinois Press, 1977.

This Negro spiritual, "O, let my people go," was the earliest spiritual to be published with both its text and music; the text had been published earlier (see no. 485). A note on the title page states: "This Song, originated among the 'Contrabands,' and was first heard sung by them on arrival at Fortress Monroe; and was introduced here by their Chaplain, Rev. L. C. Lockwood."

455 M. "Philadelphia Correspondence." NATIONAL ANTI-SLAVERY STANDARD 23 (31 May 1862): [2-3].

Letter dated Philadelphia, 26 May 1862, describing the author's visit to Washington, D. C., during the Civil War, refers to contraband slaves singing songs.

Text of 1 chorus: O, go down, Moses, away down in Egypt's land.

456 Mackay, Charles. LIFE AND LIBERTY IN AMERICA; OR, SKETCHES OF A TOUR IN THE UNITED STATES AND CANADA IN 1857-58. 2 vols. London: Smith, Elder & Company, 1859. Reprint. New York: Johnson Reprint Corporation, 1971.

English author published parts of this book earlier in the ILLUSTRATED LONDON NEWS under the title "Transatlantic Sketches." Comment on the slaves on a Mississippi steamer, who sing as they pile wood on the deck to be burned in the steamer furnace (244); on slaves singing as they work on the levee of New Orleans (267); and on the singing of slave children on a plantation in South Carolina (328).

457 Mathews, Charles. THE LONDON MATHEWS, CONTAINING AN ACCOUNT OF THIS CELEBRATED COMEDIAN'S TRIP TO AMERICA...TO WHICH ARE PREFIXED, SEVERAL ORIGINAL COMIC SONGS. Philadelphia: Morgan & Yeager, 1824. 36 pp. Reprint. Microfiche. Louisville, KY: Lost Cause Press, 1973.

English actor Charles Mathews attended the African [Grove] Theatre during his visit to New York, November 1822-May 1823, where he heard a "genuine" negro song: Opossum up a gum tree.

Text of 1 song (11): Opossum up a gum tree.

458 _____. MEMOIRS OF CHARLES MATHEWS, COMEDIAN. By Mrs. Mathews. Vol. 3. London: Richard Bentley, 1837. 650 pp.

English actor traveling in the United States during the 1820s discusses a black preacher in Boston (350) and "Black Brimstone Churches" of the Methodists in Philadelphia, including a summary of a sermon he heard (390). Also references to a black fiddler (384) and a "real negro melody": Opossum up a gum tree. (See also no. 458).

459 McKim Garrison, Lucy. "Songs of the Port Royal 'Contrabands'." DWIGHT'S JOURNAL OF MUSIC AND MUSICIANS 22 (8 November 1862): 254, 700. Reprints. LIBERATOR 32 (28 November 1862): 191. THE NEGRO AND HIS FOLKLORE IN NINETEENTH-CENTURY PERIODICALS. Edited by Bruce Jackson. Published for the American Folklore Society. Austin: University of Texas Press, 1967. THE SOCIAL IMPLICATIONS OF EARLY NEGRO MUSIC.... Edited by Bernard Katz. New York: Arno Press and the New York Times, 1969.

Letter to the editor, dated 1 November 1862, Philadelphia, discusses the work songs, boat songs, and religious music of the ex-slaves at Port Royal, South Carolina. The letter writer would later become one of the compilers of SLAVE SONGS OF THE UNITED STATES (1867). See no. 1072.

Texts of 2 couplets: 1. And massa tink it day ob doom. 2. Roll, Jordan, roll.

460 McKim, James Miller. "The Freed Men of South Carolina." Address of Mr. J. M. McKim, At Samson Hall, Philadelphia, on Wednesday evening, the 9th instant, to an audience invited by the Port Royal Relief Committee. LIBERATOR 32 (25 July 1862): 120. Also in the NATIONAL ANTI-SLAVERY STANDARD 23 (26 July 1862): [4]. Reprint.

AMERICAN MISSIONARY (MAGAZINE) n. s. 8 (April 1864): 104-05.

Report of the Philadelphia Presbyterian minister, abolitionist, and co-founder of the American Anti-Slavery Society, to the Port Royal Relief Committee of Philadelphia on the condition of the ex-slaves in Port Royal, South Carolina, where he had visited during the previous month. Discussion includes description of the quality of the slave songs, particularly of the boatmen, improvisation, and performance practice.

Texts of 2 songs: 1. Poor Rosy, poor gal. 2. No more driver call for me. Reference to 1 song: Sing and pray their souls away.

461 _____. "Songs of the Slaves." CHRISTIAN WATCHMAN & REFLECTOR (=WATCHMAN-EXAMINER) 43 (7 August 1862): [1-2]. Reprints entitled "Negro Songs." DWIGHT'S JOURNAL OF MUSIC 21 (9 August 1862): 148-49. THE SOCIAL IMPLICATIONS OF EARLY NEGRO MUSIC IN THE UNITED STATES. Edited by Bernard Katz. New York: Arno Press and the New York Times, 1969.

This report on the condition of the ex-slaves on the Sea Islands of South Carolina is drawn from an address delivered earlier (see no. 460). It includes discussion of the songs, improvisation, and performance practice.

Texts of 2 songs: 1. Poor Rosy, poor gal. 2. No more driver call for me.

462 Mead, Whitman. TRAVELS IN NORTH AMERICA.... New York: Printed by C. S. Van Winkle, 1820. 160 pp.

Comment on slave singing in Savannah, Georgia, in March 1817: "Slaves on the wharves accompany all their labor with a kind of monotonous song, at times breaking out into a yell, and then sinking in the same nasal drawl..." (13-14). Also references to a black fiddler, who amused the company (29), and to dancing (67).

463 Moore, Frank, ed. "A Contraband Refrain, Now Much in Vogue at Fortress Monroe." Vol. 1 of REBELLION RECORD: A DIARY OF AMERICAN EVENTS.... 11 vols. New York: G. P. Putnam, 1861-63; D. Van Nostrand, 1864-68.

Reference to a song sung by ex-slaves at Fortress Monroe, Virginia, in 1861.

Text of 1 song: Wake up, snakes, pelicans, and Sesh'ners (1:126, section 3).

464 "Negro Melodies." DE BOW'S REVIEW 18 (MARCH 1855): 335-36.

Editor requests readers to send him specimens of genuine songs as sung by the slaves in their cabins and on river boats on the bayous of the South. Reprints a minstrel song from the BOSTON POST that he maintains was based on an original slave song.

465 "Negro Songs." MUSICAL WORLD 40 (6 December 1862): 780.

Discussion of slave songs uses quotation from Lucy McKim's article "Songs of the Port Royal 'Contrabands'." (See no. 459.) Discussion of performance practice, voice quality, and problems arising from efforts to transcribe the songs.

466 Neilson, Peter. RECOLLECTIONS OF A SIX YEARS' RESIDENCE IN THE UNITED STATES OF AMERICA, Interspersed with Original Anecdotes, Illustrating the Manners of the Inhabitants of the Great Western Republic. Glasgow: David Robertson & William Tait, 1830. 358 pp. Reprint. Micro-opaque. Louisville, KY: Lost Cause Press, 1959.

English traveler was in the United States during the years 1818-1825 and visited New York, Philadelphia, Charleston, and New Orleans, among other places. Description of Baptist and Methodist religious services in New Orleans.

Texts of 2 songs (259): 1. Sturdy sinners, come along 2. Old Satan come before my face.

467 Olliffe, Charles. AMERICAN SCENES. EIGHTEEN MONTHS IN THE NEW WORLD. Originally published as SCENES AMERICAINES. Paris: Amyot, 1852. Translated by Ernest Falbo and Lawrence A. Wilson. Painesville, OH: Lake Erie College Press, 1964. 143 pp.

French traveler's discussion of slavery comments on tunes "invented" by the slaves (45), the banjo (46), and the vocal quality of Negro music as "marked by a kind of plaintive sadness" (46).

468 "The Peculiar Institution: The Treatment of Slaves." NATIONAL ANTI-SLAVERY STANDARD 5 (17 April 1845): 181. Reprinted from CHRISTIAN POLITICIAN.

Discussion of condition of slaves on a southern plantation owned by a Baptist Church deacon includes comments on the character of their religious songs, composed to "tunes of their own making" and sung "with much judgment." Also references to the slaves' oratory style in prayers and addresses, and to the fact that the slaves preferred to hold meetings among themselves and to listen to their own preachers, rather than to the preaching of the whites.

469 Plumer, William S. THO'TS ON THE RELIGIOUS INSTRUCTION OF THE NEGROES OF THIS COUNTRY. Savannah: Edward J. Purse Printer, 1848. 28 pp. Reprint. Microfiche. Louisville, KY: Lost Cause Press, 1983.

Discussion includes lengthy quote from the letters of Samuel Davies (11-13) about the slave's ecstatic delight in psalmody (see no. 35). Recommends that the slaves memorize good psalms and hymns "to take the place of the foolish and irreverent ones that are often in use among them" (27).

470 "Religion in a Cottage." LIBERATOR 3 (31 [sic] April 1833): 60.

Discussion of a mournful song heard by the author as he passed a slave's hut.

Text of 1 song: O poor nigga, he will go.

471 "Scene on a Mississippi Cotton Plantation." BALLOU'S PICTORIAL DRAWING-ROOM COMPANION 10 (12 April 1856): 236.

Description of the pressing and packing of cotton on a plantation in Mississippi includes reference to the slaves singing "monotonous but musical chants" as they worked.

472 [Schoolcraft, Mary Howard]. LETTERS ON THE CONDITION OF THE AFRICAN RACE IN THE UNITED STATES BY A SOUTHERN LADY. Philadelphia: T. K. and P. G. Collins, 1852. 34 pp. Reprint. Ann Arbor, MI: University Microfilms International, 1974.

Daughter of a plantation owner discusses slave life, including comment on the "wild" songs of black boatmen near Beaufort and Savannah, Georgia (13), on Christmas holiday observances of the slaves, on their singing and dancing to the music of fiddles, and on their attendance at prayer meetings (13).

473 Simms, William Gilmore. THE YEMASSEE: A ROMANCE OF CAROLINA. Rev. ed. New York: J. S. Redfield, 1853. 454 pp. Reprint. New York: Twayne Publishers, 1964.

Novel about life in the South includes the text of a "familiar negro doggrel."

Text of 1 chorus: Possum up a gum tree (50).

474 "Sketches of South-Carolina: Number Three --Merry Christmas." KNICKERBOCKER 21 (March 1843), 222-29.

Description of Christmas Day celebrations on plantations in South Carolina includes references to slaves singing hymns, Christmas ballads and playing games as part of the festivities.

475 "The Slave Deck of the Bark 'Wildfire', Brought into Key West on April 30, 1860." HARPER'S WEEKLY 4 (2 June 1860): 344-45.

Article, dated 20 May 1860, from Key West, Florida, discusses the capture of the slave vessel, the "Wildfire"; refers to the slave singing and dancing aboard ship, also to performance practice.

476 "Slavery in the United States, by an American." KNICKERBOCKER 10 (October 1837): 321-28.

Discussion of slave life in East Florida, on the St. John's River, includes description of the songs of boatmen and associated performance practice. Also refers to a slave woman imitating her mistress in dance, to religious services of the slaves, and to slave fiddlers.

477 "Songs of the Blacks." EVANGELIST AND RELIGIOUS REVIEW (New York) 27 (23 October 1856): [1]. Reprints. DWIGHT'S JOURNAL OF MUSIC 10 (15 November 1856): 51-52; 25 (3 September 1859): 179-80. MUSICAL WORLD 37 (1 October 1859): 638.

Essay about slave music in the South includes the observation that slaves are natural musicians and learn to play instruments quicker than whites. Also comment on their singing African airs as they worked along the banks of the Mississippi River, on the quality of the African voice, and on black participation in camp meetings.

478 Smith, Elias. "The Freed Men under Gen. Burnside." INDEPENDENT 14 (15 May 1862): 1.

Letter to the editor, dated 6 May 1862, from Newborn, North Carolina, discusses the condition of the slaves in the contraband camps. Refers to their singing "some of their simple chants and hymns" in celebration of their deliverance from slavery.

Reference to 1 song: Oh, ain't I glad to get out de wilderness.

479 "The Story of a Contraband." NATIONAL ANTI-SLAVERY STANDARD 22 (25 January 1862): [1]. Reprinted from the NEW YORK TIMES.

Summary of a narrative told by William Davis, ex-slave, on 13 January [1862]. Comment on the contraband slaves singing hymns and songs, and enjoying themselves on Christmas and New Year's Day, in stark contrast to their activities on previous New Year's Days, when they spent the holiday moaning the loss of their loved ones, who were sold at slave auctions on this holiday.

480 Stowe, Harriet Beecher. UNCLE TOM'S CABIN; OR, LIFE AMONG THE LOWLY. Boston: John P. Jewett & Company, 1852. 2 vols. Reprint. New York: Harper & Row, 1965.

Novel about slave life in the South includes descriptions of slave dancing (5, 239-40, 328), fiddling in the slave-auction warehouse (328), and the singing of religious slave songs and a field song.

Texts of 5 songs: 1. Die on the field of battle (Cho: Glory in my soul) (30). 2. O, I'm going to glory (Cho: Won't you come along with me) (31). 3. O, where is weeping Mary (Cho: 'Rived in the goodly land) (332). 4. Mas'r see'd me cotch a coon (Cho: High boys, high). 5. O, there'll be mourning, mourning, mourning (374-75).

481 [Strother, David.] "Virginia Illustrated: Adventures of Porte Crayon and His Cousins." HARPER'S NEW MONTHLY MAGAZINE 12 (January 1856): 158-78.

Describes the singing of Negro boatmen at night (generally accompanied by "an antic dance").

Texts of 3 songs: 1. Caesar, Caesar, bring here my horse and saddle, 2. I went to see Ginny when my work was done, 3. Juggity jug, whar's dat jug?

482 Thornton, Thomas C. AN INQUIRY INTO THE HISTORY OF SLAVERY--ITS INTRODUCTION INTO THE UNITED STATES, CAUSES OF ITS CONTINUANCE, AND REMARKS UPON THE ABOLITION TRACTS OF WILLIAM E. CHANNING, D. D. Washington, DC: William M. Morrison, 1841. 345 pp. Reprint. Detroit: Negro History Press, 196-.

President of Centenary College, Clinton, Mississippi, comments on antebellum slave preachers in the South (104, 108). Also discussion of slave "picking-match" songs (119), of a slave corn-shucking festival and corn songs (120-22).

Texts of 3 songs (120-22): 1. I loves old Virginny (Cho: So Ho! boys! ho!). 2. General Washington was a gentleman (Cho: Here goes the corn). 3. The parson say his prayers in church (Cho: It rain boys, it rain).

483 [Tucker, George]. LETTERS FROM VIRGINIA. Translated from the French. Baltimore: Fielding Lucas, Jr., 1816. 220 pp. Reprint. Ann Arbor, MI: University Microfilms International, 1979.

One letter describes a slave coffle singing "wild" hymns in Portsmouth, Virginia (29-30, 33-34). Reference to "legendary ballads, narratives of alternative dialogue, and singing" as amusements of the slave (79).

484 _____. THE VALLEY OF SHENANDOAH; OR, MEMOIRS OF THE GRAYSONS. New York: Charles Wiley, 1824. 2 vols. Reprint: Chapel Hill: University of North Carolina Press, [1970].

Novel about life along the Shenandoah River in Frederick County, Virginia, includes description of slave corn-songs and performance practice (2:116-18) and reference to slave fiddlers and a fifer playing for balls of the whites (2:121).

485 Vernon, Harwood. "The Contrabands' Freedom Hymn." NATIONAL ANTI-SLAVERY STANDARD 22 (21 December 1861): [4]. From the [New York] TRIBUNE.

Letter to the Editor, dated New York, 2 December 1861, contains the text of a freedom song supplied by Rev. L. C. Lockwood, agent of the American Missionary Association at Fortress Monroe, Virginia. Informant advises that the song was sung by slaves in Virginia and Maryland approximately fifteen or twenty years earlier.

Text of 1 song: When Israel was in Egypt's land (Cho: O go down, Moses)

486 Victor, Metta. MAUM GUINEA AND HER PLANTATION "CHILDREN"; OR, HOLIDAY-WEEK ON A LOUISIANA ESTATE. A SLAVE ROMANCE. New York: Beadle and Company, 1861. 215 pp. Reprint. Freeport, NY: Books for Libraries Press, 1972.

Fictional account of plantation life during a Christmas-week holiday period includes numerous references to slave singing, dancing, telling tales, and related performance practice. Detailed description of the Christmas Eve and Christmas Day dancing to the music of fiddle, 2 banjos, tambourine, kettledrum, and a tin pan (15-19, 35-41).

Texts of 2 songs: 1. John, come down in de holler (76). 2. By de dark lagoon (Cho: Huah, huah, huah) (108).

487 Waters, Horace. THE HARP OF FREEDOM. New York: Published by Horace Waters, 1862. 32 pp. Reprint of "O, Let my People Go" in SINFUL TUNES AND SPIRITUALS..., by Dena Epstein, 366-71. Urbana: University of Illinois Press, 1977.

This collection of "A New and Superior Collection of Anti-Slavery, Patriotic and Contraband" songs contains text and music for the first spiritual to be published, "The Song of the Contrabands," arranged by Thomas Baker. Included also is an eleven-verse, parody version of the song, which expresses abolitionist sentiments.

Text and music of 1 song (2-4): The Lord by Moses to Pharaoh said (Cho: Oh, Go down, Moses).

488 Watson, Elkanah. MEN AND TIMES OF THE REVOLUTION; OR, MEMOIRS OF ELKANAH WATSON, INCLUDING JOURNALS OF TRAVELS IN EUROPE AND AMERICA FROM 1777 TO 1842, With His Correspondence with Public Men, and Reminiscences and Incidents of the Revolution. Edited by his son, Winslow C. Watson. New York: Dana & Company, 1856. 460 pp. Reprint. Ann Arbor, MI: University Microfilms International, 1973.

Report includes references to Negro boatmen in South Carolina singing "plaintive African songs in cadence with the oars" as they rowed the writer down the Wingan River in 1777 (43).

489 Weld, Theodore Dwight, ed. AMERICAN SLAVERY AS IT IS: TESTIMONY OF A THOUSAND WITNESSES. New York: American Anti-Slavery

Society, 1839. 224 pp. Reprint. Salem, NH: Ayer Company Publishers, 1968.

This collection of articles "taken, mainly, from recent newspapers, published in the slave states" includes reprint of a song text and discussion by editor Weld of the real reasons why slaves sing (13).

Text of 1 song: Hurra, for good ole Massa (13).

490 Wiley, Calvin Henderson. ADVENTURES OF OLD DAN TUCKER, AND HIS SON WALTER; A TALE OF NORTH CAROLINA. London: Willoughby & Company, 1851. 222 pp. Also published as LIFE IN THE SOUTH.... 1852. Reprint. Microfilm. Woodbridge, CT: Research Publications, 1970.

This tale includes discussion of Wild Bill, an escaped slave and leader of a band of outlaws, who lived in caves in the swamps (54-55), and comment on the quality of Bill's singing and Negro song in general (112-13).

491 [Williams, Isaac.] AUNT SALLY; OR, THE CROSS THE WAY OF FREEDOM. A Narrative of the Slave-Life and Purchase of the Mother of Rev. Isaac Williams, of Detroit, Michigan. Cincinnati, OH: American Reform Tract and Book Society, 1858. 216 pp. Reprint. Miami: Mnemosyne Publishing Company, 1969.

Biography of "Aunt Sally," mother of Isaac Williams, includes discussion of slave life and examples of slave songs.

Texts of 3 songs: 1. Sister, far'well! I bid ye adieu (111). 2. Oh, when I'm in trouble here (153). 3. I have a place in Paradise (Cho: To praise the Lord in glory) (167-68).

THE TALE

492 "Black Version." ZION'S HERALD AND WESLEYAN JOURNAL 28 (21 October 1857): [165]

Transcription of the text of a black version of the legend about Noah, concerning the color of Noah's skin.

493 Cobb, Joseph Beckham. MISSISSIPPI SCENES; OR, SKETCHES OF SOUTHERN AND WESTERN LIFE AND ADVENTURE, HUMOROUS, SATIRICAL, AND DESCRIPTIVE.... 2d ed. Philadelphia: A. Hart, Late Carey & Hart, 1851. 250 pp. Reprint. Upper Saddle River, NJ: Literature House, 1970.

Journalist's collection of sketches about life in Mississippi includes references to the slaves telling folk tales to children of local planters and identifies tale types as those about Jack-o'-the-lantern, the whippowill, swamp oils, and animal fables (98-99, 168). Also brief description of a corn-husking festival and corn songs (83).

494 "The Slave That Sold His Master." LIBERATOR 30 (16 MARCH 1860): 44.

Text of a tale in which a slave outwits the slave-dealer.

ARTWORKS: 1700s-1862

SOCIAL ACTIVITIES

495 "At the South." [1859?]. Wood engraving. Published in HARPER'S WEEKLY (January 1860). Reprint. "Black American Music in Pictures," by Frederick Crane, 33. BLACK MUSIC RESEARCH JOURNAL [6] (1986).

Scene shows a rude cabin room; a mother, who is sitting before the hearth, scolds her child, who stands beside her. A banjo hangs on the wall, head downwards. Occasion: indoor domestic scene.

496 Bibb, Henry (?). "The Sabbath among Slaves." [1850]. Wood engraving. Published in NARRATIVE OF THE LIFE AND ADVENTURES OF HENRY BIBB, AN AMERICAN SLAVE. WRITTEN BY HIMSELF. With an introduction by Lucius C. Matlock. New York: Published by the Author, 1850. Reprint. BLACK DANCE...., by Lynne Emery, 129. Palo Alto: National Press Books, 1972.

Scene shows 20 or more men, women, and children making merry in a grassy area, which is bounded on the right by a tall fence. They play games, wrestle, and lounge about; two boys have climbed the fence. In the forefront center, a couple and a man dance to the music of a banjoist, who is leaning against a tree. The woman, whose back is turned to her partner, looks over her shoulder, lifting her skirt and pointing her toe as she dances. Her partner dances with high kicking steps, his left leg lifted high while balancing on the ball of the right foot. The solo dancer, bending from the waist, with arms held limply to the side and knees bent, executes a heel-toe step with his left foot. Occasion: outdoor recreation.

497 "The Breakdown---American Home Scenes." [1861]. Wood engraving. Published in HARPER'S WEEKLY 5 (April 1861). Reprint. "Black American Music in Pictures," by Frederick Crane, 35. BLACK MUSIC RESEARCH JOURNAL [6] (1986).

One in a series of six sketches entered on facing pages, entitled "American Home Scenes," this caricatural scene shows a group of 14 men and women (one with an infant) gathered in a large rude cabin room. In the center a couple dances to the music of a banjoist; the man presumably is dancing the break-down, with arms held akimbo to his sides and his right leg lifted high. The woman dances with considerable grace, holding her voluminous skirts in a curtsey position. The spectators watch with great interest; one man is pattin' juba. Occasion: indoor entertainment.

498 Brown, James. "'Dancing for Eels'---A Scene from the New Play of NEW-YORK AS IT IS, as Played at the Chatham Theatre, New York." 1848. Lithograph by Eliphalet M. Brown and James Brown. Washington, DC, The Collections of the Library of Congress. Published in AMERICA AS ART, by Joshua C. Taylor, 66. Washington, DC: Smithsonian Institution, 1976.

Advertisement for a current play shows 2 men in ragged attire dancing on a wharf of New York City. Face-to in the center, one of the men seems to be dancing a clog: he leaps straight upward, knees bent outward, with one hand raised and other on his hip. The other, shown in profile, is pattin' juba by way of providing accompaniment for his partner's dancing. An indefinite number of white spectators (children and men) watch with interest, as does also a lone black woman. The illustration represents a scene from the play, according to the subcaption. Occasion: theatre advertisement.

499 "A Carolina Rice Planter." [1859]. Wood engraving. Published in "The Rice Lands of the South," by T. Addison Richards. HARPER'S NEW MONTHLY MAGAZINE 19 (November 1859).

Portrait of a man playing the banjo in an outdoor setting. With one leg is lifted, resting on a tree stump, he leans forward slightly, resting his instrument on his thigh, as he plucks the four-stringed banjo. He does not sing. Plainly dressed, but with jacket, cape, and hat, he has a pleasant air and apparently is playing a sentimental piece for his own amusement. Occasion: outdoor domestic music.

500 Clonney, James Goodwyn. "Negro Boy Dancing." 1839. Wash. Study for "Militia Training." Boston, Museum of Fine Arts. Reproduced in M. AND M. KAROLIK COLLECTION OF AMERICAN WATER COLORS AND DRAWINGS, 1800-1875, 1:109. Boston: Museum of Fine Arts, 1962.

This is a study for the foremost dancer in the painting "Militia Training" (see no. 504). He seems younger and more lithe than the painting's figure in the same position. He dances with arms outstretched to the side, right palm open, and he holds a cap in the other hand. With knees bent, and his lifted right leg crossing the left one, he balances on the ball of the left foot. Occasion: domestic recreation.

501 _____. "Negro Boy Singing and Dancing." 1839. Wash drawing. Study for "Militia Training." Boston, Museum of Fine Arts. Reproduced in M. AND M. KAROLIK COLLECTION ...1800-1875, 1:107. Boston: Museum of Fine Arts, 1962.

This is the finished study for the oil painting's second dancing figure, whose back is to the viewer (see no. 504). He looks over his shoulder as he sings and dances, with arms uplifted and knees bent as he takes large steps, lifting one leg while balancing on the ball of the other foot. Occasion: domestic recreation.

502 _____. "Sketches for Dancing Men and Other Figures." [1841]. Pencil on buff paper. Boston, Museum of Fine Arts. Reference to in M. AND M. KAROLIK COLLECTION..., 1:107. Boston: Museum of Fine Arts, 1962.

This study for the painting "Militia Training" (see no. 504) shows action drawings of 4 individual dancers in the upper plane of the picture, and of 2 sets of paired dancers in the lower plane. Occasion: domestic recreation.

503 _____. Studies for "Militia Training." 1841. Wash and pencil. Boston, Museum of Fine Arts. Reference in M. AND M. KAROLIK COLLECTION..., 1:107. Boston: Museum of Fine Arts, 1962.

In addition to the three studies cited above, the artist made the following: (1) "Composition," a wash, which depicts the entire scene; (2) "Two Studies on One Sheet," in pencil, which shows a group gathered around the dancing pair and a fiddler; and (3) "Dancing Negro," pencil on buff paper, which was a preparatory sketch for the painting. Occasion: domestic recreation.

504 _____. "Militia Training." 1841. Oil on canvas. Philadelphia, Pennsylvania Academy of Fine Arts. Reproduced in THE U. S. A.: A HISTORY IN ART, by Bradley Smith, 154. New York: Thomas Y. Crowell Company, 1975. Also in AMERICA AS ART, by Joshua C. Taylor, 52. Washington, DC: Smithsonian Institution, 1976.

Depiction of a military scene against a vast landscape, with an indefinite number of men and women making merry in the foreground. Far in the distance soldiers congregate in groups, some of them marching. In the center of the picture 2 men dance back to back, accompanied by a white fiddler. Both men, with arms to the side or lifted and bent knees, are dancing vigorously. One dancer uses a heel-toe step. The bystanders include 3 more blacks, one of them a fiddler who rests his fiddle on his thigh while watching the dancers. Occasion: outdoor entertainment.

505 _____. "Study for the Central Figure from 'A Dance on a Stone Boat'." [184?]. Pencil on buff paper. Boston, Museum of Fine Arts. Reproduced: M. AND M. KAROLIK COLLECTION.

.., 1:111. Boston: Museum of Fine Arts, 1962. Also "James Goodwyn Clonney (1812-1867): American Genre Painter," by Lucretia H. Giese, 18. AMERICAN ART JOURNAL 11 (October 1979).

This sketch shows the dancer with back turned, but looking over his shoulder as he dances. His arms are extended to the side, the right hand with open palm, the left lifted up and holding a cap, and his left leg lifted high, crossing over the right leg. Occasion: domestic recreation.

506 _____. "Study for 'Dance on a Stone Boat,' Small Composition." [184?]. Pencil on brown paper. Boston, Museum of Fine Arts. Reference to in M. AND M. KAROLIK COLLECTION...1800-1875, 1:111. Boston: Museum of Fine Arts, 1962. Reproduced in "James Goodwyn Clonney (1812-1867): American Genre Painter," by Lucretia H. Giese. AMERICAN ART JOURNAL 11 (October 1979).

This preliminary sketch for an outdoor genre scene shows a black man dancing on a small, wooden, rectangular floor placed beneath a tree. To his left a fiddler plays, and to his right, a man is pattin' juba. White spectators include a seated man, another man leaning over him, and a child. Occasion: outdoor entertainment.

507 _____. "The Militia Training." 1842. Engraving by Joseph Ives Pease. Published in "The Militia Training...," by John Frost, 192. THE GIFT: A CHRISTMAS AND NEW YEAR'S PRESENT. Philadelphia: Carey & Hart, 1842.

This print is very close to the original painting (see no. 504). In the article Frost describes the dance of the two men as "a genuine African reel." Occasion: outdoor entertainment.

508 "The Coffle Gang." [1864]. Wood engraving. Published in THE SUPPRESSED BOOK ABOUT SLAVERY!, by George Carleton. New York: Carleton, Publisher, 1864. Reprints. SLAVERY TIMES IN KENTUCKY, by J. Winston Coleman, 140. Chapel Hill: The University of North Carolina Press, 1940. THE MUSIC OF BLACK AMERICANS: A HISTORY, edited by Eileen Southern, 158. 2d ed. New York: W. W. Norton, 1983.

Scene depicts 2 violinists playing as they march at the front of a slave coffle moving through the woods on the way to the slave market. Behind the slave musicians, the other slaves, men and women, follow two-by-two, their hands chained behind their backs. One man carries the American flag. Three men on horseback guard them. Occasion: outdoor procession.

509 Crowe, Eyre. "A Negro Ball, Charleston, Ga. [sic], 8 March 1853." Pen and ink. Published in WITH THACKERAY IN AMERICA, by Eyre Crowe. New York: Charles Scribner's Sons, 1893. Reprint. BLACK DANCE IN THE UNITED STATES..., by Lynne Emery, 107. Palo Alto: National Press Books, 1972.

The artist, secretary to William Makepeace Thackeray on his American lecture tour (1852-53), offers a caricatural depiction of a formal ball in a elaborately decorated ball room of Charleston, South Carolina. An indeterminate number of couples mill about and dance to the music of a 5-piece band: 2 straight trumpets, bones, tambourine, and string bass (which the bassist is bowing, not plucking). Occasion: indoor recreation.

510 "Cy or Sy Gilliat, Negro Banjo Player" (also known as "The Banjo Man"). [c.1810]. Oil on canvas. Richmond (Virginia), The Valentine Museum. Reproduced in THE PORTRAYAL OF THE NEGRO IN AMERICAN PAINTING. Exhibition Catalogue, no. 7. Brunswick, ME: Bowdoin College Museum of Art, 1964. Also in THE ART OF THE OLD SOUTH, by Jessie Poesch, 172. New York: Alfred A. Knoepf, 1983.

Simeon Gilliat (d. 1820; also known as Sy, Cy, Simon, Cyrus), a popular slave musician of Richmond (Virginia), is shown in an outdoor scene playing a banjo beneath the trees. He is surrounded by members of a white family (his owners?); all pay rapt attention, and three of the children dance to Cy's music. A smiling fellow slave stands in the background. The unusually long, thin neck of the banjo requires the full extension of Cy's raised left arm, held shoulder-high. The banjo appears to have four strings. Occasion: outdoor entertain-ment.

511 Dallas, Jacob A. "Virginia Hoe-Down." [1855]. Wood engraving. Published in "Remembrances of the Mississippi," by Thomas Bangs Thorpe, 25. HARPER'S NEW MONTHLY MAGAZINE 12 (December 1855).

The scene shows the interior of a rustic inn, with a blazing fire in the huge fireplace. In the center of the picture is a barefoot dancer, his back to the viewer, who vigorously dances a hoe-down in front of the hearth, accompanied by a white fiddler perched on a barrel. The spectators are three white men, only one of whom pays attention to the dancer. Occasion: indoor entertainment.

512 Darley, Felix Octavius Carr. "Chorus---Sing, Darkey, Sing." [1852]. Wood engraving. Elias J. Whitney and Phineas F. Annin, engravers. Published in "UNCLE TOM'S CABIN" CONTRASTED WITH BUCKINGHAM HALL, THE PLANTER'S HOME..., by Robert Criswell, opp. 64. New York: D. Fanshaw, 1852.

Scene shows 15-20 plantation workers---men, women, and children---gathered around an immense pile of corn in front of a cabin. Sitting on top of the huge mound, a man leads the workers in singing as they husk the corn, directing with his left hand. One man accompanies the music by beating on a three-legged stool. Two white men watch the corn-shucking festival. Occasion:

outdoor work festival involving music.

513 ____. "The Festival." [1852]. Wood engraving. Elias J. Whitney and Phineas F. Annin, engravers. Published in "UNCLE TOM'S CABIN" CONTRASTED WITH BUCKINGHAM HALL, THE PLANTER'S HOME..., by Robert Criswell, 112. New York: D. Fanshaw, 1852.

Scene shows an indeterminate number of merry makers gathered in a clearing, with the "big house" in the left background. Some dance, some watch the dancers, and some eat at a picnic table. In the foreground, 7 figures are sharply delineated: a dancing couple, 4 musicians, and a spectator. The couple dances vigorously, with high kicking steps, the woman with one arm around her partner's shoulder. Music is provided by a fiddler, perched high on a huge barrel; a banjoist, who sits on the ground, leaning against the barrel; a man playing the bones, also seated on the ground; and a man pattin' juba, who stands facing the dancers. Occasion: outdoor recreation.

514 Heriot, George. "Canadian Minuets." c1801. Aquatint engraving. J. C. Stadler, engraver. Reproduced in TRAVELS THROUGH THE CANADAS, by Heriot, opp. 258. London: R. Phillips, 1807. Reprint. GEORGE HERIOT, 1759-1839, by Gerald Finley, 46. Ottawa: National Gallery of Canada, 1979.

Scene depicts a ball for whites in a large, rude but spacious, ballroom. Four couples dance in the center of the room, watched by an indeterminate number of spectators seated and standing on the sides. Music is supplied by a white fiddler, seated at one end of the hall, and 3 performers standing on a raised platform against the left wall--a white tambourine player, a black tambourine player, and a black man whose head only is visible. The black tambourinist holds his instrument waist-high with his left hand and kicks it with his right foot; his right arm is lifted into the air. Occasion: indoor recreation.

515 Homer, Winslow. "Soldier Dancing." c.1861. Pencil. New York City, Cooper-Hewitt Museum of Decorative Arts and Design. Reproduced in ECHO OF A DISTANT DRUM: WINSLOW HOMER AND THE CIVIL WAR, by Julian Grossman, 29. New York: Harry N. Abrams, n.d.

This is a sketch for the dancer in "A Bivouac Fire on the Potomac" (see no. 516). Some details are different; for example, the sketch gives the dancer a cap. Occasion: outdoor recreation.

516 ____. "A Bivouac Fire on the Potomac." [1861]. Wood engraving. Published in HARPER'S WEEKLY 5 (December 1861). Reproduced in WINSLOW HOMER'S AMERICA, by Lloyd Goodrich, 56. New York: Tudor Publishing Company, 1969. Also in THE IMAGE OF THE INDIAN AND THE BLACK MAN IN AMERICAN ART, 1590-1900, by Ellwood C. Parry, 114. New York: George Braziller, 1974.

This Civil War night scene shows an indeterminate number of white Union soldiers gathered around a campfire. In the center of the circle formed by the soldiers a black soldier dances to the music of a grinning black fiddler, who sits on the ground nearby. With hands on his hips, the dancer lifts one leg high while balancing on the ball of the other foot. Occasion: outdoor entertainment.

517 "How Slavery Honors Our Country's Flag." [1835]. Wood engraving. Published in "How Slavery Honors our Country's Flag," by John Rankin. ANTI-SLAVERY RECORD 1 (February 1835). Reprints. NARRATIVE OF AMOS DRESSER..., by Amos Dresser, 7. New York: American Anti-Slavery Tract Society, 1836. Also in SINFUL TUNES AND SPIRITUALS..., by Dena J. Epstein, 149. Urbana: University of Illinois Press, 1977.

The scene shows a slave coffle in Paris, Bourbon County, Kentucky, during the summer of 1822. An indeterminate number of men and women march two abreast in chains, preceded by 2 male slaves who play violins, providing music for the march. A white slave driver watches. In the midst of the coffle, a slave hoists an American flag. Occasion: outdoor procession.

518 "Husking Corn---American Home Scenes." [1861]. Wood engraving. Published in HARPER'S WEEKLY 5/224 (April 1861). Reprint. "Black American Music in Pictures," by Frederick Crane, 35. BLACK MUSIC RESEARCH JOURNAL [6] (1986).

One in a series of six sketches entered on facing pages in the magazine, this caricatural depiction of a corn-husking bee shows 6 men at work. Sitting in a barn, almost covered by an immense pile of corn, they sing with gusto as they work. A fiddler, perched high at the top of the pile, provides accompaniment for the singing, and one man, with arm lifted high, seems to be beating time for the singing. Occasion: indoor work activity involving song.

519 "Independence Day." [1852]. Wood engraving. Published in LIFE AT THE SOUTH: OR UNCLE TOM'S CABIN AS IT IS, by William L. G. Smith, 164. Buffalo: George H. Derby & Company. 1852.

Illustration shows a small black boy marching along and beating on a large watering can as if it was a drum. Occasion: outdoor recreation.

520 "Is dat 'Hail Columbus...." [1861]. Wood engraving. Published in HARPER'S WEEKLY 5 (February 1861). Reprint. "Black American Music in Pictures," by Frederick Crane, 33. BLACK MUSIC RESEARCH JOURNAL [6] (1986).

Full caption reads: "Is dat 'Hail Columbus, Happy Lan'! you's playin', 'Sephus?" The cartoon scene depicts 2 men, Jeremiah and Josephus, in a rude cabin room: one, seated in a chair with his right leg crossing the left above the knee level, plays the banjo; the other, standing, asks questions of his friend. Occasion: indoor domestic music.

521 Jennings, Samuel. "Liberty Displaying the Arts and Sciences." 1792. Oil on canvas. Philadelphia, Collection of the Library Company of Philadelphia. Reproduced in "Liberty Displaying the Arts and Sciences: A Philadelphia Allegory by Samuel Jennings," by Robert C. Smith, figs. 1, 2, 10. WINTERTHUR PORTFOLIO 2 (1965): 84-105. Reprints. THE IMAGE OF THE INDIAN AND THE BLACK MAN IN AMERICAN ART, 1590-1900, Ellwood C. Parry, 49, 102. New York: George Braziller, 1974. SINFUL TUNES AND SPIRITUALS..., by Dena J. Epstein, 35. Urbana: University of Illinois Press, 1977.

During his residency in London, this American artist painted this allegorical scene upon the commission of the Library Company of Philadelphia, headed by Benjamin Franklin at that time. Believed to be the first abolitionist painting, it shows Miss Liberty seated in front of her palace, left center of the picture, surrounded with examples of the European arts and sciences (books, painter's easel, globe, etc.). In the right foreground a group of 4 slaves face Miss Liberty, some kneeling, a woman with arm lifted and lips parted as if speaking. In the background are musicians and dancers: a male plays a lute-like banjo; a boy with outstretched arms is singing; and several men and women dance with scarves. The patrons wished the painting to be "expressive of Ease & Joy." Occasion: patriotic representation; outdoor recreation.

522 "Jim along, Josie." Lithograph. [1838]. Sheet-music cover of an Ethiopian minstrel song. New York: Firth & Hall, 1838.

Caricatural depiction of a young boy dancing, with both hands held high in the air, bent knees stretched to the sides, and left leg lifted high while he balances on the sole of the right foot. His attire is clean but tattered: his breeches are patched, and he wears only one shoe. He grins widely as he dances. Apparently he dances for his own amusement, for there are no spectators. Occasion: outdoor domestic recreation.

523 Johnson, Eastman. "Negro Life in the South" (later known as "Old Kentucky Home"). 1859. Oil on canvas. New York City, New-York Historical Society. Reproduced in AMERICAN PAINTING FROM ITS BEGINNINGS TO THE ARMORY SHOW, by Jules David Prown, 85. Cleveland: World Publishing Company & Skira, 1969. Also in EASTMAN JOHNSON, by Patricia Hills, 30. New York: Clarkson N. Potter and Whitney Museum of American Art, 1972. Also THE IMAGE OF THE INDIAN AND THE BLACK MAN IN AMERICAN ART 1590-1900, by Ellwood C. Parry, 101. New York: George Braziller, 1974.

The scene, set in the courtyard of a quite dilapidated, two-story house, believed to be in Washington, D. C., shows 2 men, 3 women, and 6 children relaxing in rather untidy surroundings. Near the center of the picture is a young man, seated on a stepladder, pensively playing a banjo and oblivious of those about him. He holds his instrument in the standard position, his left leg lifted so as to rest on the first rung of the ladder. A small boy watches him intently. In the foreground a mother teaches her son to dance, holding both hands as he takes the dance steps. The spectators includes 2 young white women, who peek in through an open gate at the far right. Occasion: outdoor recreation.

524 _____. "Kentucky Home." [1859]. Oil on canvas. Amherst College (Massachusetts), Mead Art Museum. Reproduced in Exhibition Catalogue: AMERICAN ARTISTS IN DUSSELDORF: 1840-1865, by Brucia Witthoft and others, 30. Framingham, MA: Danforth Museum, 1982.

A young man, perched on a step-ladder, is shown playing a banjo (the short fifth string is visible), while a small boy, standing to the left, watches him intently. The banjoist is oblivious to all but his music. With a pensive look on his face, he holds his instrument low, resting it on his right thigh, and lifts his left leg to the first rung of the ladder in support of his playing hand. Although the two central figures in "Negro Life in the South" (see no. 523) are similar to those shown here, this painting is not a duplicate. Occasion: outdoor domestic music.

525 _____. "Negro Boy." c.1860. Oil on canvas. New York, National Academy of Design. Reproduced in EASTMAN JOHNSON, by Patricia Hills, 33. New York: Clarkson N. Potter and Whitney Museum of American Art, 1972.

A young boy, sitting on the stoop of a log-cabin doorway, plays a home-made flute. Occasion: outdoor domestic music.

526 "Juba at Vauxhall Gardens, London." [1848] Wood engraving. Published in the ILLUSTRATED LONDON NEWS (5 August 1848). Reprints. BLACK DANCE..., by Lynne Emery, 187. Palo Alto, CA: National Press Books, 1972. Also in BLACK PERSPECTIVE IN MUSIC 3 (Spring 1975): 98.

Master Juba (b. William Henry Lane, c.1825-52), one of the few black minstrels of the antebellum period and noted for his skills as dancer and tambourinist, played with White's Serenaders in the United States, and after 1848, with Pell's Serenaders in London. This illustration shows him dancing a Negro folk dance, which, according to the text, is one of the following: the Virginny breakdown, Alabama kick-up, Tennessee double-shuffle, or Louisiana toe-and-heel. Occasion: indoor entertainment.

527 Krimmel, John Lewis. "Dance in a Country Tavern." Before 1821. Lithograph by George

Lehman, Childs & Lehman, 1835-1836. Philadelphia, Historical Society of Pennsylvania. Reproduced in WILLIAM SIDNEY MOUNT, 1807-1868, AN AMERICAN PAINTER, by Bartlett Cowdrey and Hermann W. Williams, 9. Published for the Metropolitan Museum of Art. New York: Columbia University Press, 1944.

The German artist depicts a rural tavern scene with about a dozen men and women lolling around. A white couple is dancing, accompanied by a black fiddler. Seated in a chair with his back to the fireplace, the musician holds his fiddle tucked under his chin in the standard way, but slanting sharply downward, and taps his foot as he plays. This work was copied by other artists for many years after Krimmel's death in 1821. Occasion: indoor recreation.

528 _____. "Quilting Party." 1813. Oil on canvas. Winterthur (Delaware), Henry Francis du Pont Winterthur Museum. Reproduced in THE U.S.A.: A HISTORY IN ART, by Bradley Smith, 116. New York: Thomas Y. Crowell, 1975.

The scene shows a dozen or more white men, women, and children (along with a little black serving-girl) in a well-appointed living room. Some have begun the quilting, and others are new arrivals. At the door a black fiddler plays, his instrument positioned so that it slants sharply downward. Occasion: indoor entertainment.

529 _____. "Fourth of July Celebration in Center Square." 1819. Watercolor. Philadelphia, Historical Society of Pennsylvania. Reproduced in DIARY OF MY TRAVELS IN AMERICA, by Louis Philippe, King of France. Translated by Stephen Becker, 172. New York: Delacarte Press, 1977.

The scene represents the celebrating of the Fourth of July in Philadelphia. A marching band plays in the background and an indeterminate number of people mill about in the Square. In the lower left corner of the picture a small black boy dances, with one leg lifted high, to the music of a white fiddler seated at a nearby table. Occasion: out-door recreation.

530 Latrobe, Benjamin. Sketches of Six Musical Instruments. [1818-20]. Pen and ink. Baltimore, Maryland Historical Society, The Papers of Benjamin Henry Latrobe. Published in THE JOURNALS OF BENJAMIN HENRY LATROBE, 1799-1820.... Vol. 3. THE PAPERS OF BENJAMIN HENRY LATROBE, edited by Edward C. Carter, 203-4. New Haven: Yale University Press, 1980. Reprint. SINFUL TUNES AND SPIRITUALS..., by Dena Epstein, 98-99. Urbana: University of Illinois Press, 1977.

Sketches for six instruments which Latrobe saw slaves playing during his residency in New Orleans in 1818-1820 (see no. 121): 1. "An old man sat astride of a cylindrical drum...." The sketch shows the drum in playing position, with a portion of the player's leg showing. 2. "The other drum was an open staved thing...." This drum is shown in an upright position. 3. "The most curious instrument however was a stringed instrument which no doubt was imported from Africa...." Sketches show both frontal and side views of the instrument. 4. "One...consisted of a block cut into something of the form of a cricket bat...." The sketch presents a three-quarters side view. 5. "A square drum looking like a stool...." Again, a three-quarters view of the drum. 6. "A Calabash with a round hole in it...." Three-quarters view is depicted.

531 "The Mathew-orama for 1824. Charles Mathews in His Roles in TRIP TO AMERICA." [1824]. Lithograph. University of Texas at Austin, Hoblitzelle Theatre Arts Collection. Published in AMERICA AS ART, by Joshua C. Taylor, 46. Washington, DC: Smithsonian Institution, 1976.

Scene shows 13 white "gentlemen," standing or seated in a city square, arrayed in a variety of dress (apparently representing Mathews in thirteen of his comic roles). A corpulent and somewhat ragged black fiddler plays a tiny violin in the right forefront of the picture. Occasion: theatre advertisement.

532 Mayr, Christian. "Kitchen Ball at White Sulphur Springs." 1838. Oil on canvas. Raleigh, North Carolina Museum of Art. Reproduced in THE PORTRAYAL OF THE NEGRO IN AMERICAN PAINTING, by Sidney Kaplan, no.15. Brunswick, ME: Bowdoin College Museum of Art, 1964. Also in AMERICAN PAINTINGS TO 1900, 72. Raleigh: North Carolina Museum of Art, 1966. THE PAINTER'S AMERICA: RURAL AND URBAN LIFE, 1810-1910, by Patricia Hills, 59. New York: Praeger and Whitney Museum of Art, 1974.

Scene shows a large, rafted but commodious, room, used as a ballroom, with an indeterminate number of well-dressed black folk milling about and dancing. Two couples in the center of the room dance with considerable verve, taking quite large, complicated steps. Music is furnished by a group of three: flutist, fiddler, and cellist (who bows his instrument). The instrumentalists are seated against the wall of a large, raftered room. Occasion: indoor recreation.

533 Miller, Lewis. "Negro Dance." 1853. Wash. Petersburg, Virginia State Library Collection. Reprint. SINFUL TUNES AND SPIRITUALS ..., by Dena J. Epstein, 157. Urbana: University of Illinois Press, 1977.

The native of York, Pennsylvania, made this sketch during a trip to Virginia in 1853. Two couples dance to the music of 3 musicians: a seated banjo player (whose instrument has the fifth short string) and, standing behind him, a fiddler and a bones player. The background suggests the dancers are dancing on the ground, not a floor. Occasion: outdoor recreation.

534 Morrill, D. "Banjo Player." 1862. Oil on canvas. Hartford, Connecticut, Wadsworth Athenaeum. Reproduced in AMERICAN FOLK PAINTING, by Mary Black and Jean Lipman, 103. New York: Clarkson N. Potter, [1966]. Also in GESCHICHTE DER AMERIKANISCHEN MALEREI, by Alfred Neumeyer, fig. 135. Munich: Prestel-Verlag, 1974.

Cartoon of a banjoist in minstrel costume, with his hat cocked over the left ear. He holds his four-string banjo horizontally. The minimal background suggests he is standing on grass. Occasion: outdoor domestic music.

535 Mount, William Sidney. "Rustic Dance after a Sleigh Ride." 1830. Oil on canvas. Boston, Museum of Fine Arts. Reproduced in M. AND M. KAROLIK COLLECTION OF PAINTINGS, 1815 TO 1865, pl. 194. Boston and Cambridge: Museum of Fine Arts and Harvard University Press, 1949. Also in WILLIAM SIDNEY MOUNT, by Alfred Frankenstein, pl. 1. New York: Harry N. Abrams, 1975.

In one of his earliest paintings, the Long Island artist shows a fiddler playing for 2 white couples dancing in a living room crowded with white spectators. Seated on a chair, the musician holds his violin well below the shoulder position, and it slants downward at a sharp angle; he taps his foot as he plays. The only other black man in the picture, the sleigh driver, peeps in through the partially open door. Occasion: indoor recreation.

536 _____. "Dance of the Haymakers." 1845. Oil on canvas. Stony Brook, New York, The Museums at Stony Brook. Reproduced in WILLIAM SIDNEY MOUNT, 1807-1868, AN AMERICAN PAINTER, by Bartlett Cowdrey and Hermann W. Williams. New York: Metropolitan Museum of Art and Columbia University Press, 1944. Lithograph, with the title "Music is Contagious," by Leon Noel, 1849. Published by Goupil, Vibert & Company. New York: Long Island Historical Society, 1944.

Scene shows a boy using two sticks as a percussion instrument to drum on the side of a barn while he watches, from outside the barn, the white merrymakers inside, two of whom dance a jig to the music of a white fiddler. Occasion: indoor recreation.

537 _____. "Right and Left." 1850. Oil on canvas. Stony Brook, New York, The Museums at Stony Brook. Reproduced in THE NEGRO IN AMERICAN PAINTING. Exhibition Catalogue, no. 21. Brunswick, ME: Bowdoin College Museum of Art, 1964. Also in WILLIAM SIDNEY MOUNT, by Alfred Frankenstein, pl. 30. New York: Harry N. Abrams, 1975. Lithograph by Jean-Baptiste Adolphe Lafosse. Published by Goupil, Vibert & Company. New York: Long Island Historical Society, 1952.

Half-length portrait of a fiddler seen from the side as he looks toward viewer. He holds his instrument in position but does not play it. Occasion: portraiture.

538 _____. "The Bone Player." 1856. Oil on canvas. Boston, Museum of Fine Arts. Lithograph by Jean-Baptiste Adolphe Lafosse (see no. 537). Reproduced in M. AND M. KAROLIK COLLECTION OF AMERICAN PAINTINGS, 1815 TO 1865, pl. 197. Boston and Cambridge: Museum of Fine Arts and Harvard University Press, 1949. Also in WILLIAM SIDNEY MOUNT, by Alfred Frankenstein, 28. New York: Harry N. Abrams, 1975.

Half-length portrait of a bones player shows him with a set of decorated bones in each hand, held between second and third fingers. With elbows down, he strikes the lower, broader sections of the bones together. Occasion: domestic music.

539 _____. "The Banjo Player." 1856. Oil on canvas. Stony Brook, New York, The Museums at Stony Brook. Reproduced in WILLIAM SIDNEY MOUNT, 1807-1868, AN AMERICAN PAINTER, by Bartlett Cowdrey and Hermann W. Williams, 40. Published for the Metropolitan Museum of Art. New York, Columbia University Press, 1944. Also in WILLIAM SIDNEY MOUNT, by Alfred Frankenstein, pl. 29. New York: Harry N. Abrams, 1975. Lithograph by J. A. Lafosse (see no. 537).

Half-length portrait of a smiling banjo player in front view. He holds his instrument, which has the fifth short string, in the conventional manner. Occasion: domestic music.

540 "The Old Plantation." Late 18th c. Watercolor. Williamsburg, VA, The Abby Aldrich Rockefeller Folk Arts Center. Reproduced in AMERICAN FOLK PAINTING, by Mary Black and Jean Lipman, 97. New York: Clarkson N. Potter, 1966. Reprints. SINFUL TUNES AND SPIRITUALS..., by Dena Epstein, 37. Urbana: University of Illinois Press, 1977. THE AFRO-AMERICAN TRADITION IN THE DECORATIVE ARTS, by John M. Vlach, pl. 1. Cleveland: Cleveland Museum of Art, 1978.

The scene shows a group of 12 men and women gathered in front of two slave cabins; in the background are more cabins, the "big house," and several smaller houses. A man dances a stick dance and 2 women dance with scarves to the music of a banjoist and a drummer. The four-string banjo has a somewhat elongated neck; the drum, which is held between the knees, appears to be a skin drum. Several of the men and women wear turbans in the African style. It is believed that this painting was made on a plantation located between Columbia and Orangeburg, South Carolina. Occasion: outdoor recreation.

541 Orr, John William. "Negro Quarters." [1853]. Wood engraving. Published in "Sugar and the Sugar Region of Louisiana," by Thomas Bangs Thorpe. HARPER'S NEW MONTHLY

MAGAZINE 7 (November 1853).

Illustration depicts a distant plantation scene, showing three cabins, an old mill, and an outhouse---the whole graced with one tree and occasional shrubbery. In the distance a couple is depicted, dancing vigorously with large kicking steps, to the music of a fiddler perched on top of a barrel. The spectators include 2 men, 1 woman, and 2 children. Occasion: outdoor recreation.

542 Orr, Nathaniel. "Christmas Eve Frolic." [1861]. Wood engraving. Published in MAUM GUINEA AND HER PLANTATION CHILDREN, by Metta V. Victor, frontispiece. New York: Beadle & Company, 1861.

The scene shows 17 or more men and woman making merry in a clearing in the woods. Most watch a couple dancing in the center of the illustration: the girl, with one hand on her hip and the other hand holding her skirt in a curtsey pose, takes large steps, crossing the right leg over the left. The man leans backwards, extending his arms even further back, and kicks high with bended knees, balancing on the ball of his left foot. Music is provided by a group of 3 musicians seated on tree stumps to the right of the dancers---a fiddler, a banjoist, and a tambourine player---and by a man seated on an upturned basket to the left, who is pattin' juba. Occasion: outdoor entertainment.

543 "A Rehearsal." [1859]. Wood engraving. Published in "The Virginians," by William Makepeace Thackeray. HARPER'S NEW MONTHLY MAGAZINE 19 (October 1859). Thackeray himself may have been the illustrator. See THE HOUSE OF HARPER..., by J. Henry Harper, 115. New York: Harper & Brothers, 1912.

Illustration for a serialized version of the British author's American novel shows a black drummer boy, a large drum suspended from his neck, with an officer and four soldiers in motley colonial dress as they pause during drill practice. Occasion: military event.

544 Schussele, Christian (?). "Negro Village on a Southern Plantation." [1852]. Wood engraving by William B. Gihon. Published in AUNT PHILLIS'S CABIN, OR SOUTHERN LIFE AS IT IS, by Mary H. Eastman, frontispiece. Philadelphia: Lippincott, Crambo & Company, 1852. Reprint. THE MUSIC OF BLACK AMERICANS..., by Eileen Southern, 177. 2d. ed. New York: W. W. Norton, 1983.

Illustration depicts a plantation scene, showing the slave quarters and a group of men and women gathered under a tree in front of one of the cabins. Two men dance with gusto, lifting their arms and kicking high with bended knees. One of them plays the bones as he dances. Accompaniment for the dancing is provided by a fiddler, who sits on a barrel, and a man who beats another barrel with open palm as if it were a drum. A boy lolling on the ground, a seated woman, and a man are spectators. Occasion: outdoor recreation.

545 Slave Drum. Late 17th-early 18th century. Wood artifact. London, The British Museum. Sir Hans Sloane Bequest of 1753. Reproduced in Exhibition Catalogue: THE AFRO-AMERICAN TRADITION IN DECORATIVE ARTS, by John Michael Vlach, 20. Cleveland: The Cleveland Museum of Art, 1978. Also in SINFUL TUNES AND SPIRITUALS..., by Dena J. Epstein, 48. Urbana: University of Illinois Press, 1977.

The drum is made of a hollowed log "sculptured into a bottle shape." Musical artifact.

546 "Slavery as It Exists in America." 1850. Lithograph. Published in AMERICA ON STONE, by Harry T. Peters, 210. Garden City, NY: Doubleday, Doran, 1931.

Caricatural cartoon shows a group of 3 men, 3 women, and 2 children making merry in a clearing (on a plantation?). In the far background four white men watch. Two couples dance with large, kicking steps, the women with hands on hips, to the music of a banjo player, who sits to the right on a large stone. One of the male dancers plays the bones with his left hand, lifted in the air. The children laugh and wave their arms about. It is probable that all are singing since their mouths are open. Occasion: outdoor recreation.

547 Stephens, Henry Louis. "The Holiday Dance." [1852]. Wood engraving. Bieler, engraver. Published in THE CABIN AND PARLOR; OR, SLAVES AND MASTERS, by J. Thornton Randolph, frontispiece. Philadelphia: T. B. Peterson, 1852.

Scene shows several persons gathered under a tree in a clearing in the woods. A couple dances vigorously, the woman with hands on her hips, the man with arms extended to the side, both with bent knees and large, leaping steps. Music is provided by a fiddler, who slouches in a chair that has been placed atop a barrel, his fiddle slanting downward at a sharp angle. Six spectators include 4 slaves (1 male, 3 children) and 2 white women. Occasion: outdoor recreation.

548 Strother, David [Porte Crayon, pseud.] "Dat fiddle done ruinged [sic]." [1857]. Wood engraving. Published in "North Carolina Illustrated," by David Strother. HARPER'S NEW MONTHLY MAGAZINE 15 (August 1857).

Caricatural portrait of a fiddler, dressed in fashionable nineteenth-century attire, holding a smashed violin in his right hand. He carries his bow in a cloth sack. Occasion: portraiture.

549 _____. Marching Boys [untitled]. [1851]. Wood engraving. Richardson, engraver.

Published in SWALLOW BARN, OR A SOJOURN IN THE OLD DOMINION, by John Pendleton Kennedy, 309. Rev. ed. New York: George P. Putnam, 1851.

Scene shows 2 young boys marching to the sounds made by beating a watering can with two drum sticks. One youngster seems to be dancing: his left foot and arm are raised; the heel of his right foot is lifted. Occasion: outdoor recreation.

550 Svin'in, Pavel Petrovich. "Merrymaking at a Country Tavern." c.1812. Watercolor. New York City, Metropolitan Museum of Art. Reproduced in PICTURESQUE UNITED STATES OF AMERICA, 1811, 1812, 1813..., edited by Avrahm Yarmolinsky, pl. 12. New York: W. E. Rudge, 1930. Reprint. THE MUSIC OF BLACK AMERICANS: A HISTORY, by Eileen Southern, pl. 6. New York: W. W. Norton, 1971.

Russian diplomat Svin'in sketched this scene in New England about 1812. Depicts a fiddler (seated) playing for the dancing of two white couples in a country tavern. The fiddler, who is the only caricatured figure in the picture, taps his foot as he plays. Occasion: indoor recreation.

551 "Tuning Up." [1858]. Wood engraving. Published in "A Winter in the South: Sixth Paper." HARPER'S NEW MONTHLY MAGAZINE 17 (August 1858).

Caricatural depiction of 3 musicians who are preparing to play for a dance: the 2 fiddlers, seated, are tuning their instruments, while a tambourine player standing behind them watches intently. They are dressed in formal attire, as if engaged to play for a society ball. Occasion: indoor recreation.

552 "View on the James River Canal, near Balcony Falls.---Rebel Troops Going from Lynchburg to Buchanan, on Their Way to Western Virginia." [1861]. Wood engraving. Published in HARPER'S WEEKLY 5 (September 1861).

Depiction of a Civil War scene shows a military boat proceeding down the James River Canal, with an indeterminate number of white Confederate troops aboard. White civilians and soldiers and 1 black man watch from the shore. On board the boat black musicians, a fiddler and a banjoist, entertain the crowd; the latter also is singing. Occasion: outdoor entertainment.

553 W., T. (or T., W.). "An Oregon Fashionable Ball." [1856]. Wood engraving. Published in "Wild Life in Oregon," by William V. Wells. HARPER'S NEW MONTHLY MAGAZINE 13 (October 1856).

Scene shows a rudely constructed room filled with white dancers. A black fiddler, perched on top of a crate, which rests on a table, plays for the dancing, tapping his foot as he plays. He holds his instrument against the shoulder, and it slants sharply downward. Occasion: indoor recreation.

554 "Winter Holydays in the Southern States. Plantation Frolic on Christmas Eve." [1858]. Wood engraving. Published in "Christmas in the South," by Thomas Bangs Thorpe. FRANK LESLIE'S ILLUSTRATED NEWSPAPER 5 (January 1858). Reprint. "Black American Music in Pictures," by Frederick Crane, 31. BLACK MUSIC RESEARCH JOURNAL [6] (1986).

Caricatural scene shows a large gathering outside a cabin in the slave quarters; the big house looms in the far background. An indeterminate number of men, women, and children are making merry, watched by 4 white spectators. In the center of the picture a couple dances: the woman holding her skirt in a curtsey position and taking small steps; the man, with arms uplifted, taking huge steps, kicking waist high with the right leg while balancing on the ball of the left foot. Accompaniment for the dance is provided by 3 musicians seated on the ground: fiddler, banjoist, and bones player. Occasion: outdoor recreation.

555 "Work's Over'---Scenes among the Beaufort Contrabands." [1861]. Wood engraving. Published in HARPER'S WEEKLY 5 (December 1861).

Scene shows a large gathering of contrabands in an open space of the town; several buildings [government?] are in the background. People are conversing, taking care of chores, and milling about. In the lower right corner of the picture 2 small boys dance with great vigor, waving their arms about and kicking high. Two men watch the dancers. Occasion: outdoor recreation.

THE RELIGIOUS EXPERIENCE

556 Antrobus, John. "A Plantation Burial." c.1860. Oil on canvas. New Orleans, Louisiana, Historic New Orleans Collection. Reproduced in THE PAINTERS' AMERICA, RURAL AND URBAN LIFE, 1810-1910, by Patricia Hills, 63. New York: Praeger and Whitney Museum of American Art, 1974. "Iconography of the Black Man in American Art, 1710-1900," by James Edward Fox, pl. 5. Ph.D. diss., University of North Carolina at Chapel Hill, 1979.

The English artist depicts a burial he saw on the Tucker plantation in Carroll Parish, Louisiana. In a clearing of a deep forest, 30 or more men, women, and children are gathered around a coffin. The officiating minister is speaking;

others are in varying attitudes of attention. Some lift their hands in the air, some meditate. The shadowy figures of a white couple can be seen behind trees at the right. Occasion: outdoor religious ceremony.

557 "The Camp Meeting." 1837. Lithograph. Henry R. Robinson, printer and publisher. New York, Museum of the City of New York. Reproduced in AMERICA ON STONE, by Harry T. Peters, pl. 122. Garden City, NY: Doubleday, Doran, 1931.

Caricatural depiction of a camp-meeting service: 6 men and women are assembled in front of a wooden pulpit, in which there are 3 men: the preacher, with arms lifted high and a book in one hand, exhorts the worshippers; a second man sits with arms folded; and the third, with open mouth as if singing or shouting. The worshippers respond emotionally, with uplifted arms or hands clasped in prayer, and some with open mouths as if singing. Occasion: outdoor religious service.

558 Croome, William. "Uncle Jack Has Come." [1849]. Wood engraving. Published in THE AFRICAN PREACHER, by William Spottswood White. Philadelphia: Presbyterian Board of Publication, c.1849.

Depiction of the celebrated slave preacher of Virginia, Uncle Jack, seated on a tree trunk in a grove, preaching to 8 white listeners. Occasion: outdoor religious service.

559 Fuller, George. "Negro Funeral." 1858. Pencil on paper. Reproduced in "Images of Slavery: George Fuller's Depictions of the Antebellum South," by Sarah Burns. AMERICAN ART JOURNAL 15 (Summer 1983).

Sketch shows a clearing of a woods, in which a large gathering of mourners proceed slowly toward the burial place. Two women stand near the wagon which serves as the hearse; two men sit on the top of the wagon. This sketch was inspired by the artist's painting of 1881 (see no. 1644), but is quite different from the later painting. Occasion: outdoor religious ceremony.

560 Johnson, Eastman. "The Chimney Corner." 1863. Oil on paperboard. Utica, New York, Munson-Williams-Proctor Institute. Reproduced in EASTMAN JOHNSON, by Patricia Hills, 36. New York: Clarkson N. Potter, Whitney Museum of American Art, 1972.

Scene shows a humble kitchen dominated by a huge cupboard to the left. A shabbily dressed man sits by the fireplace, reading the Bible (?) by the light of the fire. Hunched over the huge book, which lies half-way open on his lap, he holds his place with the thumb of his left hand, covering the opposite page with his right hand. Occasion: indoor domestic religious experience.

561 "Meeting in the African Church, Cincinnati, Ohio." [c.1853]. Wood engraving. Washington, D. C., Collections of the Library of Congress. Reprint. A PICTORIAL HISTORY OF THE NEGRO IN AMERICA, by Langston Hughes, Milton Meltzer, and C. Eric Lincoln, 63. 3d ed. New York: Crown Publishers, 1968.

Scene shows a fairly large, tidy church, with an indeterminate number of worshippers standing in the pews. About 30 men and women have moved into the center aisle, where 3 or 4 sit on a bench directly in front of the pulpit. Others are kneeling or standing. The minister, leaning forward over the lectern, with arms raised and brows knit, is delivering a sermon. Members of the congregation respond emotionally to his sermon, some with one arm uplifted, some with hands clasped in prayer, and at least 1 woman seems to be possessed by the spirit. Occasion: religious service.

562 "A Negro Funeral." [1859]. Wood engraving. Published in "Rice Lands of the South," by T. Addison Richards. HARPER'S NEW MONTHLY MAGAZINE 19 (November 1859).

Scene shows a large gathering of mourners in a clearing of a deeply wooded area. In the center of the picture, the officiating clergyman with arms uplifted, his back turned to the viewer, appears to be speaking. Others are in various positions of mourning around the open grave, sitting or kneeling on the ground, or standing, some with hands in faces, or with bowed heads. Occasion: outdoor religious ceremony.

563 "Reading the Bible to the Slaves." [1841]. Wood engraving. Published in THE FAMILY MAGAZINE 6 (1841).

Scene shows a small group gathered outside a cabin door under a tree. A young white woman is reading the Bible to 2 male and 3 female slaves. Occasion: outdoor religious service.

564 "The Reverend Richard Allen." 1813. Stipple engraving. Philadelphia, Library Company of Philadelphia. Published in THE BLACK PRESENCE IN THE ERA OF THE AMERICAN REVOLUTION, by Sidney Kaplan, 91. Greenwich, CT: New York Graphic Society in association with the Smithsonian Institution.

Portrayal of the founder and first bishop of the African Methodist Episcopal Church, the world's first independent black denomination. Occasion: religious portraiture.

565 Sheppard, William L. "Prayer Meeting in a Contraband Camp---Washington, 1862." Wood engraving. Published in MY STORY OF THE WAR..., by Mary A. Livermore, 263. Hartford, CT: A. D. Worthington and Company, 1889.

Caricatural scene shows an indeterminate number of persons participating in a religious exercise in a small, dark cabin. This possibly is the artist's conception of the shout: the worshipers seem to be moving in a circle, and most are singing and dancing with one or both arms uplifted, but some do not use the characteristic shuffle step. Bystanders, some kneeling, sing and clap their hands. Occasion: indoor religious service.

566 Stephens, Henry Louis. "Reading the Bible to the Slaves." [1852]. Wood engraving, by Bieler. Published in THE CABIN AND PARLOR; OR, SLAVES AND MASTERS, by J. Thornton Randolph, title page. Philadelphia: T. B. Peterson, 1852.

Scene shows a young white woman reading the Bible to 6 slaves, who are seated outside a cabin in the slave quarters. This illustration is similar in most respects to one published in 1841 (see no. 562), except that details are reversed and another figure is added to the group, a man standing against the tree. Occasion: outdoor religious service.

567 Svin'in, Pavel Petrovich. "Negro Methodists Holding a Meeting in Philadelphia." c.1812. Watercolor. New York City, Metropolitan Museum of Art. Reproduced in PICTURESQUE UNITED STATES OF AMERICA, 1811, 1812, 1813..., edited by Avrahm Yarmolinsky, pl. 18. New York: W. E. Rudge, 1930.

Caricatural scene, sketched in Philadelphia about 1812, depicts a religious service of black Methodists (Bethel A. M. E. Church?). A minister or deacon (?) stands in the doorway of the meeting house with mouth open as if exhorting (or remonstrating with the worshippers). An indeterminate number of men and women gathered on the church grounds just outside the doorway respond in various ways: some with arms lifted high, some kneeling or lying on the ground, some jumping, many with mouths open as if singing or shouting. Occasion: outdoor religious service.

THE SONG

568 "Black Tom, the Little Sweep Ho, of New York." [1852]. Wood engraving. Published in GLEASON'S PICTORIAL DRAWING-ROOM COMPANION 2 (February 1852).

Depiction of a street crier: a boy chimney-sweep at work in New York City. Occasion: outdoor work activity.

569 Croome, William. Street Criers [untitled]. [1850]. Wood engravings. Published in CITY CRIES; OR, A PEEP AT SCENES IN TOWN BY AN OBSERVER. Philadelphia: George S. Appleton, 1850.

Twenty-four "designs" of street criers include 9 black vendors: 1. Chimney sweep (16-18), 2. White wash man (28-30), 3. Crab-man (60-62), 4. Ice-cream men (66), 5. Hot-corn woman (68-70), 6. Fishmongers (72-74), 7. Hominy-man (80-82), 8. Split-wood man (88-90), 9. Pepper-pot woman (96-98). Occasion: outdoor work activity.

570 Street Criers of New York. Prints [untitled]. [1809]. Published in THE CRIES OF NEW YORK. New York: Printed and Sold by S[amuel] Wood, 1809.

Pictures of black street criers include chimney sweeps and vendors of "Butter Mel-leck" and "Bake Pears." Occasion: outdoor work activity.

THE TALE

571 Darley, Felix Octavius Carr. "Wild Bill, Walter, and Utopia." [1852]. Wood engraving, by Leslie. Published in LIFE IN THE SOUTH. A COMPANION TO UNCLE TOM'S CABIN, by Calvin Henderson Wiley, frontispiece. Philadelphia: T. B. Peterson, 1852.

Scene shows the fearsome Wild Bill telling his story to the young white couple he has encountered in the woods. Occasion: outdoor entertainment.

III

THE POST-EMANCIPATION ERA

LITERATURE: 1863–1899

SOCIAL ACTIVITIES

572 Allen, James Lane. "Plantation Music." CRITIC 4 (5 January 1884): 9.

In a Letter to the Editor, dated 31 December 1883 from New York, this writer (formerly of Lexington, Kentucky) takes exception to Joel Chandler Harris's article "Plantation Music and the Banjo" (see no. 624). Maintains that black street musicians frequently played the banjo.

573 _____. "Mrs. Stowe's 'Uncle Tom' at Home in Kentucky." CENTURY MAGAZINE 34 (October 1887): 852-67.

Discussion of an all-black town in the South after the Civil War refers to the ex-slave preacher and his exhortations, to the fiddlers, banjoists, and percussionists. Description of the construction of folk instruments (gourd banjo, copper-still drum, and tambourine).

Reference to 1 sermon: Come unto me ye that are heavy laden (865).

574 _____. THE BLUE-GRASS REGION OF KENTUCKY, AND OTHER KENTUCKY ARTICLES. New York: Harper & Brothers, c.1892. 322 pp.

Chapter 2, "Uncle Tom at Home," is about the black man in Kentucky (47-86). References to the antebellum slave preacher and exhorter as a type (79-80) and discussion of slave instrumental music. Comment on the fiddle and the banjo as popular instruments heard in cabins. Description of the folk-crafted banjo, kettledrum, and tambourine (79-80).

575 "An Artist Selecting an Instrument." FRANK LESLIE'S ILLUSTRATED NEWSPAPER 32/818 (3 June 1871): 192.

Brief discussion of the essential qualities of a good string instrument in the opinion of a black fiddler, as distinguished from those features of the instrument that are not important to him.

576 "Banjo and Bones." SATURDAY REVIEW OF POLITICS, LITERATURE, SCIENCE AND ART (London) 67 (7 June 1884): 739-40. [Attributed to Brander Matthews in some sources.] Reprints. CRITIC 1 (28 June 1884): 308-9. THE NEGRO AND HIS FOLKLORE IN NINETEENTH-CENTURY PERIODICALS. Edited by Bruce Jackson. Published for the American Folklore Society. Austin: University of Texas Press, 1967.

Article focusing primarily upon "Ethiopian" minstrelsy discusses the banjo controversy: whether the banjo was a genuine plantation instrument (see no. 624).

Text of 1 creole slave song: Voyez ce mulet-la Musieu Bainjo (740).

577 Barrow, David Crenshaw, Jr. "A Georgia Corn-Shucking." CENTURY 24 (October 1882): 873-78. Reprint. THE NEGRO AND HIS FOLKLORE.... Edited by Bruce Jackson. Published for the American Folklore Society. Austin, University of Texas Press, 1967.

This native of Georgia describes a corn-shucking

festival of the ex-slaves and the dance that followed it. Reference to the "straw beater" who accompanied the dance fiddler.

Text and music of 2 songs: 1. Little Billy Woodcock lived o'er de mountain (Cho: Ho mer Riley ho). 2. Round up, dubble up, round up corn. Texts only of 3 songs: 1. Slip shuck corn a little while. 2. Here is yer corn-shucker. 3. Rabbit in de gyordin.

578 Bassett, A. L. "Going to Housekeeping in North Carolina." LIPPINCOTT'S MAGAZINE 28 (August 1881): 205-8.

Discussion of the religious activities of the local Negroes includes comment on the Baptists and Methodists, and the chanting of prayers by a cook. Also description of a cakewalk festival (208).

579 Benjamin, Samuel Green Wheeler. "The Sea Islands." HARPER'S NEW MONTHLY MAGAZINE 57 (November 1878): 839-61.

Artist-writer includes references to blacks in his account of his journey through the Sea Islands of Georgia, South Carolina, and Florida. Description of a band of child musicians who performed on folk-crafted instruments to entertain hotel guests in Fernandina, Florida (847). Comment on the mournful singing of hymns at night by blacks on board a vessel sailing between Cumberland and Savannah, Georgia, as they held midnight vigil over the coffin of a child (850).

580 Brackett, Jeffrey Richardson. THE NEGRO IN MARYLAND. Baltimore: Johns Hopkins University, 1889. Johns Hopkins University Studies in Historical and Political Science 6. Edited by Herbert B. Adams. 268 pp.

The discussion of slavery includes references to laws in regard to religious gatherings (199) and camp meetings (201); also references to cake walks that ended in "noise and disorder" (204).

581 Bradley, Arthur Granville. "A Peep at the Southern Negro." MACMILLAN'S MAGAZINE 39 (November 1878): 61-68.

Discussion of the social conditions and lives of country blacks in the former slave states during the Reconstruction Era includes the observation that preachings, weddings, baptisms, cakewalks, candy-stews, and corn-shuckings were important social events for the ex-slaves and that typical gatherings called for singing, dancing, and banjo-playing.

582 Brainerd, E. "Plantation Music." CRITIC 3 (29 December 1883): 534.

In a Letter to the Editor, dated 22 December 1883 from Philadelphia, the writer takes exception to Joel Chandler Harris's article about "Plantation Music and the Banjo" (see no. 624) and maintains that blacks played banjos in the antebellum South. Author concurs with Harris, however, about the disuse of tambourines and bones by blacks.

583 Brown, William J. THE LIFE OF WILLIAM J. BROWN OF PROVIDENCE, R. I., WITH PERSONAL RECOLLECTIONS OF INCIDENTS IN RHODE ISLAND. Providence, RI: Angell and Company, 1883. Reprint. Freeport, NY: Books for Libraries Press, 1972. 230 pp.

The black author (b. 1814), whose grandfather was born in Africa and was owned by the celebrated Brown brothers of Providence, gives some account of slavery in Rhode Island before emancipation in 1808. Discussion of the events of Election Day for the "colored" (13), which took place on the last Saturday in June.

584 Bruce, Phillip Alexander. "A Tobacco-Plantation." LIPPINCOTT'S MAGAZINE 36 (December 1885): 533-42.

Discussion of a Virginia tobacco plantation includes description of a night-time corn-shucking contest and its singers, of the Sunday social gatherings of slaves in the "quarters," and of a plantation party with music and dancing. Also comment on the performance practice of musicians who played banjo and accordion (540-41).

585 Cable, George W. "The Dance in Place Congo." CENTURY MAGAZINE 31/4 (February 1886): 517-32. Reprints. THE NEGRO AND HIS FOLKLORE.... Edited by Bruce Jackson. Published for the American Folklore Society. Austin: University of Texas, 1967. THE SOCIAL IMPLICATIONS OF EARLY NEGRO MUSIC IN THE UNITED STATES. Edited by Bernard Katz. New York: Arno Press and the New York Times, 1969.

Discussion by a native of New Orleans of the slave dancing in the city's Congo Square, of the slave orchestras that accompanied the dancing, the dance figures, and the music. Also references to solo vocal styles and choral forms. Detailed description of the instruments: African drums, huge wooden horns, triangles, rattles made of gourds filled with pebbles or rice, jew's-harps, keys, barrels and casks "beaten on the head with the shank-bones of cattle," four-stringed banjos, and the "Marimba brett."

Texts and music of 11 songs; 2 quill tunes (without text). See SONG COLLECTIONS (no. 1743).

586 Cable, James B. "The Banjo Controversy---Mr. Harris and the Messrs. Cable." CURRENT: POLITICS, LITERATURE, SCIENCE, AND ART (Chicago) 2 (2 August 1884): 76. Reprint. CRITIC 2, n.s. (9 August 1884): 65-66.

A Letter to the Editor from the brother of

George Cable refers to the controversy over whether the banjo or the fiddle was the most popular plantation instrument (see nos. 575, 623). Observation that he had not seen the banjo on plantations in Louisiana and Mississippi, where the violin and "rude mouth organ [made] of graded canes were common." But in New Orleans, he had watched dancing on the street to banjo music, and in Baltimore in 1875 the banjo was teamed with jawbones to produce street music.

587 "The Cake Walk." FRANK LESLIE'S ILLUSTRATED NEWSPAPER 31/796 (31 December 1870): 261-62.

Detailed description of a Cake Walk ball, a traditional festival "peculiar to the colored race" that took place during the Christmas holidays in Richmond, Virginia.

588 Cameron, Rebecca. "Plantation on 'The Neck'---Cape Fear River." LADIES' HOME JOURNAL (December 1891): 5-6. Reprint as "Christmas at Buchoi, a North Carolina Rice Plantation." NORTH CAROLINA BOOKLET 13 (July 1913): 3, 8-10.

Description of slave life on a rice plantation at Buchoi, on the Cape Fear River, North Carolina, during the antebellum period includes discussion of Christmas holidays, which lasted from Christmas Eve until the Yule log "burnt in two" after New Year's Day. Comment on the task of selecting the Yule log for the coming year and on a "coonah" song the field hands chanted as they cut down the Yule tree. Discussion of the Christmas dance of the slaves, accompanied by fiddle and banjo, and the John "Coonahs" (=John Kuners or John Canoe) festival, held on the second day after Christmas on this plantation. The John Kuners festival was distinctive for its masking and dressing in costumes, singing, and dancing, with music for the procession provided by banjo, bones, triangles, castanets, fifes, drums, and other folk-crafted plantation instruments. Description of the John Kuners dances and comment on relevent performance practice. Author speculates that the John Kuner festival may have been introduced by South Carolina slaves who accompanied Governor Sir John Yeamans from Barbados to South Carolina, and from there were taken by his descendents into North Carolina, where they settled on the Cape Fear River.

Text of 1 song: 1. Christmas comes but once a year (Cho: Ho rang du rango!).

589 Campbell, James Edwin. ECHOES FROM THE CABIN AND ELSEWHERE. Chicago: Donohue & Henneberry, 1895. 86 pp.

Black poet's collection of poems includes numerous references to folk traditions: the religious service (44), the corn shucking and corn songs (27), lullabies (33), animal folk tales (13, 34) and the dance (36). Detailed description of the "Mobile buck" dance, which the poet saw danced by longshoremen on the Ohio and Mississippi Rivers (36).

590 Chamberlain, Mary E., compiler. "Folk-Lore Scrap-Book: Negro Superstition concerning the Violin." JOURNAL OF AMERICAN FOLK-LORE 5 (October-December 1892): 329-30.

Report by the plantation owner of a decrease in fiddle and banjo playing among rural blacks after the Civil War because of the superstition that "de devil is a fiddler." Most black violinists were professional musicians; church members in the country played the lap organ or "cor'jon" [accordion], and city blacks favored the piano.

591 Chambers-Ketchum, Annie. "Music in the South...." Parts 1, 3. AMERICAN MUSICIAN (New York) 19 (1 November 1890): 7-8; (6 December 1890): 7-8.

The first essay in a series about American music in the South, from early colonial exploration through the antebellum period, includes a section devoted to the Afro-American: his songs, dances, and instrumental music on banjo, violin, mouth-organ, and jews-harp.

The third essay is devoted to comment on slave music and religion: on the plantation fiddler, with description of string performance practice (e.g., the imitation of the sounds of water, wind, beasts); and on a type of black music called "ear music" (produced by closing the mouth and sending sounds through the ear). Also description of plantation dances brought from Africa to Virginia, and references to a song allegedly dating from c.1650.

Music and text of 1 song: Run, nigger, run, de patrolah ketch you (8).

592 Chenault, John Cabell. OLD CANE SPRINGS: A STORY OF THE WAR BETWEEN THE STATES IN MADISON COUNTY, KENTUCKY. Edited by Jonathan Truman Dorris.... From the original manuscript of John Cabell Chenault. Louisville, KY: The Standard Printing Company, 1937. 259 pp.

Discussion of plantation life in Kentucky during the 1860s by a judge includes detailed description of a corn-shucking festival, of the songs, and related performance practice (42-50). Also discussion of the songs of field hands (13, 15), of a slave Christmas festival (58-59), and of burial traditions (95). Observation that there is a change in style in the songs of the Negroes (126).

Text of 1 corn-shucking song: Old Master shoot a wild goose (Cho: Ju ranzie, hio ho!) (47). Reference to 1 song: Swing low, sweet chariot.

593 "Chin Music." FRANK LESLIE'S ILLUSTRATED NEWSPAPER 32 (5 August 1871): 347.

Detailed description of the street music produced by young boys, who, by controlling the air passages into the larynx and striking their cheeks, produce sounds of a "vocal character." The chin music is accompanied by foot tapping.

594 Cooke, John Esten. "Virginia in the Revolution." HARPER'S NEW MONTHLY MAGAZINE 53 (June 1876): 1-15.

Novelist, born in Winchester, Virginia, gives a historical sketch of life in Virginia before the Revolutionary War, and refers to the banjo playing and dancing of the field hands.

595 " 'Corn Shuckin' down South." NEW YORK SUN (11 November 1895): 4.

Discussion of a corn-shucking festival in the Carolinas includes detailed description of the event, from the beginning, with the gathering of the corn huskers from miles around, to the end, when all huskers feasted and danced after the work had been completed. Description of the wooden bugles, five to six feet in length, that were used to call together the huskers and of the quills used for calling between one group and another. Also, how these instruments were made from natural materials. Detailed description of the singing and relevant performance practice.

Texts of 3 songs: 1. I will start de holler. 2. Lord, I can't stay away. 3. Lookin' fur de los' year.

596 Craighead, James B. "The Future of the Negro in the South." APPLETON'S POPULAR SCIENCE MONTHLY 26 (November 1884): 39-46.

Discussion of the social mores and the condition of freedmen in the South after the Civil War with comment on their singing and dancing at Saturday-night religious meetings.

597 Crim, Matt. "An Old-Time Love Story." INDEPENDENT 43 (18 June 1891): 930-31.

Short story set in antebellum Georgia, on a plantation near the Chattahoochee River, contains references to an old slave fiddler on this plantation who was summoned by his master in the middle of the night to play tunes on his violin and dance for the entertainment of a guest.

598 Custer, Elizabeth Bacon. TENTING ON THE PLAINS, OR GENERAL CUSTER IN KANSAS AND TEXAS. New York: Charles L. Webster & Company, 1889. 702 pp.

Autobiographical account written by the wife of Colonel George Armstrong Custer includes references to a black prayer meeting in Alexandria, Louisiana (80), and to a "Negro Ball" (233), where they "cut some pigeon-wings," danced the break-down, and all the assembly "patted juba."

599 Davis, Daniel Webster. "Echoes from a Plantation Party." SOUTHERN WORKMAN 28 (February 1899): 54-59.

Afro-American elementary-school principal, poet, and author (1862-1913) in Richmond, Virginia, reports on folklore he collected from former slaves in a paper read before the Hampton Folk-Lore Society, on 17 December 1898. Detailed comment on slave life (work activities, music, religious and social customs, the visual arts, and folklore).

Descriptions and texts of 10 dances/playgames: 1. Walk old John the blind man. 2. I don' los' de dairy keys. 3. Peep squirrel. 4. King William was King George's son. 5. Here come two drunkards. 6.Miss Susie Anna Brown. 7. Bounce the ball. 8. Jinny put de kettle on. 9. Rock Candy Joe. 10. Husko ladies turn.

600 Davis, Mollie E. Moore. "A Bamboula." HARPER'S WEEKLY 37 (21 January 1893): 53-55. Reprint. DAILY PICAYUNE 57 (29 January 1893): 19.

Short story contains a description of the creole slave dance, the bamboula, which was accompanied by a fiddler.

601 "Dinky." ATLANTIC MONTHLY 54 (August 1884): 206-12.

Short story about a black orphan from the South who is taken into the family of a white northern lawyer. At the beginning of the story, Dinky attempts to sell himself on the auction block and puts on a performance, singing a song, "cutting de pigeon wing," and "jumping Juba."

Text of 1 song: De cotton is a blowin'.

602 Earle, Alice Morse. "Early New England Holidays." CHRISTIAN UNION (=OUTLOOK) 46 (17 December 1892): 1171-72.

Discussion of holiday celebrations in New England during antebellum times includes description of 'Lection Day celebrations of the blacks in Boston and other Massachusetts communities. States that they also celebrated the 14th of July, which was called "Bobalition Day," in observance of the beginning of the anti-slavery movement in the United States. Reference to their autumn corn-huskings in Narragansett.

603 _____. "Pinkster Day." OUTLOOK 49 (28 April 1894): 743-44.

Discussion of Pinkster Day celebrations of the slaves in New York State during the late eighteenth and early nineteenth centuries includes comment on the slave 'Lection Day celebrations in the Northeast.

Descriptions of 2 slave dances: 1. Double-shuffle. 2. Heel-and-toe breakdown. Also description of an African dance: Toto dance. Reference to the refrain of 1 dance-song: Hi-a bomba-bomba-bomba.

604 _____. "A Black Politician." INDEPENDENT 46 (3 May 1894): 574-75.

Story about the slave Cuddymonk, thrice-elected black "Gov'nor" of Narragansett, includes detail about the election procedures and celebration of "Nigger 'Lection Day." Comment on the powers and responsibilities of a slave governor during the eighteenth-nineteenth centuries.

605 _____. "A Baptist Preacher and Soldier of the Last Century." NEW ENGLAND MAGAZINE n.s. 12 (June 1895): 407-14.

Biography of the life and times of New Englander John Pitman includes references to a black fiddler who played for dances in Newport, Rhode Island, in the eighteenth century.

606 _____. COLONIAL DAYS IN OLD NEW YORK. New York:Charles Scribner's Sons, 1896. 312 pp.

New Englander who settled in New York gives an account of old New York during Dutch rule. Discussion of slaves celebrations of the Pinkster festival in Albany, based on writings of Munsell and Eights (see no. 649). Comment on the musical instruments, on the eel-pots used for dancing, and on the African "Toto Dance" (195-98). Also discussion of Pinkster Day celebrations in the city of New York and on Long Island (199-200) and comment on the Nigger 'Lections held in New England in May or the first week in June (201).

607 Edwards, H. S. "De Valley an' de Shadder." CENTURY 35 (January 1888): 468-77.

Georgia-born author sets a short story on a southern plantation and introduces it with a slave dance-scene. An old fiddler leads the group in dancing and singing.

Texts of 4 dance songs: 1. Shuffl' littl' Lou (Cho: Pretty littl' Lou). 2. Turn 'er high, turn lady. 3. Knock candy, Candy gal. 4. You sif' de meal, you gimme de husk (Cho: Ole Kate, git over). Descriptions of 4 dances: 1. Shuffl' littl' Lou. 2. Turn 'er high. 3. Knock candy. 4. You sif' de meal.

608 Ellis, Edward S. "Swept Away" ---"Down the Mississippi." Chapters 5-9, ST. NICHOLAS: AN ILLUSTRATED MAGAZINE FOR BOYS AND GIRLS 10 (June 1883): 599-608.

Fictional story about the flooding of the Arkansas lowlands in 1874 includes description of plantation blacks floating down the swollen Mississippi on a raft. Comment on the songs and dances they performed to entertain themselves; also on a prayer service (with singing, prayers, and exhortations) conducted in a cabin on board a ship sailing on the Mississippi River.

Text and music of 1 song: 1. We're gwine to de camp meetin' (Cho: Sing, brudder, sing) (606).

609 Farmer, H. H. VIRGINIA BEFORE AND DURING THE WAR. Henderson, KY: Published by the Author, 1892. 102 pp.

Discussion of an ex-slaveholder includes comment on the work songs of the slaves as they stripped tobacco (6); on the slave dancing at Christmas time in Danville, Virginia, to the music of the fiddle (17); and on worship practices in a Baptist church, where the slaves sat in the gallery (19).

610 Finck, Julia Neeley. "Mammy's Song: A Negro Melody." MUSIC (Chicago) 13 (March 1898): 604-05.

Discussion of performance practice associated with a song obtained from an old family servant includes comment on the instrumental accompaniment and singing of the song: "In playing the banjo, they [blacks] never have any set accompaniment: just a succession of indicating chords, connected by the distinctly outlined melody... They nearly always accent the second beat in an accompaniment, and follow with a pause, producing a throbbing effect..."

Song text and music: 1. Oh, it's hard to lub, an' it's mighty hard to lub.

611 Fisher, J. A. "A Colored Excursion." CHRISTIAN WATCHMAN & REFLECTOR (=WATCHMAN-EXAMINER) 65 (7 August 1884): [6].

Clergyman discusses the activities of the Free Summer Excursion Society of Baltimore, Maryland, an organized charity that provided outings for the poor of that city. Description of the activities at a typical black outing, including the dancing in the pavilion, the marching of the children to the music of a string band, and the "prayer and experience meeting," where exhortations were given.

Text of 1 song: What ship is this that you talk about? (Cho: Oh, it is the Old Ship of Zion).

612 Fitts, James Franklin. "The Negro in Blue." GALAXY, AN ILLUSTRATED MAGAZINE OF ENTERTAINING READING (1 February 1867): 249-55.

Officer of the Union Army discusses the activities of black soldiers during the Civil War, the songs of the contraband slaves in the camps, and a ring-dance accompanied by a fiddler.

Text of 1 dance-song: Ole massa went to town.

613 Folsom, M. M. "Christmas at Brockton Plantation." SOUTHERN BIVOUAC n.s. 1 (January 1886): 483-89.

In a short story about Christmas celebrations on a southern plantation, there is discussion of the slaves singing songs and related performance practice. Also description of the rabbit dance.

614 Fortier, Alcee. "Customs and Superstitions in Louisiana." JOURNAL OF AMERICAN FOLKLORE 1 (July-September 1888): 136-40.

Professor at Tulane University describes New Year's Day celebrations on plantations in Louisiana, with comment on the use of folk-crafted musical instruments to accompany the singing and dancing at festivities.

Text of 1 couplet: Madame Gobar, en sortant di bal. Description of 2 dances: 1. Carabine. 2. Pile Chactas.

615 _____. LOUISIANA STUDIES. LITERATURE, CUSTOMS AND DIALECTS, HISTORY AND EDUCATION. New Orleans, F. F. Hansell & Brothers, 1894. 307 pp.

This volume includes both new studies and revisions of studies previously published in "literary and scientific journals." There is detailed discussion of the celebration of Christmas on a Louisiana plantation (125-28). Also description of sugar-cane cutting and the accompanying singing and dancing performance practice (128-29); and references to Voudou dancing (130).

Text of 1 couplet: Madame Gobar, en sortant di bal. Description of 2 dances: 1. Carabine. 2. Pile Chactas.

616 Fowler, William Chauncey. "The Historical Status of the Negro in Connecticut." A Paper Read Before the New Haven Colony Historical Society.... Copied from HISTORICAL MAGAZINE AND NOTES AND QUERIES CONCERNING THE ANTIQUITIES, HISTORY, AND BIOGRAPHY OF AMERICA (1874-1875). Edited by Henry B. Dawson. Published in the Year Book of the City of Charleston for 1900.

Discussion of the annual elections of slave "governors, some of whom were called Kings, in remembrance of the Kings in Guinea," with specific reference to Caesar of Durham (21-22). Also references to slave drummers, fifers, fiddlers, and "good whistlers" (23).

617 Gilmore, James Robert [Edmund Kirke, pseud.]. "A Merchant's Story." CONTINENTAL MONTHLY 3 (March 1863): 289-315.

Seventh article in a series about the experiences of a northern traveler in the South includes description of a Christmas-day celebration (307-8). Three fiddles and four banjos accompanied the slaves as they danced. Later, the author met an African-born conjure woman, who told him his fortune (290-93).

Description of 1 dance: break-down.

618 _____. "The Poor Whites of the South." HARPER'S NEW MONTHLY MAGAZINE 29 (June-November 1864): 115-24.

Discussion of class distinctions in the pre-Civil War South includes reminiscences about the close relations between the races and how they hauled corn together for the husking-bee. Also reference to an old black dance banjoist.

619 Glasier, Jessie C. "Ole Mammy Prissy." ST. NICHOLAS: AN ILLUSTRATED MAGAZINE FOR BOYS AND GIRLS 14 (October 1887): 916-21.

Short story about an elderly black woman, a former slave from Kentucky, includes description of a Christmas dance on the old plantation and corn-shucking festivals.

620 Gordon, Armistead C., and Thomas Nelson Page. BEFO' DE WAR. ECHOES IN NEGRO DIALECT. New York: Charles Scribner's Sons, 1891. 131 pp.

This collection of fictitious plantation tales written in dialect verses includes a detailed description of a corn shucking (98-101).

621 Green, Jacob D. NARRATIVE OF THE LIFE OF JACOB D. GREEN, A RUNAWAY SLAVE FROM KENTUCKY, CONTAINING AN ACCOUNT OF HIS THREE ESCAPES IN 1839, 1846, AND 1848. Huddersfield, MD: Henry Fielding, 1864. 43 pp. Reprint. Ann Arbor: University Microfilms International, 1971.

Ex-slave, born 1813 in Queen Anne's County, Maryland, describes a slave dance held in an old house in the woods, which formerly was a meeting house for the slaves' religious services (11-12).

622 H., E. E. "A Rice-Plantation as It Used to Be." SOUTHERN MAGAZINE 16 (March 1875): 237-49.

Nostalgic reminiscenses about life on a rice plantation in South Carolina before the Civil War include discussion of the plantation slaves and their activities. Comment on the Christmas holiday celebrations, references to the all-night dancing and to the slave fiddler.

623 Hammond, Eli S. "Slave Life on a Plantation before the War" [written about 1895]. Manuscript (pencil). Harvard University, Houghton Library, Ms. US5279.22*. Cambridge, MA. 153 pp.

District U. S. Judge of Tennessee offers comment on slave dancing (6, 47-49) and fiddling (46, 121), based on observation of his father's slaves. Also detailed description of slave cornshuckings (119-21), and log-callings (46).

References to 4 slave dances (69, 122): 1. Pattin' Juba. 2. Jig. 3. Cutting the pigeon wing. 4. Hands all around (122). Text of 1 log-calling holler: Pig-o-o-o-ey, Pig, Pig (46). Text of 1 couplet: Run, nigger, run (102).

624 Harris, Joel Chandler. "Plantation Music and the Banjo." CRITIC 3 (15 December 1883): 505-06. Reprint. THE NEGRO AND HIS FOLKLORE IN NINETEENTH-CENTURY PERIODICALS. Edited by Bruce Jackson. Published for the American Folklore Society. Austin: University of Texas Press, 1967.

Observation by the author of the Uncle Remus tales that antebellum blacks did not play banjos, bones, and tambourines on Georgia plantations, that quills, fiddles, fifes, and tin trumpets were the popular instruments among slaves. References to corn-shucking festivals, songs, and dances.

625 _____. "A Thanksgiving Story. As Told by Mr. Isaiah Winchell of Georgia." INDEPENDENT 40 (29 November 1888): 1548-49.

An elderly male ex-slave, born about 1808, reminisces about his journey in 1826 to Savannah, Georgia, in a cotton caravan. In the evenings, after dinner was cooked and the teams fed, the blacks would gather around the campfire, would sing, dance, and wrestle each other, while the white men would sit nearby and cheer them on or play cards. Reference to a black fiddler who played a "queer" serenade identified as a" heartbreaker."

626 _____. "Uncle Remus' Christmas Dance Songs." CENTURY 25 (January 1883): 480.

Discussion of the performance practice associated with "pattin' Juba."

Texts of 2 dance songs: 1. Rabbit foot quick, Rabbit foot light. 2. Hit's a mighty fur ways up de far'well Lane.

627 Hearn, Lafcadio. "Ole Man Pickett." CINCINNATI ENQUIRER, 12 February 1875. Reprint in CHILDREN OF THE LEVEE. Edited by O. W. Frost. Lexington: University of Kentucky Press, 1957.

Short story includes discussion of black levee workers who danced to the music of a black band, and of the band leader who called sets for the dance.

628 _____. "Black Varieties/The Minstrels of the Row." CINCINNATI COMMERCIAL, 9 April 1876. Reprint in CHILDREN OF THE LEVEE. Edited by O. W. Frost. Lexington: University of Kentucky Press, 1957, 84-90.

Description of the dancing of blacks at a local waterfront tavern in Cincinnati includes discussion of the performance practice of a local tambourinist and refers to other instrumental music.

References to 2 dances: 1. Break-down. 2. Jig.

629 _____. "Banjo Jim's Story." CINCINNATI COMMERCIAL, 1 October 1876. Reprint. CHILDREN OF THE LEVEE. Edited by O. W. Frost. Lexington: University of Kentucky Press, 1957: 23-31.

This short story centers on the superstitions about death held by blacks who worked on the levee at Cincinnati, Ohio, and notes especially the mysterious death of one of the locals, a roustabout, who played banjo. Observation that music for dances was provided by bass viols, banjos, and fiddles.

Text of 1 couplet: Ole Joe kickin' up ahind an' afore.

630 Herz, Henri. MY TRAVELS IN AMERICA. Originally published as MES VOYAGES EN AMERIQUE. Paris: Achille Faure, 1866. Translated by Henry Bertram Hill. Madison: State Historical Society of Wisconsin, 1963. 102 pp.

European concert pianist, who traveled in America from Boston to New Orleans during the years 1846-1851, includes in his account a long, detailed discussion of the banjo, of the rhythm of slave music, and of dancing (75-77).

631 Holdern, Joseph Bassett. "Along the Florida Reef---Fourth Paper." HARPER'S NEW MONTHLY MAGAZINE 42 (May 1871): 820-30.

Fourth in a series of descriptions of travel in Florida by an naturalist includes discussion of a black minstrel show that he attended. Observation that the personnel consisted of "real plantation darkies," that one performer from Texas played the conch shell with great virtuosity, and that another danced the jig.

632 Howell, George Rogers. BI-CENTENNIAL HISTORY OF ALBANY. HISTORY OF THE COUNTY OF ALBANY, NEW YORK, FROM 1609 TO 1886. New York: W. Munsell & Company, 1886. 997 pp.

The chapter entitled "Colored People of Albany" includes a description of Pinkster celebrations (725-26). This seems to be a reprint of the description given by Eights, which was originally published in 1857 (see no. 649).

633 Hughes, Rupert. "A Eulogy of Ragtime." MUSICAL RECORD (BOSTON) 447 (1 April 1899): 157-59.

Discussion of Negro popular songs and dances at the turn of the century states that Negroes call their clog-dancing "ragging" and the dance itself, "ragtime." Description of a rag-dance performed to accompaniment of the banjo, and discussion of the character of the music.

634 Humphreys, Mary Gay. CATHERINE SCHUYLER. Women of Colonial and Revolutionary War Times Series. New York: Charles Scribner's Sons, 1897. 251 pp.

Biography of Catherine Schuyler, wife of Philip Schuyler, Revolutionary War general, contains a description of a Pinkster Day celebration in colonial New York (39).

635 Hutton, Lawrence. "The Negro on the Stage."

HARPER'S NEW MONTHLY MAGAZINE 79 (June-November 1889): 131-45.

Discussion of the various stories that purport to pinpoint the origin of Jim Crow and of the original Jim Crow song as sung by the stable-hand Jim Crow (137-38). Also discussion of the instruments played on the plantation and comment on the making of a banjo (145).

Text of 1 chorus: Wheel about, turn about, Do jis so.

636 "In Dixie, by a Confederate Staff Officer." BENTLEY'S MISCELLANY 63 (1868): 638-62.

Article focusing upon the war activities of a Confederate officer during the autumn of 1864 contains a description of his visit to a plantation near Richmond, Virginia. References to the slaves dancing and singing on the plantation on Saturday evenings.

637 Ingersoll, Ernest. "The City of Atlanta." HARPER'S NEW MONTHLY MAGAZINE 60 (December 1879): 30-43.

Naturalist, in an historical account and travel sketch of Atlanta, Georgia, during the Reconstruction era, discusses the black community, noting the music produced by a "string band" of five black laborers, and the guitar and banjo music of another group of freedmen. Also references to a black-face minstrel show staged by black performers.

638 Ingraham, Joseph Holt [Kate Conyngham, pseud]. NOT "A FOOL'S ERRAND." LIFE AND EXPERIENCE OF A NORTHERN GOVERNESS IN THE SUNNY SOUTH. New York: G. W. Carleton & Company, 1880. 526 pp.

A series of fictional letters about life in the antebellum South includes description of slave children dancing to the music of an improvised plantation band composed of a violin, banjo, and folk-crafted drum (105-9). Describes construction of the drum. References to a "corn dance" and songs (107).

639 "Is the Coon Craze Dying Out?" NEW YORK DRAMATIC MIRROR (12 November 1898): 19.

Discussion of the coon songs and ragtime music that have been taken to the stage by vaudevillians.

640 Jay, Hamilton. "Music among the Negroes." MUSICAL RECORD (Boston), no. 263 (December 1883): 8.

Florida correspondent of the NEW YORK SUN offers comment on the blacks marching on Saturdays to music provided by drums, and describes a folk-crafted drum made from an empty nail keg and coon skin. Also comment on secular singing, and description of a revival service: mourners, exhortations, prayers, singing accompanied by hand clapping, stamping feet, swaying of bodies in time to music.

Texts of 2 songs: 1. De rabbit am a cunnin' ting (Cho: Big-eyed rabbit, boo!). 2. I'se got on de back ob de Mefodis mule (Cho: An' I'll ride right on to glory!).

641 Knox, George L. "Origin of the Cakewalk." FREEMAN 9 (27 November 1897): [3].

Black editor of this Afro-American newspaper of Indianapolis, Indiana, states the origin of the cakewalk to have been a plantation festival among French blacks in the South during the 1790s. Observes that the festival was popular as a wooing event in instances where slaves were not able to get a licensed preacher to marry them.

642 Larison, Cornelius Wilson, ed. SILVIA DUBOIS (NOW 116 YEARS OLD): A BIOGRAPHY OF THE SLAV WHO WHIPT HER MISTRES AND GAND HER FREDOM [sic]. Ringos, NJ: C. W. Larison, 1883. Reprint. New York: Negro Universities Press, 1969. 124 pp.

Narrative of a ex-slave (born c. 1768 in New Jersey) states that New Year's Day, Easter, the Fourth of July, and General Training Day (i.e., Militia Day) were popular slave holidays in the North (66-67). Reference to dancing to the accompaniment of a fiddle (53, 67).

643 Lodge, William C. "Among the Peaches." HARPER'S NEW MONTHLY MAGAZINE 41 (September 1870): 511-18.

Description of visits to peach orchards along the Delaware-Chesapeake Bay includes references to the after-dinner ball of black workers on a farm in Kenton, Kent County (Delaware). Description of the six-piece band of worker-musicians, composed of two fiddlers and four brass players and the dancing of the blacks.

644 Macon, John Alfred. UNCLE GABE TUCKER; OR, REFLECTION, SONG, AND SENTIMENT IN THE QUARTERS. Philadelphia: J. B. Lippincott, 1883. 181 pp. Reprint. Ann Arbor: University Microfilms International, n.d.

One of the prominent white southern writers who worked Negro themes into their literature, Macon is represented here with a miscellaneous collection of verses and tales about plantation life written in Afro-American dialect. References to folk traditions: to dances such as the pigdin-wing, stomp, double-shuffle, gra'-vine-twis (79-80); to corn-shuckings (73-75, 95); to the banjo and fiddle (49, 95); to worksongs (104, 124), to animal tales (117-123). Also description of religious services (108-109). Some quotation of genuine slave-song refrains in the rhymes and use of imagery associated with the slave songs and the black folk sermon.

645 Malet, William Wyndham. AN ERRAND TO THE SOUTH IN THE SUMMER OF 1862. London: Richard Bentley, 1863. 312 pp.

Brief description of the informal religious services held in cabins on the plantations (49); also comment on the use of fiddles, tambourines, or banjoes as accompaniment for dancing.

Text of 1 song: The Jews killed my Jesus (Cho: Hallelujah) (114).

646 Mallard, Ralph Quarterman. PLANTATION LIFE BEFORE EMANCIPATION. Richmond, VA: Whittel & Shepperson, 1892. Reprint. Detroit: Negro History Press, c.1969. 237 pp.

Methodist minister and missionary to the slaves, Mallard includes in his book description of slaves flailing rice with the accompaniment of improvised songs (21-22); references to a worship service "in the edge of the forest" (89), and to a funeral service (189); and to slaves dancing the "Ethiopian jig" to the music of fiddles and "quaw sticks" (162). Two folk tales are reprinted from Charles C. Jones, NEGRO MYTHS FROM THE GEORGIA COAST.... (See no. 1451).

Texts of 2 tales: 1. Buh Squirle and Buh Fox. 2. Buh Wolf, Buh Rabbit, an de Tar Baby. Text of 1 song: My brother, you promised Jesus (R: Oh, I wish I was there (163).

647 Mayer, Francis Blackwell. "Aunt Eve Interviewed." HARPER'S NEW MONTHLY MAGAZINE 46 (March 1873): 509-17.

Short story about the reminiscences of an old woman of Guinean ancestry who was a slave in Baltimore, Maryland, following the Revolutionary War. Also references to fiddlers who performed in Annapolis.

Texts of 2 dance-songs: 1. I was drunk last night (Cho: Hi dompty, dompty). 2. Where did ye come from? I come from Virginny.

648 Munroe, Kirk. "A Southern Convict Camp." INDEPENDENT 36 (28 August 1884): 1094.

Discussion of life in a state convict camp in Florida includes description of an impromptu minstrel show staged by black convicts for the entertainment of white visitors. Musical accompaniment for the dancing was provided by the chains the prisoners wore around their legs, and by a quartet of whistlers and several "patters." The dancing was followed by the singing of duets and choruses, most of which were authentic slave songs performed in "plantation style."

649 Munsell, Joel. COLLECTIONS ON THE HISTORY OF ALBANY, FROM ITS DISCOVERY TO THE PRESENT TIME. With Notices of Its Public Institutions and Biographical Sketches of Citizens Deceased. Albany, NY: J. Munsell, 1865-71. 4 vols. Reprint of selected passages in READINGS IN BLACK AMERICAN MUSIC. Edited by Eileen Southern. 2d ed. New York: W. W. Norton, 1983.

Volume 2 includes two detailed descriptions of the celebration of Pinkster festivities in Albany, New York: "Albany Fifty Years Ago" (56) and "Pinkster Festivities in Albany Sixty Years Ago" (323-27). The second of these descriptions ia s reprint of an article written by James Eights when he was eighty years old, (originally published in HARPER'S NEW MONTHLY MAGAZINE 14 [1857]). References to the African styles of dancing at the festival, to a home-made drum, to performance practice, and to "King Charley," native of Angola and leader of the dancing.

650 Murfree, William L. "How Uncle Gabe Saved the Levee." SCRIBNER'S MONTHLY 16 (October 1878): 848-57.

Short story about a flood in Mississippi by a senator from North Carolina includes description of "pattin' juba."

Text and music of 1 song: Little Billy Woodcock lib on de mountain. Text of 1 dance-song chorus: Juba dis an' juba dat, an' Juba 'round de kettle o' fat.

651 "Negro Love of Music." MUSICAL RECORD (Boston), no. 282 (July 1885): 9. Reprint. MUSICAL RECORD (Boston), no. 308 (September 1887): 9; no. 321 (October 1888): 2.

This Letter from Alabama, originally published in the PHILADELPHIA TIMES, contains a general discussion of black folk music and performance practice. Comment on the extempore songs at religious services, and on instrumental music, generally supplied on the plantation by banjoes and fiddles. References to the large brass and string bands of the blacks that are found in southern cities, and to blacks playing the harmonicon. Comment on the prohibition of church members from dancing and singing devil songs.

Reference to 1 dance tune, described as a galop: Dem jolly bredren.

652 "Night Amusement in the Confederate Camp." ILLUSTRATED LONDON NEWS 42 (10 January 1863): 44.

Discussion of camp life among soldiers in the Confederate Army during the Civil War includes comment on a slave who danced a break-down for the amusement of the camp. Observation that the onlookers beat time for him (40).

653 "A Noted Pennsylvania Prison." LESLIE'S ILLUSTRATED NEWSPAPER 56 (10 March 1883): 43.

Discussion of the Schuylkill Prison at Pottsville, Pennsylvania, includes the observation that "when the prisoners are gathered for their daily round of exercise...a couple of jolly Africans...sound the keynote with their banjos."

654 Offenbach, Jacques. ORPHEUS IN AMERICA. NOTES OF A TRAVELLING MUSICIAN.... Originally published as OFFENBACH EN AMERIQUE, NOTES D'UN MUSICIEN EN VOYAGE. Paris, 1877. Translations. New York: G. W. Carleton and Company, 1877. ORPHEUS IN AMERICA. OFFENBACH'S DIARY OF HIS JOURNEY TO THE NEW WORLD. Translated by Lander MacClintock. Bloomington: Indiana University Press, 1957.

Diary of the French composer, which he kept during his travels in the United States in 1876, includes references to black drummers playing on tom-toms at railway stations (136-38).

655 "Old-Time Fiddler." CHICAGO RECORD, 31 October 1893: 11.

Article refers to a "noted mulatto fiddler called Yallah Sam," who taught George Washington (later, president of the United States) as a boy to play the fiddle. Sam's favorite tune "still holds its popularity in the mountain country of the South," as of 1893.

Text of 1 song: Yaller Sam, he went a-hunting (Cho: Hoo-ah-hoo, Hoo-ah, hoo-ah).

656 "On Horseback." ATLANTIC MONTHLY 56 (October 1885): 540-54.

Description of the author's travels through the South includes discussion of a minstrel stage show in which "slaves of Wade Hampton" sang songs and played on the banjo and guitar.

Reference to 1 song: Mary's gone away wid de coon.

657 Page, Thomas Nelson. SOCIAL LIFE IN OLD VIRGINIA BEFORE THE WAR. New York: G. Scribner's Sons, 1897. Reprint. Freeport, NY: Books for Libraries Press, 1970. 107 pp.

Virginia-born novelist's discussion of the plantation life of the slaves includes references to the singing of field hands, to corn-shucking and hog-killing festivals (28). Also discussion of the slave celebrations of Easter, Whit-Sunday, and Christmas (80), and of a slave wedding held during Christmas week (100).

658 Phillips, Henry. MUSICAL AND PERSONAL RECOLLECTIONS DURING A HALF CENTURY. London: Charles J. Skeet, 1864. 2 vols.

Autobiography of the English concert tenor, who toured the United States in 1844-1845, includes comment on the singing of a slave congregation in Macon, Georgia, and on their singing of secular songs to banjo accompaniment (2:165-66).

659 "Pictures of the South---Marriage of a Colored Soldier." HARPER'S WEEKLY 10 (30 June 1866): 411.

Description of the wedding of a black, Civil War veteran in the South includes description of the bridal supper, held out of doors, for which a band provided music. Special reference to the black fiddler.

660 Points, Marie L. "Henriette's Christmas: An Episode of the Olden Days." DAILY PICAYUNE 55 (27 December 1891): 20.

Fictional short story about plantation life near New Orleans during the antebellum period refers to slaves singing songs in the fields as they cut sugar cane, playing banjos and beating sticks upon an empty barrel as accompaniment to plantation songs, and holding dances that lasted far into the night.

661 Potts, William John. "Plantation Music." CRITIC 4 (5 January 1884): 8-9.

In a letter, dated 31 December 1883 from Camden, New Jersey, the author takes exception to Joel Chandler Harris's article about "Plantation Music" in the CRITIC (see no. 624). Asserts that banjo music was common on plantations in the antebellum South.

662 Prescott, Harriet E. "Down the River." ATLANTIC MONTHLY 16 (October 1865): 468-90.

Account of a young slave girl, Flor, who was the best dancer among the slaves on the plantation, includes discussion of her performance practice (468, 485).

Text of 1 song: Oh, no longer bond in Egypt.

663 Ralph, Julian. "The Plantation Negro." HARPER'S WEEKLY 37 (14 January 1893):38-39.

Journalist, writing about ex-slaves in the South after the Civil War, offers comment on the chanting of boatmen along the Mississippi River and describes the Afro-American contredance, which is compared to the Virginia reel except it uses a "jig" step.

664 _____. "The Old Way to Dixie." HARPER'S NEW MONTHLY MAGAZINE 86 (January 1893):165.

Narrative of the journalist's trip down the Mississippi River from St. Louis to New Orleans includes comment on the singing of black stevedores and on a workman playing the "jew's harp."

665 Robinson, Nina Hill. AUNT DICE: THE STORY OF A FAITHFUL SLAVE. Nashville, TN: Methodist Episcopal Church, South, 1897. 144 pp.

Slaveholder recounts the life story of a family slave, Aunt Dice, who joined the family on their plantation near Nashville in 1834 when she was thirty-four years old. References to the fiddle, banjo, "flute-like canes," and "ringing clevis pins" (16, 25); description of a corn-shucking (30-39). Observation on the dearth of old-time melodies in Nashville (91).

Texts of 3 songs: 1. The mo' I pray the happier I am (17). 2. Th'ow it up, shuck it up (33). 3. Work away, boys, heave ho (34). Text of 1 couplet: Possum up a gum stump, coon up a holler (91).

666 Robinson, T. L. "The Coloured People in the United States: In the South." LEISURE HOUR 38 (1889): 54-59.

Essay focuses upon social conditions and customs particularly in Alabama. Discussion of sacred songs, including a rare description of "beating Juba" (or "Jubilee") to accompany hymn singing. Comment on camp meetings and description of the shout. Also discussion of instrumental music---the use of fiddles and banjos on plantations, the commonness of brass-and-string bands in large cities---and description of the cakewalk.

667 "Scenes at the South." LESLIE'S ILLUSTRATED NEWSPAPER 56 (3 March 1883): 29-30.

Discussion of the charms of Florida during the winter season includes description of the fog which often comes up on the St. John's River at night: "If a fog comes up...the powerful note of the fog-horn makes its way through the mists, and guides the pilot to the point where a youthful African toils at the warning instrument."

668 Seawell, Molly Elliot. "Tubal the Fiddler." HARPER'S WEEKLY 33 (10 August 1889): 642-43.

Novelist-playwright, in a fictional short story about life on an antebellum southern plantation, refers to a superstition that blacks believe the devil was a fiddler.

References to 2 songs: 1. Roll, Jordan, roll. 2. Dem golden slippers. References to 3 dances: 1. Back-step. 2. Double-shuffle. 3 Pigeon-wing.

669 Shelton, Jane de Forest. "The New England Negro: A Remnant." HARPER'S NEW MONTHLY MAGAZINE 88 (March 1894): 533-38.

General discussion of the life, customs, and social conditions of early Africans in colonial New England includes a description of 'Lection Day celebrations in Connecticut, including references to the use of fifes and drums for the parade, the "election sermon," and the supper that followed the ball. Excerpt of a letter from a "black governor," dated 11 May 1766, Hartford.

670 Sheppard, William Ludlow. "Shedrick the Fiddler." HARPER'S WEEKLY 31 (26 November 1887): 853-54.

Short story about the black fiddler Shedrick and the German violinist Steinmarck, a member of a concert troupe that was touring in the United States. The two men perform for each other, and Shedrick dances the pigeon-wing to the music of "Sugar in de Gode," played by Steinmarck.

671 Slade, Daniel Denison. "A New England Country Gentleman in the Last Century." NEW ENGLAND MAGAZINE n.s. 2 (March 1890): 3-20.

Historical account of the town of Harvard, Massachusetts, focuses upon Henry Bromfield, an eighteenth-century resident. Discussion of Bromfield's black servant, Othello, a fiddler, who was brought from Africa to the United States as a slave about 1760 and who died in 1813.

672 Smalley, Eugene V. "Sugar-Making in Louisiana." CENTURY MAGAZINE 35 (November 1887): 100-120.

Discussion of the sugar industry in South and the various methods of sugar making includes description of a music-and-dance scene witnessed by the author while he was visiting a supply store on the Belair plantation in Louisiana. Notes that the accordion, fiddle, and triangle were played to accompany the contestants competing in dancing the "double shuffle" and the "heel-and-toe."

673 Smedes, Susan Dabney. A SOUTHERN PLANTER. New York: James Pott & Company, 1890. 342 pp. Also published MEMORIALS OF A SOUTHERN PLANTER (1887).

Southern-born author describes plantation life in Mississippi during the antebellum period. Chapter 12, entitled "Holiday Times on the Plantation," includes discussion of the music of the slaves, and their dancing to the accompaniment of fiddles and banjos (161-64). Observation that these celebrations were discontinued after the whole plantation joined the Baptist Church. Comment on the festive occasion of hog-killing on the plantation, and on the songs accompanying the semi-monthly chore of corn-shelling in preparation for Saturday's grinding.

674 Smith, Harry. FIFTY YEARS OF SLAVERY IN THE UNITED STATES OF AMERICA. Grand Rapids, Michigan: West Michigan Printing Company, 1891. 183 pp. Reprint. Louisville, KY: Lost Cause Press, 1957.

Narrative of ex-slave Smith (b. 1814) contains references to preachers and praying in the slave quarters at night, and to dancing to the music of fiddles and pattin' (38). Cites festivities that accompanied a slave corn-husking festival, including dancing and wrestling (62). Comment on a former slave living in the North who sang old plantation songs and told tales of plantation possum and coon hunts (173).

675 Smith, Zachary Frederick. THE HISTORY OF KENTUCKY. FROM ITS EARLIEST DISCOVERY AND

SETTLEMENT TO THE PRESENT DATE.... Louisville, KY: Courier-Journal Job Printing Company, 1886. 824 pp.

Discussion of the first Christmas celebration at the Falls of Ohio (later named Louisville) in 1778 includes reference to the black fiddler Cato and the white company dancing black dances: jigs, hoe-downs, shuffles, and pigeon-wings (120-24).

676 "A Southern Barbecue." HARPER'S WEEKLY 31 (9 July 1887): 487.

Description of a barbecue given by blacks in the South includes discussion of the entertainment that followed, with music provided by a fiddler, accordionist, and a player on a set of bones. References to dancing.

677 "Southern Sketches---II." APPLETON'S JOURNAL OF POPULAR LITERATURE, SCIENCE, AND ART 4 (9 July 1870): 44-45.

Description of a dancing lesson. References to 2 dances: 1. Breakdown. 2. Double-twister.

678 Steiner, Bernard C. "History of Slavery in Connecticut." JOHNS HOPKINS UNIVERSITY STUDIES IN HISTORICAL AND POLITICAL SCIENCE SERIES 11/9-10 (September-October 1893): 7-84.

Discussion of the election of "black governors" in colonial Connecticut includes description of the 'Lection Day parade, where music was provided by "fifes, fiddles, clarionets, and sundry metal objects" (79).

679 Strother, David Hunter [Porte Crayon, pseud.]. "The Young Virginians." RIVERSIDE MAGAZINE FOR YOUNG PEOPLE 2 (June 1868): 261-67.

Serialized novel of Virginia-born artist/illustrator discusses life in antebellum Virginia. Chapter 4 includes discussion of a mock tournament, described as a favorite pastime of white children, where the instrumental music was performed by a slave orchestra consisting of two fiddles, fife, tambourine, and bones, led by the famous black fiddler Old Nace Coleman.

680 Stroyer, Jacob. SKETCHES OF MY LIFE IN THE SOUTH. Salem, MA: Salem Press, 1879. 51 pp. Reprints in MY LIFE IN THE SOUTH. Salem: Newcomb & Gauss, 1893. 100 pp. FIVE SLAVE NARRATIVES.... New York: Arno Press and the New York Times, 1968.

Narrative of ex-slave Stroyer, born 1849 near Columbia, South Carolina, includes description of Christmas festivities that lasted five or six days (44-46). Dancing, singing African songs, and story-telling about customs in Africa took place. The master hired fiddlers if no one on the plantation was a fiddler. Comment on fiddle playing, banjo picking, and dancing (41).

Text of 1 song: When we all meet in heaven (Cho: There is no parting there) (41).

681 Stuart, Ruth McEnery. A GOLDEN WEDDING AND OTHER TALES. New York: Harper & Brothers, 1893. 366 pp.

This collection of thirteen stories about life in the South during the antebellum and post-Civil War periods includes nine accounts of slave lifestyles. Most of the tales are set in rural Louisiana on plantations, or in New Orleans. References to wedding rites, including a wedding sermon (31); to dances---"double twis'," "cutting the pigeon wing" (55)---and description of dancing (135-38); to funeral rites (95-96); and singing performance practice (255-56).

Text of 1 song: Dey's a star in de eas' on a Chris'mus morn (135).

682 _____. "Apollo Belvedere: A Christmas Episode on the Plantation." HARPER'S NEW MONTHLY MAGAZINE 96 (December 1897): 155-58.

Fictional short story about Christmas Eve celebrations of the blacks on a southern plantation include comment on the annual dance held in the sugar-hall and on a black fiddler.

683 _____. "Thanksgiving on Crawfish Bayou." SATURDAY EVENING POST 172 (25 November 1899): 424-26.

Fictional short story about a Thanksgiving Day celebration of ex-slaves during the Reconstruction Era includes description of an impromptu dance in which some participants imitated woodwind instruments with their voices and drummed on a table with forks to provide musical accompaniment for the dance.

684 Tabb, John B. "The Banjo Controversy." CRITIC 2 (9 August 1884): 65.

Letter to the Editor in reference to the controversy over whether the banjo was the most popular plantation instrument includes the observation: "the habits and dialects of the Southern negro differed in different parts of the land." In some places the banjo was the "Negro's instrument"; in other places, the fiddle was most popular, and banjos were unknown.

685 "Terpsichore in the Flat Creek Quarters." SCRIBNER'S MONTHLY 21 (February 1881): 488.

Narrative in the form of a composed poem accompanies an illustration and describes a dance scene. A caller shouts "de figgers" for dancers: "All go forrard to de center! Balance roun' an' den go back!" A narrator describes the dance movements: "now look at dat limber Jonah tryin' to tech de fancy fling!"

References to 3 dance steps: 1. Stomp 2. Double shuffle. 3. Pidgin-wing.

686 Thomas, James. FROM TENNESSEE SLAVE TO ST. LOUIS ENTREPRENEUR: THE AUTOBIOGRAPHY OF JAMES THOMAS. Edited by Loren Schweninger. Columbia: University of Missouri Press, 1984. 225 pp.

Narrative of ex-slave Thomas (1827-1913), written during the 1890s, focuses on slave life in Nashville, Tennessee, during the 1840s (58-72). Comment on the Christmas celebrations of the slaves, the auctioning of slaves on New Year's Day, and the local African church. Also references to blacks dancing to the music of fiddles, and to the new dances improvised by some of them. Discussion in Chapter 6 (104-120), of life along the Mississippi River, with comment on the dancing on Sundays at the Place Congo in New Orleans, which the author witnessed during the 1840s (109).

687 Thompson, Maurice. "Plantation Music." CRITIC 4 (12 January 1884): 20.

Discussion of three musical instruments commonly used by slaves on plantations in Georgia and Alabama: banjo, violin, and reed pipe (a type of pan-pipes). Description of how instruments are made, of performance practice, and of the occasions when the instruments were used. The banjo is associated with the "jubah dance"; the banjo and reed-pipe are used in ensemble with boat songs.

688 "Touching the Popular Heart." MUSICAL RECORD 1 (4 January 1879): 211.

Reprint from the VIRGINIA CHRONICLE (of Nevada) refers to a black street singer and his worn banjo, which he had made of "stained sheepskin" and catgut.

689 "A True Story of Texas Life Written...by a Detective." NEW YORK CLIPPER 20 (11 January 1873): 324.

Description of the writer's visit to the town of Heame, Robert County, Texas, on a Saturday evening during April 1871 contains discussion of the activities at the local black bar and ballroom, including references to the shuffle dancing of "plantation types" to the music of two brass instruments and a small fiddle.

690 Twain, Mark, and Charles Dudley Warner. THE GILDED AGE. A TALE OF TODAY. Hartford: American Publishing Company, 1892. 574 pp.

Discussion of black folk includes a quotation from the prayer of a frightened slave (37) and comment on two small boys "breaking down a juba in approved style" (157).

691 Tyson, Bryan. THE INSTITUTION OF SLAVERY IN THE SOUTHERN STATES, RELIGIOUSLY AND MORALLY CONSIDERED IN CONNECTION WITH OUR SECTIONAL TROUBLES. Washington, DC: H. Polkinhorn, 1863. 60 pp.

Comment on slaves in North Carolina dancing after supper to music of the banjo (12). Reference to a funeral sermon preached by Ralph Freeman, an ex-slave native of Moore County, North Carolina (27-28).

692 Viele, Egbert T. "The Knickerbockers of New York Two Centuries Ago." HARPER'S NEW MONTHLY MAGAZINE 54 (December 1876): 33-43.

History of the Knickerbocker family in colonial New York, written by an army general, includes discussion of the family slaves, who were emancipated by state law in 1827. Reference to dancing and the telling of ghost tales in the slave quarters.

693 "A Virginia Tobacco Mart." HARPER'S WEEKLY 23 (3 May 1879): 345.

Discussion of scenes at a tobacco mart in Lynchburg, Virginia, includes remarks about a young black trumpeter named Gabriel, who executed a fanfare on his tin horn to announce the beginning of "the breaks" (i.e., tobacco auction).

694 Wallaschek, Richard. PRIMITIVE MUSIC. AN INQUIRY INTO THE ORIGIN AND DEVELOPMENT OF MUSIC, SONGS, INSTRUMENTS, DANCES, AND PANTOMIMES OF SAVAGE RACES. London: Longmans, Green and Company, 1893. 326 pp.

Although the author had little personal contact with so-called primitive peoples, he used reliable primary sources as bases for his arguments. Brief discussion of black-American music (60-61) and of the use of a long brass tube as a musical instrument (73). Extensive discussion of African musical culture and practices, of which many aspects relate directly to black traditions in the United States.

695 "Wandering Minstrels on Harlem Lane." FRANK LESLIE'S ILLUSTRATED NEWSPAPER 34/862 (6 April 1872): 60-61.

Discussion of the black street musicians who, in groups of four or five, traveled over the nation giving impromptu, informal concerts in barrooms, hotels, and restaurants of such large cities, as Boston, Washington, D. C., St. Louis, Charleston, and New Orleans. Playing instruments such as the flute, violin, banjo, and harmonica, they performed "the latest songs, stories, and fancy steps."

696 Washington, Ella B. "The Ebony Bridal." Parts 1, 2. FRANK LESLIE'S ILLUSTRATED NEWSPAPER 32 (19 August 1871): 388-90; (26 August 1871): 398-99.

Southern slaveholder offers detailed description of a slave wedding, beginning with the preliminaries when bride and bridegroom obtain the consent of their masters and following through to the end of the festivities, when the wedded pair enter their bedchamber after the wedding ball.

697 Webb, William. THE HISTORY OF WILLIAM WEBB, COMPOSED BY HIMSELF. Detroit: Egbert Hoekstra, Printer, 1873. 77 pp.

Slave narrative includes discussion of plantation life in the states of Mississippi and Kentucky. Reference to slaves walking approximately nine or ten miles to a Christmas ball and dancing all night (9).

698 Weise, Arthur James. HISTORY OF THE CITY OF TROY, FROM THE EXPULSION OF THE MOHEGAN INDIANS TO THE PRESENT CENTENNIAL YEAR OF THE INDEPENDENCE OF THE UNITED STATES OF AMERICA, 1876. Troy, NY: William H. Young, 1876. 400 pp.

Chapter 4, entitled "Manners and Customs of the People---1786 to 1800," refers to Pinkster Day as a favorite holiday of slaves in Troy, New York. Reference to King Charles, the slave master of ceremonies, who beat the drum and provided music for slave dancing. Description of the drum (62-63).

699 Wentworth, N. C. "The Year before the War." ZION'S HERALD 53 (29 June 1876): [201].

Northern school teacher's discussion of her visit in 1859 to Pine Grove, Virginia, during the period of John Brown's raid on Harper's Ferry, includes description of a slave corn-husking festival, which concluded with the singing of corn songs and a march. Reference to blacks singing in their own "peculiar monotone."

Text of 1 song: Far-well! far-well! These rocks and these trees all seem to say, far-well, far-well!

700 Whipple, Wade. "Jim, the Ferry Boy." HARPER'S YOUNG PEOPLE: AN ILLUSTRATED WEEKLY 2 (9 August 1881): 647-48.

Short story about a black boy, Jim, who lived in Waterview, West Virginia. Jim worked as a ferry boat boy along the Great Kanawha River and played the violin for his own amusement.

701 Williams, Isaac D. SUNSHINE AND SHADOW OF SLAVE LIFE. REMINISCENCES AS TOLD BY ISAAC D. WILLIAMS TO "TEGE." East Saginaw, MI: Evening News Printing and Binding House, 1885. Reprint. New York: AMS Press, 1975. 91 pp.

Ex-slave "Uncle Ike" Williams (1821-98), offers comment on singing performance practice (16), on camp meetings, funerals and "buryings," and the weekly prayer meetings on the plantation (65-67). Also description of how slaves made banjos and fiddles and of slave dancing on Saturday nights, with special reference to the double-shuffle (61-62). Discussion of the kind of entertainment the slaves provided for their masters when "company" came.

702 Williams, Martha McCulloch. "Silk and Tassel." COSMOPOLITAN: A MONTHLY ILLUSTRATED MAGAZINE 15 (August 1893): 440-48.

Short story about a corn-husking festival, in which both young black and white males participated, includes description of the singing of corn-songs and performance practice.

Texts of 4 songs: 1. Birdeye lady, Sooner in de mornin'. 2. Oh, Miss Maria, I want to go to 'Ria. 3. Dram! Dram! Little drap er dram, sir! (Cho: Dram! Dram! Fetch erlong de dram). 4. Cyarve dat 'possum!

703 Wilson, Robert. "At the Old Plantation. Two Papers---II." LIPPINCOTT'S MAGAZINE 17 (February 1876): 241-48.

Comment on a visit to a South Carolina plantation during the antebellum era includes description of a slave Christmas Eve celebration and the music of a fiddler and a "triangle player."

704 Woods, Henry C. "A Southern Corn-Shucking." APPLETON'S JOURNAL OF POPULAR LITERATURE, SCIENCE, AND ART 4 (12 November 1870): 571.

Description of a southern corn-husking festival witnessed by the author during the 1860s on a plantation in the South. Discussion of songs sung by blacks during a corn-husking contest and of relevant performance pratice. Also reference to the slaves dancing to the music of violin, banjo, and bones.

Texts of 2 corn-husking songs: 1. Here's your corn pile. 2. Obadiah jumped in the fire.

THE RELIGIOUS EXPERIENCE

705 A., S. J. "Louisiana Letter." CHRISTIAN WATCHMAN & REFLECTOR (=WATCHMAN-EXAMINER) 62 (7 April 1881): [2].

Discussion of events that occurred during the winter and early spring, 1881, in Leland, Louisiana, in regard to the baptism of thirteen converts at the Austerlitz Street (colored) Church.

706 "An African Missionary." SOUTHERN CHRISTIAN ADVOCATE 29 (6 April 1866): n.p.

Account of a visit to the South by Henry M. Turner, a minister of the A. M. E. Church, includes references to his rude reception at a black church in Montgomery, Alabama, and discusses a sermon on "Love thy neighbor" delivered there by a exhorter of that congregation.

707 Albert, Octavia Victoria Rogers. THE HOUSE OF BONDAGE; OR, CHARLOTTE BROOKS AND OTHER SLAVES. New York: Hunt & Eaton, 1891. 161 pp. First published as a serial in the SOUTHWESTERN CHRISTIAN ADVOCATE under the title "House of Bondage."

Written by a black woman (b. 1853), who was a minister's wife and a teacher, the book includes interviews of Aunt Charlotte and other ex-slaves. Description of the slaves singing in Virginia cane fields (5) and of secret prayer meetings held in cabins, where a washtub full of water was put in the middle of the floor to muffle the singing of hymns (11-12).

Reference to 2 songs: 1. O, where are the Hebrew children? (6), 2. Old ship of Zion. Texts of 4 songs: 1. In the valley there's a mighty cry to Jesus (26). 2. My God delivered Daniel (31). 3. O brother, where was you when the Lord came passing by (32). 4. In the morning when I rise (Cho: Give me Jesus (93).

708 Allen, William Francis. [Marcel, pseud.]. "Correspondence: Negro Dialect." NATION 1/24 (14 December 1865): 744-45.

Essay on Negro dialect heard on the plantations of the Sea Islands includes a description of the shout, with the observation that sometimes it was performed backwards, that is, in clock-wise movement.

Texts of 10 spirituals; texts of 2 couplets. See SONG COLLECTIONS (no. 1735).

709 Allston, Robert F. W. THE SOUTH CAROLINA RICE PLANTATION AS REVEALED IN THE PAPERS OF ROBERT F. W. ALLSTON. Edited by James H. Easterby. Chicago: University of Chicago Press, 1945. 478 pp.

The papers, dating from 1809 to 1896, include excerpts from the diaries of Allston's wife and daughter. Discussion of Christmas as a particular time for feasting and enjoyment on the plantation (347-48). Observation that a large number of the slaves were Methodist, and that religious services were held for the slaves "one a day on nearly every Sabbath in the year" (349).

710 American Freedmen's Inquiry Commission. "Negroes as Refugees---District of Columbia, Eastern Virginia, and North Carolina." ZION'S HERALD AND WESLEYAN JOURNAL 35 (19 August 1863): [129].

Excerpt of a report to the U. S. Secretary of War from the American Freedmen's Inquiry Commission focuses upon the social and economic impact of slavery on the freedmen. Comment on the songs of the South Carolina slaves as being of "plaintive, despondent, and religious nature."

711 _____. "Letter from Col. J. Alexander, Alabama Infantry C. Troop," dated District of Corinth, 1 September 1863. MS. Houghton Library. Harvard University, Cambridge, MA. 19 pp.

The Letter, dated September 1863 from a Command Post near the District of Corinth, discusses the condition of the contraband slaves and comments on their religious disposition, superstitions, and beliefs in dreams and visions (10-11).

712 _____. "Abstract of Mr. Eaton's Report (c.1863)." Manuscript. Houghton Library. Harvard University, Cambridge, MA. 12 pp.

References to religious rituals of the contrabands with comment on the singing, shouting of hallelujahs, and "great religious display" (8).

713 "American Negro Hymns." MUSICAL WORLD 63 (17 July 1886): 461-62.

Discussion of Afro-American religious songs, relevant performance practice, and voice quality. Texts of 11 songs. See SONG COLLECTIONS (no. 1737).

714 "THE AMERICANS AT HOME, by David Macrae." Unsigned book review. AMERICAN MISSIONARY (MAGAZINE) n.s. 14 (September 1870): 211-22.

Reviewer of Macrae's book (see no. 909) discusses oddities in black worship. Observation that much of the imagery in folk prayers was drawn from the slaves' experiences during slavery.

715 Anderson, Robert. THE LIFE OF REV. ROBERT ANDERSON. Born the 22nd Day of February, in the Year of Our Lord 1819, and Joined the Methodist Episcopal Church in 1839. This Book Shall Be Called The Young Men's Guide, or The Brother in White. Macon, GA: J. W. Burke, 1891. 116 pp. Reprint. Atlanta: Foote & Davies Company, 1900. 229 pp.

Ex-slave Anderson (born 1819 in Liberty City, Georgia) earned money as a "hired-out" slave, bought his freedom, and later became a Methodist Episcopal preacher. Comment on religious services on the plantation (61) and to a sermon given by black minister Rev. Rubin Kinlaw (227-29).

Text of 1 sermon: Origin of the white man; Adam and Eve in the Garden of Eden.

716 Andrews, Eliza Frances. THE WAR-TIME JOURNAL OF A GEORGIA GIRL, 1864-1865. New York: D. Appleton & Company, 1908. 387 pp.

Diary includes discussion of the slaves singing

in the plantation "praise house" and relevant performance practice (89-91).

Texts of 3 "speritual" songs: 1. Mary an' Marthy, feed my lambs. 2. I meet my soul at de bar of God (Cho: Run home, believer). 3. King Jesus he tell you (Cho: Christ was born on Chris'mus day). Text of 1 couplet: I knowed it was a angel.

717 Andrews, Garnett. REMINISCENCES OF AN OLD GEORGIA LAWYER. Atlanta: Franklin Steam Printing House, 1870. 104 pp.

Autobiography of a judge of the Georgia Superior Courts includes discussion of the corn-shucking festivals that he witnessed in the early nineteenth century as a child on his father's plantation (10-12). Also discussion of a black preacher's sermon on "original sin," with references to Adam and Eve and Nicodemus and Jesus. (97-98).

Text of 1 song: Did you ever hear the cow laugh? (Cho: Ha, hi, ho) (11). Excerpt of 1 sermon: Original Sin (97-98).

718 "Anecdote and Incidents of a Visit to Freedmen: II." FREEDMEN'S RECORD 1 (October 1865): 158-62.

Report prepared at the request of the Philadelphia branch of the Women's Aid Association describes a prayer meeting, including discussion of the preacher and his sermon and of performance practice associated with congregational singing. Also reference to the singing of children.

Text of 1 sermon: The Lord is my rock and my fortress.

719 Arrowood, Mary Dickson and Hamilton, T. F. "Notes and Queries: Nine Negro Spirituals, 1850-1861, from Lower South Carolina." JOURNAL OF AMERICAN FOLK-LORE 41 (October-December 1928): 579-84.

Discussion of the missionary activities of Presbyterian minister Andrew Flinn Dickson focuses on his work among the slaves and contrabands in South Carolina on James Island, in Orangeburg, and in Barnwell during the years 1858-65. Descriptions of the religious services, of congregational singing, the sermon, and Joe Hooks, the black preacher at Orangeburg.

Texts of 9 spirituals, one of which is identified as a boatman's song: Breddren, don't get weary. See SONG COLLECTIONS (no. 1735).

720 "At a Negro Camp-Meeting." ZION'S HERALD 75 (11 August 1897): 501.

This reprint from the NEW YORK TIMES describes a black camp-meeting service and discusses the singing of spirituals and their performance practice, the oratory style of the black preacher, and the vocal responses of his congregation.

Texts of 4 songs: 1. They crucified my Savior and nailed Him to the cross (Cho: He rose, He rose). 2. Oh, I'll be there when Gabriel blows his horn. 3. Roll, Jordan, roll. 4. Oh, how I love Jesus. Text of 1 sermon: The Love of God and His desire to save sinners.

721 Austin, Emily L. "Reminiscences of Work among the Freedmen." Parts 1, 2. SOUTHERN WORKMAN 26 (July 1897): 128-30; 27 (August 1897): 148-50.

Posthumously published memoirs of a white missionary who worked among the ex-slaves in Greenville, South Carolina, and Knoxville, Tennessee, refers to their folk song, prayers, and sermons. Discussion of Samuel, a black folk preacher of Greenville, and excerpts from two of his sermons.

Reference to 1 song: Oh, the chariot of the Lord (130). Excerpts of 2 sermons: 1. Abraham and Isaac (129). 2. Daniel in the lion's den (129).

722 Avon [pseud.]. "Our Washington Correspondent." NATIONAL ANTI-SLAVERY STANDARD 23 (10 January 1863): [3].

Letter, dated 4 January 1863, describes a grand prayer-meeting of contraband slaves held in Washington, D.C.

723 B. "Inside Southern Cabins. Georgia.---No. 1." HARPER'S WEEKLY 24 (13 November 1880): 733-34.

Discussion of a visit among former slaves in Georgia during the Reconstruction era refers to their practice of singing spirituals "sotto voce" in cabins during the antebellum period in order to hold prayer meetings undetected by the masters, and to performance practice associated with the songs.

Text of 1 couplet: Steal away to Jesus.

724 _____. "Inside Southern Cabins. II---Georgia." HARPER'S WEEKLY 24 (20 November 1880): 749-50.

Discussion of religious worship in Georgia includes description of the singing and performance practice associated with spirituals and ring-shout songs, of the holy dance, and the preaching. Reference to the "Amen Corner."

Texts of 2 songs: 1. When I was down in de Egypt land (Cho: Love, love for me). 2. Old Satan is a liar, and a conjurer too (Cho: Oh, my Lord). References to 2 sermons: 1. God raining down water in the wilderness. 2. God in the concatination of His wisdom caused the angels to swing rapidly around His throne.

725 _____. "Inside Southern Cabins. III---Charleston, South Carolina." HARPER'S WEEKLY 24 (27 November 1880): 765-66.

Travel memoir focuses upon the social conditions, work, and customs of the ex-slaves in Charleston, South Carolina. Discussion of street peddlers and of religious practices includes references to the shout and to a sermon.

Text of 1 street cry: Strawberries, superfine strawberries. Reference to 1 street cry and 1 shout-song: 1. Beans and potatoes. 2. Let us walk in the light of God. Reference to 1 sermon: David, the son of Jesse.

726 _____. "Inside Southern Cabins. IV.---Alabama, Agricultural Negroes." HARPER'S WEEKLY 24 (4 December 1880): 781-82.

Description of a visit among blacks in Alabama includes references to their music, and the observation that they did not break out in impromptu song as did blacks in the Carolinas and Georgia. Description of a church service in rural Alabama and the blowing of "long, tin horns" to gather together the congregation.

727 B., E. "General Howard, at Edisto Island, S. C." INDEPENDENT 17 (7 December 1865): 7.

Discussion of General Oliver Howard's visit to the Edisto Island contraband camp by one of the female teachers there includes a description of a church service of the freedmen.

References to 2 songs: 1. Wandering in the wilderness of sorrow and gloom, 2. Nobody knows the trouble I see.

728 B., F. W. "From Hilton Head: The Pioneer Negro Colony in South Carolina." LIBERATOR 35 (12 May 1865): 76.

Discussion of a visit to an experimental colony of freedmen in Mitchelville, South Carolina, includes a reprint of the charter of the self-governing body. Comment at length on the local church and description of a religious service held there, with special attention to "a plaintive hymn peculiar to plantation worship."

Text of 1 song: Simon Peter, feed my lambs (Cho: Sitting on the golden altar). Reference to 1 song: The day of Jubilee hab come.

729 B., H. H. "Reminiscences of a Southern Plantation." Parts 1, 2. INDEPENDENT 26 (16 April 1874): 13-14; (23 April 1874): 14-15.

Discussion of a visit to a cotton plantation in Georgia, during August 1831, refers to plantation slave preachers and traces the "calling to preach" of one of them. Description of the religious services of the ex-slaves, including a summary of one exhortation and comment on the singing of religious songs, as well as the "plaintive minor wail" of slaves as they work. References to making banjos from little gourds.

Text of 1 song: She have tuck her thousand ober.

730 Bacon, Alice Mabel. "Work and Methods of the Hampton Folk-Lore Society." JOURNAL OF AMERICAN FOLK-LORE 11 (January-March 1898): 17-21. Reprint. BLACK PERSPECTIVE IN MUSIC 4 (July 1976): 151-55.

This paper, read at the Ninth Annual Meeting of the American Folk-Lore Society, 29 December 1897, in Baltimore, reports on the ways Hampton gathered Negro folk materials. Discussion of transcription problems, of the importance of obtaining the "place and history" of each item as it is added to the collection. Comment on the "hag" stories, and on the "intoned" sermons and prayers of "nighthawks" (i.e., night preachers). Also discussion of religious-services practice.

731 Banks, Elizabeth L. "The American Negro and His Place." NINETEENTH CENTURY (London) 46 (September 1899): 459-74.

Discussion focuses upon racism and the color line in the United States during the late-nineteenth century. References to the distinctive qualities of black singing, preaching, and praying as a reason why blacks should not seek admittance to white churches.

Text of 1 song: If yo' want ter go ter heaben (463).

732 Barr, Lillie E. "Three Months on a Cotton Plantation." INDEPENDENT 33 (30 June 1881): 1-2; 33 (14 July 1881): 4-5.

Discussion of a visit to a cotton plantation on John's Island, South Carolina, includes comment on the social life and religious practices of blacks, and on the duties of the "church mother" in that community. Cites a curious practice associated with the funeral services for ordained ministers: black hoods are passed out to the mourners. Discussion of the various song-types of the blacks---boat songs, secular songs, spirituals, and funeral songs---and of relevant performance practice.

Texts of 11 songs. See SONG COLLECTIONS (no. 1739).

733 _____. "Negro Sayings and Superstitions." INDEPENDENT 35 (17 September 1883): 1222-23.

Discussion of superstitions and funeral practices on John's Island, South Carolina, includes references to the mourners gathering around a coffin, singing songs and clapping their hands, singing lively songs on their return from grave site, and relevant performance practice.

Text of 1 burial song: What de matter here? (Cho: Sister Martha done gone home).

734 Barron, Elwyn Alfred. "Shadowy Memories of Negro-Lore." FOLK-LORIST (Chicago) 1 (July 1892): 46-53.

Discussion of Negro superstitions includes description of a funeral "celebrated" for a woman who had died four years earlier.

735 Barton, William E. OLD PLANTATION HYMNS: A COLLECTION OF HITHERTO UNPUBLISHED MELODIES OF THE SLAVE AND THE FREEMAN, WITH HISTORICAL AND DESCRIPTIVE NOTES. Boston: Lamson, Wolffe & Company, 1899. Reprint. THE SOCIAL IMPLICATIONS OF EARLY NEGRO MUSIC IN THE UNITED STATES. Edited by Bernard Katz. New York: Arno Press and the New York Times, 1969.

This volume gathers together three song collections that Congregational minister Barton had published in NEW ENGLAND MAGAZINE in December 1898, January 1899, and February 1899. See nos. 736, 737, 738. The songs were gathered during the years 1880-1887. See SONG COLLECTIONS (no. 1740).

736 Barton, William Eleazar. "Old Plantation Hymns." NEW ENGLAND MAGAZINE n.s. 19/4 (December 1898): 443-56. Reprints. See no. 735

Description of the religious dance "Marching 'round Jericho" and comment on socio-religious aspects of the sacred music of black Christians in the South.

Texts and music of 27 songs; texts of 6 songs. See SONG COLLECTIONS (no. 1740)

737 _____. "Hymns of the Slave and the Freeman." NEW ENGLAND MAGAZINE n.s. 19/5 (January 1899): 609-24. Reprints. See no. 735.

Discussion of the theology and musical character of Negro religious songs and of the narratives that were collected from ex-slaves.

Texts and music of 27 songs; texts of 2 songs. See SONG COLLECTIONS (no. 1740).

738 _____. "Recent Negro Melodies." NEW ENGLAND MAGAZINE n.s.19/6 (February 1899): 707-19. Reprints. See no. 735.

Discussion of performance practice, song structure, and description of a Negro prayer-meeting service, including comment on the oratory style of the preacher and congregational responses.

Texts and music of 13 songs. See SONG COLLECTIONS (no. 1740).

739 Bassett, John Spencer. SLAVERY IN THE STATE OF NORTH CAROLINA. Johns Hopkins University Studies in Historical and Political Science, 17, nos. 7, 8. Baltimore: Johns Hopkins Press, 1899. 111 pp.

This historical account includes references to slave preachers, reputed to be active as early as 1773 at the Baptist Sandy Run Church in Bertie County, North Carolina (61). Among the preachers identified by name are folk preachers Henry Evans (d. 1810), Ralph Freeman, and John Charles (57-59). Also references to the slaves singing African songs.

740 Bates, Lizzie. "Religion on the Plantation." LADIES' REPOSITORY 25 (December 1865): 707-11.

Description of religious services witnessed by the author on a southern plantation during the fall of 1859 (place not indicated) includes discussion of a plantation slave preacher named Jackson. Comment on a wake for, and burial of a slave child.

741 Beach, Ida M. WORK AMONG THE COLORED PEOPLE OF THE SOUTH---A Paper Read at the Woman's Meeting of the American Missionary Association, October 31, 1883. New York: American Missionary Association, 1883. 4 pp.

Northern black school teacher working among ex-slaves in Savannah, Georgia, describes a revival prayer-meeting and discusses the sermons of local preachers.

References to texts of 2 sermons: 1. And he opened the bottomless pit and there arose smoke, 2. Pray without ceasing. Excerpt of 1 sermon text: Daniel in the lion's den.

742 Beecher, Henry Ward. "Henry Ward Beecher's Visit to South Carolina." LIBERATOR 35 (26 May 1865): 84. Reprinted from the INDEPENDENT, 11 May 1865.

Travel narrative of the minister's trip to South Carolina and his contact with freedmen includes discussion of the religious activities of blacks, their singing, and relevant performance practice.

Reference to 1 song: Roll, Jordan, roll.

743 Beecher, Thomas K. "Brother Anderson." SOUTHERN WORKMAN 23 (October 1894): 181.

Minister discusses the impromptu sermon of a black folk preacher, which was about St. Paul's Letter to the Corinthians, and which took its inspiration from the third stanza of a hymn lined-out by the congregation, "Let saints below in concert sing."

Text of 1 sermon: Let saints below in concert sing.

744 Bennett, H. S. "The Religion of the Negro." INDEPENDENT 27 (15 July 1875): 12-13.

Minister's discussion of the moral and religious life of blacks in the South acknowledges the existence of so-called "extravagances" in black worship services and states that the excellence of a preacher's sermon is measured by his ability to evoke vocal responses from his congregation. Comment on the fact that blacks take their religion seriously, sing their religious songs everywhere, and converse about religious matters wherever they meet.

745 Beyer, J. S. "Virginia Conference." ZION'S HERALD 54 (30 August 1877): 280.

Discussion of the progress of black Methodists in the Virginia Conference in a letter, dated 13 August 1877, includes a reference to prayer meetings held annually for two-week periods in Falls Church, Virginia. Observation that the songs heard at these meetings were mostly of a type sung by the Jubilee Singers, although the worshipers knew the old Methodist hymns and sang them at their regular services.

746 Bishop, Julia Truitt. "Easter Morn in a Colored Convent." LADIES HOME JOURNAL (April 1899): 10.

Detailed description of the voice quality of the black singers and relevant performance practice in a cathedral of New Orleans, Louisiana: "All the singers are women and they have brought to the song service the rich quality of the Negro voice, musical in its wildest state, and now trained to the most perfect melody. But the voices have also brought with them that pathetic touch which lingers around their gayest notes...."

747 Blacknall, O. W. "The New Departure in Negro Life." ATLANTIC MONTHLY 52 (November 1883): 680-85.

Discussion of the passing of the old folkways among former slaves in the South and the growing importance of religion and knowledge of the Bible for them. References to the decline in popularity of corn-shucking festivals, at which time blacks sang "weird" corn-shucking songs. Detailed description of a Baptist revival service and discussion of "negro preachers...larnt and unlarnt."

748 Boardman, Mary W. "Among the Southern Negroes." INDEPENDENT (New York) 31 (5 June 1879): 27.

Texts of a farewell sermon delivered by black preacher "Uncle Joe" (place not indicated), and of a prayer made by a small boy under punishment.

Text of 1 sermon: Darkness was over all the land.

749 Bolton, Henry Carrington. "Decoration of Graves of Negroes in South Carolina." JOURNAL OF AMERICAN FOLK-LORE 4 (July-September 1891): 214.

Discussion by a chemist, one of the founders of the American Folklore Society, of the decoration of the graves of blacks in Columbia, South Carolina (overlooking the Congaree River), with objects composed of oyster shells, broken crockery, glass, and bottles.

750 Botume, Elizabeth Hyde. FIRST DAYS AMONGST THE CONTRABANDS. Boston: Lee & Shepard Publishers, 1893. Reprint. New York: Arno Press and the New York Times, 1968. 286 pp.

Account of the author's experiences as a teacher in Beaufort, South Carolina, includes references to performance practice (73, 74, 135-136, 206, 256) and to funeral traditions (108, 222-23).

Texts of 7 choruses: 1. We must fight for liberty in that new Jerusalem (9, 76). 2. Roll, Jordan, roll (135). 3. Oh, believer, go ring that bell (135). 4. Nobody knows the trouble I feel (256). 5. I can't stay behind, my Lord (256). 6. Keep your lamps trimmed and burning (208). 7. I am bound for the land of Canaan (208).

751 Brackett, Anna C. "Charleston, South Carolina (1861)." HARPER'S NEW MONTHLY MAGAZINE 88 (May 1894): 941-50.

Educator of Massachusetts, who taught the school year 1860-1861 in Charleston, South Carolina, includes in her discussion of the city description of religious services where blacks and whites worshipped at the same church, the blacks sitting in segregated gallery pews. Observation that the blacks provided the only music at these services. Also references to their singing for Christmas Eve celebrations.

752 Bradford, Sarah. SCENES IN THE LIFE OF HARRIET TUBMAN. Auburn: W. J. Moses, 1869. 132 pp.

Biography of Tubman (c.1821-1913), the black abolitionist conductor of the Underground Railroad, includes discussion of the use of song as means of communication for slaves in South (16-19). Description in Tubman's own words of her use of spirituals and hymns as alerting songs and aids in helping the slaves to escape (26-27) and description of the shout (44).

Texts of 6 songs: 1. When dat ar old chariot comes (Cho: I'm gwine to lebe you) (17). 2. I'm sorry I'm gwine to lebe you (Cho: Farewell, oh farewell) (18). 3. I'll meet you in the mornin' (Cho: I'm bound for de promise land) (18). 4. Moses, go down in Egypt, tell ole Pharo' let my people go (27). 5. Glory to God and Jesus too (Cho: One more soul got safe) (34). 6. My sis'r Mary's bound to go (44). Text of 1 sermon: Funeral oration (43-44).

753 Bradford, Sarah. HARRIET TUBMAN, THE MOSES OF HER PEOPLE. 1869. 2d exp. ed. privately printed by Mrs. Bradford, 1886. 149 pp. Reprint. New York: Corinth Books, 1961.

Biography written "chiefly from Harriet's own recollections," of the ex-slave who led more than 300 slaves to freedom via the "underground railroad" includes an appendix which provides documentation in the form of letters from contemporaries. She communicated her plans to the slaves by singing songs which by "telling of the heavenly journey and the land of Canaan...conveyed to their brethren and sisters in bondage something more than met the ear" (27). Description of a funeral service (103-05).

Texts of 6 songs: 1. When dat ar ole chariot comes, I'm gwine to lebe you (28). 2. Oh, go down, Moses (37). 3. I'm sorry friends to lebe you (28). 4. I'm on the way to Canada (Cho: Farewell, ole Master, don't think hard of me) (49-50). 5. Glory to God and Jesus too (51). 6. My sis'r Mary's boun' to go (104). Excerpt of 1 sermon text: Prepare to lie dead (104).

754 Brine, C. L. "The Promised Prayer (A True Incident of the South)." NEW ENGLAND MAGAZINE 6 (March 1888): 264-65.

Narrative poem about the religious life of a slave on an antebellum plantation in the South, purportedly based upon a true incident.

Text of 1 song: Oh, yes, de ole religion am good enuff fer me.

755 Brooks, Esta. "Lowly Southern Life." CHRISTIAN WATCHMAN & REFLECTOR (=WATCHMAN-EXAMINER) 68 (10 March 1887): [6].

Discussion of a northerner's exposure to life among southern blacks includes references to a church service of colored Methodists, and comment on the "sing-song, quasi-unintelligible oratory" of black preachers. Also description of a church wedding service.

756 Brown, William Wells. THE NEGRO IN THE AMERICAN REBELLION. Boston: Lee & Shepard, 1867. 380 pp. Reprint. New York: The Citadel Press, 1971. 389 pp. Page references below are to the reprint edition.

Ex-slave author (1815-1884) offers a historical survey of the role of black soldiers and freedom fighters in the United States, from the Revolutionary War through the Civil War. Discussion includes description of a corn-husking festival (29-30); comment on the funeral of a black soldier and on black preachers and exhorters (133-35), and discussion of the religious services held on the eve of Emancipation, "the last night in December, 1862," in Boston, New York, Philadelphia, and at the Contraband Camp in Washington, D. C. (111-19).

Texts of 6 songs: 1. Oh, go down Moses, way down in Egypt's land (111). 2. If de debble do not ketch Jeff Davis (113). 3. Massa gone, Missy too, cry nigger, cry (Cho: Hi!Hi! Yankee shot 'im) (115). 4. Go down, Abraham, away down in Dixie's land (118). 5. De Lord, he make us free indeed (306). 6. We heard de proclamation (308). References to 2 songs: 1. I am a free man now (111). 2. Glory, glory, hallelujah (117).

757 _____. MY SOUTHERN HOME; OR, THE SOUTH AND ITS PEOPLE. Boston: A. G. Brown & Company, 1880. Reprint. Upper Saddle River, NJ: Gregg Press, 1968. 253 pp.

Insightful discussion of black life in the South includes comment on songs, street cries, dancing in New Orleans (121-23), and religious practices (68-69, 192-93, 203-07). Also discussion of the Rev. John Jasper and paraphrase of one of his sermons (205-207), De Sun Do Move.

Texts of 9 songs and 4 street cries. See SONG COLLECTIONS (no. 1741).

758 Bruce, Henry Clay. THE NEW MAN. TWENTY-NINE YEARS A SLAVE. TWENTY-NINE YEARS A FREE MAN.... York, PA: P. Anstadt & Sons, 1895. Reprint. Miami, FL: Mnemosyne Publishing Company, 1969. 176 pp.

Ex-slave Bruce (1836-1902), born in Prince Edward County, Maryland, was frequently "hired out" and consequently had a relatively independent life style. His autobiography, which pertains primarily to slavery in Missouri, includes discussion of black preachers (72-73) and description of a slave wedding (74).

759 Bryant, M. Winifred. "Negro Services." AMERICAN MISSIONARY (MAGAZINE) n.s. 46 (September 1892): 301-2.

Description of a Methodist Love Feast in the South includes comment on the ritual communion of bread and water, the singing of a religious folk song and its performance practice, and the sermon of the "illiterate" pastor.

Text of 1 song: I wish that heaven were mine (Cho: When I come to die I want to be ready). Summary of 1 sermon: And He will destroy in this mountain the face of the covering cast over all people (Isaiah 15:7).

760 Buel, James William. METROPOLITAN LIFE UNVEILED; OR THE MYSTERIES AND MISERIES OF AMERICA'S GREAT CITIES, EMBRACING NEW YORK, WASHINGTON CITY, SAN FRANCISCO, SALT LAKE CITY, AND NEW ORLEANS. St. Louis, MO: Historical Publishing Company, 1882. 600 pp.

Journalist's account includes chapters on "Negro Life and Superstitions" in the section about New Orleans (497-606). Discussion of author's visit to a revival meeting, with quotations from the sermon given by the black preacher (501-09), and to a voodoo ceremony in an abandoned brick yard (520-29). Also description of dancing (514-16) and the calinda (528), of instrumental performance practice associated with voodoo ceremonies---the use of drums, bones, calabash or rattle, tom-tom, and banjo (524-25, 529)--and performance practice associated with songs (532-35). Author's discussion of the voodoo ceremonies is identical to Marie B. Williams, "A Night with the Voudous" (published 1875; see no. 1055), except that Williams's description is shorter than Buel's. It is not clear whether Buel "borrowed" from Williams, or whether they both borrowed from an earlier source not yet identified. On the other hand, Buel's material was widely plagiarized by writers who came after him.

Texts of 2 songs: 1. Oh, de Lawd has cotch me under de arm (Cho: Gelory, hallelugerum) (506). 2. Heron mande, heron mande (533). Reference to 1 song: 1. Houm! dance Calinda (528). Text of 1 sermon: 1. Isaiah 18: 1-7 (501-9).

761 Burrill, David James. "At a Negro Meeting." ZION'S HERALD 63 (18 September 1895): 594.

Clergyman's description of his visit to a black prayer-meeting includes comment on their singing of hymns, the oratory style of the preacher, and related performance practice.

Excerpts of 1 sermon text: The Law is given by Moses, but grace and truth came by Jesus Christ (John 1: 17).

762 Burwell, Letitia M. [Page Thacker, pseud.] PLANTATION REMINISCENCES. N. p.[Owensboro, KY?]: 1878. 69 pp.

Slaveholder's discussion of slave life on the plantation includes references to the marriage ceremony (4), to work songs in the fields, and to dancing accompanied by the banjo or fiddle (46). Detailed description of dances, "cornshuckings," and "religious rites performed around the death bed" (57). Also reference to the practice of religious rites similar to those "practiced before the idols in Africa" (64).

763 C. "A Novel Sabbath in Charleston." INDEPENDENT 17 (27 April 1865): 3.

Letter to the editor, dated 16 April 1865 from Charleston, South Carolina, includes description of a Sabbath service and comment on the black worshippers singing "some of their own peculiar religious choruses, whose dialect a dozen glossaries could not entangle, and whose rhythm Hayden [sic] and Mozart would hardly criticize."

764 C. "Appeal against an Old Charge." SOUTHERN WORKMAN 12 (May 1883): 53.

Letter to the Editor, from Newburyport, Massachusetts, dated 27 March 1883, discusses the imprisonment of William Lloyd Garrison in Baltimore for his denunciation in the press of Captain Brown (of Newburyport) for transporting a cargo of slaves to New Orleans. Reference to the singing of the slaves.

765 C., A. M. "Plantation Preaching." INDEPENDENT 16 (31 March 1864): 2.

Letter to the Editor, dated 1 March 1864, from Alexandria, Virginia, includes character sketch of a contraband preacher, "Uncle Lebard," and comment on his oratory style, which had a "rough and somewhat stormy eloquence."

Excerpts from the text of 1 funeral oration: I am the Resurrection.

766 C., J. D. "Old Jenny's 'Woods Meeting'." CHRISTIAN WATCHMAN & REFLECTOR (=WATCHMAN-EXAMINER) 48 (18 July 1867): [4].

Letter focussing on the need for religious instruction for the young and untutored includes an example of an illiterate old black woman who attended camp-meeting services and was enthralled by the singing and praying, though she could not understand the sermons.

Text of 1 camp-meeting song: I hears a rumblin' in de skies.

767 Cabell, I. C. "A Plantation Funeral." HARPER'S NEW MONTHLY MAGAZINE 72 (March 1886): 653-54.

Description of a plantation slave funeral in Virginia during June 1864 includes comment on the singing of the mourners and on the unusual rites. Also an excerpt from the funeral sermon delivered by the black preacher.

Texts of 2 songs: 1. We are walkin' in de light (Cho: Walkin' in de light ob God) 2. On Canaan's calm and peaceful shore, We ain't gwine die no more. Text of 1 sermon: Funeral oration.

768 Calkins. "A Poor Negro's Prayer." AMERICAN MISSIONARY (MAGAZINE), n. s. 8 (April 1864): 89.

This report by a surgeon in a Massachusetts regiment includes comment on the strong imagery in a prayer offered by a black preacher at a funeral service and its use of motifs from hymns, the Bible, and spirituals.

769 "The Capture of a Negro Prayer Meeting." ZION'S HERALD AND WESLEYAN JOURNAL (=ZION'S HERALD) 35 (2 September 1863): [137].

Correspondent of Helena, Arkansas, discusses the exodus of a slave congregation to freedom under direction of Lieut. Col. DeCosta of the U. S. Second Arkansas (Colored) Regiment. Reference to the prayer of a slave preacher.

770 Car-Wheel Tourist [pseud.]. "Swing Low, Sweet Chariot." ZION'S HERALD 73 (3 April 1895): 242.

Discussion of a meeting at the Central Missouri Conference of the Methodist Episcopal Church refers to the singing of the blacks who were there.

Texts of 2 songs: 1. Roll, Jordan roll. 2. Swing low, sweet chariot.

771 Carleton, William McKendree. "The Funeral." HARPER'S WEEKLY 30 (28 August 1886): 545, 550.

Poem written by this American poet/journalist about the funeral of a small black boy in Savannah, Georgia, imitates the style and content of the sermon of a local black preacher and uses Afro-American folk images and dialect.

772 Castellanos, Henry C. NEW ORLEANS AS IT WAS: EPISODES OF LOUISIANA LIFE. 1895. 2d ed. New Orleans: L. Graham & Sons, 1905. Reprint of 2d ed. New Orleans: Pelican Publishing Company, 1961. 345 pp.

Description of slave dancing and related performance practice in the Place Congo in New Orleans (297-98). Also discussion of the voodoo cult in New Orleans, with comment on religious rituals, performance practice associated with the Calinda and the Bamboula, and voodoo dances (90-101).

Text of 1 voodoo song: Eh! Bomba, hen, hen! Canga bafio te (94).

773 Champney, Lizzie Williams. "Three Thunderbolts." HARPER'S NEW MONTHLY MAGAZINE 57 (October 1878): 704-09.

Short story about life in the South during the Reconstruction Era includes references to a camp-meeting service, describes the sermon delivered by the local black preacher, and discusses the "Amen Corner."

Texts of 3 songs: 1. Trials, hard trials, an' tribulations 2. De gospel train's a-comin' 3. Shout an' nebber tire. Reference to 1 song: Sheep know shepherd's voice. Reference to 1 sermon: 1. So run dat ye may obtain.

774 Chaplin, Jane Dunbar. "Aunt Seraph on Forgiveness." ZION'S HERALD 52 (22 July 1875): [225].

A story about the religious exhortations of an elderly black woman includes references to her singing improvised hymns of her own composition.

775 ____. "Out of the Wilderness---Chapter 10." CHRISTIAN WATCHMAN & REFLECTOR (=WATCHMAN-EXAMINER) 50 (8 July 1869): [4].

Discussion of life on a southern plantation includes description of a black prayer-meeting service, with references to the sermon, singing, and the shout.

776 Chase, Mary C. "Foot-Washing in Georgia." CHRISTIAN WATCHMAN & REFLECTOR (=WATCHMAN-EXAMINER) 49 (3 May 1888): [6].

In a Letter to the Editor, dated 16 April 1888 from Macon, Georgia, the black teacher describes the religious foot-washing rites found among black sects in Georgia. Comment on the oratory style of the preacher and the responses of his congregation.

Text of 1 couplet: Rather than be a slave, I'd be buried in my grave.

777 [Chase, Sarah, and Lucy Chase.] DEAR ONES AT HOME: LETTERS FROM CONTRABAND CAMPS. Edited by Henry L. Swint. Nashville: Vanderbilt University Press, 1966. 274 pp.

Collection of letters written by Lucy and Sarah Chase, New England school teachers who worked among the freedmen in the South from 1863 until about 1869, includes discussion of black lifestyles in the South. References to "boisterous Amens," dancing, and the sing-song delivery of prayers at black religious services (58, 124-25).

Texts of 5 songs (125-26): 1. Oh, happy is the child who learns to read (Cho: When I get over). 2. You must watch the sun and see how she run (Cho: I hope for to get up into Heaven) 3. If I had uh died when I was young (Cho: De prettiest thing dat ever I dun) 4. My Lord 'liver Daniel. 5. So Jesus listen all 'ee night.

778 [Chesnut, Mary Boykin.] A DIARY FROM DIXIE. Edited by Isabelle D. Martin and Myrta Lockett. New York: Appleton, 1905. Reprints. A DIARY.... Edited by Ben Ames Williams. Boston: Houghton Mifflin, 1949. MARY CHESNUT'S CIVIL WAR. Edited by C. Vann Woodward. New Haven: Yale University Press, 1981. The 1981 publication includes an edition of Chesnut's Journal.

The Diary entry for 13 October 1861 gives a detailed description of a worship service in a black Methodist church on Mulberry Plantation (Camden, South Carolina), including discussion of a prayer offered by "driver" Jim Nelson, and of the congregational responses. References to the singing of "camp meeting hymns" as the "saddest of all earthly music" (148-149).

779 "A Church House." SOUTHERN WORKMAN 26 (August 1897): 160.

Discussion of folk religious practices (song, dance, and congregational responses) in a rural black church in Alabama. Observation that the shout is described as "getting happy."

780 Church, Pharcellus [pseud.]. "What I found in Florida. II---The Freedmen, The Baptist Churches." CHRISTIAN WATCHMAN & REFLECTOR (=WATCHMAN-EXAMINER) 60 (20 March 1879): [1].

Minister's discussion of a sermon he heard at a "come outer" black church (that is, a church that had separated from its parent body) in St. Augustine, Florida, includes the assertion that it consisted of "an indigested detail of a few gospel facts." Notes that the hand-shaking ceremony was dispensed with in this church.

Reference to 1 sermon: Many are called, but few are chosen.

781 "Church-Going in Plantation Days." DAILY PICAYUNE 56 (4 September 1892): 8.

Discussion of the church attendance in the ante-bellum South includes references to black exhorters and preachers, describes the singing of religious songs and related performance practice.

Reference to 1 song: De ole ship o' Zion.

782 Clarke, W. L. "A Call to Preach." AMERICAN MISSIONARY (MAGAZINE) n.s. 13 (February 1869): 28.

Teacher of Georgia comments on an uneducated ante-bellum preacher who had memorized the Bible and based the texts of his sermons upon the Scriptures.

783 Clay-Clopton, Victoria. A BELLE OF THE FIFTIES; MEMOIRS OF MRS. CLAY, OF ALABAMA, COVERING SOCIAL AND POLITICAL LIFE IN WASHINGTON AND THE SOUTH, 1853-66. Edited by Ada Sterling. New York: Doubleday, Page & Company, 1904. 386 pp.

Memoirs include detailed description of a baptism ceremony in the Big Spring near Huntsville, Alabama (162-63), and comment on slave worship services, with references to "exciting Negro preachers" and the "religious excesses" of the congregation (219). Also description of slaves singing while "chopping out cotton," including related performance practice (220-21) and of slave dancing, particularly the "turkey-buzzard" dance (217).

784 Cleef, A. van. "The Hot Springs of Arkansas." HARPER'S NEW MONTHLY MAGAZINE 56 (January 1878): 193-210.

Traveler describing events in Hot Springs, Arkansas, in the 1870s includes comment on the popularity of revival meetings among local black Baptists in that area during the summer months.

Texts of 2 songs: 1. Soul shall shine like a star in de mornin'. 2. I'll meet my modder at de new buryin'-groun'.

785 Coan, W. L. "Among the Contrabands." SOUTHERN WORKMAN 13 (April 1884): 46.

Missionary, describing a prayer meeting conducted by contrabands at Camp Hamilton, Virginia, on Christmas day in 1861, refers to two hymns that the ex-slaves lined-out. Also excerpts of several exhortations and prayers offered by both male and female members of the group.

786 Coffin, Charles Carleton. "The First Sabbath of Freedom." CHRISTIAN WATCHMAN & REFLECTOR (=WATCHMAN EXAMINER) 45 (21 July 1864): [1]. Reprint. NATIONAL ANTI-SLAVERY STANDARD 25 (13 August 1864):[4].

An officer in the Union Army describes the spontaneous worship services of the contrabands who were behind the Union lines at Richmond, Virginia, during the Civil War. Detailed description of the shout, with special note of the young man standing in the center of the circle, who seemed to be the leader.

Text of 1 shout song: We are going to the other side of Jordan (Cho: So glad!).

787 _____. FOUR YEARS OF FIGHTING: A VOLUME OF PERSONAL OBSERVATION WITH THE ARMY AND NAVY. From the First Battle of Bull Run to the Fall of Richmond. Boston: Ticknor & Fields, 1866. Reprint. New York: Arno Press and the New York Times, 1970. 558 pp.

Chapter 15 of this book, entitled "The Atlantic Coast," is given over to discussion of black music and religious practices, including comment on hymns sung in the African Baptist Church at Port Royal and on a plantation; and description of a shout. The chapter also includes an account of Harriet Beecher Stowe's inverview with Sojourner Truth, the "original Libyan Sibyl." Other discussion includes description of a secular dance (345), of the shout (230-31), and of the singing of black soldiers (434-35, 507).

Text and music of 1 song (230): Little children sitting on the tree of life (Cho: O roll, Jordan, roll). Texts only of 2 songs: 1. We are going to the other side of Jordan (Cho: So glad) (345). 2. Ye's long been a-comin' (478). References to 2 songs: 1. There's a meeting here tonight (231). 2. I wish I was back in old Caroline (342).

788 Coffin, Levi. REMINISCENCES OF LEVI COFFIN, THE REPUTED PRESIDENT OF THE UNDERGROUND RAILROAD.... Cincinnati: Western Tract Society, c.1876. 2d ed. Cincinnati: Robert Clarke & Company, 1880. New York: Arno Press and the New York Times, 1968. 732 pp.

Account includes references to a religious service held by slaves in 1821 at New Garden, North Carolina, where a black exhorter, Uncle Frank, delivered the sermon, and to the singing of plantation songs (70-71).

789 Collins, C. C. "Education of Colored Ministers." AMERICAN MISSIONARY (MAGAZINE) n.s. 47 (May 1893): 156-57.

Clergyman of Troy, North Carolina, discusses the grammatical syntax of the speech of uneducated black preachers he has heard deliver sermons.

790 "Colored Revivals in Virginia." LESLIE'S ILLUSTRATED NEWSPAPER 61 (12 September 1885): 54.

Description of "African worship" at a religious revival witnessed in Virginia includes comment on the four preachers who offered the opening prayers, each singing and exhorting in turn, as groups of "mourners" stood before the pulpit. Many worshipers were seized with ecstasy in the setting of jubilant song and exhortation.

791 Comings, E. J. "Uncle Robert." AMERICAN MISSIONARY (MAGAZINE) n.s. 8 (April 1864): 100-101.

Biographical sketch of a slave preacher includes comment on the sermons he has delivered.

792 "A Contraband Prayer Meeting." NATIONAL ANTI-SLAVERY STANDARD 25 (25 June 1864): 4.

Description of an ex-slave prayer meeting at Belle Plain, Virginia, reprinted from the Burlington FREE PRESS, includes the text of 1 exhortation: The prodigal son.

793 "Contrabands in Camp." CHRISTIAN WATCHMAN & REFLECTOR (=CHRISTIAN EXAMINER) 44 (17 December 1863): [4].

Discussion of a Methodist slave preacher includes excerpts of his exhortations and sayings regarding slave life and the Emancipation Proclamation.

794 "The Contrabands' Gratitude." CHRISTIAN WATCHMAN & REFLECTOR (=WATCHMAN-EXAMINER) 44 (22 October 1863): [1].

A Union Army soldier's description of a prayer meeting of contrabands in Florida during the Civil War includes references to the preacher "reading a hymn." Also excerpts from exhortations about "deliverance out of bondage."

795 Cook, Isaac P. "Black Harry." ZION'S HERALD 57 (21 October 1880): 337.

Discussion of the correspondence of Bishop Francis Asbury includes references to the slave exhorter Harry [Hoosier]. The Bishop writes that Black Harry, who traveled throughout the former British provinces preaching to black and white people, spoke eloquently at a Methodist Conference in Baltimore in April 1781.

Reference to 1 sermon: The barren fig tree.

796 Cooley, J. H. "Religious Matters in New Orleans." ZION'S HERALD AND WESLEYAN JOURNAL (=ZION'S HERALD) 35 (17 June 1863): [93].

A Letter dated 13 May 1863 from Baton Rouge, Louisiana, includes discussion of the conditions under which black Methodists in New Orleans worshipped before the Civil War and after the Union soldiers captured the city. Sketch of George Gordan, a former slave of Maryland, who served as a preacher without compensation because black preachers in the South were not allowed to accept money for their services. Comment on his sermons.

797 Curry, Jabez L. M. "A Study in Community Life." NEW ENGLAND MAGAZINE 18 (April 1898): 177-81.

Baptist clergyman and chaplain during the Civil War discusses life in Alabama in the pre-war years. Recalls that there were some black preachers for the slaves, but more often blacks and whites worshipped in the same house but in segregated pews. Description of a corn-husking festival, of slaves singing and telling tales.

798 D., R. M. "Letter from Kentucky." CHRISTIAN WATCHMAN & REFLECTOR (=WATCHMAN-EXAMINER) 68 (1 September 1887): [5].

A native of Georgetown, Kentucky, in a letter dated 18 August 1887, discusses the 19th Annual Meeting of the General Association of Colored Baptists of Kentucky, including comment on singing performance practice associated with the taking of the collection.

799 Davis, Charles Henry S. HISTORY OF WALLINGFORD, CONNECTICUT. Meriden, Connecticut: Published by the Author, 1870. 956 pp.

Discussion of black fiddlers in colonial Connecticut (341, 344) and of slave baptisms (342).

800 Deming, Clarence. BY-WAYS OF NATURE AND LIFE. New York: G. P. Putnam's Sons, 1884. 383 pp. Miscellaneous collection of articles that originally were published in the NEW YORK EVENING POST.

Three articles of the collection are given over to discussion of the Negro in the South (343-83), including detailed description of folk practices at funerals, prayer meetings, and weddings. Also comment on the singing of religious songs and on the songs of the stevedores, and discussion of the oratory style of folk preachers.

Texts of 10 songs; text and music of 1 song. Excerpt of 1 sermon: Horse a-pawin' in de valley. See SONG COLLECTIONS (no. 1746).

801 "DIDDLE, DUMPS AND TOT." Unsigned book review. HARPER'S NEW MONTHLY MAGAZINE 64 (February 1883): 484-85.

Discussion of the book (see no. 968) includes a Biblical story told to the white "chil'en" by Uncle Bob, and refers to the singing of Dumps.

Texts of 3 songs: 1. Efn 'ligion was er thing that money could buy (Cho: O reign Marse Jesus). 2. Dan'l wuz er prayin' man. 3. All folkses, Lord, all folkses, Lord, O Lord bless all de same. Text of 1 sermon: Daniel in the lions' den.

802 Dingley, Frank. "The Negro Creed and Hymnology." MUSICAL RECORD (Boston) 128 (12 March 1881): 382.

Reprint of a letter originally published in the LEWISTON JOURNAL discusses the religion of blacks in Arkansas. Distinguishes between the preacher (who takes his text from the Bible) and the exhorter (who speaks on any subject). Reference to a Baptist prayer meeting.

Texts of 2 songs: 1. Satan came hoppin' long same as a flea (Cho: If you kotch me I'll git up again). 2. An' I wear my bran new shoes.

803 Dobbs, A. S. "Our Southern Work." ZION'S HERALD 58 (4 August 1881): 242.

In a letter written from Charleston, South Carolina, dated 4 July 1881, a minister refers to the similarities between the religious exercises of southern black Baptists and those of the "howling dervishes of Asia and Africa."

804 Douglass, Frederick. "The Progress of Blacks Twenty Years after Emancipation." HARPER'S WEEKLY (8 December 1883). Reprint. FREDERICK DOUGLASS: THE NARRATIVES AND SELECTED WRITINGS. Edited by Michael Meyer. New York: Random House, 1984. 391 pp. Page references below are to the reprint edition.

Discussion of race progress and problems by the black abolitionist Douglass (c.1817-1895) includes comment on the traditions of the old-time preachers (385-86).

805 Duganne, Augustine Joseph Hickey. CAMPS AND PRISONS. TWENTY MONTHS IN THE DEPARTMENT OF THE GULF. New York: J. P. Robens, 1865. 424 pp.

Officer of the Union Army describes his experiences as a prisoner-of-war in Mississippi and Texas during the Civil War. Discussion of the singing of a boatman (73-74), religious services of the blacks, and of an illiterate folk preacher, who recited the Scriptures from memory. Comment on the preacher's sermon and the communal responses of his congregation (79-83).

Text of 1 plantation song: De cane is in de sugar-biler (74). Text of 1 couplet: Ole massa's runn'd, aha! de darkeys stays (Cho: An' de year of Jubilo) (349). Excerpt from text of 1 sermon: Bress de Lord for His mercy (81-83).

806 Dunbar, Alice. THE GOODNESS OF ST. ROCQUE AND OTHER STORIES. New York: Dodd, Mead & Company, 1899. 224 pp.

Collection of stories about creoles, white and colored, includes reference to the "rhythmic song of the stevedores" as they heaved cotton-bales (118) and a story about a street peddler, the Praline Woman (175-79).

Text of 1 song: Tu l'aimedes trois jours (178). Text of 1 work cry: Oh-ho-ho-humph...(118).

807 Dunbar, Paul Laurence. "Anner 'Lizer's Stumblin' Block." INDEPENDENT 47 (23 May 1895): 706-07.

Short story about plantation blacks on an estate in Fayette County, Kentucky, written by black-American poet-novelist Dunbar (1872-1906), contains a description of a church service with excerpts written in the idiomatic style of the black preacher, comment on the performance practice associated with singing spirituals (including hand clapping and feet tapping), and comment on ecstatic seizure.

Texts of 2 songs: 1. Sabe de mounah jes' now (Cho: He'p de sinnah jes' now). 2. Git on bo'ad-ah, little childering. Text of 1 couplet: Loose him and let him go, Let him shout to glory.

808 _____. "A Mess of Pottage." SATURDAY EVENING POST 172 (16 December 1899): 516-17.

Fictional story about a political rally held by members of a congregation at Bethel Chapel in "Little Africa" includes dicussion of the preacher's address to the gathering.

809 "The Earthquake at Charleston." HARPER'S WEEKLY 30 (18 September 1886): 610.

Report about the earthquake that struck Charleston, South Carolina, on 31 August 1886, includes discussion of the victims of the disaster. Observation that the black population passed the nights in lamentation and "indescribable" psalm-singing.

810 Edwardes, Charles. "A Scene from Florida Life." MACMILLAN'S MAGAZINE 50 (August 1884): 261-70.

Discussion of the Englishman's visit to a black church in Jacksonville, Florida, on 4 January 1884, includes description of religious practices, including the singing of hymns, the "bread-and-water forgiveness festival," and the religious dance. Reference to the moaning and rocking to and fro.

Summary of 1 New Year's sermon: Starting anew. Also texts of exhortations given by lay members.

811 Ela, Elwood. "Southern Sketches." ZION'S HERALD 57 (10 June 1880): 186.

References to the lively worksongs of the black stevedores and description of a funeral wake and the the singing of songs pertaining to death.

812 Ellis, A. "On Vodu-Worship." APPLETON'S POPULAR SCIENCE MONTHLY 38 (March 1891): 651-63.

Army Major discusses the origin and rites of voodoo worship among blacks along the Slave Coast of West Africa and in Haiti. Reference to voodoo practices in Louisiana, with note of similarities in the dances and rituals of blacks there to those in West Africa and Haiti.

813 Emery, E. B. LETTERS FROM THE SOUTH, ON THE SOCIAL, INTELLECTUAL, AND MORAL CONDITION OF THE COLORED PEOPLE. Boston: Beacon Press, 1880. 19 pp.

Description of a northerner's visit to an African Methodist Church in Charleston, South Carolina, in 1880 includes discussion of the singing of "strange" songs and the related performance practice. References to the sermon, ecstatic seizures of members of the congregation, and the religious dance (5-7).

814 Eveleth, E. B. "Florida---Negro Preaching." AMERICAN MISSIONARY (MAGAZINE) n.s. 14 (March 1870): 55.

Native of Gainesville, Florida, discusses the preaching of black clergymen at a local Sabbath School. Observes that the elderly ministers delivered their sermons loudly, in a high key, and in a manner almost unintelligible.

815 [Everts, Orphus.] "A Negro's Theology." INDEPENDENT 16 (6 October 1864): 1.

Letter to the editor written from the Headquarters Birney Division, Second U. S. Army Corps, dated 1 August 1864, includes discussion of an ex-slave who held prayer meetings in the servants' quarters, and with whom the writer had discourse on the subject of sin. Also comment on the singing and "loud praying" of the colored attendants.

816 Everts, W. W. "Fifth Letter from Dr. Everts." CHRISTIAN WATCHMAN & REFLECTOR (=WATCHMAN-EXAMINER) 68 (9 June 1887): [3].

Clergyman's discussion of Baptists and religious institutions in Richmond, Virginia, gives a history of its black clergy, including anecdotes and discussion of sermons delivered by the Rev. John Jasper.

Synopses of 3 sermons: 1. The Sun Do Move. 2. The Resurrection of Lazarus. 3. The Earth Has Four Corners.

817 F., C. H. "Negro Worship and Music: Notes of a Foot Traveler.---The Influences of a Black Parson's Sermon---the Remarkable Music of a Colored Congregation---Expression of Religious Sentiment of the Race." NEW YORK TIMES, 25 February 1877: 5.

Correspondent visiting in Montgomery, Alabama, describes the religious service at a local black Baptist church. Discussion of the oratory style of the preacher and reference to the text of his sermon: John 14. Also discussion of the performance practice associated with the lining-out of hymns and the congregation's responses to the sermon.

818 Felix [pseud.]. "Uncle Andy's Theology." DAILY PICAYUNE 56 (29 May 1892): 19.

Character sketch of an antebellum plantation exhorter includes an excerpt from one of his sermons. Text of 1 sermon: The fall of Satan.

819 "Fetish Follies." AMERICAN MISSIONARY (MAGAZINE) n.s. 19 (January 1875): 17-18.

Description of a new ceremony evolving among blacks in Augusta, Georgia, called "Marching out of Egypt": participants pace around and around the room and sing from sunset to sunrise as an act of religious piety.

820 Fitzhugh, Daisy. "De Sun Do Move." LESLIE'S ILLUSTRATED WEEKLY 73 (16 January 1892): 414.

Sketch of the life of the Rev. John Jasper (1812-1901), the ex-slave preacher of the Sixth Mount Zion Baptist Church of Richmond, Virginia, includes comment on the congregational singing and the preacher's oratory style.

Excerpt of 1 sermon: De Sun Do Move.

821 Floyd, Mary Rose. "Uncle Adam's Funeral Feast." SOUTHERN BIVOUAC n.s. 1 (March 1866): 616-19.

Short story about the funeral celebration for a deceased plantation slave, which was held one month after his interment. Includes songs written in the style of folksongs and excerpt of the funeral oration.

822 Foote, Julia A. J. A BRAND PLUCKED FROM THE FIRE. AN AUTOBIOGRAPHICAL SKETCH.... Cleveland, OH: Printed for the Author by W. F. Schneider, 1879. 124 pp. Reprint. SISTERS OF THE SPIRIT. THREE BLACK WOMEN'S AUTOBIOGRAPHIES OF THE NINETEENTH CENTURY. Edited by William L. Andrews. Bloomington: Indiana University Press, 1986. 245 pp.

This narrative of black evangelist Foote (1823-1900) offers insight into the experiences and difficulties of the females who became exhorters, preachers, and missionaries. She preached "santification" long before blacks began to organize their own Holiness churches.

823 Frederick, Francis. AUTOBIOGRAPHY OF REV. FRANCIS FREDERICK. Baltimore: J. W. Woods, Printer, 1869. 40 pp.

Narrative of ex-slave (b. 1809), who escaped via the Underground Railroad in 1855 and later became a Presbyterian minister, includes comment on a plantation party where the guests "promenaded in couples, putting on remarkable and grotesque airs" (21), and description of a slave wedding (28).

824 French, Austa Malinda. SLAVERY IN SOUTH CAROLINA AND THE EX-SLAVES; OR, THE PORT ROYAL MISSION. New York: Winchell M. French, 1862. 312 pp. Reprint. New York: Negro Universities Press, 1969.

Discussion includes references to two plantations where slaves held prayer meetings every evening among themselves (235) and to a speech delivered by one "Deacon" Jones about slavery (240-41).

825 Fuller, Richard F. CHAPLAIN FULLER: BEING A LIFE SKETCH OF A NEW ENGLAND CLERGYMAN AND ARMY CHAPLAIN. Boston: Walker, Wise, and Company, 1864. 342 pp.

Biography of Arthur B. Fuller includes references to the religious services of the "contrabands," to a funeral service, and to the mournful quality of their religious songs (199-200).

826 G., L. G. "Uncle Johnson: In Memoriam." NATIONAL ANTI-SLAVERY STANDARD 25 (21 May 1864): [4].

Obituary notice reprinted from the NEW YORK EVANGELIST for Johnson Harrison (1745-1864), an antebellum slave preacher of Virginia, includes reference to an itinerant minister who visited a plantation once a year to preach a funeral sermon for all the slaves who had died during the previous year.

827 Gage, Frances D. "Religious Exercises of the Negroes of the Sea Islands." INDEPENDENT 15 (15 January 1863): 6.

Discussion of the religious traditions of the freedmen in the Sea Islands of South Carolina includes comment on their singing religious songs while at work in the fields and rowing boats, as well as during religious services. "Many of their melodies seem like a wail of anguish." Detailed description of the shout, which lasted two hours and involved from forty to fifty persons.

Text of 1 song: I want to go home.

828 Gannett, W. C. "The Freedmen at Port Royal." NORTH AMERICAN REVIEW 101 (July 1865): 1-28.

Discussion of the importance of religion in the lives of the ex-slaves includes comment on their "plaintive songs" and their religious practices, and description of the shout and "striving." Observation that praise-meetings are held three evenings of the week and three times on Sundays (12).

829 Gilmore, James R. [Edmund Kirke, pseud.]. "A Merchant's Story." CONTINENTAL MONTHLY 3 (February 1863): 206-22.

Serialized story is the true account of a northern writer and his experiences with planters, merchants, and slaves in the South. In the sixth article of the series, discussion of the activities of slaves on a turpentine plantation in South Carolina: a church service, its singing performance practice, fiddle music, and a sermon given by a local preacher.

Text of 1 sermon: Joseph and the Ishmaelites.

830 _____. MY SOUTHERN FRIENDS. ALL OF WHICH I SAW, AND PART OF WHICH I WAS. New York: Carleton Publisher, 1863. 308 pp.

Fictional story about the South is based on facts the author gathered during sixteen years of business and social intercourse with planters and merchants in the South. Chapter 11 is devoted to "The Negro Meeting" and Chapter 19, to "The Negro Wedding," including excerpts from the wedding sermon. Also references to the plantation preacher (112), the singing of worksongs by the slaves (107), the singing of an African song by a slave born in Africa (153), and dancing to the music of the "big fiddle," small fiddles, and the banjo (191, 208).

831 _____. "Charcoal Sketches." COSMOPOLITAN: A MONTHLY ILLUSTRATED MAGAZINE 6 (January 1889): 300-302.

Character sketches of two former slaves living in the South include discussion of John Cobble, who improvised melodies on his banjo or violin, and excerpt from a sermon by a black preacher.

Text of 1 sermon: Old man Enoch's grit.

832 Graves, Frederick Burrill. "Southland Studies." Part 1. ZION'S HERALD 71 (15 February 1893): 50.

Minister's discussion includes references to sermons he heard in four black churches of Jacksonville, Florida, and observation that the sermons were adapted to the needs of the people. Comment that some black church choirs were unwilling to sing their melodies for northern white visitors.

833 _____. "Southland Studies." Part 2. ZION'S HERALD 71 (22 February 1893): 57.

Discussion of student life at Claflin University in Orangeburg, South Carolina, includes comment on the students' rhythmic singing of work songs and on the performance practice associated with the singing of religious songs.

834 "The Great South: A Ramble in Virginia---On the Railroad." AMERICAN MISSIONARY (MAGAZINE) n.s. 18 (May 1874): 97-102.

The writer's train journey includes stops in Lynchburg, where he comments on the singing of "eccentric hymns" by black workers in the tobacco factories, and to a revival meeting held near Richmond, where his description includes comment on the preacher's oratory style.

Text of 1 sermon: Christ is the Creating Power of God.

835 Gris, Cheveux [pseud.]. "A Peculiar People." SOUTHERN MAGAZINE 13 (August 1873): 172-76.

Description of a Negro funeral service in the South, including excerpts from the sermon.

Text of 1 sermon: No man liveth to himself, and no man dieth to himself. Text of 1 song: Def [death] is a mighty conqueror (Cho: Lay low, lay low). Text of 1 couplet: We're jining the heavenly hosts above.

836 Guial, E. L. "Among the Sable Singers." WESTERN MONTHLY (=LAKESIDE MAGAZINE) 2 (December 1869): 421-26.

Visitor to a large metropolitan city along the Ohio River offers a description of a "colored revival" and a Sabbath morning service held at a local church in the upper loft of an abandoned tobacco house. Comment on the oratory style of the preacher and the responses of the congregation, on the singing of improvised songs and remnants of "almost forgotten plantation ditties," and on a Love Feast. Excerpts of exhortations.

Texts of 2 songs: 1. Dar is a city far away (Cho: Glory, glory, hallelujah). 2. You and I will go to heav'n, singin' brother, singin' sister. Texts of 3 couplets: 1. O Zion, O Zion, when the bridegroom comes. 2. When rocks and mountains all fade away, we'll have a hidin' place that day. 3. When I get in trouble I know who to go to.

837 H., E. J. "The Invasion of the North." HARPER'S WEEKLY 7 (18 July 1863): 459.

This report on responses in Philadelphia to the news that Harrisburg, Pennsylvania, was in danger of falling to Rebel forces includes references to a meeting of black men at the Mother Bethel A.M.E. Church to discuss this danger. One resolution called on "all ministers of the Gospel, preaching to colored congregations" to "teach their several charges that the days of our bondage in this land are at an end, and that God is saying to us...Be Free."

838 H., G. E., Jr. "The Sunny South." CHRISTIAN WATCHMAN & REFLECTOR (=WATCHMAN-EXAMINER) 74 (23 March 1893): [1].

Discussion of a prayer-meeting service held at a hotel in Richmond, Virginia, in March 189-, by waiters in their own dining room, which was filled with colored people and a few white guests of the establishment. Comment on the sermon of a local black preacher as "crude" but orthodox.

839 Hagood, Atticus. OUR BROTHER IN BLACK: HIS FREEDOM AND HIS FUTURE. New York: Phillips & Hunt, 1881. 252 pp.

Description by a white minister of a sermon given by a black preacher and summary of the text (222-23).

Text of 1 sermon: The fiery furnace and the three Hebrew children.

840 Hallowell, Florence B. "Aunt Mely's Insurance." LESLIE'S ILLUSTRATED NEWSPAPER 57 (10 November 1883): 182.

Short story includes description of a church service and its sermon. (Place not indicated.)

Text of 1 song: Oh, sinnah, yo' bettah gittin' ready. Text of 1 sermon: He that giveth to the poor, lendeth to the Lord.

841 Hammond, C. "A Love-Feast among the Colored People." ZION'S HERALD 59 (29 March 1882): 90.

Minister, in describing a black Love Feast held at a Methodist Episcopal Church in Austin, Texas, refers to "quaint songs" and exhortations.

Texts of 5 songs: 1. But we are going home to live with Jesus (Cho: I'll die in this army). 2. I looked at the world and the world looked new. 3. I want to go to heaven when I die (Cho: Walk in the light). 4. The Union band is the band (Cho: I belong to this band). 5. We have had hard trials every day (Cho: But we are going to live with Jesus). Texts of 2 couplets: 1. Is there anyone here that loves my Jesus. 2. O, brethern, wa'n't that a mighty day when Jesus Christ was born?

842 Hampton Folk-Lore Society. "Folk-Lore and Ethnology: Contributions from Correspondents." SOUTHERN WORKMAN 12 (August 1894): 210.

Discussion of religious practices among the ex-slaves includes description of their "getting religion," and discussion of the "seeker" who "sets out to pray" after having been converted.

843 _____. "Religious Experience." SOUTHERN WORKMAN 24 (April 1895): 59-60.

Essay focuses upon Afro-American folk religious practices in the rural South during the antebellum period, particularly the "conversion" experience and the "seeker."

Text of 1 song: I am going to walk on de sea of glass (Cho: Go tell the holy angels).

844 _____. "Sermons and Prayers." SOUTHERN WORKMAN 24 (April 1895): 60-61.

Transcriptions of three Afro-American folk sermons from the antebellum period and discussion of the performance practice associated with the delivery of the sermons.

Texts of 3 sermons: 1. Epiphany. 2. Noah and the ark. 3. Who is worthy to drink the cup.

845 _____. "Beliefs and Customs Connected with Death and Burial." SOUTHERN WORKMAN 26 (January 1897): 18-19.

Description of a wake and burial service among rural blacks in Gloucester County, Virginia, and of folk singing.

Reference to 1 song: I don't want to die in a storm, good Lord.

846 _____. "The Watch Meeting." SOUTHERN WORKMAN 28 (April 1899): 151-54. Reprint. BLACK PERSPECTIVE IN MUSIC 4 (July 1976): 141-44.

Discussion of a watch meeting on New Year's Eve night includes description of the "awakening," the service, the "spiritual enthusiasm" of the congregation, and its conclusion.

Text of 1 prayer. Music and texts of 3 songs: 1. Jesus, Jesus is my Frien' (Cho: Don't leave me Lord). 2. Praise God, Hallelujah. 3. Walk togedder, children. Text only of 1 song: 'Tis a Happy New Year, Hallelujah.

847 Harland, Marion. "Christmas on the Old Plantation." CHRISTIAN UNION (=OUTLOOK) 46 (17 December 1892): 1173-74.

Article focusing upon holiday celebrations among whites, includes comment on the slaves' celebration of the "Watch Night," a religious service held on Christmas Eve. Notes that the leader of the service prostrated himself, facing east, at the stroke of midnight to give thanks for the birth of the Christ Child. Other members followed suit.

848 Harper, Frances E. W. IDA LEROY, SHADOWS UPLIFTED. 3d ed. Boston: James H. Earle, 1892. 282 pp.

Novel by black author includes references to the religious experience: description of prayer meetings held in wooded areas, where pots filled with water were used to deaden the sound (12); of a religious service and of a woman who "come throo" at the service (13, 179-81). Also reference to a Guinea slave who retained her African traditions (22-23).

849 Harrison, Jonathan Baxter. "Studies in the South: VIII." ATLANTIC MONTHLY 50 (October 1882): 476-88.

References to black school children singing revival melodies, and to the fact that the educated black clergy discouraged them because the "strange, wild songs" were regarded as "relics and badges of the old condition of slavery and heathenism." Description of a devotional service held at a local church, with reference to a sermon delivered in plantation dialect.

850 Harrison, Samuel. REV. SAMUEL HARRISON: HIS LIFE STORY TOLD BY HIMSELF. Pittsfield, MA: Eagle Publishing Company, 1899. 47 pp.

Afro-American clergyman from Philadelphia (b. 1811) discusses his activities as an agent of the Freedman's Relief Society during the years 1861-1863. Comment on his six-weeks stay on the Sea Islands of South Carolina and his work there as a chaplain to Negro soldiers during the Civil War (25-31). Reference to his preaching to ex-slaves in their praise-meeting houses. Observes that ex-slaves held four religious services on the Sabbath, with the first service (at 6 a.m.) lasting two hours (26).

851 Harrison, William Pope. THE GOSPEL AMONG THE SLAVES: A SHORT ACCOUNT OF MISSIONARY OPERATIONS AMONG THE AFRICAN SLAVES OF THE SOUTHERN STATES. Nashville: Publishing House of the M. E. Church, South, 1893. Reprint. New York: AMS Press, 1973. 394 pp.

Detailed account of Methodist missionary activity in the South during the antebellum period includes references to the occasional survival of African practices, called "gree gree worship" (252, 306); to unusual congregational singing practice (292-93, 339); to famous slave exhorters: Henry Evans (139), Punch (178), Henry Adams (281), Uncle Emmanuel (290), Emanuel Mask (341), and Lucius Holsey (350). Excerpt from a sermon heard in 1843 at Huntsville, Alabama, on a text of Revelation (338-40).

Text of 1 sermon: Behol' I stan' at de door n' knock.

852 Haskell, Marion Alexander. "Negro Spirituals." CENTURY 58/4 (Aug. 1899): 577-81. Reprint. THE SOCIAL IMPLICATIONS OF EARLY NEGRO MUSIC IN THE UNITED STATES. Edited by Bernard Katz. New York: Arno Press and the New York Times, 1969.

Discussion of the origin and social-religious aspects of the Negro spiritual by this white author, who recalls her childhood experiences in attending religious services of the ex-slaves.

Reference to 1 sermon. Texts and music of 11 songs. See SONG COLLECTIONS (no. 1753).

853 Hearn, Lafcadio. "Dolly/An Idyl of the Levee." CINCINNATI COMMERCIAL, 27 August 1876. Reprints. THE SELECTED WRITINGS OF LAFCADIO HEARN. Edited by Henry Goodman. New York: Citadel Press, 1949. CHILDREN OF

THE LEVEE. Edited by O. W. Frost. Lexington: University of Kentucky Press, 1957.

References to a black preacher in a short story about life on the levee in Cincinnati, Ohio.

Text of 1 song: Here comes my pilgrim Jesus, a-riding a milk-white horse (Cho: Oh, ain't I mighty glad my Jesus arose).

854 Heart [pseud.]. "Letter from Mississippi." CHRISTIAN WATCHMAN & REFLECTOR (=WATCHMAN-EXAMINER) 49 (13 August 1868): [1].

Article about Lake County, Mississippi, includes discussion of the life of the freedmen in that region. Description of a Sunday service among blacks, conducted by an elderly preacher called Old Uncle Will. References to the singing of sacred songs and performance practice.

Texts of 2 choruses: 1. We have our trials every day. 2. There's none but the righteous. Text of 1 sermon: De lazy bird dat buil' her nes' four thousand miles up.

855 "Heathenism in New Orleans---A Young White Girl among the Fetish Worshippers." DAY'S DOINGS 2 (24 April 1869): 323.

Description of the annual meeting of Voudoo worshippers, held on St. John's Day in New Orleans, includes discussion of the rites, of the ceremonial attire, the chanting of songs, the dancing in a circle around a basket holding a dozen hissing snakes, and spirit possession.

856 Hepworth, George Hughes. THE WHIP, HOE, AND SWORD; OR, THE GULF-DEPARTMENT IN '63. Boston: Walker, Wise, and Company, 1864. 298 pp. Reprint. Freeport, NY: Books for Libraries Press, 1971.

New England minister, who served as a chaplain in the Union army, refers to the Saturday afternoon dancing of the blacks to the "twang of the banjo" (139) and offers a detailed description of a worship service in Carrollton, Louisiana, including discussion of the quality of the singing with its "wild, mournful chorus," and a summary of the sermon (163-69).

857 Hewetson, W. T. "The Social Life of the Southern Negro." CHATAUQUAN 26 (December 1897): 295-304.

Discussion of the life and social customs of southern blacks following the Civil War includes description of a camp-meeting, the singing of religious songs, and the oratory of minister. Comment on the religious songs as "senseless combinations of words set to music, having neither rime nor meter," songs that "abound in vain repetitions, and are usually strung out to an interminable length."

858 Higgins, R. C. "The Rice Negro as an Elector." NATION 15 (11 July 1872): 2-3.

Discussion of the ex-slaves on a rice plantation near Charleston, South Carolina, includes detailed description of their religious traditions, including the rites involved when the backslider who has "fallen from grace" wishes to be readmitted to the congregation.

859 Higginson, Thomas Wentworth. "Piety of the Black Soldier." NATIONAL ANTI-SLAVERY STANDARD 25 (10 December 1864): 4.

Letter, dated 14 December 1863, reprinted from the ATLANTIC MONTHLY, describes the funeral of a black soldier. References to a deacon lining out a hymn, to exhorters, and to a sermon: This poor man cried and the Lord heard him and delivered him out of his troubles.

860 _____. "Leaves from an Officer's Journal." Parts 1-3. ATLANTIC MONTHLY 14 (November 1864): 521-29; 14 (December 1864): 740-48; 15 (January 1865): 65-73. Reprint in ARMY LIFE IN A BLACK REGIMENT, by Thomas Wentworth Higginson. Boston: Fields, Osgood & Company, 1870.

Colonel of the First South Carolina (Colored) Union Volunteers, an ex-slave regiment, in discussion of the life-style of his black recruits in the Union Army during the Civil War, includes description of the shout and shout songs (526-27, 740). References to an elderly slave telling tales around the campfire at night (524), to dancing to the music of a fiddler (740), and to exhorters. Also a description of the funeral of a black recruit (741).

Texts of 3 plantation songs: 1. I can't stay behind, my Lord (529). 2. We'll fight for liberty (Cho: Till de Lord shall call us home) (745). 3. I know moon-rise, I know star-rise (Cho: Lay dis body down) (70).

861 _____. "The First Black Regiment." OUTLOOK 59 (2 July 1898): 521-31.

Commander of the First South Carolina (Colored) Union Volunteers, a regiment of ex-slaves, describes the military engagements of his troops during the Civil War. Comment on music and dance in the camp, and description of the shout.

862 A HISTORY OF THE PARISH OF TRINITY CHURCH IN THE CITY OF NEW YORK. Edited by Morgan Dix. New York: G. P. Putnam's Sons, 1898. 261 pp.

Discussion of the religious instruction given to the slaves in New York, particularly by Elias Neau (162-63, 188).

863 Holley, Sallie. A LIFE FOR LIBERTY: ANTI-SLAVERY AND OTHER LETTERS OF SALLIE HOLLEY. Edited by John White Chadwick. New York: G. P. Putnam's Sons, 1899. 292 pp.

Letters of this New England abolitionist and founder of a school for freedmen at Lottsburgh, Virginia, include discussion of prayer meetings of the ex-slaves (221) and of Christmas holiday celebrations (229). Also discussion of the singing and dancing at religious meetings (232). Reference to the horn used to awaken slaves on plantations in the antebellum period (232).

864 Holsey, Lucius H. AUTOBIOGRAPHY, SERMONS, ADDRESSES, AND ESSAYS OF BISHOP L. H. HOLSEY, DD. Atlanta, GA: The Franklin Printing and Publishing Company, 1898. 288 pp. Reprint. Englewood, CO: Microcard Editions, 1971.

Ex-slave Holsey, born 1842 near Columbus, Georgia, compiled a collection of fifteen of his sermons and thirteen addresses and essays. Discusses the style of the folk preacher and related performance practice (13-14), and the training of a slave preacher (17-19). Also references to a slave wedding of "house servants" (11-12) and discussion of the origin of the Colored Methodist Episcopal Church (14, 20).

865 Hopkins, Isabella T. "In the M. E. African Church." SCRIBNER'S MONTHLY 20 (July 1880): 422-29.

Discussion of a visit to a Methodist Episcopal African church in rural South Carolina includes references to the congregational singing of "spirityubble" songs and related performance practice, comment on the voice quality of the singing, and description of the shout. Excerpts from a sermon about King Davis and from a prayer delivered by the plantation preacher.

Texts of 6 songs: 1. You come now, ef you comin'. 2. Feel like I'm on my journey home. 3. 'Zekiel saw a valley. 4. Oh, who all dem come dress' in white? (Cho: Oh, what you say, John?). 5. Oh, look at de Moses (Cho: Oh, de ole ferry-boat stan' a-waitin' at de landin'). 6. Oh, what you reckon de debbil say? (Cho: Keep inchin' a-long). Texts of 3 couplets: 1. Now de bones begin to move. 2. Ef you want to catch de heavenly breeze. 3. Wise man! Wise man! Don't delay.

866 Hopley, Catherine Cooper. LIFE IN THE SOUTH FROM THE COMMENCEMENT OF THE WAR, BY A BLOCKADED BRITISH SUBJECT. London: Chapman & Hall, 1863. 2 vols. Reprint. New York: Da Capo Press, 1974.

British visitor in Virginia discusses slave life on the plantation (1:103) and describe a worship service she attended in the African Church of Richmond, Virginia (1:188-89).

867 Howland, Eliza Woolsey. "Homosassa." INDEPENDENT 34 (9 March 1882): 5-6.

Discussion of life along the Homosassa [Springs?] in Hernando County, Florida, includes discussion of blacks on the Old Yulee Plantation, their songs, and their religious practices. Description of the shout at Sunday services and night prayer meetings, particularly one conducted by a plantation preacher. References to secular dances held three or four times a week.

References to 2 songs: 1. Roll, Jordan, roll. 2. When de bridegroom comes. Excerpt from 1 sermon: He [Christ] denied Himself.

868 Hughes, Louis. THIRTY YEARS A SLAVE. FROM BONDAGE TO FREEDOM....Milwaukee, WI: South Side Printing Company, 1897. 210 pp. Reprint. Westport, CT: Negro Universities Press, 1969.

Ex-slave Hughes, born 1832 near Charlottesville, Virginia, describes religious meetings of the slaves held in their cabins (52-54).

Text of 1 song: There'll be no more talk about Monday, by and by (146).

869 Hunt, Sara Keables. "A Camp-Meeting in Virginia." ZION'S HERALD 54 (1 November 1877): 850.

Description of a visit to the eastern shores of Virginia includes comment on one of the "colored uncles" who sings improvised songs as he drives his cart through the traffic on boat day. Also description of a Negro camp-meeting.

References to 2 songs: 1. Swing low, sweet chariot. 2. Roll, Jordan, roll.

870 Hunter, W. H., compiler. "The Pathfinders of Jefferson County." OHIO ARCHAEOLOGICAL AND HISTORICAL PUBLICATIONS 6 (1898): 95-383.

Chapter 20 focuses on discussion of the manumitted-slave colony called Hayti, which was founded on McIntyre Creek, County of Jefferson, Ohio, in 1829 by Nathaniel Bedford, a former slaveholder of Charles City County, Virginia (274-85). Description of a "bush" prayer meeting held by the residents, with comment on their "weird" plaintive singing, on the practice of lining-out hymns and adding an ad libitum chorus, on the shout, and on the preacher and his prayers.

871 HYMN BOOK OF THE AFRICAN METHODIST EPISCOPAL CHURCH, BEING A COLLECTION OF HYMNS, SACRED SONGS AND CHANTS, DESIGNED TO SUPERSEDE ALL OTHERS HITHERTO MADE USE OF IN THAT CHURCH. SELECTED FROM VARIOUS AUTHORS. Collected by Henry M. Turner. Philadelphia: Publication Department A.M.E. Church, 1876.

A. M. E. minister Turner (later A. M. E. Bishop) was appointed at the General Conference of the Church in 1868 to compile a new hymnal. He completed his work in 1873, having selected hymns "from 32 of the very best and most orthodox hymn books extant...[drawing] largely upon the Wesleys," according to his Compiler's Remarks. Only texts and meters are given, with no indication of the appropriate tunes for the singing of the texts. Observation that "We have a wide spread custom of singing on revival occasions, especially, what is commonly called spiritual songs, most of which are devoid of both sense and reason....To obviate the necessity of recurring to these wild melodies," he included a number of "old Zion Songs" in the section entitled Revivals. Two songs have a typical structure of the spiritual.

Texts of 2 songs: 1. Say, brothers will you meet us? (no. 852). 2. I'll try to prove faithful (Cho: Till we all shall meet above) (no. 866).

872 HYMN BOOK OF THE AFRICAN METHODIST EPISCOPAL CHURCH, BEING A COLLECTION OF HYMNS.... Philadelphia: Published by the A. M. E. Book Concern, 1897.

A. M. E. Church appointed a committee in 1888 to plan for the publication of an official "music hymnal," which in 1897 became the first music hymnal in the history of the Church. Most of the work was done by Bishop J. C. Embry and John Turner Layton, a songwriter-hymnist. Music is provided for approximately one-half of the hymns; for some hymns the titles of appropriate tunes are given. One hymn has the typical structure of a spiritual; no tune is indicated for it.

Text of 1 song: Say, brothers, will you meet us (no. 616).

873 "Incidents in Negro Religion." NATIONAL ANTI-SLAVERY STANDARD 24 (10 October 1863): [4].

Discussion of the antebellum slave preacher includes description of slave religious-conversion experiences.

874 Ingersoll, Ernest. "Decoration of Negro Graves." JOURNAL OF AMERICAN FOLK-LORE 5 (January-March 1892): 68-69.

American naturalist discusses graveyard decorations he found in the black cemetery in Columbia, South Carolina, c.1881.

875 Ingle, A. L. Bassett. "Religion in the South: A Negro Revival in Virginia." FRANK LESLIE'S ILLUSTRATED NEWSPAPER 36 (9 August 1873): 346-47.

Discussion of a revival meeting in Virginia includes references to the practice of "seeking" and to the baptism that followed the meeting.

876 J. "Folk-Lore and Ethnology: The Ceremony of 'Foot Wash' in Virginia." SOUTHERN WORKMAN 25 (April 1896): 82.

Description of a ritual Foot Wash, which was held annually during the fall in rural black churches of Virginia, includes discussion of the Biblical readings that refer to "foot-washing," to the singing of songs, the prayers, and the distinctive attire of the participants. Detailed description of the "Christian shout," which takes place after the ceremonies.

877 Jasper, John. DE SUN DO MOVE. Richmond, VA:, 188-. Pamphlet. 4 pp.

Synopsis of the celebrated sermon of ex-slave minister Jasper (1812-1901), pastor of the Sixth Mt. Zion Baptist Church in Richmond, Virginia.

878 [_____.] "Personal." HARPER'S WEEKLY 33 (30 March 1889): 239.

News item about the Rev. John Jasper, of the First African Church of Richmond, Virginia, whose sermon "The Sun Do Move" made him nationally famous in the 1890s, includes comment on the allegorical wedding conducted in his church, based upon the parable of "the Wise and Foolish Virgins." Also reference to holy dancing.

879 Jocelyn, Caroline E. "South Carolina." AMERICAN MISSIONARY (MAGAZINE) n.s. 8 (August 1864): 238-40.

Northern school teacher, working among the freed slaves on Hilton Head, South Carolina, describes a plantation funeral, commenting on the mourners singing a plaintive dirge as they followed the cart carrying the crude coffin.

880 Jocelyn, S. S. "A Visit to the Freedmen in East Virginia." INDEPENDENT 15 (16 July 1863): 8.

Description of a Love Feast attended by the author at Fortress Monroe, Virginia, at which about 250 ex-slaves were present. Also description of a religious service witnessed at the Bute-Street Baptist Church in Norfolk, Virginia. Comment on the prayers and exhortations, which were "remarkable for their pertinency, depth of experience and the knowledge of divine things manifested." Reference to the black clergyman Rev. Mr. Parker of Norfolk.

881 Johnson, M. "The Georgia Negro before, during, and since the War." AMERICAN CATHOLIC QUARTERLY REVIEW 6 (1881): 353-67.

Focus upon the consequences of the abolition of slavery in South, including discussion of plantation life. Description of the corn husking and the great "laying-by" barbecues that took place in the summers. Also discussion of the various attitudes towards religion, the preference of some Negroes for black preachers rather than white. References to the oratory of the black preacher at funerals and to the lining out of hymns.

882 Johnson, Plato. "Free Cirkelatin' Liberies." INDEPENDENT 34 (23 February 1882): 3.

Discussion by a black preacher of the need for New York to make free circulating libraries available to colored citizens and other poor.

883 ____. "No Color Line in Heaven." FOLIO (Boston) 19 (January 1880): 2.

Excerpt of a sermon: No color line in heaven. Brudders, de lub ob de Lord am a wonderful ting.

884 Joseph, Frances. "Prison Reform Work in New Orleans." A. M. E. CHURCH REVIEW 15 (1899): 827-35.

Afro-American missionary Joseph, describing her work among the inmates at the State Prison at Baton Rouge, Louisiana, discusses weekly prayer-meeting services, the singing of hymns, and religious conversions.

885 K., C. "Virginia." ZION'S HERALD 50 (24 April 1873): 133.

Discussion of proceedings of the Virginia Conference of the A. M. E. Church at Portsmouth, Virginia, during 187-. Observation that the preachers were mainly from Virginia. Reference to a resolution passed by the assembly condemning the practice of A.M.E. congregations singing songs without meaning or sense. Reference to song performance practice.

Texts of 3 songs: 1. Good morning to you, stranger. 2. A child may get converted. 3. Swing low, chariot in the East.

886 Kealing, H. T. "The Colored Ministers of the South---Their Preaching and Peculiarities." A. M. E. CHURCH REVIEW 1 (1884): 139-44.

Black professor of Waco, Texas, discusses the oratory of black preachers of the South. Cites examples of both learned and self-made orators, who relied more upon sound and "stentorian lungs" than upon reasoned discourse. Comment on the eloquence of the preacher, his philosophy, and dramatic presentation. Analysis of a sermon, with comment on its themes and imageries.

Excerpt of 1 sermon text: Gabriel, blow your horn.

887 Kemble, Frances Anne. FURTHER RECORDS: 1848-1883. A Series of Letters by Frances Anne Kemble, Forming a Sequel to RECORDS OF A GIRLHOOD and RECORDS OF LATER LIFE. London: Richard Bentley & Son, 1890. 2 vols.

References to the survival of African traditions among the ex-slaves, particularly "Obi-Worship in a great many curious forms of what they consider evil omen, unlucky, uncanny" (2:32).

888 Kilham, Elizabeth. "Sketches in Color." PUTNAM'S MONTHLY 5 (March 1870): 304-11.

Fourth in a series of articles written by a northern schoolteacher about her experiences in the South after the Civil War includes description of black church services and discussion of their liturgy and hymns. One sermon text is accompanied by the description of the congregation testifying to various "experiences," after which a praise service was held.

Texts of 9 songs. See SONG COLLECTIONS (no. 1771).

889 King, Edward Smith. "A Ramble in Virginia: From Bristol to the Sea." SCRIBNER'S MONTHLY 7 (April 1874): 645-47.

Massachusetts-born journalist, discussing his travels, includes description of a Sunday revival meeting held in Richmond, Virginia---the preacher and the responses of his congregation (666-70). Also discussion of factories and the marketplace of Lynchburg, Virginia, where he notes: "The plaintive sound of a horn was heard above the bustle of traffic; it was in the hands of a negro, summoning tobacco buyers to an auction" (646).

Excerpt of 1 sermon text: Christ is the creating power of God.

890 ____. THE SOUTHERN STATES OF NORTH AMERICA: A RECORD OF JOURNEYS IN LOUISIANA, TEXAS, THE INDIAN TERRITORY, MISSOURI, ARKANSAS, MISSISSIPPI, ALABAMA, GEORGIA, FLORIDA, SOUTH CAROLINA, NORTH CAROLINA, KENTUCKY, TENNESSEE, VIRGINIA, WEST VIRGINIA, AND MARYLAND. London: Blackie & Son, 1875. 789 pp. Also published as THE GREAT SOUTH: A RECORD.... Hartford, CT: American Publishing Company, 1875. Reprint. Baton Rouge: Louisiana State University, 1972.

The author and the artist J. Wells Champney were commissioned by SCRIBNER'S MONTHLY MAGAZINE to write articles about "The Great South" after the Civil War. This book includes all the SCRIBNER'S articles "re-written and rearranged" with "more description and illustrations." Detailed discussion of blacks singing worksongs (69), of the songs of roustabouts in St. Louis, with special reference to their curious practice of ending refrains with a "characteristic "wail" (257); of Negro prayer meetings in Georgia and Virginia, with comment on performance practice associated with the singing of "wild hymns" (521-22, 583-86); of performance practice associated with the singing of Negro spirituals (616-17) and of the musical character of the spirituals. Chapter 68 is given over to "Negro Songs and Singers." Also comment on a folk preacher, Father Jupiter, (585-86) and reprint of an article about the shout from the NATION (618).

Texts of 26 spirituals; texts of 2 couplets. Excerpt from the text of a revival sermon: Christ is the Creating Power of God (584-86). See SONG COLLECTIONS (no. 1772).

891 King, Grace E. NEW ORLEANS, THE PLACES AND THE PEOPLE. New York: Macmillan & Company, 1895. Reprint. New York: Negro Universities Press, 1968. 404 pp.

This history of New Orleans, written by a native, devotes Chapter 14 to discussion of slaves and free "men of color" and refers to blacks in other sections. Description of plantation singing (337), of creole songs and relevant performance practice (339-40), and of voodoo (342-44). References to blacks dancing the Bamboula and the Calinda in Congo Square (342).

Text of 1 song: Di temps Missie d'Artaguette (Cho: He! Ho! He!). Texts of 2 choruses: 1. Dansey Calinda! Badoum! Badoum! 2. Bonsoir, danse, soleil, couche!

892 Kipling, Rudyard. AMERICAN NOTES. Philadelphia: Henry Altemus, 1899. 184 pp.

English author describes a worship service he attended at a black church in Philadelphia (49-50). Reference to the worshippers dancing up the aisle to the mourner's bench and likens the dance to a "Zanzibar stick dance."

893 L. "Extracts from Letters from among the Freedmen." CHILDREN'S FRIEND (Philadelphia) 1 (1866): 63-66.

Report on a woman's work among the freedmen on St. Helena Island, South Carolina, includes an account of an illiterate preacher who requested the missionaries to read specific chapters from the Bible to him. Though neither he nor any of his congregation could read, he applied the readings well in his sermons.

894 L., D. F. "Uncle Ben Johnson." CHRISTIAN WATCHMAN & REFLECTOR (=WATCHMAN-EXAMINER) 55 (29 October 1874): [4].

Character sketch of an illiterate black preacher in rural North Carolina, written by a northern minister and agent of the Home Missionary Society, includes excerpts of his interview with the preacher, with comment on singing and praying.

895 Laney, Lucy C. "The Burden of the Educated Colored Woman." SOUTHERN WORKMAN 28 (September 1899): 341.

Afro-American principal of the Haines School in Augusta, Georgia, in discussing the economic hardships of, and discrimination against black women, comments on a plantation minister and on his congregation's practice of lining out hymns.

896 Langhorne, Orra. "A Funeral at the African Church." SOUTHERN WORKMAN 12 (April 1883): 38.

Comment by a former slaveholder of Virginia on the dual preaching styles of Mr. Homor, pastor of the A. M. E. Church in Lynchburg, Virginia. One preaching style was intended for white southerners, another for his black congregation.

897 _____. "Colored Religion." INDEPENDENT 35 (30 August 1883): 1091.

Discussion of religious practices at a revival meeting held at a local black church in Lynchburg, Virginia, as told to the author by a servant. Reference to preachers "shouting" in the pulpit.

898 _____. "Southern Sketches: Goin' to the Baptism." SOUTHERN WORKMAN 20 (October 1891): 234.

Description of a baptism service of a local black congregation near Culpeper, Virginia, includes comment on the passing of traditional performance practice associated with baptism services. Description of the shout.

Text of 1 song: Ef you want go to Heaven an' set aroun' de throne. Text of 1 couplet: Go on, go on to Jesus' arms.

899 "Laying the Foundations." SOUTHERN WORKMAN 24 (September 1895): 139-43.

Excerpts from a letter written by the Rev. L. C. Lockwood of the American Missionary Association, dated Fortress Monroe (Virginia), 4 September 1861, provide primary-source information about the singing of spirituals by blacks, about their prayer meetings, and their religious practices in the South. Observation that the ex-slaves sang songs "of their own making" and description of relevant performance practice.

Text of 1 song: Go down to Egypt.

900 Leach, D. F. "The Freedmen on the Plantations." CHRISTIAN WATCHMAN & REFLECTOR (=WATCHMAN-EXAMINER) 54 (1 May 1873): [1].

Description of the life-style of former slaves living in and about Yatesville, Virginia, after the Civil War, written by a white native of the area, includes references to their religious practices, to the shout, which he compares to a Shaker dance, and its performance practice. Also comment on "ecstatic seizure" and spirit possession, on the illiteracy of the ex-slave preacher; and on performance practice associated with the singing of sacred folksongs.

Texts of 4 songs: 1. Sister, hold your light high. 2. Before I would lie in hell one day, I'd pray and sing myself away (Cho: I have nothing else to do, But to sing Jerusalem). 3. Mary, tune your harp. 4. Moses smote the water.

901 Leedom, Benjamin J. WESTTOWN UNDER THE OLD AND NEW REGIME BY AULD LANG SYNE. Wuerzburg: Bonitas-Bauer, 1883. 300 pp.

Written in 1869, this book recounts the author's

school-days experiences during the years 1817-18? at the Westtown school in Chester County, Pennsylvania. Description of the visit of about 100 white school boys to a colored camp meeting held in the woods near West Chester (166-72).

Text of 1 chorus: We're traveling to Immanual's land. Glory! Hallelujah!

902 Leigh, Frances Butler. TEN YEARS ON A GEORGIA PLANTATION SINCE THE WAR. London: Richard Bentley & Son, 1883. 347 pp.

Discussion, by the daughter of Frances Kemble, of her stay on a Georgia plantation during the years 1866-67 and later, includes detailed description of the shout as performed on St. Simon Island (59-60) and refers to the songs of boatmen on the Island (172-73, 344). Also discussion of the ex-slave funeral traditions, where the funeral comes three weeks later than the burial (165); of a church wedding (247-48); a religious ring dance (254); and the singing of hymns and plantation songs (322-23).

903 Lewis, T. Willard. "Missionary Letter from the South." ZION'S HERALD AND WESLEYAN JOURNAL (=ZION'S HERALD) 35 (27 June 1864): [117].

Clergyman of the New England (Methodist) Church, serving as a missionary to the Department of the South, in a letter dated 6 July from Beaufort, South Carolina, describes the missionary work among blacks on the Florida Sea Islands. Comment on the funeral services of a boy, at which a hymn was lined out.

904 Livermore, Mary Ashton. MY STORY OF THE WAR: A WOMAN'S NARRATIVE OF FOUR YEARS PERSONAL EXPERIENCE AS NURSE IN THE UNION ARMY. Hartford, CT: A. D. Worthington & Company, 1889. Reprint. New York: Arno Press and the New York Times, 1971. 700 pp.

Written by a native of Boston, these memoirs of her experiences as a nurse in the Union Army during the Civil War include discussion of life in contraband camps and religious services held there in the evenings (257-79, 350-55). Comment on the shout and the performance practice associated with singing (262-65, 355).

Texts of 2 songs: 1. I see de angels beck'nin' (Cho: Oh, I'm gwine home to Glory) (262). 2. An' I hope to gain de prommis' land (333). Text of 1 couplet: Go tell Moses, go down into Egypt (267).

905 _____. THE STORY OF MY LIFE; OR, THE SUNSHINE AND SHADOW OF SEVENTY YEARS. Hartford, CT: A. D. Worthington & Company, 1899. 730 pp.

The author, who spent three years as a tutor on a plantation in Virginia, includes in these memoirs discussion of Christmas festivities (210, 346-48), of religious services with reference to performance practice (253-55, 348), of dancing to the music of banjos and fiddles (210, 255-58), and the corn-shucking festival (332-41).

Texts of 5 songs: 1. An' I hope to gain de promis' lan' (183). 2. I's gwine t' Mas'r Jesus (185). 3. Oh, brethern pray, for cloudy is my way (254). 4. Religion's like a bloomin' rose (339). 5. We're gwine home t' die no mo' (Cho: We'll meet ag'in in de mawning) (340). Reference to 1 dance: the pigeon-wing (333).

906 Lockwood, Lewis C. "Capacity of Slaves for Freedom and Soldiery: As Seen in a Year's Experience among the Ex-Slaves." INDEPENDENT 15 (5 February 1863): 2-3.

Missionary clergyman working among the freedmen at Fortress Monroe, Virginia, during the Civil War, includes in his discussion comment on their "fitness for freedom and soldiery," observing that "many of their songs were inspired by the spirit of liberty." Observation that one of the songs, "O, go down, Moses," had been sung by slaves for thirty or forty years before it was "introduced to the ears of the nation." Also discussion of Mary S. Peake, a colored women, who was the first teacher of contrabands.

Texts of 2 songs: 1. Stolen we were from Africa (Cho: There's a better day a-coming). 2. The Lord by Moses to Pharaoh said (Cho: O, go down, Moses).

907 M. (=McAdoo, Orpheus Myron?). "Letters from Hampton Graduates." Nos. 1, 2. SOUTHERN WORKMAN 7/Supplement (October, November 1878): 76, 92.

Letter No. 1, addressed to General Armstrong at Hampton Insitute, dated 24 August 1878, includes comment of a Hampton graduate on his work among rural blacks in Accomac County, Virginia. Observation that they had religious services only once a month and that the singing was in plantation-style. Letter No. 2 discusses further his work and refers to a spiritual sung by his students: In dat great gettin'-up morning.

908 MacDowell, Katherine S. B. [Sherwood Bonner, pseud.]. "Christmas Eve at Tuckeyho." LIPPINCOTT'S MAGAZINE 33 (January 1884) 51-65.

This short story of romance and intrigue on a plantation includes comment on the "wild negro melody" of the boatmen and, as others joined in, the sound of "a hundred voices swelled out in a deep...harmony" (53); and on a Christmas Eve sermon preached in the "quarters" (63).

Text of 1 song: De Lord he giv de cotton an' de corn. Excerpt of 1 sermon text: Sin and hell.

909 Macrae, David. THE AMERICANS AT HOME. Edinburgh: Edmonston and Douglas, 1870. 2 vols. Reprint. New York: Dutton, 1952. 606 pp. Page references below are to the reprint.

Scottish clergyman's account of his visit to America after the Civil War includes a chapter, entitled "Black Christianity" (353-375) given over to discussion of religion. Comment on the typical religious services of the blacks, on the rude oratorical style of black preachers, the "excitements" called "shoutings," and the direct quality of the prayers. Detailed discussion of the "original hymns" sung in the worship services.

Texts of 2 sermons: 1. The regulations of John (the Book of Revelation). 2. Man's creation and Satan's expulsion from heaven (368-69). Melodies (without texts) of 4 songs; texts of 8 songs. SEE SONG COLLECTIONS (no. 1774).

910 _____. AMONGST THE DARKIES, AND OTHER PAPERS. c.1876. Glasgow: John S. Marr & Sons, 1880. 118 pp.

Discussion of the condition of blacks in the United States focuses upon life for them after the Civil War, as witnessed during the author's travels in the South during 1868. Description of a New Year's Eve service at a contraband camp near Washington, D. C., in December 1862 (16-17), with reference to the singing and the preaching of a plantation preacher, and description of the shout (18).

Texts of 2 songs: 1. Go down, Abraham, way down into Dixie's land (16). 2. O, poor sinners, watch and pray (22). Reference to 1 song: My fader died a shoutin' (18). References to 2 sermons: 1. And in those days came John de Baptis' (17). 2. One faith, one Lord, one baptism (17).

911 Malcolm, Thomas S. "Six Men for Africa." CHRISTIAN WATCHMAN & REFLECTOR (=WATCHMAN-EXAMINER) 63 (16 March 1882): 82.

Discussion by a white American minister of the black missionaries sent to Liberia, West Africa, includes a character sketch of ex-slave Lott Cary [=Carey], a Baptist preacher who conducted prayer-meetings among the blacks on plantations near Richmond, Virginia, in the early 1800s. Through Cary's efforts, the African Baptist Missionary Society was founded at Richmond in 1815.

912 Martson, S. M. "Freedmen's Missions." CHRISTIAN WATCHMAN & REFLECTOR (=WATCHMAN-EXAMINER) 60 (1 April 1880): [2].

Discussion of the religious education of black preachers in the South by a white minister of Natchez, Mississippi, includes the observation that some prefer to remain in "ignorance," are unable to read, denounce the Bible as the work of men and not of God, and are unwilling to share their pulpits with any preacher who uses "books" (i.e., the Bible and hymnals). Cites the example of Rev. J. S. Campbell, a black preacher of Galveston, Texas, who was barred from preaching at a rural church when it was learned that he used a hymnal and a Bible in preparing his sermons.

913 Mason, Isaac. LIFE OF ISAAC MASON AS A SLAVE. Worcester, MA: The Author, 1893. 74 pp. Reprint. Miami, FL: Mnemosyne Publishing Company, 1969.

Autobiography of a slave (b. 1822) who escaped from Maryland and finally settled in Worcester, Massachusetts, reports on a slaveholder who attended the colored Methodist Church, where he would "jump, shout and sing" like the slaves (27), and discusses a camp meeting of colored people held near Albany, New York, in July 1851.

914 McCabe, Linda R. "Colored Church Work in New York." OUTLOOK 54 (22 August 1896): 327-29.

This history of black churches in the City of New York and their pastors includes the observation that the "old-time funeral customs" should be retained as a means of reaching the "lower-classes," as should also the preservation of the "Amen Corner" on the first Sunday of each month. Also discussion of the old-time exhortation.

915 McCulloch-Williams, Martha. "A Black Settlement." HARPER'S NEW MONTHLY MAGAZINE 93 (October 1896): 767-78.

Discussion of an all-black settlement in the interior of Tennessee, founded by ex-slaves from Kentucky, Virginia, and the Carolinas, includes comment on their religious singing and describes the "Dead March," a walk-around religious dance similar to the shout.

Texts of 2 songs: 1. Jerusalem! My happy home! I want ter go dar too! 2. When I gits my new house done.

916 Michaux, Richard Randolph. SKETCHES OF LIFE IN NORTH CAROLINA, EMBRACING INCIDENTS AND NARRATIVES, AND PERSONAL ADVENTURES OF THE AUTHOR DURING FORTY YEARS OF TRAVEL. Culler, NC: W. C. Phillips, Printer, 1894.

Chapter 3 (21-32), which focuses on the religious activities of black folk in North Carolina, includes a brief description of congregational singing (26) and references to Uncle Lige of Guilford County (29) and to Livingston College (for colored) in Salisbury, North Carolina.

917 Mead, Mary N. "From House to House." SOUTHERN WORKMAN 25 (April 1896): 80.

Essay about the religious experiences of an elderly black woman of Hampton, Virginia.

Text of 1 song: I am building on de rock.

918 Miller, Joaquin. "From New Orleans to Vera Cruz: Barataria." INDEPENDENT 37 (7 May 1885): 578-79.

Travelogue includes description of a plantation

in Louisiana and comment on a religious service and oratory style of the black preacher, a common field-hand, who "exhorted" without notes and read with difficulty from the Bible.

919 Minton, T. J. "Northern Correspondents: In the South.---The Sort of Men They Are and Always Have Been." NEW YORK GLOBE (3 February 1883): [1].

Letter to the Editor, dated 29 January 1883, Washington, D. C., includes comment on the series of articles published by the GLOBE on the condition of the ex-slaves in the South and on the white newspaper reporters. Quotation of a passage from the Rev. Hamilton Pierson's book IN THE BUSH (see no. 960) about the sermons of antebellum Negro preachers and discussion of their oratory style.

920 "More Southern Notes." CHRISTIAN WATCHMAN & REFLECTOR (=WATCHMAN-EXAMINER) 49 (3 May 1888): [2].

Discussion of three institutions for the religious training of blacks: Shaw University in Raleigh, North Carolina; Richmond Theological Seminary in Virginia; and the Weyland Seminary in Washington, D. C. Also discussion of black churches in Richmond, Virginia, with comment on the celebrated Rev. John Jasper, ex-slave Baptist pastor of that city.

921 Morehouse, Julia Hunt. "Sunday among the Freedmen." ZION'S HERALD 57 (15 April 1880): 126.

Description of a worship service of black Methodists at Sumter, South Carolina, includes comment on their singing of "weird" Negro melodies, on performance practice, and the shout.

Text of 1 sermon: And Saul yet breathing out threatenings and slaughter (Acts 9:1).

922 Mosby, Ella F. "A Negro Quarter." INDEPENDENT 34 (15 June 1882): 6-7.

Discussion of the death-rites custom of "sitting up" with the body and singing at the wake.

923 Mott, Abigail. NARRATIVES OF COLORED AMERICANS. Compiled by Alexander Mott and M. S. Wood. New York: William Wood & Company, 1877. Reprint. Freeport, NY: Books For Libraries Press, 1971. 276 pp.

Biographical sketches for the slave preacher "Uncle Jack" (46-48) and a female slave fiddler (144), and description of a religious service of contrabands held near Washington, D. C. (266).

Summary of 1 sermon: I commanded you to go into all the world and preach the gospel.

924 Nason, C. "Religious Matters in South Carolina." ZION'S HERALD AND WESLEYAN JOURNAL (=ZION'S HERALD) 34 (18 March 1863): 42-43.

Chaplain in the Union Army, 8th Maine Volunteers, writes from Beaufort, South Carolina, on 2 March 1863, urging that missionary work be undertaken by Methodists in that region. Observes that there are about 200 Methodist contrabands, who seek to form a church, their only religious instruction being provided by an unordained, fugitive slave of Charleston.

925 "Negro Dances in Arkansas." JOURNAL OF AMERICAN FOLK-LORE 1 (April-June 1888): 83.

Originally published in the BOSTON HERALD, 7 May 1887, this article reports on a dance that was performed around the grave of a dead pastor by his colored congregation, which lasted for three nights. Comparison of the ceremony to African rites and interpretation of it as an effort to conjure the pastor back to life.

926 "The Negro Marms Having a Hard Time of It." DE BOW'S REVIEW n.s. 11 (July 1866): 94-95.

Discussion of the work of northern black school teachers in the South after the Civil War includes description of a typical, black camp meeting, with references to the shout and the oratory style of the preacher.

927 "A Negro Methodist Conference." CORNHILL MAGAZINE 33 (March 1876): 338-48. Reprint. LITTELL'S LIVING AGE 129 (8 April 1876): 106-13.

Discussion of church services attended by the writer in Western New York State and in Virginia includes comment on the choral singing and congregational responses to the sermon. Comment on a curious melody identified as an African tune.

928 "A Negro Pastor in New Orleans." CHRISTIAN WATCHMAN & REFLECTOR (=WATCHMAN-EXAMINER) 44 (3 September 1863): [4].

White traveler's discussion of black religious services in New Orleans in 1847 includes comment on the black pastor and the singing of his congregation, composed mostly of slaves, and on a deacon's "raising of a tune" in the wrong meter.

Text of 1 sermon: Gabriel blowin' de trumpet.

929 "Negro Preachers at the South." ILLUSTRATED CHRISTIAN WEEKLY 1 (3 June 1871): 61-62.

Discussion of a sermon delivered at the African Meeting House in Richmond, Virginia.

Text of 1 sermon: De hireling fleeth, I am a Good Shepherd.

930 "Negro Preachers.---Original Sin." ILLUSTRATED CHRISTIAN WEEKLY 1 (22 July 1871): 117-18.

Character sketch of Ashby McGuire, an antebellum black preacher, includes a transcription of a sermon that he preached on Original Sin.

Text of 1 sermon: The Fathers have eaten sour grapes: the children's teeth are set on edge.

931 "Negro Preaching." CHRISTIAN WATCHMAN & REFLECTOR (=WATCHMAN-EXAMINER) 45 (7 July 1864): [1].

Description of a religious service at the African church in Nashville, Tennessee, includes references to the singing of "monotonous" tunes by a row of colored brethern, who kept time by the swaying of their bodies"; to the oratory style of the preacher; and to the congregation's communal responses to the preaching.

Text of 1 sermon: The Crucifixion of Christ.

932 "Negro Religion." AMERICAN MISSIONARY (MAGAZINE) n.s. 32 (July 1878): 217.

Discussion of the character of religious worship in black churches includes a description of the religious chanting and dancing of an elderly woman. References to the black preacher and the singing of "quaint hymns."

Text of 1 sermon: There is no use hiding, for you cannot hide from the grave.

933 "A Negro's Gratitude." WATCHMAN & REFLECTOR (=WATCHMAN-EXAMINER) 48 (28 February 1867): [1].

Discussion includes an account of a preacher whom the writer taught to read the Bible and comment on the preacher's gratitude for finally being able to read about the Deity he had preached about all his life.

934 "Negro-Prayers." CHRISTIAN WATCHMAN & REFLECTOR (=WATCHMAN-EXAMINER) 46 (11 May 1865): [1].

Excerpts of two prayers delivered by slave preachers after being informed by soldiers of the Union Army that they had been freed.

935 "New Year's Day in Richmond." INDEPENDENT 18 (18 January 1866): 6.

Description of a service held at the African Church of Richmond, Virginia, on 1 January, at which 4,000 freedmen assembled to honor the memory of the slain President Lincoln. Includes comment on the prayer and speech on freedom delivered by the Rev. John Oliver, "a colored citizen of the Frederick Douglass class and for eighteen years a resident of Boston," and the singing of a freedom song by black servicemen.

Text of 1 couplet: We look like men of war.

936 N., C. [=Nordhoff, Charles]. "The Freedmen of South Carolina." Parts 1, 2. NATIONAL ANTI-SLAVERY STANDARD 24 (2, 23 May 1863): [4]; [4]. Reprinted from the EVENING POST.

Part 1: The Schools---Character of the People---The Administrative System." Discussion includes comment on the songs of the contrabands on the Sea Islands of South Carolina. References to songs of the boatmen and the general religious basis of slave song texts.

Reference to 1 song: Roll, Jordan, roll. Text of 1 couplet: I'll follow Jesus's way. Text of 1 song: Old massa death, he's a very little man (Cho: Good Lord, remember me).

Part 2: "Their Moral Condition---Religious Sentiments---Smalls, [sic] of the Planters." Discussion of the ex-slaves' fondness for singing, attending religious meetings, and their display of emotionalism during the worship service. Description of the shout.

937 _____. THE FREEDMEN OF SOUTH-CAROLINA: SOME ACCOUNT OF THEIR APPEARANCE, CHARACTER, CONDITION AND PECULIAR CUSTOMS. New York: Charles T. Evans, 1863. 27 pp.

Discussion of the singing heard at Port Royal, South Carolina, includes comment on the quality of the voices and the subjects of the texts (10). References to the "curious excitability" exhibited in devotional meetings and comparison of the shout to the "jerks" of white worshipers, as seen in the West and South West (23).

Texts of 2 songs: 1. I'll follow Jesus's ways (Cho: No man can hinder me) (10). 2. Old massa Death, he's a very little man (Cho: Good Lord, remember me) (10).

938 _____. THE COTTON STATES IN THE SPRING AND SUMMER OF 1875. New York: D. Appleton & Company, 1876. 112 pp. Reprint. New York: B. Franklin, c.1971.

Report on the social, political, and industrial conditions in six southern states includes references to a black church in Arkansas with cotton-farmer preachers (39) and to the "peculiar" worship services of black Baptists and Methodists in Louisiana (73).

939 Odana [pseud.]. "Jack and His Sermon." NATIONAL ANTI-SLAVERY STANDARD 24 (6 February 1864): [4]. Reprint from NEW YORK OBSERVER.

Summary of the sermon of an antebellum slave preacher of Tennessee: Whar de chillum of Izzul war tryin' to leab de lan' of Egypt.

940 "An Old Landmark." HARPER'S WEEKLY 18 (27 JUNE 1874): 545.

History of the First African Church of Richmond, Virginia. Originally built by whites in 1802, the church building was turned over to the black congregation in the early 1800s. References to the singing of the congregation and choir.

941 "Origin of the White Trash." DRAMATIC NEWS AND SPORTING JOURNAL 11 (4 May 1872): 14.

Excerpt from the text of a funeral discourse delivered by a black preacher: Origin of the species.

942 P., L. A. "Contrasts: The Past and the Present." AMERICAN MISSIONARY (MAGAZINE) 33 (1879): 335-37.

Discussion of the activities in an evening school for freedmen includes the transcription of a prayer, which contains phrases and motifs found also in the texts of spirituals.

Text of 1 prayer.

943 Page, Walter Hines [Nicholas Worth, pseud]. "Religious Progress of the Negroes." INDEPENDENT 33 (1 September 1881): 7.

Journalist-writer of Greenville, South Carolina, compares the religious instruction and practices of slaves in the antebellum South to practices of ex-slaves since the Civil War, particularly in Virginia and South Carolina. Comment on a camp meeting he attended in 1866, with its sermon "full of ignorance," extemporaneous singing and exhortations, shout, and "mourner's bench," and observation that such practices were on the decline in many black urban churches.

Text of 1 song: You may bury my body in de middle of de ocean.

944 _____. "The Biography of a Negro---IV." INDEPENDENT 35 (15 February 1883): 176.

Fictional biography of an ex-slave named Primus includes discussion of religious practices in a black church, the oratory of the preacher, the singing of a "corrupt" version of the hymn "The Old Ship of Zion," and the moaning and shouting of the congregation.

Reference to 1 song: The Old Ship of Zion.

945 Parker, Allen. RECOLLECTIONS OF SLAVERY TIMES. Worcester, MA: Charles W. Burbank and Company, 1895. 96 pp.

Slave narrative includes discussion of Christmas festivities on the plantation, with references to performance practice associated with pattin' Juba (66-67), and description of a prayer meeting held in a cabin (68-69) and a burial service (79-80).

Text of 1 song: You see dat falcon a-lighting (Cho: Roll, Jordan, roll).

946 Parrish, Joseph. "Correspondence." PENNSYLVANIA FREEDMEN'S BULLETIN (June 1866): 1-8.

Written by a physician visiting the Sea Islands of South Carolina after the Civil War, a letter dated 17 May 1866, from Beaufort, South Carolina, describes a plantation praise-meeting. References to the "chief man" on the plantation (who conducted the services), to prayers, and to plantation songs.

947 Partridge, H. E. "Meetings among the Hills and at a Convict Camp." AMERICAN MISSIONARY (MAGAZINE) n. s. 50 (June 1896): 186-88.

Description of a religious service at a black convict camp includes comment on the black prisoners singing "weird religious songs" of "their own race."

948 Payne, Daniel Alexander. THE SEMI-CENTENARY AND THE RETROSPECTION OF THE AFRICAN METHODIST EPISCOPAL CHURCH IN THE UNITED STATES OF AMERICA. Baltimore: Published by the Author, Sherwood & Company, c.1866. 189 pp. Reprint. Freeport, NY: Books for Libraries Press, 1972.

Historical survey of the African Methodist Episcopal Church, its publications and educational institutions, by Payne (1811-1893), who served the church as minister, historian, bishop, and college president (of Wilberforce University). Includes reference to a resolution passed by the Church at the Annual Conference in 1841 that preachers should "strenuously oppose" the people singing "hymns of their own composing" at public meetings and in church (45).

949 _____. "Journal, 1877-78." Manuscript. Moorland-Spingarn Collection, Howard University. Washington, D. C.

In an entry dated 10 July 1877 Payne comments on the "spiritual" folk preacher.

950 _____. RECOLLECTIONS OF SEVENTY YEARS. Edited by C. S. Smith. Nashville, TN: Publishing House of the A. M. E. Sunday School Union, 1888. 335 pp. Reprints: New York: Arno Press and the New York Times, 1968. Selected passages in READINGS IN BLACK AMERICAN MUSIC. Edited by Eileen Southern. 1971. 2d ed. New York: W. W. Norton, 1983.

These memoirs of Bishop Payne include discussion of formal music in the black church and also references to folk practices: to "spiritual songs of the people" (94) and to "praying and singing bands," a bush meeting, and the shout (253-255).

Texts of 2 couplets: 1. Ashes to ashes, dust to dust 2. I was way over there where the coffin fell (255).

951 _____. HISTORY OF THE AFRICAN METHODIST EPISCOPAL CHURCH. Nashville, TN: Publishing House of the A. M. E. Sunday School Union, 1891. 502 pp. Reprint. Englewood, CO: Microcard Editions, 1971.

This is Part 1 of the history of the A.M.E. Church, covering the years up to 1856 (see no. 1975 in regard to Part 2). Includes the observation that congregations cannot read the hymnbooks "correctly" and therefore "introduce disorder and confusion in our singing, [and] make fuge [sic] tunes for themselves" (194). Also reference to William P. Jones, the A. M. E. traveling book agent during the years 1852-56, who published "thousands of cornfield ditties" during the 1850s (334).

952 Pearson, Elizabeth Ware, ed. LETTERS FROM PORT ROYAL [1862-1868] WRITTEN AT THE TIME OF THE CIVIL WAR. Boston: W. B. Clarke Company, 1906. Reprint. New York: Arno Press and the New York Times, 1969. 345 pp.

Collection of letters written by the daughter of Charles Ware to relatives and friends associated with the Port Royal Settlement for "contraband slaves" of the Civil War includes references to boatmen's songs and performance practice (19, 134); to baptism ceremonies in the creek (268-69); to the shout among soldiers (124); the praise-service shout (26-28); a Saturday-evening shout (34); and a children's shout (292-93). Also discussion of the religious service she attended one Sunday, with special comment on the voice quality of the singing (49-50), and of burial practices (65-66, 252-53).

Text of 1 song: Oh, Jacob's ladder climb higher (26).

953 Pendleton, Louis. "Salmagundi: 'Black' Corinth Church." SOUTHERN BIVOUAC n. s. 2 (November 1886): 391-92.

Description of a black church service (in Virginia?--place not indicated) includes comment on the oratory of the preacher and on the singing. Reference to the dancing of the worshippers on the church benches as "stompin' on de Old Boy."

Text of 1 song: Fox dig hole een de groun', Bird mek nes' in the air (Cho: Chillun, 'tis hard---trial---great tribulation).

954 Phi [pseud.]. "Our Washington Letter." CHRISTIAN WATCHMAN & REFLECTOR (=WATCHMAN-EXAMINER) 63 (12 May 1882): [4].

Discussion of the black population in Washington, D. C., and its surrounding communities of Virginia and Maryland includes the observation that the older ministers and church members still practice the "Old Virginia religion," which many blacks interpret as abandonment to "fanatical religious excitement" and use of "plantation methods of revivalism."

955 Phillips, A. L. "The Development of the Negro Ministry---First Stage." Parts 1, 2. HOMILETIC REVIEW 36 (1898): 21-22; "Stage Second": 502-504.

Discussion of the origin and development of the Negro ministry in the United States from slavery through Emancipation by the Secretary of the Executive Committee of Colored Evangelization of the Presbyterian Church (South) in the United States. Discussion of the religious instruction of slaves in the antebellum South, of the plantation preacher, his character, method of discourse, oratory style, and dramatic presentation of sermon. References to responses of the congregation and ecstatic seizure.

956 Phillips, W. S. "The Revival in South Carolina." CHRISTIAN WATCHMAN & REFLECTOR (=WATCHMAN-EXAMINER) 44 (14 May 1863): [2].

Description of a religious service of the ex-slaves on St. Helena Island, South Carolina.

Text of 1 song: Jesus lives and reigns forever (Cho: On Canaan's happy shore).

957 _____. "Going to a Wedding under Difficulties." NATIONAL ANTI-SLAVERY STANDARD 24 (11 July 1863): [4]. Reprinted from the SPRINGFIELD REPUBLICAN.

Description of the wedding of a contraband couple, conducted on the Sea Islands by a white, northern, Baptist clergyman, includes reference to the slaves' concept of living in sin, which was called "the lonesome valley."

Texts of 2 songs: 1. Brudder Sancho, do you want to get religion? (Cho: Go down in de lonesome valley). 2. I take my text from Matthew (Cho: There's a meeting here tonight.

958 _____. "Letter from South Carolina." CHRISTIAN WATCHMAN (=WATCHMAN-EXAMINER) 44 (20 August 1863): [2].

Missionary's discussion of his work among the ex-slaves on St. Helena Island, South Carolina, in a letter dated 31 July 1863, refers to a baptism service and the singing of sacred songs and hymns.

Text of 1 song: Good Lord, me are the one (Cho: Old Jordan's stream is a happy stream).

959 "Philologists in Session." CRITIC 4 (18 July 1885): 30-31.

A paper presented by J. A. Harrison, of Washington and Lee University, at the meeting of the American Philological Association (1885, Yale University) addresses the subject of "Negro English," and includes discussion of the black folk sermon, its contents, and performance practice.

960 Pierson, Hamilton W. IN THE BUSH; OR, OLD-

TIME SOCIAL, POLITICAL, AND RELIGIOUS LIFE IN THE SOUTHWEST. New York: D. Appleton and Company, 1881. 321 pp.

Clergyman and agent for the American Bible Society refers to the ex-slaves singing "breaking songs" at the close of prayer-meetings and marching past the pulpit to shake hands with the preacher (253). Also discussion of black folk preachers (262-77), of hymn singing (283), and of performance practice associated with the improvising of religious songs (284-86).

Reference to 3 sermon texts: 1. Duty to keep hearts pure and free (264). 2. De Methodis' is like de grasshopper (267-68). 3. For de great day of his raff is come (270).

961 "Plain Preaching." CHRISTIAN WATCHMAN & REFLECTOR (=WATCHMAN-EXAMINER) 60 (20 February 1879): [2].

Text of the sermon of a black Georgia preacher: The practice of religion makes man acceptable in heaven.

962 Pollard, Edward Alfred. "The Romance of the Negro." GALAXY, AN ILLUSTRATED MAGAZINE OF ENTERTAINING READING 12 (October 1871): 470-78. Reprint. THE AMERICAN MISSIONARY n.s. 15 (November 1871).

Discussion of the character of black life in the South after the Civil War refers to a preacher who, though limited in his mastery of language, often astonished his educated white listeners.

References to 2 songs: 1. The old ship of Zion. 2. Swing low, sweet chariot.

963 Pool, Ruth. "A 'Sitting-Up' Meeting in the South." ZION'S HERALD 57 (1 January 1880): 6.

Description of a New Year's Eve watch-meeting at a southern black church includes references to the singing of "weird" spiritual songs and song performance practice. Also references to exhortations and prayers.

964 Porter, Mary W. "Aunt Betsey's Funeral Sermon." INDEPENDENT 30 (17 January 1878): 3.

Description of the graveside rites for an old ex-slave woman, where each friend present threw a clod of earth into the open grave, and of the funeral sermon, which was preached in the village church several months after entombment. Includes references to the singing of hymns.

Text of 1 sermon: Blessed is de dead what lies in de Lord (Revelation).

965 _____. "Some Genuine Negro Songs." INDEPENDENT 30 (9 May 1878): 1.

This northerner, visiting Franklin, St. Mary's Parish, Louisiana, discusses the singing at the local black church on a Saturday evening, including comment on the relevant performance practice.

Texts of 4 songs: 1. Watch dat sun, see how she run (Cho: True believer, run home). 2. Come run along home to my Jesus. 3. Oh! Joshuay fought de battle at Jericho, An' de wall come a-tumblin' down!. 4. Little children, you better believe I'm most done wagging wid de cross. Reference to 1 sermon: Let not your hearts be troubled. Text of 1 couplet: Glory and honor, praise King Jesus.

966 _____. "In Memoriam." INDEPENDENT 30 (19 September 1878): 1-2.

Description of the funeral service of a black man, known as Uncle George Payne, at a local plantation church in St. Mary's Parish, Louisiana, includes reference to the fact that the congregation stood to sing "official" church hymns and sat when singing "their own songs."

Text of 3 songs: My Lord walking in de garden (Cho: Hail, oh! hail! Hallelujah!) 2. Oh! Where is brother George? (Cho: He died in the field of battle) 3. I've been in a strange land, so far from home (Cho: Fur de Lord done sanctify me). Text of 1 sermon: Death a-coming.

967 "Prayer." INDEPENDENT 19 (30 May 1867): 2.

Text of a "quaint but genuine prayer," delivered by a "colored woman at Richmond," Virginia, includes phrases and imagery that appear in spirituals of the period.

968 Pyrnelle, Louise-Clarke. DIDDIE, DUMPS, AND TOT; OR, PLANTATION CHILD LIFE. New York: Harper and Brothers, 1882. 217 pp. Reprint. Gretna, LA: Pelican Publishing Company, c.1963.

Discussion of plantation life includes description of a worship service and transcription of the sermon (168-77). Also description of play-party games along with texts of the dance/game songs. Discussion of Negro folk tales.

Texts of 4 dance/game songs (128-33): 1. I ac' monkey moshun. 2. Lipto, lipto, jine de ring. 3. De one I like de bes'. 4. Cotton-eyed Joe, cotton-eyed Joe. Texts of 4 songs: 1. Ef' 'ligion was er thing that money could buy. 2. Dan'l wuz er prayin' man. 3. My marster, Lord (Cho: O bless us, Lord). 4. Oh, pray, my brudder, pray (Cho: Roll, Jordan, roll).

Text of 1 sermon: Burhol', I'll punish um! Dey young men shall die by de s'ord. Texts of 8 tales. See TALE COLLECTIONS (no. 1734).

969 Quis est? [pseud.]. "From New Orleans---Worship in Colored Churches in the South." CHRISTIAN WATCHMAN & REFLECTOR (=WATCHMAN-EXAMINER) 62 (10 November 1881): 357.

Description of a Sunday-morning service in a large southern city includes comment on the performance practice associated with the singing of religious songs, and discussion of the oratory style of the preacher and the congregation's responses.

Text of 1 sermon: Christians should not glorify themselves, but seek to be glorified by God (based on Heb. 5:5).

970 R. "Letters from Hampton Graduates---A Scared Stump Speaker." SOUTHERN WORKMAN 9 (February 1880): 18.

Description by a black teacher of the shout, which was performed during the praise-meetings of a rural black community in the Blue Ridge Mountains of Virginia on Wednesday and Sunday evenings.

971 Ralph, Julian. "How a Tourist Sees Richmond." HARPER'S WEEKLY 38 (24 February 1894): 179-80.

Journalist-author, writing about Richmond, Virginia, includes comment on the African Church of that city and its former pastor, the Rev. John Jasper, an antebellum slave preacher.

Reference to 1 sermon: De Sun Do Move.

972 Raymond, Charles A. "The Religious Life of the Negro Slaves." Parts 1-3. HARPER'S NEW MONTHLY MAGAZINE 27 (September 1863): 479-85; (October 1863): 676-82; (November 1863): 816-25.

Discussion of slaves in the cotton-growing states, particularly South Carolina, Louisiana, Virginia, and Georgia, includes references to hymns singing (479, 482, 678-79) and other devotional singing (482), to worship at regular services and at prayer meetings (676-79, 680-82), and to "spirit possession" (818-19).

Texts of 2 songs: 1. I want to go where Jesus gone. 2. For all dere lies. Texts of 2 sermons: 1.The temptation of Abraham (482-483). 2. Funeral oration (679).

973 Reed, William Howell. HOSPITAL LIFE IN THE ARMY OF THE POTOMAC. Boston: William V. Spencer, 1866. 199 pp.

Discussion of the condition of the freed slaves at Port Royal, South Carolina, during the Civil War includes description of their singing "plaintive" evening hymns (49-50, 96) and of a sermon preached by a Negro chaplain of the 43rd United States Colored Troops. Also references to religious performance practice (100-101).

Text of 1 sermon: And bearing His cross, he went forth into a place....(95-100).

974 Reeves, D. M. "The Holy Dance of the Freedmen." CHRISTIAN WATCHMAN & REFLECTOR 49 (26 November 1868): [4].

Southern clergyman living in Tarrytown, New York, describes a performance of the "shout" that he observed at a black church in 1867. Discussion of shout songs and relevant performance practice in front of the altar.

975 Reid, Whitelaw. AFTER THE WAR: A SOUTHERN TOUR. MAY 1, 1865, TO MAY 1, 1866. New York: Moore, Wilstach, and Baldwin, 1866. 589 pp.

Former Librarian of the House of Representatives discusses the tour he made of the South immediately following the Civil War. References to blacks include description of a black church service in Beaufort, South Carolina, and the singing of a spiritual by an old African and the congregation (103-106). Also description of a church service in Louisiana (519-23) and comment on singing performance practice and the oratory of the black preacher. Discussion of the difference between a "burying" and "funeral" (523).

Text of 1 song: 1. Massa Fullah a sittin' on de tree ob life (104-5). Reference to 1 song: We'll hang Jeff Davis on a sour apple tree (158, 162). Text of 1 sermon: White man might tink dey could get 'long, because dey was rich (521).

976 "Religious Enthusiasts at Atlanta." INDEPENDENT 31 (28 August 1879): 28.

Description of a revival meeting held at the Wheat Street Methodist Church (Colored) in July 1879, in Atlanta, Georgia, includes references to ecstatic seizure and religious dancing, which the author identifies as "prancing."

977 "The Religious Sentiment of the Colored People." INDEPENDENT 17 (31 August 1865): 6.

Correspondent of the BOSTON TRANSCRIPT, living in Richmond, Virginia, discusses the devotional services of the ex-slaves, with comment on their singing of "rude hymns," which consoled the hearts of the aged. Observation that the Revelation of John was a favorite source of phrases that appear in improvised spirituals.

Texts of 3 couplets: 1. An' eff I blow my lungs away. 2. De angels stan' aroun' my bed. 3. When de reapin' day shall come. Reference to 1 song: In de mornin' I'se gwine away.

978 Reynard [pseud.]. Part 1. "God-Illumined Ebony." Part 2. "Ebony Unpolished and Gnarled: Second Paper." ZION'S HERALD 56 (16 January 1879): [17]; (6 February 1879): [4].

Part 1. Description of a black Love-Feast c.1859 with excerpts of exhortations and folk prayers.

Part 2. Discussion of black dialect in South

Carolina includes comment on the survival of African dialects among some preachers of the A. M. E. Church and description of a sermon that was delivered on St. John's Island.

Text of 1 sermon: based on John 21:17.

979 Romeyn, Henry. "Little Africa: The Last Slave Cargo Landed in the United States." SOUTHERN WORKMAN 26 (January 1897): 14-17.

Army Captain Romeyn, of the Fifth U.S. Infantry (Fort McPherson, Georgia), offers an account of the origin of the colony called "Little Africa" near Mobile, Alabama, and describes its folk practices. The community, which retained its African language and culture, descended from slaves illegally imported from Dahomey during the years 1858-1860 by Captain Timothy Meaher.

980 Rowe, George C. "Letter from Rev. Geo. C. Rowe." SOUTHERN WORKMAN 12 (September 1883): 94.

In a letter dated 10 July 1883, Congregational minister discusses life among the blacks in Cypress Slash, McIntosh, Georgia, and a sermon delivered by the local black preacher.

Text of 1 sermon: based on Zechariah.

981 Roy, Joseph E. "Studies in the South." AMERICAN MISSIONARY (MAGAZINE) n.s. 36 (October 1882): 299-302.

White clergyman and Field Superintendent of the American Missionary Association at Atlanta, Georgia, discusses black preachers in South, with special reference to their oratory style.

982 Rumley, Robert Parker. DE DRY BONES IN DE VALLEY. Ashville, NC: Purman and Messler, 1896. Reprint. SOUTHERN FOLKLORE QUARTERLY 20 (June 1956).

This sermon, "De dry bones in de valley," based on Ezek. 37:1-10, includes texts and music of 2 songs: 1. All dese dry bones ob mine (Cho: What you goin' do when de judgement day?). 2. Joseph had a vision (Cho: Rise, shine like de stars).

983 Russell, Henry Everett. "Negro Troops." CONTINENTAL MONTHLY 6 (August 1864): 191-98.

Discussion of black soldiers during the Civil War includes references to their religious practices, including baptisms in the river, prayer-meeting services, and singing.

984 Russell, Henry. CHEER, BOYS, CHEER; MEMOIRS OF MEN AND MUSIC. London: John Macqueen, 1895. 276 pp.

Travel narrative of the English singer and composer, who toured the United States from 1838 to 1841, contains description of a slave congregation singing lined-out psalms in Vicksburg, Mississippi, and of the sermons of slave preachers in that city.

Texts of 2 sermons: 1. Repudiation (85-89). 2. Whether the black man's chances of getting to heaven are equal with that of the white man (89-91).

985 Russell, Irwin. "Christmas-Night in the Quarters." POEMS BY IRWIN RUSSELL. New York: Century Press, 1888. Reprint. ONE HUNDRED CHOICE SELECTIONS. Edited by Phineas Garrett, no. 16, 15-20. Philadelphia: Penn Publishing Company, 1923.

Credited with being among the first writers, if not the very first, to introduce the theme of "the Negro" into American literature, Russell in this long narrative poem draws on the stereotypes of the black man that were current during his time. Oral traditions are represented by the preacher's "blessing" given to the Christmas festivities, the fiddling that accompanies the traditional Christmas dance, and the banjo (home-crafted) used to accompany the singing.

986 Russell, William Howard. MY DIARY, NORTH AND SOUTH. London: Bradbury and Evans, 1863. 2 vols. Also published in New York: Harper and Brothers, 1863. Reprint (abridged version). MY CIVIL WAR DIARY. Edited by Fletcher Pratt. London: Hamish Hamilton, 1954. Page references below are to the London 1863 edition.

British war correspondent for the TIMES (London) toured in the United States in 1861; this book is a digest of the correspondence he sent to the TIMES. His discussion of slave life and customs on plantations in the Sea Islands of South Carolina includes description of a canoe trip, with comment on the oarsmen singing in unison "a real Negro melody" (202); of boatmen singing as they rowed (211); a plantation church and its preacher (213); and slaves dancing the double-shuffle step (374) in a plantation sugar house.

Reference to 1 song: Passing over Jawdan. Text of 1 song: Oh, your soul, Oh, my soul/I'm going to the church yard to lay this body down (202).

987 S. "Letters from Hampton Graduates." SOUTHERN WORKMAN 7 (April 1878): 28.

A graduate of Hampton's Normal School discusses socio-religious customs of blacks in his rural Virginia community: "They marry here on Sundays, and have prayer-meetings Saturdays. It opens at nine, and closes Sunday morning about five. This is the place for shouts...."

988 S., G. W. (=Smalley, George Washington?). "Negro Sermons." GOOD WORDS 8 (March 1867): 186-89. Reprint. LITTELL'S LIVING AGE 93 (13 April 1867).

Northern clergyman, in describing his visits to black churches in the South in 1864-1865, discusses antebellum black preachers, who were "generally uneducated but manifested astonishing ability to memorize and quote passages verbatim from the Scriptures." Special comment on the preachers he heard in Chattanooga and Tullahoma, Tennessee. Also references to religious singing.

Texts of 4 sermons: 1. Reading the time, because the days are evil. 2. Oh give thanks unto the Lord (Psalms of David). 3. Humility. 4. For the Grace of God dat bringeth salvation hath appeared to all men (Titus 2: 11).

989 S., H. L. "Negro Sketches: What is the Best Earthly Heritage for Our Children?" ILLUSTRATED CHRISTIAN WEEKLY 1 (7 October 1871): 205-6.

Character sketch of an antebellum slave preacher includes discussion of a funeral sermon he preached.

Text of 1 sermon: And what den is to be dun fur her? (2 Kings: 4).

990 S., M. R. "Notes from a Pleasant Journey." PENNSYLVANIA FREEDMEN'S BULLETIN (February 1867): 10-11.

Discussion of ex-slaves on the Sea Islands of South Carolina includes comment on the praise-meetings, the shout, and singing performance practice.

Text of 1 song: De tallest tree in paradise.

991 S., T. "Letter from Nashville." CHRISTIAN WATCHMAN & REFLECTOR (=WATCHMAN-EXAMINER) 46 (6 May 1875): [2].

Survey of Baptist churches in Nashville, Tennessee, notes that there are five black Baptist churches and includes a description of baptisms at the largest one, the First African Church, pastored by the Rev. Nelson Merry.

992 Saxton, Gen. Rufus. "The Religious Life of the Negroes." INDEPENDENT 19 (5 September 1867): 1.

Letter to the Editor from the Commander of the Union Army at Port Royal, South Carolina, dated 22 August 1867, Atlanta, Georgia, includes discussion of the religious fervor of an elderly, female ex-slave with whom he came in contact. Comment on the large "capacity for religious development" of the emancipated people.

Text of 1 exhortation.

993 "A Scene from Richmond." CHRISTIAN WATCHMAN & REFLECTOR (=WATCHMAN-EXAMINER) 49 (9 July 1868): [1].

Description of the baptism of 240 converts at the African Baptist Church in Richmond, Virginia, about 1868.

994 "Scenes on a Cotton Plantation." HARPER'S WEEKLY 11 (2 February 1867): 69.

Discussion of activities on a cotton plantation in Clarke County, Alabama, includes references to the burial of the dead, to plantation prayer meetings, to dancing, and to the way workers were called to work in the mornings by the blowing of a horn.

995 Scott, John. "North Carolina---An All Night Contest with Superstition." AMERICAN MISSIONARY (MAGAZINE) n.s. 16 (June 1872): 121-22.

Description of two variant performances of the shout as observed in North Carolina, and comment on the quality of the singing.

996 Scott, O. W. "A Middle State Colored Conference." ZION'S HERALD 56 (9 October 1879): 322.

Comment on a Love-Feast at the A. M. E. Church in Wilkes Barre, Pennsylvania, in 1879 refers to the singing of religious songs, to the shout, and to performance practice.

References to 2 songs: 1. This old religion is good enough for me. 2. My Lord is threading the wine-press alone.

997 Scoville, Annie Beecher. "The Negro and the Bible." SOUTHERN WORKMAN 24 (September 1895): 145-47.

Instructor at Hampton Institute, in discussing the meaning of the Bible for blacks, identifies it as the origin of Afro-American spirituals and folk hymns, maintaining that no missionary taught religion to the slaves. Slaves borrowed from the Biblical stories and made up texts for songs of their own composition, which they sang to old African melodies.

Texts of 2 songs: 1. De Lord delivered Daniel (Cho: Didn't my Lord deliver Daniel). 2. He broke the Roman Empire down (Cho: He is King of Kings).

998 "A Sermon from Our Colored Brethern." CHRISTIAN WATCHMAN & REFLECTOR (=WATCHMAN-EXAMINER) 49 (18 June 1868): [1].

Discussion of the traditional communal responses of black audiences or congregations to black speakers, and references to the "Amen Corner" in black churches, with the observation that a black bishop in Baltimore objected to this kind of performance. Excerpt from the text of the bishop's admonition.

999 Seymour, William H. "A Voudou Story."

DAILY PICAYUNE 56 (3 July 1892): 14.

Fictional (?) tale about a white creole of New Orleans and her black attendant, a voodoo priestess includes description of a voodoo dance.

Text of 1 dance song: Houm, dance Calinda.

1000 Showers, Susan. "A Wedding and a Buryin' in the Black Belt." NEW ENGLAND MAGAZINE n.s. 18 (June 1898): 478-83. Reprint. THE NEGRO AND HIS FOLKLORE IN NINETEENTH-CENTURY PERIODICALS. Edited by Bruce Jackson. Published for the American Folklore Society. Austin: University of Texas Press, 1967.

Description by a white teacher in Alabama of a marriage and a funeral among blacks includes discussion of related performance practice. Also comment on the lining out of hymns, and on the black preacher and his funeral orations, which sometimes were "preached" several months or even a year after the "buryin'" in order to allow the mourners time to assemble from distant places. Discussion of the ring-game songs performed at the wedding.

Texts of 2 songs: 1. Lonesome without you. 2. Run dem keys, Loud, Loud. Text of 1 couplet: Back o'me, Sophy.

1001 Simmons, William J. "Rev. John Jasper," in MEN OF MARK. Cleveland: George M. Rewell and Company, 1887. Reprint. Chicago: Johnson Publishing Corporation, 1970. 829 pp.

Afro-American scholar and President of the State University for Colored at Louisville, Kentucky, includes in his biographical sketch of the Rev. John Jasper, antebellum preacher of Richmond, Virginia, a synopsis of 1 sermon (1067-1072).

Text of 1 sermon: The Sun Do Move (Exodus 15:3).

1002 Simms, James M. THE FIRST COLORED BAPTIST CHURCH IN NORTH AMERICA. CONSTITUTED AT SAVANNAH, GEORGIA, JANUARY 20, A.D. 1788. Philadelphia: J. B. Lippincott Company, 1888. 264 pp.

Although primarily a history of the church and its pastors, Chapter 6 (63-75) is devoted to description of the conditions and routines of Sunday worship, and of the evening prayer meetings held by members of the congregation. They were regulated by curfews enforced by the city's patrol guard.

1003 Slaughter, Linda Warfel. THE FREEDMEN OF THE SOUTH. Cincinnati, OH: Elm Street Printing Company, 1869. Reprint. New York: Kraus Reprint Company, 1969. 201 pp.

Discussion of the origin of American slavery, the status of the freedmen after the Civil War, and missionary work among the freedmen. Reprints of letters of the missionaries, which include description of a prayer-meeting service and the singing of religious songs (123). Also references to burial customs (135).

Texts of 9 songs. See SONG COLLECTIONS (no. 1780).

1004 "Slave Songs of the United States." Anonymous review of the book (see no. 1072). FREEDMEN'S RECORD 3 (December 1867): 185-86.

Discussion of the songs of the ex-slaves, with special reference to the shout.

1005 "Slaves at Worship on a Plantation in South Carolina." ILLUSTRATED LONDON NEWS 42 (5 December 1863): 574.

Description of the slave worship service, with focus on a cotton-plantation service in Port Royal, South Carolina, includes a sketch of the slave preacher who was able to read from the Bible but could not write. Also discussion of extemporaneous preaching.

1006 Smiley, Portia. "The Foot-Wash in Alabama." SOUTHERN WORKMAN 25 (1 May 1896): 101-2.

Description of two foot-washing ceremonies, one held in a black Baptist church in Alabama and the other, in a black church (denomination not given) in North Carolina. Comment on the singing of spirituals and performance practice. Description of the "Christian shout," which took place after the foot-washing ceremony.

Text of 1 song: Give me your hand. Text of 1 chorus: I look at my hand, my hand look new.

1007 Smith, Amanda Berry. AN AUTOBIOGRAPHY: THE STORY OF THE LORD'S DEALINGS WITH MRS. AMANDA SMITH, THE COLORED EVANGELIST. Chicago: Meyer and Brother, 1893. 506 pp. Reprint. Noblesville, IN: Newby Book Room, 1964.

Smith (1837-1915), born a slave, was called "the Singing Pilgrim." She traveled widely for ten years as an evangelist in England, Africa, and India. Her narrative includes references to her hymn singing (77).

1008 Smith, David. BIOGRAPHY OF REV. DAVID SMITH OF THE A.M.E. CHURCH; BEING A COMPLETE HISTORY EMBRACING OVER SIXTY YEARS' LABOR....INCLUDING THE HISTORY OF THE ORIGIN AND DEVELOPMENT OF WILBERFORCE UNIVERSITY. Xenia, OH: Printed at the Xenia Gazette Office, 1881. Reprint. Freeport, NY: Books for Libraries Press, 1971. 135 pp.

Black preacher (b. 1784) discusses the early black Methodist church in Baltimore and its exhorters (18-19), singing in the church (36), and "quarterly meetings," to which people traveled in wagons (38). The history of Wilberforce University was written by Bishop Daniel Payne (99-132).

1009 Smith, James L. AUTOBIOGRAPHY OF JAMES L. SMITH, INCLUDING, ALSO, REMINISCENCES OF SLAVE LIFE, RECOLLECTIONS OF THE WAR, EDUCATION OF FREEDMEN, CAUSES OF THE EXODUS, ETC. Norwich, CT: Press of the Bulletin Company, 1881. 150 pp. Reprint. FIVE BLACK LIVES.... Edited by Arna Bontemps. Middletown, CT: Wesleyan University Press, 1971.

Ex-slave author, born in Northern Neck, Northunberland County, Virginia, offers detailed descriptions of prayer meetings in plantation cabins, including comment on singing performance practice, in which there was an "ectasy of motion, clapping of hands, tossing of heads...(26-27, 33-34). Also discussion of revival services at the Fairfield Church, which lasted eight days and nights without ceasing (31).

1010 "Some New Book: THE LIFE OF JOHN JASPER." Unsigned book review. NEW YORK GLOBE (6 September 1884): 1.

Discussion of ex-slave minister Jasper and the fame he received because of his sermon "The Sun Do Move" includes a brief biographical sketch and summaries of some of Jasper's sermons.

1011 Somers, Anna M. "Mississippi: From a Teacher." AMERICAN MISSIONARY (MAGAZINE) n.s. 12 (January 1868): 8.

Letter, dated November 1867 from Natchez, Mississippi, states that the writer (white) attends a black church service each Sabbath, and offers extracts from some sermons and prayers.

Texts of 2 songs: 1. I want to go to Heaven. 2. I hears a rumbling in de skies. Text of 1 sermon: Dar ain't no room in Heavan for you.

1012 Southern Contributor. "At a Colored Camp-Meeting." ZION'S HERALD 63 (6 October 1886): [313].

This resident of Lookout Mountain, Tennessee, reminisces about the camp-meeting services of the A. M. E. Church and the African Zion Methodist Church that he observed as a boy in the 1830s. Comment on the slaves singing home-made songs and choruses at the services. References to sermons, exhortations, the singing of hymns, and related performance practice.

Reference to 1 sermon text: As I live, saith the Lord, I have no pleasure in the death of him that dieth.

1013 "Southern Sketches.---III." APPLETON'S JOURNAL OF POPULAR LITERATURE, SCIENCE, AND ART 4 (23 July 1870): 108-10.

Discussion of the oratory of black preachers, with special references to revivalist preachers at camp meetings.

1014 "Southern Sketches.---IV." APPLETON'S JOURNAL OF POPULAR LITERATURE, SCIENCE, AND ART 4 (6 August 1870): 164-66.

Discussion of religion among southern blacks includes comment on the custom of "seeking," which the author describes as a "forlorn probation of sighings and groanings" undertaken in the belief that they lead to an understanding of "divine truth." Reference to a black preacher who delivered a missionary sermon.

1015 Spaulding, H. G. "Under the Palmetto." CONTINENTAL MONTHLY 4 (August 1863): 188-203. Reprints. THE NEGRO AND HIS FOLKLORE IN NINETEENTH-CENTURY PERIODICALS. Edited by Bruce Jackson. Published for the American Folklore Society. Austin: University of Texas Press, 1967. Selected passages reprinted in THE SOCIAL IMPLICATIONS OF EARLY NEGRO MUSIC IN THE UNITED STATES. Edited by Bernard Katz. New York: Arno Press and the New York Times, 1969.

Discussion of the life-style of the freedmen on the South Carolina Sea Islands during 1863 includes the observation that the ex-slaves retained the old style of singing plantation hymns and chants. Reference to two black preachers; description of the shout and its performance practice. Description of a show staged in Beaufort, South Carolina, by a "band of genuine negro minstrels" (200).

Texts and music of 6 songs (198-200): 1. I'd like to die as a Jesus die (Cho: O, Lord, remember me). 2. I wonder why Satan do follow me so (Cho: Hold your light, hold your light). 3. Dar's a meeting here tonight (Cho: Roll, Jordan, roll). 4. Done wid driber's dribin'. 5. Down in de lonesome valley (Cho: O, brudder William, you want to get religion). 6. O, Death he is a little man. Text of 1 exhortation (196).

1016 Stearns, Charles. THE BLACK MAN OF THE SOUTH AND THE REBELS. New York: Sold by the American News Company, 1872. 562 pp. Reprint. Englewood, CO: Microcard Editions, 1971.

Chapter 33 (345-78) is given over to discussion of the religion of the ex-slave in the South, with description of religious practices such as the shout, and of the shout songs, prayers, and exhortations. Also comment on the black preacher.

Reference to 1 song: May I die like the Virgin Mary (352).

1017 Stetson, George Rochford. THE SOUTHERN NEGRO AS HE IS. Boston: Press of George H. Ellis, 1877. 32 pp.

Essay focusing upon the depravities of the

freedmen of the South offers as an example the "shout," also called the "holy dance" or "walk to Egypt," which is described as "a relic of African barbarism." Comment on performance practice associated with the shout (9). Detailed description of a baptism ceremony, which lasted a full day, "gradually increasing in fervor" and climaxing with the holy dance (9-10). Also comment on the singing of spirituals.

1018 Stillman, C. A. "The Freedman in the United States." CATHOLIC PRESBYTERIAN (London) 1 (January-June 1879): 119-27.

General survey of the social conditions of the freedmen in the South includes discussion of the protracted religious meetings of blacks, of the excesses allowed in the divine worship service, and of the singing of songs at these meetings. Also comment on the black preacher.

1019 Stowe, Harriet Beecher. "A Negro Prayer-Meeting---Letter from Florida." CHRISTIAN WATCHMAN & REFLECTOR (=WATCHMAN-EXAMINER) 48 (18 April 1867): [1].

Description by the author of UNCLE TOM'S CABIN of two prayer meetings held in Jacksonville, Florida---one Baptist and the other Methodist---includes comment on the oratory of one preacher, on the communal responses of his congregation, and the singing of religious songs. Observation that two styles can be distinguished: one imitative of white people; the other, reserved by blacks for performance among themselves and apparently African in origin. Also detailed description of a variant performance practice associated with the shout.

Texts of 3 songs: 1. We'll camp awhile in de wilderness. 2. I want to climb up Jacob's ladder. 3. Who's dat a-standin' dere?

1020 _____. "Letter from Florida---Plantation Life." CHRISTIAN WATCHMAN & REFLECTOR (=WATCHMAN-EXAMINER) 48 (9 May 1867): [1].

Comment on plantation life in a letter dated 1 April 1867 from St. Johns River, Florida, by the author of UNCLE TOM'S CABIN includes comment on the sermon and oratory style of a local preacher.

Text of 1 sermon: In the Judgement Day...when Gabriel will blow his horn.

1021 _____. "Correspondence." SOUTHERN WORKMAN 8 (February 1879): 14. Reprint. (June 1879): 63.

Letter written to General Samuel C. Armstrong, founder and first principal of Hampton Institute, on 13 December 1878, informs him of Stowe's desire to enroll the son of her headman at Hampton. Discussion of the education of rural preachers in Florida includes the observation that "for a long time yet, in the country, the preacher must be only an educated farmer, laboring weekdays and preaching Sundays...."

1022 Strother, David [Porte Crayon, pseud.]. "On Negro Schools." HARPER'S NEW MONTHLY MAGAZINE 49 (September 1874): 457-68.

General survey of the state of education among blacks in the United States in 1870 includes comment on the preacher as religious leader and teacher combined, refers to his oratory style, and describes the singing of men, women, and children in the tobacco factories of Richmond, Virginia.

1023 Stuart, Ruth McEnery. "The Second Wooing of Salina Sue." HARPER'S NEW MONTHLY MAGAZINE 98 (December 1898): 49-61.

Short story about a plantation couple first wedded by common law, who later remarry in the local church, includes discussion of the wedding sermon of the black minister and the singing of sacred songs.

1024 Stubbert, J. R. "The Sunny South." CHRISTIAN WATCHMAN & REFLECTOR (=WATCHMAN-EXAMINER) 67 (22 July 1886): [2].

Clergyman of Putnam, Connecticut, comments on the life-style of southern blacks he observed in traveling through Georgia and South Carolina. Observes that the old plantation songs were being supplanted by new songs in the black cabins of South Carolina. Comment on a baptismal service he witnessed on the banks of the Savannah River (Georgia), and references to the singing of religious songs at the service.

1025 "A Summer on a Southern Plantation." INDEPENDENT 31 (11 December 1879): 3-4.

Discussion of the freedmen on a plantation in Alabama during the fall/winter of 1879 includes the observation that the ex-slave was less fond of the violin, banjo, and dancing than before emancipation. Comment on the fondness for "protracted" prayer meetings, revivals, and funeral services, and that the "old plantation wail" was still favored by the older blacks. Comment on the shout, and the burial of a former slave, whose funeral sermon would be preached at a later date.

Text of 1 exhortation: If we could all see into our hearts as God do. References to 3 songs: 1. Hold the fort. 2. Ninety and nine. 3. Sweet bye and bye.

1026 "Sunday School Meeting in Beaufort." LIBERATOR 33 (22 May 1863): [81].

Description of a Negro Sunday School meeting at Beaufort, South Carolina, includes comment on the fact that services included the singing of hymns, an improvised prayer by a church elder, two addresses by members of the South Carolina (Colored) Regiment, and the singing of a song.

Text of 1 song: I have a father in the slavery land (Cho: My father calls, and I must go).

1027 Symmes, Elmore. "Aunt Eliza and Her Slaves." NEW ENGLAND MAGAZINE n. s. 14 (January 1897): 528-37.

Discussion of the slaves of a free black woman known as Aunt Eliza, who owned slaves and founded a black settlement near Louisville, Kentucky, in the 1830s. Description of the black church of this settlement.

Texts and music of 3 songs: 1. You will dance---I will sing. 2. Jingo my lango, hey! 3. Farwell, Miss Julia, farwell (Cho: Hey ho high-o twing twang de banjo). Text of 1 song: Oh! Shuck dat corn, you niggers. Texts of 2 sermons: 1. Is it right to be "drawed off" on the Sabbath, O Lord? 2. Funeral sermon.

1028 Tanner, Benjamin Tucker. AN APOLOGY FOR AFRICAN METHODISM. Baltimore: Printed for the Author, 1867. 468 pp.

Black Methodist minister refers to the "emotional demonstrations which our zeal assumes in our prayer and class meetings" (110-11). Characterizes the A.M.E. preacher: "They are as a whole, self-made men" (123).

1029 _____. HINTS TO MINISTERS, ESPECIALLY THOSE OF THE AFRICAN METHODIST EPISCOPAL CHURCH. Wilberforce, OH: Industrial Student Printers, [c.1900]. 96 pp.

Bishop Tanner's admonitions include rules for reading the Bible: "Don't chant it on a high and holy key..." (73); and for avoiding the "raving of the mystic..." (52) and the singing of songs "which do not tend to the knowledge of God" (64).

1030 Thomas, William Hannibal. "Religious Characteristics of the Negro." A. M .E. CHURCH REVIEW 9 (1893): 388-402.

Black author's theological discussion of the religious education of blacks in the antebellum period includes the observation that whites view the religion of the Negro as "an entirely sensuous physical type." Discussion of the extraordinary ability of slave preachers to memorize the New Testament and prophecies. References to the slave songs as "weird, plaintive and expressive, unique in character and original in composition."

1031 Tillman, Katherine Davis. "Clancy Street. ---Chapter I. The Newly Freed." A. M. E. CHURCH REVIEW 15 (1898): 643-45.

Story about ex-slaves living in Louisville, Kentucky, includes comment on their belief in Israel's God, which they expressed in "ludicrous prayers and plaintive songs." Negro churches in the South described as training schools for freedom. Also discussion of the Negro preacher as being generally illiterate or partly educated, but as one who exerted moral leadership on the former slaves.

1032 Todd, Robert W. METHODISM OF THE PENINSULA; OR, SKETCHES OF NOTABLE CHARACTERS AND EVENTS IN THE HISTORY OF METHODISM IN THE MARYLAND AND DELEWARE PENINSULA. Philadelphia: Methodist Episcopal Book Rooms, 1886. 336 pp.

Discussion includes description of a camp meeting attended by blacks, of the quality of their singing in front of their tents, of the "grand march 'round de campment" (179-82), and of the blacks' congregational responses to the preaching of the whites (183-85). References to black preachers by name in Chapter 8: "Uncle Stephen, the Slave Preacher" (202-37), Frost Pollet (187), and Black Harry [Hosier] (307, 316-17).

Text of 3 songs: 1. O sinner, run to Jesus (Cho: Den you will get free) (181). 2. We's a-marchin' away to Cana-ann's land (Cho: O, come and jine de army) (181). 3. De gospel train am a-comin' (Cho: Git on board, childring) (233). Text of 2 sermons: 1. Go and shew John agin de things which ye do. 2. And, without controversy, great is the mystery of godliness (188-93).

1033 Tonsor, Johann. "Negro Music." MUSIC (Chicago) 3 (December 1892): 119-22.

Discussion of folk songs the author heard in the South during his childhood includes comment on their melodic and rhythmic characteristics, and on the singing and religious fervor of religious revivals. Observation that the old folk melodies were disappearing with the advent of "gospel hymns."

Melodies of 2 songs: 1. Lullaby. 2. Melody without title. Text and melody of 1 song: O far' you well old mistis. Text of 1 song: O, de mugwump roots on de hollow log. Reference to 1 song: Swing low, sweet chariot.

1034 Trumbull, H. Clay. WAR MEMORIES OF AN ARMY CHAPLAIN. New York: Charles Scribner's Sons, 1898. 421 pp.

Chaplain in the U. S. Army, 10th Regiment of the Connecticut Volunteers, devotes Chapter 14 of his book to discussion of slavery and the emancipation of the slave. Description of the singing of spirituals by contraband children and the singing of black boatmen (387-88); comment on the religious life of southern blacks, with description of a funeral sermon delivered by an itinerant black evangelist in memory of one who had died several months previously (389-91).

Texts of 2 songs (387-88): Death is a little man (Cho: Good Lord, remember me). 2. My Jesus made the blind to see (Cho: No man can hinder me). Text of 1 sermon: Low, I come (based on Mark 5).

1035 V., G. L. "An African in Whom Was No Guile." INDEPENDENT 17 (23 March 1865): 3.

Discussion of Francis Cummings, an ex-slave exhorter, includes comment on his active role in leading congregations in prayer and on his "broken, ungrammatical sentences, and the figurative character of his ideas."

Text excerpt of 1 prayer.

1036 Vacuus Viator [pseud.]. "A Negro Revival." LITTELL'S LIVING AGE 171 (30 October 1886): 318-20.

Article reprinted from the SPECTATOR, dated 11 September 1886 from Rugby, Tennessee, describes a prayer-meeting service in that city. Observation that the blacks sing hymns to tunes unlike those the author knew in Protestant white churches; references to the moan, the moaner's bench, and to the oratory style of the preacher.

References to 3 songs: 1. Say, poor sinner, lov'st thou me?. 2. Come along, poor sinner, glory is drawing near. 3. When I was a sinner, just like you, I was in hell till I got thro'.

1037 Vassar, D. N. "Present Status of the Negro." CHRISTIAN WATCHMAN & REFLECTOR (=WATCHMAN-EXAMINER) 49 (7 June 1888): [2].

Transcript of an address by a black clergyman of Richmond, Virginia, about the religious training and education of southern blacks, includes the observation that the black man had "thrown off the heathen worship of his African fetish," and that the day had passed when "the man who made the most noise was the preferred preacher...."

1038 "Virginia Watch Meeting." LESLIE'S ILLUSTRATED NEWSPAPER 49 (10 January 1880): 351.

Description of a New Year's Eve watch meeting in the woods of Virginia includes references to musical performance practice.

1039 "A Voodoo Festival near New Orleans." JOURNAL OF AMERICAN FOLK-LORE 10 (January-March 1897): 76. Reprinted from the NEW ORLEANS TIMES-DEMOCRAT, 24 June 1896.

Description of a Voodoo ceremony held near Bayou St. John, Louisiana (near New Orleans), includes comment on the ritual lighting of the fire, the dance of the Voudon (=Voodoo priest), and the destruction of a black cat.

Text of 1 song: Au joli cocodri.

1040 W., J. E. "Ole Aunt Betsy." INDEPENDENT 19 (21 November 1867): 2.

An elderly, female slave of Kentucky, while describing her "religious conversion" to a visitor, began to grow excited. Her "feet began to grow uneasy, her body to sway backward and forward... and if not checked...she would have gone into one of those strange rhapsodies."

1041 "Waifs." MUSICAL WORLD (New York) 51 (26 April 1873): 273.

Description of the singing, religious dancing, and performance practice at the Old African Church in Richmond, Virginia, in the 1870s.

1042 Walworth, Jeannette H. SOUTHERN SILHOUETTES. New York: Henry Holt and Company, 1887. 376 pp.

These sketches, which were first published in the NEW YORK EVENING POST, include description of a slave wedding (186-90) and a "big baptizing" (341-43).

1043 Warner, Charles Dudley. "A Voudoo Dance." HARPER'S WEEKLY 31 (25 June 1887): 454-55.

Discussion of voudoo rites in Louisiana, regarded as originating among African blacks who were imported into New Orleans by way of San Domingo, includes comment on religious practices in the Place Congo, New Orleans, in the early nineteenth century. Description of one ceremony, with comment on the songs, dances, prayers, and performance practice that accompanied the rites.

Description of 2 dances: 1.Calinda. 2. the Canga dance. Texts of 2 Creole dance-songs: 1. Danse, Calinda, boudoum, boudoum! 2. Eh! Eh! Bomba, hen, hen.

1044 _____. STUDIES IN THE SOUTH AND WEST. New York: Harper and Brothers, 1899. 484 pp.

Description of voudoo dancing in New Orleans (64-74).

Text of 1 Louisiana Creole dance song: Eh! eh! Bomba, hen! hen! (71). Text of 1 couplet: Danse Calinda, boudoum, boudoum! (69).

1045 Warren, Edward. A DOCTOR'S EXPERIENCES IN THREE CONTINENTS. Baltimore: Cushings and Bailey, 1885. 613 pp.

Physician of Edenton, North Carolina, writing from Somerset Place on Lake Phelps in the state, refers to a slave exhorter and briefly describes his sermons (118-19). Also discussion of the "Guinea Negroes" that he observed during his youth, with detailed description of their John Koonering at festivals, which were characterized by masking, singing, instrumental music, and dancing (200-203). Description of a musical instrument called the "gumba box" (201).

Text of 1 song: My massa am a white man, juba! (Cho: Juba, juba! O, ye juba!) (202).

1046 Washington, Ella B. "A Colored Funeral in the South." FRANK LESLIE'S ILLUSTRATED NEWSPAPER 32 (24 June 1871): 242-43.

Southern slaveholder offers a detailed description of the night funeral of her "Mammy." Also description of the group funeral that took place some time after the interment of the body, called the "false burying," and various customs associated with it, such as a "burying cake."

1047 "A Watch-Night Meeting." AMERICAN MISSIONARY (MAGAZINE) n.s. 44 (March 1890): 82-84.

Discussion of a New Year's Eve Watch-Service in the rural South includes a description of the shout, which is accompanied by the chanting of a plantation hymn. Also references to the preacher and "mourners."

1048 Waterbury, Maria. SEVEN YEARS AMONG THE FREEDMEN. 1890. 2d ed. Chicago: T. B. Arnold, 1891. 198 pp.

Northern missionary school teacher, in describing her experiences among ex-slaves in the South, comments on the performance practice associated with the singing of religious songs (43), on a funeral wake (181-82), and on two antebellum slave preachers (167-70, 185-89). Also description of the "heavenly dance," which "usually began when the preaching was nearly done" (195-96).

Texts of 9 songs; refrain texts of 6 songs. Text of 1 sermon: The Lord knows who is a backslider (170). See SONG COLLECTIONS (no 1784).

1049 Watterson, Henry. "Oddities of Southern Life." CENTURY MAGAZINE 23 (April 1882): 886-87.

Article written by a journalist and Civil War officer includes the transcription of a sermon he heard given by a black preacher, who was a flat-boat captain who happened to "lay up" by a Mississippi River landing, and described himself as a self-educated Hardshell Baptist.

Text of 1 sermon: An' he played upon a harp of a thousand strings---sperrits of just men made perfick.

1050 Wentworth, E. "The Great We-Wi-Val Preacher." ZION'S HERALD 59 (2 August 1882): [241].

Account of a black Methodist revival meeting, obtained by the author from a black janitor working at South College in Dickinson, Pennsylvania, from 1853 to 1854, includes comment on a revivalist preacher and his sermon, which was unintelligible to his auditors, and on the singing and religious dancing that followed the sermon.

Reference to 1 sermon: The Great White Horse and his rider (Revelation).

1051 Whinton, J. S. "Virginia." AMERICAN MISSIONARY (MAGAZINE) n. s. 10 (May 1866): 102-3.

Clergyman describes a prayer-meeting of freedmen at Fortress Monroe, Virginia. Reference to the singing of old plantation songs.

Text of 1 song: I am hunting for a city, Where pleasure never dies.

1052 Whitman, F. T. "Morals of the Negroes." CHRISTIAN WATCHMAN & REFLECTOR (=WATCHMAN-EXAMINER) 64 (31 May 1883): [2].

Comment on a speech given by the Rev. J. L. Tucker of Jackson, Mississippi, about the freedmen refers to the perpetuation of, and confusion of ancient African rites with those of the Christian worship service in Beaufort County, South Carolina---an area where the last shipload of native Africans was imported into the United States.

1053 Wilkinson, William Cleaver. "A New Orleans Negro 'Funeral'." INDEPENDENT 37 (14 May 1885): 614.

Discussion of funeral customs among blacks in New Orleans, Louisiana, by a white clergyman includes the observation that there the "funeral" was a memorial occasion, and that it seemed to be a movable feast. Discussion of other aspects of funeral customs, including a memorial service for six individuals who had died within a certain time frame. Comment on the "testimonies" about the deceased, the preaching of a dozen or so ministers, their oratory style, and the communal responses of the congregation.

1054 Williams, Marie B. "Voudoued Woman." INDEPENDENT (New York) 25 (2 October 1873): 1230-31.

Discussion of a plantation on Bayou Boeuf, Rapides Parish, Louisiana, includes comment on the superstitions of the ex-slaves. Also discussion of an elderly woman named Aunt Elsie, who believed she had been cursed by an African Voudou priest and who attempted to break the curse by singing religious songs. Description of the dance and incantation sung over the woman by an old African man.

Text of 1 song: It's de good ole ship of Zion.

1055 ______. "A Night with the Voudous." APPLETON'S JOURNAL 13 (27 March 1875): 403-4.

A "bona-fide account of the rites of Voudouism fifty years ago in Louisiana." Although this article is signed by a woman, the story is told in the first person by a fifteen-year-old boy. This is word-for-word the same material that later appears in an article by James Buel (see no. 760), except that the Buel description is longer. Both authors may have copied their texts from an earlier source as yet not known.

Text of 1 song: Houm! dance Calinda.

1056 Wilson, Robert. "At the Old Plantation. Two Papers---1." LIPPINCOTT'S MAGAZINE 17 (January 1876): 118-24.

Discussion of a visit to a southern plantation during the antebellum period includes description of a religious service and its singing.

Text of 1 song: De angel cry out, Amen.

1057 Winkler, E. T. "The Colored Preacher." CHRISTIAN WATCHMAN & REFLECTOR (=WATCHMAN-EXAMINER) 52 (13 July 1871): [1].

Extract of a sermon delivered in Chicago by white clergyman Winkler includes comment on the education of the black ministry. Observation that the black preacher has a natural advantage as a leader in worship and discipline inasmuch as he speaks and thinks in the style of his people.

1058 _____. "The Negroes in the Gulf States." INTERNATIONAL REVIEW 1 (September 1874): 577-94.

Discussion of blacks in the Gulf States and South Carolina coastal region, particularly the freedmen, includes comment on folk customs in South Carolina, referring to the practice of concluding funerals with a "dance upon the grave, after which a rag is burned," and similar activities, such as "jumping through fire," and "hunting for Jesus in the bushes."

1059 Winslow, M. B. "Letter from Florida." ZION'S HERALD 53 (10 February 1876): [41].

Description of New Year's Day festivities in Florida after the war includes comment on a covenant meeting at a black Baptist church and the exhortations heard there. Observation that old colored "Aunties" performed a dance around the altar to invisible music during the service.

1060 Winston, Celia M. "Genuine Negro Melodies---Weird Hymnology of the Colored People of the South." NEW YORK TIMES (8 August 1887): 6.

Discussion of the religious songs composed by Negroes in Eastern Virginia includes comment on the character of the music. Also references to a preacher's sermon on the text of the "Parable of the Ten Virgins," with description of the extemporaneous way in which the minister improvised a song on this text and expected his congregation to quickly "catch up the chorus."

Texts of 2 songs: 1. Who'll be the leader when the bridegroom comes? (Cho: Who'll be the leader?). 2. Who am dese all dressed in white? (Cho: Red Sea, Lord).

1061 Wood, Henry Cleveland. "Negro Camp-Meeting Melodies." NEW ENGLAND MAGAZINE n.s. 6 (March 1892): 61-64. Reprint. THE SOCIAL IMPLICATIONS OF EARLY NEGRO MUSIC IN THE UNITED STATES. Edited by Bernard Katz. New York: Arno Press and the New York Times, 1969.

Business-executive author places the origin of the camp-meeting in southern Kentucky. His description of a camp-meeting service conducted by blacks after the Civil War includes comment on the singing of hymns and other religious song, and on performance practice associated with the delivery of folk sermons.

Music and texts of 8 songs; texts of 5 songs. See SONG COLLECTIONS (no. 1785).

1062 Woodbridge, W. G. "Aunt Easter." CHRISTIAN WATCHMAN & REFLECTOR (=WATCHMAN-EXAMINER) 71 (6 March 1890): [6].

Account of a white clergyman about a black cook named Aunt Easter, who worked for his family during his youth, includes discussion of prayer-meeting services that Aunt Easter hosted in his family's home. Description of the oratory style of the preacher, the reponses of those in attendance, the "raising of a tune," and the lining out of hymns.

Reference to 1 song: We are a-marching home to glory.

1063 Woods, W. H. "'Lisher's Bears: A Camp-Meeting Story." INDEPENDENT 46 (19 July 1894): 939-41.

Short story about a black camp-meeting service includes description of the "preaching place" erected on the site, of the hymns "half chanted" and "touched with those minor chords [that] haunt the music of the Negro race." Summary of an exhortation delivered by a local black preacher.

Text of 1 song: Hit's a-comin'! Don't you yer it, A rollin' thro' the skies? (Cho: O dat jedgment cyar). Text of 1 exhortation.

1064 Woodsmall, H. "Letter from Tennessee." CHRISTIAN WATCHMAN & REFLECTOR (=WATCHMAN-EXAMINER) 58 (15 February 1877): [1].

Clergyman writes from Selma, Alabama, about the distribution of religious books and tracts at the colored Baptist Convention held in Nashville, Tennessee, citing the poverty of religious literature among blacks in Alabama and Georgia, and noting that many preachers, teachers, and deacons in Alabama do not have Bibles and religious books.

1065 Woodville, Jennie. "Rambling Talk about the Negro." LIPPINCOTT'S MAGAZINE 22 (November 1878): 621-26.

Description of a post-funeral service of blacks includes reference to 1 song: Dead and gone (625).

1066 Woolson, Constance Fenimore. "The Ancient City: Part II." HARPER'S NEW MONTHLY MAGAZINE 50 (January 1875): 165-85.

Discussion of a visit to St. Augustine, Florida, includes a reference to children singing religious songs at a local black Methodist church.

1067 Wyman, Lillie B. Chace. "Colored Churches and Schools in the South." NEW ENGLAND MAGAZINE n.s. 3 (February 1891): 785-96.

Discussion of the religion and education of blacks in South during the Reconstruction era includes description of services in local black churches and of performance practice associated with singing.

Reference to 1 song: Ring those charming bells. Summaries of 2 sermons: 1. Called to preaching. 2. The resurrection of Christ.

THE SONG

1068 Abbott, Allen O. PRISON LIFE IN THE SOUTH: AT RICHMOND, MACON, SAVANNAH, CHARLESTON, COLUMBIA, CHARLOTTE, RALEIGH, GOLDSBOROUGH, AND ANDERSONVILLE, DURING THE YEARS 1864 AND 1865. New York: Harper and Brothers, 1865. 374 pp.

Memoirs of a Union Army officer, who was a prisoner of the Confederate Army during the Civil War, include comment on an interview he had with a slave woman (210) and references to women singing in the slave quarters at night (272).

Text of 1 couplet: De Kingdom am a-coming (215).

1069 Advertisement. "Slave Songs of the United States." NATION (New York) 5 (19 September 1867): 241.

Advertisement includes the texts and music of 2 slave songs from the published collection, SLAVE SONGS OF THE UNITED STATES (see no. 1072): 1. Little children, then won't you be glad?. 2. I know member, know Lord, I yedde de bell da ring.

1070 Advertisement. "Specimen Page from JUBILEE AND PLANTATION SONGS." MUSICAL RECORD (Boston), no. 308 (September 1887): 23.

Advertisement for the anthology of 120 songs sung by the Hampton Students, Jubilee Singers of Fisk University, and other concert companies.

Text and music of 1 song: Didn't my Lord deliver Daniel? Reference to 11 songs: 1. I'm troubled in mind. 2. Weep a-low. 3. Some of these mornings. 4. Fighting on! Hallelujah. 5. I ain't got weary. 6. Chilly water. 7. Dust and ashes. 8. My way's cloudy. 9. Run, Mary, run. 10. Been a-listenin'. 11. John saw.

1071 Advertisement. "Specimens---SLAVE SONGS OF THE UNITED STATES." AMERICAN FREEDMEN 2 (September 1867): 287-88.

Advertisement for SLAVE SONGS OF THE UNITED STATES (see no. 1072) contains examples of songs from the collection.

Texts and music of 4 songs: 1. Poor Rosy, poor gal. 2. I'm gwine to Alabamy, Oh!. 3. Little children, then won't you be glad? 4. I know member, know Lord, I yedde de bell da ring.

1072 Allen, William Francis; Charles Pickard Ware; and Lucy McKim Garrison, eds. SLAVE SONGS OF THE UNITED STATES (with Preface by Allen). New York: A. Simpson, 1867. 115 pp. Reprints. Freeport, NY: Books for Libraries Press, 1971. Reprint of Preface in LITTELL'S LIVING AGE 96 (25 January 1868): 230-42. Reprint of selected passages in READINGS IN BLACK AMERICAN MUSIC. Edited by Eileen Southern. 1971. 2d ed. New York: W. W. Norton, 1983.

This historic collection of 152 songs---the first collection of slave songs to appear in print---was compiled by white northerners who lived among the ex-slaves in the Sea Islands off the coast of South Carolina and Georgia as teachers and missionaries. Many persons contributed songs, the largest number of texts coming from Thomas W. Higginson (see no. 1215) after the compilers themselves, but not all the songs contributed appear in the published collection. The 38-page Preface offers valuable insight into performance practice (v-viii, xvii-xviii), voice quality (iv), song types (x, xvii), the shout (xii-xv), and other aspects of the slave songs. The detailed Table of Contents indicates the geographical sources of the songs and the names of the contributors, and notes are attached to many of the songs.

Music and texts of 152 songs (including 19 variants). See SONG COLLECTIONS (no. 1736).

1073 _____. "Musical Excerpts from the MS Diaries of William Francis Allen." Taken from the William Francis Papers, State Historical Society of Wisconsin. Published in SINFUL TUNES AND SPIRITUALS, by Dena Epstein, 349-58. Urbana: University of Illinois Press, 1977.

Discussion of much the same musical matter as later appeared in Allen's introduction to SLAVE SONGS OF THE UNITED STATES, including comment on the boatmen's singing (352-53), the children's singing (350-53), the "chanted" sermon (357), and the shout (351). Music and texts of 21 songs (published in SLAVE SONGS; see no. 1072).

1074 Andrews, Maude. "The Georgia Barbecue." HARPER'S WEEKLY 39 (9 November 1895): 1072.

Discussion of the black cooks at the Atlanta Exposition of 1895 includes comment on the songs the cooks sang as they worked.

Texts of 3 songs: 1. An' we shell have some rabbit stew. 2. Satan am er liar, hallelujah!. 3. De sun went down in de purple extreme.

1075 Armstrong, Edith. "An Inside View of the Cantata." SOUTHERN WORKMAN 22 (February 1893): 36.

Discussion of the American tour of the Hampton Institute Singers in the North by an instructor of vocal music at Hampton Institute.

References to 2 songs: 1. Camping in the wilderness. 2. De ole sheep dun know de road.

1076 _____. "A Visit to the New York Colored Home and Hospital." SOUTHERN WORKMAN 24 (May 1895): 80.

Discussion of spirituals by an instructor of vocal music at Hampton Institute includes comment on the singing of ex-slaves in the Colored Home and Hospital in New York City.

Text of 1 song: Hark, baby, hark! The slave is a moanin' (Cho: If there's any place in heaven). References to 2 songs: 1. The old sheep done know de road. 2. Rise and shine.

1077 Armstrong, Mary Frances Morgan, and Helen W. Ludlow. HAMPTON AND ITS STUDENTS, BY TWO OF ITS TEACHERS, MRS. M. F. ARMSTRONG AND HELEN W. LUDLOW. With Fifty Cabin and Plantation Songs, Arranged by Thomas P. Fenner. New York: G. P. Putnam's Sons, 1874. 255 pp. Reprint. Freeport, NY: Books for Libraries Press, 1971.

Discussion of the work of the American Missionary Association among the ex-slaves and of the founding of Hampton Institute (1-69). Comment on "Interior Views of the School and the Cabins" and on the singing campaign of the Hampton Students (71-158). A final section, which has a preface, consists of fifty plantation songs arranged by Thomas Fenner, of Providence, Rhode Island, who taught at the New England Conservatory of Music before going to Hampton in June 1872 (171-256). Also included are the narratives of nine, ex-slave student singers. Comment on boat songs (11), sermons and the singing of "wild, rude hymns" (101-4), corn-shucking songs (112), and performance practice (172).

Music and texts of 51 songs. See SONG COLLECTIONS (no. 1750).

1078 Armstrong, Samuel Chapman. "The Enlisted Soldiers." SOUTHERN WORKMAN 18 (April 1889): 47. Reprint. SOUTHERN WORKMAN 46 (September 1917): 479.

Text of the "Negro Battle Hymn," which General Armstrong reports he first heard sung by men of the 9th Regiment of U. S. Colored Troops at Benedict, Maryland, during the winter of 1863-1864: Hark! listen to the trumpeters (Cho: They look like men of war).

1079 Aughey, John H. TUPELO. Lincoln, NE: State Journal Company, 1888. 595 pp. Reprint. Freeport, NY: Books for Libraries Press, 1971.

Discussion of the incarceration of a northern missionary in a Confederate prison at Tupelo during the Civil War refers to imprisoned slaves and their spiritual songs (114-16).

Texts of 2 songs: 1. Oh, poor Negro, he will go some day (Cho: Far away) (116). 2. My ole missus promise me, dat when she die, she'd set me free (244). Texts of 2 couplets: 1. De pore white trash dey lives an' grows (245). 2. My name's Sam, I don't care a d--n (245).

1080 Ayers, Nelson. "On the Busy Street: Remarkable Types of Character, a Motley People of Polyglot Noises---Men and Women Who Peddle and Bargain at Large." DAILY PICAYUNE 56 (7 August 1892): 17.

Discussion of the black street vendors in New Orleans includes texts of 3 cries: 1. Stra-a-aberries! Three-e-e-ee fer a di-i-i-me. 2. Cawn, cawn, nice green cawn. 3. Clo'es, po-or-o-a.

1081 B., A. B. "The South Carolina Negro Soldiers." ZION'S HERALD AND WESLEYAN JOURNAL (=ZION'S HERALD) 35 (24 June 1863): 98.

Discussion of the character of the black troops commanded by this officer of the First South Carolina Regiment includes comment on the songs and worship services of the black soldiers and contraband slaves.

1082 B., C. "The Jubilee Singers." Concert review. DWIGHT'S JOURNAL OF MUSIC 33 (29 November 1873): 131-32. Reprinted from the NORTH BRITISH DAILY MAIL (Glasgow) 27 October [1873].

Discussion of the slave songs performed by the Fisk Jubilee Singers in Scotland by a reviewer of Andersonian University. Comment on the character of the music (especially the scales, text settings, and rhythms).

Text of 1 couplet: Bury me in the East, bury me in the West. References to 11 songs: 1. Children, we shall all be free. 2. No more auction block for me. 3. Turn back Pharaoh's army, Hallelu. 4. O, sinner man, where are you going?. 5. My good Lord's been here. 6. Keep me from sinking down. 7. Go down Moses, tell old Pharaoh let my people go. 8. Did not Pharaoh's army get lost?. 9. Nobody knows the trouble I see. 10. Steal away. 11. O, sinner man, been a-listening.

1083 B., E. H. "New Year's with the Freedmen at Beaufort." NATIONAL ANTI-SLAVERY STANDARD 25 (4 February 1865): [4].

Reprint of a letter originally published in the COMMONWEALTH, from Beaufort, South Carolina, dated 6 January 1865, describes New Year's Day celebrations of the ex-slaves.

Text of 1 song: In that new Jerusalem (Cho: We must fight for liberty).

1084 B., L. E. "Life in Charleston." INDEPENDENT 31 (18 September 1879): 5.

Sketches of life in Charleston, South Carolina, contain description of black street peddlers at the Charleston Market.

Texts of 3 street cries: 1. Big House, look out of de window (Cho: Snap-beans gwine by). 2. Now's yer chance (Cho: Strawberries gwine by). 3. Taters, Irish taters! Squash, Irish squash.

1085 Backus, Emma. Miscellaneous Folksongs. JOURNAL OF AMERICAN FOLK-LORE (1894-1899).

Instructor at Hampton Institute and president of the Institute's Folk-Lore Society, Backus published isolated examples of Negro folksongs in the JOURNAL OF AMERICAN FOLKLORE during the years 1894-99, mostly without comment except that in some instances the town or community of origin is named along with the state.

(1) "Cradle-Songs of Negroes in North Carolina." v. 7 (October-December 1894): 310. 1. Dar'll be no mo' sighing (Cho: An' befo' I'll be a slave, I'll be carried to my grave). 2. De ole Mosa, he am trabeling. [Songs collected at High Point.]

(2) "Negro Hymns from Georgia." v. 10 (April-June 1897): 116. 1. Wuz yo dar when dey crucified de Lord (Cho: O, sometimes it causes me to tremble). 2. One day I wuz a-walking (Cho: Rockaway home to Jesus). [Songs collected in Columbia County.]

(3) "Negro Hymns from Georgia." v. 10 (October-December 1897): 202, 216, 264. 1. I John see de good time comin' (Cho: Holy number, holy number). 2. I'se gwine on er journey, tell yo' (Cho: O blow, blow, old Massa, blow de cotton horn). 3. If yo' gets ter heaben befo' I do. (Cho: O, glorious time 'ill soon be ober) [song collected in Columbia County].

(4) "Negro Hymn from Georgia." v. 11 (January-March 1898): 22. 1. Peter an' Paul wuz boun' in jail (Cho: Den shout yo' glory yonda).

(5) "Negro Song from North Carolina." v. 11 (January-March 1898): 60. 1. O, my pious old daddy I done lub him dear (Cho: O da's a crown fo' me, reign, Jesus, reign). [Song collected in Polk County.]

(6) "Christmas Carols from Georgia." v. 12 (October-December 1899): 272. 1. De lettle cradle rocks tonight in glory (Cho: Peace on earth). 2. De Christ-chile am passin'.

1086 Bacon, Alice Mabel. "Silhouettes: Over the Hill to the Poorhouse." SOUTHERN WORKMAN 15 (April 1886): 41.

Discussion of Afro-American folk singing as observed in Virginia by a teacher at Hampton Institute includes references to performance practice.

1087 _____. "Silhouettes: The 'Whittier'." SOUTHERN WORKMAN 19 (April 1890): 40.

Text of 1 song described as a plantation hymn sung by children at the Whittier School: O, de fox have hole in de groun' (Cho: Ain't dem hard trials).

1088 _____. "The Dixie, Its Progress and Its Needs." SOUTHERN WORKMAN 23 (February 1894): 30-32.

Discussion of Hampton Institute's Training School for Nurses by a former teacher at Hampton Institute and president of the school's Folk-Lore Society includes the text of 1 shout song: I will meet you in the city of the New Jerusalem.

1089 _____. "Memories of Old Hampton: A Glimpse of Hampton, Winter of '70-'71." SOUTHERN WORKMAN 23 (March 1894): 40-42, 46.

Text of 1 chorus of a song sung by students at Hampton Institute in the early 1870s: Sweet red flowers (46). References to 3 songs: 1. Nobody knows the trouble I'se seen (41). 2. De winter'll soon be over (41). 3. My Lord delivered Daniel (41).

1090 _____. "A Trip through the South: Part II." SOUTHERN WORKMAN 22 (May 1894): 80-82.

Discussion of the differences between the plantation songs sung by students in Virginia and and in Alabama. Observation that students at the Calhoun School (Alabama) sang "wilder and quainter" songs than did Hampton students, although the Hampton songs were known at Calhoun.

1091 Banks, Mary Ross. BRIGHT DAYS IN THE OLD PLANTATION TIME. Boston: Lee and Shepard, 1882. 266 pp.

Fifteen short stories based upon the author's experiences as a child in the antebellum South include description of a slave corn-husking festival (114-32) and a Wednesday-night prayer meeting, with its "untutored preacher" (169-72).

Texts of 4 songs: 1. Oh! Chullun, in de mornin' (R: Den take up de shovel an' de hoe) (127-28). 2. Oh! Mr. Reid iz er mighty fine man (130). 3. Shout, little chillun (R: Way in de kingdom) (171). 4. Oh, do let me out! I'z in dis lady's gyarden (175-6).

1092 Barr, Lillie E. "Colored Factory Hands." INDEPENDENT 34 (5 January 1882): 2-3: 34 (12 January 1882): 5.

Article on the social conditions of black workers in tobacco factories at Richmond, Virginia, includes discussion of the songs of workmen. Also comment on their graveyard decorations, particularly the placement of "rude" dolls and broken pieces of china around the graves of children.

Texts of 2 songs: 1. An' when you p'rade through de heabenly street (Cho: Oh! ter hear Jerusalem mourning) (2-3). 2. Oh! I've got eighteen sides of bacon! (5).

1093 Barrett, W. A. "Negro Hymnology." MUSICAL TIMES 15 (1 August 1872): 559-61.

This discussion of the musical features of the plantation songs and of peculiarities in their performance practice, secular and spiritual, includes quotation from the writings of Thomas Higginson (see nos. 1214-1215) and Lucy McKim (see no. 460), and reprint of the description of the shout that was published in the NEW YORK NATION (30 May 1867).

Texts and music of 4 songs: 1. De tallest tree in paradise (Cho: Blow your trumpet, Gabriel). 2. Poor Rosy, poor gal. 3. And de moon will turn to blood. 4. O, me no weary yet. Texts only of 2 songs: 1. I saw the beam in my sister's eye. 2. O, fare you well, my brudder.

1094 Bedford, R. C. "Another Tribute to the Negro Melodies." SOUTHERN WORKMAN 23 (March 1894): 45.

Northern minister, a trustee of Tuskegee Institute, contributes the text of 1 song sung by the Hampton Institute Singers in Andover, Massachusetts, about 1870: I hope my mother will be there.

1095 "BEHIND THE LINES; OR, A YANKEE PRISONER LOOSE IN DIXIE, by Capt. John James Geer, Late of Gen. Bucklands' Staff." Unsigned book review. NATIONAL ANTI-SLAVERY STANDARD 24 (5 September 1863): [2-3].

Review of the war memoirs of an officer of the Union Army includes an excerpt from the author's description of slaves singing a plantation song.

Text of 1 song: We'll soon be done wagging with the crosses (Cho: And wing with the angels).

1096 Beman, Jennie Howard. "Milly." INDEPENDENT 33 (29 December 1881): 28.

Short story about a young white girl, Milly, who sang Negro songs taught to her by a black woman.

One couplet text: Gwine to ride up in de chariot.

1097 Bergen, Fanny D. "On the Eastern Shore." JOURNAL OF AMERICAN FOLK-LORE 2 (October-December 1889): 295-300.

Collection of folklore gathered from blacks in the Chesapeake Bay region (Maryland) includes comment on folk customs, such as avoiding the crossing the feet during the holy dance.

Texts of 3 songs: 1. Canaon, Canaon, 'tis a my happy hom'. 2. Jesus died for you an' me, Hang yo' bonnet on a tree. 3. Way down yander to de sunrise. Text of 1 ghost tale: The jay bird and the buzzard.

1098 Berwick, (?). Review of SLAVE SONGS OF THE UNITED STATES (see no. 1072). ZION'S HERALD 45 (8 October 1868): 482.

Discussion of the context in which the songs were sung and how they were used in accompanying the shout on the Sea Islands of South Carolina.

Texts of 5 songs: 1. Poor Rosy, poor gal. 2. My brudder sittin' on de tree of life (Cho: Roll, Jordan, roll). 3. Nobody knows the trouble I've seen: 4. Go down in de lonesome valley). 5. My father, how long poor sinner suffer here? Text of 1 couplet: Jesus die on Calvery.

1099 _____. "Scenes in Charleston." NATIONAL ANTI-SLAVERY STANDARD 25 (11 March 1865): [1]. Reprinted from the TRIBUNE.

Excerpt of a letter from Charleston, South Carolina, dated 20-22 February 1865, includes a reference to the singing of an elderly woman in celebration of her deliverance from slavery.

Text of 1 song: Ye's been long a-coming (Cho: For to take the land).

1100 Bonner, Sherwood [Katherine Sherwood Bonner McDowell]. "Dr. Jex's Predicament." HARPER'S WEEKLY 24 (18 December 1880): 816-17.

Short story about a southern white woman in Kentucky and her black servants.

Text of 1 song: Wish I was in Tennessee, a-settin' in my cheer.

1101 _____. SUWANEE RIVER TALES. Boston: Roberts Brothers, 1884. 303 pp.

Six tales of Gran'mammy, ex-slave and nurse of the writer when she was a child, include references to plantation traditions. The old woman's story about the meteoric shower of 1833 has parallels in black folksong literature (13-21).

Texts of 2 songs: 1. You may back-bite me jes' as much as you please (6). 2. Satan's such a liar and a kunjurer too (51).

1102 Brace, Charles Loring. "Hampton Anniversary, Commencement Day with the Colored Students." NEW YORK TIMES, 15 June 1875: 5. Reprints. SOUTHERN WORKMAN 4 (July 1875): 50-51. THE BOOKER T. WASHINGTON

PAPERS, VOL. 2, 1860-89. Edited by Louis R. Harlan et al, 55-60. Urbana: University of Illinois Press, 1972.

Philanthropist's discussion of Commencement Day celebrations at Hampton Institute refers to Joseph Towe, a graduating senior from North Carolina, who gave a commencement address about Afro-American folksong and performance practice.

1103 Bradford, Joseph. OUT OF BONDAGE. 1876. Four-act play. Typescript at the Library of Congress, Washington, D. C. 67 pp.

Musical drama written by the white journalist-novelist for the (black) Hyers Sisters' dramatic troupe calls for plantation songs and dances in addition to requisite ballads and minstrel songs. References to 12 plantation songs and spirituals that were sung in the first-year productions of the musical in 1876: 1. O yes, I'm gwine up. 2. Nobody knows what trouble I see. 3. Gwine to ride up in de chariot. 4. Carve dat possum. 5. There's a great camp-meeting. 6. Peter, go ring dem bells. 7. I don't want to stay here no longer. 8. Angels meet me at the cross road. 9. One more ribber to cross. 10. Ain't I glad to get out the wilderness. 11. Heavenly home up yonder. 12. Rise and shine.

1104 Bradley, Arthur Granville. "Some Plantation Memories." BLACKWOOD'S EDINBURGH MAGAZINE 161 (March 1897): 331-41.

Discussion of plantation life in Virginia at the close of the Civil War includes comment on the fact that the plantation banjo was not the same as the one heard on the minstrel stage.

Texts of 2 songs: 1. Oh, my lovely Lemma. 2. Away up in de mountain.

1105 Brewster, Anne M. "Lucy's Letters." ATLANTIC MONTHLY 17 (January 1866): 64-69.

Story of a black housekeeper, Lucy, whose husband was in the army, and who became greatly depressed after receiving notice of his death. Writer offers comment on the song Lucy sang.

Text of 1 song: I know there's room in heaven for me.

1106 Brock, John C. "Music---Its Origin and Development." A. M. E. REVIEW 5 (July 1899): 128-34.

Black clergyman's discussion of music from biblical times through the late nineteenth century attributes the black man's racial preservation to his "wild, weird songs" of slavery.

References to 3 songs: 1. Steal away. 2. I'm bound for the Land of Canaan. 3. Don't you hear those charming bells.

1107 Brown, John Mason. "Songs of the Slave." LIPPINCOTT'S MAGAZINE 2 (December 1868): 617-23. Reprint. THE SOCIAL IMPLICATIONS OF EARLY NEGRO MUSIC IN THE UNITED STATES. Edited by Bernard Katz. New York: Arno Press and the New York Times, 1969.

Discussion by a former colonel of the Union Army includes comment on the dramatic powers of the slave songs and their use of vivid imagery. Also discussion of the "river songs" of the steamboat firemen, which ended with a howl; also of the harvest songs of the "cradlers, who sang as they worked, and of other song types. Reference to the turkey-buzzard jig (622).

Texts and music of 6 songs: 1. Oh, what ship is that you are sailing (619). 2. Pray on, pray on, pray on (619). 3. Oh, wake the nations underground (619). 4. What boat is that, my darling honey (620). 5. Rise up in due time. 6. Oh, Suzann, fare you well (621).

1108 Burwell, Letitia M. A GIRL'S LIFE IN VIRGINIA BEFORE THE WAR. 2d ed. New York: Frederick A. Stokes Company, 1895. 209 pp.

Nostalgic reminiscences of life on a plantation in antebellum Virginia include references to the slaves singing, dancing, playing the banjo (1, 3), and and telling tales in their cabins (14). Description of a corn-shucking festival and the improvisation of corn songs (131-32).

1109 Bush, G. Gary. "Florida Sketches.---III. The Black Man." ZION'S HERALD 62 (16 December 1885): 400.

Discussion of a black school and church visited by the author in Florida includes the text of 1 freedom song sung by the children: Before I'd be a slave, I'd be buried in my grave.

1110 C., J. "Emancipation Day in Boston." INDEPENDENT 21 (7 January 1869): 1.

Letter to the editor, dated 2 January 1869, Boston, Massachusetts, includes comment on the observance of the Emancipation Proclamation in that city. References to the ex-slaves and to a song they sang.

Text of 1 couplet: And your soul and my soul shall meet.

1111 Cable, George Washington. "Creole Slave Songs." CENTURY MAGAZINE 31/6 (April 1886): 807-28. Reprints. THE NEGRO AND HIS FOLKLORE. Edited by Bruce Jackson. Published for the American Folklore Society. Austin: University of Texas Press, 1967. THE SOCIAL IMPLICATIONS OF EARLY NEGRO MUSIC IN THE UNITED STATES. Edited by Bernard Katz. New York: Arno Press and the New York Times, 1969.

Discussion of the content and language of slave songs by a native of New Orleans. Sections of the article are entitled: "The Quadroons," "The

Love-Song," "The Lay and the Dirge," "The Voodoos," and "Songs of Wood and Waters.

Descriptions of 4 dances: 1. Bamboula. 2. Counjaille. 3. Calinda. 4. Voodoo dance. Music and texts of 11 songs; texts only of 9 songs. See SONG COLLECTIONS (no. 1742).

1112 ____. "A Negro Folk-Song." FOLK-LORIST (Chicago) 1 (July 1892): 54.

Comment on the performance practice associated with ring-game songs sung on plantations in the South.

Text and music of 1 ring-game song: O me! pity po' me, I'm in dem ladies gya'din (Cho: Bow to de ladies, Susan Gray).

1113 Canedy, Anne C. G. "Letter." FREEDMEN'S RECORD 1 (March 1865): 39-40.

Letter from New Berne, North Carolina, dated 11 February 1865, describes a New Year's Day celebration of ex-slaves. Observation that they are unaccustomed to singing any songs except their own "native" hymns.

1114 Champney, Lizzie Williams "Polly Pharaoh." HARPER'S NEW MONTHLY MAGAZINE 53 (July 1876): 195-99.

Short story set in Arkansas during 1862 includes comment on a slave fiddler. Also description of a slave baptism, the singing of religious songs in slave cabins at night, and the "walk-around."

Texts of 5 songs: 1. Did you ebber hear de hammers ring? (Cho: Chilleren, dey nailed our Sabeyer down). 2. My sister's gone to hebben, an' I want to go too. 3. Didn't you promise de Lord to take care ob de lambs. 4. Den hold out, pilot, leetle longer. 5. I do believe widout a doubt.

1115 "Charcoal Sketches." APPLETON'S JOURNAL OF POPULAR LITERATURE, SCIENCE, AND ART 3 (12 February 1870): 176-78.

Discussion of the poor in the South includes 1 text of a watermelon-peddler's street cry: Here dey are, fresh and fine, jest come from de vine.

1116 Chase, Mrs. T. N., "Honorable William E. Dodge and Atlanta University." AMERICAN MISSIONARY (MAGAZINE) n.s. 36 (May 1882): 141.

Report on the address of a New York speaker at Atlanta University notes that a spiritual was sung at its conclusion.

Text of 1 song: We are climbing Jacob's ladder.

1117 Christensen, Abigail M. Holmes. "Spirituals and 'Shouts' of Southern Negroes." JOURNAL OF AMERICAN FOLK-LORE 7 (April-June 1894): 154-55.

New England folklorist's discussion of the shout, which she witnessed in the South in 1893, includes detailed description of the dancers and the responses from the onlookers.

1118 "Chromatics: Negro Melodies and National Music." MUSIC REVIEW (Chicago) 2 (July 1893): 514-16.

Discussion of the Negro folksong includes adverse criticism of Antonin Dvorak's stance (see nos. 1142, 1143) that Negro melodies should serve as the foundation for establishing a national school of musical composition in the United States. "The melodies of the Negro are as foreign to the Americans as [to] the Bohemians, and to call them American folksongs is as little reasonable as calling them Bohemian."

1119 Clarke, Mary Olmsted. "Song-Games of Negro Children in Virginia." JOURNAL OF AMERICAN FOLK-LORE 3 (1890): 289-90.

New Englander, discussing the songs her black nurse sang to white children, includes the texts of 9 ring-game songs, of which 2 have verses found in Negro folksongs: 1. Mosquito he fly high (Cho: Boil the cabbage down). 2. Go on, Liza (Cho: Go on, Liza Jane).

1120 Collins, M. A. "A Vicar in Ebony." LIPPINCOTT'S MAGAZINE 29 (February 1882): 175-85.

A romance about life on the tobacco plantations includes comment on the work songs sung by the black field hands while cutting wheat.

1121 "Concerts." MUSICAL WORLD (London) 62 (19 April 1884): 246.

Review of a concert given in London by the Canadian Jubilee Singers includes comment on the vocal quality of the singers, particularly in singing spirituals.

References to 2 songs: 1. Steal away to Jesus. 2. Roll, Jordan, roll.

1122 Cooke, John Esten. "Christmas Time in Old Virginia." MAGAZINE OF AMERICAN HISTORY WITH NOTES AND QUERIES 10 (December 1883): 443-59.

Description of Christmas celebrations in Virginia during the colonial and antebellum eras includes comment on the holiday observances of "the local Africans" and "an old African hymn."

Text of 1 song: Oh, chillun, Christ is come (448).

1123 Cooley, Stoughton. "The Mississippi Roustabout." NEW ENGLAND MAGAZINE n. s. 11

(November 1894): 290-301.

Description of the life and work of black boatmen along the Mississippi River includes references to their improvised songs. Discussion of the structure of the couplets and refrains of the songs, and comment on song performance practice.

1124 Cromwell, S. C. "Editor's Drawer: Corn-Shucking Song." HARPER'S NEW MONTHLY MAGAZINE 69 (October 1884): 807.

Presumably S. C. Cromwell was the collector of this song: Shuck erlong, niggers, shuck dis co'n (Cho: Shuck a ruck a shuck!).

1125 Crounse, L. L. "The Army Correspondent." HARPER'S NEW MONTHLY MAGAZINE 27 (October 1863): 627-33.

Correspondent for the Union Army, writing about army life during the the Civil War, comments on a song sung by a slave from Manassas.

Text of 1 song: Me messa on his trabbels gone.

1126 Davis, Mollie E. M. "The Sinkin' Brake." HARPER'S YOUNG PEOPLE 12 (24 March 1891): 350-55.

Short story about life on a plantation in the South during the antebellum era includes the text of 1 song: Dey nailed my Lord upon er tree.

1127 Davis, Rebecca Harding. "Thanksgiving at Vogel's." INDEPENDENT 40 (29 November 1888): 1522-23.

Short story set in Vogel's Ferry (Georgia?) during the post-war era includes the text of 1 couplet: De Lohd, he stannin' at de doah.

1128 Day, Charles H. FUN IN BLACK; OR, SKETCHES OF MINSTREL LIFE, by Charles H. Day.... WITH THE ORIGIN OF MINSTRELSY, by Col. T. Allston Brown. New York: Robert DeWitt, Publisher, 1874. 70 pp.

Discussion of the origin of Ethiopian minstrelsy includes references to genuine Negro songs and the text of 1 song: I went down to creek (Cho: First on the heel top) (5-7).

1129 Dayre, Sydney. "Phrony Jane's Lawn Party." HARPER'S YOUNG PEOPLE 3 (22 August 1882): 679-80.

Short story about a young girl, Phrony Jane, who cared for a white infant, refers to a lullaby she sang to the child and to a spiritual: Nobody knows de trubble I hab.

1130 Denison, Mary A. "A Letter from Florida." CHRISTIAN WATCHMAN & REFLECTOR (=WATCHMAN-EXAMINER) 65 (12 JUNE 1884): [1].

Discussion of life in a black settlement of Janesville, Florida, includes comment on the local Baptist church and the religious fevor and emotionalism of the inhabitants.

Texts of 2 songs: 1. Oh, de pure gold 'ligion (Cho: I wants more 'ligion in dat Jedgement day). 2. My Lord a-sleeping in de grave (Cho: De bressed Jesus).

1131 Dennett, John Richard. THE SOUTH AS IT IS: 1865-1866. Edited by Henry M. Christman. New York: The Viking Press, 1965. 370 pp.

This book consists of a series of articles originally published in the NATION, written by a special correspondent who formerly was superintendent of a plantation in Port Royal, South Carolina. Includes a reference, published in an article dated 17 November 1865, to a shout song: Hold your light (207).

1132 Depew, Chauncey Mitchell. "Speech of the Hon. Chauncey M. Depew at Hampton Institute, Virginia." SOUTHERN WORKMAN 21 (April 1892): 63-64.

U. S. Senator from New York refers in his speech to a song students sang at Hampton Institute: King of Kings, Lord of Lords, broke the Roman kingdom down.

1133 Deveaux, Eugene. "Yellow Ned and His Freedom Papers." NEW ENGLAND MAGAZINE n.s. 16 (June 1897): 432-43.

Short story based upon the true life history of an ex-slave includes the text of 1 couplet: O, de halle-hallelujah days is heah!

1134 "Dinah's Wrestling." ZION'S HERALD 57 (5 August 1880): 254.

Short story includes discussion of the blacks singing religious songs in a minor key.

Text of 1 song: I'se be'n a-wrestlin' wid de Lord. Texts of 3 couplets: 1. De sperrits lef' de sinner now. 2. De Lord He come with mighty power. 3. Sabe us, Lord, mighty Lord.

1135 Dodge, Mary Elizabeth. "Our Contraband." HARPER'S NEW MONTHLY MAGAZINE 27 (August 1863): 395-403.

This story of a contraband girl, a native of Virginia living in Boston, includes references to the singing of hymns and contraband songs by blacks. Reference to a dance, the pigeon-wing.

Texts of 3 songs: 1. All good people when dey die. 2. Oh, I'se goin' to be an angel. 3. Massa gone, missy too. Reference to 1 song: 1. I'se boun' fur de lan' ob Canaan.

1136 Doughty, Frances A. "The Music Lesson: A Story of the South." MUSICAL RECORD (Boston) 14 (September 1890): 8.

Short story includes references to ex-slaves playing the banjo and singing songs.

Texts of 2 songs: 1. Look-a-look a heah, look-a-look a whar! (Cho: Unh unh um, a low down! Johnny come down de hollow!). 2. Oh, Susie, wouldn't you like to go way up in de mountains? Reference to 1 song: Old ship of Zion.

1137 Douglass, Dennis F. "Letters from Hampton Graduates: In the Wire Grass Region." SOUTHERN WORKMAN 25 (September 1896): 195.

Black teacher's discussion of a rural black community in Richmond County, Georgia, includes comment on a well-liked song in his region.

Text of 1 song: Though I cannot sing like Silas (Cho: There is a balm in Gilead).

1138 Douglass, Frederick. LIFE AND TIMES OF FREDERICK DOUGLASS, WRITTEN BY HIMSELF. His Early Life as a Slave, His Escape from Bondage, and His Complete History to the Present Time, Including His Connection with the Anti-Slavery Movement. Introduction by George L. Ruffin. Hartford, CT: Park Publishing Company, 1881. Reprint. Rev. ed. Boston: DeWolfe, Fiske, 1892. Reprint (of 1892 ed.). New York: Collier Books, 1962. 640 pp.

This third and final autobiography of black abolitionist Douglass includes reprints of passages in the two earlier books about the meaning of the slave songs (54) and about holiday celebrations (146). See nos. 237, 429.

1139 Dromgoole, Will Allen. "Aunt Angeline's Triumph." ARENA 11 (February 1895): 391-98.

Short story about an elderly woman from Virginia includes text of 1 song: Fur you can't stan' de fiyah, sinner.

1140 DuBois, W. E. Burghardt. "Strivings of the Negro People." ATLANTIC MONTHLY 80 (August 1897): 194-98.

Black scholar's discussion of the condition of the black men in the United States in the late nineteenth century, especially his "longing to attain self-conscious manhood." Comment on the black man's contribution to American music: "We come not altogether empty-handed: there is today no true American music but the sweet wild melodies of the Negro slave...." (197).

Text of 1 song: Shout, O children! Shout, you're free! The Lord has brought your liberty!

1141 "The Dvorak Symposium." MUSICAL RECORD (Boston) no. 379 (August 1893): 4.

Editorial(?) observation: "Had a musician less eminent than Antonin Dvorak promulgated the idea that the negro melodies of the Southern States should form the basis for an American school of music, the opinion would doubtless have obtained but little attention from the musicians of the United States." Discussion of the controversial reaction to Dvorak's statements by nine white composers from Boston (among them, John Paine, George Whiting, George Osgood, B. J. Lang, Bernard Listemann, Mrs. H. H. A. Beach, and Napier Lothian).

1142 Dvorak, Antonin. "Dvorak on Negro Melodies." MUSICAL RECORD (Boston) no. 378 (July 1893): 13. Reprinted from the NEW YORK HERALD (25 May 1893).

Bohemian composer resided in New York during the years 1893-95 as director of the National Conservatory of Music. Asked in an interview about his opinion in regard to the founding of a "national school of musical composition in this country," he revealed that he had given the matter much thought: "I am now satisfied that the future music of this country must be founded upon what are called negro melodies. This must be the real foundation of any serious and original school of composition to be developed in the United States...."

1143 _____. "Music in America." HARPER'S NEW MONTHLY MAGAZINE 90 (February 1895): 428-34. Reprint. MUSICAL RECORD (Boston), no. 407 (December 1895): 12-13.

Dvorak suggests that American composers establish a national school of American music based on the use of Negro melodies and Indian chant, stating, "the most potent as well as the most beautiful among them, according to my estimation, are certain of the so-called plantation melodies and slave songs, all of which are distinguished by unusual and subtle harmonies, the like of which I have found in no other songs but those of old Scotland and Ireland."

1144 Dyer, Mrs. D. B. "Some Types in Dixieland." COSMOPOLITAN: A MONTHLY ILLUSTRATED MAGAZINE 22 (January 1897): 235-46.

References to songs of the blacks in a discussion of their life-styles in Augusta, Georgia.

Text of 1 song: Oh, de sun des shine an' shine. Texts of 2 street cries: 1. Fresh shrimp!. 2. Hyar yo' mullet. Reference to 1 song: I am a-rolling through an unfrien'ly world.

1145 Dyer, Oliver. "What I Have Seen about New York---A Lecture." INDEPENDENT 20 (8 October 1868): 2.

Text of a lecture delivered by the author at the Cooper Institute in New York City on 24 September 1868 includes discussion of the narratives of two ex-slaves who took refuge in the city. One of them, Aunt Rachel, was a fine singer of plantation and camp-meeting songs. One of her favorite songs was performed by a chorus of children at the lecture.

Text of 1 song: Sometimes I'm up, sometimes I'm down (Cho: Nobody knows de trouble I see).

1146 Edmonds, S. Emma E. NURSE AND SPY IN THE UNION ARMY, COMPRISING THE ADVENTURES AND EXPERIENCES OF A WOMAN IN HOSPITALS, CAMPS, AND BATTLE-FIELDS. Hartford, CT: W. S. Williams & Company, 1865. 384 pp.

Canadian, reporting on her experiences as a spy for the Union Army during the Civil War, refers to contraband slaves singing in camps near Washington, D. C. (240-340).

Text of 1 chorus: Massa run, ha! ha! Darkie stay ho! ho! (77). Text of 2 songs: 1. Oh! We're de bully soldiers of de "First of Arkansas" (Cho: Glory, glory hallelujah!) (383). 2. Oh, praise an' thanks. De Lord he come (340).

1147 "Educating the Freedmen.---Colored Schools in Florida---Capacity of the Negro Mind---Anecdotes and Incidents." NATIONAL ANTI-SLAVERY STANDARD 24 (29 August 1863): [4].

Discussion of the schools for ex-slaves in Fernandina, Florida, includes comment on plantation songs.

Text of 1 song: My mother, how long? (Cho: It won't be long).

1148 Edwards, Charles L. BAHAMA SONGS AND STORIES. A CONTRIBUTION TO FOLK-LORE. Boston: Houghton, Mifflin & Company, 1895. 111 pp. Reprint. Millwood, NY: Kraus International Publications, c1976.

Although the songs and stories in this collection are Bahamian, the appendix, "Negro Music" (103-11), focuses on the music of the black man in the United States. Discussion of the characteristic features of this music, with extensive references to important publications of the period, such as the writings of William Allen, John Mason Brown, and George Cable. The Bahamian songs share a common musical and textual vocabulary with slave songs of the United States.

1149 Elcho, Dr. [pseud.]. "The Songs of Slavery." FOLIO (Boston) 18 (December 1879): [445].

Translation from the German of an essay about slavery in the United States, and discussion of a ten-year-old child, whose mother had been sold.

Text of 1 couplet: Rock me to sleep, mother, all day, all day.

1150 Elson, Louis C. "The Negro Melodies Again." MUSICAL VISITOR (Cincinnati), July 1893: 177.

Response to the Dvorak statements, that Negro melodies of the South should be employed as the foundation for an American school of music (see nos. 1142, 1143), includes the observation that the "sweet hymns" and the "strange improvisations of the plantation" would not have evolved if blacks had remained in Africa. Comment on the various types of black folksong: work songs of the roustabouts on the levees of New Orleans, songs of the sailors, creole music.

1151 Engel, Carl. AN INTRODUCTION TO THE STUDY OF NATIONAL MUSIC: COMPRISING RESEARCHES INTO POPULAR SONGS, TRADITIONS, AND CUSTOMS. London: Longmans, Green, Reader, and Dyer, 1866. 435 pp.

Detailed discussion and analysis of folk musics of the world include considerable comment on the music of various sub-Saharan African nations and examples of their melodies. Also comment on slave music in the United States (85, 182, 362-363). Some of the discussion of African performance practice applies as well to black-American music (89, 136).

1152 Eustis, Isabel B. "Second Historical Meeting of the Armstrong League: Reminiscences." SOUTHERN WORKMAN 23 (May 1894): 77.

Instructor at Hampton Institute during the years 1875-1894 or thereafter recalls songs sung by the Hampton Institute Singers in 1875.

Texts of 2 choruses: 1. Slavery's chain done broke at las'. 2. John saw, I John saw. Reference to 1 song: Oh, walk togedder children.

1153 Evans, Albert G. "Randolph of Roanoke and His People." NEW ENGLAND MAGAZINE n. s. 5 (December 1891): 442-48.

Discussion of John Randolph's manumitted slaves, who emigrated to Ohio from Virginia after his death, includes discussion of their music.

Texts of 3 songs: 1. Stand back, Satan, an' let me come by (Cho: Then I'll shout glory, glory). 2. Seek Him, see Him truly (Cho: My Lord, I feel like I'm new-born again). 3. I'll never turn back no more.

1154 Everts, Grace Mitchell. "The Christ-Day Gift." CHRISTIAN WATCHMAN & REFLECTOR 73 (22 December 1892): 6.

Short story includes references to a band of members of the local African church singing as they progressed homeward.

Text of 1 chorus: Nobody knows the trouble I see.

1155 Fairbank, Calvin. REV. CALVIN FAIRBANK DURING SLAVERY TIMES: HOW HE "FOUGHT THE

GOOD FIGHT" TO PREPARE "THE WAY." Chicago: R. R. McCabe & Company, 1890. 207 pp. Reprint. Westport, CT: Greenwood Press, 1969.

Autobiography of abolitionist Methodist clergyman includes discussion of singing he heard in West Virginia in 1837.

Text of 1 song: De col' frosty mornin' make er nigger feel good (12).

1156 "The Faith of the Poor." HALE'S WEEKLY (Raleigh, NC) 18 November 1879: 1.

Description of the life of destitute blacks in urban ghettos around 52nd Street in New York Street includes comment on dancing and singing.

Text of 1 song: Ef yo' git dar befo' I do (Cho: Good-by, I'm goin' home).

1157 Fedric, Francis. SLAVE LIFE IN VIRGINIA AND KENTUCKY; OR, FIFTY YEARS OF SLAVERY IN THE SOUTHERN STATES OF AMERICA BY FRANCIS FEDRIC, AN ESCAPED SLAVE. London: Wertheim, Macintosh, and Hunt, 1863. 115 pp. Reprint. Microfiche. Louisville, KY: Lost Cause Press, 198-.

This narrative of a slave who escaped to Canada via the Underground Railroad and finally settled in London devotes the fourth chapter, "Corn Songs in Harvest-Time-Conversion," to detailed description of a corn-husking festival, including the slaves' march to the farm where the corn-husking took place, the associated competitive activity, and the singing of songs and related performance practice (47-51). Also reference to a female singing psalms and hymns as she worked (97).

Texts of 2 songs: 1. Fare you well, fare you well (Cho: Well, ho). 2. I've just come to let you know (Cho: I'll bid you, fare you well). Text of 1 couplet: Fare you well, Miss Lucy (Cho: John come down de hollow).

1158 Fenner, Thomas P., arr. CABIN AND PLANTATION SONGS AS SUNG BY THE HAMPTON STUDENTS. New York: G. P. Putnam's Sons, 1876, 1877, 1879. 82 pp. (See no. 1077 in regard to the first publication of the Hampton songs in 1874.)

Songs sung by the students of Hampton Institute, Virginia, on their tours in the United States and abroad, were gathered from the students, many of whom were ex-slaves. Edited by Fenner, white instructor of music at Hampton, the book includes occasional notes about the source of a song and comment on musical features and performance practice. Also: "The most characteristic of the songs are left entirely or nearly untouched...to those who wish to sing them the best advice is...go listen to a native."

Texts and music of 51 songs. See SONG COLLECTIONS (nos. 1750-1752).

1159 Fenner, Thomas P., and Frederick P. Rathbun, arrs. CABIN AND PLANTATION SONGS, AS SUNG BY THE HAMPTON STUDENTS. Enl. ed. New York: G. P. Putnam's Sons, 1891. 126 pp.

This is identified as the second edition of the Hampton songs, but there were several reprintings since the first edition of 1874. This book includes new songs and songs from the Tuskegee and Fisk collections, used by permission. Discussion of the songs and their features includes the comment that the freedmen tend to be ashamed of the "songs of slave time."

Texts and music of 72 plantation songs. See SONG COLLECTIONS (nos. 1750-1752).

1160 Fenner, Thomas Putnam. "Memorial Letter, Joseph B. Towe." SOUTHERN WORKMAN 9 (September 1880): 91.

Obituary for Towe, an original member of the Hampton Student Singers (Class '76), includes comment on three of his favorite spirituals.

References to 3 songs: 1. You hear de lambs a-crying. 2. Yonder comes my Jesus. 3. Great camp meeting in the promised land.

1161 "The Fisk Jubilee Singers." Unsigned review of THE JUBILEE SINGERS.... (see no. 1304). NEW YORK MUSICAL GAZETTE 7 (March 1873): 38.

Discussion of the conditions of slave life and the origin of the Fisk Jubilee Singers.

Text of 1 song: Didn't the Lord deliver Daniel?

1162 "The Fisk Jubilee Singers." Unsigned review of THE JUBILEE SINGERS.... (see no. 1304). FOLIO 8 (May 1873): 134.

Review, dated Boston, Massachusetts, 26 March [1873], includes references to 2 songs: 1. Old Pharaoh. 2. Ain't them hard times?

1163 Fly by Night [pseud.]. "Origin of Shoo Fly." FOLIO 2 (1870): 35.

Identification of "Shoo, Fly" as a genuine Negro melody that originated in the South "among the colored population." Discussion of its origin and its popularity in the United States and abroad.

1164 Folksongs, Miscellaneous. "Swing low sweet chariot." ILLUSTRATED CHRISTIAN WEEKLY 2 (4 MAY 1872): 210.

Text and music of 1 song: I looked over Jordan, and what did I see (Cho: Swing low, sweet chariot).

1165 Folksongs, Miscellaneous. DEXTER SMITH'S MUSICAL, LITERARY, DRAMATIC, AND ART PAPER

2 (July 1873): 20. Originally published in the ILLUSTRATED CHRISTIAN WEEKLY 2 (4 May 1872): 210.

Folksongs were published occasionally in periodicals without commentary. Here are texts and music of 3 songs: 1. Gwine to write to Master Jesus (Cho: To turn back Pharaoh's army). 2. When Israel was in Egypt's land (Cho: Go down, Moses). 3. I looked over Jordan and what did I see (Cho: Swing low, sweet chariot).

1166 Folksongs, Miscellaneous. JOURNAL OF AMERICAN FOLK-LORE 9 (July-September 1896): 210; 11 (October-December 1898): 272.

Text of 1 song (Negro Hymn of the Judgement Day): Don' yo' see de chariot ridin' on de clouds? (Cho: O dat mornin' you'll hyar a mighty roarin'). Text and music of 1 song: O, what is on dat tree? (Cho: Down in de beautiful green).

1167 Forten Grimke, Charlotte. THE JOURNAL OF CHARLOTTE L. FORTEN: A FREE NEGRO IN THE SLAVE ERA. Edited by Ray Allen Billington. New York: The Dryden Press, 1953. 248 pp.

Black teacher Charlotte Forten (1838-1914), a native of Philadelphia, began her journal on 24 May 1854 when she went to Salem, Massachusetts. The last entry was 15 May 1864 at Port Royal, South Carolina. A graduate of Salem Normal School, she taught in the contraband settlement on St. Helena Island, South Carolina, from October 1862 to May 1864. Her discussion includes description of the boatmen's singing (128, 151, 173), and children singing "their own beautiful hymns" (133), although she "couldn't understand all the words" (136). References to several children shout songs (149, 151, 185, 191), and to a regular shout, a "new song" of the children in the piazza (141). Also description of a child's "burying" (145).

References to 11 songs: 1. Roll, Jordan, roll (128). 2. Down in the lonesome valley (133). e. De bell am bell am ringing (136), 4. Hold the light (136), 5. Christ build the church widout no hammer nor nail (136). 6. Jehovah, Hallelu-hiah (136). 7. Look upon the Lord (151). 8. Religion so sweet (151). Jacob would not let me go (166). 10. Gabriel blow the trumpet (185). 11. The talles' tree in Paradise (191).

Texts of 5 songs: 1. Jesus make de blind to see (Cho: No man can hender me) (128). 2. Old elder, old elder, where hab you been (141). 3. My mudder's gone to glory (Cho: Cinda gnaw my sin, hallelujah) (142). 4. I wonder where my mudder gone (142). 5. Praise believer, praise God (173).

1168 _____. "Life on the Sea Islands." Parts 1, 2. ATLANTIC MONTHLY 13 (May 1864): 587-96; (June 1864): 666-76.

Part 1. Discussion of Forten's experiences on St. Helena Island, South Carolina, includes description of a children's shout and discussion of singing, including a rowing song.

Texts of 4 songs: 1. Jesus make de blind to see. 2. My sister, you want to git religion. 3. Mr. Fuller settin' on de tree ob life. 4. What makes ole Satan follow me so?

Part 2. Description of the New Year's Day celebration of the black First Regiment of South Carolina Volunteers, commanded by Colonel Thomas Higginson, at Camp Saxton, South Carolina. Discussion of songs that were sung at a Christmas celebration on St. Helena's Island, and at a church service.

Texts of 3 songs: I wonder where my mudder gone. 2. De foxes hab holes and de birdies have a nest. 3. De tallest tree in Paradise.

1169 _____. "New-Year's Day on the Islands of South Carolina, 1863," in THE FREEDMEN'S BOOK. Edited by Lydia Maria Child, 251-57. Boston: Ticknor and Fields, 1866.

Discussion of the freedmen living on the Sea Islands of South Carolina includes references to their singing of patriotic songs and dancing during their New Year's Day celebrations. Also mention of the "wild" hymns of black boatmen from Beaufort, South Carolina.

1170 _____. "Folksongs of the Sea Island Negroes." INDEPENDENT 46 (1 Nov. 1894): 1401-02.

Discussion of song and dance among the contrabands on the Sea Islands off the coast of South Carolina: the songs of Negro boatmen, worksongs, and the shout.

Texts of 18 songs. See SONG COLLECTIONS (no. 1747).

1171 Fortier, Alcee. BITS OF LOUISIANA FOLK-LORE. Extracted from TRANSACTIONS OF THE MODERN LANGUAGE ASSOCIATION OF AMERICA 3 (1887). Baltimore, Maryland, 1888. 69 pp.

Miscellaneous collection of creole folklore obtained in lower Louisiana includes texts of 17 songs and couplets; texts of 9 folk tales, of which 6 are rabbit tales. Translations included for the tales (39-61).

See SONG COLLECTIONS (no. 1748); see TALE COLLECTIONS (no. 1728).

1172 Fortune, T. Thomas. "Melissa's Christmas Surprise." NEW YORK AGE (20 December 1890): 3.

Story written by a black college professor about a young slave couple in the fictitious town Morgantown just before Fort Sumpter was fired upon. Insight into slave life and culture.

Text of 1 chorus: Run, nigger, run.

1173 "The Freedmen's Songs: The Original Negro

Minstrelsy of the War." LITTELL'S LIVING AGE 83 (1 October 1864): 47-48. Reprint of an article published originally in the NEW YORK POST.

Discussion of the "new and quaint species of literature, heretofore almost wholly unknown," which was brought to public attention by the war. This small collection of nine songs, which were gathered in Port Royal, South Carolina, and New Orleans, Louisiana, is one of the earliest publications of a group of slave songs, as distinguished from one or two songs. (See also nos. 199-201.). Comment on the character of the songs, on the significance of the texts, and on performance practice.

Texts of 10 songs. See SONG COLLECTIONS (no. 1749).

1174 "The Freedmen's Songs." AMERICAN MISSIONARY (MAGAZINE) n.s. 12 (December 1868): 272.

Observation that the plantation songs of the freedmen were improvised and never written down.

Texts of 2 songs: 1. By and by gwine to tell God how you abruse me. 2. Sisters hold out just a little while longer (Cho: For we are going to live with God).

1175 Frissell, Hollis Burke. "Miss Dillingham's Life at Hampton." SOUTHERN WORKMAN 23 (November 1894): 187-88.

Principal of Hampton Institute refers to songs sung by black students of the Calhoun School (Alabama) at the funeral of Miss Dillingham, a founder of that institution.

References to 3 songs: Steal away. 2. My Lord, what a morning. 3. My Lord calls me.

1176 G., H. M. "From Egypt." CHRISTIAN WATCHMAN & REFLECTOR (=WATCHMAN-EXAMINER) 69 (26 April 1888): [2].

Travel narrative contributed by a writer on board the houseboat "Dahabeah Ibis" along the Nile in Egypt, commences with the text of a chorus from an Afro-American song: Way down in Egypt's land.

1177 Gage, Frances D. "Character and Condition of the Freedmen." DOUGLASS' MONTHLY 5 (February 1863): 794-95.

Excerpt from a letter, dated 26 December 1862, from Beaufort, South Carolina, refers to the religious songs of the freedmen.

1178 _____. "Letters from Mrs. Gage." NATIONAL ANTI-SLAVERY STANDARD 24 (5 December 1863): [2].

Letter to the Editor, dated 25 November 1863, from Mount Vernon, New York, includes discussion of the condition of the ex-slaves on the Sea Islands of South Carolina.

Text of 2 choruses: 1. Don't get weary waiting, brothers. 2. For He's coming, Satan's kingdom to put down.

1179 Garrison, William Lloyd. "Speech: The New England Anti-Slavery Society." NATIONAL ANTI-SLAVERY STANDARD 25 (18 June 1864): [1, 4].

Abolitionist's speech concludes with the text of 1 song of the contrabands: De massa run---ha, ha! De darkies stay, ho, ho!

1180 Geer, John James. BEYOND THE LINES; OR, A YANKEE PRISONER LOOSE IN DIXIE. Philadelphia: J. W. Daughaday, 1863. 285 pp.

Memoirs of an officer in the Union Army include comment on the singing of the slaves (123-24).

Text of 1 song: We'll soon be done wagging with the crosses (Cho: And wing with the angels in the new Jerusalem).

1181 Godman, W. D. "Some Things That Are Passing." INDEPENDENT (1 February 1894): 5-6.

Minister's discussion of the changes in the South includes comment on the plantation songs "now in a large measure extinct," and on the performance practice associated with the singing.

References to 3 songs: 1. I can't stay here no longer. 2. Dere's room enough in heaven for us all. 3. David! Play on yer golden harp. Text of 1 song: Lazarus is dead, O bless God!

1182 Gough, John Bartholomew. "Temperance." INDEPENDENT 35 (12 July 1883): 874-76.

Speech contains references to an address given by the author at the [African?] Baptist Church in Richmond, Virginia, in 1847, before approximately 2,500 slaves and about eight to ten whites. Comment on a song sung by a slave on the occasion.

Text of 1 song: I'ze bound for de land of Canaan. Text of 1 slave exhortation.

1183 Grady, Henry W. "Cotton and Its Kingdom." HARPER'S NEW MONTHLY MAGAZINE 63 (October 1881): 719-34.

Journalist's discussion of the cultivation of cotton in the South in the antebellum and post-Civil War years includes comment on the role of blacks in the work force. References to black folk festivals (corn-shuckings, log-rollings, quilting-bees, threshing jousts), singing, and the telling of tales.

1184 "The Great South: The South Carolina Problem---The Epoch of Transition." AMERICAN MISSIONARY (MAGAZINE) n.s. 18 (July 1874): 145-50.

Discussion of a visit to rice plantations in South Carolina includes comment on the singing.

Text of 1 song: De bottom rail's on de top, And we's gwine to keep it dar (148).

1185 Griffin, George H. "The Slave Music of the South." AMERICAN MISSIONARY (MAGAZINE) n. s. 36 (March 1882): 70-72.

New England clergyman of Milford, Connecticut, discusses the musical character of the southern slave music and relevant performance practice.

References to 5 songs: 1. Roll, Jordan, roll. 2. Run to Jesus. 3. Nobody knows the trouble I see. 4. You may bury me in the East. 5. Go down, Moses, way down in Egypt land.

1186 H. (=John Wheeler Harding?). "Hampton Anniversary: Commencement Day with the Colored Students." NEW YORK TIMES (15 June 1875): 5. Reprint. THE BOOKER T. WASHINGTON PAPERS, VOL. 2, 1860-89. Edited by Louis R. Harlan et al, 60-66. Urbana: University of Illinois Press, 1972. Page reference is to the reprint edition.

Detailed discussion of the talk given by black student Joseph B. Towe on "Old Time Music" includes comment on the performance practice of the student singers on the Commencement program. Also references to song leader John Jones and to the quality of the singing (65).

Text of 1 chorus: O walk together, children.

1187 H., R. J. "Notes from the Capital---Personal and Literary." NATIONAL ANTI-SLAVERY STANDARD 28 (21 December 1867): [3].

Short review of SLAVE SONGS OF THE UNITED STATES (see no. 1092) includes references to 2 songs: 1. Roll, Jordan, roll, 2. Poor Rosey.

1188 Hadley, John Vestal. SEVEN MONTHS A PRISONER. New York: Charles Scribner's Sons, 1898. 258 pp.

Soldier in the Union Army, reporting on his capture and imprisonment by Confederates during the Civil War, discusses the folksongs of the slaves (114-128).

Text of 1 song: Massa don't know nothin' (118).

1189 Hague, Parthenia Antoinette. A BLOCKADED FAMILY: LIFE IN SOUTHERN ALABAMA DURING THE CIVIL WAR. Boston: Houghton, Mifflin, & Company, 1888. 176 pp. Reprint. Freeport, NY: Books for Libraries Press, 1971.

Schoolteacher's narrative of life in Alabama during the Civil War includes comment on the slaves singing "corn songs" on their way to work (125), on their dancing to music of the fiddle (126), and singing "old-time songs" at their religious services in the quarters (126-27).

Text of 1 song: Where, oh, where is the good old Daniel? (Cho: By and by we'll go home to meet him, way over in the promised land) (127).

1190 Hall, Newman. "Mr. Gladstone and the Jubilee Singers." INDEPENDENT 25 (21 August 1873): 1036-37.

Clergyman's letter from London, England, dated 30 July 1873, includes discussion of the special performance of the Fisk University Jubilee Singers at the private residence of the British Prime Minister, which included slave songs.

References to 2 songs: 1. O, how I love Jesus. 2. Good-bye brother, good-bye sister.

1191 Hallock, Charles. "A Southern Gentleman's Estate." NEW ENGLAND MAGAZINE n.s. 9 (February 1894): 692-97.

History and discussion of a southern plantation near the Chewan River, North Carolina, includes description of the "John Coona" celebrations of the black field hands on this estate during the Christmas holidays. Comment on the use of song, musical instruments, effigies, pageantry, and masks.

1192 Hamilton, F. E. "Tribberlation." INDEPENDENT 31 (30 January 1879): 27-28.

Short story about a slave boy from Kentucky includes the text of 1 song: Oh! De trouble all is ober (Cho: Ober in de happy land).

1193 "HAMPTON AND ITS STUDENTS, by Mrs. M. F. Armstrong and Helen W. Ludlow." Unsigned review of the book (see no. 1077). NATION (New York) 18 (16 April 1874): 254-55.

Reviewer, in discussing the careers of the Hampton Singers, includes reference to 1 song: Swing low, sweet chariot.

1194 Hampton Folk-Lore Society. "Christmas Day at Hampton Institute." SOUTHERN WORKMAN 28 (December 1899): 477-80.

References to 2 songs sung by students at Hampton Institute during Christmas Day festivities: 1. Steal away to Jesus. 2. Canaan's happy land.

1195 _____. SOUTHERN WORKMAN 26 (August 1897): 163.

Narrative about slave life contains discussion by one student of the origin of the song "Run, nigger, run."

1196 _____. "Superstitions about Animals." SOUTHERN WORKMAN 25 (January 1896): 15-16.

Contains 2 variant text-couplets of a children's song about the snail: 1. Snail, snail, poke out you horn, Give me a peck of corn. 2. Snail, snail, poke out your horn, Ding a ding a darden dead and gone.

1197 _____."American Folk-Lore Society." SOUTHERN WORKMAN 24 (February 1895): 30-32. Reprint as "Negro Folk Songs." BLACK PERSPECTIVE IN MUSIC 4 (July 1976).

Report on the annual meeting of the American Folk-Lore Society on 27-28 December 1894 includes discussion of the paper sent by the Hampton Folk-Lore Society, which was read by Robert R. Moton (1867-1940) and illustrated with songs by a Hampton student quartet: William E. Daggs, J. H. Wainwright, F. D. Banks, and Captain Moten. Identifies four classes of Negro folksong: corn-songs, dance-songs, spirituals, and shout-songs. Description of the juba dance.

Texts of 4 songs: 1. What in de worl' is de marter here? . 2. Run, nigger, run, patteroler' ketch yer. 3. Master had a yaller man (Cho: Juba). 4. Our bondage'll have an end, by and by (Cho: From Egypt's yoke set free.)

1198 "Hampton School Record." [Memorial Service for Frederick Douglass]. SOUTHERN WORKMAN 24 (March 1895): 40.

Comment on songs sung by the Hampton students at a memorial service for Frederick Douglass at Hampton Institute.

References to 3 songs: 1. No more auction block for me. 2. Mother, is massa gwine to sell us tomorrow? 3. O, Freedom.

1199 _____. Unsigned review. SOUTHERN WORKMAN 19 (September 1890): 96.

Reprint of the South African CAPE TIMES' review of a concert staged in that city by the McAdoo Jubilee Singers (also known as the Virginia Jubilee Singers) on 30 June 1890. Comment on the group's performance of the "simple but fervid melodies which were their forefathers."

1200 "The Hampton Students." Unsigned reviews of concerts given by the Hampton Institute Students when touring in the North. Published in the SOUTHERN WORKMAN 2 (April, May, June 1873): [2]; [2]; [2].

(1) April: Three reviews of performances in Philadelphia and New York include the text of 1 song: Blow your trumpet, Gabriel (Cho: In dat great gittin'-up morning, Fare you well). References to 5 songs: 1. I hope my mother will be there. 2. Roll me, chariot, roll me. 3. Oh, wasn't dat a wide riber?. 4. Nobody knows de trouble I see. 5. Glory, glory, new born again.

(2) May: Reviews of concerts given in New York include comment on the "wild, crude" slave songs and camp-meeting melodies that the Hampton Students sang. Observation that the songs show kinship to the lamentations of the children of Israel when they were in bondage.

(3) June: Three reviews of concerts given in New Bedford and Haverhill, Massachusetts, and other places in New England contain references to 7 songs: 1. Peter, go ring dem bells. 2. Swing low, sweet chariot. 3. In dat great gittin'-up morning. 4. I hope my mother will be there. 5. Nobody knows the trouble I've seen. 6. Sound the loud timbrel. 7. Go down, Moses.

1201 Handy, Mrs. M. P. "On the Tobacco Plantation." SCRIBNER'S MONTHLY 4 (October 1872): 651-55.

Description of the cultivation of tobacco on a plantation in Virginia includes discussion of a folksong popular among blacks, and sung by them on flat-boats as they conveyed the tobacco crop to market.

Text of 1 song: 1. Oh, I'm gwine down to town.

1202 Harris, Joel Chandler. "Two Plantation Songs." CENTURY 24 (May 1882): 160.

Discussion of two folk songs by the Georgia-born author of the "Uncle Remus" tales, one of which is attributed to Harbert, a hog feeder on the Turner Plantation in Putnam County, Georgia.

Texts of 2 songs: 1. (Hog-feeder's song) Oh, rise up, my ladies! Lissen unter me!. 2. Track in de paff whar rabbit bin play'n' (Cho: Hey, my Lily! go down de road!).

1203 Haven, Gilbert. "Seeking a Home." ZION'S HERALD 50 (9 January 1873): [9].

Southern Methodist minister refers to a freedom song in his travel narrative: Go tell Pharaoh.

1204 Haviland, Laura Smith. A WOMAN'S LIFE-WORK: LABORS AND EXPERIENCES. Chicago: Publishing Association of Friends, 1889. 559 pp. Reprint. New York: Arno Press and the New York Times, 1969.

Abolitionist's description of a black Love Feast in New Orleans in 1864 (320-21) includes the text of 1 couplet: The Jubilee has come and we are free (321)

1205 Hearn, Lafcadio. "Levee Life." CINCINNATI COMMERCIAL, 17 March 1876. Reprints. THE SELECTED WRITINGS OF LAFCADIO HEARN, edited by Henry Goodman, 215-33. New York: The Citadel Press, 1949. CHILDREN OF THE LEVEE, ed. by O. W. Frost, 61-83. Lexington, University of Kentucky Press, 1957. Page references below are to the Goodman edition.

Discussion of the songs and dances of the black roustabouts and firemen working on the levee in Cincinnati, Ohio, after the Civil War. Comment on how "the echoes of the old plantation life still live in their songs and pastimes" (217). Discussion of the "melancholy" and "plaintive" quality of the songs and performance practice, particularly the exchange betweens soloist and chorus. Observation that the chorus often was accompanied by "that wonderfully rapid slapping of thighs and hips known as patting Juba" (224). Texts of 11 songs. See SONG COLLECTIONS (no. 1754).

1206 _____. "Some Pictures of Poverty." CINCINNATI COMMERCIAL, 7 January 1877. Reprint. THE SELECTED WRITINGS OF LAFCADIO HEARN. Edited by Henry Goodman, 250-59. New York: The Citadel Press, 1949.

Discussion of poor Negroes in Cincinnati, Ohio, includes comment on a death-bed scene, where the dying old woman was attended by a black preacher.

Text of 1 chorus: Dese old bones of mine will all come together in de morning.

1207 _____. "Genius Loci." CINCINNATI COMMERCIAL, 12 August 1877. Reprint. CHILDREN OF THE LEVEE. Edited by O. W. Frost, 104-111. Lexington: University of Kentucky, 1957.

Short story about black roustabouts of Cincinnati, Ohio, includes the text of 1 song chorus: I'm Rag-a-back Sam, And I don't care a d--n, Fur I sooner be a nigger dan a poor white man.

1208 _____. "Voices of Dawn." NEW ORLEANS ITEM, 5 October 1879. Reprint. THE SELECTED WRITINGS OF LAFCADIO HEARN, ed. by Henry Goodman, 266-68. New York: The Citadel Press, 1949.

Description of the street cries sung by Italian, Negro, French, and Spanish peddlers in New Orleans.

Text of 1 black peddler's cry: Cantel-lope-ah! Fresh and fine.

1209 _____."The Creole Patois." HARPER'S WEEKLY 29 (10 January 1885): 27.

Discussion of the origin of the creole dialect among African slaves in Latin America and in Louisiana includes reference to the research of George Cable. Comment on the extant repertory of creole songs, rhythms, proverbs, and tales.

1210 _____."The Creole Patois." HARPER'S WEEKLY 29 (17 January 1885): 43.

In discussion of black Creole songs of Louisiana, author observes that the poetry contains "quaint" construction of stanzas, simplicity of images, and systematic repetitions of phrases.

References to 3 dances: 1. Bamboula. 2. Congo. 3. Calinda. Text of 1 song: 1. Belle Amerikaine, no l'aimin toi!

1211 _____. CREOLE SKETCHES. Edited by Charles Woodward Hutson. Boston: Houghton Mifflin, 1924. 201 pp.

Miscellaneous collection of articles written by Hearn for the NEW ORLEANS ITEM during the years 1879-1881 includes several that have references to black creole culture.

Texts of 2 songs: 1. Pitis' sans papa (11-13). 2. Cantellope---ah! fresh and fine (199). Reference to 1 song: Des perches (86-87). Text of 1 tale: Why crabs are boiled alive (59).

1212 Henry, Guy V. "Adventures of American Army and Naval Officers. IV---A Sioux Indian Episode." HARPER'S WEEKLY 40 (26 December 1896): 1273-75.

U. S. Brevet Brigadier-General and former commander of Troop D, Ninth Cavalry, in reminiscences about war maneuvers against hostile Sioux Indians in the Dakotas during 1890-1891, discusses the black soldiers attached to his regiment and their singing.

1213 Higginson, Thomas Wentworth. "Out on Picket." ATLANTIC MONTHLY 19 (March 1867): 271-81.

Colonel in the Union Army, and commander of the first slave troops to be mustered into the Union Army during the Civil War (the First Regiment of South Carolina Volunteers), discusses the singing of his soldiers.

Texts of 2 songs: 1. All true children gwine in de wilderness. 2. We're gwine to de ferry (Cho: De bell done ringing).

1214 _____. "Negro Spirituals." ATLANTIC MONTHLY 19 (June 1867): 685-94. Reprints. ARMY LIFE IN A BLACK REGIMENT. Boston: Fields, Osgood & Company, 1870. THE SOCIAL IMPLICATIONS OF EARLY NEGRO MUSIC IN THE UNITED STATES. Edited by Bernard Katz. New York: Arno Press and the New York Times, 1969. READINGS IN BLACK AMERICAN MUSIC. Edited by Eileen Southern. 1971. 2d ed. New York: W. W. Norton, 1983.

Discussion of the "plaintive...quaint" songs sung by the servicemen in Higginson's regiment, the First South Carolina Volunteers (see no. 1216), includes comment on the circumstances under which the songs were sung, on improvisation, and the shout. Observation that the songs could be compared to Scottish ballads.

Texts of 41 songs. See SONG COLLECTIONS (no. 1755).

1215 _____. ARMY LIFE IN A BLACK REGIMENT. Boston: Fields, Osgood & Company, 1870.

296 pp. Chapter entitled "Negro Spirituals" reprinted from the ATLANTIC MONTHLY 19 (June 1867): 685-94. "Leaves from an Officer's Journal" reprinted from the ATLANTIC MONTHLY 14 (November 1863): 521-529. Reprint of book: Boston: Houghton, Mifflin & Company, 1900.

This account of the colonel's experiences includes detailed description of the shout (22-24, 32), references to the lining-out of hymns (32), the telling of tales around the camp fire (15-17), and a prayer meeting (343). Contains the same collection as in no. 1214. See SONG COLLECTIONS (no. 1755).

1216 _____. "Drummer Boys in a Black Regiment." YOUTH'S COMPANION (27 September 1888): 465

Discussion of the boys' drum corps that was attached to the colonel's black regiment during the Civil War includes comment on their singing.

Texts of 2 songs: 1. All true believers gwine in de wilderness. 2. O! we're gwine to de Ferry.

1217 _____. LETTERS AND JOURNALS OF THOMAS WENTWORTH HIGGINSON, 1846-1906. Edited by Mary Thacher Higginson. Boston: Houghton Mifflin Company, 1921. 358 pp. Reprint. New York: Da Capo Press, 1969.

Letters written by Higginson during his years of service in the Union Army as Colonel of the ex-slave regiment, the First South Carolina Volunteers, include references to performance practice (219-220) and to singing.

Texts of 2 songs: 1. What make old Satan for follow me so? (Cho: Hold your light) (219). 2. I see de old man sitting! (Cho: Glory Hallelujah) (220).

1218 Hopkins, Pauline E. PECULIAR SAM; OR, THE UNDERGROUND RAILROAD. A Musical Drama in Four Acts. 1879. Manuscript. Special Collections, Fisk University Library. Nashville, Tennessee. 27 pp.

Musical play written by the black novelist for black minstrel-star Sam Lucas in the leading role calls for plantation songs and dances in addition to the customary minstrel songs and ballads. For the premier production in 1879, directions in the manuscript indicated that spirituals should be sung at various points in the play.

References to 5 spirituals: 1. Ain't got long to stay here. 2. Gospel train. 3. Rise and shine. 4. Way over in Jordan. 5. Dar's only one more riber to cross.

1219 Howland, Emily. "Tribute to John D. Read." NATIONAL ANTI-SLAVERY STANDARD 25 (12 November 1864): [2].

Letter pertaining to the murder of John Read at Fall's Church, Virginia, by guerillas includes comment on the victim and his daughter, who taught black children in a local Sabbath school.

Text of 1 chorus: Go down, Moses, go 'way down.

1220 "The Hymnody of the Blacks." Unsigned review of SLAVE SONGS OF THE UNITED STATES (see no. 1072). INDEPENDENT 19 (28 November 1867): 2.

Discussion of the various channels by which the slave songs moved northward includes comment on the fact that "the names of the editors of the collection are sufficient vouchers for its genuineness." Extensive quotation from William Allen's introductory essay to SLAVE SONGS OF THE UNITED STATES.

1221 "In Carnival Time." HARPER'S WEEKLY 28 (8 March 1884): 155.

Description of a street procession in New Orleans, Louisiana, during Carnival celebrations includes references to singing of black revelers.

1222 "It Might as Well Be Me." ZION'S HERALD 45 (15 October 1868): 495.

Narrative of a fugitive slave includes the text of 1 song that he chanted as he rowed his boat: O, my soul, arise in heaven (Cho: Roll, Jordan, roll, Jordan, roll).

1223 J. "Letters from Hampton Graduates: A Northern School House." SOUTHERN WORKMAN 14 (May 1885): 52.

Letter written by a black school teacher living in New Jersey, dated 19 March 1885, comments on the fondness of his pupils for singing plantation songs.

1224 Jennings, John J. THEATRICAL AND CIRCUS LIFE; OR, SECRETS OF THE STAGE, GREEN-ROOM AND SAWDUST ARENA. New York: William H. Sheppard, 1882. 608 pp.

Dicussion of Negro minstrelsy (367-81) includes observations that the early minstrel stars---"Daddy" Thomas Dartmouth Rice, George Nichols, Barney Burns, Joe Blackburn---all sang songs that "were taken from hearing the Southern darkies singing in the evenings on their plantations" (368).

1225 Johnston, Richard Malcolm. "Moll and Virgil." Chapter 1. HARPER'S NEW MONTHLY MAGAZINE 75 (September 1887): 583-92.

Serialized novel about a slave brother and his sister, written by a Georgia-born author and educator, includes discussion of their activities as house servants on a plantation in the antebellum South.

Text of 1 song: In hopes of dat immorchil crown.

1226 JUBILEE AND PLANTATION SONGS. CHARACTERISTIC FAVORITES, AS SUNG BY THE HAMPTON STUDENTS, JUBILEE SINGERS, FISK UNIVERSITY STUDENTS, AND OTHER CONCERT COMPANIES. Also a Number of new Pleasing Selections. Boston: Oliver Ditson Company, 1887. Reprint. Philadelphia: Oliver Ditson Company, 1915. 80 pp.

Collection contains texts and music of 98 songs; includes notes about function, origin, and variant texts of the songs, and performance practice.

1227 "Jubilee Hall.---Dedication." AMERICAN MISSIONARY (MAGAZINE) n. s. 20 (February 1876): 32-37.

Discussion of the dedication service for Jubilee Hall at Fisk University refers to George L. White's role in organizing the Fisk Jubilee Singers and to the use of slave, plantation, and camp-meeting melodies on the fund-raising concerts given to raise money for building Jubilee Hall.

References to 2 songs: 1. Steal away to Jesus. 2. The year of Jubilee.

1228 "The Jubilee Singers." Unsigned reviews of concerts published in AMERICAN MISSIONARY n.s. during the years 1872-1876.

(1) "The Jubilee Singers." 16/Supplement (February 1872): 1-4.

Reprints from three reviews of performances of the Fisk Jubilee Singers include reference to the songs as "wild, plaintive hymns."

Texts of 5 songs: 1. You may bury me in the East (Cho: But I'll hear the trumpet in that morning). 2. Didn't my Lord deliver Daniel?. 3. Gwine to write Massa Jesus (Cho: To turn back Pharaoh's army, hallelu). 4. When Israel was in Egypt Land (Cho: Go down Moses). 5. O, brothers, don't stay away (Cho: My Lord says there's room enough , don't stay behind). References to 3 songs: 1. We'll die in the field. 2. Steal away to Jesus. 3. Roll, Jordan, roll.

(2) "The Jubilee Singers; England's Welcome---Press Notices." 17 (July 1873): 145-147.

Reprints of reviews of performances of the Fisk Jubilee Singers in England includes reference to the songs as "wild" and plaintive.

References to 4 songs: 1. Steal away. 2. Turn back, Pharoah's army. 3. Didn't my Lord deliver Daniel?. 4. Keep me from sinking low.

(3) "The Jubilee Singers." 18 (January 1874): 1-4:

Reprinted reviews of performances in Scotland include comment on the character of the slave songs.

References to 7 songs: 1. Steal away to Jesus. 2. Turn back Pharaoh's army. 3. Gwine to ride up in a chariot. 4. Gwine shoutin' home to glory. 5. The angels waiting at the door. 6. I'll hear the trumpet sound. 7. Now ain't them hard trials and tribulations.

(4) "The Jubilee Singers." 19 (April 1875): 89-90.

Reviews include references to the worksongs sung by blacks along the levees of Louisiana.

Texts of 2 songs: The fare is cheap and all can go. 2. Keep inching along (Cho: Jesus will come by an' by).

(5) "Meetings with Mr. Moody." 19 (April 1875): 90.

Reprinted reviews of performances of the Fisk Jubilee Singers in Great Britain include discussion of the character of the slave songs.

Texts of 2 refrains: 1. Nobody knows the trouble I see, Lord. 2. You may bury him in the East.

1229 "The Jubilee Singers." Unsigned review of Jubilee concerts. DRAMATIC NEWS AND SPORTING JOURNAL 11 (25 May 1872): 14.

Discussion includes text of 1 song: Gwine to write to Massa Jesus. Also texts of 2 couplets: 1. Didn't my Lord deliver Daniel? 2. Go down, Moses.

1230 "The Jubilee Singers." Unsigned review of Jubilee concerts. MUSICAL STANDARD n.s. 4 (17 May 1873): 312.

Discussion includes texts of 4 songs sung during the tour of England in 1873: 1. Gwine to write to Master Jesus (Cho: To turn back Pharoah's army). 2. Yes, He delivered Daniel from the lion's den. 3. My Lord calls me (Cho: Steal away). 4. Brothers, will you pray for me? (Cho: Nobody knows the trouble I see, Lord.

1231 "The Jubilee Singers." Unsigned review of Jubilee concerts. MUSICAL WORLD (London) 51 (7 June 1873): 375-76.

Detailed discussion of the folksong repertory of the Jubilee Singers during the London concerts in 1873.

Texts of 3 songs: 1. No more rain fall for to wet you. 2. O, Lord, I want some valiant soldier. 3. Bendin' knees a achin' (Cho: I'd git home bime-by). References to 19 songs, all of which are published in SLAVE SONGS OF THE UNITED STATES.

1232 "Keep Your Lamps Trimmed." MUSICAL RECORD (Boston), 92 (3 July 1880): 626.

Discussion of the dedication of a new church for ex-slaves at Cypress Slash, Georgia, includes the text of 1 song: Brothers, don't grow weary (Cho: Keep your lamps trimmed and a-burning).

1233 Kendrick, Helen F. "Daddy." INDEPENDENT 37 (9 July 1885): 897.

Essay (fictional?) about an old man who escaped from slavery and a little waif girl that he had adopted includes reference to a corn-shucking song of antebellum times in the South.

Text of 1 song: I'm trubbled in de mountin' (Cho: An trubble gwine ca'y me home).

1234 King, Edward. "The Great South---Old and New Louisiana." SCRIBNER'S MONTHLY 7 (December 1873): 651-75.

Discussion of social and economic conditions in New Orleans, Louisiana, before and after the Civil War includes references to the songs of black stevedores, whose arms and limbs kept time to songs they sang as they worked. Reference to one stevedore work song, described as a "rude chant": Oh, I los' my money dare.

1235 _____. "The Great South---The South Carolina Problem; The Epoch of Transition." SCRIBNER'S MONTHLY 8 (June 1874): 129-60.

Discussion of social and economic conditions in South Carolina before and after Civil War includes the text of a Carolinian couplet: De bottom rail's on de top (151).

1236 Kingsland, Mrs. Burton. "Reminiscences of Old New York." OUTLOOK 49 (3 March 1894): 404-6.

This octogenarian writer, reminiscing about life in New York in the early nineteenth century, discusses black street peddlers and chimney-sweeps and their street cries.

Reference to 1 street cry: Butt-milk (406).

1237 Krehbiel, H. Edward. "Folk Music in America." MUSIC REVIEW (Chicago) 2 (September 1893): 603-8.

Address delivered before the meeting of the Musical Congress in 1893 includes discussion of the features of Negro folk songs: the content, improvisation, character of rhythm and melodic structure, and African retentions.

Texts and music of 2 plantation songs: 1. Gwine to mourn an' nebber tire (Cho: O, walk togedder, childron don't yer get weary). 2. 'Twas just about the break of day (Cho: Come trembling down, go shouting home). Text of 1 creole slave song: Pov' piti Lolotte a mouin. Text of 1 chorus: Nobody knows the trouble I see. Reference to 1 song: Go down, Moses.

1238 _____. "American Music---The Nationality of the Slave-Songs, and Their Relation to Other Lands." MUSICAL RECORD (Boston), no. 414 (July 1896): 2.

Reprint of an article originally published in the NEW YORK SUN includes discussion of the African origin of the slave songs, peculiarities of melody and rhythm of the songs, and comment about the American context in which the music evolved.

1239 "The Labor Question South." SOUTHERN WORKMAN 7 (February 1878): 10-11.

Article includes the text of a three-line work song sung by black workers in the Black Belt of the South: Nought's a nought, figure's a figure.

1240 Langhorne, Orra. "Southern Sketches: An African Philanthropist." SOUTHERN WORKMAN 5 (January 1886): 4.

Discussion by the daughter of an ex-slaveholder of an old black peddler of Virginia, who left his fortune to his church. Text of 1 street cry: Buttermilk fresh an' coo-ool.

1241 _____. "Southern Sketches: Living in Two Centuries." SOUTHERN WORKMAN 15 (December 1886): 124.

Discussion of the field cries sung by farm workers while hauling tobacco from a plantation in Bedford, Virginia, to Lynch's Ferry includes the text of 1 song: I'm gwine along down to Lynchburg town.

1242 Lanier, Sidney. FLORIDA: ITS SCENERY, CLIMATE AND HISTORY.... Philadelphia: J. B. Lippincott & Company, 1876. 336 pp.

Poet's discussion includes comment on the whistling of his boatman, Dick, as they moved up the Ocklawaha River, with special reference to its quality and syncopations (29-30). Also discussion of congregational singing in a black church, with special comment on the modes used in the songs---they "sing a whole minor tune without once using a semitone" (31).

Transcriptions of 2 whistling tunes (30-31).

1243 _____. THE SCIENCE OF ENGLISH VERSE. 1880. 2d ed. New York: Charles Scribner's Sons, 1888.

Discussion of the rhythms of poetry includes detailed description of "pattin' juba" and transcription of the note values of pattin' patterns (186-89, 247). Also detailed description of the "typical negro sermon," with its gradual transition from "pure musical poetic recitative to the speech-tune, or more refined recitative" (276). Transcription of several phrases of a sermon (which begins with the words: "Yes, my bretherin and sisterin") into musical notation (276-77).

1244 Lemon, John W. "Extracts from Commencement Essays---Industrial Education." SOUTHERN WORKMAN 19 (July 1890): 79.

Son of an ex-slave discusses the importance of education for black people, citing songs that were sources of inspiration for blacks during their "moments of tribulation."

Texts of 2 songs: 1. Nobody knows the trouble I see, Lord. 2. Didn't my Lord deliver Daniel.

1245 "Letter to the Editor." INDEPENDENT (New York) 34 (24 August 1882): 19.

Writer requests concordances for a song he heard at a black camp-meeting in New Jersey: I had a praying father.

1246 "Light in a Dark Corner." AMERICAN MISSIONARY (MAGAZINE) n. s. 46 (September 1892): 302-3.

Discussion of a visit to a black school near Savannah, Georgia, includes description of a ring-game song performed by the children and text of the chorus: Of all the girls I ever did saw, I'd rather marry you.

1247 Linton, William James. POETRY OF AMERICA. SELECTIONS FROM ONE HUNDRED AMERICAN POETS FROM 1776 TO 1876. WITH AN INTRODUCTORY REVIEW OF COLONIAL POETRY, AND SOME SPECIMENS OF NEGRO MELODY. London: George Bell & Sons, 1878. 387 pp.

English writer has added a Supplement to his volume (379-87), which contains examples of the plantation songs and editorial notes culled from commentary found in the contemporary collections of slave songs published by Thomas W. Higginson, William Allen, Charles Ware, and Lucy McKim Garrison (see nos. 1072, 1216).

Texts and music of 5 songs; texts only of 9 songs; 1 musical incipit. See SONG COLLECTIONS (no. 1773).

1248 Lockwood, Lewis C. MARY S. PEAKE, THE COLORED TEACHER AT FORTRESS MONROE. Boston: Published by the American Tract Society, 1863. 64 pp. Reprint. TWO BLACK TEACHERS DURING THE CIVIL WAR. New York: Arno Press and the New York Times, 1969. 86 pp. The reprint includes also two articles by Charlotte Forten (see no. 1168), which were originally published in the ATLANTIC MONTHLY. Pages references below are to the reprint.

The biography of Peake, the first black teacher of the contrabands at Fortress Monroe, Virginia, does not include specific references to black oral traditions. Forten's discussion of her experiences on St. Helena's Island includes description of the singing of the children and related performance practice (69, 76-77), and of the singing of boatmen (68). Also discussion of the shout (73, 79), religious services (69-70, 82), and a Fourth of July celebration (85).

Texts of 7 songs. See SONG COLLECTIONS (no. 1747).

1249 Lucas, Sam. SAM LUCAS' PLANTATION SONGSTER. Boston: White, Smith & Company, [c1876]. 48 pp.

Black minstrel-star Lucas (1840-1916) wrote many of the "character songs" in this collection of 40 minstrel songs, which also includes a brief biographical sketch of Lucas.

Texts of 7 songs are parodies or variants of plantation songs: 1. De possum meat am good to eat (Cho: Carve dat possum). 2. When I was down in Egypt land (Cho: I'se gwine in de valley to meet my Lord). 3. I think I hear the angels sing (Cho: Shew fly, don't bother me). 4. If I had a wife and a little baby (Cho: Dar's a meeting here to-night). 5. I went to de church de other night (Cho: Old Aunt Jemima, Oh! oh! oh!). 6. I hope I may jine de band (Cho: So early in de morning). 7. Oh, Hannah, boil dat cabbage down (Cho: Hannah, boil 'em down).

1250 Ludlow, Fitz Hugh. "If Massa Put Guns into Our Han's." ATLANTIC MONTHLY 15 (April 1865): 504-12.

Discussion of the activities of abolitionists among the slaves during the Civil War era.

Text of 1 song: O! O! Him hab face jus' like de crow, But de Lor' gib him heart like snow (506).

1251 Ludlow, Helen W. "The Hampton Normal and Agricultural Institute." HARPER'S NEW MONTHLY MAGAZINE 47 (October 1873): 672-85.

Hampton instructor's discussion of the industrial training for students at the institution includes comment on the singing of the students and the contra-dances they performed during holiday celebrations.

Texts of 4 songs: Did you hear my Jesus when he called you?. 2. When de moon puts on a purple robe, De sun refuse to shine (Cho: Jesus he will be mine). 3. Yonder comes my sister!. 4. I'm gwine to climb up Jacob's ladder (Cho: I'm gwine to climb up higher and higher).

1252 _____, ed. TUSKEGEE NORMAL AND INDUSTRIAL SCHOOL, FOR TRAINING OF COLORED TEACHERS AT TUSKEGEE, ALABAMA: ITS STORY AND ITS SONGS. Hampton, Virgina: Normal School Steam Press, 1884. 47 pp. The Supplement is entitled CABIN AND PLANTATION SONGS, AS SUNG BY THE TUSKEGEE SINGERS. Arranged by R. H. Hamilton. 21 pp.

Miscellaneous collection of essays includes the narrative of an octogenarian ex-slave preacher, Father Thomas Perry, who was opposed to "studied oratory" or any "extreme" in the "natural way of preaching (28-31). The Preface to the music supplement includes discussion of the problems involved in "reducing the melodies to writing" and performance practice associated with the singing of the songs. Observation that the "songs have not, to our knowledge, been reduced to music before."

Music and texts of 12 songs. See SONG COLLECTIONS (no. 1773).

1253 M. "In a Colony of Slaves." SATURDAY EVENING POST 171 (12 March 1898): 13.

Discussion of an African colony in Texas, located near the lowlands of the Brazos River, whose members originally were imported from Africa as slaves, but having arrived in the United States during the Civil War, were given their freedom. Some returned to Africa. Those who remained founded the colony, living apart from the native-born blacks and preserving their tribal customs, songs, and dances.

1254 M'K., C. M. [=McKim, Charles M.?]. "Aunt Becky's Troubles: The Short and Simple Annals of the Poor." CHRISTIAN WATCHMAN & REFLECTOR (=WATCHMAN-EXAMINER) 49 (10 December 1868): [4].

Discussion of a destitute ex-slave of Petersburg, Virginia, includes the texts of 2 songs: 1. Shall we meet again?. 2. De bell done ring.

1255 Magill, Mary Tucker. "Sis." HARPER'S NEW MONTHLY MAGAZINE 72 (January 1886): 257-63.

Story about a black nurse in antebellum Virginia includes the text of 1 song: Sister, dus you want to git aligion?

1256 "Major and Minor." MUSICAL RECORD (Boston), no. 275 (December 1884): 8.

Description of a camp-meeting religious service. Texts of 3 couplets: 1. If onct I get inside the door. 2. When I am dead an' gone. 3. Daniel's got in the lion's den, I r'aly do belieb.

1257 "Margaret Miller." HARPER'S WEEKLY 8 (31 December 1864): 838-39.

Fictional story about the South during the Civil War era includes the text of 1 song: Dar'll be no more sorrow dar!

1258 Marrowfat, Max. "Visit to a Georgia Sugar Camp: Sugar Boiling in Southwest Georgia." APPLETON'S JOURNAL OF POPULAR LITERATURE, SCIENCE, AND ART 9 (25 January 1873): 137-40.

Description of children playing and dancing in a a sugar-making camp in Georgia includes text of 1 children's song: Dar's ur rat (Cho: Dar he go! Hoo-ray!).

1259 Marsh, J. B. T. THE STORY OF THE JUBILEE SINGERS, WITH THEIR SONGS. London: Hodder and Stoughton, 1876. 232 pp. 1877 ed. 248 pp. Reprint of 1877 ed. New York: Negro Universities Press, 1969.

This book combines two earlier histories of the Fisk Jubilee Singers written by the Rev. G. D. Pike (see nos. 1304, 1305). Includes biographies of the nine original members (104-18) and discussion of the character of the folksongs and performance practice (121-22) by Theodore Seward. The 1877 edition includes an introduction by E. M. Cravath, president of Fisk University.

Texts and music of 112 songs. See SONG COLLECTIONS (no. 1764).

1260 _____. THE STORY OF THE JUBILEE SINGERS, WITH THEIR SONGS. Rev. ed. Boston: Houghton, Mifflin and Company, [1882]. 265 pp.

This edition combines the two earlier histories of the Fisk Jubilee Singers written by the Rev. G. D. Pike (see nos. 1304, 1305) and adds an updated narrative about the group's tour of Germany in 1877-1878. Also includes biographies of the nine original members of the Jubilee Singers and their chaperon, Susan Gilbert White.

Texts and music of 122 songs. See SONG COLLECTIONS (nos. 1767, 1768).

1261 _____. THE STORY OF THE JUBILEE SINGERS BY J. B. T. MARSH, WITH SUPPLEMENT CONTAINING AN ACCOUNT OF THE SIX YEAR'S TOUR AROUND THE WORLD, AND MANY NEW SONGS, BY F. J. LOUDIN. Cleveland: Cleveland Printing and Publishing Company, 1892. Reprint. London: Hodder and Stoughton, 1903. 311 pp.

Revised edition of the 1877 publication, combining two earlier histories of the Fisk Jubilee Singers written by the Rev. G. D. Pike (see nos. 1304, 1305) with the Marsh editions. Addition of a Supplement written by black singer-impresario Frederick J. Loudin, which offers the history of the reorganized Jubilee Singers. Loudin, one of the early Jubilee Singers, became director in 1878 after Fisk University dropped its sponsorship and the troupe turned professional.

Texts and music of 139 songs. See SONG COLLECTIONS (no. 1769).

1262 Martin, Rev. Sella. "My Slave Life." GOOD WORDS 8 (May 1867): 314-21; 8 (June 1867): 393-99.

Ex-slave preacher's narrative about his youth in the South includes discussion of the sale of himself, his mother, and siblings from a plantation in Virginia to the cotton fields of Georgia. Vivid description of a slave coffle and the circumstances under which the slaves were forced to sing.

Text of 1 song: Oh, fare ye well, my bonny love (315).

1263 "Massa Charles' and the Silver Dollar." HARPER'S WEEKLY 8 (29 October 1864): 699.

Short story about a black boatman who lived near Charleston includes the text of 1 boat song: Ole Maum Dinah, O, he hab 'leben chillen.

1264 Mathews, William Smythe Babcock. "The Jubilee Slave-Songs." NEW YORK MUSICAL GAZETTE 7 (October 1873): 147-48.

Discussion of the music of the slaves during the years 1850-1860 and comparison of this music with the songs published in the Fisk Jubilee Singers Anthology. Description of the singing performance practice, of the black preacher, and of prayer-meetings.
Texts of 6 songs: 1. I'm a-rolling thro' an unfriendly world. 2. Swing low, sweet chariot. 3. From all that dwell below the skies (Cho: Oh! happy day). 4. When Israel was in Egypt's land. 5. Been a-listening all the night long. 6. Some say that John the Baptist was nothing but a Jew.
References to 2 songs: 1. Oh, for a thousand tongues to sing. 2. Oh, rise up, children, get your crown.

1265 McKay, Charlotte Elizabeth Johnson. STORIES OF HOSPITAL AND CAMP. Philadelphia: Claxton, Remsen, & Haffelfinger, 1876. Reprint. Freeport, NY: Books for Free Libraries, 1971. 230 pp.

Discussion of the author's missionary work among freedmen at Popular Springs, Virginia, during the winter of 1865-1866 includes description of a prayer meeting of some ex-slaves and refers to performance practice associated with the songs and the religious dance (170-72).

Texts of 3 songs: 1. I thank God I'm bound to die (171). 2. Shall we meet again? (Cho: I'll meet you in heaven to part no more) (211). 3. Sister Phoebe gone to heaven (Cho: De bell done ring) (212).

1266 McKenzie, Andrew. "The Glory of His Shame." NEW ENGLAND MAGAZINE n. s. 16 (April 1897): 245-52.

Short story about race relations in a prison includes reference to 1 song: Swing low, sweet chariot.

1267 McKinstry. "Negro Melodies." MUSICAL VISITOR (Cincinnati) July 1888, 177-78.

Journalist's comment on the movement towards "artistic" music in black churches in the South includes the caution that the plantation songs are in danger of becoming "obsolete." Discussion of the successes of the Fisk Jubilee Singers and the "weird" plantation songs they sing, with the observation that these songs can only be preserved by the children of bondsmen.

1268 Meekins, Lynn Roby. "The Maryland Oyster Business." HARPER'S WEEKLY 33 (2 March 1889): 167.

Journalist's discussion of the oyster industry in Baltimore, Maryland, after the Civil War includes description of a black oyster peddler and his street cries.

Text of 1 song: Here I have oysters to sell.

1269 Meikleham, Randolph. "A Negro Ballad." JOURNAL OF AMERICAN FOLK-LORE 6 (October-December 1893): 300-301.

Discussion of songs collected from an elderly black women in Albemarle County, Virginia, and of related performance practice includes the text of 1 song: Old Women, she do me so (Cho: Who, wow, wow! Hooray blow).

1270 Miehling, Charles. "American Folk Songs." ETUDE 11 (November 1893): 233.

Discussion focuses on the importance of distinguishing between authentic folk songs of the American black, which evolved out of religious revivals and camp meetings, and the parody minstrel songs heard on the American stage. Observes that many "peculiarities" in the spirituals can be traced to African traditions. Traces 3 sources for Afro-American music in the United States: 1. Imitation of Irish and Scotch ballads, reels, and jigs heard on steamers or in dance halls. 2. Imitation of Baptist and Methodist hymns. 3. African models, described as "recitative style." References to the shout.

Text of 1 song: In de days of the great tribulation (Cho: O, come down, John).

1271 "The Mississippi River." HARPER'S WEEKLY 11 (9 November 1867): 716-17.

Discussion of a river-boat incident on the Mississippi River at the close of the Civil War includes comment on black boatmen and their songs.

1272 Moore, Ella Sheppard. "Needs of the Colored Woman and Girls." AMERICAN MISSIONARY (MAGAZINE) n.s. 43 (January 1889): 22-25.

Organist-pianist of the original Fisk Jubilee Singers discusses the educational needs of black women in the South.

Texts of 5 choruses: 1. Nobody knows the trouble I see. 2. O, Lord, oh my good Lord (Cho: Keep me from sinking down). 3. Didn't my Lord deliver Daniel? 4. March on, and you shall gain the victory. 5. O, brethern, rise and shine and give God glory.

1273 Moore, Frank, ed. ANECDOTES, POETRY, AND INCIDENTS OF THE WAR, NORTH AND SOUTH: 1860-1865. New York: Printed for the Subscribers, 1866. 560 pp. Reprint as THE

CIVIL WAR IN SONG AND STORY. Collected and arranged by Frank Moore. New York: P. F. Collier, Publisher, 1889.

Miscellaneous collection of previously published literature about the Civil War includes four articles that discuss the songs and dances of slaves in South Carolina and Florida: (1) "Music of the Port Royal Negroes," by Lucy McKim (98). (2) "The Schools of Fernandina, Florida," by an anonymous correspondent (116-18). (3) "Worship of the Negroes," by an anonymous writer of Port Royal (146-47). (4) "Christmas of the Slaves," by an anonymous writer of Port Royal (465-66). Descriptions of songs and dances, their performance practice, and the context in which they were performed. Comment on a religious festival held on Christmas Eve, called a "Serenade to Jesus." Two descriptions of the shout (146-47, 466). Also summaries of a slave sermon based on Nicodemus and Hezekiah (225-26) and a funeral prayer offered by a black exhorter (289).

Texts of 6 songs: 1. My mother! how long will sinners suffer here? (Cho: It won't be long) (117). 2. We'll soon be free (Cho: My brother, do sing de praises ob de Lord (117), 3. Little children sitting on the tree of life (Cho: O, roll, Jordan, roll) (146). 4. My sister, don't you want to get religion? (Cho: Go down in the lonesome valley, my Lord (146). 5. Ole massa he come dancin' out (309) 6. Say brothers, will you meet me (466). References to 2 songs: 1. O, poor sinner, can't stand de fire. 2. We'll wait till Jesus comes.

1274 Mosby, Ella F. "Old Virginia Legends." POTTER'S AMERICAN MONTHLY 14 (February 1880): 139-42.

Essay about black legends and superstitions in Virginia includes description of the slave songs as "wild" and performed in a "weird" manner.

Text of 1 song: O, give me wings and I'll fly to New Jerusalem. Reference to 1 song: De coming ob de Lord.

1275 Monroe, Kirk. "Wakulla." Parts 1, 2. HARPER'S YOUNG PEOPLE 5 (30 September 1884): 754-56; 6 (18 November 1884): 39-42.

Serialized novel about the journey of an American family down the eastern sea coast of the United States to their plantation in Key West, Florida, contains discussion of the activities of the blacks, including description of a dance (42) and of the singing (755).

Text of 1 boat song (755): Oh, dey put John on the islan' (R: When de bridegroom come).

1276 Murphy, Jeannette Robinson. "The Survival of African Music in America." APPLETON'S POPULAR SCIENCE MONTHLY 55 (September 1899): 660-72. Reprint. THE NEGRO AND HIS FOLKLORE IN NINETEENTH-CENTURY PERIODICALS. Edited by Bruce Jackson. Published for the American Folklore Society. Austin: University of Texas Press, 1967.

Discussion of the retention of African traditions in the songs, dances, and performance practice of southern blacks includes excerpts of interviews with three ex-slave women, who describe the context in which the songs were sung. Comment on the custom of "singing to the soul of the departed" and how to sing the spirituals. Discussion of the stock animal characters of folk tales and text of an excerpt from a folk tale about Noah's ark. Texts of 4 African songs.

Texts and music of 5 songs: 1. Who dat yonder dressed in white? Must be de chillun ob de Israelite (Cho: Come along, done found dat new hidin' place). 2. Mary and Marthy had a cha-ain, walk Jerus'lem jis like Job (Cho: When I comes ter die, I want ter be ready). 3. See my mudder, oh, yes! tell her for me (Cho: Ride on, Jesus, Ride on, conq'ring king). 4. Fadding, gidding, fadding go. 5. Gawd bless dem Yankees, dey'll set me free! (Cho: 'Most done toilin' heah!). Reference to 1 song: I don't want to be buried in de storm.

1277 N., H. "Negroes and Negro Melodies. The Real Music Is to Be Found at a Camp Meeting or Revival." AMERICAN ART JOURNAL 62 (24 March 1895): 477-78.

Discussion of a letter written by G. Wilfred Pearce to the NEW YORK SUN, dated 15 February 1894, includes refutation of Pearce's statement that "the jubilee songs, music and words, of most all the so-called negro melodies, were written by keen-witted New Englanders." Detailed description of a camp-meeting service, where "real negro music" was heard, includes description of the improvisation of a song and relevant performance practice. Also comment on the fact that the fourth and seventh scale degrees are absent in Negro melodies, but there is use of "the flatted seventh continuously" and occasional use of the flatted fourth.

1278 "A Negro Camp-Meeting Hymn." HARPER'S NEW MONTHLY MAGAZINE 70 (May 1885): 982.

Discussion of an improvised "camp-meeting hymn" that the author heard in Georgia and its related performance practice.

Text of 1 song: Oh, Lady, pull de string! When de heab'n bell ring (Cho: Shout, shout, I's a heab'n-boun' soul).

1279 "Negro Folk Songs: Slave Melodies of the South---The Jubilee and Hampton Singers." Unsigned review. DWIGHT'S JOURNAL OF MUSIC 32 (5 April 1873): 411-13. Reprinted from the NEW YORK WEEKLY REVIEW.

Reviewer's discussion of religious songs of the ex-slaves sung by the Fisk Jubilee and Hampton Institute Singers refers to the context in which the songs originated and to the character of the music. Observes that although slave songs and performance practice underwent modification when performed by the college students, the music generally remained "strikingly wild."

Texts of 10 songs. References to 5 songs. See SONG COLLECTIONS (no. 1775).

1280 "Negro Hymn of the Judgement Day." JOURNAL OF AMERICAN FOLK-LORE 9 (July-September 1896): 210.

Text of 1 song collected in North Carolina: Don' yo' see de chariot ridin' on de clouds? (Cho: O dat mornin' you'll hyar a mighty roarin').

1281 "Negro Hymns, etc." ATLANTIC MONTHLY 42 (September 1878): 371-73.

Discussion of performance practice associated with Negro sacred and secular folksongs. Discussion of one play-game, Peep, Squirrel, and its accompanying song.

Texts of 2 songs: 1. A mighty war in heaven (Cho: Don't you grieve after me). 2. I hear a-rumbling under the ground. Texts of 2 couplets: 1. Say, Jonah, you's de man. 2. You can't fool dis child, go along, Jesus.

1282 "Negro Music." MUSICAL VISITOR (Cincinnati) 24 (July 1895): 179.

Article focuses upon the "imitative faculty" of blacks for performing European music. Comment on the song "Juba," which the writer states is a "pure African" song that is half-chanted, half-sung.

1283 Nevin, Robert P. "Stephen C. Foster and Negro Minstrelsy." ATLANTIC MONTHLY 20 (1867): 608-16.

Discussion includes a description of the black stage-driver who originated the "Jump, Jim Crow" song in Cincinnati, Ohio, in 1829, the song made famous by Thomas Dartmouth Rice.

Text of 1 chorus: Turn about an' wheel about an' do jis so.

1284 NEW ORLEANS UNIVERSITY. THE ONLY ORIGINAL NEW ORLEANS UNIVERSITY SINGERS. A Colored Double Quartette. Voices Unrivalled. Philadelphia: Wm. Syckelmoore, 1881. 22 pp.

Notes in the collection include information about New Orleans University, a black school "conducted by" the Freedmen's Aid Society of the M. E. Church, and give the names of the singers.

Texts of 21 songs. See SONG COLLECTIONS (no. 1776).

1285 "The New Times in Richmond." NATIONAL ANTI-SLAVERY STANDARD 25 (15 April 1865): [2]. From the Richmond correspondence of the TIMES.

Description of the Jubilee Meeting held at the African Church in Richmond, Virginia, includes comment on the congregation's peculiar performance practice in lining out a hymn.

Text of 1 chorus: I am going to join in this army of my Lord.

1286 Newell, William Wells. "Waste-Basket of Words: Calinda." JOURNAL OF AMERICAN FOLK-LORE 4 (January-March 1891): 70.

Bibliographical essay by the JOURNAL'S editor on a Louisiana creole folk dance.

Text of 1 couplet: 1. Dance, Calinda, Bon-djoum! Bon-djoum!

1287 Nichols, George. "Down the Mississippi." HARPER'S NEW MONTHLY MAGAZINE 41 (November 1870): 835-45.

American marine painter's narrative of a journey he made by boat down the Mississippi River, from St. Louis, Missouri, to New Orleans, includes discussion of the black deck-hands who sang a "parting song" and of the performance practice associated with their singing.

1288 Nordhoff, Charles. "West Virginia: Horse-back Ride through the Wilderness." AMERICAN MISSIONARY (MAGAZINE) n.s. 16 (January 1872): 1-4.

Travel narrative contains text of 1 slave song: Getting late, getting late, Get up! get up! get up!

1289 "North Carolina Singers." Unsigned concert review. WATCHMAN & REFLECTOR (=WATCHMAN-EXAMINER) 54 (28 May 1873): [2].

Reviewer's discussion of the fund-raising tour of black student singers of the Shaw Collegiate Institute in Raleigh, North Carolina, taken through New England in 1873, includes comment on the religious songs they sang.

References to 7 songs: 1. The general roll call. 2. Did you ever see such a man?. 3. Pick up de young lambs. 4. Jonah. 5. Didn't my Lord deliver Daniel?. 6. One more river to cross. 7. Glory in my soul.

1290 Ober, Sarah Endicott. "The Strivings of Red Clay Gully." INDEPENDENT 44 (27 October 1892): 1534-36.

Short story about the temperance movement in a black community, spearheaded by a local, woman teacher (colored) includes the text of 1 song: 'Tis the old time religion.

1291 "The Old African Church, Richmond." LESLIE'S ILLUSTRATED NEWSPAPER 32 (3 June 1871): 195.

Discussion of the First African Church of Richmond, Virginia, includes comment on the various types of congregational songs sung there.

Texts of 2 songs: 1. Oh, had I wings like a dove. 2. Riding on a rail.

1292 "Old Shady." MUSICAL VISITOR (Cincinnati) December 1888: 315.

Discussion of the ex-slaves employed by officers of the Union Army during the war includes comment on a cook called Old Shady, who would gather together a group of ex-slaves each night to entertain the white officers. Reference to a song that Old Shady himself composed.

Text of 1 song: Yah! Come laugh wid me (Cho: Den away, I can't stay here no longer).

1293 Oldham, Edward A. "Mammy's Churning Song." CENTURY 40 (October 1890): 960.

Short story includes the text of 1 work song: Set still, honey, let ole Mammy tell yer 'bout de churn (Cho: Jiggery, jiggery, jiggery, jum).

1294 "Opening at Hampton Institute of the Armstrong-Slater Trade School." SOUTHERN WORKMAN 25 (December 1896): 231-45.

References to 2 songs sung by Hampton Institute students on the occasion: 1. Walking in the light (242). 2. Let the heaven light shine on me (242).

1295 Page, Thomas Nelson. "Rachel's Lover." HARPER'S NEW MONTHLY MAGAZINE 88 (December 1893): 159-61.

Ghost story written by the novelist and diplomat relates the adventure of a black man who, on the eve of his wedding, encounters a rat he believes is possessed by the devil.

Text of 1 song: I went down to Hell town.

1296 Palmer, John Williamson. "Old Maryland Homes and Ways." CENTURY 49 (December 1894): 244-61.

Baltimore editor's discussion of life-styles on Maryland estates in the late eighteenth century includes references to songs and dances of the blacks associated with the Christmas season. Description of 1 dance: Juba (260).

Texts of 2 songs (260): 1. Hooray, hooray, ho! (Cho: Round de corn, Sally!). 2. Juba up and juba down, juba all aroun' de town.

1297 Parker, William. "The Freedman's Story." Parts 1, 2. ATLANTIC MONTHLY 17 (February 1866): 152-66; 18 (March 1866): 276-95.

Ex-slave narrator of Anne Arundel County (Maryland) gives an account of his life as a slave and his escape to freedom. Offers comment on the activities of abolitionists and citizen groups in preventing the kidnapping and re-enslavement of blacks in North.

Text of 1 song: Leader, what do you say.

1298 Perkins, Frances Johnson Beecher. "Two Years with a Colored Regiment: A Woman's Experience." NEW ENGLAND MAGAZINE n.s. 17 (January 1898): 533-43.

Reminiscences by the widow of Colonel James C. Beecher of her experiences with her husband's black regiment, the First North Carolina Volunteers (Colored), during the Civil War includes comment on the singing of the soldiers.

1299 "Philadelphia Correspondence." NATIONAL ANTI-SLAVERY STANDARD 24 (10 October 1863): [3].

Article, dated 5 October 1863, describes a serenade given by Negro recruits at a Union Army camp near Washington, D. C., during the Civil War. Comment on the soldiers singing one of "their" own anthems.

Text of 1 chorus: They look like men of war.

1300 "Philadelphia Street Characters." HARPER'S WEEKLY 20 (8 April 1876): 292.

Description of three black street peddlers includes texts of 3 street cries: 1. Cra-a-abs! Crab all alive! (Crab man). 2. De hominy ma-a-an. 3. Pep-pree-ee-ee pot, all hot (Pepper pot woman)

1301 Phillips, Wendell. "The State of the Country: A Lecture." NATIONAL ANTI-SLAVERY STANDARD 24 (30 May 1863): [4].

Transcript of a speech by the president of the American Anti-Slavery Society has a commentary by William Lloyd Garrison, in which there is discussion of the slave songs in Port Royal, South Carolina.

Text of 1 song: Dun no what de people want ob me.

1302 ____. "Speech." LIBERATOR 34 (10 June 1864): 93-94.

Phillips's address to the New England branch of the American Anti-Slavery Society, on 27 May 1864, concludes with the text of a contraband song: De massa run---ha, ha!

1303 Pierce, Edward L. "The Freedmen at Port Royal." ATLANTIC MONTHLY 12 (SEPTEMBER 1863): 291-315.

Discussion of the condition of the freedmen at Port Royal, South Carolina, during the Civil War.

Reference to 4 songs: 1. The wrestling Jacob. 2. Down in the lonesome valley. 3. Roll, Jordan, roll. 4. Heab'n shall-a be my home. Texts of 2 songs: 1. In de mornin' when I rise (Cho: Tell my Jesus, huddy oh). 2. I would not let you go, my Lord (Cho: Dere's room enough).

1304 Pike, Gustavus D. THE JUBILEE SINGERS AND THEIR CAMPAIGN FOR TWENTY THOUSAND DOLLARS. Boston: Lee & Shepard, 1873. Also London: Hodder and Stoughton, 1873. 219 pp. Reprint. New York: AMS Press, 1974. See also nos. 1258-1260, 1346-1347.

Secretary of the American Missionary Association offers a detailed history of the Fisk Jubilee Singers' tours through the United States from October 1871 to April 1872. Includes biographies and portraits of the nine original members of the group (49-72) and a group portrait (insert 164-5). Discussion of the musical character of the songs and performance practice in the Preface to the collection (163-64).

Texts and music of 61 songs. See SONG COLLECTIONS (no. 1760).

1305 _____. THE SINGING CAMPAIGN FOR TEN THOUSAND POUNDS; OR, THE JUBILEE SINGERS IN GREAT BRITAIN. London: Hodder and Stoughton, 1874. Boston: Lee & Shepard, 1874. 202 pp.

This edition has no music. Discussion of the tours of the Fisk Jubilee Singers in Europe and biographical sketches for the eight members of the original troupe who were born slaves.

References to 2 spirituals: 1. Steal away (39). 2. Go down, Moses (39). Text of 1 couplet: There are angels hovering round (153). Text of 1 song: Way over in Egypt land (Cho: March on, and you shall gain the victory) (182)

1306 _____. THE SINGING CAMPAIGN FOR TEN THOUSAND POUNDS: OR, THE JUBILEE SINGERS IN GREAT BRITAIN, WITH AN APPENDIX CONTAINING SLAVE SONGS. Rev. ed. New York: American Missionary Association, 1875. Reprint. Freeport, NY: Books for Libraries Press, 1971. 272 pp.

This edition offers an up-dated history of the Fisk Jubilee Singers' tours abroad, including the tour in England in 1875. Its Preface to the Music (as in the other Pike editions) includes discussion of the musical qualities of the slave songs and states they were: "taken down from the singing of the band...and no line or phrase was introduced that did not receive full endorsement from the singers."

Music and texts of 71 songs. See SONG COLLECTIONS (no. 1762).

1307 "Plantation Song." [Editor's Drawer] HARPER'S NEW MONTHLY MAGAZINE 62 (February 1881): 479.

Text of 1 plantation song: Oh, whar shill we go w'en de great day comes.

1308 "Poll Tax: A Song of North Carolina Freedmen." NATIONAL ANTI-SLAVERY STANDARD 28 (9 November 1867): [2].

Contributed by a correspondent living in North Carolina, text of 1 song: De black man's gittin' awful rich (Cho: Den jis fork up de little tax).

1309 "Polly-Voo in Criticism." FOLIO (Boston) 13 (July 1875): 5.

Comment on the singing of an elderly woman includes the text of 1 song: I hear a rumblin' in de skies (Cho: Jews screws de-fi-dum).

1310 Porter, Mary W. "Some Negro Melodies." INDEPENDENT 30 (8 August 1878): 2-3.

Discussion of the songs and performance practice of Negro boatmen in Louisiana.

Texts of 5 songs: 1. Glory and honor, praise King Jesus. 2. Christ while walking on earth (Cho: Free pass over Jordan). 3. Oh! de Book of Revelation (Cho: Oh! Zion's wheel 'fuse to trabel). 4. I, John saw the holy numbers. 5. Doubting Thomas, doubt no more (Cho: For de angel's awaiting at de gate).

1311 _____. "At the Sugar-House." INDEPENDENT 31 (11 September 1879): 3-4.

Description of the singing and related performance practice of secular and religious songs of blacks on a sugar plantation in Louisiana.

Texts of 4 songs: 1. Stand steady, children. 2. One day as I was walking (Cho: Let us cheer the weary traveler). 3. Pick up John's resolution. 4. Jubilee, jubilee, jubilee.

1312 _____. "Genuine Negro Hymns." INDEPENDENT 32 (22 July 1880): 4-5.

Texts of 7 songs that were sung to the author by an elderly ex-slave: 1. Oh, de Gospel train am comin' (Cho: Now git on board, chillen). 2. When I was a sinner, I loved my distance well (Cho: Die in de field o' battle, gloryin' my soul). 3. When we see Master Jesus come ridin' out on de bow (Cho: Yes, we'll run and go to meet him). 4. Injine pudding and pumpkin pie (Cho: Walk, Jawbone, walk). 5. I want to be like old wrastlin Jacob into the days of old (Cho: Gwine home! Come pray with de heavenly mind). 6. My sister talk about me (Cho: Rock me, member, rock!). 7. Oh! Who's that coming over yonder? Hallelujah!

1313 Preston, Margaret J. "Cuckoo's Christmas." INDEPENDENT 33 (22 December 1881): 31-32.

Short story about a black boy living on a plantation near James River in the Old Dominion

(=Virginia) includes the text of 1 song: De Lord, he come to Befle'em.

1314 Pyle, Howard. "A Peninsular Canaan: II---Maryland." HARPER'S NEW MONTHLY MAGAZINE 59 (June 1879): 63-75.

Narrative about the author's travels through Maryland in the 1870s, which focuses primarily upon a description of fishing and agricultural industries, includes discussion of Afro-American folk singing as observed in Virginia.

Text and music of 1 song: My soul, no use bein' 'fraid of the rainbow (69).

1315 R., P. "Scraps of Plantation Songs---Picked up in de Quarter." MUSICAL RECORD (Boston), no. 189 (13 May 1882): 540.

Texts of 5 songs: 1. When de stars of de yallerments a fallin', when the moon drips away with blood. 2. Daniel, po' Daniel, Oh, de Lawd he 'livered po' Daniel. 3. I axed my sister how she do (Cho: Satum is a fallin' fuller sand). 4. Brur John he saw de lan', so losser in de suth'n sea. 5. Have oil in yo' vessels when de bridegroom comes (Cho: Come up a little higher!).

1316 R., S. S. "Negro Psalmody, or Religious Songs." AMERICAN NOTES AND QUERIES 4 (1 March 1890): 208-9.

Discussion of the religious songs of ex-slaves from Maryland and Virginia who settled along the Susquehanna River in Pennsylvania during the early nineteenth century focuses on the character and performance practice of the songs.

Texts of 3 songs: 1. O, brudders, be determined for to jine me in de battle (Cho: I am bound to die in de army). 2. Come, brudders in de Lord, come, rise, shine, and go wid me. 3. Send for de doctor, and he'll come a ridin (Cho: Sin sick, O, halleluya).

1317 Ralph, Julian. "An Angel in a Web: Chapter XII---Through a Break in the Web." HARPER'S NEW MONTHLY MAGAZINE 97 (November 1898): 938-61.

Serialized novel by this journalist includes the text of 1 song: Some folks say dat a preacher can't lie.

1318 Ranger [pseud.]. "Letters from the Army." CHRISTIAN WATCHMAN & REFLECTOR 44 (25 January 1863): [2].

Discussion of contrabands by a correspondent at Fort Monroe, Virginia, includes the observation that the "noisy, illiterate songs, which form so prominent a feature in Negro worship, are being gradually eradicated."

1319 Rankin, J. E. "The Aesthetic Capacity of the Afro-American." OUR DAY 13 (July-August 1894): 289-97.

White professor at Howard University offers comment on the creativity of blacks, pointing to the indigenous body of folksongs and tales they created during slavery.

Reference to 1 song: Steal away to Jesus.

1320 Rathbun, Frederick G. "Negro Music of the South." SOUTHERN WORKMAN 22 (November 1893): 174. Reprint. BLACK PERSPECTIVE IN MUSIC 4 (July 1976): 138-40.

This reprint of a Letter to the Editor, written by the director of music at Hampton Institute and originally published in the NEW YORK HERALD, discusses the character of the music and texts of Negro spirituals, including comment on the potential use of these songs in classical symphonic forms. Observation that the old style of singing is slowly dying out.

Text of 1 song: Dere's a better day a-comin' (Cho: In dat great gettin' up mornin'). Reference to 2 songs: 1. Church of God. 2. Some o' dese morning.

1321 Read, Opie P. "Cotton Is All Dun Picked." HARPER'S NEW MONTHLY MAGAZINE 75 (November 1887): 971.

Editor of the ARKANSAS TRAVELER contributes the text of 1 work song: I's gwine up ter town an' spen' my money (Cho: Cotton is all dun picked).

1322 "The Reminiscences of an Egoist." NEW ENGLAND MAGAZINE n.s. 4 (April 1891): 241-50.

Daughter of a country clergyman, recalling incidents from her childhood, discusses her father's participation in the Underground Railroad and the fugitive slaves who sang songs for her family.

1323 Rexford, Eben E. "Negro Music." MUSICAL VISITOR (Cincinnati) 21 (April 1897): 85-86.

Discussion of black folk music points to the use of vivid imageries in the religious songs.

Texts of 4 songs: 1. Methodis', Methodis' I was born, Methodis' gwine to die. 2. Raccoon up a 'simmon-tree, possum in de holler. 3. Ol' Aunt Lukey an' ol' Aunt Sal, gwine ter git a home bymeby! 4. Dar's a low, sweet music (Cho: From de ol' church-yard).

1324 Reynard [pseud.]. "Ebony: Quaint and Semi-Inspired. Third Paper." ZION'S HERALD 56 (27 February 1879): 65. See also nos. 977, 978.

Description of a black jubilee in Charleston,

South Carolina, following the fall of the city during the Civil War includes references to the blacks singing and marching through the streets.

1325 Rideing, William H. "Chimney-Sweeps, Past and Present." ST. NICHOLAS, AN ILLUSTRATED MAGAZINE FOR BOYS AND GIRLS 2 (February 1875): 211-14.

General discussion of chimney sweeps in Europe and the United States includes the text of 1 street cry sung by a black chimney sweep in Charleston, South Carolina: O weep, wee-ep.

1326 [Ridley, Florida Ruffin?]. "Society for the Collection of Negro Folk Lore in Boston". WOMAN'S ERA (September 1894): 37.

Article published in this black journal by one of the founders (reportedly) of the Boston Negro Folk-Lore Society, focuses on contemporary attitudes towards the group: "There have been and are two strong sides as to the value of...[preserving Negro folklore]. There are those who believe firmly that the sooner the colored man loses and forgets his characteristics, the better it will be for himself and other Americans-good of the race is served by preserving all characteristics worth preserving....It can not but help to dignify the race to preserve its anecdotes and songs, the work that is being done here by the [Negro] Folk-Lore Society."

1327 Ritter, Frederick Louis. MUSIC IN AMERICA. New York: Charles Scribner's Sons, 1883. 423 pp. Reprint. New York: Burt Franklin, c.1972.

This first history of music in the United States includes discussion of the musical traditions of the slave songs (392-400) with comment on the influence of African traditions on the songs. Lengthy quotation from an article that was published in the EVENING POST [no date given] that offers detailed description of "the Negro's characteristic manner of singing and hymn-composing." Comment on vocal qualities, rhythmic "precision," antiphonal style, and melodic features (392-94).

Text of 1 song: In de days of great tribulashun (393). Texts and music of 2 songs: 1. Old Satan told to me to my face (Cho: True believer, I know when I gwine home)(415). 2. I am a troubled in de mind (415).

1328 Robarts, L. W. "The Darky of the Rice-Lands." CHRISTIAN WATCHMAN & REFLECTOR (=WATCHMAN EXAMINER) 71 (16 October 1890): [6]. Reprinted from POPULAR SCIENCE MONTHLY, October 1890.

Discussion of the ex-slaves on rice plantations along the tidelands of Georgia, the Carolina coast, and adjacent islands includes the observation that they are a distinct type and their dialect differs from that of blacks in the interior. References to their songs.

1329 Robinson, M. G. "The Chimney Sweep." ILLUSTRATED CHRISTIAN WEEKLY 2 (30 November 1872): 576.

Short sketch about a black chimney sweep includes the text of 1 street cry: Hark, Ho-oo---swee---e---eep.

1330 Ryder, Charles J. "The Theology of the Plantation Songs." AMERICAN MISSIONARY (MAGAZINE) 46 (January 1892): 9-16.

Secretary of the Eastern district of the American Missionary Association, and former business manager of the Fisk Jubilee Singers, discusses the religious theology of the slave songs.

Texts of 13 songs. See SONG COLLECTIONS (1778).

1331 _____. "Christian Truth in Slave Songs." AFRO-AMERICAN ENCYCLOPEDIA; OR, THE THOUGHTS, DOINGS, AND SAYINGS OF THE RACE, EMBRACING ADDRESSES, LECTURES, BIBLIOGRAPHICAL SKETCHES, SERMONS, POEMS, NAMES OF UNIVERSITIES, COLLEGES, SEMINARIES, NEWSPAPERS, BOOKS, AND A HISTORY OF DENOMINATIONS....Edited by James T. Haley, 254-64. Nashville, TN: Haley & Florida, 1895. Reprint. Ann Arbor, MI: University Microfilms International, 1976.

Article traces the impact of slavery upon nations through examination of the folksongs of the people. Draws an analogy between the plight of the Israelites in Egypt and the conditions of the black slave in America. Examines texts of plantation hymns and spirituals for evidence of a slave theology.

Texts of 12 refrains; texts of 7 songs. See SONG COLLECTIONS (no. 1777).

1332 _____. "Fifty Years of the American Missionary Association." NEW ENGLAND MAGAZINE n.s. 15 (October 1896): 225-44.

Clergyman's discussion of his missionary work in helping to educate blacks includes comment on a song improvised by an old ex-slave working in a cotton field: This yer sun am so hot.

1333 S., J. T. "Literary: ARMY LIFE IN A BLACK REGIMENT, by Thomas Wentworth Higginson, late colonel of the 1st South Carolina Volunteers." Book review. NATIONAL ANTI-SLAVERY STANDARD 30 (2 October 1869): [3].

Review includes discussion of a ballad sung by black recruits during the Civil War about the U. S. government's default in paying them their wages.

Text of 1 song: Ten dollar a month, tree ob dat for clothin'.

1334 S., K. G. "Negroes' Spirituals." LIPPINCOTT'S MAGAZINE 7 (March 1871): 331-34.

Discussion of the slave music includes comment on the shout and related performance practice.

Texts and music of 2 songs: 1. I have no friend but Jesus. 2. Mary weep, Marta moan. Text only of 1 song: You may carry me to de grabeyard (Cho: Every day's a Sunday, by 'n' by).

1335 S., M. R. "A Pleasant Story." PENNSYLVANIA FREEDMEN'S BULLETIN (February 1868): 2-3.

Reference to the chorus of a plantation greeting song: I rise up soon in de mornin'.

1336 _____. "A Visitor's Account of Our Sea Island Schools." PENNSYLVANIA FREEDMEN'S BULLETIN (October 1866): 5-8.

Discussion of school children singing a "wild, droning chant" at the freedmen's school near Beaufort, South Carolina, and description of the shout they performed.

Texts of 2 songs: 1. Nobody knows the trubble I sees. 2. We a-hunting fo' a city to stay a while (Cho: Oh! Lord, de believer got a home at last).

1337 _____. "Our Sea Island Schools." PENNSYLVANIA FREEDMEN'S BULLETIN (December 1866): 2-6.

Reference to a plantation song and text of its chorus: Let all de old tings done all away.

1338 Sala, George Augustus. MY DIARY IN AMERICA IN THE MIDST OF WAR. London: Tinsley Brothers, 1865. 2 vols.

English novelist and correspondent for the LONDON DAILY TELEGRAPH reports on his experiences in the United States during the Civil War. Comment on the folksongs of black Americans, both slave and free.

Text of 1 song: Chase de debbil round the stump (Cho: Glory, hallelujah) (2:332).

1339 _____. AMERICA REVISITED: FROM THE BAY OF NEW YORK TO THE GULF OF MEXICO, AND FROM LAKE MICHIGAN TO THE PACIFIC. 3d. ed. London: Vizitelly & Company, 1883. 2 vols.

This record of the novelist's second visit to the United States in 1879 includes comment on his contacts with black Americans, particularly in Baltimore, Maryland; Richmond, Virginia; and New Orleans, Louisiana.

Text of 1 song: 1. When de brimstone's ladled out (1:210).

1340 Satterthwait, Elizabeth Carpentier. A SON OF THE CAROLINAS: A STORY OF THE HURRICANE UPON THE SEA ISLANDS. Philadelphia: Henry Altemus, 1898. Reprint. Freeport, NY: Books for Libraries Press, 1972. 273 pp.

Novel about black life-styles on the Sea Islands of South Carolina includes comment on songs of the boatmen, dance-songs, and religious songs.

Texts of 5 songs: 1. I'm gwine ter cross ole ocean by mys'ef (Cho: Lord, I cannot stay here by mys'ef) (133). 2. Hard times in ole Faginia [=Virginia] (142). 3. Death ain't got no shame (164). 4. When I lay on a sick bed, nobody visit me (168). 5. I'se r'ady fo' ter die (239). Description of a ring-dance (141-42).

1341 Sawyer, Jacob J., arranger. JUBILEE SONGS AND PLANTATION MELODIES (WORDS AND MUSIC) SPECIALLY ARRANGED BY PROF J. J. SAWYER, AND SUNG BY THE ORIGINAL NASHVILLE STUDENTS, THE CELEBRATED COLORED CONCERT CO. Introduction by H. B. Thearle, Proprietor. N.p.: J. J. Sawyer, 1884. 14 pp.

The introduction to the collection includes discussion of the origin, compositional process, and musical characteristics of the songs.

Texts and music of 14 songs. See SONG COLLECTIONS (no. 1779).

1342 Scharf, John Thomas, and Thompson Westcott. HISTORY OF PHILADELPHIA, 1609-1884. 3 vols. Philadelphia: L. H. Everts & Company, 1884.

Comprehensive history of the city includes detailed discussion of music and musicians, with comment on black street vendors and their songs, and songs of the black stevedores on the waterfront of Philadelphia's port (2:929-31). Comment on the Old Hominy Man, who first made his appearance on the city streets about 1828.

Text of 1 street cry: Hominy man came out today, For to sell his hominay. Text of 1 stevedore song: Nancy Bohannan, she married a barber (Cho: Shave her away! shave her away!).

1343 Scruggs, Lawson Andrew. WOMEN OF DISTINCTION. Raleigh, NC: L. A. Scruggs, 1893. 382 pp.

Collection of biographies of distinguished Afro-American women in the nineteenth century, compiled by black author Scruggs, includes a sketch of the life of Harriet Tubman (c. 1821-1913), conductor of the Underground Railroad, and comment on the songs she sang.

Text of 1 song (68): I am gwine away to leab you (Cho: We'll sing and shout ag'in).

1344 "The Second Historical Meeting of the Armstrong League." Part 1: "An Incident of the Beginning." Part 2. "Some Old Songs." SOUTHERN WORKMAN 23 (May 1894): 72-76; 76.

Part 1. Discussion of the first tour of the Hampton Institute Singers in the North during the years 1873-1874. References to 6 songs: 1. Dat great get-tin' up mornin (73). 2. Dust and ashes (75). 3. My Lord what a morning (75). 4. Church of God (74). 5. Wide river (74). 6. Swing low, sweet chariot (76).

Part 2. References to 2 plantation songs: 1. Bright sparkles. 2. Travelling to de grave.

1345 Semple, Patty Blackburn. "In a Border State." ATLANTIC MONTHLY 62 (October 1888): 464-82.

Short story about the Civil War includes comment on the singing of the black cook, Aunt Gin.

Text of 1 song: Oh, the raccoon's tail is ring'd all round (471).

1346 Seward, Theodore. JUBILEE SONGS: AS SUNG BY THE JUBILEE SINGERS OF FISK UNIVERSITY, UNDER THE AUSPICES OF THE AMERICAN MISSIONARY ASSOCIATION. Compiled by Theo. F. Seward. New York: Biglow & Main, 1872. 32 pp.

Seward, the compiler of this very first edition of the Jubilee Songs, who was also editor of the NEW YORK MUSICAL GAZETTE, discusses the origin, composition, and character of the slave music in his preface. The Introduction, dated 1 March 1872, written by E. M. Cravath, field secretary of the American Missionary Association (and later president of Fisk University), includes further discussion of the origin of the spirituals and of the quality of the music, how it was recorded in notation by George White (the white music teacher at Fisk) and Seward. Also discussion of the nine singers and their background, of Fisk University, and of "Notices from the Press."

Music and texts of 23 songs. See SONG COLLECTIONS (no. 1758).

1347 _____. JUBILEE SONGS: COMPLETE. AS SUNG BY THE JUBILEE SINGERS OF FISK UNIVERSITY (NASHVILLE, TENN.). Compiled by Theo. F. Seward. New York: Biglow & Main, 1872. 64 pp.

This expanded edition of the Jubilee songs includes further discussion of the origin, composition, and characteristics of the songs as performed by the Fisk Jubilee Singers. Also includes the Cravath introduction (see no. 1346).

Texts and music of 61 songs. See SONG COLLECTIONS (no. 1759).

1348 Seward, William H. "The Army and the Negroes." NATIONAL ANTI-SLAVERY STANDARD 23 (3 January 1863): [3].

Dispatch dated 25 December [1862] includes discussion of the condition of the black regiments in the Union Army during the Civil War. An entry dated 3 December [1862] pertains to the recruitment of black soldiers from among the contrabands at Beaufort, South Carolina. References to the singing and dancing of ex-slaves.

Text of 1 song: Room enough in heaven, my Lord (Cho: Oh, I can't stay behind).

1349 _____. "The Army and the Negroes." NATIONAL ANTI-SLAVERY STANDARD 24 (13 June 1863): [3].

Description of the reception given Union Army soldiers by slaves in Louisiana includes the text of 1 song chorus: Massa run away, hi, hi!

1350 _____. "The Army and the Negroes: Songs of the Colored Soldiers." NATIONAL ANTI-SLAVERY STANDARD 25 (15 April 1865): [3].

Discussion of the singing of the Negro infantry as it marched through Petersburg and Richmond, Virginia, during the Civil War includes the text of 1 song: Say darkies, hab you seen massa? (Cho: De massa run, ha! ha! De darkey stay, ho! ho!).

1351 Shaler, N. S. "An Ex-Southerner in South Carolina." ATLANTIC MONTHLY 26 (July 1870): 53-61.

Description of the singing of a religious chant by black boatmen en route from Bull River to Beaufort, South Carolina, includes comment on performance practice.

1352 Shanley, C. D. "Street Cries of New York." ATLANTIC MONTHLY 25 (February 1870): 199-204.

Discussion of street criers and vendors includes references to black peddlers of hot corn and chimney-sweeps. Comment on song performance practice.

Text and music of 1 cry: 1. Hot corn, here's your fine hot corn (200).

1353 Sheldon, George. "Negro Slavery in Old Deerfield." NEW ENGLAND MAGAZINE n.s. 8 (March 1893): 49-60.

Discussion of slavery in Deerfield, Massachusetts, during the period c.1673-1781 by the historian and abolitionist contains character sketches of 2 slaves: Cato, a singer, and Luce Bijah, who was famous in the town as a story teller. Discussion of the religious instruction of slaves.

1354 Sheppard, Andrew. SHEPPARD'S JUBILEE SINGERS (program notes for a concert given on 8 November 1875).

The four-page program gives the history of the eight-person, ex-slave singing group, led by Andrew Sheppard, formerly a slave of Robert E. Lee at Arlington, Virginia. Included is a list of 88 songs, from which songs were selected for performance, and press notices that include description of performance practice.

1355 Shipman, Clara Wood. "A Loyal Traitor." NEW ENGLAND MAGAZINE n.s. 14 (June 1896): 411-18.

Short story about an ex-slave who joined the Union Army during the Civil War, but remained loyal to his former slaveowner.

Text of 1 song: I went to the river an' what did I see.

1356 Siebert, Wilbur H. THE UNDERGROUND RAILROAD FROM SLAVERY TO FREEDOM. London and New York: The MacMillan Company, 1898. 478 pp. Reprint. New York: Arno Press and the New York Times, 1968.

Historical account includes reference to Harriet Tubman and the text of her favorite song, which was associated with her activities as a "conductor" of the Underground Railroad (186): Dark and thorny is de pathway.

1357 "Silhouettes." SOUTHERN WORKMAN 20 (April 1891): 172.

Discussion of the singing of black students at a sewing school in Slabtown, Virginia.

Texts of 4 songs: 1. Some go to meeting to laugh and talk (Cho: Oh, de angel done change my name). 2. Go down my soul and suffer shame (Cho: Jesus locked the lion's jaw. 3. Run, mourner, run (Cho: Day is breakin'). 4. Jesus in the valley on his knees (Cho: We will all rise together and view the rising sun).

1358 Simond, Ike. OLD SLACK'S REMINISCENCE AND POCKET HISTORY OF THE COLORED PROFESSION FROM 1865 TO 1891. Chicago, [1891]. 33 pp. Reprint. Edited by Francis Lee Utley, with introduction by Robert Toll. Bowling Green, OH: Bowling Green University Press, 1974. 123 pp.

This primary source of information about professional black minstrelsy in the late nineteenth century, written by black minstrel Simond (1847-189?), calling himself a "banjo comique," is of historic importance because the author was an eye-witness of the events he chronicled.

References to 2 songs: 1. Dem bones would rise again (11, 32). 2. Old ark moving (14).

1359 "Singing in the Cotton Fields." NEW ORLEANS TIMES DEMOCRAT [clipping], n.d. Boston Public Library. A. A. Brown Scrapbooks, "Musical Topics." 7:209.

Discussion of black cotton-pickers in Louisiana, who sang as they worked, includes comment on relevant performance practice and their voice quality.

1360 Slave Songs of the South." FOLIO (Boston) 13 (July 1875): 5. Reprinted from GOOD WORDS.

Text and music of 1 song: Nobody knows the trouble I've had.

1361 "Slave Songs of the United States." Unsigned review. LIPPINCOTT'S MAGAZINE 1 (March 1868): 341-43.

Review discusses the content and value of "Negro music" in an editorial column. Comment on music in Dahomey (Africa) and on a "festas" in Brazil, which high-lighted dancing, drumming, and the playing of indigenous African instruments. Comment on the American-based "negro melodies," with the assertion that many of the songs were taken from the music of Europeans.

1362 "Slave Songs of the United States." Unsigned review. NATION (New York) 5 (21 November 1867): 411.

Reviewer of William Allen's SLAVE SONGS OF THE UNITED STATES (see no. 1072) discusses the origin and performance practice of the songs. Description of the shout.

Text of 1 couplet: Nobody knows the trouble I've had. References to 19 songs: 1. The old ship of Zion. 2. Almost over. 3. Poor Rosy. 4. Becca Lawton. 5. Jehovah, halleluia. 6. De foxes have a hole, and de birdies have a nest. 7. Blow your trumpet, Gabriel. 8. Praise, member. 9. The lonesome valley. 10. O deat', he is a little man. 11. Oh, Lord, remember me. 12. Graveyard. 13. Meet, O Lord. 14. Day of judgement. 15. Nobody knows. 16. Let God's saints come in. 17. The gold band. 18. I want to die like-a Lazarus die. 19. God got plenty o' room.

1363 Slayton, M. G., ed. JUBILEE SONGS, AS SUNG BY THE SLAYTON'S JUBILEE SINGERS. Chicago: Thayer & Jackson Stationery Company, c.1882. 16 pp.

The cover page of this collection offers a group photograph of the nine-member troupe (four men, four women, and the director) and identifies the sponsor as the Slayton Lyceum Bureau. An introductory note on the first page gives brief suggestions for singing the songs.

Texts and music of 14 songs. See SONG COLLECTIONS (no. 1781).

1364 Smith, Dexter. "An African-American School of Music." MUSICAL RECORD (Boston), no. 381 (October 1893): 13.

In this reprint from the LONDON MUSICAL TIMES, the editor of Boston's MUSICAL RECORD challenges Antonin Dvorak's statement that black-American folksong could constitute the foundation for an American school of composition (see nos. 1142, 1143). He disputes the originality of the songs, citing tunes sung by black workers in tobacco factories in Richmond, Virginia. Maintains that America has folksongs that did not originate with the blacks.

1365 "The Songs of the Freedmen." Unsigned review. DWIGHT'S JOURNAL OF MUSIC 27 (20 July 1867): 71-72.

Reviewer of the SLAVE SONGS....(see no. 1072) discusses the chronology of the collection of songs and its compilers. Includes a quotation from a book review in NATION, 30 May [1867].

1366 "Songs of the Races Gathered at Hampton Institute." SOUTHERN WORKMAN 20 (March 1891): 160.

Texts of two songs originally published in CABIN AND PLANTATION SONGS AS SUNG BY HAMPTON STUDENTS (1879): 1. Oh, my young Christians, I got lots for to tell you all (Cho: Live humble, humble yourselves, de bell done rung). 2. When the general roll is called, yes, I'll be there (Cho: I'll be there in the morning).

1367 SPIRITUELLES. UNWRITTEN SONGS OF SOUTH CAROLINA. Sung by the Carolina Singers, During Their Campaigns in the North in 1872-73. N.p., [1873?]

The following statements about the Carolina Singers appear on the title page of this collection: "They are students of the Fairfield Normal Institute, near Columbia, S. C. Their object is to raise funds to meet its pressing wants. They sing the weird songs of the colored people, as they learned them in the days of slavery. Written for the First Time, From Memory, By the Carolina Singers."

Texts of 54 songs. See SONG COLLECTIONS (no. 1744).

1368 Spratt, Dora E. W. "Sea-Island Cotton Respun." LIPPINCOTT'S MAGAZINE 53 (June 1894): 780-86.

Discussion of the ex-slaves living on the Sea Islands of South Carolina in 1861-1862 includes the text of 1 song: Say, darkies, hab yo' seen ole maussa (Cho: De maussa run---ha, ha!).

1369 Stansbury, Mary A. P. "Tony." NEW ENGLAND MAGAZINE n.s. 8 (June 1893): 454-60.

Short story about an invalid white woman and a small lonely black boy, who find solace in each other. He shows his appreciation of her interest by singing plantation songs and playing his banjo for her.

Text of 1 song: Steal away, steal away to Jesus. Texts of 2 couplets: 1. Oh, Jordan's riber I'se bound to cross (Cho: Come old, come young, come rich, come poor). 2. Gwine to ride up in the chariot (Cho: Sooner in de mawnin'). Reference to 1 song: Swing low, sweet chariot.

1370 "The Story of the Jubilee Singers, with Their Songs." Unsigned review of the book of the same title (see no. 1258). MUSICAL STANDARD n. s. 9 (17 December 1875): 393-94.

Reviewer refers to 3 songs performed in London by the Fisk Jubilee Singers [1873?]: 1. Oh, how I love Jesus. 2. Go down Moses. 3. Steal away.

1371 Stowe, Harriet Beecher. MEN OF OUR TIMES; OR, LEADING PATRIOTS OF THE DAY. BEING NARRATIVES OF THE LIVES AND DEEDS OF STATESMEN, GENERALS, AND ORATORS. INCLUDING BIOGRAPHICAL SKETCHES AND ANECDOTES.... Hartford, CT: Hartford Publishing Company, 1868. 575 pp. Reprint. Freeport, NY: Books for Libraries Press, 1973.

The chapter on Frederick Douglass (380-404) in this book written by the author of UNCLE TOM'S CABIN (see no. 480) includes extensive quotation of passages from Douglass's autobiographies about the meaning of the slave songs and the vocal quality of the singing.

Text of 1 chorus: I am going away to the great house farm (Cho: O yea! O yea! O yea!) (394-95).

1372 _____. "Sojourner Truth, the Libyan Sibyl." ATLANTIC MONTHLY 11 (April 1863): 473-81.

Description of the author's visit to black abolitionist Truth (c1821-1913) includes comment on her slave narrative.

Reference to 1 song: O glory, glory, glory, Won't you come along with me? Texts of 2 songs: 1. There is a holy city. 2. I'm on my way to Canada.

1373 Strieby, M. E. "Jubilee Hall, Fisk University." ILLUSTRATED CHRISTIAN WEEKLY 3 (5 April 1873): 161.

Minister's discussion of slavery in the United States includes comment on the building of Jubilee Hall at Fisk University with money raised by the singing campaigns of the Fisk Jubilee Singers.

Texts of 2 choruses: 1. Go down, Moses, way down in Egypt Land. 2. Didn't my Lord deliver Daniel?

1374 _____. "The American Freedmen as Factors in African Evangelization." AMERICAN MISSIONARY (MAGAZINE) n.s. 42 (December 1888): 367-73.

Minister includes the text of 1 song: Way over in Egypt land (Cho: March on, and you shall gain the victory) (370).

1375 Strother, David H. [Porte Crayon, pseud.]. "Personal Recollections of the War by a Virginian---Sixth Paper." HARPER'S NEW

MONTHLY MAGAZINE 34 (MARCH 1867): 423-49.

Discussion of the author's Civil War experiences in the South refers to slaves singing spirituals near Williamsport [Maryland] in an entry dated 25 May [1862].

Reference to 1 song: Jordan is a hard road to travel.

1376 ____. VIRGINIA ILLUSTRATED: CONTAINING A VISIT TO THE VIRGINIAN CANAAN, AND THE ADVENTURES OF PORTE CRAYON AND HIS COUSINS. New York: Harper & Brothers, 1871. 300 pp. Reprint. Ann Arbor, MI: University Microfilms International, 1966.

Discussion of the songs of boatmen on the James River in Virginia, whose "melodies [were] wild and plaintive, [and] occasionally mingled with strange, uncouth cadences," accompanied by banjos and fiddles (232-34).

Texts of 3 songs: 1. Caesar, Caesar, bring here my horse and saddle. 2. I went to see Jenny. 3. Juggity jug, whar's dat jug.

1377 Tanner, Benjamin T. "Richard Randolph Disney." A. M. E. CHURCH REVIEW 2 (1885): 2.

Black-churchman Tanner's editorial includes the text of a song sung by black boatmen on the Susquehana River: Row the boat, take her home.

1378 Taylor, Marshall W. A COLLECTION OF REVIVAL HYMNS AND PLANTATION MELODIES. MUSICAL COMPOSITION BY MISS JOSEPHINE ROBINSON. COPIED BY MISS AMELIA C. AND HETTIE G. TAYLOR. Cincinnati: Marshall W. Taylor and W. C. Echols, 1882. 262 pp.

In his preface, black clergyman Taylor discusses the socio-historical context in which the slave songs evolved (3-7). In the introduction, F. S. Hoyt, editor of the WESTERN CHRISTIAN ADVOCATE, observes that the songs were transcribed by ex-slaves, who were "well acquainted with all the characteristics of the music." The songs fall into two categories: "Revival Songs," which were sung by both blacks and whites in the South, and "Plantation Songs," which originated with the blacks (i-vi). Also discussion of the worship services of the slaves (259).

Music and texts of 62 plantation songs; texts only of 3 plantation songs. See SONG COLLECTIONS (no. 1783).

1379 "Teacher's Festival." FREEDMEN'S RECORD 3 (August 1867): 129-30.

Description of a festival that took place in Boston on 11 July 1867 includes the text of 1 plantation song: I think I see Sister Hannah, I know her by her garments.

1380 Thanet, Octave. "Folk-Lore in Arkansas." JOURNAL OF AMERICAN FOLK-LORE 5 (April-June 1892): 121-25.

Discussion of Negro tales, superstitions, and songs.

Texts of 3 songs: 1. O mourner, give up your heart to die: 2. O Ziney, Ziney, Ziney, now (Cho: I wonder what's the matter of Ziney): 3. Jestice setting on the spangles of the sun.

1381 "Thanksgiving among the Contrabands at Washington." LIBERATOR 33 (16 January 1863): [9].

Northern abolitionist's discussion of his visit to a contraband camp in Washington, D. C., includes comment on the singing of the "Moses Song," which slaves were forbidden to sing.

Text of 1 song: Oh, Pharoah said he would go cross (Cho: Oh, go down, Moses).

1382 Thomas, Henry Goddard. "The Colored Troops at Petersburg." CENTURY 34 (September 1887): 777-82.

Recollections of Colonel Thomas, who commanded U. S. colored troops of the Union Army during the Civil War, include description of the "Battle of the Crater" at Petersburg, in which black soldiers fought heroically. Comment on the song the soldiers sang before going into battle.

Text and music of 1 song: We looks like men a marchin' on, we looks like men er war.

1383 Thompson, Joseph P. "A Talk with the Telephone: A Thanksgiving Address in Berlin." INDEPENDENT (New York) 30 (24 January 1878): 4-6.

Clergyman refers to 2 slave songs in his talk: 1. Yes, Gabriel's trumpet's going to blow, by and by. 2. We are almost home (Cho: To ring those charming bells).

1384 Tobias, D. E. "A Negro on the Position of the Negro in America." NINETEENTH CENTURY (London) 46 (December 1899): 957-73.

Black scholar's discussion of the social, economic, and political situation of the black man in America at the turn of the twentieth century includes such topics as education, lynchings, and racial problems in the North and the South.

Text of 1 freedom song: Shout, O, shout, children, shout, you're free (968).

1385 "The Town and Fortifications of Savannah." ILLUSTRATED LONDON NEWS 42 (18 April 1863): 432.

Discussion of life in Savannah, Georgia, during the Civil War refers to the slave workers and the songs they sang.

Text of 1 song: I don't like the lowland gal.

1386 Towne, Laura Matilda. LETTERS AND DIARY OF LAURA M. TOWNE. WRITTEN FROM THE SEA ISLANDS OF SOUTH CAROLINA, 1862-1884. Edited by Rupert Sargent Holland. Cambridge, MA: Riverside Press, 1912. 310 pp. Reprint. New York: Negro Universities Press, 1969.

White native of Pittsburgh, Pennsylvania, volunteered in April 1862 to go to South Carolina to work with the ex-slaves and remained in the Sea Islands, mainly on St. Helena Island, thirty-eight years. She includes detailed description of life among the ex-slaves in her diary and letters over the years 1862-84. Descriptions of the shout are found mostly in the diary entries dated 1862 (20).

References to 7 songs: 1. We're bound to go (4). 2. Oh yes, ma'am (4). 3. No man can hinder me (26). 4. The bell done ring (26). 5. Bound to go (26). 6. Come to Jesus (26). 7. Roll, Jordan, roll (73). Texts of 2 couplets: 1. De bells done rung. 2. Poor Rosie, poor gal.

1387 Trotter, James M. MUSIC AND SOME HIGHLY MUSICAL PEOPLE....SKETCHES OF THE LIVES OF REMARKABLE MUSICIANS OF THE COLORED RACE. WITH PORTRAITS, AND AN APPENDIX CONTAINING COPIES OF MUSIC COMPOSED BY COLORED MEN. Boston: Lee & Shepard, 1878. 152 pp. Reprint. New York: Johnson Reprint Corporation, 1968. Reprint of selected passages in READINGS IN BLACK AMERICAN MUSIC. Edited by Eileen Southern. 2d. ed. New York: W. W. Norton, 1983.

This landmark publication was the first survey of American music to be published in the United States. Black author Trotter (1842-1892) states that his aim was "to trace the footsteps of the remarkable colored musician wherever they might lead" (274); consequently, he discusses the Georgia Minstrels and the Fisk Jubilee Singers as well as concert artists and groups. His discussion of black folksong as a genre is limited primarily to philosophical observations about the meaning of the songs and performance practice (324-327).

1388 "A Troupe of Colored Singers" AMERICAN MISSIONARY (MAGAZINE) n.s. 15 (December 1871): 282.

Reprint of an excerpt from a review of a performance of the Fisk Jubilee Singers that was published in the DAILY REPUBLIC (Springfield, Ohio) 21 October 1871.

Reference to 5 songs: 1. We'll die in the field. 2. My Lord says there's room enough. 3. Roll, Jordan, roll. 4. Go down Moses. 5. Turn back Pharoh's army.

1389 "Unwritten Negro Melodies." MUSICAL RECORD (Boston), no. 404 (September 1895): 10.

Discussion of the passing of the plantation tunes includes the conjecture that it is doubtful that an American school can be built upon black melodies as the foundation.

Text of 1 song: It's hard to love, it's mighty hard to love.

1390 Venable, W. H. "Down South before the War." OHIO ARCHAEOLOGICAL AND HISTORICAL QUARTERLY 2 (March 1889): 488-513.

Travel memoirs of the author's journey through Kentucky, Mississippi, and Louisiana during the years 1855-1857 includes discussion of the improvised songs of the slave iron workers in Maysville, Kentucky, on Christmas Eve (490). Also references to black children gathering in the public square in Panola, Mississippi, to sing, dance, and pat "juber" (497), and to the fiddle and the banjo (498).

Text of 1 couplet: Oh, Lord! have mercy on my soul (490). Text of 1 song: Fare ye well, ye white folks all! (Cho: Wo-o-o-o-o-o) (490).

1391 "A Virginia Song." MUSICAL RECORD (Boston), no. 78 (27 March 1880): 403.

Discussion of Negro melodies of the South refers to a song reputedly sung by slaves in Jamestown, Virginia.

Text of 1 song: I shake de dus' off ob my feet, An' walk bar'-foot on de golden street.

1392 W., J. S. "A Pathetic Reminiscence." SOUTHERN WORKMAN 8 (May 1879): 50.

Description of the return of the body of General Robert Anderson's only son to Fortress Monroe, Virginia, in 1862 by the U. S. Navy. Comment on the black students of Hampton, who rowed the boats to pick up the body from the warship Guerriere, singing a plaintive spiritual as they rowed: Dust and ashes lie over me.

1393 Warner, Charles Dudley. "The Industrial South: The New Lynchburg." HARPER'S WEEKLY 30 (4 December 1886): 791.

Discussion of life in Lynchburg, Virginia, after the Civil War includes comment on the singing of a black worker as he hauled tobacco to market.

Text of 1 couplet: I's gwine down to Lynchburg Town.

1394 Washington, Booker T. THE BOOKER T. WASHINGTON PAPERS. VOL. 2, 1860-89. Edited by Louis R. Harlan. Urbana: University of Illinois Press, 1972. 557 pp.

Reprint of various kinds of documents relating to Washington (1856-1915), race leader and founder of Tuskegee Institute, includes references to performances of the Hampton Institute Singers

(45, 85, 145, 239, 246) and to the singing of plantation songs at Tuskegee (247, 266).

1395 Wayman, Alexander W. MY RECOLLECTIONS OF AFRICAN M. E. MINISTERS; OR, FORTY YEARS' EXPERIENCE IN THE AFRICAN METHODIST EPISCOPAL CHURCH. By...One of the Bishops of the A.M.E. Church. With an Introduction by Rev. B. T. Tanner. Philadelphia: A. M. E. Book Rooms, 1881. 259 pp.

Memoirs of black churchman Wayman (1821-1895) include discussion of songs "composed by the colored people."

Texts of 2 songs: 1. Poor Moses, poor Moses, sailing on the ocean (4). 2. Fare you well, fare you well (92).

1396 Webster, Albert, Jr. "A Jaunt in the South." APPLETON'S JOURNAL OF POPULAR LITERATURE, SCIENCE, AND ART 10 (30 August 1873): 263-66; (6 September 1873): 297-99; (13 September 1873): 322-25.

References to street cries of black peddlers in Charleston, South Carolina.

1397 Wentworth, E. "The Tennesseeans." ZION'S HERALD 51 (12 February 1874): [49].

Discussion of an attempt to build a black school in Tennessee by raising money through a concert tour of "Dr. Rust's student singers." Description of the "plaintive, peculiar" plantation songs the students sang, and reference to the shout. Later, a black school was named after white abolitionist Richard Rust.

1398 Wentworth, N. C. "Slave Telegraphy." ZION'S HERALD 52 (16 September 1875): [289].

Discussion of the espionage system of antebellum slaves in the South includes an example of an alerting call used by slave sentries to warn those who had assembled illegally that the slave patrollers were approaching.

Reference to 1 song: 1. Run, nigger, run, the patrol'll catch you.

1399 Whitney, Annie Weston. "De Los' Ell an' Yard." JOURNAL OF AMERICAN FOLK-LORE 10 (October-December 1897): 293-98.

A member of the Baltimore Folk-Lore Society describes a plantation corn-husking festival with comment on the singing, accompanied by the banjo, and the "crude form of shuffling dance."

Text of 1 couplet: Fer de los' ell an' yard is a huntin' fer de mornin'.

1400 "Whittier Day at the Whittier." SOUTHERN WORKMAN 18 (January 1889): 5.

Description of a birthday celebration held at Hampton Institute's Normal School and Whittier School in honor of the poet John Whittier.

References to 5 folk songs: 1. Rise and shine. 2. Gwine jine de saints above. 3. Little Eliza Jane. 4. Am I born to die? 5. Sweet Canaan's happy land I am bound for.

1401 Wilson, Calvin Dill. "Through an Old Southern Country." NEW ENGLAND MAGAZINE n.s. 20 (April 1899): 161-76.

Presbyterian clergyman comments on the worksongs of black laborers in the Chesapeake Bay area of Maryland.

1402 "Word Shadows." ATLANTIC MONTHLY 67 (February 1891): 143-44.

Discussion of the idioms and sayings of the black Americans includes comment on their use of lively lyrics, such as "sinner-songs," "corn-hollers," "jump-up songs," or "chunes dat skip wid de banjo." References to religious songs as "member-songs" or "hymn-chunes," and to long chants as "spirituelles." Individuals not belonging to church are described as "settin' on de sinner seat," or "still in de open fiel'".

1403 Wyeth, Mary E. D. "Sister Angela's Roses." INDEPENDENT 36 (13 March 1884): 346-47.

Short story about life on the lower Mississippi River includes comment on the boatmen's songs.

Text of 1 song: One mo' river to cross.

1404 Wyman, Lillie B. Chace. "Harriet Tubman." NEW ENGLAND MAGAZINE n.s. 14 (March 1896): 110-18.

Account of the black, abolitionist conductor of the Underground Railroad, Harriet Tubman (c.1821-1913), includes discussion of how slaves used songs as signals to alert slaves to prepare for escapes.

Texts of 3 songs: 1. When dat ere old chariot comes (Cho: I'm gwine to leabe you). 2. Oh, I heard Queen Victoria say. 3. Glory to God and Jesus too, One more soul got safe.

THE TALE

1405 Allen, William Francis. "Southern Negro Folk-Lore." Book review. DIAL (January 1881): 183-85.

Review of Joel Chandler Harris's UNCLE REMUS: HIS SONGS AND SAYINGS....(see no. 1439) includes comment on the publication of the first examples of Negro folk tales "a few years ago" in the Riverside Magazine and Harper's Monthly. Observation that the dialect in the Riverside stories from the Sea Islands region differed from that in the Uncle Remus stories, which were set in the region of Atlanta, Georgia.

Excerpt from 1 tale: Story of the Deluge.

1406 Anderson, W. T. "Jack and the King. "SOUTHERN WORKMAN 28 (June 1899): 232-33.

A Master-John folk tale involving trickery by the slave John.

1407 Babe: The Tale of a Tailless Hound that Found Food for a Family." DAILY PICAYUNE 56 (14 August 1892): 16.

Short story about a poor, ex-slave, widowed mother in post-Civil War Mississippi, about her children, and the family's pet dog.

Text of 1 funeral song: Oh! if God had er bin like er natral man. Text of 1 couplet: Bow ter de bussid, an' den ter de crow.

1408 Backus, Emma M. "Negro Ghost Stories." JOURNAL OF AMERICAN FOLK-LORE 9 (July-September 1896): 228-30.

Texts of 2 Master-John folk tales in which deceased slaves return as ghosts and haunt their former masters.

1409 _____. "Animal Tales from North Carolina." JOURNAL OF AMERICAN FOLK-LORE 11 (October-November 1898): 284-91.

Texts of 7 animal tales: 1. When Brer Rabbit and Brer Terrapin runned a race. 2. When Mr. Terrapin went riding on the clouds. 3. Why the spider never got in the ark. 4. How come Brer Bar sleep in the winter. 5. How come Mr. Buzzard to have a bald head. 6. The woolly crows. 7. How come the pigs can see the wind.

1410 _____. "Tales of the Rabbit from Georgia Negroes." JOURNAL OF AMERICAN FOLK-LORE 12 (April-June 1899): 108-15.

Texts of 6 folk tales about Brer Rabbit and his animal friends: 1. How the rabbit practiced medicine. 2. Why the people tote Brer Rabbit foot in their pocket. 3. Brer Rabbit born to luck. 4. Why Mr. Dog runs Brer Rabbit. 5. How Brer Rabbit bring dust out of the rock. 6. Why Brer Rabbit save the pig.

1411 Bacon, Alice Mabel. "Folk-Lore and Ethnology." SOUTHERN WORKMAN 24 (September 1895): 154-56.

An open letter to friends and alumni of Hampton Institute discusses the goals and aims of that institution's folklore society. Writer informs readers of the kinds of materials that have been collected by the society (tales, customs, African traditions, proverbs, superstitions, and folk songs), and requests contributions. Focus upon a "footwashing ceremony," which was still practiced in some black churches of Virginia, on folk tales, and on ring-game songs.

References to 5 ring-game songs: 1. King William was King George's son. 2. London Bridge is burning down. 3. Peep-squirrel. 4. Gimme de gourd to drink water. 5. Rain a little bit, snow a little bit. References to 8 tales: 1. The witch cats. 2. Why the tiger is striped. 3. Old Hag and Jack Lantern. 4. Where de owl fus' come from. 5. How Brer Rabbit won de case. 6. The conquest of a hag. 7. Brer Rabbit tries to get even with Brer Rooster. 8. Why some men are black.

1412 Barnette, V. G.; C. H. Herbert; and Susan Showers. "Folk-Lore and Ethnology." SOUTHERN WORKMAN 27 (February 1898): 36-37.

Collection of miscellaneous folklore contributed by three graduates of Hampton Institute includes superstitions and tales.

Texts of 2 tales: 1. Why the dog cannot talk, and why the rabbit has a short tail. 2. Why the clay is red.

1413 Bergen, Fanny D. "Two Witch Stories." JOURNAL OF AMERICAN FOLK-LORE 12 (January-March 1899): 68-69.

Tales about women who possessed supernatural powers, obtained from a black girl of Chestertown, Maryland.

Texts of 2 tales: 1. The brothers who married witches. 2. The snake-wife.

1414 _____. "Louisiana Ghost Story." JOURNAL OF AMERICAN FOLK-LORE 12 (April-June 1899): 146-47.

Tale about a female ghost collected from an ex-slave originally from Louisiana.

1415 Bolden, T. J. "Brer Rabbit's Box: With Apologies to Joel Chandler Harris." SOUTHERN WORKMAN 28 (January 1899): 25-26.

Adaptation of an Afro-American folk tale to contemporary life by a Hampton Institute graduate.

Text of 1 animal tale: Brer Rabbit's box.

1416 Bullock, Mrs. Walter R. "The Collection of Maryland Folk-Lore." JOURNAL OF AMERICAN FOLK-LORE SOCIETY 11 (January-March 1898): 7-16.

Miscellaneous folklore collected by members of the Baltimore Folk-Lore Society includes reference to a black superstition regarding dancing, which the author states was in current usage among Virginia blacks.

Texts of 3 folk tales: 1. The origin of the black man. 2. How the Negro got the name of Coon. 3. How Mr. Hare proved that Mr. Fox was his riding-horse.

1417 Chesnutt, Charles W. THE CONJUR WOMAN. Boston: Houghton, Mifflin, and Company, 1899. 229 pp. Reprint. New York: Dell Publishing Company, 1973.

Collection of seven short stories written by the Afro-American novelist (1854-1932), which focus upon folk superstitions and tales about conjuring and witchcraft.

1418 Christensen, Abigail M. Holmes. This collector published four tale texts (without comment) in the INDEPENDENT over a period of two years.

(1) The Elephant and the Rabbit. (2 September 1875): 27:25-26.

(2) The Rabbit Desires a Long Tale. (9 March 1876): 28:26.

(3) The Rabbit, the Wolf, and the Keg of Butter. (18 November 1875): 27:27.

(4) A Story-Teller. (28 October 1875): 27:26]. The fourth tale is about the terrapin, the cooter, and the deer.

1419 _____. AFRO-AMERICAN FOLK LORE, TOLD ROUND CABIN FIRES ON THE SEA ISLANDS OF SOUTH CAROLINA. Boston: J. G. Cupples Company, 1892. 116 pp. 2d ed. Boston: The Author, 1898. Reprint. Freeport, NY: Books for Libraries Press, 1971.

Collection of mostly Br'er Rabbit tales obtained from black informants on the Sea Islands of South Carolina, and published verbatim. Includes an introductory chapter about the storytellers.

Texts of 17 tales. See TALE COLLECTIONS (no. 1727).

1420 The Contributors' Club. "A Negro Witch Story." ATLANTIC MONTHLY 75 (May 1895): 715-17.

Story about how Levine Williams became involved with two witches and their witchcraft.

1421 "The Coon Hunt." HARPER'S WEEKLY 16 (14 December 1872): 974.

Description of a coon hunt includes discussion of the men who sit around a campfire, telling tales about the raccoon and singing songs.

1422 Crane, T. Frederick. "Plantation Folk-Lore." APPLETON'S POPULAR SCIENCE MONTHLY 18 (April 1881): 824-33.

Critique by a college professor on the subject of Negro animal tales focuses primarily on the tales published by Joel Chandler Harris in UNCLE REMUS: HIS SONGS AND HIS SAYINGS (see no. 1439) and by William Owens in "Folk-Lore of the Southern Negroes" (see no. 1463). Attempts to trace these plantation tales to foreign variants published by C. F. Hartt in AMAZONIAN TORTOISE MYTHS (1875).

Synopses of 6 rabbit tales: 1. Old Mr. Rabbit, he's a good fisherman. 2. Mr. Rabbit nibbles up the butter. 3. How Mr. Rabbit lost his fine bushy tail. 4. The awful fate of Mr. Wolf. 5. A story about the little rabbits. 6. The sad fate of Mr. Fox. References to 5 tales: 1. Uncle Remus. 2. Buh Rabbit, Buh Wolf, and the pears. 3. Buh Rabbit frightens Buh Wolf. 4. The rooster and the cornbread. 5. Buh Elephant and Buh Lion.

1423 Davis, Daniel Webster. 'WEH DOWN SOUF AND OTHER POEMS. Cleveland: The Helman-Taylor Company, 1897. 136 pp. Reprint. Washington, DC: Microcard Editions, 1972.

Collection of poems by black poet Davis (1862-1913) includes quotation of a phrase from a spiritual, "Keep inchin' along" (12-13), references to lining out (54-56), to dance tunes (76-77), to banjo playing (103-104), and to the religious meetings of the slaves in cabins, where they placed water-filled pots on the floors to deaden the sound (123).

Excerpts from 2 sermons (72-74, 110-111). Reference to 1 dance: the pijin-wing.

1424 Devereux, George M. "Southern Ghost Stories." SOUTHERN BIVOUAC n.s. 1 (June 1885): 1-5.

Discussion of the ghost stories told by blacks on the plantations.

Excerpts from 3 tales: 1. Monkey impersonates master. 2. The preacher and the ghost. 3. Ghost haunts victim.

1425 Dorsey, J. Owen. "OLD RABBIT, THE VOODOO, AND OTHER STORIES, by Mary Alicia Owen." Book review. JOURNAL OF AMERICAN FOLK-LORE 6 (October-December 1893): 322-24.

Reviewer of the Owen book (see no. 1461) discusses the possibility of a relationship between Negro tales and Indian narratives in general, and observes that such a relationship does exist between the folk tales of the Negroes of Missouri and some of the Indian myths.

1426 Ellis, A. B. "Evolution in Folklore: Some West African Prototypes of the 'Uncle Remus Stories'." APPLETON'S POPULAR SCIENCE MONTHLY 48 (November 1895): 93-104.

Collection of 9 West African tales that relate to the Uncle Remus tales of Joel Chandler Harris.

1427 Felix [pseud.]. "Uncle Andy's Talk." DAILY PICAYUNE, 26 June 1892.

Text of 1 animal tale explaining why the alligator has no tongue: Mr. Dog and Mr. Alligator.

1428 Fortier, Alcee. "Louisiana Nursery-Tales." Parts 1, 2. JOURNAL OF AMERICAN FOLK-LORE 1, 2 (July-September 1888): 140-45; (January-March 1889): 36-40.

Part 1: Texts of 2 Louisiana creole folk tales in dialect with parallel English translations: 1. La Graisse. 2. De zif ki parle (the talking eggs).

Part 2: Texts of 2 creole tales in dialect with parallel English translations: 1. The golden fish. 2. Give me.

1429 _____. LOUISIANA FOLK-TALES. IN FRENCH DIALECT AND ENGLISH TRANSLATION. Memoirs of the American Folk-Lore Society, vol. 2. Boston: Houghton, Mifflin and Company, 1895. Reprint. Millwood, NY: Kraus Reprint Company, 1976.

Collection of 27 tales includes 15 animal tales, some of African origin, and "vaudevilles where the song is more important than the plot." Discussion of the dialect of "negroes in Lower Louisiana." See TALE COLLECTIONS (no. 1729).

1430 Fowke, Gerard. "Brer Rabbit and Brer Fox: How Brer Rabbit Was Allowed to Choose His Death." JOURNAL OF AMERICAN FOLK-LORE 1 (July-September 1888): 148-49.

Tale contributed by an archaeologist at the Bureau of Ethnology about a theft of food and escape through deception.

Text of 1 tale: Brer Rabbit and Brer Fox.

1431 Gerber, A. "Uncle Remus Traced to the Old World." JOURNAL OF AMERICAN FOLK-LORE 6 (October-December 1893): 245-57.

Discussion of the African and European roots of the Uncle Remus stories of the American slave. Observation that tales learned from the slave masters underwent greater changes than the tales brought from Africa. References to 54 tales. Discussion of tale types, motifs, and origins.

1432 Hampton Folk-Lore Society. "Folk-Lore and Ethnology." SOUTHERN WORKMAN 12 (October 1884): 179-80.

Tales presented to the Society by Mr. Patterson, Mr. Clayton, and Miss Spennie include ghost tales and a preacher tale.

Texts of 3 tales: 1. The cat's scratch. 2. Why an old man was so ugly. 3. Preacher's story.

1433 _____. SOUTHERN WORKMAN 23 (1894). The Society periodically published tale texts, often without comment, in a column titled "Folk-Lore and Ethnology." The entries that follow are arranged chronologically.

(February): 27. Text of 1 tale: Capture of a Hag.

(August): 149-50. Texts of 3 tales: 1. Brer Rabbit and Brer Elephant. 2. The donkey, the dog, the cat, and the rooster. 3. The fish hawk and the eagle.

(October): 179-80. Texts of 3 tales: 1. Devil story. 2. Devil story. 3. Preacher story.

1434 _____. SOUTHERN WORKMAN 24 (1895).

(March): 50. Text of 1 tale: Hag lore.

1435 _____. SOUTHERN WORKMAN 25 (1896).

(March): 61-62. Text: Brer Rabbit outdone.

(April): 82. Text: Why the tiger is striped.

(May): 102. Text: Why the fox's mouth is sharp.

(October): 205-06. Texts of 2 tales: 1. How Brer Wolf divide de hog. 2. How Brer Wolf caught Brer Rabbit.

1436 _____. SOUTHERN WORKMAN 26 (1897).

(March): 58. Texts of 3 tales: Why the terrapin has red eyes. 2. Why the mole has no eyes. 3. Where de owl fus' come from.

(April): 78-79. Texts of 2 tales: 1. A race for a wife. 2. The hog thief.

(June): 122-23. Texts of 2 tales: The possessed cow. 2. Wrestling with ghosts.

(October): 210. Texts of 2 tales: 1. Uncle Abraham and his Christmas Eve supper. 2. Slave unwittingly entertains master.

(November): 229-30. Texts of 3 tales: 1. Fish story. 2. Fish story. 3. Come back, Sambo.

(December): 249. Texts of 2 tales contributed by a black Hampton graduate residing in Calhoun, Alabama: 1. The rabbit and the busard. 2. The rabbit and the girl.

1437 _____. SOUTHERN WORKMAN 27 (1898).

(January): 17-18. Text of 2 tales contributed by Susan Showers: 1. How the jays saved their souls. 2. The jay and the martin.

(February): 37-38. Texts of 4 tales: 1. Tricking a steamboat. 2. Amenities of the profession [conjuring]. 3. A false Messiah. 4. Devil worship.

(April): 76-77. Texts of 2 tales contributed by J. C. Walker: 1. Why the rabbit has a short tail and the dog a wide mouth. 2. The goose and the drake.

(June): 124-25. Texts of 2 tales: 1. Ghost tale. 2. The fox and the pig.

(November): 230. Text of 1 tale: How the rabbit and the frog caught the deer.

1438 _____. SOUTHERN WORKMAN 28 (1899).

(January): 32. Texts of 5 tales: Why the crab has no head. 2. Why the buzzard eats carrion. 3. Why there are moles. 4. Why hens are afraid of owls. 5. The snail's smartness.

(March): 112-13. Texts of 3 tales: The trick bone of a black cat. 2. Why the warren does not fly high. 3. Brer Rabbit beats Brer Fox.

(November): 449. Text: A Negro ghost story.

1439 Harris, Joel Chandler. UNCLE REMUS, HIS SONGS AND SAYINGS: THE FOLK-LORE OF THE OLD PLANTATION. New York: D. Appleton & Company, 1880. 231 pp. Rev. ed. New York: D. Appleton-Century Publishing Company, 1908. 270 pp.

Miscellaneous collection of tales, songs (camp-meeting hymns, play-party, corn songs, work songs), and sayings in folk dialect. Texts of 34 animal tales.

1440 _____. Harris periodically published tale texts (sometimes without introductory or expanatory comment) in contemporary periodicals during the years 1881-1892. The entries that follow are arranged first by periodical source, and chronologically within that category.

"Nights with Uncle Remus." Parts 1-3. CRITIC [1] (26 February 1881): 45-46; [2] (23 April 1881): 104; [3] (17 December 1881): 347-48.

Part 1: How Mr. Fox failed to get his grapes.
Part 2: Mr. Fox figures as an incendiary.
Part 3: A dream and a story.

1441 _____. "A Rainy Day with Uncle Remus." Parts 1-3. SCRIBNER'S MONTHLY 22 (June, July, August 1881): 241-48, 443-53, 608-16.

Each part, which contains 5 tales, begins with an introduction that sets the stage for Uncle Remus to tell tales to a small white boy,

Part 1: 1. Mr. Fox catches Mr. Horse. 2. Mr. Fox catches Mr. Horse. 3. Mr. Rabbit and the Little Girl. 4. How Mr. Fox was a little too smart. 5. Mr. Rabbit's astonishing prank.

Part 2, "Afternoon": 1. Mr. Rabbit secures a mansion. 2. Mr. Lion hunts for Mr. Man and finds him. 3. The story of the pigs. 4. Mr. Benjamin Ram and his wonderful fiddle. 5. Mr. Rabbit's riddle.

Part 3, "Evening": 1. How Mr. Rooster lost his dinner. 2. Mr. Rabbit breaks up a lynch party. 3. Brother Fox, Brother Rabbit and King Deer's daughter. 4. Brother Terrapin deceives Brother Buzzard. 5. Mr. Fox covets the quills. Also text of 1 song: Come under (609).

1442 _____. "Nights with Uncle Remus." Parts 1-3. CENTURY 26 (July, August, September 1883): 340-49, 611-23, 772-81.

Part 1. Introduction sets the scene for Uncle Remus to tell tales to the small white boy who lives in the "big house." Texts of 6 tales: 1. The moon in the mill pond. 2. Brother Rabbit takes some exercise. 3. Why Brother Bear has no tail. 4. How Brother Rabbit frightened his neighbors. 5. Mr. Man has some meat. 6. How Brother Rabbit got the meat.

Part 2. Introduction sets the scene for Uncle Remus to tell tales to the small white boy and the slave house-girl Tildy. Texts of 5 tales: 1. African Jack. 2. Why the alligator's back is rough. 3. Brother Fox says grace. 4. A ghost story told by Tildy. 5. Brother Rabbit and his famous foot.

Part 3. Introduction sets the scene for Uncle Remus to tell tales to Daddy Jack, Aunt Tempy, and the small white boy. Texts of 6 tales: 1. Oh, Blue, go 'way! You shall not stay. 2. In some lady's garden. 3. Brother 'Possum gets in trouble. 4. Why the guinea fowls are speckled. 5. Brother Rabbit's love charm. 6. Brother Rabbit submits to a test.

1443 _____. NIGHTS WITH UNCLE REMUS: MYTHS AND LEGENDS OF THE OLD PLANTATION. Boston: Houghton, Mifflin & Company, 1883. 416 pp.

Miscellaneous collection of tales, songs (play party, corn songs, work songs), and sayings in dialect includes texts of 34 animal tales.

1444 _____. "Plantation Fables." DAILY PICAYUNE. The tales were published weekly during 24 July--30 October 1892.

(24 July):13. Brother Bear and the honey orchard.

(31 July): 16. Why the Hawk catches the Chickens.

(7 August): 13. Brer Rabbit at the ferry.

(14 August): 16. Death and the Negro man. Where the Harrycane comes from.

(21 August): 13. Why Brer Wolf didn't eat the small rabbits. Mrs. Partridge has a fit.

(28 August): 13. Brother Fox smells smoke.

(4 September): 19. Brother Fox still in trouble.

Why Brother Fox's legs are black.

(11 September): 16. Why Brother Bull growls and grumbles.

(18 September): 16. The man and the wild cattle.

(25 September): 13. Brer Rabbit frightens Brer Tiger.

(2 October): 18. Brother Billy Goat eats his dinner. The king that talked biggity.

(9 October): 18. Brother Rabbit's money mint. Why the moon's face is smutty.

(16 October): 21. According to how the drop falls.

(23 October): 18. Brother Rabbit conquers Brother Lion. Heyo House.

(30 October): 19. The man and his boots. Brother Mud-Turtle's trickery.

1445 _____. UNCLE REMUS AND HIS FRIENDS. OLD PLANTATION STORIES, SONGS, AND BALLADS WITH SKETCHES OF NEGRO CHARACTER. Boston: Houghton, Mifflin & Company, 1892. 357 pp.

Collection includes 24 stories about "Uncle Remus and the Little Boy"; 16 songs (none appear to be concordant with other Negro folksongs); 21 stories about "His Home Folks and Friends."

1446 _____. ON THE PLANTATION. A STORY OF A GEORGIA BOY'S ADVENTURES DURING THE WAR. New York: D. Appleton & Company, 1897. 233 pp.

This "mixture of fiction and fact" includes comment on the slave Harbert, who told tales to the plantation folk (74-79, 141-61), and offers a detailed description of "hog calling" (80).

Text of 1 hog-feeder's song: Oh, rise up my ladies. Texts of 4 tales: 1. The story of the owl and the birds. 2. The story of the sheep. 3. How de mountains come about. 4. Brer Rabbit and de overcoat.

1447 Hawkins, John. "An Old Mauma's Folk-Lore." Parts 1, 2. JOURNAL OF AMERICAN FOLK-LORE 9 (January-March 1896): 129-31; (April-June 1896): 129-31.

Part 1: Discussion primarily of plantation superstitions and ghost stories by a native of Newberry, South Carolina. Excerpts of a passage from Joel Chandler Harris's NIGHTS WITH UNCLE REMUS (see no. 1440).

Part 2: Discussion of an antebellum nanny includes an excerpt from 1 tale: The hag out of her skin, identified as a variant of the Daddy Jack tale.

1448 Holmes Christensen, Abigail M. "The Story Aunt 'Tilda Told." INDEPENDENT 26 (5 November 1874): 14.

Ex-slave Aunt Tilda consents to tell her former white charge, Alice, now a young woman and attending a school in the North, one of the tales she told Alice as a child.

Text of 1 tale: De rabbit an' de alligator.

1449 Hunter, Rosa, et al. "Folk-Lore and Ethnology." SOUTHERN WORKMAN 27 (March 1898): 57.

Discussion of ghost stories collected in western Virginia and southern Alabama.

Texts of 2 tales: 1. The rich ghost. 2. The boy and the ghost.

1450 Johnston, Mrs. William Preston. "Two Negro Tales." JOURNAL OF AMERICAN FOLK-LORE 9 (July-September 1896): 194-98.

Wife of a former Confederate officer discusses the context in which her slave nurse told her folk tales as a child on a plantation on Avery Island in southwestern Louisiana.

Texts of 2 tales: 1. Mr. Deer's my riding horse. 2. Trouble, trouble, Brer Alligator.

1451 Jones, Charles C., Jr. NEGRO MYTHS FROM THE GEORGIA COAST, TOLD IN THE VERNACULAR. Boston: Houghton, Mifflin & Company, 1888. 171 pp. Reprint. Detroit: Singing Tree Press, 1969.

Miscellaneous collection of Afro-American folklore collected by the editor from the Sea Island areas of Georgia and South Carolina includes 57 folktales, primarily animal tales about such stock characters as Brer Rabbit, Fox, Cooter, and Deer. See TALE COLLECTIONS (no. 1730).

1452 L. "Letters from Hampton Graduates: Superstition Is of All Colors---Ten Witch-Cats." SOUTHERN WORKMAN 10 (February 1881): 18.

Text of 1 folk tale about witch-cats submitted by a Hampton graduate.

1453 McLennan, Marcia. "Origin of the Cat, a Negro Tale." JOURNAL OF AMERICAN FOLK-LORE 9 (January-March 1896): 71.

Text of 1 tale about superstitions relating to the cat.

1454 Moton, Robert Russa, and F. D. Banks, contributors. "Folk-Lore and Ethnology." SOUTHERN WORKMAN 25 (September 1896): 185-86.

Tales collected by Hampton Institute graduates.

Texts of 3 folk tales: 1. To talk at the big gate. 2. The marsh light, or the Will-o'-the wisp. 3. Brer Rabbit and Brer Wolf.

1455 Newell, William Wells. "AFRO-AMERICAN FOLK-LORE. TOLD ROUND CABIN FIRES OF THE SEA ISLANDS OF SOUTH CAROLINA, by Abigail M. Holmes Christensen." Book review. JOURNAL OF AMERICAN FOLK-LORE 5 (July-September 1892): 258-60.

Reviewer of Christensen's book (see no. 1419) suggests that the tales are of African origin, though "European elements may have mingled themselves with some of them." Discussion of the author's informant, who regarded the rabbit tales with great respect, "evidently considering them types of human experience in general, and his own in particular."

Synopsis of 1 tale: De Tiger an' de Nyung Lady.

1456 "Negro Fables." RIVERSIDE MAGAZINE FOR YOUNG PEOPLE 2 (November 1868): 505-07; 3 (March 1869) 116-18; 4 (April 1870): 163.

Possibly the earliest publication of Brer Rabbit tales in history, this collection of Negro folk tales includes texts of 9 tales about Brer Rabbit, 1 tale about Brer Coutah. See TALE COLLECTIONS (no. 1731).

1457 Norris, Thaddeus. "Negro Superstitions." LIPPINCOTT'S MAGAZINE 6 (July 1870): 90-95. Reprint. THE NEGRO AND HIS FOLKLORE IN NINETEENTH-CENTURY PERIODICALS. Edited by Bruce Jackson. Published for the American Folk-Lore Society. Austin: University of Texas Press, 1969.

Article focuses primarily upon slave superstitions and Hoodoo. Texts of 2 tales: 1. Brer Rabbit and the tar baby. 2. Conjur man.

1458 Oldham, Edward A. "Brer Fox en de Ole Black Duck." CENTURY 43 (November 1891): 159.

Discussion of the author's sentimental attachment to his childhood nurse, "Mammy 'Riah," includes comment on the tradition of storytelling carried on by the older slaves on the plantation.

Text of 1 tale: Brer Fox jumped up one moonshine night.

1459 Owen, Mary Alicia. "Ole Rabbit and de Dawg He Stole." JOURNAL OF AMERICAN FOLK-LORE 3 (April-June 1890): 135-38.

Tale published in the Gullah dialect by a collector of Cambridge, Massachusetts.

1460 _____. "Three Stories." FOLK-LORIST 1 (July 1893): 101-05.

Folk tales collected from a black inmate of the Poor House in Buchanan County, Missouri, and one song.

Text of 1 song: 1. Oh! li'l gal, won't you be my wife? (Cho: Oh! nigga, now yo' dancin'). Texts of 3 tales: 1. The trees and the hunter. 2. The young man and the tree wife. 3. How the bear lost his tail.

1461 _____. OLD RABBIT, THE VOODOO, AND OTHER SORCERERS. Also published as VOODOO TALES AS TOLD AMONG THE NEGROES OF THE SOUTHWEST. New York: G. P. Putnam's Sons, 1893. Reprint. Freeport, NY: Negro Universities Press, 1969. 310 pp.

Miscellaneous collection of animal tales collected from Negroes in the southwestern states, principally along the Missouri border, about the rabbit, fox, woodpecker, skunk, and snake.

Texts of 31 tales. See TALE COLLECTIONS (1732).

1462 _____. "Voodooism." ARCHIVES OF THE INTERNATIONAL FOLK-LORE ASSOCIATION 1 (1898): 313-26.

This paper, which was presented at the International Folk-Lore Congress in London, 1891, offers a general discussion of voodooism and includes summaries of several tales about the origin of voodoo. The paper was read also at the International Folk-Lore Congress of the World's Columbian Exposition in Chicago, July 1893.

Texts of 2 tales: The origin of Voodoo. 2. The joke Fish-hawk played on the old boy.

1463 Owens, William. "Folk-Lore of the Southern Negroes." LIPPINCOTT'S MAGAZINE 20 (December 1877): 748-55.

One of the earliest writers to publish on the Negro folk tale, Owens focuses in this article on various aspects of the folklore, including comment on specific features, such as, for example, the taboo among religious people about crossing the legs: "crossing the legs is the same as dancing, and dancing is a sin."

Texts of 7 tales: 1. Buh Rabbit and Tar Baby. 2. Buh Rabbit and Buh Frog's foot-race. 3. Buh Wolf's funeral. 4. Buh Rabbit and Buh Wolf riding horse. 5. Buh Fox and Tiny Pig. 6. Buh Rooster and the corn bread dinner. 7. Buh Lion and the man.

1464 Page, Thomas Nelson. IN OLE VIRGINIA, MARSE CHAN, AND OTHER STORIES. New York: Charles Scribner's Sons, 1887. 275 pp.

This collection of tales includes four in Negro dialect as told by slaves, but only one is about the slave experience. Also discussion of the plantation Christmas dance and description of the music provided by the fiddlers and "de clappers" and of "de back-steppers" (83-84, 88).

1465 Pendleton, Louis. "Negro Folklore and Witchcraft in the South." JOURNAL OF AMERICAN FOLKLORE 3 (July-September 1890): 201-7.

Southerner offers comment on variant versions of the Tar-baby tale, the one collected in middle Georgia, and the other in southern Georgia. Also discussion of voodoo, conjuring, and witchcraft.

Summaries of 4 tales: 1. Tar-baby story. 2. Tar-baby story. 3. The bride and the Old Boy. 4. The little girl and the devil.

1466 Penick, C. C. "Negro Music and Folk Lore." NEW YORK SUN (1894). Clipping in the Boston Public Library, A. A. Brown Scrapbooks, "Musical Topics." Vol. 2, 132.

Penick, formerly the Bishop of Cape Palmas (West Africa), in discussing the Brer Rabbit stories identifies Brer Rabbit with the African nar, a small deer. His discussion of Negro folk music of the South compares it to African folksong in regard to function and performance practice. Writer lived in Africa for three-and-a-half years during the 1870s-80s.

1467 Pickett, Lasalle Corbell. "In de Miz." ARENA (Boston) 8 (October 1893): 642-46.

Negro folk tale about the creation, which the author obtained as a child from her black nurse: In de miz.

1468 Porter, Anna. "Negro Stories." INDEPENDENT 30 (11 April 1878): 27-28.

Texts of 5 tales: 1. The biggest fool. 2. Brer Rabbit in the briar patch. 3. Brer Rabbit and Tar-baby. 4. Why rabbits have short tails. 5. De wrong hog.

1469 Rabbit, Budd [pseud.]. "Why the Rabbit has a Short Tail." INDEPENDENT 31 (6 February 1879): 27.

Discussion of a Negro tale teller and the children who listen to his tales includes the text of 1 tale: Why the rabbit has a short tail.

1470 Scarborough, William Sanders. "Compair Bouki and Compair Lapin---Creole Folk-Tale." SOUTHERN WORKMAN 25 (September 1896): 186.

Discussion by black professor Scarborough (later president of Wilberforce University), centers on a creole folktale collected by Alcee Fortier, a Tulane University professor, about Brer Goat, Brer Rabbit and the theft of food.

Text of 1 tale: Compair Bouki and Compair Lapin.

1471 _____. "Negro Folk-Lore and Dialect." ARENA 17 (December 1896): 186-92.

Discussion of Afro-American folklore focusing on folk dialect includes references to the singing and exhortations involved in the "foot-wash" ceremony. Discussion also of folk superstitions and sayings.

Excerpt of 1 tale: Hag-riding.

1472 Shepard, Eli."Superstitions of the Negro." COSMOPOLITAN: A MONTHLY ILLUSTRATED MAGAZINE 7 (March 1888): 47-50.

Discussion includes an excerpt from 1 tale: The creation of man.

1473 Thompson, James Maurice. "The Intellectual Future of the Negro." INDEPENDENT 43 (16 April 1891): 550.

Essay questioning the intellectual and learning abilities of blacks of pure African ancestry includes the observation, however, that the pure-blood black was an excellent teller of tales. Cites the Bre'r Rabbit stories, and notes that the black corn-husking songs were models "of rhythm and meter" though their meaning was often obscure.

1474 "Trouble, Brudder Alligator, Trouble." HARPER'S NEW MONTHLY MAGAZINE 73 (August 1886): 483.

Text of 1 tale: Bre'r Rabbit and Bre'r Alligator.

1475 "Two Negro Witch-Stories." JOURNAL OF AMERICAN FOLK-LORE 12 (April-June 1899): 145-46.

Two folk tales about witch-cats collected from a black stewardess of Baltimore, Maryland.

1476 Vance, Louis Joseph. "Plantation Folk-Lore." Parts 1-3. OPEN COURT 2 (14 June 1888): 1028-32; (5 July 1888): 1074-1076; (12 July 1888): 1092-95.

This review of black folk tales published in the nineteenth century by American writers focuses primarily upon the collection of Charles C. Jones, Jr., NEGRO MYTHS FROM THE GEORGIA COAST (see no. 1451). Compares the animal tales in Jones's collection to those compiled by other folk-tale collectors, particularly Crane, Harris, and Owens (see nos. 1422, 1439-1445, 1463). Examines the characteristics of stock animal characters in folk tales, such as Brer Rabbit, Fox, Wolf, and Terrapin.

Texts of 3 tales. Excerpts of 12 tales. References to 8 tales. See TALE COLLECTIONS (no. 1734).

1477 Watson, Annah Robinson. "Comparative Afro-American Folk-Lore." THE INTERNATIONAL FOLK-LORE CONGRESS OF THE WORLD'S COLUMBIAN EXPOSITION. 1893. Chicago: Charles H. Sergel Company, 1898. Reprint. ARCHIVES

OF THE INTERNATIONAL FOLK-LORE ASSOCIATION 1 (1898): 327-40.

Discussion of Negro folklore and comment on the similarities between themes found in American Indian folklore and in Afro-American folklore.

Texts of 2 tales: 1. Witches. 2. Soo-loo, the witch (334-7).

1478 Wells, David Dwight. "Evolution in Folk-lore: An Old Story in a New Form." APPLETON'S POPULAR SCIENCE MONTHLY 41 (May 1892): 45-54.

Discussion of two tales about dogs, one obtained from the slaves of an English planter living in British Guiana, and the second, an Uncle Remus tale of Afro-American origin, obtained from a Joel Chandler Harris tale published in the LOUISVILLE COURIER-JOURNAL. Writer attempts to prove that the tales had a common African origin.
Text of 1 tale: The little boy and his dogs (49)

1479 Whitney, Anne Weston. "Items of Maryland Belief and Custom." JOURNAL OF AMERICAN FOLK-LORE 12 (October-December 1899): 273-74.

Text of 1 tale : Why the devil never wears a hat.

1480 Wyman, Lillie B. Chace. "A Southern Study." NEW ENGLAND MAGAZINE n.s. 4 (June 1891): 521-31.

Discussion of black life in a small southern town includes references to the telling of Br'er Rabbit and ghost stories, such as why the blue jay disappears on Friday.

ARTWORKS: 1863-1899

SOCIAL ACTIVITIES

1481 Abbey, Edwin Austin. "Slaves' Quarters in the Cellar of the Old Knickerbocker Mansion." [1876]. Wood engraving by French. Published in "The Knickerbockers of New York Two Centuries Ago," by Egbert T. Viele. HARPER'S NEW MONTHLY MAGAZINE 54 (December 1876).

Illustration depicts slave dancing in colonial New York in the seventeenth century. Eight slaves (3 males, 1 female, 4 children) are gathered in front of a huge fireplace in their cellar quarters. A small boy dances on the hearth to the music of a fiddle. Both hands of the dancer are lifted in the air, one leg is lifted, and he balances himself on the ball of the other foot. The fiddler, seated on the hearth, his instrument tucked under his chin, holds it in shoulder position, but slanting downwards at a sharp angle. A second man accompanies the dancing by pattin' juba. He shows the traditional stance of the patter, with bent body, bent knees, and the hands in clapping position just over the thighs. Occasion: indoor entertainment.

1482 Arms, H. P. "An 'Election Parade' of a Negro Governor." [1899]. Wash drawing. Published in "Negro Slavery in Connecticut," by Frederick Calvin Norton. CONNECTICUT MAGAZINE 5 (June 1899).

Illustration of an 'Lection Day parade of slaves in colonial Connecticut depicts the elected slave governor parading through the street on horseback, followed by 2 male attendants, also on horseback. Indeterminate number of spectators line the street. Occasion: outdoor procession.

1483 Baker, J. E. "Great Musical Drama 'Out of Bondage'." Lithograph. [1876]. Advertisement for the Hyers Sisters' Combination. Published in the CIRCULAR OF THE REDPATH LYCEUM BUREAU. Boston, Season of 1876-77.

The illustration represents a scene from the musical drama "Out of Bondage." Scene shows the interior of a rude cabin with a group of three men and three women, five of whom are standing near a table. The sixth, an elderly man, is seated at the table. All watch a young woman who is dancing, with one hand lifted to her brow, one leg stretched to the side, and balancing on the heel of the other. Occasion: indoor entertainment (formal and professional).

1484 The Banjo Player [untitled]. Mixed media. [1887]. HARPER'S WEEKLY 31 (12 February 1887).

Cartoon depicts 2 men, one pointing to a banjo resting horizontally across his lap, who are engaged in conversation over the "ole-time feelin'" of the banjo. Occasion: domestic music.

1485 Barker, George. "Gems of American Society." Late 19th c. Stereograph. Washington, D. C., Collections of the Library of Congress, Prints Division.

Three young men dance to the music of a fiddler on the front porch and steps of a large frame house. The youngest of the men, positioned in front of the steps in the foreground of the scene, is bent over at the waist, with arms held akimbo, knees bent outwards, and feet crossed. The other 2 men dancing on the porch position themselves as if dancing with an imaginary partner, their arms extended. The fiddler, who stands on the steps, bows his fiddle in the standard manner. Spectators include 3 men and 3 small boys. Occasion: outdoor recreation.

1486 Becker, Joseph, and John N. Hyde. "Pennsylvania--Scene in the Schuylkill County Prison at Pottsville--The 'Prisoners' March' for Exercise in the Corridor." [1883]. Wood engraving. Published in "A Noted Pennsylvania Prison." LESLIE'S ILLUSTRATED NEWSPAPER 56 (March 1883).

Based on a sketch by Becker, "special artist" for LESLIE'S, Hyde's engraving shows a prisoners' procession in double file moving through the corridors of the prison. All are white except for the leading couple, 2 black men who sing and play on banjos as they walk. The other prisoners, 10 men and 2 boys, also sing as they walk. A prison official stands watch. Occasion: indoor processional.

1487 [Benjamin, Samuel Green Wheeler?]. "The Juvenile Band, Fernandina." [1878]. Pen and ink. Published in "The Sea Islands," by Samuel Green Wheeler Benjamin. HARPER'S NEW MONTHLY MAGAZINE 57 (November 1878). Reprint. THE SOCIAL IMPLICATIONS OF EARLY NEGRO MUSIC IN THE UNITED STATES. Edited by Bernard Katz, 68. New York: Arno Press and the New York Times, 1969.

Illustration, apparently drawn by the author, who was also an artist, of a band composed of 8 young boys performing on folk-crafted instruments at a hotel in Fernandina, on Amelia Island, Florida. The band instruments include 2 drums (constructed from square and rectangular cardboard boxes), 5 small tin trumpets (straight with flared bell, one made from an animal bone), and a pair of cymbals (made from tin cans). Occasion: outdoor entertainment.

1488 "The Bow-Arm Stopped." [1871]. Mixed media. Published in "A Fish Story," by Innes Randolph. APPLETON'S JOURNAL OF POPULAR LITERATURE, SCIENCE, AND ART 6 (October 1871).

Caricatural illustration accompanies a poem composed by the author about Old Ned the violinist. The scene depicts Ned playing his fiddle while adrift in a boat on the Chesapeake Bay. His head is bent over his instrument, which is tucked under his chin but slants downward at a sharp angle. Occasion: outdoor domestic music.

1489 Brown, D. R. "Rebels Moving South from Atlanta." [1864]. Wood engraving. Published in HARPER'S WEEKLY 8 (October 1864).

Civil War illustration shows Confederate troops evacuating citizens and their slaves from Atlanta, Georgia. Men load wagons as women and children watch or, in some instances, help. Two boys dance in the lower left corner of the picture, both with sharply bent knees, balancing on the ball of one foot while kicking the other leg. One holds his arms slightly behind his body and slightly akimbo; the other raises one arm and holds the other at his waist. Few persons watch the dancers. Occasion: outdoor recreation.

1490 Buchser, Frank. "Guitar Player." 1867. Oil on canvas. New York City, Kennedy Galleries. Reproduced in Exhibition Catalogue: PORTRAYAL OF THE NEGRO IN AMERICAN PAINTING, by Sidney Kaplan, no. 49. Brunswick, ME: Bowdoin College Museum of Art, 1964.

The Swiss artist, who lived in the United States during the years 1866-71, depicts a guitar player seated in a cane chair before a small fireplace. He sings to his bird in a cage placed on a shelf over the fireplace, accompanying himself on the guitar, which is held in the conventional position, resting on his left leg, which crosses the right leg at knee level. Occasion: indoor domestic music.

1491 _____. "Lesender Neger im Fass," 1869. Oil on canvas. Private collection. Reproduced in FRANK BUCHSER 1828-1890, LEBEN UND WERK, by Gottfried Waelchli, fig. 63. Zurich and Leipzig: Orell Fuessli Verlag, 1941.

Scene shows a boy reading a paper, who is pushed down into the top end of a barrel and steadied by propping his feet on the wall just in front of the barrel. A banjo lies nearby on the floor. Occasion: indoor domestic music.

1492 "Callender's Minstrels: The Past. The Origin of Minstrelsy: The First Rehearsal." [1870s]. Lithograph. Cambridge, Massachusetts, Harvard University Theatre Collection.

Advertisement flyer shows a caricatural depiction of merry makers gathered outside the door of a log-cabin. Lined up before an elderly banjoist, who is sitting on an upturned basket, are 6 children (5 boys and 1 girl), who dance and sing with gusto, each with bent knee and one leg lifted high. The girl holds her hands on her hips; the boys (2 of whom play the bones) hold their arms to the side with bent wrists or lifted in the air. Behind the dancers is a second line, composed of 5 boy musicians who play various home-crafted instruments: tambourine, drums made of cooking pans, sticks, and a natural horn. At the left of the picture an adult male directs the children forcefully, stomping his right foot on the ground. A woman stands in the cabin door with open mouth as if singing. Occasion: outdoor rehearsal for professional entertainment.

1493 "Camp Life." [1874]. Wood engraving. Published in THE GILDED AGE, A TALE OF TODAY, by Mark Twain and Charles Dudley Warner, facing 156. Hartford, CT: American Publishing Company, 1874. Discussed in "Black Images in Nineteenth-Century American Literature: An Iconological Study of Mount, Melville, Homer and Mark Twain," by Karen M. Adams, fig. 76. Ph.D. diss., Emory University, 1977.

Outdoor scene shows 2 boys dancing in a Union army camp, accompanied by a white banjoist. One boy bends his knees and crosses his feet; the other boy kicks one foot in the air, balancing on the ball of the other foot. Occasion: outdoor recreation.

1494 Chalfant, Jefferson David. "Sketch for 'Envious Criticks'." c.1894. Oil on board. New York City, Hirschl and Adler Galleries. Reproduced in AMERICAN PAINTINGS FOR PUBLIC AND PRIVATE COLLECTIONS, no. 76. New York: Hirschl and Adler Galleries, 1967-68.

Painting depicts a sparsely furnished, middle-class room, in which 2 black boys, both seated on chairs, admiringly watch a white boy play the violin. The larger black boy holds a large, triple-coil natural horn, with its bell resting on the floor. Occasion: indoor domestic music.

1495 _____. "Sketch for 'The Hornblower'." c.1895. Oil on board. New York, Hirschl and Adler Galleries in 1967. Reproduced in AMERICAN PAINTINGS FOR PUBLIC AND PRIVATE COLLECTIONS, no. 77. New York: Hirschl and Adler Galleries, 1967-1968.

Scene shows one of the black boys represented in an earlier painting (no. 1494). Perched on a table with one foot on a chair, he puffs on the large, triple-coil, natural horn. Occasion: indoor domestic music.

1496 Champney, J. Wells. "Come to de Auction." [1874]. Wood engraving. Published in "Glimpses of Texas," by Edward Smith King. SCRIBNER'S MONTHLY MAGAZINE 7 (February 1874). Reprint in THE GREAT SOUTH, by Edward Smith King, 408. Hartford, CT: American Publishing Company, 1875.

Full-length portrait of a man who swings a bell in one hand as he walks along, and holds a flag over his shoulder, on which the words "Auction Sale" are printed. His mouth is open as if he is singing. Occasion: outdoor work activity involving song.

1497 _____. "The Summons to a Tobacco Sale." [1874]. Mixed media. Published in "A Ramble in Virginia: From Bristol to the Sea," by Edward Smith King. SCRIBNER'S MONTHLY MAGAZINE 7 (April 1874). Reprints with new title, "Summoning Buyers to a Tobacco Sale." THE GREAT SOUTH, by Edward King. Hartford, CT: American Publishing Company, 1875. THE SOUTHERN STATES OF NORTH AMERICA, by Edward King, 560. London: Blackie and Son, 1875.

Full-length portrait of a man, standing, who blows a long (about 6 feet), straight trumpet held by an attached handle. Wearing hat and apron, he summons buyers to a tobacco sale. Occasion: outdoor work activity involving music.

1498 _____. "The Cheery Minstrel." [1874]. Wood engraving? Published in THE GREAT SOUTH, by Edward Smith King, 255. Hartford, CT: American Publishing Company, 1875.

Full-length portrait of a young street musician, who "makes music" on the railroad cars. He plays a "harmonicon" and triangle simultaneously. His left hand holds the harmonica to his mouth and holds a string to which is attached the triangle. He beats the triangle with his right hand. No spectators are included in the picture. Occasion: indoor entertainment.

1499 _____. "A Jolly Raftful--Taking the Flood Good-Naturedly". [1883]. Pen and ink. Published in "Swept Away"--"Down the Mississippi," Chapter 5, by Edward S. Ellis. ST. NICHOLAS: AN ILLUSTRATED MAGAZINE FOR BOYS AND GIRLS 10 (June 1883).

Scene shows 12 or more men, women, and children on a raft drifting down the river. Three boys dance: 2 in a couple dance with one hand grasping that of the partner, and with one leg lifted high, while balancing on the other foot. The other boy lifts one leg waist-high in a kicking step, and holds one arm high over his head. Others on the raft watch with obvious enjoyment. A man, perched high on a box, provides an accompaniment by clapping his hand. Occasion: outdoor entertainment.

1500 Colburn, Mrs. R. "Monday Morning, or The Tender Passion." 1877. Pen and ink (?). Washington, D. C., Collections of the Library of Congress.

Illustration depicts 2 small boys dancing, facing each other. One has bent knees with one leg lifted; the other literally leaps in the air with both feet off the ground. Others on the scene, a washer woman, another hanging washed clothes on a line, a young man, and a child, pay no attention to the dancers. Occasion: outdoor recreation.

1501 Colburn, Mrs. K. (or C. H. Harris, illustrator?) "The Colored Band." 1887. Pen and ink (?). Washington, D. C., Collections of the Library of Congress.

Four adolescent girls dance about the major domo of a band and his baton. Each balances on the ball of one foot, lifting the other foot high in the air. Two of the girls also lift their arms high, and one bends over sharply at the waist. Others in the scene include members of the band playing brass instruments, 4 boys, and shadowy figures in the background. Occasion: outdoor procession.

1502 Coolidge, Cassius Marcellus. "Street Music." [1872]. Wood engraving. Published in HARPER'S WEEKLY (Supplement) 16 (November 1872).

Scene depicts 2 male musicians performing on a wharf. One sings, accompanying himself on a banjo. His companion plays a fiddle, tucked under his chin but slanting sharply downwards. No spectators are included in the picture. Occasion: outdoor entertainment.

1503 Currier and Ives. "The Old Barn Floor." 1868. Lithograph. New York City, Museum of the City of New York, Harry T. Peters Collection. Reproduced in CURRIER AND IVES, PRINTMAKERS TO THE AMERICAN PEOPLE, by Harry T. Peters, 2:309. Garden City, NY: Doubleday, Doran and Company, 1931. Also in THE GREAT BOOK OF CURRIER AND IVES' AMERICA. Edited by Walton Rawls, 185. New York: Abbeville Press, 1979.

Just inside a barn a child dances to music produced by a smiling banjo player, while a beaming white farmer, his wife, and baby watch. The dancing boy, also smiling broadly, is shown in a leaping position with one foot lifted high in the air and balancing on the toe of the other foot. The banjo player is seated in a chair that tilts forward, and he beats time to the music with one foot as he plays. Occasion: indoor entertainment.

1504 _____. "On the Mississippi: Loading Cotton." 1870. Lithograph. New York City, Museum of the City of New York, Harry T. Peters Collection. Reproduced in CURRIER AND IVES, PRINTMAKERS TO THE AMERICAN PEOPLE. Edited by Harry T. Peters, 1:119. Garden City, NY: Doubleday, Doran and Company, 1929. Also THE GREAT BOOK OF CURRIER AND IVES' AMERICA. Edited by Walton Rawls, 219. New York: Abbeville Press, 1979.

Scene shows a river landing where workers are loading cotton on the steamship New Orleans Packet Eclipse. In the lower right foreground, 2 boys dance face to face, each with one leg lifted and balancing on the other foot, one on his heel and the other on the ball of the foot. One holds both hands outstretched to his partner, the other lifts one arm over his head, and holds the other by his side to the rear. A girl watches from behind a pile of logs. It is not clear whether the white passengers on the ship are also watching. Occasion: outdoor recreation.

1505 _____. "The Old Plantation Home." 1872. Lithograph. Reproduced in THE GREAT BOOK OF CURRIER AND IVES' AMERICA. Edited by Walton Rawls. New York: Abbeville Press, 1979. Reprint. "Black American Music in Pictures," by Frederick Crane, 37. BLACK MUSIC RESEARCH JOURNAL [6] (1986).

Inferior copy of a detail from a painting by Fanny Palmer (see no. 1576) shows a group recreating in front of a neat little cottage in the foreground, and shows the "big house" in the background. Two couples (boys and girls) and a tot dance to the music of a banjoist, who sits on a stool. A woman seated on a log claps her hands in time to the music, or is perhaps pattin' juba. A woman standing in the cottage doorway watches the dancing. Occasion: outdoor recreation.

1506 D., G. [=Georgiana A. Davis?]. "Courtyard of a Rice Mill. The Noon Hour." [1883]. Mixed media. Published in "Georgia--The Cultivation of Rice--Work in the Field and Mill." FRANK LESLIE'S ILLUSTRATED NEWSPAPER 56 (May 1883).

One of five outdoor scenes about rice production published in LESLIE'S ILLUSTRATED in 1883. A man and a woman dance in the center of the courtyard, face to face. Both raise the left leg, balancing on the ball of the right foot. The woman holds a huge basket under her left arm and her right arm akimbo at her waist. The man holds both arms at his side. Spectators include 7 men and women, also out for the lunch hour. Occasion: outdoor entertainment.

1507 Davis, John S. "A Freighters' Camp, West Virginia." [1875]. Wood engraving. Published in THE GREAT SOUTH, by Edward King. Hartford, CT: American Publishing Company, 1875.

A camp scene, with covered wagons and the travelers idling about, depicts in the foreground 2 boys dancing---one of whom snaps his fingers apparently in accompaniment to the athletic dance of the other, who balances himself with his right hand on the ground, while lifting the left arm and his two legs in the air. A man clapping his hands, or perhaps pattin' juba provides more accompaniment. Occasion: outdoor recreation.

1508 Davis, Theodore Russell. "Camp of Negro Refugees." [1865]. Wood engraving. Published in HARPER'S WEEKLY 9 (July 1865).

Illustration of a contraband camp depicts 2 men dancing, face to face, in a clearing of the camp. Both men lift one leg, balancing on the ball of the other foot. One bends forward from the waist, with arms held slightly arched to his sides; the other leans backwards, with arms arched behind his body. The spectators include 5 men, 1 woman, and a child in the foreground, and shadowy figures in the background. Occasion: outdoor entertainment.

1509 "The Departure for Liberia of Freedmen from Columbia, S. C." [1867]. Wood engraving. Published in FRANK LESLIE'S ILLUSTRATED NEWSPAPER 25 (December 1867).

This outdoor scene shows a procession led by 2 drummers, followed by a player on a "flageolet" and a man carrying the American flag. A large crowd of men, women, and children fill the picture, some marching, others obviously spectators. Some have mouths open wide as if singing. Occasion: outdoor procession.

1510 Dumond, Frank Vincent. "A Bamboula." [1892]. Mixed media. Published in "A Bamboula," by Mollie E. Moore Davis. HARPER'S WEEKLY 37 (January 1893). Reprint (of dancing figure only). THE DAILY PICAYUNE 57 (January 1893).

Scene shows a woman dancing the bamboula in the parlor of a middle-class white home, accompanied by a fiddler seated on a chair nearby. The spectators include 6 or more black servants, and 5 white guests in addition to the host and hostess. Occasion: indoor entertainment.

1511 Durkin, John. "Old Gabe." [1886]. Wood engraving. Published in "A Tobacco 'Break' at Lynchburg, Virginia." HARPER'S WEEKLY 30 (December 1886).

One of six scenes entered on a single page depicting aspects of tobacco auctions in Lynchburg, Virginia, shows a full-length portrait of Old Gabe, who is announcing the "breaks" (i.e., the opening of the auction) by blowing a fanfare on a natural tin trumpet (approximately four to six feet in length). Occasion: outdoor work activity involving music.

1512 Eakins, Thomas. "The Banjo Player." c.1878. Oil on canvas mounted on cardboard. Collection of Mr. and Mrs. Paul Mellon. Reproduced in EAKINS WATERCOLORS, edited by Donelson F. Hoopes, 46. New York: Watson-Guptill, 1971.

This is an oil sketch for the banjo player in "Negro Boy Dancing" (see no. 1514). Seated in a chair, the young banjoist leans forward over his instrument in deep concentration; his right leg is lifted high in support of the banjo, resting only on the ball of the foot. Occasion: indoor domestic music.

1513 _____. "Study for Negro Boy Dancing." c.1878. Oil on canvas. Collection of Mr. and Mrs. Paul Mellon. Reproduced in EAKINS WATERCOLORS. Edited by Donelson F. Hoopes, 48. New York: Watson-Guptill, 1971.

Study for the boy in "Negro Boy Dancing" depicts him with body held erect, knees bent, and heels lifted with the weight on one foot. One arm hangs limply at his side, the other is raised to waist level. He concentrates deeply on what he is doing, staring stonily ahead and biting his lower lip. Occasion: domestic dancing.

1514 _____. "Negro Boy Dancing." 1878. Watercolor. New York City, Metropolitan Museum of Art. Reproduced in EAKINS WATERCOLORS. Edited by Donelson F. Hoopes, 44. New York: Watson-Guptill, 1971.

Scene shows a young boy dancing to the music of a seated banjo player, who bends over his instrument but focuses his eyes on the dancer (see nos. 1512, 1513). An older man (his instructor?) whose top hat lies in a nearby chair, watches intently. Occasion: indoor domestic music/dance.

1515 "The Ebony Bridal--Marching to the Feast." [1871]. Wood engraving. Published in "The Ebony Bridal," by Ella B. Washington. FRANK LESLIE'S ILLUSTRATED NEWSPAPER 32 (August 1871).

The scene shows 2 musicians standing outside a rather large cabin, one playing a small natural trumpet (with soundholes) and the other playing a cello, furnishing music for the newly-weds and guests to march from the cabin on their way to site of the wedding feast. The spectators include white and black men, women, and children, who watch the informal procession with interest. Occasion: outdoor entertainment.

1516 "The Ebony Bridal--The Ball." [1871]. Wood engraving. Published, "The Ebony Bridal," by Ella B. Washington. FRANK LESLIE'S ILLUSTRATED NEWSPAPER 32 (August 1871).

The scene shows a large room of a cabin filled with animated dancers, mostly couples, some of whom leap high in the air. A single man dances alone vigorously with legs crossed and balancing on one foot. Musical accompaniment is provided by 2 musicians, one is playing a small, natural trumpet (with soundholes), and the other plays a cello. In the foreground, a woman and a man, both seated, clap their hands in time to the music. Occasion: indoor recreation. (See also nos. 1515, 1639.)

1517 Ehninger, John Whetten. "Old Kentucky Home." 1863. Oil on canvas. Shelburne (Vermont), Shelburne Museum. Reproduced. PAINTINGS AND DRAWINGS AT THE SHELBURNE MUSEUM, 62. Shelburne: Shelburne Museum, 1976. Exhibition Catalogue: AMERICAN ARTISTS IN DUESSELDORF: 1840-1865, by Brucia Witthoft, Anneliese Harding, Joy L. Gordon, 23. Framingham, MA: Danforth Museum, 1982.

The American painter, a native of New York, shows here the scene of a fiddler giving an informal concert in the back yard of a cabin. Perched on a large barrel, the fiddler plays for a seated woman and a small white girl, who leans on her lap. A second musician, an adolescent boy seated on a stool in front of the fiddler, plays a string instrument that seems to be a banjo (the artist has covered most of the instrument with the back of the boy's body). Occasion: outdoor entertainment.

1518 _____. "Music Hath Charms." [1873]. Wood engraving. Published in THE ILLUSTRATED CHRISTIAN WEEKLY 3 (October 1873).

Illustration shows 7 men, women, and children (including 1 small white boy) gathered in the backyard of a cabin. A banjoist, standing with one foot lifted to rest on a keg, sings as he plays. Occasion: outdoor entertainment.

1519 Elder, John Adams. "A Virginny Breakdown." c.1877. Oil on canvas. Richmond, The Virginia Museum of Fine Arts. Reproduced in Exhibition Catalogue: PAINTING IN THE

SOUTH: 1564-1980, 89, 256. Richmond: The Virginia Museum of Fine Arts, 1983. Reprint. "Black American Music in Pictures," by Frederick Crane, 39. BLACK MUSIC RESEARCH JOURNAL [6] (1986).

Virginia-born artist depicts a scene inside a cabin. An adolescent boy dances the breakdown while another boy, seated on a chair near the door, plays a jew's-harp, and two women, one holding a baby, watch admiringly. The dancer, silhouetted by sunlight from the open door, leans slightly backwards as he dances, balancing on the ball of one foot while lifting the other, and extending his arms forward but low. The musician holds the tongue (or lamella) end of his tiny instrument in his left hand, activating it with the index finger of his right hand.

1520 Eytinge, Solomon. "De Jubilee Am Come---Fourth of July, 1876." 1876. Wood engraving. Published in HARPER'S WEEKLY 20 (July 1876).

Caricatural depiction of a Fourth of July parade of Civil War veterans (in ragged uniforms) in a rural area. The procession, led by a trombonist and a drummer (playing a snare drum), includes a "general" on horseback, men holding various kinds of staffs in the air, and little boys prancing along the side, forming a "second line." By-standers include several children perched on a fence, two women standing behind the fence, and persons waving handkerchiefs from the window of a cabin. Occasion: outdoor procession.

1521 The Fiddler [untitled]. [1898]. Pen and ink. Published in AFRO-AMERICAN FOLK LORE, TOLD ROUND CABIN FIRES ON THE SEA ISLANDS ..., by Abigail Holmes Christensen, 62. 2d ed. Boston: The Author, 1898.

A cabin scene (untitled) shows an elderly man, seated near a blazing fire, playing a fiddle. His chair is pushed backwards on its rear legs, and he holds the instrument in the conventional folk fashion. Spectators include 3 seated figures: a woman in the center of the room, a girl who gazes at the fire, and a white boy in a corner near the fireplace. Occasion: domestic entertainment.

1522 "The Fiddler." [1875]. Pen and ink (?). Published in "The Land of the Sky--Or, Adventures in Mountain By-Ways," by Christian Reid. APPLETON'S JOURNAL OF POPULAR LITERATURE, SCIENCE, AND ART 15 (January 1876).

Illustration for a short story depicts a man sitting atop a bale of cotton, who is playing the violin vigorously. His fiddle rests on his shoulder and slants downward sharply. One foot is lifted as if he is stomping his foot in time to the music. Occasion: outdoor domestic music.

1523 "The Fiddler." [1897]. Pen and ink. Published in "The Social Life of the Southern Negro," by W. T. Hewetson. THE CHAUTAUQUAN 26 (December 1897).

Scene depicts a fiddler, who is sitting in a chair, holding his instrument in a rest position against his left thigh. He holds the bow in his right hand. Occasion: indoor portraiture.

1524 Frost, Arthur Burdett. "There's Music in the Air." [1879]. Wood engraving. Published in "The City of Atlanta," by Ernest Ingersoll. HARPER'S NEW MONTHLY MAGAZINE 60 (December 1879). Reprint. THE SOCIAL IMPLICATIONS OF EARLY NEGRO MUSIC..., edited by Bernard Katz, 138. New York: Arno Press and the New York Times, 1969.

Scene shows 5 musicians (flutist, banjoist, 2 violinists, and accordionist) providing musical entertainment for patrons at a local bar on a summer evening. The accordionist, with head thrown back and mouth open very wide, seems to be singing. He and one of the fiddlers sit within the room; the banjoist and flutist sit on the stoop of the wide opening to the barroom, and the second fiddler sits just outside the door. In the foreground, to the left, a man is dancing, leaning slightly backwards, his hands held limply before him from bent elbows, and balancing on the ball of one foot. Occasion: indoor entertainment.

1525 _____. "The Music for the Dance." [1891]. Wash. Published in HARPER'S WEEKLY 35 (December 1891). Reprints. AMERICAN ILLUSTRATORS, by Francis Hopkinson Smith, Part 2. New York: Charles Scribner's Sons, 1892. Reprint. THE MUSIC OF BLACK AMERICANS: A HISTORY, by Eileen Southern, 186. 2d ed. New York: W. W. Norton, 1983.

Four plantation musicians (2 violinists, a banjoist, and a cellist) are shown walking across a snow-covered field, engaging in conversation with each other as they walk. They either are on their way to play for a dance, or have completed their work and are on the way home. They hold their instruments carefully under their arms. Occasion: outdoor group portraiture.

1526 _____. "The Cake Walk." [1892]. Wash. Published in "Jessekiah Brown's Courtship," by Ruth McEnery Stuart. HARPER'S NEW MONTHLY MAGAZINE 84 (May 1892). Reprint. A GOLDEN WEDDING AND OTHER TALES, by Ruth M. Stuart, frontispiece. New York: Harper and Brothers, 1916.

Scene depicts 6 or more dancing couples, dressed in their finest, high-stepping it clock-wise around the room in a circle. A fiddler and a bones player provide music for the cake-walk. An indeterminate number of spectators, some seated, some standing, watch the procession with interest. Occasion: indoor recreation.

1527 Fuller, George. "The Banjo Player." 1876. Oil on canvas. Collection of Mrs. Emily

Abercrombie. Reproduced in "Images of Slavery: George Fuller's Depictions of the Antebellum South," by Sarah Burns, 52. THE AMERICAN ART JOURNAL 15 (Summer 1983).

The banjoist represented in the painting posed for the artist in Montgomery, Alabama, in 1857-1858. Depiction of a boy sitting on a stool in a cabin room; with legs spread wide, he plays on a large banjo, which he holds in the standard position. He faces the hearth, where his mother is cooking, as if entertaining her with his music. Occasion: indoor entertainment.

1528 The Guitarist [untitled]. [1892]. Pen and ink. Published (without title) in "The Old Way to Dixie," by Julian Ralph. HARPER'S NEW MONTHLY MAGAZINE 86 (January 1893).

Full-length portrait of a young man, seated on a chair, playing a guitar. He holds his instrument in the standard position as he strums, his left leg lifted with his foot hooked on the rung of the chair, and the instrument steadied on his right thigh. He may be singing; his mouth is slightly open. Occasion: indoor domestic music.

1529 Hampton Institute Camera Club. "A Banjo Song." [1899]. Photograph. Published in POEMS OF CABIN AND FIELD, by Paul Laurence Dunbar, 116. New York: Dodd, Mead and Company, 1899. Reprint. "Solving the Problem in a Christian Way," by W. F. Mallalieu, 171. ZION'S HERALD 80 (February 1902).

Scene shows 5 children (boys and girls) dancing a ring dance in the yard of a rude cabin, accompanied by the music of a banjoist. Spectators include a woman and a small girl. Occasion: outdoor recreation.

1530 _____. "A Banjo Song." [1899]. Photograph. Published in POEMS OF CABIN AND FIELD, by Paul Laurence Dunbar, 114. New York: Dodd, Mead and Company, 1899.

Scene shows a large group of men, women, and children gathered outside the door of a rude cabin. Two banjoists, seated on benches near each other, sing as they play. Some on-lookers are seated, others stand. Occasion: outdoor entertainment.

1531 _____. "A Banjo Song." [1899]. Photograph. Published in POEMS OF CABIN AND FIELD, by Paul Laurence Dunbar, 120. New York: Dodd, Mead and Company, 1899.

Scene shows a group of 2 adults and 4 children gathered in the back yard of a rude cabin. Two banjoists, leaning against the back and side walls of the cabin at some distance from each other, play what seems to be a duet on their banjos. The same figures appear in another photograph (see no. 1530). Occasion: outdoor domestic music.

1532 _____. "Chris'mus Is A-comin'." [1899]. Photograph. Published in POEMS OF CABIN AND FIELD, by Paul Laurence Dunbar, 64. New York: Dodd, Mead, and Company, 1899.

Full-length portrait of a young man, seated on a barrel, singing and accompanying himself on a banjo. The leg supporting his instrument is propped up on a wooden crate. Occasion: outdoor domestic music.

1533 _____. "The Hunting Song--Rural South." [1899]. Photograph. Published in POEMS OF CABIN AND FIELD, by Paul Laurence Dunbar, 36. New York: Dodd, Mead, and Company, 1899.

Scene of an open field shows a man, with two hunting dogs, blowing on a hunting horn made from an animal's horn. Occasion: work activity that includes song.

1534 Haskell, F. M. and Company. Illustrations for the sheet-music cover of "James Bland's Three Great Songs." 1879. Lithograph. Boston: White, Smith and Company, 1879. Lithographed sheet music. Cambridge, Massachusetts, Harvard University Theatre Collection. Reprint. THE MUSIC OF BLACK AMERICANS: A HISTORY by Eileen Southern, 235. 2d ed. New York: W. W. Norton, 1983.

The song cover has a portrait of the black composer in the center, surrounded by small scenes that illustrate his songs. For "Pretty Little South Carolina Rose"--a boy dances with one foot raised high in the air and both arms outstretched. "Father's Growing Old" shows a fiddler sitting in front of a cabin, resting his fiddle on his lap. Occasion: domestic music and dancing.

1535 Hatfield, Joseph H. "A Few Low, Sweet Chords Vibrated upon the Moonlit Air." [1893]. Wash. Published in "Tony," by Mary A. P. Stansbury. NEW ENGLAND MAGAZINE n.s. 8 (June 1893).

Scene depicts a well-appointed room, with a white woman lying on a chaise lounge listening to the singing of 4 small children, 3 girls and a boy. The boy accompanies the singing on his guitar. Occasion: indoor entertainment.

1536 Helmick, Howard. "The Juba Dance." [1894]. Wood engraving by E. H. Del'Orme. Published in "Old Maryland Homes and Ways," by John Williamson Palmer. CENTURY MAGAZINE 49 (December 1894).

An indoor scene shows a large, sparsely furnished room with 5 women and 4 men seated or standing against the walls. All watch an adolescent boy dancing in the center of the room. He bends forward sharply from the waist, with one arm arched over his head and one leg lifted high in the air, balancing himself on the ball of the other foot. A second dancer is cut out of the scene; only his raised foot and outstretched hand are seen on the right edge of the picture. Accompaniment is provided by a fiddler, seated on a stool, who gazes upwards as he plays, and by a woman, standing against the wall, who is clapping her hands. Two men wave their hands high over their heads in gestures of approval. Occasion: indoor entertainment.

1537 _____. "Giving the Bridal Couple a Good Send Off." [1897]. Pen and ink. Published in THE STORY OF MY LIFE, by Mary A. Livermore, 258. Hartford, CT: A. D. Worthington & Company, 1897.

The scene show a group of about 13-15 persons (men, women, and children) gathered in front of a cabin to give the newly married couple a "good send-off." Music is provided by a fiddler, a banjoist, and a man shaking a tambourine, who stand near the cabin door, while a boy in the foreground claps his hands in time to the music. Occasion: outdoor entertainment.

1538 _____. "A Plantation 'Corn-Shucking'." [1897]. Gouache. Published in THE STORY OF MY LIFE, by Mary A. Livermore, 185. Hartford, CT: A. D. Worthington & Company, 1897.

The sub-caption of the illustration is "Social Meeting of Slaves." A song leader stands at the center of the picture, beside a huge mound of corn shucks. Men and women sing as they husk the corn, some seated on the ground, some standing, all accompanying their work with song. One man plays the bones, held in his right hand, as he sings. Occasion: outdoor work activity involving song.

1539 _____. "Uncle Henson Cuts the Pigeon Wing." [1897]. Pen and ink. Published in THE STORY OF MY LIFE, by Mary A. Livermore, 333. Hartford, CT: A. D. Worthington & Company, 1897.

Scene depicts an elderly man dancing the pigeon-wing in the living/bedroom of a cabin. One arm is lifted over his head, the other outstretched by his side, and the left leg is lifted high while he balances on the ball of the right foot. An elderly woman watches, and a white boy snaps his fingers by way of accompaniment. Occasion: indoor entertainment.

1540 Hicks, Thomas. "The Musicale, Barber Shop, Trenton Falls, New York." 1866. Oil on canvas. Raleigh, North Carolina Museum of Art. Reproduced in AMERICAN PAINTINGS TO 1900, 48-49. Raleigh: North Carolina Museum of Art, 1966. Reprint. "Thomas Hicks at Trenton Falls," by David Tatham, 12. AMERICAN ART JOURNAL 15 (Autumn 1983).

This scene of the barber shop in a New York hotel shows a concert group of 4 men performing together: a black singer, identified elsewhere as the barber William Brister, who wears his apron, and sings with lips slightly parted; a black violinist, who holds his instrument in the conventional concert style; a white cellist; and a white guitarist, who stands to the rear of the group. Seated or standing inside the room and outside the door are 11 whites (men, women, and children) and a black woman who all listen quietly to the music. Occasion: indoor entertainment.

1541 Homer, Winslow. "Our Jolly Cook." 1863. Lithograph. New York City, New York Public Library, Prints Division. Published in CAMPAIGN SKETCHES (the artist's portfolio). Boston: L. Prang and Company, 1863. Reproduced in ECHO OF A DISTANT DRUM: WINSLOW HOMER AND THE CIVIL WAR, by Julian Grossman, 150. New York: Harry N. Abrams, [1974]. Also in WINSLOW HOMER'S AMERICA. Edited by Lloyd Goodrich, 74. New York: Tudor Publishing Company, 1969.

A Civil War scene of a Union camp shows a man dancing around a fire, accompanied by music provided by the company fifer, a white boy. The dancer leaps wildly, his arms outstretched in arch form, his left leg high in the air, balancing on the ball of his right foot, and his mouth open wide as if singing. An indeterminate number of white soldiers watch. Occasion: outdoor entertainment.

1542 _____. "Defiance: Inviting a Shot before Petersburg, Virginia." 1864. Oil on canvas. Two versions are extant: Detroit Institute of Arts. New York City, Whitney Museum of American Art. Reproduced in ECHO OF A DISTANT DRUM: WINSLOW HOMER AND THE CIVIL WAR, by Julian Grossman, 176-77. New York: Harry N. Abrams, [1974]. Also in WINSLOW HOMER, by Forbes Watson, 56. New York: Crown Publishers, 1942. The annotation below refers to the Detroit Institute painting.

The Civil War night scene shows a young white man standing silhouetted against the sky on the top of trenches in order to draw the fire of the enemy. Behind the trench, a black banjoist plays to attract the attention of the enemy, to delude them into thinking that the Union troops, which are concealed by the trenches and are in readiness for battle, are off guard and relaxing. Occasion: Outdoor war scene.

1543 _____. "The Carnival." 1877. Oil on canvas. New York City, Metropolitan Museum of Art. Reproduced in WINSLOW HOMER, by Lloyd Goodrich, fig. 35. New York: George Braziller, 1959.

A man in carnival costume shows something to 2 women as 6 children watch. The adults requested that the artist paint them in their Christmas costumes. Occasion: outdoor portraiture.

1544 Huddle, William Henry. "The Slave." 1889. Oil on canvas. Dallas, Texas, Dallas Museum of Fine Arts. Reproduced in PAINTING

IN TEXAS, by Pauline A. Pinckney, 197. Austin: University of Texas for the Amon Carter Museum of Western Art, 1967.

Virginia-born painter offers a naturalistic portrayal of an elderly man, who is seated and holds his fiddle in a resting position. Occasion: portraiture.

1545 Hyde, John N. "Life Sketches in the Metropolis.--Wandering African Minstrels Performing at a Noted Place of Resort on Harlem Lane." [1872]. Wood engraving. Published in FRANK LESLIE'S ILLUSTRATED MAGAZINE 34 (April 1872).

The scene depicts a bar in Smith's Club House on Harlem Lane in New York City. Entertainment is offered by 4 black musicians for the ten white patrons gathered there. They play bones, violin, banjo, and tambourine. The bones player, his arms extended forward, sings with gusto, leaning back in his chair and rolling his eyes as he sings. The fiddler tucks his instrument under his chin, but holds it in such manner that it slants sharply downward. The banjoist also holds his instrument in unorthodox manner, its neck high in the air and the body resting on his lap. Occasion: indoor entertainment.

1546 "In Ole Virginny." [1876]. Wood engraving. Published in "Virginia in the Revolution," by John Esten Cooke. HARPER'S NEW MONTHLY MAGAZINE 53 (June 1876). Reprint. THE SOCIAL IMPLICATIONS OF EARLY NEGRO MUSIC IN THE UNITED STATES. Edited by Bernard Katz, 1. New York: Arno Press and the New York Times, 1969.

Scene depicting plantation life in Virginia before the Revolutionary War shows a group of 11 persons (men, women, and children) gathered in front of a cabin. All watch the central figure, a man sprawled out in a chair, who is singing and accompanying himself on the banjo. Two boys dance to the music, both with outspread arms and one leg lifted high while balancing on the sole of the other foot. A woman claps her hands to the music. Occasion: outdoor entertainment.

1547 Johnson, Eastman. "Fiddling His Way." 1866. Oil on canvas. New York City, Coe Kerr Gallery. Reproduced in EASTMAN JOHNSON, by Patricia Hills, 42. New York: Clarkson N. Potter and Whitney Museum of American Art, 1972. Also in THE PAINTER'S AMERICA; RURAL AND URBAN LIFE, 1810-1910, by Patricia Hills, 73. New York: Praeger Publishers, 1974.

The scene shows a fiddler playing for a white family (men, women, and children) in a well-furnished living room. The fiddler sits on a chair, legs crossed at the knees, his left arm resting on his left thigh, and his violin slanting sharply downward. Occasion: indoor entertainment.

1548 _____. "Old Kentucky Home." 1866. Wood engraving. Published in "The Century--Its Fruits and Its Festival," by Edward C. Bruce. LIPPINCOTT'S MAGAZINE 18 (October 1867).

This is an inferior copy of a painting by Eastman Johnson, originally entitled "Negro Life in the South" (see no. 525). The scene shows 2 men, 5 women (2 of them white), and 6 children in the backyard of a quite dilapidated two-story house. A young man, perched on a short ladder, plays a banjo with a pensive air, apparently oblivious to those about him. A small boy watches him intently, and in the foreground a kneeling woman holds both hands of her little son, teaching him to dance to the music. Occasion: outdoor recreation.

1549 _____. "The Banjo Player." 1894. Oil on canvas. New York City, Hirschl and Adler Galleries. Reproduced in AMERICAN PAINTINGS FOR PUBLIC AND PRIVATE COLLECTIONS, no. 62. New York: Hirschl and Adler, 1967-1968. Discussed in "Iconography of the Black Man in American Art" by James Edward Fox, 5/34. Ph.D. diss., University of North Carolina at Chapel Hill, 1979.

Full-length portrait of a man playing the banjo with serious mien. He leans forward in his chair, feet set wide, holding the banjo in an unorthodox position, cradled under his right arm and held horizontally. Occasion: domestic music.

1550 Kemble, Edward Windsor. "The Bamboula." 1885. Pen and ink. Published in "The Dance in Place Congo," by George W. Cable. CENTURY MAGAZINE 31 (February 1886). Reprints. THE CENTURY---SELECTED PROOFS. New York: Century Magazine and St. Nicholas, 1893. BLACK DANCE..., by Lynne Emery, 161. Palo Alto: National Press, 1972. THE MUSIC OF BLACK AMERICANS: A HISTORY, by Eileen Southern, 136. 2d ed. New York: W. W. Norton, 1983.

Outdoor scene depicts a man and woman dancing in a clearing in the Place Congo of New Orleans, surrounded by an indeterminate number of spectators, who form a semi-circle around the couple. He steps backwards, holding the woman's right hand in his, and leading her forward into the open space. Both extend their left arms to the side and lift one foot, balancing on the full sole of the other. At the right 4 drummers seated on the ground straddle their instruments, beating with their hands long, cylindrical skin-drums. Another drummer squats behind them, and another player, standing, swings widely over his head a percussion instrument made of a gourd rattle attached to a long stick. Almost all the figures have wide open mouths as if singing or shouting. Occasion: outdoor recreation.

1551 _____. "Blowing the Quills." [1886]. Wood engraving by James Tynan. Published in "The Dance in Place Congo," by George W. Cable. CENTURY MAGAZINE 31 (February 1886). Reprint. "Black American Music in Pictures," by Frederick Crane, 40. BLACK

MUSIC RESEARCH JOURNAL [6] (1986).

Outdoor scene depicts a young boy tending cattle in a clearing next to a corn field. He blows on the quills (=pan pipes) as he walks behind the cows. Occasion: outdoor domestic music-making.

1552 _____. "The Love Song." [1885]. Pen and ink. Published in "The Dance in Place Congo," by George W. Cable. CENTURY MAGAZINE 31 (February 1886). Reprint. BLACK DANCE..., by Lynne Emery, 155. Palo Alto: National Press Books, 1972.

Depiction of a man and woman dancing: they step forward with the right foot, the man slightly behind the woman. She has both hands on her hips; he holds his right hand on his hip, and lifts his left arm behind his partner. Both appear to be singing. No spectators nor setting. Occasion: domestic dancing.

1553 _____. "The Fiddler." 1886. Pen and ink. Published in "Creole Slave Songs," by George W. Cable. CENTURY MAGAZINE 31 (April 1886).

Full-length portrait of a musician, who stands on a platform. Very erect, he rests his instrument upright against his left leg, holding the bow in his right hand. Occasion: portraiture.

1554 _____. "The Fiddler." [1887]. Mixed media. Published in "Mrs. Stowe's 'Uncle Tom' at Home in Kentucky," by James Lane Allen. CENTURY MAGAZINE 34 (October 1887).

Full-length portrait of a fiddler, dressed in formal attire, seated outdoors in a chair on a platform. His violin tucked under his left arm, he rosins his bow. In the background are four whites in formal dress. Obviously the fiddler is waiting for the dancing to begin, for which he will be playing. Occasion: portraiture.

1555 _____. "In the Store." 1886. Crayon. Published in "Sugar-Making in Louisiana," by Eugene V. Smalley. CENTURY MAGAZINE 35 (November 1887). Reprint. BLACK DANCE..., by Lynne Emery, 88. Palo Alto, CA: National Press Books, 1972.

Scene shows a man dancing the pigeon-wing (?) in a country store. He holds his neck stiffly, his arms extended (one to the front, the other to the side with the hand bent backwards), and the right leg raised while balancing on the ball of the left foot. His lips are pursed as if he is whistling or making a bird sound. Musicians seated on benches accompany him, one playing a cello, the other playing an small accordion. Spectators include a white man behind the counter and five or more (black and white) silhouetted in an open doorway. Occasion: indoor entertainment.

1556 _____. "Libely Times We All Use to Hab down t' dat ole Plantation." [1887]. Pen and ink. Published in "Ole Mammy Prissy," by Jessie C. Glasier. ST. NICHOLAS: AN ILLUSTRATED MAGAZINE FOR BOYS AND GIRLS 14 (October 1887).

Scene depicts 4 couples (3 adult, 1 pair of children) dancing at a Christmas Day party, all dressed in their finest. A fiddler, seated in a chair that is elevated upon a table, provides music for the dance. Occasion: indoor recreation.

1557 _____. The Fiddler [untitled]. 1891. Pen and ink. Published in "Christmas on an Old Plantation," by Rebecca Cameron. LADIES HOME JOURNAL (December 1891).

Full-length portrait of a seated fiddler, who is shown resting his instrument on his lap. Occasion: portraiture.

1558 _____. "Grand Ball in de Qua'ters." 1891. Pen and ink. Published in "Christmas on an Old Plantation," by Rebecca Cameron. LADIES HOME JOURNAL (December 1891).

Scene shows a dance in progress in a large room of a cabin. Several couples move forward, holding hands, in a double-file formation. Each of the men is lifts his right foot, while balancing on the ball of the other, and raises his left arm in the air. The foot movement of the women is not visible, being covered by their dresses; they hold their right hands are on their hips. Music is provided by a 3-man orchestra, two violins and a banjo, seated on a dais centered against the right wall. Indeterminate number of spectators include men and women. Occasion: indoor recreation (formal).

1559 _____. "De John Connahs Comin'." 1891. Pen and ink. Published in "Christmas on an Old Plantation," by Rebecca Cameron. LADIES HOME JOURNAL (December 1891).

Scene shows an indeterminate number of men marching in an outdoor procession, in costumes and masked, with mouths open as if they are singing. Three leaders are depicted in detail: The first has a huge pair of ox horns attached to his head gear and flourishes a whip. The second has his head covered totally with a beast-head mask (a boar?). The third, equally heavy-masked and wearing a dunce-head cap, plays the banjo for the marching. Occasion: outdoor procession (recreation).

1560 _____. "The Fiddler." [1892]. Mixed media. Engraved by J. H. E. Whitney. Published in "Middle Georgia Rural Life," by Richard M. Johnston. CENTURY MAGAZINE 43 (March 1892).

Torso portrait of an old man who is tuning his violin. He passes the bow across the strings with his right hand as he turns the peg with his left. Occasion: domestic music-making.

1561 ____. "On with the Dance." 1892. Watercolor. Reproduced in AMERICAN ILLUSTRATORS, by Francis Hopkinson Smith, 57. New York: Charles Scribner's Sons, 1892.

Scene shows 2 boys facing each other in a dance in the side yard of a cabin. Both dancers lean backwards. One claps upraised hands as he advances, with bent knees, one foot resting on its ball and the other flat on the ground. The other kicks up dust with his leaping. His knees also are bent, one arm extends to the front, and one behind, with both bent at the elbow. Spectators include 1 woman and 3 small girls; one of the girls claps by way of providing accompaniment for the dancing. Occasion: outdoor recreation.

1562 ____. "The Breakfast Horn." [1897]. Pen and ink. Published in THE ADVENTURES OF HUCKLEBERRY FINN (TOM SAWYER'S COMRADE), by Mark Twain, 322. New ed. New York and London: Harper and Brothers, 1897.

Scene shows a small girl standing in the doorway of a cabin, blowing a large curved horn, similar in shape to a hunting horn, made from the horn of an animal. A woman, working inside the cabin, is visible. Occasion: outdoor work activity that includes music.

1563 Knaffl and Brothers. "Blackville Gallery--No. III.--The Black Cotillon." 1897. Photograph. Published in LESLIE'S ILLUSTRATED WEEKLY 86 (January 1898).

Caricatural depiction of a dance in progress in a rude room serving as a dance hall. The 4-piece band, which is seated on an elevated platform, consists of a fiddler, banjoist, string bassist, and trombonist, and is augmented by a patter, who performs vigorously. Two of the 3 couples in the room are dancing, and a third couple is about to dance. The sub-caption indicates the band is playing a popular ragtime song of the time: "Mr. Johnsing, turn me luse" ["Mr. Johnson, turn me loose"]. Occasion: indoor recreation.

1564 "Lucindy." Pen and ink. [1892]. Published in "Lucindy," by Ruth M. Stuart. HARPER'S NEW MONTHLY MAGAZINE 84 (April 1892). Reprint. A GOLDEN WEDDING AND OTHER TALES, by Ruth M. Stuart, 365. New York: Harper and Brothers, 1893.

Illustration for a poem written by the author shows a couple dancing side by side. The woman extends her left hand to the man, holding her skirt in a curtsey position with the right hand. He bends slightly backwards, extending his right arm to his partner. Both raise the left leg, balancing on the ball of the right foot. No musical accompaniment is shown, nor are there spectators. Occasion: indoor recreation.

1565 Mangold, J. G. "The Jug Band of Palatka, Fla." 1891. Photograph. Published in LESLIE'S ILLUSTRATED NEWSPAPER 72 (March 1891).

Photograph show 5 boys lined up facing the photographer. Three blow over the mouths of large jugs (of different sizes), which they hold within their arms. Another jug sits on the ground near the boys, and yet another jug is held by a boy who is playing a harmonica. The fifth boy adds a percussive sound by beating two sticks together. Occasion: outdoor entertainment.

1566 Mayer, Frank (=Francis). "Jack Ashore." [1880]. Wood engraving. Published in "Old Baltimore and Its Merchants." HARPER'S NEW MONTHLY MAGAZINE 40 (January 1880). Reprint. BUILDING THE NATION: EVENTS IN THE HISTORY OF THE UNITED STATES, by Charles C. Coffin, 274. New York: Harper and Brothers, 1883.

Scene shows 2 boys dancing in front of a general store/inn of Baltimore in the 18th century for the amusement of 6 white sailors and their female companions. One leans backwards, his arms somewhat extended at his side; the other bends forward from the waist, holding his hands in front of him. Both have one leg lifted, balancing on the full sole or ball of the other foot. Occasion: outdoor entertainment.

1567 Moser, James Henry. "Corn-Shucking Song." 1880. Wood engraving. Published in UNCLE REMUS, HIS SONGS AND SAYINGS, by Joel Chandler Harris, 158. New York: D. Appleton and Company, 1893.

The Canadian artist offers a caricatural depiction of a corn festival at night on a plantation. Indeterminate number of workers (men, women, and boys) are shown, about 15 in the foreground. Those sit in a circle around a big pile of corn husks, singing as they husk the corn. A "general," who stands on top of a pile of corn, directs the work activities and, at the same time, leads the singing with one arm lifted in the air. A waterboy stands near the huskers with bucket and ladle in his hands. Occasion: outdoor work activity that includes song.

1568 ____. "Old Plantation Play-Song, Putnam County, 1856." 1880. Wood engraving. Published in UNCLE REMUS, HIS SONGS AND SAYINGS, by Joel Chandler Harris, 164. New York: D. Appleton and Company, 1893.

Caricatural depiction of a night scene on the plantation with an indeterminate number of persons (men, women, and adolescents) making merry in a clearing outside a cabin. In the foreground, 5 dancers move about in a circle, and 1 elderly man dances alone. One couple dances decorously, arms hanging to the sides, with feet close to the ground. The other 4 bend forward from the waist, swing their arms vigorously, and kick high. There is no evidence of instrumental musical accompaniment, but some persons appear to be singing. Occasion: outdoor recreation.

1569 ____. "Dats de lick, little Ellick." 1881. Wood engraving. Published in BRIGHT

DAYS ON THE OLD PLANTATION, by Mary Ross Banks, frontispiece. Boston: Lee and Shepard, Publishers, 1882.

Caricatural depiction of a corn-husking festival on the plantation at night shows a man dancing on top of a huge pile of corn and leading the workers in song. A number of men and women sit in a circle around the pile, husking the corn and singing songs by the firelight, while others carry bales into three log buildings. Occasion: outdoor work activity that involves song.

1570 _____. "The Whistler." [1887]. Wood engraving. Published in HARPER'S YOUNG PEOPLE 8 (May 1887).

Full-length portrait of an adolescent boy, seated on a stool, who is whistling and accompanying himself on a banjo. His left leg crosses the right at knee level, thus securing the instrument, which he holds in the standard position. Occasion: outdoor domestic music-making.

1571 "Mr. and Mrs. Newlywed's Next 'French' Cook." Late 19th century. Stereograph. New York City, the New York Public Library, Schomburg Center for Research in Black Culture.

A smiling woman plays the mandolin in the midst of kitchen clutter. Occasion: indoor domestic music.

1572 Nast, Thomas. "Entrance of the Fifty-Fifth Massachusetts (Colored) Regiment into Charleston, S. C., February 21, 1865." 1865. Pencil, wash, and oil. Boston, Museum of Fine Arts. Reproduced in M. AND M. KAROLIK COLLECTION OF AMERICAN WATER COLORS AND DRAWINGS 1800-1875, 2:78. Boston: Museum of Fine Arts, 1962.

Illustration portrays the ragged march of Col. Bennett's tired soldiers (Union Army) through streets of ruins in Charleston during the Civil War. An indeterminate number of spectators crowd the scene. Two of them, a man in the foreground and a small boy in the middleground, are depicted in dance attitudes with arms waving about and legs kicking high. Occasion: outdoor war scene.

1573 _____. "'Marching On!' The Fifty-Fifth Massachusetts Colored Regiment Singing John Brown's March in the Streets of Charleston." 1865. Wood engraving. Published in HARPER'S WEEKLY 9 (March 1865).

The first troops to occupy Charleston, South Carolina, are led by Colonel Bennett past buildings in ruins. The soldiers sing with gusto as they march along. An indeterminate number of slaves (freed?) line the streets to cheer the victorious black regiment, waving their arms and reaching out toward the troops. This is a different view of the event painted in no. 1572. Occasion: outdoor war scene.

1574 Newell, Peter Sheaf. "Negro Minstrels." 1887. Charcoal. Published in HARPER'S YOUNG PEOPLE 8 (April 1887).

Scene shows a boy, seated on a wooden bench, playing a banjo (4 strings), which he holds in the standard position. His mouth is open, so he may be singing as well. Standing near him is a young girl, holding a hoop and a stick, who listens intently. Occasion: indoor domestic music.

1575 "On the Observation Platform of a Vestibule Train, Entering Charleston, S. C., Music by the 'Bottle Band'." [1889]. Pencil. Published in FRANK LESLIE'S ILLUSTRATED NEWSPAPER 68 (February 1889).

Scene depicts a "bottle band" performance at a train-stop for 3 white passengers standing on the observation platform. The band consists of 5 boys who blow across the tops of bottles of assorted sizes, a 6th boy who plays a mouth-organ, and a 7th who collects change (holding outstretched a tambourine) from the passengers. Other spectators include 5 adults and a baby standing behind the boys. Occasion: outdoor entertainment.

1576 Palmer, Frances Flora Bond. "Low Water in the Mississippi." 1868. Lithograph, by Currier and Ives. New York City, Museum of the City of New York, Harry T. Peters Collection. Reproduced in CURRIER AND IVES, PRINTMAKERS TO THE AMERICAN PEOPLE, by Harry T. Peters, 1:pl.75. Garden City, NY: Doubleday, Doran and Company, 1929.

The English-born artist, one of the few professional women artists of the period, depicts a small cabin in the foreground, in front of which a family is entertaining itself, against the larger setting of a plantation scene, which includes the "big house" and two steam boats and a raft on a river. Two couples dance energetically, one consisting of a young boy and girl, the other of older dancers. A fifth dancer (male) has no partner, and a tot also dances alone. The males, in particular, kick high; all balance on the ball of one foot. Musical accompaniment for the dancing is pro-vided by a banjoist, who sits on a bench just outside the cabin door. The spectators include a woman sitting in the doorway and a woman seated on a log, who claps her hands in time to the music. Occasion: outdoor recreation.

1577 Penfield, Edward. The Fiddler [untitled]. 1892. Mixed media. Published (without title) in "A Great Speculation," by James Otis. HARPER'S YOUNG PEOPLE 14 (January 1893).

Depiction of a barn-yard scene shows a full-length study of a fiddler engaged in conversation with 2 white adolescent boys. He holds his instrument under the left arm and the bow by his side in his right hand. Occasion: outdoor portraiture.

1578 Pennell, Joseph. "In Carnival Time." [1884]. Wood engraving. Published in HARPER'S WEEKLY 28 (March 1884).

Caricatural illustration depicts a torch-light procession moving through a street of New Orleans, Louisiana, during Carnival time. Indeterminate number of revelers, dressed in long, flowing robes, sing, dance, and haul a float. Occasion: outdoor recreation.

1579 Phillips, J. Campbell. "Ragtime." 1899. Pen and ink. PLANTATION SKETCHES (published in the artist's portfolio). New York: R. H. Russell, 1899. New York City, New York Public Library, Prints Division.

Scene shows 6 boys dancing on the front porch of a decrepit cabin to the music of an adult male banjoist, who sits on a wooden box. The boys, who range in age from eight or nine years through the mid-teens, dance with bodies bent from the waist, hands to the side, bent knees, and generally with one leg lifted, except that one boy has crossed his feet, and a second boy is beginning to do so. Although only 2 boys face the viewer--3 have their backs to the viewer and a fourth is in side profile--it is obvious that all are deeply concentrating on their dance steps. The banjoist plays with his head bent closely over his instrument, totally ignoring the dancers. Occasion: outdoor recreation.

1580 "Picking the Nuts." [1885]. Mixed media. Published in "Scenes and Incidents of a Southern Tour--Peanut-Culture on the Battlefield of Petersburg." FRANK LESLIE'S ILLUSTRATED NEWSPAPER 61 (December 1885).

This is one of six outdoor scenes about peanut culture entered on a single page of the magazine, the only one that depicts music-making. Of the 5 workers (3 women and 2 men) tending the rows of harvested peanut plants, at least 1 woman appears to be singing. In the foreground a seated man sings, accompanying himself on a banjo. Occasion: outdoor work activity involving music.

1581 Reinhart, Charles Stanley. "The Ball after Supper." [1870]. Wood engraving. Published in "Among the Peaches," by William C. Lodge. HARPER'S NEW MONTHLY MAGAZINE 41 (September 1870).

Caricatural representation of an after-supper dance (indoors?) involving an indeterminate number of dancers, who wave their arms with great energy, kick high, and have wide open mouths as if singing. In the foreground, 3 are pictured in detail: a young man, an older woman, and a quite elderly man. Occasion: indoor recreation.

1582 Rogers, William Allen. "Music Hath Charms." [1878]. Wood engraving. Published in "The Sea Islands," by Samuel Green W. Benjamin. HARPER'S NEW MONTHLY MAGAZINE 57 (November 1878). Reprints. BUILDING THE NATION: EVENTS IN THE HISTORY OF THE UNITED STATES, by Charles Carleton Coffin, 419. New York: Harper and Brothers, 1883. THE SOCIAL IMPLICATIONS OF EARLY NEGRO MUSIC IN THE UNITED STATES, edited by Bernard Katz, 24. New York: Arno Press and the New York Times, 1969.

Scene depicts a boy seated on a bench outside the door of a cabin, who plays a home-crafted fiddle (with 3 strings), made from a cigar box, using a home-crafted bow. Occasion: domestic music-making.

1583 _____. "Quorum Dances a Break-Down." [1892]. Mixed media. Published in "Canoemates: A Story of the Everglades," by Kirk Munroe. HARPER'S YOUNG PEOPLE 13 (April 1892).

Cartoonist for the NEW-YORK DAILY GRAPH, later for HARPER'S WEEKLY, depicts a gathering of 12 or more seamen and stevedores (black and white) in an area below deck on a ship in the Florida Everglades. An elderly stevedore dances a breakdown for the men, accompanied by 4 white musicians playing banjo, guitar, fiddle, and fife. The dancer is shown with open mouth (singing?), arms extended to the sides akimbo, bent knees, and jumping high with both feet off the floor. Occasion: indoor entertainment.

1584 _____. "I'se Ringin' fo' de Cake-Walk." [1895]. Pen and ink. Published in "Scenes on the Midway---Cotton States and International Expositions, Atlanta, Georgia." HARPER'S WEEKLY 39 (November 1895).

One of eight scenes representing Midway attractions of the Exposition of Cotton States at Atlanta in 1895 depicts The Old Plantation exhibit, which is staged in a log cabin. An elderly woman, seated to the left of the ticket window, rings a large bell hung above the ticket window, holding its rope in her hand, to attract the attention of passers-by. To the right of the ticket window a musician plays a banjo, and another bows a bass fiddle. Occasion: outdoor entertainment.

1585 Schell, Francis H. "Yanks Expedition---Extempore Musical and Terpsichorean Entertainment at the U. S. Arsenal, Baton Rouge. Under the patronage of the 41st Mass., the 131st N. Y. and 25th Conn. Volunteers--Contraband Children Dancing the Breakdown." [1862]. Wood engraving. Published in FRANK LESLIE'S ILLUSTRATED NEWSPAPER 15 (January 1863). As lithograph entitled "Extempore Musical...." Washington, D.C., Collections of The Library of Congress.

Pennsylvania-born artist offers here a caricatural depiction of an armory, crowded with an indeterminate number of white soldiers and 18 or more contrabands (men, women, and children), who form a rough circle around 2 dancing children.

The boy and girl dance energetically, face to face, waving their arms about and kicking high with bent knees. Music is provided by a fiddler, seated on an upturned tub, who stomps one foot as he plays. He holds his instrument in the old way, cradled in his left arm rather than tucked under his chin. Occasion: indoor entertainment.

1586 Schell, Fred B. "A New Year's Day Contraband Ball at Vicksburg, Miss." 1864. Wood engraving. Published in FRANK LESLIE'S ILLUSTRATED NEWSPAPER 17 (January 1864).

Caricatural depiction of a dance-hall scene shows 23 or more dancing couples, dressed in their finest, and an indeterminate number of revelers in the background. In the foreground, 3 couples are depicted in detail. Two of the men arch one arm over their head, holding, with the opposite hand, their partner's hand. The women hold their skirts in curtsey position with their free hands. All appear to be taking leaping steps. Seated on a raised platform, a fiddler and banjo player provide music for the dancing. Occasion: indoor recreation (formal).

1587 Sheppard, William Ludlow. "Dinner-Time at the Tobacco-Factory." [1870]. Wood engraving by John Filver. Published in "Southern Sketches--II." APPLETON'S JOURNAL OF POPULAR LITERATURE, SCIENCE, AND ART 4 (July 1870).

Caricatural depiction of a dancing lesson taking place outside the doors of a tobacco factory during the dinner-hour break. A man teaches two adolescent boys how to dance. The teacher, bending from the waist and with bent knees, demonstrates how to lift the leg and to hold one arm arched to the back, the other in front with bent wrists. No musical accompaniment is in evidence. Occasion: outdoor recreation.

1588 _____. "Holiday Games at Richmond, Va.---'The Cake Walk'." [1870]. Wood engraving. Published in FRANK LESLIE'S ILLUSTRATED NEWSPAPER 31 (December 1870).

Scene shows a ballroom with 9 or more persons depicted in detail in the foreground and an indeterminate number in the background, black and white. All eyes are centered on 3 woman, dressed in their finest, who prance toward the front of the room, competing for the prized cakes. They must make three complete turns around the ballroom. In the back of the room are 5 judges seated or standing on a raised platform. At the right can be seen a long table, which is covered with cakes. No musical accompaniment is in evidence. Occasion: indoor entertainment.

1589 _____. "An Artist Selecting an Instrument." [1871]. Wood engraving. Published in FRANK LESLIE'S ILLUSTRATED NEWSPAPER 32 (June 1871). Reprint (entitled "Selecting a Banjo"). AMERICA REVISITED, by George A. Sala, 1:198. London: Vizitelly & Company, 1883.

Scene shows a white instrument dealer and a banjoist in a storeroom, where the latter is testing a banjo prior to purchasing it. Perched on a crate, he strums the instrument, while the dealer holds another in readiness to be tested. A smiling boy, leaning on the top crate, watches intently. Occasion: indoor domestic music.

1590 _____. "Negro Life in the South." [1872]. Wood engraving. Published in HARPER'S WEEKLY 16 (May 1872). Reprint (entitled "The Old Darkey's Last Love"). METROPOLITAN LIFE UNVEILED..., by James W. Buel, 559. St. Louis: Historical Publishing Company, 1882.

Outdoor scene shows a fiddler, seated in a chair outside the door of his cabin, playing his violin for the enjoyment of his wife and 2 children. He holds his fiddle in the old way, resting it against his chest, and taps his foot as he plays. All 4 may be singing as their mouths are open. Occasion: outdoor domestic music.

1591 _____. "Bond and Free." [1873]. Wood engraving. Published in HARPER'S WEEKLY 17 (December 1873).

Scene depicts 3 children (1 black and 2 white street musicians) standing on a city street in front of the entrance steps to a building. The boot-black sings and dances, leaning backwards, with arms arched at his side, bent knees, and one leg lifted. The other children watch him closely: the girl, holding her violin in her arms, and the boy, whose harp rests on the sidewalk beside him, waving a scarf in time to the singing. Occasion: outdoor recreation.

1592 _____. "The Dance." [1882]. Wood engraving by J. Clement. Published in "A Georgia Corn-Shucking," by David C. Barrow. CENTURY MAGAZINE (October 1882). Reprint. BLACK DANCE..., by Lynne Emery, 113. Palo Alto: National Press Books, 1972.

Outdoor night scene shows workers (18 or more men and women) making merry in a clearing in the slave quarters. Attention is centered on 3 dancers, a couple and a man dancing alone. The latter, kicking knee high with arms outstretched before him in arch form, looks over his left shoulder and turns in that direction as he dances. The man and woman dance face to face. She holds her skirt in curtsey form with both hands, kicking with her right leg. The man, leaning towards her, lifts his right leg, balancing on the ball of the left foot. In the background a fiddler and a strawbeater, standing above the crowd, provide musical accompaniment for the dancing. Others clap hands, tap feet, and sing. Occasion: outdoor entertainment.

1593 _____. "The Shucking." [1882]. Wood engraving. Published in "A Georgia Corn-Shucking," by David C. Barrow. CENTURY MAGAZINE 24 (October 1882).

Scene shows an indeterminate number of corn huskers (men and women and including at least 1 white) husking corn in a clearing on the plantation. There are two groups, each with its own song leader, who compete in trying to be first in finishing the husking of the pile of corn before them. The song leaders stand on top of the piles, singing and pressing their groups to win. Many of the huskers also are singing, or shouting, and corn husks fly through the air. An overseer stands apart , with arms folded, watching the workers. Occasion: outdoor work activity that includes song.

1594 _____. "Echoes of Old Plantation Melodies." [1884]. Wood engraving by R. Staudenbaur. Designed by J. W. Published in HARPER'S WEEKLY 28 (January 1884).

Scene depicts 3 men and a girl gathered in the bedroom-sitting room of an humble cabin. The men, seated in chairs, sing with zest; the girl, standing behind a chair watches with great interest. The youngest of the men accompanies the singing on a banjo (the peg for the short fifth string is visible). In the background a woman ascends the stairs. Occasion: indoor recreation.

1595 _____. "I kain stand hit no longer." [1887]. Pen and ink. Published in "Shedrick the Fiddler," by William Ludlow Sheppard. HARPER'S WEEKLY 31 (November 1887).

Scene depicts 2 men (1 black, 1 white) in a humble cabin room in which a fire burns brightly. The former dances to the music of the white fiddler. He leans backwards as he dances, holding his arms to the side with bent wrists and crossing his legs in a kicking step. Occasion: indoor recreation.

1596 _____. "'The Fourth' at Blackville--Parade of the Lincoln Guards' Cadets." [1893]. Pen and ink. Published in HARPER'S YOUNG PEOPLE 14 (July 1893).

Scene shows 9 young boys, decked out in costumes of a sort, standing in a mock military line-up, preparatory to staging a Fourth of July parade. Some boys carry sticks as if they were rifles, one boy carries the American flag, and in front of the line-up a boy beats on a drum. The spectators include 3 or more children, 1 girl, and 1 male adult. Occasion: outdoor recreation (procession).

1597 _____. The Dancers [untitled]. [1897]. Pen and ink drawing. Published in "Ol' Virginny Reel". WEH DOWN SOUF AND OTHER POEMS, by Daniel Webster Davis, 74-75. Cleveland: Helman-Taylor Company, 1897.

This illustration has a caption: "Ol' Lijah wuz de bes' man; he'd cut de pigin-wing.." Scene shows 10 or more men and women making merry in a barn lighted by candles. Several dance, with high kicking steps, arms waving about, and with open mouths as if singing. A couple in the foreground is drawn with great detail. The woman holds her arm outstretched to the side and balances on the ball of her left foot; the man, turned sidewise, crosses his leg in a high kick. No musical accompaniment is in evidence. Occasion: indoor recreation.

1598 Sheppard, William Ludlow, and J. Wells Champney. "The Carnival---White and Black Join in Its Masquerading." [1875]. Wood engraving by F. Juengling. Published in THE GREAT SOUTH, by Edward King, 38. Hartford, CT: American Publishing Company, 1875.

Night scene shows a square in New Orleans, crowded with an indeterminate number of masquerading Carnival revelers (white and black). In the foreground a black banjoist plays for the dancing of a black couple. The man, holding his left hand on his hip, waves the right arm in the air and kicks high with his right leg. The woman holds her skirt with both hand in a curtsey position and raises her right leg in a kicking step. Occasion: outdoor recreation.

1599 Smillie, James D. "Black Joe, The Fiddler." [1881]. Pen and ink drawing published in "Phil's Fairies," by Mrs. W. F. Hays. HARPER'S YOUNG PEOPLE 2 (February 1881).

Full-length portrait of an elderly fiddler, seated on a chair, playing a violin. He appears to be in a pensive mood, looking into space as he draws the violin bow downward. Occasion: domestic music.

1600 Snyder, Willard Poinsette. "Some One Produced a Fiddle, and They Danced." [1884]. Pen and ink. Published in "Wakulla," by Kirk Munroe. HARPER'S YOUNG PEOPLE 6 (November 1884).

Scene shows an indeterminate number of workers gathered outside their workplace at the close of the work day. Many are dancing. Women dance with hands on hips, one arm arched over the head, or holding their skirts in curtsey fashion, while extending one hand to a partner. Men hold one arm arched at the side, extending the opposite hand to a partner. All dance with lively, leaping steps. One vivacious young man waves a scarf over his head, places a hand on his hip, and crosses his legs at knee level as he dances. In the lower right of the picture a caller (?) stomps his foot and claps his hands. Despite the title of the illustration, no fiddle is in evidence. In the background, a young white man has climbed into a tree in order to watch the dancing. Occasion: outdoor recreation.

1601 "The South as Secession Found It and as It Leaves It." [1863]. Wood engraving. Published in FRANK LESLIE'S ILLUSTRATED NEWSPAPER 17 (December 1863).

Depiction of a city scene with an indeterminate

number of persons in the background (black and white) and dancers and other revelers in the foreground. In a grassy clearing, 2 men dance, face to face, with arms thrust in front of them and taking lively kicking steps, while balancing on the ball of one foot. A fiddler, perched high on a huge barrel, plays for the dancing, along with a banjoist, who is seated below the fiddler. Some of the numerous spectators watch the dancing. Occasion: outdoor recreation.

1602 [Strother, David Hunter] [Porte Crayon, pseud]. The Tournament [untitled]. [1868]. Wood engraving. Published without title in "The Young Virginians," by David H. Strother. THE RIVERSIDE MAGAZINE FOR YOUNG PEOPLE 2 (June 1868).

Illustration, presumably by the author, shows a mock tournament being staged by small boys (white and black) in a woodlands setting. Music is provided by 5 black males seated on a raised platform: 2 fiddlers, a fifer, a bones player, and a tambourinist, who holds his instrument high over his head. Spectators include children and adults watching the performance from the sidelines. Occasion: mock military activity.

1603 Tanner, Henry Ossawa. "The Banjo Lesson." c.1893. Oil on canvas. Hampton, Virginia, Hampton University Art Museum. Reproduced in TWO CENTURIES OF BLACK AMERICAN ART, by David Driskell, 52. Los Angeles: Los Angeles County Museum of Art, 1976. Also in THE PAINTER'S AMERICA; RURAL AND URBAN LIFE, 1810-1910, by Patricia Hills, 83. New York: Praeger Publishers, 1974.

One of the few black-American artists of the nineteenth century who attracted international attention depicts here an elderly man teaching a boy in the kitchen of a cabin, which is brightly lit up by a blazing fire in the fireplace. The boy, standing between his teacher's legs, actually plays the banjo, with his left hand on the fingerboard (about midway) and his right hand plucking the strings. The teacher steadies the instrument, holding it at the top of the fingerboard with his left hand. The short, fifth string of the banjo is visible. For another Tanner painting with a similar theme, see no. 1604. Occasion: indoor domestic music.

1604 _____. "Dis heah's a fus'-class thing ter work off bad tempers wid." c.1893. Oil on canvas. Reproduced in "Uncle Tim's Compromise on Christmas," by Ruth M. Stuart. HARPER'S YOUNG PEOPLE 15 (December 1893). Reprint. SOLOMON CROW'S CHRISTMAS POCKETS AND OTHER TALES, by Ruth M. Stuart, frontispiece. New York: Harper & Brothers, 1897.

Scene shows an elderly man, seated on a bench, giving a banjo lesson to a small boy who stands between his teacher's legs. The teacher steadies the banjo neck for the boy; both closely watch the boy's right hand strumming the banjo (see also no. 1603). Occasion: indoor domestic music.

1605 Tarbell, John H. "My Gal Is a High-Born Lady." [1897]. Photograph. Published in "The New Generation down in Dixie." LESLIE'S WEEKLY ILLUSTRATED NEWSPAPER 85 (December 1897).

Photograph shows a boy, seated on a high bench, plucking a mandolin; a girl seated beside him listens intently. Occasion: domestic music.

1606 Taylor, F. H. "Calling to the 'Breaks.'" [1879]. Wood engraving. Published in "A Tobacco Market in Lynchburg, Virginia." HARPER'S WEEKLY 23 (May 1879).

One of six sketches about a tobacco market entered on a single page in HARPER's depicts a trumpeter playing a long tin horn (approximately four to six feet long) to announce the beginning of the tobacco auction. Occasion: outdoor work activity involving music.

1607 "Terpsichore in the Flat Creek Quarters." [1881]. Mixed media. Published in SCRIBNER'S MONTHLY 21 (February 1881). Reprint (entitled "An Old-Fashioned Negro Dance"). METROPOLITAN LIFE UNVEILED, by James W. Buel, 515. St. Louis: Historical Publishing Company, 1882. Reprint (entitled "Terpsichore in the Quarters"). UNCLE GABE TUCKER; OR, REFLECTION, SONG, AND SENTIMENT IN THE QUARTERS, by John Alfred Macon, frontispiece. Philadelphia: J. B. Lippincott Company, 1883.

Caricatural depiction of a rather formal dance taking place in the large room of a cabin. Seven couples participate vigorously in a Virginia-reel style dance, positioned in two facing lines, alternating men and women. Holding hands along the lines, they leap in the air, some with feet crossed. Music is provided by a fiddler, who sits to the left of the dancers in the foreground, tapping his foot as he plays. To the right sits the caller, an elderly man, who calls the figures obviously with considerable authority and also stomps his foot in time to the music. Indeterminate number of shadowy party-participants are in the background. Occasion: indoor recreation.

1608 Thompson, Alfred Wordsworth. "Registration at the South---Scene at Asheville, North Carolina." 1867. Wood engraving by John C. Karst. Published in HARPER'S WEEKLY 11 (September 1867).

Illustration of an election-day scene in Ashville depicts a large, indeterminate number of black and white men gathered before the building that houses the registration headquarters. In the foreground a man dances, accompanied by a banjoist. With head thrown back, he holds his arms akimbo to the sides with his hands turned inward, and kicks high, balancing on the ball of his left foot. Occasion: outdoor recreation.

1609 _____. "Scene on a Southern Plantation."

[1868]. Wood engraving. Published in HARPER'S WEEKLY 12 (February 1868).

Scene shows a fiddler leaning against a tree-stump in a clearing near a cabin and tuning his violin. A woman seated on a huge log, a man standing with his foot on the log, and 3 small children watch the fiddler intently. Occasion: outdoor domestic music.

1610 "Uncle Pete's Bony Fingers Skipped Joyously over the Strings." [1890]. Pen and ink. Published in "De Chillun's Cup," by Mollie E. Moore Davis. HARPER'S YOUNG PEOPLE 12 (December 1890).

Scene shows young people gathered in the back yard of a cabin. Three girls and 4 boys dance to the music of an elderly banjoist, who sits on a wooden bench outside the cabin door. Some of the dancers kick their legs high and fling their arms about; a small girl thrusts her arm, bent at the elbow, to the back; an adolescent girl, bent over from the waist, dances with feet flat on the ground. Occasion: outdoor recreation.

1611 Upham, C. "The New South---Scenes in North Carolina, Georgia and Florida." Part 1. "The Fog Horn---St. John's River." [1883]. Wood engraving. Published in FRANK LESLIE'S ILLUSTRATED NEWSPAPER 56 (March 1883).

Illustration depicts a night scene: a man silhouetted against the sky, seated high on a pier, is blowing a fog-horn (a long straight trumpet about four feet long). Another man leans against the pier at the bottom. Occasion: outdoor work activity involving music.

1612 _____. "The New South... Part 2. Log Raft. Cape Fear River." [1883]. Wood engraving. Published in FRANK LESLIE'S ILLUSTRATED NEWSPAPER 56 (March 1883).

Night scene shows 7 workmen on a huge raft, lounging or standing by a blazing fire, which burns at one end of the raft under a makeshift canopy. One man, standing aside with his back to the fire, strums a banjo. A man seated nearby on a wooden box plays an instrument that seems to be playing a mouth organ. The other men pay no attention to the music makers. Occasion: outdoor domestic music.

1613 _____. "Virginia---A Night Scene in Lynchburg during the Tobacco Season---Negro Tobacco Farmers Making Merry." [1883]. Wood engraving. Published in FRANK LESLIE'S ILLUSTRATED NEWSPAPER 57 (October 1883).

Outdoor night scene shows 7 men and 1 boy, gathered around a campfire, celebrating the end of the harvest season and the opening of the tobacco market. One man dances, with head thrown back, right arm arched over his head, and right leg lifted high, balancing on the ball of the left foot. Musical accompaniment is provided by a banjo player, seated on a wooden box, along with a bones player, who stands behind the banjoist. Both sing as they play. Two men watch the musicians; 3 others are absorbed in a card game. Occasion: outdoor recreation.

1614 Vizetelly, Frank. "Night Amusements in the Confederate Camp." [1862]. Wood engraving. Published in THE ILLUSTRATED LONDON NEWS 42 (January 1863). Reprint. THE WAR ILLUSTRATORS, by Pat Hodgson, 66. New York: MacMillan, 1977.

Night scene depicts a Confederate camp during the Civil War. A large indeterminate number of white soldiers fill the picture. In the foreground 23 or more (including 2 blacks) stand or sit around a campfire, watching a dancer. He holds one arm limply to the side, lifts the other chest-high, and kicks wildly, balancing on the ball of one foot. A white soldier, sitting nearby on the ground in an open tent, provides music on a banjo. Occasion: outdoor entertainment.

1615 W. "Jim, the Ferry Boy." Wood engraving. [1881]. Published in "Jim, the Ferry Boy," by Wade Whipple. HARPER'S YOUNG PEOPLE: AN ILLUSTRATED WEEKLY 2 (August 1881).

Illustration depicts a small barefoot boy playing a violin as he sits in a flat boat beached on the shore of the Kanawha River at Waterville, West Virginia. Occasion: outdoor domestic music.

1616 _____. "Evening at the quarters." [1887]. Wood engraving. Published in "Here and There in the South: IV--Among the Bayoux," by Rebecca Davis. HARPER'S NEW MONTHLY MAGAZINE 75 (October 1887). Reprint. THE MUSIC OF BLACK AMERICANS: A HISTORY, by Eileen Southern, 165. 2d ed. New York: W. W. Norton, 1983.

A depiction of the slave quarters of a Louisiana plantation shows 12 men and women in the background performing a ring-game dance, holding hands and moving in a counter-clockwise circle. Indeterminate number of spectators. Occasion: outdoor recreation.

1617 "Walking for the Cake." [1889]. Pen and ink. Published in "The Coloured People in the United States: In the South," by T. L. Robinson, 58. LEISURE HOUR 38 (1889).

Scene shows a rudely constructed dance-hall, decorated with flower garlands and lanterns, and filled with an indeterminate number of dancers and spectators. Dressed in their finest, 9 couples walk sedately around the room; musical accompaniment is offered by 3 musicians, who sit on a raised platform. The fiddler and banjo player sit on chairs; the cornetist stands. The banjoist is reading from the music on a stand before him. In addition to the other spectators, 2 sit on the musicians' platform, and 5 in a balcony overhead. Occasion: indoor recreation (formal).

1618 "The War in Louisiana--Scene at Tarleton's Plantation, Bayou Teche." 1864. Wood engraving. Published in FRANK LESLIE'S ILLUSTRATED NEWSPAPER 18 (September 1864).

Plantation scene shows a gathering of 18-20 persons (men, women, and children) under a tree in the foreground; in the background can be seen tents and a riverboat. In the center of the crowd 2 boys dance, face to face, accompanied by a fiddler, who sits on a tree stump. One boy leans forward, the other leans backwards, both with arms outstretched to the side, bent knees, and one leg lifted while balancing on the flat foot of the other leg. Some white soldiers watch from a distance. Occasion: outdoor entertainment.

1619 Waud, Alfred R. "The Call to Labor." [1867]. Wood engraving. Published in "Scenes on a Cotton Plantation." HARPER'S WEEKLY 11 (February 1867).

The English-born staff artist for HARPER'S made thirteen sketches representing life on a cotton plantation in Clarke County, Alabama, of which three refer to music (see also nos. 1620, 1688). This scene depicts a man blowing an instrument (made from a cow's horn), which has the appearance of a hunting horn, to summon the plantation workers to the fields. Occasion: outdoor work activity involving music.

1620 _____. "Saturday Evening's Dance." [1867]. Wood engraving. Published in "Scenes on a Cotton Plantation." HARPER'S WEEKLY 11 (February 1867).

Illustration shows an indeterminate number of workers and children assembled in front of the "big house." Two couples dance to the music of a fiddler, who stands not too far away. The dancers leap in the air, the women with hands on hips, the men with arms outstretched to the side. Most of those present watch the dancers, including 5 whites standing on the porch of the big house. See also no. 1619. Occasion: outdoor recreation.

1621 _____. "The Levee at New Orleans." [1869]. Wood engraving. Published in APPLETON'S JOURNAL OF POPULAR LITERATURE, SCIENCE, AND ART 1, Art Supplement (May 1869).

Illustration shows a crowded levee with city buildings and ships in the background, and an indeterminate number of workers, stevedores, vendors, ship passengers, merchants, military officers, and others (black and white) in the foreground. In the bottom left of the picture 2 boys dance, face to face, watched by another boy and a woman holding a baby. Both dancers hold arms akimbo to the side; one raises the left leg, balancing on the flat foot of the other leg, and the other boy has both feet in the air. No musical accompaniment is in evidence. Occasion: outdoor recreation.

1622 "Way Down upon the Swanee Ribber." [1873]. Wood engraving. Published in HARPER'S WEEKLY 17 (JUNE 1873). Reprint. "Black American Music in Pictures," by Frederick Crane, 38. BLACK MUSIC RESEARCH JOURNAL [6] (1986).

Illustration shows an old fiddler, violin in his hands and violin case on the ground nearby, dozing in his cabin near the stove. His dream, which is depicted in the upper half of the picture, shows his old cabin by the river, in front of which 2 women dance to the music of a banjoist. Holding their skirts in curtsey fashion and bent over from the waist, they leap high in the air. Occasion: outdoor recreation.

1623 Weathervane. 19th century. Collection of Mrs. Terry Dintenfass. Painted iron sculpture. Photograph published in TWO CENTURIES OF BLACK AMERICAN ART, by David C. Driskell, 114-115. New York: Los Angeles County Museum of Art and Alfred A. Knopf, 1976.

This unusual weathervane, made of a flat sheet of iron, depicts a man (or boy) dancing vigorously atop a high iron pole. Made in profile, he kicks one leg straight forward and stretches both arms before his face, with one hand touching his nose (suggesting a derisive gesture, which may be unintentional in the sculptor's effort to reinforce the metal). Occasion: outdoor representation of domestic dance.

1624 Webber, Charles T. "The Underground Railroad." c.1890. Oil on canvas. Cincinnati, Ohio, Cincinnati Art Museum. Reprint. Washington, D.C., Collections of the Library of Congress. Discussion of the painting in "Charles T. Webber," by James H. Rodabaugh, 59. MUSEUM ECHOES (27 August 1954).

Painting shows a winter scene with snow-covered fields and a dilapidated house in the background. The Rev. Levi Coffin, "President" of the Underground Railroad, his wife, and Mrs. Hannah Haydok are shown helping 8 fugitive slaves get down from a cart, in which presumably they have been traveling. At the lower right, a young man unpacks his banjo. Occasion: domestic music.

1625 Worth, Thomas. "A Mule Train on an Up Grade; A Mule Train on a Down Grade." 1881. Lithograph, by Currier & Ives. New York City, Museum of the City of New York. Reprint. CURRIER AND IVES, PRINTMAKERS TO THE AMERICAN PEOPLE, by Harry T. Peters, 1:29 (pl). Garden City, NY: Doubleday, Doran & Company, 1929.

Caricatural depiction of a family (man, wife and baby) travelling West by mule. They protect their banjo by rolling it in a mattress with the baby. Sub-captions of the scenes: 1. "Golly, Where is dis yere promis' land"; 2. "Clar de track for we's a comin." Occasion: domestic music.

1626 Zogbaum, Rufus F. "Reveille Found These Jolly Fellows Still Laughing." [1896]. Wash. Published in "Adventures of American Army and Navy Officers. IV.---A Sioux Indian Episode," by Guy V. Henry. HARPER'S WEEKLY 40 (December 1896).

Camp scene in the Dakotas during the winter of 1890-1891 shows 3 soldiers of Troop D, Ninth Cavalry (Colored), standing in front of a tent. The regimental trumpeter holds his instrument poised in his right hand as he jokes with the other 2 soldiers. Occasion: outdoor military activity.

THE RELIGIOUS EXPERIENCE

1627 "Baptizing in the Pool." [1891]. Mixed media. Published in SEVEN YEARS AMONG THE FREEDMEN, by Maria Waterbury, 169. 2d ed. Chicago: T. B. Arnold, 1891.

Outdoor scene depicts a number of male and female candidates for baptism standing beside the pond that serves as the baptismal pool, and the clergyman standing knee-deep in the water. The church is visible in the background. A large indeterminate number of spectators, some of whom are singing, includes 3 or more whites. Occasion: outdoor religious ceremony.

1628 Becker, Joseph. "The Contraband Camp at City Point--An Evening Prayer Meeting." [1864]. Wood engraving. Published in FRANK LESLIE'S ILLUSTRATED NEWSPAPER 19 (October 1864).

Night outdoor scene depicts a prayer meeting being conducted in a clearing (with huts and tents in the background), led by a man who stands, hands folded, behind a rudely constructed altar. The altar has a canopy covering and is lit by 2 candles in bottles. Thirty or more men, women, and children, many with heads lowered, surround the altar; some are seated on wooden crates, some stand. A comment in the brief text identifies the speaker as Brother John, a contraband in Gen. Grant's camp at City Point, VA. Occasion: outdoor religious service.

1629 _____. "A Fireman's Funeral." [1871]. Wood engraving. Published in "A Colored Funeral in the South," by Ella B. Washington. FRANK LESLIE'S ILLUSTRATED NEWSPAPER 32 (June 1871).

Scene shows a vast gathering in front of a large church. Four pall-bearers carry a casket, which contains a deceased fireman, out of the church, accompanied by a man carrying the fire company's banner. Two rows of mourners in firemen's uniforms flank the pall bearers, and a single fireman stands before a large cart, which will transport the casket to the grave. The large crowd includes others in uniform in addition to mourners and spectators in ordinary dress. Occasion: outdoor religious ceremony.

1630 Becker, Joseph, and Georgiana Davis. "Virginia Watch Meeting." [1880]. Wood engraving. Published in FRANK LESLIE'S ILLUSTRATED NEWSPAPER 49 (January 1880). Reprint (entitled "Gelory Hallelujah"). METROPOLITAN LIFE UNVEILED, by James W. Buel, 508. St. Louis: Historical Publishing Company, 1882.

Sub-caption: "Virginia.--'De Lord Will Take Care ob de Colored Folk.' Seeing the Old Year Out and the New Year In--Scene in the Colored Church at Grafton, near Yorktown, during the Watch Meeting on New Year's Eve." Illustration shows a large number of people assembled in a plain meeting house for a New Year's Eve watch meeting. Men, women, and children of all ages compose the group. Most are singing--some with upraised arms, some on bended knees; 2 women in the foreground stand on the podium with the seated minister, who leans forward with clasped hands, watching the gathering. His mouth is not opened in song, but he may be praying softly. Others in the foreground include a man kneeling near the podium and clapping his hands as he sings, and another seated on the edge of the podium, his face buried in his hands. A child seated on the steps of the podium appears to be bewildered. Occasion: indoor religious service.

1631 Berkeley, Carter N. "Virginia---Scene at a Colored Revival Meeting...." [1885]. Wood engraving. Published in "Colored Revivals in Virginia." FRANK LESLIE'S ILLUSTRATED NEWSPAPER 61 (September 1885).

Full caption is "Virginia.... 'Oh! come down from heben, en ride roun' in de hearts uv des sinners'." Indoor scene of a small meeting room shows in the foreground 9 men and women and a child sitting or lying on the floor near the preacher's pulpit. Three women stand over the others, who appear to be "possessed," fanning them and singing. The minister leans over his pulpit with one arm extended, either singing or speaking to the assembled gathering. In the middle ground of the picture, 5 men are singing, and behind the minister on the pulpit sit 2 elders, who also are singing. In the background an indeterminate number of shadowy figures participate in the religious exercise, some with hands clapsed over their chests and singing with gusto. Occasion: indoor religious service.

1632 Bricher, Alfred T. "Religious Dancing of Blacks, Termed Shouting." [1892]. Engraving, either by Alban J. Conant or by Bricher and Conant. Reproduced in THE BLACK MAN OF THE SOUTH AND THE REBELS, by

Charles Stearns, 370. New York: American News Company, 1892.

Caricatural depiction of a religious service in a praise cabin shows 15-18 men and women moving counter-clockwise in a circle formation. Most have the stance of the "shouter," with bodies bent forward from the waist, knees bent, and feet moving in the shuffle step. Some, however, have one foot lifted in the process of stepping forward. Some lift arms in the air, one of the shouters is clapping his hands, and several are singing. One woman is jumping high in the air with both arms lifted. There are 3 on-lookers. Occasion: indoor religious ceremony.

1633 Brooke, Richard Norris. "A Pastoral Visit." 1881. Oil on canvas. Washington, D.C., Corcoran Gallery of Art. Reproduced in Exhibition Catalogue: THE PORTRAYAL OF THE NEGRO IN AMERICAN PAINTING, by Sidney Kaplan, no. 58. Brunswick, ME: Bowdoin College Museum of Art, 1964. Also in "Preview: The Negro in American Art," by Marvin S. Sadik, 81. ART IN AMERICA 52 (June 1964). There is a wood engraving of the scene (entitled "The Pastor's Visit") by R. Staudenbaur. Published in HARPER'S WEEKLY 26 (October 1882).

The artist painted from life this scene of a young black family in his home town, Warrenton, Virginia. The family entertains their minister at dinner. The mother serves; the father and 2 children listen intently to the minister's discourse; the youngest child leans on her father's knees. A banjo rests on a stool near the father. Occasion: indoor domestic religious experience.

1634 Carlton, William Tolman. "Watch Meeting, December 31, 1862." 1863. Oil on canvas. New York City, Hirschl & Adler Galleries. Discussed in "Iconography of the Black Man in American Art (1710-1900)," by James Edward Fox. Ph.D. diss., The University of North Carolina at Chapel Hill, 1979.

Scene shows a group of 15 men and women gathered for a religious service in a large room on the night before the Emancipation Proclamation becomes the law of the land. A banjo hangs on the wall. Occasion: indoor religious service.

1635 Champney, J. Wells. "Negro Prayer Meeting." 1874. Wood engraving, mixed media. Published in "Southern Mountain Rambles," by Edward King. SCRIBNER'S MONTHLY 8 (May 1874). Reprint. THE GREAT SOUTH, [entitled "Let us address the Almighty wid pra'r"], by Edward King, 520. Hartford, CT: American Publishing Company, 1875. "Studies in the South," by Joseph E. Roy. AMERICAN MISSIONARY (MAGAZINE), n. s. 36 (October 1882).

Scene shows 8 men and women kneeling outside the door of a praise cabin, and an indeterminate number of worshippers inside the cabin, visible through the open doorway. Most of those inside are kneeling in prayer, but one man stands with both arms lifted upwards and mouth open wide. Another stands outside the door, with his right hand on the lintel, observing the scene. Occasion: indoor/outdoor religious service.

1636 _____. "The Exhorter." [1883]. Pen and ink. Published in "Swept Away, Down the Mississippi, Chapter V," by Edward S. Ellis. ST. NICHOLAS: AN ILLUSTRATED MAGAZINE FOR BOYS AND GIRLS 10 (June 1883).

Bust portrait of an elderly black preacher. Occasion: religious portraiture.

1637 "Dar, now! I had a thought." [1880]. Wood engraving. Published in "Inside Southern Cabins. Georgia---II." HARPER'S WEEKLY 24 (November 1880).

Scene shows an elderly preacher standing before a table, on which there are crumpled notes. Occasion: religious portraiture.

1638 Durkin, John. "A Voudoo Dance." [1887]. Wood engraving by H. Goetze. Published in HARPER'S WEEKLY 31 (June 1887). Reprint. BLACK DANCE..., by Lynne Emery, 169. Palo Alto, CA: National Press Books, 1972.

Scene shows a voodoo ceremony in New Orleans, Louisiana. The ritual trappings depicted include a statue of the Virgin Mary elevated on a makeshift altar, which holds three lighted candles, four portraits, and two small vessels. Offerings of wine, candies, sugar cubes, and fruit are on the floor. A voodoo priest dances in front of the altar while balancing a flaming plate of sugar cubes upon his head. His extended left hand touches the head of a female worshiper, who kneels before him holding a lighted candle with both hands. The 20 worshippers include black and white men and women, of whom 8 kneel in a semicircle around the dancer, holding lighted candles. Some of those present have open mouths as if they are singing. A man standing near a door in the background sings and claps his hands. There is no other accompaniment for the dancing. Occasion: indoor religious ceremony.

1639 "The Ebony Bridal--Wedding Ceremony in the Cabin." [1871]. Wood engraving. Published in "The Ebony Bridal," by Ella B. Washington. FRANK LESLIE'S ILLUSTRATED NEWSPAPER 32 (August 1871).

Scene shows an indeterminate number of persons gathered in a large cabin for a wedding ceremony. Bride and groom stand before the minister, surrounded by bridesmaids and guests, which include men, women, and children. In the foreground are 2 musicians sitting on low benches: one holds a cello; the other tucks his straight trumpet under his arm. Occasion: religious ceremony.

1640 Eytinge, Solomon, Jr. "A Negro Camp-Meeting in the South." [1872]. Wood engraving.

Published in HARPER'S WEEKLY 16 (August 1872).

Scene depicts a religious gathering in a wooded area. In the foreground are 7 men, 5 women, and 4 children, some of whom are praying aloud with upstretched arms, others clasping their hands, 2 reading from the Bible (?), and 1 woman in a prostrate position. In the middle ground of the picture, a preacher or exhorter, standing in a makeshift pulpit, addresses an assembly of worshippers. Tents and an indeterminate number of shadowy figures are visible in the background. Occasion: outdoor religious service.

1641 "Father Perry--80 Years Old." [1884]. Wood engraving. Published in TUSKEGEE NORMAL AND INDUSTRIAL SCHOOL, FOR TRAINING OF COLORED TEACHERS AT TUSKEGEE, ALABAMA: ITS STORY AND ITS SONGS, edited by Helen W. Ludlow, 32. Hampton, VA: Normal School Steam Press, 1884.

Full-length portrait of an ex-slave preacher from Tuskegee, Alabama. Occasion: religious portraiture.

1642 Frost, Arthur Burdett. "A Negro Funeral in Virginia." [1880]. Wood engraving. Published in HARPER'S WEEKLY 24 (February 1880). Reprint. AMERICA REVISITED, by George Augustus Sala, 1:240. London: Vizetelly & Company, 1883. THE MUSIC OF BLACK AMERICANS: A HISTORY, by Eileen Southern, 154. 2d. ed. New York: W. W. Norton, 1983.

Scene shows a plantation funeral cortege. The deceased (in a wooden coffin) lies in an open wagon drawn by a horse. The mourners include the driver, 2 grave diggers, 2 women, 4 men, and a child. All walk slowly alongside or behind the wagon, with the grave diggers in the lead. Occasion: outdoor religious ceremony.

1643 ____. "He p'int at me." [1898]. Mixed media. Published in "The Second Wooing of Salina Sue," by Ruth M. Stuart. HARPER'S NEW MONTHLY MAGAZINE 98 (December 1898).

Portrait of a minister preaching from his pulpit. One hand is lifted, pointing at someone beyond the confines of the picture. Occasion: indoor religious service.

1644 Fuller, George. "Negro Funeral." 1881. Oil on canvas. Boston, Museum of Fine Arts. Bequest of Anna Perkins Rogers. Reproduced in Exhibition Catalogue: THE PORTRAYAL OF THE NEGRO IN AMERICAN PAINTING, by Sidney Kaplan, no. 59. Brunswick, ME: Bowdoin College Museum of Art, 1964.

The artist, a native of Deerfield, Massachusetts, depicts an Alabama funeral at sunset. Silhouetted on a bleak rise of land, the distant mourners gather around the speaker, whose arms are upraised. A woman bends over the coffin as a man adjusts it. There is an indeterminate number of mourners, some with heads bowed, some with arms upraised, some kneeling. Occasion: outdoor religious ceremony.

1645 "Gospel Singer." Figural vessel, red ware. Late 19th century. New York City, John Gordon Gallery. Photograph published in Exhibition Catalogue: THE AFRO-AMERICAN TRADITION IN DECORATIVE ARTS, by John Michael Vlach, 93. Cleveland: the Cleveland Museum of Art, 1978.

Ceramic jug, thirteen inches high, in the shape of a torso figure, is thought to have been a cemetery decoration in eastern Alabama. Has the image of a singer, with arms folded over his stomach and mouth open in song. Occasion: religious imagery.

1646 Helmick, Howard. "The Burial of a Family Servant." [1894]. Wood engraving by C. W. Chadwick. Published in "Old Maryland Homes and Ways," by John Williamson Palmer. CENTURY MAGAZINE 49 (December 1894).

Outdoor winter scene shows a white preacher reading from the Bible to a group of 8 or more men, women, and children gathered around an open grave. Occasion: outdoor religious ceremony.

1647 ____. "The Broomstick Wedding." [1897]. Pen and ink drawing. Published in THE STORY OF MY LIFE, by Mary A. Livermore, 257. Hartford, CT: A. D. Worthington and Company, 1897.

Depiction of a group of 8-10 persons gathered around the bridal couple in a cabin room. A man and woman hold a broom about two feet above the floor, and an exhorter instructs the couple how and when to jump over the broomstick. Occasion: indoor religious ceremony.

1648 ____. "Uncle Aaron, the Preacher." [1897]. Pen and ink. Published in THE STORY OF MY LIFE, by Mary A. Livermore, 254. Hartford, CT: A. D. Worthington and Company, 1897.

A torso portrait in profile of an elderly, bespectacled preacher, who is shown seated with a cane in hand. Occasion: religious portraiture.

1649 ____. "Uncle Aaron's Advice from the Pulpit." [1897]. Pen and ink. Published in THE STORY OF MY LIFE, by Mary A. Livermore, 255. Hartford, CT: A. D. Worthington and Company, 1897.

Caption: "Martin, quit youah stealing." Scene shows a service in progress in a praise cabin. The preacher leans forward on his rudely constructed altar and points an accusing finger at a young man seated in the congregation, who turns away. The other 8 persons present (women, men, and children) look at him or stare stolidly ahead. Occasion: indoor religious service.

1650 Homer, Winslow. "Sunday Morning in Virginia." 1877. Oil on canvas. Cincinnati (Ohio) Art Museum. Reproduced in WINSLOW HOMER, A RETROSPECTIVE EXHIBITION, no. 37. Boston: Museum of Fine Arts, [1959].

The Boston-born painter depicts a woman reading the Bible to 3 children in a cold, bare, cabin room. She points to the words with her finger, and the older boy follows her hand. The 5th person in the picture, an old woman, pays no attention to the others. Occasion: indoor religious experience.

1651 Hovenden, Thomas. "Sunday Morning." 1881. Oil on canvas. San Francisco, California, the Fine Arts Museums of San Francisco. Reproduced in THE PAINTERS' AMERICA; RURAL AND URBAN LIFE, 1810-1910, by Patricia Hills, 81. New York: Praeger Publishers, 1974.

Scene shows an elderly couple in the bedroom-sitting room of a cabin, perhaps making the necessary preparations for going to church later. The man, standing, is about to shave; his wife, seated, is mending a sock. On the wall hangs a hunting horn, the kind used for calling plantation workers to assemble for one reason or another. Occasion: indoor religious experience.

1652 "In a Negro Church." Wood engraving. [1883]. Published in AMERICA REVISITED, by George Augustus Sala, 1:126. London: Vizetelly & Company, 1883.

Scene shows a religious service in progress in a large church of Baltimore, Maryland. Two men are in the pulpit, one seated and the other standing with mouth open as if singing from a book he holds in his right hand. The congregation includes more than 30 men, women, and children, most with open mouths as if singing, some holding open hymnals (?). Occasion: indoor religious service.

1653 Kappes, Alfred. "The Funeral." [1886]. Wood engraving. Published in "The Funeral," by Will Carleton. HARPER'S WEEKLY 30 (August 1886). Reprint. MORIAH'S MOURNING, by Ruth M. Stuart, 134. New York: Harper & Brothers, 1898.

Scene shows the pulpit section of a well-appointed church in Savannah, Georgia, with the preacher presiding over the funeral of a young boy. The casket rests on a stand in front of the altar. Only 5 grieving family members and friends of the deceased are included in the picture. Occasion: indoor religious ceremony.

1654 Kemble, Edward Windsor. "The Voodoo Dance." 1885. Pen and ink. Published in "Creole Slave Songs," by George W. Cable. CENTURY MAGAZINE 31 (April 1886). Reprint. THE MUSIC OF BLACK AMERICANS: A HISTORY, by Eileen Southern, 139. 2d. ed. New York: W. W. Norton, 1983. BLACK DANCE ..., by Lynne Emery, 59. Palo Alto, CA: National Press Books, 1972.

Scene shows a large cabin room filled with 15 or more persons, male and female--dancers, musicians, and other worshippers. Three men dance in the center of the room, moving around a square cloth on the floor that has a lighted candle at each corner. They wave their arms wildly and move with short shuffle steps. Against the back wall are 3 musicians, seated on their knees. Two drummers beat with their hands on small, skin drums, which are placed between their legs. The other musician bows a lute-like instrument with a very long neck. The other participants sit on the floor or stand near the walls, except for 1 woman (the voodoo queen?) who sits in a chair on a platform at the right. All except the queen have wide-open mouths as if singing. Occasion: indoor religious ceremony.

1655 _____. "The Preacher." 1886. Pencil. "Mrs. Stowe's Uncle Tom at Home in Kentucky," by James Lane Allen. CENTURY MAGAZINE 34 (October 1887). Reprint. THE BLUE-GRASS REGION OF KENTUCKY AND OTHER ARTICLES, by James L. Allen, 81. New York: Harper & Brothers, 1892.

Full-length portrait of a clergyman, shown knocking at the door of a log cabin, who is making a pastoral visit to a member of his congregation. Occasion: outdoor religious experience.

1656 _____. "Round, Round They Go." 1895. Crayon. Published in "A Black Settlement," by Martha McCulloch-Williams. HARPER'S NEW MONTHLY MAGAZINE 93 (October 1896). Reprint (with title "Salvation's Kyar Is Moving") in MORIAH'S MOURNING AND OTHER HALF-HOUR SKETCHES, by Ruth McEnery Stuart, 148. New York: Harper & Brothers, 1898.

Depiction of the Dead March, a holy dance similar to the shout, performed by an indeterminate number of men and women, who sing and shuffle about in a circle. Occasion: indoor religious service.

1657 Knaffl & Brothers. "The Blackville Gallery.--No. III--A Blackville Wedding." [1897]. Photograph. Published in LESLIE'S ILLUSTRATED WEEKLY 87 (January 1898).

Caricatural depiction of a wedding ceremony in progress. The bride and a rather elderly groom stand before the minister, who, with open book in his right hand and his left hand raised, asks, "Honey, does yo' lub yo' man." The attendants include a couple, both of whom hold flowers, and a young girl holding the bridal train. Occasion: indoor religious ceremony.

1658 Moser, James Henry. "Read er chapter fer de ederfurkashun of de 'sembled sinners." [1882]. Wood engraving. Published in

BRIGHT DAYS ON THE OLD PLANTATION, by Mary Ross Banks, 168. Boston: Lee and Shepard Publishers, 1882.

Caricatural depiction of a prayer meeting in progress in a praise cabin, which is lighted by a roaring fire in the fireplace. The participants include 5 men, 7 women, and 3 children; some sitting on rude benches, others standing. Some have open mouths as if singing. Occasion: indoor religious service.

1659 [Nast, Thomas]. "Family Worship on a Plantation in South Carolina." [1863]. Wood engraving by Mason Jackson. Published in "Slaves at Worship on a Plantation in South Carolina." THE ILLUSTRATED LONDON NEWS 43 (December 1863). Reprint. FROM SLAVERY TO FREEDOM: A HISTORY OF THE NEGRO AMERICAN, by John Hope Franklin, 152. 4th ed. New York: Alfred A. Knopf, 1974.

Scene shows a religious service in progress in a praise cabin on a plantation of Port Royal, South Carolina. Standing on a platform, on which a table serves as altar, the preacher lifts his left hand in the air and points with his right hand to the place in the Bible on which his sermon is based. His small congregation includes 11 men, 6 women, and 1 boy, and as well, the white slaveholder, his wife, and two children. Occasion: indoor religious service.

1660 _____. "What the Colored Race Have to Be Thankful For." [1886]. Pen and ink? Published in HARPER'S WEEKLY 30 (November 1886).

Full-length portrait of a well-dressed clergyman delivering a sermon in a large, well-appointed church. Standing back a bit from the altar, he raises his eyes upwards and stretches out his hand. In the background, a large number of shadowy figures are visible in a balcony. Occasion: religious portraiture.

1661 Newell, Peter. "An Unfortunate Misunderstanding." [1886]. Pen and ink. Published in HARPER'S WEEKLY 30 (December 1886).

Torso portrait of a preacher standing at his altar, delivering a sermon. Occasion: religious portraiture.

1662 Pettie, John, and Dalziel. "Kalampin, the Negro." [1863]. Pen and ink? Published in "Kalampin," by Countess de Gasparin. GOOD WORDS 4 (1863).

Depiction of an elderly man sitting by the bedside of a sick little girl, to whom he is reading the Bible. He points to each word with his left-hand finger and guides her finger to each word with his right hand. Occasion: indoor religious experience.

1663 Phillips, J. Campbell. "The Gospel." 1899. Pen and ink. Published in PLANTATION SKETCHES (artist's portfolio). New York: R. H. Russell, 1899.

Scene shows the interior of a humble meeting place, where 9 worshippers, dressed in their Sunday attire, are assembled for a religious service. Three persons in the foreground (man, woman, young girl), sitting on a bench before the pulpit, have their backs to the viewer; 3 others (elderly man, young man, girl), also sitting on a bench, present side profiles to the viewer. In the background the preacher stands before his lectern, on which there is an open Bible, facing the viewer directly. Obviously speaking in stentorian tones, he points a finger at the worshippers. Two deacons (?) sitting behind him in the pulpit listen intently, as do apparently the others, except for the elderly man, who reads his Bible. Occasion: indoor religious service.

1664 Potthast, Edward. "Brother Lazarus, des er minute fo' yer fling dat line." [1899]. Ink wash. Published in CENTURY MAGAZINE 58 (July 1899). Collection of Mr. and Mrs. Alan Goffman (as a drawing). Reprint. TWO HUNDRED YEARS OF AMERICAN ILLUSTRATION, by Henry C. Pitz, 113. New York: Random House, 1977.

Scene depicts a religious service in progress in a rather shabby church auditorium. The minister, standing beside the altar with watch in hand, calls time on a member who has been addressing the congregation, to the great amusement of some. Participants include 17 or more men and women, most of them seated on long benches, three standing against a side wall. Occasion: indoor religious service.

1665 Powers, Harriet. Pictorial Bible Quilt [untitled]. c.1886. Cotton. Washington, D.C., The National Museum of History and Technology, Smithsonian Institution. Photograph published in Exhibition Catalogue: THE AFRO-AMERICAN TRADITION IN DECORATIVE ARTS, by John Michael Vlach, 46. Cleveland: The Cleveland Museum of Art, 1978.

Quilt consisting of eleven panels or squares includes ten that represent Biblical scenes: two of Adam and Eve; two of Cain and Abel; one each about Jacob's dream, the Crucifixion, Judas, the baptism of Christ, the Last Supper, and the Holy Family. Occasion: artifact.

1666 _____. Pictorial Quilt. c.1895-1898. Cotton. Boston, Museum of Fine Arts, M. and M. Karolik Collection. Photograph published in Exhibition Catalogue: THE AFRO-AMERICAN TRADITION IN DECORATIVE ARTS, by John Michael Vlach, 47. Cleveland: Cleveland Museum of Art, 1978.

Quilt consisting of fifteen panels or squares includes eleven that represent Biblical scenes, and four that represent historical or current events. Occasion: artifact.

1667 "Preacher Man." Figural vessel, red ware. Late 19th century. New York City, John Gordon Gallery. Photograph published in Exhibition Catalogue: THE AFRO-AMERICAN TRADITION IN DECORATIVE ARTS. Exhibition catalogue, by John Michael Vlach, 93. Cleveland: the Cleveland Museum of Art, 1978.

Ceramic jug in the shape of a torso figure of a preacher. More than sixteen inches high, it is thought to have been a cemetery decoration in Eastern Alabama. The hands are folded across the chest, and the mouth is open as if he is speaking. Occasion: artifact.

1668 Reinhart, Charles Stanley. "A Colored Preacher." 1889. Crayon. Published in HARPER'S WEEKLY 34 (November 1890).

Torso portrait of an elderly preacher depicts him reading from a psalter as he stands in the pulpit. A large Bible lies open on the altar, resting on a large velvet cushion. Occasion: religious portraiture.

1669 Remington, Frederic; A. J. Gustin; William Allen Rogers; Willard Poinsette Snyder. "Negro Prayer-Meeting." [1886]. Wood engraving, based on sketches by Remington and Gustin. Published in HARPER'S WEEKLY 30 (September 1886).

Caricatural depiction of a nocturnal prayer-meeting in progress in an open field following the earthquake in Charleston, South Carolina, 31 August 1886. The 12 or more worshippers center their attention on the preacher, who stands in the center near a campfire clapping his hands and vigorously conducting the singing of hymns. Most of the men and women, some kneeling, some standing, sing and clap hands. Two lie prostrate on the ground. Occasion: outdoor religious service.

1670 "Rev. Ezekiel Moses." [1897]. Pen and ink. Published in "The Social Life of the Southern Negro," by W. T. Hewetson. THE CHAUTAUQUAN 26 (December 1897).

Depiction of a country preacher riding a mule on his way to his rural church, which appears in the background. Occasion: outdoor religious portraiture.

1671 "Rev. H. M. Turner." [1863]. Wood engraving. Published in HARPER'S WEEKLY 7 (December 1863).

Torso portrait of the Rev. Henry McNeal Turner, the first black chaplain to be appointed to Union troops (later a bishop of the A. M. E. church): the First U. S. Colored Regiment. Pastor of Israel Bethel Church in Washington, D. C. Occasion: religious portraiture.

1672 "Rev. John Jasper." [1887]. Engraving. Published in MEN OF MARK, by William J. Simmons, 1065. Cleveland, OH: George M. Rewell & Company, 1887. Other portraits of the Rev. Jasper are in "De Sun Do Move," by Daisy Fitzhugh. LESLIE'S ILLUSTRATED MAGAZINE 73 (January 1892). "The Life and Work of the Rev. John Jasper," by P. Thomas Stanford. THE COLORED AMERICAN MAGAZINE (July 1901).

Bust portrait of the Rev. John Jasper, celebrated antebellum preacher and pastor of Sixth Mt. Zion Baptist (Colored) Church of Richmond, Virginia. Occasion: religious portraiture.

1673 "Rev. R. D. S." [1891]. Wood engraving. Published in SEVEN YEARS AMONG THE FREEDMEN, by Maria Waterbury, 48. 2d ed. Chicago: T. B. Arnold, 1891.

Full-length portrait of a southern black preacher in a formal pose. Occasion: Religious portraiture.

1674 Rogers, William Allen. The Prayer-Meeting [untitled]. [1890]. Wood engraving. Published in CITY LEGENDS, by Will Carleton, 131. New York: Harper & Brothers, 1890.

Illustration has the caption: "But there sudden[ly] rose among them one of earth's untutored kings." Night scene shows an outdoor prayer meeting being held after the earthquake in Charleston, South Carolina (August 1886), in front of the wreckage of a building. A preacher, praying aloud with outstretched hand, stands on a wooden box above the gathering of 8 or more men and women, who kneel in agonized prayer about him. One woman prostrates herself at his feet, and some have open mouths as if also praying aloud. Occasion: outdoor religious service.

1675 Sheppard, William Ludlow. "Seeking." [1870]. Wood engraving by John Filmer. Published in "Southern Sketches---IV." APPLETON'S JOURNAL OF POPULAR LITERATURE, SCIENCE, AND ART 4 (August 1870).

Caricatural depiction of a man deeply engrossed in thought as a part of the religious experience called "seeking." He sits outdoors on a wooden bench, his head held between his hands and a with a gloomy expression on his face. Occasion: outdoor religious experience.

1676 _____. "The Sunny South.---A Negro Revival Meeting---A Seeker 'Getting Religion'." [1873]. Wood engraving. Published in "Religion in the South. A Negro Revival in Virginia," by A. L. Bassett Ingle. FRANK LESLIE'S ILLUSTRATED NEWSPAPER 36 (August 1873).

Scene shows a revival meeting in progress in a praise cabin, involving 17 men and women and 2 children. One woman, who apparently is "possessed" by the Holy Spirit, lies unconscious on the floor; the minister bends over her, touching her on the forearm. Another woman, with both hands lifted over her head, is shouting. Others are singing, some clapping hands as they sing. Occasion: indoor religious service.

1677 _____. "A Baptizing." Wood engraving. Published in "An Old Landmark." HARPER'S WEEKLY 18 (June 1874).

Scene shows a ceremony involving baptismal rites in the First African Church of Richmond, Virginia. The church is filled to overflowing with an indeterminate number of worshipers, who not only sit in the pews but also stand in the aisles. In the center of the picture, the minister has just baptized a woman in the church's pool, which is situated in the front of the podium. At the left, another woman, awaiting baptism, stands at the edge of the pool, assisted by a church deacon. At the right, 2 deacons assist a woman, who has been baptized and is wrapped in a sheet, ascend the 3 steps that lead from the pool to the floor of the sanctuary. Other candidates are lined up awaiting their turns. Occasion: indoor religious ceremony.

1678 _____. "Interior of the Church from the Western Wing." [1874]. Mixed media. Published in "An Old Landmark." HARPER'S WEEKLY 18 (June 1874).

Scene shows a religious service in progress at the First African Church of Richmond, Virginia; the minister stands at the altar, preaching with hand outstretched to the congregation. The large commodious church is filled to overflowing with an indeterminate number of persons sitting in pews on the main floor of the sanctuary and in the two balconies. Occasion: indoor religious service.

1679 _____. "The Rev. James Holmes." [1874]. Wood engraving. Published in "An Old Landmark," HARPER'S WEEKLY 18 (June 1874).

Bust portrait of the Rev. James Holmes, pastor of the First African Church of Richmond, Virginia. Occasion: religious portraiture.

1680 _____. "An Old-Time Midnight Slave Funeral." [1881]. Wood engraving by Schults. Published in IN THE BRUSH..., by Hamilton W. Pierson, 284. New York: D. Appleton & Company, 1881. Reprint. AMERICAN MISSIONARY (MAGAZINE) n.s. 36 (April 1882).

Night scene shows a group of 15-20 or more persons gathered around an open grave in the woods, many of them holding torches lifted high over their heads. From the rear men carrying the wooden coffin move toward the grave. Some of those present appear to be singing. Occasion: outdoor religious ceremony.

1681 _____. "Brotherly Encouragement." [1897]. Pen and ink. Published in THE STORY OF MY LIFE by Mary A. Livermore, 347. Hartford, CT: A. D. Worthington and Company, 1897.

Depiction of a religious service in a cabin shows 7 persons seated on benches near the improvised pulpit. The exhorter, with one arm lifted high, leans on the small table that serves as an altar, addressing the group with great animation. But the group refuses to accept his message; 3 men try to "talk him down," waving their arms about and interjecting comments with obviously loud voices. Occasion: indoor religious service.

1682 "Shout, Sisters." [1880]. Pen and ink. Published in "Inside Southern Cabins. Georgia.---II." HARPER'S WEEKLY 24 (November 1880).

Scene shows a religious service underway in a praise cabin. In the foreground, 4 or more women sit, kneel, or lie prostrate in front of the pulpit, obviously in a state of "possession." The minister, leaning far over the pulpit to talk to them (or to sing?), reaches toward them with both arms; 2 women stand over them, fanning the air with their hands. In the background an indeterminate number of worshippers sing, some with uplifted arms. Occasion: indoor religious service.

1683 "Southern Types--Going to Church." [1874]. Mixed media. Published in THE SOUTHERN STATES OF NORTH AMERICA..., by Edward King, 780. London: Blackie & Son, 1875.

Illustration depicts an elderly couple on the way to an evening religious service service; the man carries a brightly shining lantern to clear their path through the fields. In the backgrond an indeterminate number of individuals are shown entering the church. Occasion: outdoor religious activity.

1684 Strother, David Hunter [Porte Crayon, pseud.], "The Negro Preacher." [1874]. Wood engraving. Published in "On Negro Schools," by David Strother. HARPER'S NEW MONTHLY MAGAZINE 49 (September 1874). Reprints. NORD-AMERIKA: SEINE STAEDTE UND NATURWUNDER, by Ernest V. Hesse-Wartegg, 4:45 (entitled "Eine Neger-Kirche"). Leipzig: G. Weigel, 1879-80. OTHER DAYS..., by James W. Leigh, 154. London: T. Fisher Unwin, 1921.

Caricatural depiction of a worship service in a well-appointed church shows the minister delivering his sermon, leaning over the pulpit with one arm stretched out to the congregation. The sanctuary is partially full, with 12 or more men, women, and children in the foreground and an indeterminate number in the background. A woman in the first pew may be saying "Amen." Occasion: indoor religious service.

1685 Tanner, Henry Ossawa. "The Thankful Poor."

1894. Oil on canvas. Collection of Dr. and Mrs. William H. Crosby, Jr., Greenfield, Massachusetts. Reproduced in THE IMAGE OF THE INDIAN AND THE BLACK MAN IN AMERICAN ART, 1590-1900, by Elwood Parry, 168. New York: George Braziller, 1974. Reprint. EBONY PICTORIAL HISTORY OF BLACK AMERICA, by the EBONY Editors, 2:75. Chicago: Johnson Publishing Company, 1971.

Afro-American painter Tanner depicts an old man and a young girl seated at the dinner table, both with bowed heads for the blessing being given by the man. Occasion: indoor religious experience.

1686 "Uncle Harvey." [1891]. Wood engraving. Published in SEVEN YEARS AMONG THE FREEDMEN, by Maria Waterbury, 62. 2d ed. Chicago: T. B. Arnold, 1891.

Bust portrait of an ante-bellum slave preacher. Occasion: religious portraiture.

1687 "The Voudou Meeting in the Old Brick-Yard." [1882]. Wood engraving. Published in METROPOLITAN LIFE UNVEILED..., by James W. Buel, 523. St. Louis: Historical Publishing Company, 1882.

Caricatural representation of an outdoor night scene shows a blazing fire at the right in the background and an indeterminate number of voodoo dancers, who kick vigorously and wave their arms about wildly. Some dance on their hands, and a few writhe on the ground. At the top of the illustration a man beats on a small drum with a stick, and in the top center, another strums a banjo. Occasion: outdoor religious ceremony.

1688 Waud, Alfred R. "Prayer-meeting." [1867]. Wood engraving. Published in "Scenes on a Cotton Plantation." HARPER'S WEEKLY 11 (February 1867).

One in a series of thirteen sketches of life on a cotton plantation in Clarke County, Alabama, published in HARPER'S, of which three relate to music (see also nos. 1619, 1620). Scene shows a rather large room of rude construction (a praise cabin?), in which 30 or more men, women, and children listen to a preacher's sermon. He stands beside the pulpit with arms outstretched to the congregation. Occasion: indoor religious service.

1689 "The Wedding, Long Ago." [1893]. Pen and ink. Published in A GOLDEN WEDDING AND OTHER TALES, by Ruth McEnery Stuart, 10. New York: Harper & Brothers, 1893.

Depiction of a wedding shows the bridal couple and party in a small cabin room, standing before a white minister. The bride wears a white gown and a bridal wreath of orange blossoms. The guests include two men, seated to the left of the couple, and five women, seated to the right. Occasion: indoor religious ceremony.

THE SONG

1690 "The Band of Hampton Singers Who 'Sang Up' Virginia Hall." [1874]. Photograph. Published in "Singing Up Virginia Hall," by Sallie Davis Thoroughgood, 127. SOUTHERN WORKMAN 57 (March 1928).

Photograph of the Hampton Institute Student Singers c.1874. The group portrait includes 11 men and 7 women. Occasion: group portraiture.

1691 "Beans and Potatoes." [1880]. Mixed media. Published in "Inside Southern Cabins III. -- Charleston, South Carolina." HARPER'S WEEKLY 34 (November 1880). Reprint. SOLOMON CROWS' CHRISTMAS POCKETS AND OTHER TALES by Ruth McEnery Stuart, 94. New York: Harper & Brothers, 1897.

Depiction of a street peddler with a huge basket on her head, shown singing about her wares on a street in Charleston, South Carolina. Occasion: outdoor work activity involving song.

1692 Becker, Joseph. "Song of the Oystermen." [1880]. Wood engraving. Published in FRANK LESLIE'S ILLUSTRATED NEWSPAPER 51 (October 1880).

Sub-caption: "Maryland.---'In de Mornin' by de Bright Light.'---Negro Oystermen of Annapolis on Their Way to the Fishing-Ground in Chesapeake Bay." Scene shows 5 men relaxing in a dilapidated sailboat at sea, one playing the banjo and two others joining him in song. The young banjoist sits on the gunwale. One singer stands leaning against the boom, one lolls against the rudder. Occasion: outdoor work activity involving music.

1693 Becker, Joseph, and William Ludlow Sheppard. "Jacksonville, Fla.---Professors of 'Chin-Music' Displaying Their Accomplishments in Front of the Market." [1871]. Wood engraving. Published in FRANK LESLIE'S ILLUSTRATED NEWSPAPER 32 (August 1871).

Scene shows a marketplace filled with an indeterminate number of market folk in the background. In the foreground 2 boys perform in the middle of a semicircle formed by an admiring group of 7 men (black and white), 1 woman, and 2 children. They stand face to face, feet apart and swaying, holding up both hands on either side of their cheeks, puffed out with air, in preparation for striking their cheeks to make "chin-music." Occasion: outdoor entertainment.

1694 Buchser, Frank. "The Song of Mary Blaine." 1870-71. Oil on canvas. Solothurn, Switzerland, Kunstmuseum. Reproduced in FRANK BUCHSERS AMERIKANISCHE SENDUNG, 1866-1871, by H. Luedeke, 91. Basel: Holbein Verlag,

1941. "Frank Buchser---A Forgotten Chapter of American Art," by H. Luedeke, 194. ART IN AMERICA 35 (July 1947).

The title of the painting derives from an American ballad about a slave's tragic love story. The scene shows a back yard of a frame house, with a cornfield in the background. A young man is singing a ballad with serious expression on his face, accompanying himself on a banjo. He is surrounded by 7 listeners---4 girls, 2 boys, and a child---who lie or sit on the ground around him. One of the boys, perched on a barrel, plays a mouth organ. All give the singer rapt attention except a tot lying on the ground in the foreground of the scene. Occasion: outdoor entertainment.

1695 Clinedinst, Benjamin West. "A Southern Oyster Peddler." [1889]. Wood engraving. Published in HARPER'S WEEKLY 33 (March 1889). Reprint. THE MUSIC OF BLACK AMERICANS: A HISTORY, by Eileen Southern, 125. 2d. ed. New York: W. W. Norton, 1983.

Full-length portrait of a street crier in Baltimore, Maryland, carrying two pails of oysters. Others in the picture include an elderly woman standing on a door stoop and 3 white spectators. None pays attention to the peddler. Occasion: outdoor work activity involving song.

1696 "Clothes Poles." [1892]. Wood engraving. Published in "On the Busy Street...," by Nelson Ayers. DAILY PICAYUNE 56 (August 1892).

Full-length portrait of a street vendor of old clothes, who sings cries in selling his wares in New Orleans. Occasion: outdoor work activity involving song.

1697 Durkin, John. "The Leading Soprano in a Tobacco Factory." [1886]. Mixed media. Published in "Scenes in Virginia." HARPER'S WEEKLY 31 (January 1887).

One of eight sketches showing tobacco factory workers, this one depicts a woman sitting at a table, who sings as she rolls the tobacco. Occasion: indoor work activity involving song.

1698 Eytinge, Solomon, Jr. "Mrs. Smallbreed's Kettledrum--A Little Black Tea at Blackville." [1879]. Wood engraving. HARPER'S WEEKLY MAGAZINE 23 (August 1879).

Caricatural depiction of a tea party with a gathering of 10-12 men and women and 1 child in a large room of a humble house. A female singer, accompanying herself on a guitar, offers entertainment to the mostly inattentive guests. Occasion: indoor entertainment.

1699 _____. "A Blackville Serenade." [1883]. Wood engraving. Published in HARPER'S WEEKLY 27 (June 1883).

Caricatural parody on the Romeo and Juliet theme depicts a young man singing a serenade to his sweetheart beneath her window on a moonlight night, accompanying himself on a banjo. The girl leans out an upstairs window; her father emerges from the house carrying a stick. Occasion: outdoor domestic music.

1700 "The Fisk Jubilee Singers." [1875]. Photograph. Published in THE STORY OF THE JUBILEE SINGERS, WITH THEIR SONGS, by J. B. T. Marsh, frontispiece. 5th ed. London: Hodder & Stoughton, 1876. Reprint. THE MUSIC OF BLACK AMERICANS: A HISTORY, by Eileen Southern, 225. 2d ed. New York: W. W. Norton, 1983.

Group photograph of the original Fisk Jubilee Singers c.1875: 3 male students and 5 women, one of whom sits at a reed organ (melodeon?). A caption gives the name of each singer. Beginning in 1876 group photographs of the Singers appear regularly in the editions of their songs. Over the years, the photographs reflect the changing membership of the group, as the original members drop out and others join the group to replace them. Occasion: indoor group portraiture.

1701 The Fisk Jubilee Singers [untitled]. [1892]. Photograph. Published in THE STORY OF THE JUBILEE SINGERS....WITH SUPPLEMENT ...BY F[REDERICK] J. LOUDIN, by J. B. T. Marsh. Cleveland: Cleveland Printing and Publishing Company, 1892.

Group photograph of the reorganized Jubilee Singers (c.1892) under the direction of Frederick J. Loudin. The troupe consisted of 6 women and 4 men at the time the photograph was made. Occasion: indoor group portraiture.

1702 Frost, Arthur Burdett. "Hieronymus Sings a Soothing Ditty." [1880]. Mixed media. Published in "Hieronymus Pop and the Baby." HARPER'S NEW MONTHLY MAGAZINE 61 (June 1880).

Scene shows a young boy, holding a baby in his arms, seated on a bench in a cabin. His head is thrown back as he sings what is obviously a lively song, and his feet are lifted in the movement of stomping on the floor. Occasion: indoor domestic music.

1703 Hampton Institute Camera Club. "The Hunting Song/Rural South." [1899]. Photograph. Published in POEMS OF CABIN AND FIELD, by Paul Laurence Dunbar, 32. New York: Dodd, Mead, and Company, 1899.

Scene depicts 4 hunters and a dog standing in a clump of tree at the edge of an open field. One man sings; the other hunters look up a tree as if seeking an animal that has run up the tree. Occasion: outdoor recreation.

1704 Havel, Edmund. "Praise Him in Song." 1873.

Oil on canvas. Nashville, Tennessee, Fisk University Jubilee Hall, Appleton Room. Reproduced in BLACK MAGIC..., by Langston Hughes and Milton Meltzer, 126. Englewood Cliffs, NJ: Prentice-Hall, Inc., 1967. THE MUSIC OF BLACK AMERICANS: A HISTORY, by Eileen Southern, pl. 8. New York: W. W. Norton, 1971.

The Court Painter to Queen Victoria painted this huge canvas from life, without fee, during the Fisk Jubilee Singers' stay in London while on a concert tour abroad, and the canvas was sent back to Fisk. The singers (4 men, 6 young women) are arranged in picturesque positions: the women seated in graceful poses, except one who stands at the left, and the men standing in a second row behind the women. At the right front is the troupe's chaperon, Susan Gilbert, later to become Mrs. George White, wife of the troupe's director. The pianist sits beside a grand piano, her left arm draped on the keyboard. Occasion: group portraiture.

1705 "Heh is yo' Green Cawn." [1892]. Mixed media. Published, "On the Busy Street..., by Nelson Ayers. DAILY PICAYUNE 56 (August 1892).

Depiction of 2 female street criers in New Orleans, who sing as they balance their wares on the top of their heads. Occasion: outdoor work activity involving song.

1706 Helmick, Howard. "The Departing Guests." [1897]. Pen and ink. Published in THE STORY OF MY LIFE by Mary A. Livermore, 340. Hartford, CT: A. D. Worthington and Company, 1897.

Sub-caption: "Their torches were borne aloft, and their melodious voices rang out in song as they marched away." Scene shows a group of 6-8 slaves walking down a woods path, singing as they leave their hosts after enjoying a party in a cabin. Some carry torches. Occasion: outdoor recreation.

1707 _____ (?). "Plantation Slave Singers." [1897]. Pen and ink. Published in THE STORY OF MY LIFE, by Mary A. Livermore, 185. Hartford, CT: A. D. Worthington and Company, 1897.

Sub-caption of illustration: "All clapped hands in unison, until the air quivered with melody." Indeterminate number of men, women, and children clap their hands, some with hands lifted in the air, as they sing together in a group outdoors. Occasion: outdoor recreation.

1708 Kemble, Edward W. "Mammy's Churning Song." [1890]. Pen and ink. Published in "Mammy's Churning Song," by Edward A. Oldham. CENTURY MAGAZINE 40 (October 1890).

Scene shows an elderly woman, sitting on a bench in an open doorway, who is working a butter churner and singing as she works. A small white girl stands by, looking on. Occasion: outdoor work activity involving song.

1709 _____. "The Field Hands Were Singing As They Picked the Opening Cotton." [1896]. Pen and ink. Published in DADDY JAKE THE RUNAWAY, AND SHORT STORIES TOLD AFTER DARK BY "UNCLE REMUS," by Joel Chandler Harris, 18. New York: Century Company, 1896.

Scene depicts a large cotton-field. In the foreground a woman carries a huge basket of cotton bolls (?) on her right shoulder. In the background 4 men pick cotton, one bent over, the others standing erect. All appear to be singing. Occasion: work activity involving song.

1710 Knaffl & Brothers. "The Blackville Gallery---No. I---Rehearsal of the Blackville Choir." 1897. Photograph. Published in LESLIE'S ILLUSTRATED WEEKLY 75 (December 1897).

Caption concludes with 'Grandpap, Gib Us de Base!' Scene shows a small group of singers (3 men, 2 women) at a choir practice in a simple country church, led by an elderly choir director, who sings from a thick book. All sing with wide open mouths from hymnals. Others present include a girl and an older man, who is snoozing. Occasion: indoor religious experience.

1711 Mueller, Rose. "A Lullaby." [1882]. Wood engraving. Published in "Phrony Jane's Lawn Party," by Sydney Dayne. HARPER'S YOUNG PEOPLE 3 (August 1882).

Scene depicts a girl swinging vigorously in an out-door swing against a background of open fields and a brook, and cradling a white infant in her arms. She sings loudly with wide open mouth as she swings high in the air. Occasion: outdoor domestic music.

1712 "The Parting Song." [1870]. Wood engraving. Anonymous artist used figures and motifs from Alfred Waud's engraving carrying the same title (see no. 1718). Published in "Down the Mississippi," by George Nichols. HARPER'S NEW MONTHLY MAGAZINE 41 (November 1870).

Riverboat scene shows a large group of 15-20 stevedores and other workers gathered around a singer, who stands high above the others on a rather elaborately designed stool. His left arm is lifted high, as if leading a song, but his mouth is not open. Several workers are singing, some with raised arms as if beating time to their singing. Occasion: outdoor recreation.

1713 Potthast, Edward. "By the Fireplace." [1899]. Charcoal and wash. Published in "Negro Spirituals," by Marion Alexander Haskell. CENTURY MAGAZINE 58 (August 1899).

Scene shows a woman, with a baby in her arms, seated in a rocking chair near a blazing fireplace. The woman leans back and sings; a small girl lying at her feet gazes into the fire. Occasion: indoor domestic music.

1714 Schell, Francis H. "Philadelphia Street Characters." [1876]. Mixed media. Published in HARPER'S WEEKLY 20 (April 1876).

The Pennsylvania artist includes 3 black street criers in his sketches of street peddlers. The crab man hawks his wares, watched by a child. The hominy man carries baskets under both arms as he walks through the snow. The pepper pot woman holds out her pot of peppered tripe to a child, who is eating from a bowl. Occasion: outdoor work activity that includes song.

1715 "Sheppard's Jubilee Singers." 1870s. Playbill. Pen and ink. Washington, D. C., Howard University, Moorland-Spingarn Collection.

Advertisement shows bust sketches of 8 singers, 4 men and 4 women, and their leader in the center. A drawing at the bottom of the sheet depicts a work scene on the plantation. Occasion: advertisement.

1716 Sheppard, William Ludlow. "Old Hominy Man." [1884]. Pen and ink. Published in HISTORY OF PHILADELPHIA, 1609-1884, by John Thomas Scharf and Thompson Westcott, 2:930. Philadelphia: L. H. Everts & Company, 1884.

Portrait of a street vendor of hominy singing about his wares as he strides along. His left hand cups his mouth to increase his volume. Occasion: outdoor work activity involving song.

1717 ____. "The Colored Choristers." [1891]. Pen and ink. Published in "The Week of Sport in Central North Carolina." HARPER'S WEEKLY 35 (February 1891).

Scene shows a choir, composed of 12 singers and the choral director, giving an outdoor evening performance for guests of local hotels in Southern Pines, North Carolina. They all sing from hymnals with mouths open wide. Occasion: indoor entertainment.

1718 Waud, Alfred R. "Scene on a Mississippi Steamer--The Parting Song." [1867]. Wood engraving. Published in HARPER'S WEEKLY 11 (November 1867). Reprint. THE MUSIC OF BLACK AMERICANS: A HISTORY, by Eileen Southern, 147. 2d. ed. New York: W. W. Norton, 1983.

Scene shows the lower deck of a Mississippi River steamer, where 17 or more stevedores and other workers are gathered around a song leader, who directs them in singing a parting song. He stands aloft on some bales of cotton, directing with his left hand. All sing with wide-open mouths. Just below him a man holds an American flag in his hand. Spectators include 5 or more whites, who listen intently. Occasion: outdoor recreation.

THE TALE

1719 "African Jack." [1883]. Pen and ink. Published in NIGHTS WITH UNCLE REMUS, by Joel Chandler Harris, 136. 21st ed. New York: Houghton Mifflin & Company, c.1883.

Illustration for the folk tale "African Jack." Two elderly men, seated on stools, are in a cabin room in the slave quarters with a young white boy. Uncle Jack has just completed telling a tale, and Uncle Remus, holding both hands of the boy, is commenting on the tale. Occasion: indoor entertainment.

1720 Brooke, Richard Norris. "The 'Coon Hunt---Telling Stories round the Camp Fire." [1872]. Wood engraving. Published in HARPER'S WEEKLY 16 (December 1872).

The Virginia-born artist shows a night scene with 5 men and an adolescent boy seated on the ground or on logs around a camp fire. They listen raptly to a story of a middle-aged man, who uses sharp gestures as he talks. Three hunting dogs lie near the fire. Occasion: outdoor entertainment.

1721 Dalziel and Markley. "A Cross-Road Lounger." [1883]. Mixed media. Published in AMERICA REVISITED, by George Augustus Sala, 1:222. 3d. ed. London: Vizetelly & Company, 1883.

Outdoor scene shows a man telling a story to 2 entranced white couples standing near a log fence. The tale teller uses sharp gestures. Occasion: outdoor entertainment.

1722 Kemble, Edward W. "The Story-Teller." [1892]. Pen and ink. Published in "Middle Georgia Rural Life," by Richard M. Johnston. CENTURY MAGAZINE 43 (March 1892).

Scene depicts an old man telling a tale, with expansive gestures, to a small white boy who listens attentively. Both are seated on benches just outside the door of a cabin. Occasion: outdoor entertainment.

1723 ____. "Poor Old Sue Tells Her Story." [1896]. Pen and ink. Published in DADDY JAKE THE RUNAWAY, AND SHORT STORIES TOLD AFTER DARK BY "UNCLE REMUS," by Joel Chandler Harris, 62. New York: The Century Company, 1896.

Scene depicts an elderly woman, seated on the ground, telling a story about her life experiences to 2 white children. Her knees are pulled up to her chest, and one hand waves in the air. The girl sits on the ground, listening intently, as does also the boy, who lies on his side with his hand under his chin. Occasion: outdoor entertainment.

1724 _____. "In the Cave." 1884. Pen and ink. Published in THE ADVENTURES OF HUCKLEBERRY FINN (TOM SAWYER'S COMRADE), by Mark Twain, 66. New York: Charles L. Webster & Company, 1891.

Scene depicts Jim telling tales to Huck inside the cave. Jim sits cross-legged, with wide eyes and mouth and extended hand, palm up, thus suggesting that he is telling a ghost story. Huck, lying on the ground in front of the narrator, listens with open mouth and rapt expression. Occasion: outdoor entertainment.

1725 Kline, William F. The Tale-teller [untitled]. [1894]. Gouache? Published in "A Real Uncle Remus Story." ST. NICHOLAS: AN ILLUSTRATED MAGAZINE FOR BOYS AND GIRLS 21 (July 1894).

Scene depicts an elderly man telling a folk tale to 6 white children, boys and girls. The children listen intently, watching the gestures of the old man. A dog lies at his feet. Occasion: indoor entertainment.

1726 Moser, James H. "Yon go dat po' Grimshaw gang, movin' ergin." 1881. Wood engraving. Published in BRIGHT DAYS ON THE OLD PLANTATION, by Mary Ross Banks, 68. Boston: Lee and Shepard, Publishers, 1882.

Depiction of a kitchen scene shows a woman polishing silver and telling a tale to a young white girl as she works. Occasion: indoor entertainment.

COLLECTIONS OF TALES AND SONGS: 1863–1899

THE TALE

1727 Christensen, Abigail M. AFRO-AMERICAN FOLK LORE. TOLD ROUND CABIN FIRES ON THE SEA ISLANDS OF SOUTH CAROLINA. 1892. 2d ed. Boston: By the Author, 1898. 116 pp. Texts of 17 tales.

Br'er Rabbit an' Br'er Wolf plant, 94
Br'er Rabbit an' Br'er Wolf, 81
Br'er Rabbit an' Br'er Wolf, 87
Cooter an' deer, 5
De rabbit an' de alligator, 42
De rabbit an' de elephant tushes, 19
De rabbit desires a long tail, 36
De rabbit, de wolf an' de alligator, 58
De rabbit, de wolf an' de keg of butter, 73
De rabbit, de wolf an' de tar baby, 62
De rabbit...an' de locus' tree, 23
De reason Br'er Rabbit wears a short tail, 26
De reason why de 'gator stan' so, 54
De reason why dog hates cat, 15
De tiger an' de nyung lady, 10
De wolf, de hog an' de lion, 101
De wolf, de rabbit an' de whale's eggs, 108

1728 Fortier, Alcee. "Bits of Louisiana Folk-lore." TRANSACTIONS OF THE MODERN LANGUAGE ASSOCIATION OF AMERICA 3 (1887): 39-61. Texts of 9 tales.

Compair Bouki and Compair Lapin (6 tales), 52-59
Ein vie zombi malin, 59
Ein fame ki tournin macaque, 60
Piti bonhomme Godron, 61

1729 _____. LOUISIANA FOLK-TALES. IN FRENCH DIALECT AND ENGLISH TRANSLATION. Boston: Houghton Mifflin Company. 1895. Texts of 27 tales.

The basket of flowers, 87
Compair Bouki and Compair Lapin (6), 109-115
Compair Bouki and the monkeys, 25
Compair Bouki...and the birds' eggs, 31
Compair Lapin and Compair L'Ours, 19
Compair Lapin and Madame Carencro, 23
Compair Lapin and Mr. Turkey, 25
Compair Lapin and the earthworm, 13
Compair Lapin's godchild, 33
Compair Taureau and Jean Malin, 7
The cunning old wizard, 116
The Devil's marriage, 69
The dog and the tiger, 33
The elephant and the whale, 3
Give me, 121
The golden fish, 120
The good little servant, 87
Grease, 119
The horse of God, 110
The Irishman and the frogs, 21
Jean Sotte, 63
John Green Peas, 89
King Peacock, 57
The little boys and the giants, 83
The little finger, 75
Marriage of Compair Lapin, 39
The men who became birds, 85
Miss Mockingbird...and Mr. Owl, 35
Mr. Monkey, the bridegroom, 27
A poor little boy, 91
The singing bones, 61
The statue of St. Anthony, 83
The talking eggs, 117
The tar baby, 98
The tortoise, 29
A woman changed into a monkey, 117

1730 Jones, Charles C. NEGRO MYTHS FROM THE GEORGIA COAST, TOLD IN THE VERNACULAR. Boston: Houghton Mifflin Company, 1888. 171 pp. Texts of 57 tales.

Buh Rabbit, Buh Pattridge, an de cow, 128
Buh Alligatuh, Buh Rabbit..., 123
Buh Alligatur an Buh Mash-Hen, 23
Buh Bear an Buh Tiger, 36
Buh Elephant an Buh Rooster, 41
Buh Fowl-Hawk an Buh Rooster, 11
Buh Fowl-Hawk an Buh Turkey Buzzud, 25
Buh Goat an Buh Wolf, 133
Buh Lion an Buh Goat, 35
Buh Lion, Buh Rabbit, Buh Fox..., 73
Buh Monkey an de bull-dog, 38
Buh Owl an Buh Rooster, 33
Buh Pattridge an Buh Rabbit, 19
Buh Rabbit an Buh Elephunt, 91
Buh Rabbit an Buh Wolf funeral, 113
Buh Rabbit an de cunjur man, 99
Buh Rabbit an de groun-mole, 60
Buh Rabbit an de king darter, 117
Buh Rabbit an de rock-soup, 63
Buh Rabbit an de tarruh beastises, 49
Buh Rabbit and de crawfish, 90
Buh Rabbit, Buh Wolf, an Buh Possum, 94
Buh Rabbit, Buh Wolf, an de porpus, 78
Buh Rabbit, Buh Wolf...an de goose, 107
Buh Rabbit...an de buckra man, 110
Buh Rabbit...an de holler tree, 97
Buh Rabbit...an de yearlin, 106
Buh Roccoon an Buh Possum, 120
Buh Sparruh, 21
Buh Squirle an Buh Fox, 109
Buh Turkey Buzzud an de king crab, 14
Buh Turkey Buzzud an de rain, 4
Buh Wolf an Buh Rabbit, 27
Buh Wolf an de two dinner, 31
Buh Wolf, Buh Rabbit, an de butter, 53
Buh Wolf, Buh Rabbit, an de rain, 121
Buh Wolf, Buh Rabbit, an de tar baby, 7
De cat, de rat, de cheese..., 48
Chanticleer an de ban-yad rooster, 58
De debble an May Belle, 82
De dyin bull-frog, 127
De eagle an eh chillun, 57
De Fiddler, Buh Tiger, an Buh Bear, 130
How Buh Cooter fool Buh Deer, 5
How come Buh Alligatur..., 1
De King an eh ring, 68
De king, eh darter, Buh Wolf..., 17
Leely gal, Buh Alligatur..., 46
De new nigger an eh mossa, 115
De ole king an de young king, 131

De ole man an Det, 66
De ole man an de coon, 89
De ole man an de gallinipper, 20
De po man and de snake, 42
De single ball, 119
De two fren and de bear, 65

1731 "Negro Fables." THE RIVERSIDE MAGAZINE FOR YOUNG PEOPLE 2 (November 1868): 505-07; 3 (March 1869): 116-18; 4 (April 1870): 163. Texts of 10 tales.

Br. Deer and Br. Coutah, the ten-mile race, 507
Br. Rabbit, Br. Wolf, Br. Dog and Br. Goose, 505
Br. Rabbit and Br. Wolf, de brier-bush, 505
Br. Rabbit, Br. Wolf, the hollow-tree, 117
Br. Rabbit, Br. Wolf, and Br. Coutah, 506
Br. Rabbit and de King, 163
Br. Rabbit catch Br. Wolf, 116
Br. Rabbit, Br. Wolf, and de Fisherman, 118
Br. Rabbit, Br. Wolf, and de cow, 117
Br. Rabbit, Br. Wolf, and de little gal, 117

1732 Owen, Mary A. VOODOO TALES AS TOLD AMONG THE NEGROES OF THE SOUTHWEST. New York: G. Putnam's Sons, 1893. Texts of 31 tales.

The Bee-king and the aunties, 1
Bills of fare--The crows, 39
Blacksnake's illness, 239
Blue Jay and his "gwines-on", 120
Cow-suckers and bunting, 266
Doves, 307
The eagle who became a girl, 305
The fuss between Woodpecker and Blue Jay, 59
The hand of stone, 297
How Blacksnake made trouble for Woodpecker, 94
How Red Fox lost Prairie-Wolf's daughter, 160
How Redbird came by his brilliant plumage, 91
How Woodpecker made a bat, 70
How Woodpecker took a boy to raise, 102
How the bluebird came by his color, 31
How the skunk became the terror, 190
Jack-me-lantuhns, "Wuller-wups", 139
Luck balls, Voodoo doctor, 169
More about Woodpecker, 52
Old King-Bee, 294
Ole Rabbit an' de dawg he stole, 138
Rabbit and the old woman, 202
Rabbit tale, 193
Snake stories, 223
The snake-egg, 245
The snipe, 261
The story of the bad goose, 29
De tale ob de gol'en ball, 185
The woodpecker and Grey Wolf, 79
Woodpecker and the young man, 301
A woodpecker story, 291

1733 Pyrnelle, Louise Clarke. DIDDLE, DUMPS, AND TOT; OR, PLANTATION CHILD-LIFE. New York: Harper & Brothers, 1882. Texts of 8 tales.

Dan'l in de lion's den, 81-85
How the woodpecker's head came to be red, 151-57
The Owl, 220-25
O, po' Nancy Jane, 116-24
The Tar baby, 77-80
Who made the first Indian, 228-30
Why the Negro's skin is black, 226-28
The wishun' stone, 37-44

1734 Vance, Louis Joseph. "Plantation Folk-Lore." THE OPEN COURT 2, 14 June 1888: 1028-32;, 5 July 1888: 1074-76;, 12 July 1888: 1092-95. Texts of 15 tales.

Brer Alligator and Buh Mash-hen, 1029
Buh Lion and Buh Goat, 1076
Buh Lion, Buh Rabbit, Buh Fox, an' Buh Roccoon, 1093
Buh Rabbit, Buh Wolf, an' de porpus, 1093
Buh Wolf, Buh Rabbit, and the tar baby, 1075
De cat, de rat, de cheese, and de fox, 1076
De Debble an' May Belle, 1093
How Buh Cooter fool Buh Deer, 1075
De King an' eh ring, 1092
De king, eh darter, Buh Wolf, Buh Rabbit, 1076
De ole king and de noung king, 1094
De ole man an' de coon, 1094
De po' man an' de snake, 1076
De two fren' and de bear, 1076
Why Brer Alligator never sleeps, 1031
Why Brer Elephant's ears hang down, 1031
Why Brer Rabbit has no tail, 1031

THE SONG

1735 Allen, William Francis [Marcel, pseud.]. "Negro Dialect." NATION 1 (14 December 1865): 744-45. 10 texts.

Chorus firstlines:

Blow your trumpet, Gabriel, 745
I can't stay behind my Lord, 745
I know member, know Lord, 745
I wait upon the Lord, 745
In dat mornin' all day, 744
O, my body rock 'long fever, 745
Run to meet him, 745

Verse firstlines:

If you want to find Jesus, 745
In de mornin' when I rise, 744
Jesus die, shall I die, 745
Meet, oh Lord, on de milk-white horse, 744
O, where d'ye tink I fin' 'em, 745
Pray a little longer, 745
De talles' tree in paradise, 745
There's room enough, 745
Want to go to meetin', 745
Way my brudder, better true belieb, 745

1736 Allen, William Francis, Charles Pickard Ware, and Lucy McKim Garrison, eds. SLAVE SONGS OF THE UNITED STATES. New York: A. Simpson, 1867. Reprints. New York: John Ross & Company, 1871. New York: Books for Libraries Press, 1971. Texts and music of 155 songs (including 19 variants). The numbers below refer to numbers given the songs in the source, not to page numbers.

Chorus firstlines:

Aine, trois, Caroline, 133
Almost over, 97
Along come an old man riding by, 109
Aunty, did you hear when Jesus rose, 91
Aurore Bradaire, belle ti fille, 132
Blow your trumpet, Gabriel, 4
Brudder, guide me home an' I am glad, 107
Build it widout a hammer or a nail, 40
Come along, Moses, don't get lost, 126
Come down, angel, and trouble the water, 99
Danse Calinda, boudoum, boudoum, 134
Dere's a meeting here tonight, 11
Dis is de trouble of de world, 122
Do come along, do let us go, 38
Don't be weary, traveller, 98
For I'm going home, 105
Glorious morning, glorious morning, 13
God got plenty o' room, 128
Good Lord, in de manshans above, 799
Good news, member, good news, member, 119
Gwine to walk about Zion, 89
He's a blessing here tonight, 11a
Hold out to the end, 76
Hold your light, 12
Hurry on my weary soul, 03
I asked my Lord, 125a
I ax all dem brudder round, 44
I can't stay behind, 8a
I can't stay behind, my Lord, 8
I don't feel weary and noways tired, 90
I know, member, know Lord, 46
I wait upon de Lord, 19
I want Aunty Mary for to go with me, 127
I want to die like-a Lazarus die, 120
I want to go to heaven when I die, 83
I wish I been dere, 39
I'm a-troubled in de mind, 42
I'm in trouble, Lord, 113
In dat mornin' all day, 56
Jehoviah, Hallelujah, de Lord is perwide, 2
John saw-r-O, John saw-r-O, 100
Keep prayin', I do believe, 93
Let me tell you what is nat'rally de fac', 75
De Lord knows de world's gwine to end up, 81
March on, member, bound to go, 30
March on, member, bound to go, 30a
Mo deja roule tout la cote, 130
My brudder, don't you give up de world, 37
My brudder, want to get religion, 7
My fader's done wid de trouble of de world, 124
My father, how long, 112
Nobody knows de trouble I've had, 74
O, come-e go wid me, 77
O, de Lamb done been down here an' died, 106
O, de vinter'll soon be ober, 101
O, don't you hear my true lub sing, 121
O, don't you hear the Heaven bells, 102
O, fare you well, my brudder, 63
O, femme Romulus, 131
O, hail, Mary, hail, 59
O, hallelu, O hallelu, 84
O, march, de angels, march, 01
O, me no weary yet, 16
O, mourner, let's go down, 104
O, my Lord delivered Daniel, 114
O, my body rock 'long fever, 45
O, my body's rocked wid de fever, 45a
O, no man...can hinder me, 14
O, run, nigger, run, 110
O, say, ain't you done wid de trouble, 10
O, shout, O, shout, O, shout away, 92
Oh, Lord, I want some valiant soldier, 67
Oh, Lord, remember me, 15
Oh, what a mournin', 34
One cold freezing morning I lay dis body down, 78
Pauve piti Lolotte a mouin, 135
Poor Rosy, poor gal, 9
Praise member, praise God, 5
Pray on, dem light us over, 118
Rain fall and wet Becca Lawton, 29
Round the corn, round the corn, 87
Sail, O, believer, sail, 32
Sail, O, believer, sail, 32a (T)
Shock along, John, 86
Sinner, what you gwine to do dat day, 103
So blow de trumpet, Gabriel, 4a
'Tis the old ship of Zion, 125
'Tis well and good I'm comin' here tonight, 25
Trabel on, trabel on, 43
True believer, I know when I gwine home, 41
Voyez ce mulet la, Musieu Bainjo, 136
Walk 'em easy round de heaben, 58
We'll land on Canaan's shore, 115
When we do meet again, 53
Wrastl' on, Jacob, Jacob, day is a-breakin', 6
You must be pure and holy, 129

Verse firstlines:

All dem Mount Zion member, 76
And de moon will turn to blood, 72
And it won't be long, 112
And when 'twas night I thought 'twas day, 92
As I walked down the new cut road, 109
As I went down in de valley to pray, 104
Been back holy, I must come slowly, 29
Believer, O shall I die, 52
Bendin' knees a achin', 93
Bow low, Mary, bow low, Martha, 32a (T)
Brethren, I have come again, 128
Bright angels on the water, 127
Bro' Joe, you ought to know my name, 48a
Brother Billy, fare you well, 53
Brudder George is a-gwine to glory, 66
Brudder Moses gone to de promised land, 65
Calalou porte madrasse, 135
Canaan land is the land for me, 99
Chapeau sur cote, Musieu Bainjo, 136
Dere's no rain to wet you, 61
Dere's room enough, 8
Dese all my fader's children, 124
Don't you see that ship a sailin', 125a
Done wid dribers dribin', 59a
Every hour in de day, cry holy, 78
Fier my Saviour, fier, 36
Five can't ketch me, 87
For I weep, I can't hold out, 67
De foxes have a hole, 2
Go down in de lonesome valley, 7
Good-bye, brother, good-bye, brother, 62
Good-bye, my brudder, good-bye, 70
Gwine to march away in de gold band, 103
Heave away, heave away, 82
Heaven bell a ring, I know de road, 38
Hunt till you find him, 18
The hypocrite and the concubine, 91
I am a-troubled in de mind, 42
I am huntin' for a city, 24

1737 "American Negro Hymns." THE MUSICAL WORLD 58 (17 July 1886): 461-62. 9 texts.

Chorus firstlines:

Verse firstlines:

1738 Arrowood, Mary Dickson and Hamilton, T. F. "Nine Negro Spirituals, 1850-1861, from Lower South Carolina." JOURNAL OF AMERICAN

FOLK-LORE 41 (October-December 1928): 579-84. Texts and music of 9 songs.

Chorus firstlines:

Breddren, don' git weary, 582
Fader, how long an' I wander here, 584
O, belieber, won't you rise, 584
O, come home, my Fadder's children, 581
O, stan' yo' storm, 582
Oh, roll, Jordan, roll, 583
When Judgement, Judgement, Judgement Day, 583
Wrestle, Jacob, Jacob, 580

Verse firstlines:

Dere's a golden crown in de heaven fo' me, 583
Hail, belieber, hail, 582
Keep yo' lamp trim an' a burning, 582
My brodder, you ought to been dere, 583
A new band a risin' an' I want to go, 584
O, he calls you by de lightnin', 581
De ship is in de harbor, 584
We will walk dose golden streets, 581
Wrestlin' Jacob, seek de Lord, 580

1739 Barr, Lillie E. "Three Months on a Cotton Plantation." INDEPENDENT 33/1700 (30 June 1881): 1-2; 33/1702 (14 July 1881): 4-5. 11 texts.

Chorus firstlines:

Gwine to hang up de sword in Zion, 1
When de hammer roll, 5

Verse firstlines:
Christ comin', 4
Don't you hear God's trumpet sound, 2
Low, chillen, low is de way, 2
My fader is gone, 5
My soul, Master Jesus, 2
O, Lord, do Lord, 4
Oh, Elsie's gwine to de fancy ball, 2
Say, graveyard, you ought to know me, 4
De sea gwine to gib up de dry bone, 1
De tomb say he can't hold him, 5
'Twas all I done, a diddle dum di, 4

1740 Barton, William Eleazar. OLD PLANTATION HYMNS. Boston: Lamson, Wolffe and Company, 1899. Reprint. THE SOCIAL IMPLICATIONS OF EARLY NEGRO MUSIC IN THE UNITED STATES, edited by Bernard Katz. New York: Arno Press and the New York Times, 1969. Music and texts of 67 songs. The numbers below refer to pages in the 1899 edition.

Chorus firstlines:

Amazing grace, how sweet the sound, 12
An' a Lawd, dese dry bones of mine, 11
Away over Jordan, 16
Before I'd be a slave, 25
De coffin to bind me down, 22
Come along, come along, 13
Cryin', O, Lord, O, my lord, 8
For I'll be there, 19
Gwine to git on de evening train, 33
Hallelujah, an' a hallelujah, 44
Hallelujah, newborn again, 7
De heabenlye lan', 42
I know, I know, my Lord, 32
I want to go where Jesus is, 13
I'll be there in the morning, 29
I'm a comin', yes, Lord, 23
I'm a goin' in Zion, I believe, 37
I'm a soldier for Jesus, 27
I'm goin' up home soon in de morning, 6
I'm no ways weary, 23
I'se a gwine ter jine de band, 28
Is there anybody here, 21
Les go down to Jordan, 31
Little David, play on your harp, 26
Lord, I'm almost home, 15
No harm, no harm, 5
Now I'm troubled in mind, 24
O, de heav'n bells ringin', 10
O, didn't Jesus rule death, 22
O, dis union band, 29
O, dis union, 28
O, how long, watch-a-man, 36
O, I'm goin' to sing, 27
O, I'm jes' a-goin' over, 5
O, Pray on, brothers, 14
O, Satan comes like a busy ole man, 11
O, stay in the field, childerenah, 27
O, the winter, the winter, 14
O, wake up, children, 13
O, wasn't that a mighty day, 20
O, where you going sinner, 32
O, who's dat yandah, 45
Oh, sweet heaven, 10
Oh, whah you runnin', 43
'S went down in the valley, 4
Sinner, behold the Lamb, 31
Sinner, you better get ready, 26
Thank God, she's got religion, 8
There's a comfort in heaven, 12
This world is not my home, 9
We will crownd him Lord of all, 29
We'll walk thro' the valley, 7
We're some of the praying people, 16
Why brethering, po' me, 24
Yes, we'll gain this world, 13

Verse firstlines:

Am I a soldier of the cross, 9
Am I a soldier of the cross, 27
Am I a soldier of the cross, 29
An' a howdy, howdy brother, 4
An' if those mourners would believe, 19
And if those mourners would believe, 13
And must I be to judgement brought, 16
The angel's wings were tipped with gold, 21
Brothers, we will walk thro' the valley, 7
Come along, my brother, 15
De coffin, de coffin to bind me, 22
Did Christ o'er sinners weep, 9
Don't you hear your Saviour call, 43
Free grace, free grace, 7
Gwine to glory, 35
Gwine to see my father, 29
Hain't but one thing that grieves my mind, 28
Heaven is a high and lofty place, 32
Hit's a mighty rocky road, 6
How long did it rain, 36
I am goin' to walk with Jesus by myself, 30
I dunno what my brother wants, 6
I want to know if you love my Lord, 21
I was but young when I begun, 13

I washed my head in the midnight dew, 14
I'm gwine away, 5
I'm trav'ling thro' the wilderness, 23
I've got my breastplate, sword, and shield, 27
In the morning I am troubled, 24
Jerusalem, my happy home, 12
Jesus, my all to heaven is gone, 13
Little David was a shepherd boy, 26
My Lord told-a me so, 33
My good old auntie's gone away, 8
Nobody knows who I am, 10
O, brother, don't you want to go, 31
O, brother, le's go down, 4
O, de heav'n bells a-ringin', 20
O, little did I think, 45
O, my Lord, good and kind, 35
O, repent, sinner, 39
O, sinnah, ain' you tired, 5
O, sinner, you be careful, 8
O, sinner, you'd better pray, 8
O, sometimes I feel like a motherless child, 18
O, we are going to wear a crown, 16
O, what preachin', 25
O, who will drive the chariot, 44
O, won't those mourners rise and tell, 44
Old Satan tho't he had me fast, 13
One day I'se walking along, 31
Peter, Peter, on the sea, 40
Satan tried my soul to stay, 28
Some people think that I have no grace, 10
The Lord is on the giving hand, 24
The tallest tree in paradise, 26
Them Methodists and Baptist, 14
'Tis the old ship of Zion, 23
Walk Jerusalem, jes' like John, 34
We want no cowards in our band, 27
Were you there when they crucified my Lord, 40
What kind of shoes is dem you wear, 11
When God commanded Michael, 22
When John first came out of Egypt, 37
Yes, the book of Revolution's to be, 20
Yes, you must have that true religion, 32
You can hinder me here, 42
You kin hinder me here, 29

1741 Brown, William Wells. MY SOUTHERN HOME; OR, THE SOUTH AND ITS PEOPLE. Boston: A. G. Brown & Company, 1880. Reprint. Upper Saddle River, New Jersey: Gregg Press, 1968. 13 texts.

Chorus firstlines:

Go send dem angels down, 156
Rise, shine, give God glory, 175

Verse firstlines:

All dem puty gals will be dar, 92
De big bee flies high, 66
De happiest day I ever did see, 43
Here's yer chitlins, 172
Hurra, for good ole massa, 96
I live fore miles out of town, 211
Now's yer time to git snap-beans, 209
Oh, bretheren, my way's cloudy, 156
Oh, Hannah, boil dat cabbage down, 210
De possum meat am good to eat, 93
Sing yo' praises Bless de Lam, 175
A storm am brewin' in de Souf, 159
When I was a mourner just like you, 90

1742 Cable, George Washington. "Creole Slave Songs." CENTURY MAGAZINE 31 (April 1886): 807-28. Reprint. THE SOCIAL IMPLICATIONS OF EARLY NEGRO MUSIC IN THE UNITED STATES, edited by Bernard Katz. New York: Arno Press and the New York Times, 1969. Texts and music of 12 songs (some with English translations); 8 texts (indicated by T).

Chorus firstlines:

Ah, suzette, 824
An-he, qui ca qui rive, 815 (T)
Eh, eh; Bomba, honc, honc, 819 (T)
M'ape Zongle, bon tan qui passe, 826
Pitis sans popa, 812 (T)
Pov' piti, Momzel Zizi, 825
Prise tobac jambette a couteau, 824
Vini, zami, pou' nous rire, 826

Verse firstlines:

Aie zein zens, vini fe ouarra, 814 (T)
C'est Miche Cayetane, 812 (T)
Calalon pote madrasse, 825
Come, young man, what chews tobacco, 812
Dans tan mo te zene, 826
Day zab, day zab, day koonoo wi wi, 827
Fizi z'Angle ye fe bim, 815 (T)
Heron mande, Heron mande, 820
In zou' in zene Criole Candjo, 826
Milatrasse courri dans bal, 809
M'alle haut montagne zamie, 824
Neg' pas capa' marche sans mais dans poche, 824
No courri l'aut' bord pou', 812 (T)
O, Zeneral Florido, 823
Quand mo 'te dans grand chimin, 824
Si to te tit zozo, 811 (T)
Sing, lads, our master bids us sing, 821
Tremblant-terr' vini 'branle, 813 (T)

1743 Cable, George Washington. "The Dance in Place Congo." CENTURY MAGAZINE 31 (February 1886): 517-32. Reprint. THE SOCIAL IMPLICATIONS OF EARLY NEGRO MUSIC IN THE UNITED STATES, edited by Bernard Katz. New York: Arno Press and the New York Times, 1969. Texts and music of 11 songs (some with English translations); 2 quill tunes.

Chorus firstlines:

Aurore Padere, belle 'ti' fille, 531
Dance, Calinda, bondjoum, bondjoum, 528
I done been 'roun' to evvy spot, 526 (T)
Inne, trois, Caroline, 526
Mo parle Remon, Remon, 530
Voyez ce mulet la, 515

Verse firstlines:

Annoque, Annobia, 523
Chapeau sur cote, Miche Bainjo, 515
Eh, pou' la belle Layotte, 518
En bas he, en bas he, 526
I done hunt all dis settlement, 526 (T)
Michie Preval li donne youn bal, 528
Mo connin, zins zens, ma mourri, 531
Mo deja roule tout la cote, 530
Mo l'aime toe, 526
O, femme Romolus, 530

Quand patate la cuite na va mange li, 529
Well, I know, young men, 527 (T)
Ya moun qui dit li trop zolie, 531

Melodies without words:

Quill tunes, 518, 529

1744 The Carolina Singers, compilers. SPIRITUELLES (UNWRITTEN SONGS OF SOUTH CAROLINA), SUNG BY THE CAROLINA SINGERS, DURING THEIR CAMPAIGNS IN THE NORTH, IN 1872-73. [Philadelphia, 1872]. 54 texts.

Chorus firstlines:

Ain't that hard trial, 10
Are your lamps a-burning, 34
Been a-listening all the night long, 24
Been all my life-time climbing, 44
Children, we all shall be free, 37
Didn't my Lord deliver Daniel, 25
Don't stay away, 8
Get on board, poor sinner, 3
Go down my son and die for sin, 31
Go down, Moses, way down in Egypt land, 26
I want my sister to go with me, 39
I'm troubled in the mind, 33
Jerusalem morning, Jerusalem morning, 23
Jesus rose, Jesus rose, 40
Keep inching along, 16
Lord, shall I be there, 11
My Lord, what a morning, 42
My way is cloudy, 40
No more, no more, thank God, 45
O, just behold that number, 22
O, Lord, O my Lord, O my good Lord, 17
O, sinner can't you lean on Jesus, 35
O, sinner, O sinner man, 18
O, there will be weeping, 29
Oh, ride on, blessed Jesus, 33
Oh, that bleeding Lamb, 27
Oh, who that raised me out of that mire, 44
Old massa run away, 47
Over Jordan River I'm bound to cross, 20
Rise, Christians, rise, 14
Roll, Jordan, roll, 20
Shout independent, shout bold, 15
Sisters, don't get weary, 24
Sooner one morning, 37
Steal away, steal away to Jesus, 6
Swing low, sweet chariot, 19
There's a lily in the valley, 9
To turn back Pharoah's army, 14
Trim your lamps, keep them bright, 42
Trouble over, trouble over, my Lord, 7
What make I bow so low, 30
What makes old Satan follow me so, 38
Where have you been so long, 8
Where shall I go, 12

Verse firstlines:

Before the heaven gate shut, 30
Children, there were three dreadful hours, 31
The Christian takes the bible, 39
The Devil thought he had me fast, 42
Do you think I'll make a soldier, 32
Doubting Thomas doubt no more, 28
The foxes have holes in the ground, 10
Going to write to Master Jesus, 14
The gospel train is coming, 3
He delivered Daniel from the lions' den, 25
I do love to sing, and I do love to pray, 27
I have a little book, that I read every day, 37
I looked over Jordan, and what did I see, 19
I looked up yonder, 17
I ran to the rocks for a hiding place, 12
I want to go to heaven, like a feather in the wind, 24
I want to go to heaven, like the poor inching worm, 16
I'm going to meet my brothers there, 22
If I had died when I was young, 44
If you got Jesus, hold him fast, 33
In the resurrection morning, 34
Jesus says there's room enough, 8
Judgment, judgment, Judgment Day, 10
Just let me get on my robe, 45
Just wait a little while, 41
My sister carry the news home, 15
No more horn blow here, 22
O, Jesus, my Saviour, on thee I'll depend, 33
O, come back sinner, and don't go there, 18
O, my sister, you don't know, 44
O, praise and tanks! De Lord he come, 53
Oh, preacher you ought to been there, 20
One day as I was walking along, 20
Parents and children will part that day, 29
The prettiest thing that ever I did, 7
Religion is just like a blooming rose, 9
Run, poor sinner, run, 43
Satan is a liar, hallelujah, 45
Say, darkies, have you seen old massa, 47
See my father walking there, 11
Sinners, you better get ready, 13
Sisters, sisters, you better be praying, 37
Some people go to meeting, 14
The soul says to the body, 8
Sweet turtle dove, sing so sweet, 23
There is fire in the East, 40
There was a search in heaven, 24
This ain't the home, 6
We want no cowards in our band, 37
When I go to my prayers, 38
When Israel was in Egypt's land, 26
When they crucified my Saviour, 40
You may bury me in the East, 36
You will hear the thunder roll, 42

1745 Coleman, Z. A., editor. THE JUBILEE SINGERS: A COLLECTION OF PLANTATION MELODIES. Cincinnati: John Church & Company, 1883. Texts and music of 19 songs.

Chorus firstlines:

And I ain't got weary yet, 11
Get you ready, there's a meetin', 18
Getting reading to die, 15
I will die in the field, 10
Keep a-inching along, 14
March on, and you shall gain the victory, 14
My ship is on the ocean, 20
Now ain't them hard times, 6
O, Zion, O, Zion, 24
Oh, I am the Door, 23
Rise, shine, an' give God de glory, 16
Roll, Jordan, roll, 17
Swing low, sweet chariot, 22
There's a heav'nly land up yonder, 4
There's a love-feast in heaven, 8

We'll camp a little while in the wilderness, 13
Why, nobody knows the trouble I see, 12

Verse firstlines:

Been praying for the sinner so long, 11
Camp-meetin' down in the wilderness, 18
Come, all ye Christian parents, 23
Do you think I'll make a soldier, 16
Five of them were wise, 24
The foxes have holes in the ground, 6
Good-by, fathers, good-by, mothers, 3
I looked over Jordan, what did I see, 22
I'm going away to see the good old Daniel, 20
O, brothers you ought t'have been there, 17
Oh, run up, children, get your crown, 8
Oh, sisters, will you pray for me, 12
Oh, stand the storm, it won't be long, 21
Oh, what do you say, seekers, 10
Old Pilate says I wash my hands, 4
'Twas a inch by inch I sought the Lord, 5
Way over in the Egypt land, 14
When I set out I was but young, 15
You'd better b'lieve de Bible, 13

1746 Deming, Clarence. BY-WAYS OF NATURE AND LIFE. New York: G. P. Putnam's Sons, 1884. Text and music of 1 song (music indicated by M); 7 texts.

Chorus firstlines:

Den come along, sinnah, 377
Den run along on to Jesus, 375 (M)
See me here, believe me, 376

Verse firstlines:

As I was a walkin' out one day, 376
In de days of de great tribulashun, 372
O, massa, how tired I be, 378
O, Moses, Moses don't git lost, 376
Oh, whar will ye be, 377
Oh, his name is John de Baptis', 375 (M)
Some join de church to put on pretents, 373
When de stars from de elemunts is fallin', 376

1747 Forten Grimke, Charlotte. "Folksongs of the Sea Island Negroes." INDEPENDENT 46 (1 November 1894): 5-6 (1401-1402). 18 texts.

Chorus firstlines:

Blow, Gabriel, trumpet, blow louder, 6
Do, Lord, remember me, 6
Go down in de lonesome valley, 5
Hallelujah, till dis warfare's over, 6
Jehovyah, Hallelujah. De Lord he will purvide, 6
No man can hinder me, 5
O, roll, Jordan, roll, 5
O, wrastlin' Jacob, Jacob, day's a breakin', 6
Praise, believer, praise, 6
So blow your trumpet, Gabriel, 6
Tiddy Rosa, hole your light, 4,
We'll soon be free, 6

Verse firstlines:

Bow low, Mary, bow low, Marta, 6
De foxes hab holes, 6
I hold my brudder wid a tremblin' hand, 6
I wonder where my mudder gone, 6
Jesus make de blind to see, 5
Mr. Fuller settin' on de Tree ob Life, 5
My brudder, how long, 6
My mudder's gone to glory, 6
My sister, you want to git religion, 5
O, Death he am a little man, 6
Oh, Jordan stream is a good ole stream, 6
Oh, de ole nigger-driver, 6
Oh, must I be like de foolish mans, 6
Oh, walk 'em easy round de heab'n, 6
Ole elder, where hab you been, 6
De prettiest ting dat ever I done, 6
De tallest tree in Paradise, 6
What make old Satan foller me so, 6

1748 Fortier, Alcee. BITS OF LOUISIANA FOLK-LORE. Extracted from TRANSACTIONS OF THE MODERN LANGUAGE ASSOCIATION OF AMERICA 3 (1887). Baltimore, 1888. 16 texts.

Chorus firstlines:

Aie! Toucoutou, yo connin vou, 68
Danse, Calinda, boumboum, 66
Mape couri dan bal, 67
Voyez ca mulet la, Miche Bainjo, 63

Verse firstlines:

Can moin Caillou parti marron l'Afrique, 67
Chapeau sur cote, Michie Bainjo, 63
Coman va fe vaillan djabaille, 68
En ho zarbe dan manche, 68
Joli son la plairi, 66
Maringouin quitte chivreil la plain, 66
Michie Mazureau, ki dan so bireau, 66
Michie Mogene, leve bo matin, 64
Mo cher zami, male di zote tou, 64
Mo gagnin piquan dan mo doi, 66
Morceau cassave dan bouillon posson, 64
Ramasse dicanne à riban, 65
Si to lainmin li, 67
Si vou contan colomme cila-la, 65
Vie Michie, Ah bon Djie, 65

1749 "The Freedmen's Songs: The Original Minstrelsy of the War." LITTELL'S LIVING AGE 83 (1 October 1864): 47-48. 10 texts.

Chorus firstlines:

De darkeys laugh, ho, ho, 47
Den, yah, oh glory come along, 48
Go down in de lonesome valley, 48
My way is dark and cloudy, 48
O, dar'll be mournin', 48
O, go down, Moses, 48
O, roll, Jordan, roll, 47

Verse firstlines:

I no weary yet, 47
If you want to make old Satan run, 48
Little children sitting on the tree of life, 47
De Lord am coming, 48
The Lord am in His chariot car, 48
The Lord by Moses to Pharaoh said, 48

Oh, Lord o' Israel, sanctify my soul, 48
Pore ole slave dar', Jesus tell, 48
Say, darkeys, have you seen de master, 47
Sister Sarah, do you want to get religion, 48

1750 [Hampton Students]. Armstrong, Mary Alice Ford, and Ludlow, Helen W. HAMPTON AND ITS STUDENTS, BY TWO OF ITS TEACHERS, MRS. M. F. ARMSTRONG AND HELEN W. LUDLOW. With Fifty Cabin and Plantation Songs Arranged by Thomas P. Fenner. New York: G. P. Putnam's Sons, 1874, 1875, 1878. Texts and music of 51 songs.

Chorus firstlines:

Bright sparkles in de churchyard, 200
Children, hail, hail, hail, 177
De church of God, 199
Den my little soul's gwine to shine, 173
Did you hear my Jesus, 230
Good news, de chariot's coming, 224
Gwine to mourn an' nebber tire, 222
He rose from the dead, 251
I heard from heaven today, 174
I'm bound to carry my soul to my Jesus, 215
I've been a list'ning all de night long, 247
If ye love God, serve Him, 178
In dat great getting-up morning, 235
Jerusalem mornin', 240
John saw, John saw, 196
Judgement day is a-rolling' around, 206
Look away in de heaven, 190
Lord, I don't feel noways tired, 228
My bretheren, don't get weary, 180
My Lord delibered Daniel, 193
My Lord, what a morning, 176
Now ain't dat hard trials, 213
Oh, Babylon's fallin', 248
Oh, de King Emanuel, 197
Oh, de band of Gideon, 242
Oh, de hebben is shinin', 219
Oh, de land I am bound for, 234
Oh, de ole sheep done know de way, 198
Oh, de winter'll soon be ober, 244
Oh, give way, Jordan, 195
Oh, hallelujah, hallelujah, 220
Oh, I will be there, 218
Oh, leaning on de Lord, 184
Oh, Lord, O my Lord, 245
Oh, nobody knows de trouble I've seen, 181
Oh, Peter go ring dem bells, 174
Oh, rise and shine, 212
Oh, sing all de way, 246
Oh, sinner, you'd better get ready, 208
Oh, swing low, sweet chariot, 183
Oh, wait till I put on my robe, 186
Oh, wasn't dat a wide riber, 194
Oh, way over Jordan, 182
Oh, yes, I'm gwine up, 216
De ole ark a-moverin', 249
Run, Mary, run, 188
Swing low, sweet chariot, 179
Walk you in de light, 238
You hear de lambs a-crying, 210
Zion, weep a-low, 232

Verse firstlines:

Dont ye view dat ship a come, 226
Dust, dust, an' ashes, 251
Ef you want to get to hebben, 230
Ef you want to see Jesus, 184
Fire in de east, an' fire in de west, 188
De fox hab hole in de groun', 213
Good mornin', brother trav'ler, 178
Gwine to get up in de chariot, 224
Gwine to see my mother, 190
I am seekin' for a city, 228
I done been to heaven, 183
I hail to my sister, 242
I hope my mother will be there, 218
I met a pilgrim on de way, 193
I tell ye, bretheren, a mortal fac', 186
I tell you what I mean to do, 245
I wonder where my mother is gone, 174
I'm a gwine to tell you, 235
I'm born of God, I know I am, 182
I'm gwine to jine de great 'sociation, 173
I've a good ole mudder in de heaven, 206
Jes' wait a little while, 249
Jesus carry de young lambs in his bosom, 212
May the Lord, He will be glad of me, 200
My Jesus Christ, a-walkin', 232
My lovely bretheren, how ye do, 220
Oh, children, do you think it's true, 238
Oh, de good ole chariot swing so low, 179
Oh, fare-you-well, friends, 219
Oh, I heard a sweet music up above, 195
Oh, look up yander, what I see, 177, 199
Oh, look up yonder what I see, 244
Oh, my brother, did you come for to help me, 234
Oh, my mudder's in de road, 215
Oh, religion is a fortune, 189
Oh, saints an' sinners will-a you go, 216
Oh, sinner man, you had better pray, 208
Oh, sooner in de mornin' when I rise, 198
Oh, walk togedder, children, 222
Oh, who do you call de King Emanuel, 197
Oh, you got Jesus, hold Him fast, 194
Our Saviour spoke dese words so sweet, 210
Pure city, Babylon's fallin', 248
Some said that John de Baptist, 247
Sometimes I'm up, sometimes I'm down, 181
Sweet turtle dove, she sing-a so sweet, 240
We're marchin' up to Hebben, 246
Worthy, worthy is the Lamb, 196
You'd better be a praying, 180
You'll hear de trumpet sound, 176

1751 ____. Fenner, Thomas P., arranger. CABIN AND PLANTATION SONGS, AS SUNG BY THE HAMPTON STUDENTS. New York: G. P. Putnam's Sons, 1876, 1877, 1879. 53 songs. Same repertory as in the 1874 edition with the addition of 2 songs, nos. 52, 53.

Chorus firstlines:

O, the stars in the elements, 84
'Tis the old ship of Zion, 85

Verse firstlines:

Come along and let's go home, 85
Don't you hear those Christians a-praying, 84

1752 ____. Fenner, Thomas P., and Frederic C. Rathburn, arrangers. CABIN AND PLANTATION SONGS, AS SUNG BY THE HAMPTON STUDENTS. Enlarged edition. New York: G. P. Putnam's

Sons, 1891. Music and texts of 72 songs.

Same repertory as in the 1879 edition (see no. 1751) with the addition of 19 songs, nos. 54-72. Six songs taken from the Fisk Jubilee Collection and 5 from the Tuskegee Collection, both sets used "by permission." See also no. 2033.

Chorus firstlines:

Fighting on, hallelujah, 93
Going to heaven, 92
I'll be there in the morning, 104
I'll be there, 91
I'm a trav'ling to the grave, 95
I'm a-rolling, I'm a-rolling, 94
Live humble, humble yourself, 87
O, bretheren, my way's cloudy, 97
O, he sees all you do, 98
Seek and ye shall find, 101
Stay in de field, 103
We are walking in de light, 102
Why, He's the Lord of Lords, 96

Verse firstlines:

De book of revelation, 92
Dere's a little wheel a-turnin', 100
Farewell, farewell to my only child, 90
Hallelujah to de Lamb, 102
Hallelujah to the Lamb, 93
I will not let you go, my Lord, 96
Mine eyes are turn'd to de Hebbenly gate, 103
Mother, is massa gwine to sell us, 86
My brother, de Lord has been here, 101
My massa died a-shouting, 95
No more auction block for me, 95
O, brothers, won't you help me, 94
O, come, my brethren, one an' all, 91
Oh, my young Christians, 87
Peter, Peter, Peter on the sea, 88
There were ten virgins, 90
There's fire in the east, 97
When I was down in Egypt's land, 98
When the gen'ral roll is called, 104

1753 Haskell, Marion Alexander. "Negro Spirituals." CENTURY 58 (August 1899): 577-81. Reprint. THE SOCIAL IMPLICATIONS OF EARLY NEGRO MUSIC IN THE UNITED STATES, edited by Bernard Katz. New York: Arno Press and the New York Times, 1969. Texts and music of 11 songs.

Chorus firstlines:

An' sometime my trouble mek me trimble, 578
Been list'nen all de day long, 578
Beliebah, some ob dese days, 579
Jesus, Mahstah, dy'n' on de cross, 580
Oh, reborned ag'in, 579
Y'all heah. Do dyse'f no harm, 578

Verse firstlines:

Dey is a tree in Paradise, 580
Ef you want to go to heaben, 579
Got a lettah dis mawnin', 578
He said to Petah, Jeems, an' John, 578
I wuz deah when dey went to Calbaree-ee, 578
Lawd, I tech one string, 580
Sometime I feel like a mo'nin' dove, 580
We'll be done wid de hard trial, 579
When you see de stahs a-fallin', 581
Whut dat sinnah-man gwine do, 581

1754 Hearn, Lafcadio. "Levee Life." CINCINNATI COMMERCIAL (17 March 1876): 2. Reprint. THE SELECTED WRITINGS OF LAFCADIO HEARN, edited by Henry Goodman, 215-33. New York: Citadel Press, 1949. Page references below are to the Goodman edition. 11 texts.

Chorus firstlines:

Farewell, 'Liza Jane, 221
Limber Jim, Shiloh, 224
Oh, ain't I gone, gone, 218
Shawneetown is burnin' down, 219
Stow'n sugar in de hull below, 222

Verse firstlines:

Belle-a-Lee's got no time, 221
Cythie, my darlin' gal, 219
I am a wandering steamboatman, 222
I come down the mountain, 221
I hev a roustabout for my man, 223
I wish I was in Mobile Bay, 222
I'm going away to New Orleans, 220
If I've a wife at New Orleans, 223
Molly was a good gal, 219
Nigger an' a white man playing seven-up, 224
You may talk about yer railroads, 218

1755 Higginson, Thomas W. ARMY LIFE IN A BLACK REGIMENT. Boston: Fields, Osgood & Company, 1870. 41 texts.

Chorus firstlines:

Come along, and let us go home, 214
Cry holy, holy, 206
Go wait upon de Lord, 212
Hold your light, Brudder Robert, 199
My army cross over, 201
O, blow your trumpet, Gabriel, 212
O, do Lord, remember me, 210
O, good news, 216
O, remember, let me go to Canaan, 203
O, won't you go wid me, 216
O, wrestlin' Jacob, Jacob, 209
One more valiant soldier here, 200
We'll run and never tire, 205

Verse firstlines:

All true children gwine in de wilderness, 133
As grief from out my soul shall fly, 216
Bow low, Mary, bow low, Martha, 208
Brudder, keep your lamp trimmin', 203
Dere's no rain to wet you, 203
Dis de good ole ship o' Zion, 214
De gospel ship is sailin', 215
He have been wid us, 210
I know moon-rise, I know star-rise, 209
I meet little Rosa early in de mornin', 211
I want to go to Canaan, 203
I wants to go where Moses trod, 204
If you want to die like Jesus, 210
In de mornin', in de mornin', 213

Jesus call you, 212
Jordan River, I'm bound to go, 199
De little baby gone home, 210
My true believers, fare ye well, 213
No more peck o' corn for me, 218
O, Jordan bank was a great old bank, 204
O, de old nigger-driver, 219
O, dey call me Hangman Johnny, 220
O, hail, Mary, hail, 200
O, I hold my brudder wid a tremblin' hand, 208
O, must I be like de foolish mans, 208
O, my mudder is gone, 200
O, walk 'em easy round de heaven, 207
De prettiest ting dat ever I done, 212
Ride in, kind Saviour, 202
She has landed many a tousand, 214
Sweet music in heaven, 215
Way down in de valley, 205
We'll cross de mighty river, 201
We'll fight for liberty, 34
We'll soon be free, 217
We're gwine to de ferry, 133
What make ole Satan for follow me so, 199
When I get dar, 206
Yonder's my old mudder, 207
You may talk of my name, 216

1756 _____. "Negro Songs." Harvard University, Cambridge, Massachusetts. Higginson Papers, Houghton Library Ms. fMS. 1162.7. 30 texts. In regard to Charles Ware as the collector of the songs, see SINFUL TUNES AND SPIRITUALS..., by Dena Epstein, 312-14. Urbana: University of Illinois, 1977.

Chorus firstlines:

And de bell done ring, 32
Come along, I nebber get to heaben, 8
Down in the lonesome valley, 3
Dying sinner, you too late, 19
For you shall gain the victory, 15
Give me Jesus, 14
Good Lord, remember me, 4
Hallelujah, when dis warfare's ober, 17
Hold your light on Canaan's shore, 23
Hurry on my weary soul, 16
I want to go home, 6
In de oder bright world, 7
Meeting here tonight, 24
Oh, Lord, oh, Lord, 33
Poor Rosie, poor gal, 21
Religion so sweet, 5
Roll, Jordan, roll, 9, 30
Still my soul's a movin', 13
Widout a hammer or a nail, 12
Zion's sons and daughters, 28

Verse firstlines:

Believer, build a house in paradise, 12
Brother Billy got a house, 13
Brudder Richard, don't get weary, 6
Death is a little man, 4
Early sinner, you too late, 19
Harken member, harken member, 33
I ax old Satan, why follow me so, 23
I build my house upon de rock, 11
I cannot stay in hell one day, 21
I don't care what dey call me, 29
I take my text in Matthew, 24
I want to be my fader's childern, 30
I want to go to meetin', 32
I weep for Mary, I weep for Martha, 5
In the morning when I rise, 14
Jehovah, hallelujah, de Lord will pervide, 31
Join um member, join um so, 20
Lord, I curse Sister Lydia widout a cause, 8
Member, march along, 15
Michael, row de boat asho', 25
My body racked wid de feber, 26
My mother's gone to glory, 17
My mudder, is you comin' tonight, 28
My sin is forgiven and my soul set free, 16
O, lay my body in de graveyard, 18
O, see what wonder Jesus done, 27
O, trebbel Jordan, long road, 22
Oh, I no weary yet, Lord, 10
Parson Fuller settin' on de tree ob life, 9
Rain fall and wet Becky Lawton, 2
Sister Libby, your name called, 7
Sister, do you want to get religion, 3
Walk easy till you get ober Jordan, 1

1757 JUBILEE AND PLANTATION SONGS. CHARACTERISTIC FAVORITES, AS SUNG BY THE HAMPTON STUDENTS, JUBILEE SINGERS, FISK UNIVERSITY SINGERS, AND OTHER CONCERT COMPANIES.... Edited by James C. Macy. Boston: Oliver Ditson Company, 1887. Reprint. 1915. Texts and music of 98 songs.

Chorus firstlines:

A few more years, 58
All I want is a little more faith, 40
And I ain't got weary yet, 42
And I will die in the field, 4
Been a listening all night long, 16
Bright sparkles in the churchyard, 66
By and by we'll all go down, 33
Children, we all shall be free, 8
Chilly water, 38
Come down, angels, trouble the water, 80
Crying, free grace and dying love, 26
Did not old Pharaoh get lost, 40
Didn't my Lord deliver Daniel, 56
Fighting on, hallelujah, 53
Get on board, children, 19
Get you ready, 67
Getting ready to die, 63
Give me Jesus, 13
Go down, Moses, 4
Going to mourn and never tire, 64
He rose, He rose, 30
He's the lily of the valley, 25
Hold the light, 52
Humble, humble, humble yourself, 48
I want to be ready, 74
I'm a rolling, I'm a-rolling, 8
I'm so glad there's no dying there, 18
I'm troubled, I'm troubled, 57
If you want to see Jesus, 14
In that great getting-up morning, 68
In that morning, my Lord, 10
John saw, John saw, 12
Jordan, o my soul, 72
Judgment day is rolling around, 34
Just behold that number, 11
Look away in the heaven, 54
March on, and you shall gain the victory, 28
My Lord delivered Daniel, 24

Verse firstlines:

We want no cowards in our band, 7, 8
We'll raise the Christian banner, 61
What kind of shoes you going to wear, 3
What ship is that a sailing, 18
When I set out I was but young, 63
When Israel was in Egypt's land, 4
Whenever we meet you here we say, 40
Where do you think I found my soul, 70
Where you been, poor mourner, 24
Worthy, worthy is the Lamb, 12
Yes, He's taken my feet out of the miry clay, 27
You may bury me in the East, 10
You'll hear the trumpet sound, 72

1758 [Jubilee Singers]. [Seward, Theodore F.]. JUBILEE SONGS: AS SUNG BY THE JUBILEE SINGERS OF FISK UNIVERSITY (NASHVILLE, TENN.). New York: Biglow & Main, 1872. Texts and music of 23 songs.

Chorus firstlines:

And I will die in the field, 21
Been a-listening all night long, 25
Children, we all shall be free, 13
Didn't my Lord deliver Daniel, 16
For my Lord says there's room enough, 7
Give me Jesus, 19
Go down, Moses, 22
I'm a trav'ling to the grave, 27
I'm a-rolling, I'm a-rolling, 14
In that morning, my Lord, 15
Just behold that number, 12
Nobody knows the trouble I see, Lord, 5
O, Lord have mercy on me, 20
O, brothers, I love Jesus, 18
O, redeemed, redeemed, 8
Oh, Lord, my Lord, 16
Oh, the rocks and mountains, 24
Roll, Jordan, roll, 9
Steal away, steal away, 28
Swing low, sweet chariot, 6
To turn back Pharaoh's army, 10
When this warfare'll be ended, 19
Yes, he's taken my feet out of the miry clay, 11

Verse firstlines:

Although you see me going along so, 8
Brothers, will you pray for me, 5
Children, you'll be called on, 19
Going to meet the brothers there, 12
Gwine to ride up in the chariot, 20
Gwine to write to Massa Jesus, 10
He deliver'd Daniel from the lion's den, 16
I looked over Jordan and what did I see, 6
I tell you what I mean to do, 26
I've just come from the fountain, 18
My Lord calls me, 28
My massa died a shouting, 27
No more auction block for me, 27
O, brothers, don't stay away, 3, 7
O, brothers, wont you help me, 14
O, brothers, you ought t'have been there, 9
O, what do you say, seekers, 21
O, when I come to die, 19
Rise, mourners, rise mourners, 7, 11
Seeker, seeker, give up your heart to God, 24
Some say that John the Baptist, 25
We want no cowards in our band, 13
When Israel was in Egypt's land, 22
You may bury me in the East, 15

1759 _____. Seward, Theodore F. JUBILEE SONGS: COMPLETE, AS SUNG BY THE JUBILEE SINGERS OF FISK UNIVERSITY (NASHVILLE, TENN.). New York: Biglow & Main, 1872. Music and texts of 61 songs.

Chorus firstlines:

All I want, all I want, 63
And I will die in the field, 21
And I wish that heav'n was-a mine, 46
Been a-listening all night long, 25
By and by we'll all go down, 42
Children, we all shall be free, 13
Crying free grace and dying love, 56
Did not old Pharaoh get lost, 64
Didn't my Lord deliver Daniel, 16
Do you think that she is able, 55
For my Lord says there's room enough, 30
Get on board, children, 36
Getting ready to die, 53
Give me Jesus, 19
Go chain the lion down, 59
Go down, Moses, 22
He arose, He arose, 45
He's the lily of the valley, 48
I'll be there, 53
I'm a rolling, I'm a rolling, 14
I'm a trav'ling to the grave, 27
I'm going to live with Jesus, 58
I'm so glad, I'm so glad, 40
I'm troubled in mind, 58
In that morning, my Lord, 15
Judgment, judgment, Judgement day, 34
Just as you live, 47
Just behold that number, 4, 12
March on, and you shall gain, 51
My good Lord's been here, 62
My ship is on the ocean, 50
No more, no more, 59
Nobody knows the trouble I see, 1, 9
O, brothers, I love Jesus, 9, 18
O, Lord, have mercy on me, 20
O, redeemed, redeemed, 31
O, Zion, O Zion, 44
Oh, Lord, my Lord, 26
Oh, ain't I glad, 57
Oh, bretheren, my way's cloudy, 52
Oh, holy Lord, holy Lord, 43
Oh, sinner, sinner man, 61
Oh, stand the storm, 39
Oh, the rocks and mountains, 24
Oh, this old time religion, 41
Oh, Zion's children coming along, 42
Pray on, pray on, pray on, 38
Prepare me, prepare me, Lord, 49
Reign, oh reign, oh reign, my Saviour, 55
Ride on King Jesus, 54
Roll, Jordan, roll, 32
Shine, shine, I'll meet you in the morning, 37
Steal away, steal away, 28
Swing low, sweet chariot, 29
These are my father's children, 54
To turn back Pharaoh's army, 10
When Moses smote the water, 60
When this warfare'll be ended, 19
Why, he's the Lord of Lords, 33
Yes, he's taken my feet out of the miry clay, 11

Verse firstlines:

Although you see me going along so, 31
And I soon shall be done, 54
As I go down the stream of time, 49
As I went down in the valley to pray, 42
Brothers, will you pray for me, 9
Children, you'll be called on, 19
Do you see that good old sister, 59
Five of them were wise, 44
Going to meet the brothers there, 12
Going to meet those happy Christians, 57
The gospel train is coming, 36
Gwine to ride up in the chariot, 20
Gwine to write to Massa Jesus, 10
He deliver'd Daniel from the lion's den, 16
I called to my father, 46
I hail my mother in the morning, 42
I looked over Jordan and what did I see, 29
I tell you what I mean to do, 26
I was but young when I begun, 54
I will not let you go, my Lord, 33
I'll tell you how I found the Lord, 40
I'm going away to see the good old Daniel, 50
I'm going to sit at the welcome table, 37
I've a good old mother in the heaven, 34
I've just come from the fountain, 18
In the river of Jordan John baptized, 38
Isaac a ransom, while he lay, 64
It is good for the mourner, 41
The Jews killed poor Jesus, 45
King Jesus in his chariot rides, 48
Mary and a Martha's just gone 'long, 56
My Lord calls me, 28
My massa died a shouting, 27
My ship is on the ocean, 39
No more auction block for me, 27
O, brethren, watch and pray, 47
O, brothers won't you help me, 14
O, children ain't you glad, 60
O, what do you say, seekers, 21
O, when I come to die, 19
Oh, brothers don't stay away, 30
Oh, brothers, where were you, 62
Oh, brothers, you ought t'have been there, 32
Oh, come back sinner, and don't go there, 61
Oh, hallelujah to the Lamb, 53
Oh, Jesus, my Saviour, 58
Oh, just let me get up, 59
Oh, rise up children, get your crown, 43
Oh, when you get there remember me, 58
Rise, mourners, rise mourners, 11
Seeker, seeker, give up your heart to God, 24
Some say that John the Baptist, 25
Takes an humble soul to join us, 55
There's a fire in the East, 52
Way over in the Egypt land, 51
We want no cowards in our band, 5, 13
What ship is that a sailing, 35
When I set out, I was but young, 53
When Israel was in Egypt's land, 22
Whenever we meet you here we say, 63
You may bury me in the East, 7, 15

1760 _____. Pike, Gustavus D. THE JUBILEE SINGERS AND THEIR CAMPAIGN FOR TWENTY THOUSAND DOLLARS. Boston: Lee, Shepard, & Dillingham, 1873. London: Hodder & Stoughton, 1873. Music and texts of 61 songs. Same repertory as the Seward edition of 1872 but different order of arrangement (see no. 1759). 1874 ed. Same repertory and order of arrangement as in the Pike edition of 1873.

1761 _____. SLAVE SONGS OF THE JUBILEE SINGERS, WITH BIOGRAPHICAL, ILLUSTRATIVE, AND CRITICAL NOTES. The American edition complete. London: W. H. Guest, 1874. 66 songs, of which 61 are identical to those in the Pike edition of 1873; 2 are additions and 3 are not spirituals.

Chorus firstlines:

Now ain't them hard trials, 35

Verse firstlines:

The foxes have holes in the ground, 35
Massa, I know nothing, 54

1762 _____. Pike, Gustavus D. THE SINGING CAMPAIGN FOR TEN THOUSAND POUNDS; OR, THE JUBILEE SINGERS IN GREAT BRITAIN, With an Appendix Containing Slave Songs. Rev. ed. New York: American Missionary Association, 1875. Texts and music of 71 songs. Same repertory and order of arrangement as in Pike edition of 1873 but with the addition of 10 songs, nos. 62-71.

Chorus firstlines:

And I ain't got weary yet, 269
Farewell, my brother, farewell forever, 267
Get you ready, there's a meeting here tonight, 266
Keep a inching along, 268
Keep your lamps trimmed and a-burning, 272
Run to Jesus, shun the danger, 270
Tell all my father's children, 271
There's a heavenly home up yonder, 265
There's a love feast in the heaven, 264
Wrestling Jacob, Jacob, 262

Verse firstlines:

Been praying for the sinner so long, 269
Brothers, don't grow weary, 272
Camp-meeting down in the wilderness, 266
He will be our dearest friend, 270
Let me go, Jacob, 262
My sister's took her flight and gone home, 271
Oh, goodbye, goodbye, 267
Oh, run up, children, get your crown, 264
Old Pilate says, I wash my hands, 265
'Twas inch by inch I sought the Lord, 268

1763 _____. TEN NEW AND POPULAR AMERICAN SLAVE SONGS, BEING THE ADDITIONAL NEW SONGS OF THE JUBILEE SINGERS. Reprinted from the American Edition, Now Selling in London. London: W. H. Guest, [1875]. 15 pp. 10 songs, which are identical to the 10 "new" songs added to the American edition of 1875.

1764 _____. Marsh, J. B. T. THE STORY OF THE

JUBILEE SINGERS; WITH THEIR SONGS. London: Hodder and Stoughton, [1876]. 227 pp. 104 songs. Same repertory and same order of arrangement as in the 1875 edition published by the American Missionary Association (see no. 1762), but with the addition of 33 songs, nos. 72-104. Not included in the list below are 4 songs that are not slave songs (e.g., The Lord's Prayer).

Chorus firstlines:

Anchor, believer, anchor, 221
Deep river, 196
Done changed my name, 227
He rose, He rose, 208
I've been redeemed, 192
In bright mansions above, 198
Let us move along, 226
My Lord, what a mourning, 199
Now, ain't them hard trials, 207
Oh, bretheren, rise and shine, 217
Oh, my little soul's going to shine, 220
Oh, wait till I get on my robe, 212
Oh, wasn't that a wide river, 200
Oh, way over Jordan, 202
Oh, we'll wait til Jesus comes, 205
Swing low, sweet chariot, 210
'Tis Jordan's river, 214
Wait a little while, 206
Way over in the heavens, 196
We are almost home, 204
We are climbing the hills of Zion, 200
We shall walk thro' the valley, 194
We'll overtake the army, 203
What a happy new year, 213

Verse firstlines:

Am I a soldier of the Cross, 214
Been wash'd in the blood of the Lamb, 192
Brother, have you come to show me the way, 191
Don't you want to be a soldier, 217
The foxes have holes in the ground, 207
Gabriel's trumpet's going to blow, 195
Good old chariot, swing so low, 210
Good-bye brothers, good-bye sisters, 215
I come this night for to sing, 212
I don't care where you bury my body, 220
I want to go to heaven when I die, 202
I went to the hill side, 227
I'm running thro' grace, 213
I've 'listed, and I mean to fight, 203
The Jews crucified Him, 208
Lord, I wish I had a come, 196
My father's gone to glory, 198
My heavenly home is bright and fair, 206
Now we take this feeble body, 219
Oh, brethern, do get ready, 200
Oh, come along, brothers, 204
Oh, don't you want to go, 196
Oh, hallelujah to the Lamb, 205
Oh, the river of Jordan is so wide, 200
Oh, who is that a coming, 216
Throw it to my dear mother's door, 221
We are on the ocean sailing, 226
We shall meet those Christians there, 194
Where do you think I found my soul, 225
You'll hear the trumpet sound, 199

1765 _____. THE STORY OF THE JUBILEE SINGERS, WITH THEIR SONGS. London: Hodder & Stoughton, 1876. 104 songs. Same repertory as in the English edition of 1875 but in different order of arrangement.

1766 _____. SONGS SUNG BY THE JUBILEE SINGERS. Enlarged ed. London: J. Clarke, c.1876. 33 songs, of which 32 are spirituals that are identical to songs in the Marsh edition of 1876 (apparently selected at random).

1767 _____. THE STORY OF THE JUBILEE SINGERS, WITH THEIR SONGS. London: Hodder & Stoughton, 1877. 112 songs. Reprint. Boston: Houghton, Mifflin & Company, 1881. Reprint of 1881 edition. New York: Negro Universities Press, 1969. Same repertory and arrangement order as in the 1876 edition with the addition of 8 songs, nos. 105-112.

Chorus firstlines:

Bright sparkles in the churchyard, 228
Come down angels, trouble the water, 234
I heard from heaven today, 236
I'm so glad the angels brought the tidings, 235
In that great getting-up morning, 240
Oh, I know, I know, my Lord, 242
Oh, the band of Gideon, 238
Oh, the land I am bound for, 243
Oh, the twelve white horses, 238

Verse firstlines:

I hail to my sister, 238
I love to shout, I love to sing, 234
I'm a-going to tell you, 240
Just stand right still, 242
May the Lord, He will be glad of me, 228
Oh, my brother, did you come, 243
Oh, Peter, go ring them bells, 236
You'll not get lost in the wilderness, 235

1768 _____. THE STORY OF THE JUBILEE SINGERS, WITH THEIR SONGS. Boston: Houghton, Mifflin & Company, [1882]. 128 songs. Reprint. London: Hodder & Stoughton, 1885. Same repertory and order of arrangement as in the 1881 edition with some substitutions in the original repertory (e.g., nos. 25, 56) and the addition of 18 songs, nos. 25, 113-128. Not included in the list below is a non-spiritual (Benediction).

Chorus firstlines:

Chilly water, 264
Come, all of God's children, 258
Go, chain the lion down, 174
Going to mourn and never tire, 246
Good news, the chariot's coming, 248
Hail, hail, I'll tell you, 261
I want to be ready, 259
I've been in the storm so long, 174
Look away in the heaven, 250
O, reign, O reign, my Saviour, 253
Oh, I'm a-going to sing, 244
Oh, childeren the work's being done, 260

Oh, give me the wings, 263
Oh, he sees all you do, 148
Oh, make a-me holy, holy, 256
Oh, rise, shine, and give God the glory, 254
Oh, rise, shine, for thy light is a-coming, 262
They led my Lord away, 257
Yes, yes, my Lord, 168

Verse firstlines:

Come down, come down, My Lord, 148
Do you see that good old sister, 174
Going to ride up in the chariot, 248
Going to see my mother, 250
I know that water is chilly and cold, 264
I tell you now as I told you before, 253
The Jews and Romans in one band, 257
John said the city was just four-square, 259
John the Baptist did declare, 261
Oh, brothers, are you getting ready, 254
Oh, let me tell my mother, 174
Oh, methodist it is my name, 263
Oh, the preachers want warriors, 258
Oh, walk together, children, 246
Oh, wet or dry, I intend to try, 262
We need more workers in the field, 260
We'll raise the Christian banner, 244
What kind of shoes you going to wear, 168
Young people, I tell you, 256

1769 ____. THE STORY OF THE JUBILEE SINGERS BY J. B. T. MARSH, WITH SUPPLEMENT CONTAINING AN ACCOUNT OF THE SIX YEAR'S TOUR AROUND THE WORLD, AND MANY NEW SONGS, BY F. J. LOUDIN. Cleveland: The Cleveland Printing and Publishing Company, 1892. 139 songs. Reprints. London: Hodder & Stoughton, 1897, 1899-1903. Same repertory and order of arrangement as the 1882 edition with the addition of 11 songs, nos. 129-139, and some replacements.

Chorus firstlines:

Den my little soul's gwine to shine, 305
Hallelujah now, 304
Hallelujah to the Lamb, 300
If ye love God, serve Him, 306
Keep a-moving, keep a-moving, 303
Live humble, humble, humble yourself, 301
My Lord delibered Daniel, 308
Oh, come and let us know, 309
Oh, sing all de way, 307
Oh, the old ark's a-moving, 310

Verse firstlines:

Elder, you say you love King Jesus, 309
Good mornin', brother trav'ler, 306
I met a pilgrim on de way, 308
I tried to live humble, 301
I'm gwine to jine de great 'sociation, 305
O, I know, yes indeed I know, 300
Way down yonder on Jordan's stream, 304
We're marchin' up to Hebben, 307
Were you there when they crucified my Lord, 302
When Jesus Christ converted my soul, 310
You may cast me here, 303

1770 Kilham, Elizabeth. "Sketches in Color." PUTNAM'S MONTHLY 5/27 (March 1870): 304-11. 8 texts.

Chorus firstlines:

Jesus said He wouldn't die no mo', 7
Shall we know each other, 9

Verse firstlines:

God bress de President, 1
Hell is a dark an' a drefful affair, 9
I looked inside ob Heaben, 8
I'll tell you what de Lord done fer me, 4
John saw, John saw, 3
King Jesus sittin' on de tree ob life, 6
De Lord tole Moses what ter do, 7
Oh, de way ter Heaben is a good ole way, 5

1771 King, Edward Smith. THE SOUTHERN STATES OF NORTH AMERICA: A RECORD.... London: Blackie & Son, 1875. Also published as THE GREAT SOUTH: A RECORD.... Hartford, CT: American Publishing Company, 1875. Reprint. Baton Rouge: Louisiana State University, 1971. 26 texts.

Chorus firstlines:

Bright sparkles in de churchyard, 609
Didn't my Lord deliber Daniel, 615
Go chain de lion down, 615
Go down, Moses, 615
Gwine to live wid God, 611
Gwine to sit down in de kingdom, 615
He rose, He rose, 613
Hunt till you find him, Hallelujah, 619
Hurry on, my weary soul, 618
I wish I ben dere, 620
In dat great gettin'-up mornin', 610
Nobody knows de trouble I see, 610
O, de ole ark a-moverin', 614
O, Lord, O, my Lord, 611
Oh, Lord, remember me, 618
Oh, swing low, sweet chariot, 614
Pure city, Babylon's fallin', 614
Swing low, sweet chariot, 615

Verse firstlines:

A baby born in Bethlehem, 618
Brudders, will you pray for me, 610
Dere's a better day comin', 611
Do you see dat good ole sister, 615
Dust, dust an' ashes, 613
Forty days an' forty nights, 614
He delibered Daniel from de lion's den, 615
Heaven bell a-ring, I know de road, 620
I saw de beam in my sister's eye, 619
I tell you what I mean to do, 611
I'm a gwine to tell yo', 610
May de Lord, He will be glad of me, 609
Michael, row de boat ashore, 620
My mudder, you follow Jesus, 620
O, de good ole chariot swing low, 614
O, John, my Jesus' comin', 612
O, me not weary yet, 619
O, walk Jordan long road, 619
Oh, deat' he is a little man, 618
Oh, Jesus tell you once befo', 614
Oh, rock away chariot, 612

Oh, shout, shout, de deb'l is about, 615
Oh, yonder come my Jesus, 612
Whar ye ben, young convert, 615
When Israel was in Egypt's land, 615

1772 Linton, W. J. POETRY OF AMERICA. SELECTIONS FROM ONE HUNDRED AMERICAN POETS FROM 1776 TO 1876. WITH AN INTRODUCTORY REVIEW OF COLONIAL POETRY, AND SOME SPECIMENS OF NEGRO MELODY. London: George Bell & Sons, 1878. Supplement (379-87) contains music and texts of 5 songs, 9 additional texts, and 1 musical incipit.

Chorus firstlines:

Dere's room in dar, 379 (T)
Keep praying, I do believe, 300 (T)
Nobody knows the trouble I've had, 380 (T)
O, Zion, O, Zion, 385
Poor Rosy, poor gal, 379 (T)
Roll, Jordan, roll, 386
Steal away, steal away, 384

Verse firstlines:

As I walk'd down the new-cut road, 381 (T)
Bendin' knees a-achin', 380 (T)
Brethren, I have come again, 381 (T)
Five of them were wise, 385
God got plenty o' room, 381 (T)
Heave away, heave away, 382 (T)
I cannot stay in hell one day, 379 (T)
I'm gwine to Alabamy--Oh, 382 (T)
My Lord calls me, 384
No more auction block for me, 387
O, brothers, you ought t'have been there, 386
O, massa take dat new bran coat, 387
O, my mudder is gone, 379 (T)
One morning I was a-walking down, 380 (T)
Rain fall and wet 'Becca Lawton, 382 (T)

Musical incipit, 383

1773 Ludlow, Helen W., ed. TUSKEGEE NORMAL AND INDUSTRIAL SCHOOL, FOR TRAINING OF COLORED TEACHERS AT TUSKEGEE, ALABAMA; ITS STORY AND ITS SONGS. Hampton, Virginia: Normal School Steam Press, 1884. Song Supplement entitled CABIN AND PLANTATION SONGS as sung by the TUSKEGEE SINGERS. Arranged by R. H. Hamilton. Texts and music of 12 songs.

Chorus firstlines:

Children, sound the jubilee, 12
Elder, we will die in the field, 18
Follow me, follow me, 3
Go, Mary, and toll the bell, 8
Good Lord, I wonder, 9
I believe in the God of Elijah, 10
I'm going home, children, 4
Jesus locked the lion's...jaw, 5
Oh, shout and let us know, 15
Oh, the old ark's a moving, 20
Stay in the field, 19

Verse firstlines:

Elder, you say you love King Jesus, 15
I think I heard my Saviour say, 12
I'm a Methodist bred and a Methodist born, 5
One day as I was walking along, 4
Simon and Peter were fishermen, 3
Some call me a Sunday Christian, 10
There's a bold little preacher in my heart, 17
The very first blessing sister Mary had, 18
When I was a mourner just like you, 19
When Jesus Christ converted my soul, 20
Who's that yonder, dress'd in black, 8
You see them children dying ev'ry day, 9

1774 Macrae, David. THE AMERICANS AT HOME. Edinburgh: Edmonston and Douglas, 1870. Reprint. New York: Dutton, 1952. Texts and music of 3 songs; 8 texts. (The letter M is used to indicate songs with music.)

Firstlines:

Come along, old fader, 359
Go down, Moses, 360
I've no time to tarry, 361, 364
If de debble do not catch Jeff Davis, 361
Jordan's River, 363 (M)
Nobody knows de trouble I see, 361
Nobody knows the trouble I see, 363 (M)
Oh, Fader Abraham, 360
When I was a mourner, 362 (M)
When I was a mourner, 365
Wish I'd died when I was a baby, 361

1775 "Negro Folk Songs: Slave Melodies of the South---The Jubilee and Hampton Singers." DWIGHT'S JOURNAL OF MUSIC 32/26 (5 April 1873): 411-13. 9 texts.

Chorus firstlines:

Didn't my Lord deliver Daniel, 412
Go down, Moses, 412
O, Lord, have mercy on me, 412
Roll, Jordan, roll, 412
Steal away to Jesus, 412

Verse firstlines:

Go chain the lion down, 412
He deliver'd Daniel from the lions den, 412
I gwine to ride up in the chariot, 412
I'm a travelling to the grave, 412
Judgment day is rolling around, 413
My Lord calls me, 412
No more auction block for me, 412
Oh, brothers, you ought t'have been there, 412
When Israel was in Egypt's land, 412

1776 NEW ORLEANS UNIVERSITY SINGERS. The Only Original New Orleans University Singers. A Colored Double Quartette. Philadelphia: Press of William Syckelmoore, 1881. 21 texts.

Chorus firstlines:

Bretheren land on the shore, 15
De ole ark's a movin', 11
Dere's no use talking, 9

Get on board, children, 19
It's way over Jordan, 5
Judgement, judgement, judgement, 16
March on, and you shall gain, 22
Nobody knows de trouble I see, Lord, 21
Oh, bretheren, my way's cloudy, 5
Oh, de King Emmanuel, 14
Oh, it's a way over Jordan, 10
Oh, Lord, have mercy on me, 7
Oh, this old time religion, 18
Oh, will you lead me to the Lamb, 4
Roll, Jordan, roll, 20
Steal away, steal away, 20
Swing low, sweet chariot, 8
To turn back Pharaoh's army, 6
Wasn't dem hard trials, tribulations, 13
We're all here, 17
Why He's the Lord of Lords, 11
Wrestling Jacob, Jacob, 3

Verse firstlines:

Been a list'ning all de night long, 13
Brothers will you pray for me, 21
Children, who dat a mournin' soul, 15
For Paul and Silas bound in jail, 17
The gospel train is coming, 19
Gwine to ride up in de chariot, 7
Gwine to write to Massa Jesus, 6
I looked over Jordan and what did I see, 8
I will not let you go, my Lord, 11
I'se a good ole mudder in de heaven, 16
If you love God, children, 4
It is good for the mourner, 18
Jes' wait a little while, 11
Let me go, Jacob, I will not let thee go, 3
Mary and Martha's just gone along, 10
My Lord calls me, 20
Oh, brothers, you ought to'a been there, 20
Oh, white folks, listen, will you know, 9
Oh, who do you call de King Emmanuel, 14
There's a fire in the east, 5
Way over in de Egypt land, 22
What kind of shoes is them you wear, 5

1777 Ryder, Charles J. "Christian Truth in Slave Songs." THE AFRO-AMERICAN ENCYCLOPEDIA..., edited by James T. Haley, 254-64. Nashville, TN: Haley & Florida Company, 1895. 7 texts; 12 chorus texts.

Chorus firstlines:

And turned back Pharoah's army, 263
The angels done changed my name, 259
I've been redeemed, 254
In bright mansions above, 263
Jesus will come by-and-by, 260
Just stand right still and steady yourself, 255
Keep inching along, 260
Keep me from sinkin' low, 257
My Lord, what a mourning, 256
Old Satan thinks he'll get us, 255
Old Satan, he wears de hypocrite shoe, 259
View the land, view the land, 260
Why, he's the Lord of Lords, 264

Verse firstlines:

I bless the Lord, I'm gwine to die, 257
I went to the hillside, I went to pray, 259
Shine, shine, I'll meet you in the morning, 262
'Twas inch by inch I sought the Lord, 260
Wait a little while, then we'll sing, 261
When Moses smote the water, 263
You say you're aiming for the skies, 260
I looked over Jordan, and what did I see, 258

1778 _____. "The Theology of the Plantation Songs." AMERICAN FREEMAN 46 (January 1892): 9-16. 13 texts.

Chorus firstlines:

Childrens, we all shall be free, 15
Didn't my Lord deliver Daniel, 10
Keep inching along, 12
My Lord, what a mourning, 13

Verse firstlines:

Don't you want to be a soldier, 11
For my Lord says there's room enough, 15
I bless the Lord I'm gwine to die, 10
I looked over Jordan, and what did I see, 15
I went to the hillside, 12
Just stand right still and steady yourself, 11
Shine, shine, I'll meet you in the morning, 14
Those bright mansions above, 14
Twas inch by inch I sought the Lord, 12
Wait a little while, then we'll sing, 14
When Moses smote the water, 15
Why, He's the Lord of Lords, 11
You say you're aiming for the skies, 13

1779 Sawyer, Jacob J., arr. JUBILEE SONGS AND PLANTATION MELODIES (WORDS AND MUSIC), as Sung by the Original Nashville Students, the Celebrated Colored Concert Company. Introduction by H. B. Thearle, Proprietor. N.p. J. J. Sawyer, 1884. Music and texts of 12 songs.

Chorus firstlines:

De chariot am coming, 7
Crying holy, holy, 10
Dar's a jubilee, 3
Den on, my little children, 7
Get on board, children, 9
March on, and you shall gain, 5
Move along, pray along, 12
O, you rock when I rock, 12
Roll, Jordan, roll, 6
Steal away, steal away, 11
Swing low, sweet chariot, 4
When the rocks and mountains shall all pass, 8

Verse firstlines:

De devil tho't he had us fast, 3
Doubter, give up your heart to God, 8
The gospel train is coming, 9
I looked over Jordan and what did I see, 4
I went down de hill, 12
I'll tell you what I like the best, 12
I've left my old pea-jacket, 13
King Jesus on de mountain top, 5
My Lord calls me, 11
Oh, brothers, you ought t'have been there, 6
Sometimes I'm up, sometimes I'm down, 7

De tallest tree in Paradise, 10

1780 Slaughter, Linda Warfel. THE FREEDMEN OF THE SOUTH. Cincinnati: Elm Street Printing Company, 1869. Reprint. New York: Kraus Reprint Company, 1969. Texts and music of 8 songs.

Chorus firstlines:

Glory, hallelujah, we are free today, 134

Verse firstlines:

All Israel love feast in heaven to-day, 137
Brother Daniel don't sing no longer, 135
Free, we are free, 134
I'll hoist my flag in the wilderness, 135
Oh, do come along, we'll see Jesus, 136
Oh, Israel, in that great day, 136
Oh, just behold that number, 136
Oh, mother, let's go down, 136

1781 Slayton, M. G., ed. JUBILEE SONGS, AS SUNG BY SLAYTON'S JUBILEE SINGERS. Chicago: Thayer and Jackson, [1882]. Texts and music of 14 songs.

Chorus firstlines:

A few more years, 7
By and by we'll wear de golden crown, 8
Dar's a jubilee, 1
Get on board, children, 5
Hallelu, hallelu, hallelujah to de Lamb, 16
Joshua fought the battle of Jericho, 15
O, children, come along, 8
Oh, de King Immanuel, 12
Peter, go ring dem bells, 14
Roll, Jordan, roll, 3
Steal away, steal away, 6
Swing low, sweet chariot, 2
We'll shout and sing, 14
When de rocks and mountains, 4
Yes, my Lord, I'm going to join, 10

Verse firstlines:

Bretherin, a long time I lived in sin, 7
Come, my sisters, and brethren too, 16
De Devil tho't he had us fast, 1
Doubter, doubter, give up your heart to God, 4
Good morning, brother pilgrim, 15
De gospel train is coming, 5
I looked over Jordan and what did I see, 2
Look over yonder, what I see, 8
My Lord calls me, 6
O, brothers, you ought t' have been there, 3
Was you there when they crucified my Lord, 11
Well, I heard a mighty rumbling, 14
What kind of shoes you going to wear, 10
Who do you call the King Immanuel, 12

1782 Stedman, Clarence, and Ellen Mackay Hutchinson, compilers. "Negro Hymns and Songs," 8:265-70. A LIBRARY OF AMERICAN LITERATURE FROM THE EARLIEST SETTLEMENT TO THE PRESENT TIME. New York: Charles L. Webster & Company, 1889. Texts of 13 songs.

Chorus firstlines

Bright sparkles in de churchyard, 66
Hi, ho, for Charleston gals, 70
In dat great gittin' up mornin', 68
In de morning, in de morning, 66
Keep prayin', I do believe, 67
O, don't you hear my true lub sing, 69
Oh, what a morning, sister, 68

Verse firstlines

As I walked down the new-cut road, 70
Bendin' knees achin', body racked wid pain, 67
Don't you hear de trumpet sound, 66
Gen'al Jackson, mighty man, 69
Heave away, heave away, 69
I know moon-rise, I know star-rise, 67
I tink I hear my brudder say, 68
I'm a-gwine to tell you 'bout de comin' ob de Saviour, 68
May de Lord, He will be glad of me, 66
My brudder sittin' on de tree of life, 65
No more peck o' corn for me, 70
O, Massa take dat new bran coat, 69
Oh, de good ole chariot swing so low, 65

1783 Taylor, Marshall W., comp. A COLLECTION OF REVIVAL HYMNS AND PLANTATION MELODIES. Musical Composition by Miss Josephine Robinson. Copied by Miss Amelia C. and Hettie G. Taylor. Cincinnati: Marshall W. Taylor and W. C. Echols, 1882. 157 songs, of which 64 are plantation songs. Texts and music for 62 songs and texts for 2.

Chorus firstlines:

All I want, all I want, 26
Before I'd be a slave, 214
Brethern, rise and shine, 153
Come down, angel, trouble the water, 207
Didn't old Pharaoh get lost, 29
Done took my Lord away, 225
Get on board, children, 158
Go down, Moses, 148
Go home and tell my Jesus, 22
He healed the sick and raised the dead, 34
He rose, He rose, 136
He set my soul free, 27
I have a little time, 18
I know the time, 231
I wish I was there, 54
I'm going away, 42
I'm in a strange land, 79
I'm so glad, I'm so glad, 20
I've been listening all the night long, 62
In this band we'll have sweet music, 47
Keep a praying, 215
Let us blow the gospel trumpet, 32
Let us cheer the wearied traveler, 21
Little children, you'd better believe, 45
Live humble, humble yourself, 103
My God delivered Daniel, 38
Now I'm going home, 233
O, hallelujah to the Lamb, 135
O, hallelujah, I've been in the grave, 204
O, Joshua fought the Battle of Jericho, 70
O, Lord, O, my Lord, 25
O, Lord, my Lord, 202
O, Lord, suffering Lamb, 244

O, ring dem charming bells, 254 (T)
O, some lie buried in the graveyard, 197
O, you must be a lover of the Lord, 39
O, Zion, O, Zion, 218
The old ark's a-moving, 54
Our lamps are burning, 33
Reign, O, reign, my Lord, 28
Ride on, conquering Jesus, 141
Rise and shine and give God glory, 253 (T)
Roll, Jordan, roll, 216
Run, mourners, run, 152
She's gone up, she's gone up, 239
Some for Paul, some for Silas, 245
Steal away, steal away, 200
Swing low, sweet chariot, 206
That great day, 223
We'll rejoice, rejoice, 162
When I come down to die, 120
When this warfare is ended, 49
Why, gilead is a healing band, 40
Why, my Jesus is a rock, 209

Verse firstlines:

The brightest day that ever I saw, 206
Christian, you'll be called on, 49
Come along, my brother, come along, 254 (T)
Did you ever hear the hammer ring, 242
Do you think I'll make a soldier, 253 (T)
Get you ready, there's a meeting, 135
Go and call the bishops in, 27
Go and tell my disciples, 47
Go read the third of Matthew, 62
Going to pray like good old Daniel, 215
Good morning, brother Pilgrim, 153
Gospel train is moving, 158
Great Jehovah, Great Jehovah, 214
Hail, O, hail, I'm on the hunt of Jesus, 40
Hark, listen to the trumpeters, 70
He was cradled in a manger, 136
High up in heaven I'll take my seat, 197
I bless the Lord, I'm born to die, 202
I found free grace in the wilderness, 233
I'll blow the gospel trumpet, 32
I'm sometimes up and sometimes down, 20
I've been coming up all this time, 204
If you get there before I do, 42
Isaac a ransom while he lay, 29
Jesus done just as he said, 223
Jesus while walking on the earth, 34
Jesus, my all, to heaven is gone, 244
John, John, what do you say, 28
Mary wears a golden chain, 120
My father's gone a journey, 45
My Lord calls me, 200
My mother died a-shouting, 245
My Saviour's name I'll gladly sing, 141
Noah built an Ark, 54
O, brethern, ain't you glad, 162
O, preacher, you ought t'have been there, 216
O, where you going, preacher, 39
Oh, preachers, can't you praise God, 22
The old ship's coming just like a whirl, 207
One day as I was walking, 21
Preaching soon in the morning, 18
Run on, my brother, 103
Shout, shout, for you are free, 79
The sinner sees a mote, 209
There was ten virgins, 218
There's trouble here, 152
They took my Lord to Pilate's bar, 225
Trouble in the morning, 8, 25
Way in heaven I'll take my seat, 54
Way over yonder in the harvest field, 231
We'll see our elders' glory, 33
When I was mourning just like you, 26
When Israel was in Egypt land, 148
Where is my mother gone, 239
Who is this a-coming, 46
Ye servants of the living God, 38

1784 Waterbury, Maria. SEVEN YEARS AMONG THE FREEDMEN. 2d ed., revised and expanded. Chicago: T. B. Arnold, 1891. 8 texts.

Chorus firstlines:

Hallelujah to Jesus, 92
Hold out, your troubles will be over, 20
I'm going down Jorden, 63
Oh, just to behold that number, 68
Roll, Jordan, roll, 65
Sinner, you'd better watch an' pray, 47
We'll walk an' talk with Jesus, 88
Zion's ship is on the ocean, 49

Verse firstlines:

I hear my Jesus say, 68
Peter was of doubting mind, 20

1785 Wood, Henry Cleveland. "Negro Camp-Meeting Melodies." NEW ENGLAND MAGAZINE n.s. 6 (March 1892): 61-64. Reprint. THE SOCIAL IMPLICATIONS OF EARLY NEGRO MUSIC IN THE UNITED STATES. Edited by Bernard Katz. New York: Arno Press and the New York Times, 1969. Music and texts of 8 songs; texts of 6 songs.

Chorus firstlines:

Ain't dat lovely, 62
Brethren, rise and shine, 61
Done took my Lord away, 64
Oh, I'm jes' from de founting, 62
Little David, play on yer harp, 62 (T)
Praise Jesus, hallelujah, 63 (T)
Yes, go tell de news, 61 (T)

Verse firstlines:

Dar's a camp meeting in de wild'rness, 61
Dis is de way de Baptis' mourn, 63
Eberybody's talkin' bout de good ole way, 62 (T)
I went down in de valley fer ter pray, 62
Keep yo' house clean, 62
De Lord don't speak like a nat'ral man, 64
Mary had one only son, 62 (T)
My body's bound fer ter moulder, 63 (T)
O, sister, do you love Jesus, 62
Oh, dying Lamb, 63 (T)
Oh, sinner, let's go down, 63
Ole Satan's camped aroun' my house, 63
Ole Sat'n can't git his grip on me, 64

IV

THE WPA SLAVE NARRATIVE COLLECTION

LITERATURE

1786 RAWICK, George P., ed. THE AMERICAN SLAVE: A COMPOSITE AUTOBIOGRAPHY. Westport, CT: Greenwood Press, 1972. Vol. 1. FROM SUNDOWN TO SUN-UP: THE MAKING OF THE BLACK COMMUNITY. 205 pp.

Introductory volume to the published collection of slave narratives that were gathered from ex-slaves by interviewers employed in the WPA Writers Project in the South and Southwest during the period 1936-1938. Editor focuses upon the creativity of the black community under slavery, exploring such topics as the African heritage, slave religion, and the black family.

Description of slave prayer meetings held clandestinely in the "brush arbor church" or slave cabins, and their rituals (39-41). Comment on slave preaching (35) and the religious ring dance (34); on the use of the spiritual as an "alerting song" (41). Discussion of the folktale as a vehicle for expressing social insights and interpreting views on human life (97).

Text of 1 song: Run, nigger, run (62). Text of 1 Br'er Rabbit tale: Br'er Patridge hides from Br'er Rabbit (99-100).

1787 _____. Vol. 2. SOUTH CAROLINA NARRATIVES. Part 1, 348 pp. Part 2, 346 pp.

Part 1. Discussion of a slave fiddler who taught himself to play violin (76) and description of slaves making whistles out of sugar cane (152). Description of the practice of blowing horns to awaken the slaves, send them into fields, and send them to bed (157-158, 191). References to the burial practice of shaking hands and marching around the grave (196); to slaves dancing to the music of a fiddler (222, 302) and dancing the jig in a circle (327).

Texts of 15 songs, including a dance-song, a lullaby, and 2 funeral songs. Couplet text of 1 juba dance-song. See Rawick SONG COLLECTIONS (no. 1827).

Part 2. Discussion of slave burials at night on the plantation (15-16, 89, 240). Description of one funeral procession where there was singing of hymns during the slow walk to the grave site, followed by the singing of livelier hymns on the way back (51). References to dancing to fiddle music (147, 215), pattin' juba (175), and use of tambourine, wash tubs, wooden sticks (169) as well as blowing of cane (pan pipes) to provide music for dancing (175).

Texts of 19 songs, including a lullaby, 2 freedom songs and a field holler. Texts of 5 couplets; reference to 1 song. See Rawick SONG COLLECTIONS (no. 1827)

1788 _____. Vol. 3. SOUTH CAROLINA NARRATIVES. Part 3, 286 pp. Part 4, 275 pp.

Part 3. References to the singing of work songs (274-75, 278, 279), dancing the jig (25), the juba dance and the "hack-back" (278). Comment on dancing to fiddle music (97), and the use of buckets and tin cans as instrumental music for dancing (160); on sermons of the antebellum slave preachers (61) and "shouting" during worship services (19, 109, 248). Description of 1 dance (278).

Texts of 9 songs; texts of 5 couplets. See Rawick SONG COLLECTIONS (no. 1828)

Part 4. References to the use of the mouth organ as musical instrument (107) and to 'Lection Day dances (238). Text of 1 Br'er Rabbit tale: Buh

Rabbit and Buh Patridge (68). One sermon excerpt [funeral oration]: Paul and Silas layin' in jail (179).

Texts of 9 songs and 1 couplet. See Rawick SONG COLLECTIONS (no. 1828)

1789 _____. Vol. 4. TEXAS NARRATIVES. Part 1, 308 pp. Part 2. 295 pp.

Part 1. Discussion of the extemporaneous composition of songs (139-40). References to dancing the jig, pigeon-wing, and round dance (10, 153); to dancing to the music of fiddle and banjo (286), of the jew's harp and accordion (158); and to pattin' juba (262). Discussion of sermons of black preachers (51, 239).

Texts of 9 songs. See Rawick SONG COLLECTIONS (no. 1829).

Part 2. Discussion of dancing to the music of fiddle and banjo (137, 234, 238, 286), of making gourd fiddles (7), of blowing quills (7, 155), and of dancing the cakewalk (243). Description of 3 dances: 1. Jig (238). 2. Pigeon-wing (243). 3. Ring-shout (294).

Texts of 40 songs and of 5 couplets. See Rawick SONG COLLECTIONS (no. 1829).

1790 _____. Vol. 5. TEXAS NARRATIVES. Part 3, 274 pp. Part 4, 237 pp.

Part 3. Discussion of slaves dancing to the music of the fiddle (234). Comment on slave preachers who took their texts from the Gospel (69), and on slaves sitting on the floor and lowering their heads to muffle sound during prayer-meeting services in their cabins (69, 240). Description of 1 ring-game (7) and 3 dances: 1. Skip frog (7). 2. Round dance (108). 3. Voodou dance (142).

Texts of 14 songs. See Rawick SONG COLLECTIONS (no. 1830).

Part 4. References to spirituals used by slaves as codes when they slipped away at night to attend prayer-meeting services (198); to dancing and singing to the music of fiddles (59, 74), and to the impromptu use of sheep's ribs, mule jaw bones, sticks, kettles, gourd fiddles, buffalo horns, and folk-crafted drums as musical instruments (198). Discussion of the slaves dancing 16-figure round sets (18) and doing the shout at "brush arbor" meetings, but without crossing the feet (198).

Texts of 18 songs and 3 couplets. See Rawick SONG COLLECTIONS (no. 1830)

1791 _____. Vol. 6. ALABAMA AND INDIANA NARRATIVES. Part 1 (Alabama), 436 pp. Part 2 (Indiana), 217 pp.

Part 1 (Alabama). Discussion of slaves stealing away at night to hold prayer-meetings in arbors (184). References to singing improvised "hymns"; dancing the shout (22, 27); to slave preaching (45, 75); and to the use of pots to muffle the sounds of prayer in the slave quarters (427). Reference to the practice of marching before the corpse in the funeral procession and singing "hymns" en route to the grave (155). References to the blowing of horns to summon slaves from the fields (134). Comment on Saturday-night dances on the plantation (111, 239), to music of banjo (111, 239), fiddle (155, 249), or gourd-fiddle (361). Description of singing at corn-shucking festivals (193-216, 360-61). Identification as popular dances the buck-dance, 16-hand reel, cake walk (280), and pigeon-wing (394).

Excerpts of 1 sermon: Don't nobody rob God (75), and 1 ghost tale (142). Texts of 24 songs and 7 couplets. See Rawick SONG COLLECTIONS (no. 1831).

Part 2 (Indiana). References to black roustabouts singing on board ship during recreation or work hours (5, 39); to the slaves singing songs in unison while working in fields (12); and to the use of pots to muffle sounds of singing and prayers during prayer-meeting ser-vices in slave quarters (53). Observation that blacks held revival- and prayer-meetings in the woods, where preaching and the shout all day (209). Mention that the telling of folk tales was censured.

Text of 1 song: Hear the trumpet sound (Cho: Come jine the roust-a-bout band!) (93).

1792 _____. Vol. 7. OKLAHOMA AND MISSISSIPPI NARRATIVES. Part 1 (Oklahoma), 362 pp. Part 2 (Mississippi), 174 pp.

Part 1 (Oklahoma). References to plantation slave preachers (78-79); to the use of pots to muffle sounds of singing, dancing the shout, and praying (308); and to the slaves lying in holes dug in the ground to muffle the sounds of prayer (308). Comment on the employment of large bottles, skillets, sticks, bones, and cane flutes as musical instruments (224), and on the blowing of horns to awaken the slaves before dawn (238). Description of 1 ring-game and its accompanying song (98-99).

Texts of 2 Master-John folk tales: 1. The talking terrapin (100-101). 2. Master John Booker (101). Texts of 10 songs and 1 couplet. See Rawick SONG COLLECTIONS (no. 1832).

Part 2 (Mississippi). Discussion of the tradition of the plantation wake, with comment on the practice of "Walking Egypt"--i.e., chanting, clapping hands, and keeping time to music with feet in order to "funeralize" the departed (86). References to the slave preacher (58). Also to slaves dancing to the music of fiddles (92, 146) and to the shuffle step (69).

Excerpt of 2 lines of a plantation sermon: Pull down de line and let de spirit be a witness (5). Texts of 8 songs, texts of 4 couplets. See Rawick SONG COLLECTIONS (no. 1832).

1793 _____. Vol. 8. ARKANSAS NARRATIVES. Part 1, 351 pp. Part 2, 354 pp.

Part 1. References to the slaves singing spirituals while working (18). Description of making quills and blowing quills (65). References to dancing to music of the fiddle (142, 158), to playing the banjo and melodion (295).

Texts of 2 songs: 1. I am climbin' Jacob's ladder (Cho: For the work is almost done) (18). 2. Hop light, lady, Cake was all dough (254). Couplet text of 1 patteroller song: 1. Run, nigger, run, the patyroles will get you (15).

Part 2. Short character sketch of an antebellum preacher of North Carolina (3). Description of the making of the folk-crafted banjo (81) and cane quills (141). References to a slave who played fife, drums, and brass horns (116). Description of the funeral of a child in Georgia, with reference to burial practices and singing funeral songs (124). Discussion of singing songs at corn-husking festival (141).

Texts of 8 songs; of 2 couplets. See Rawick SONG COLLECTIONS (no. 1833)

1794 _____. Vol. 9. ARKANSAS NARRATIVES. Part 3, 393 pp. Part 4, 310 pp.

Part 3. Reference to a plantation (slave) fiddler teaching another slave to play the violin (12). Discussion of the practice of slipping away to hold secret prayer-meeting services (40), to the use of pots to muffle sounds of singing and praying (40, 364). Description of corn-shucking festivals (97, 291), dance music provided by hand-saw and tin pan (97) as well as the fiddle (237, 291). Reference to 1 dance: Juland dance [=juba?] (237).

Texts of 3 songs: 1. Mus' Jesus bear de cross alone? (Cho: Oh, backslider, don't stay away) (175). 2. My old Mistis promised me, Dat when she died, she gwine set me free (175). 3. You can't do wrong en git by, No matter how hard yo try. Texts of 2 couplets: 1. Black Judy wus er good gal (174). 2. Sho' pity Lawd forgive that ar' pentant rebel live (297).

Part 4. Narratives include discussion of the prohibition of slave preaching (179, 271). References to clog dancing on plantations (208), playing jew's harp, making fiddles and banjos (230). Note that slaves were required to entertain masters by singing on Sunday evenings (257). References to dancing to the fiddle (258, 262).

Texts of 5 songs: 1. Dar's golden streets and a pearly gate somewhars (115). 2. Lie on him if you sing right (257). 3. The ark was seen at rest upon the hill (Cho: Sanctify to God upon the hill) (257-58). 4. I'm a-goin' to tell my Lord (Cho: Daniel in de lion's den) (265). 5. Big bells a-ringin' in de army of de Lord (Cho: My soul's a-shoutin' in de army) (265). Text of 1 couplet: Give me Jesus (257). Excerpt of 1 sermon: Marvel not you must be born again (118-19).

1795 _____. Vol. 10. ARKANSAS NARRATIVES. Part 5, 368 pp. Part 6, 310 pp.

Part 5. Discussion of slave worship services and the use of pots to muffle sound of prayer during cabin prayer-meetings (259); description of the physical plan of the "arbor" church (252). References to blowing a conch shell as a bell on plantations (181). Discussion of the corn-shucking festival, in which a prize was awarded to the person who shucked the most corn (161-162). Description of 2 ring-games (162, 320-21).

Texts of 5 songs, of 5 couplets. See Rawick SONG COLLECTIONS (no. 1834).

Part 6. References to the use of wash pots to muffle sounds of singing and praying during cabin prayer-meeting services (126-27) and to slave preaching (224). Reference to the blowing of a short, bugle-shaped horn to summon slaves (40). Comment on quilting parties that ended with dancing (327), to banjo and fiddle playing (443-44), and dancing to music of fiddle (326-27).

Excerpts from 2 ghost tales: 1. Ghost haunts building (6). 2. Witch cats (6). Texts of 2 songs and 1 couplet. See Rawick SONG COLLECTIONS (no. 1834).

1796 _____. Vol. 11. ARKANSAS NARRATIVES, PART 7, AND MISSOURI NARRATIVES. Part 1 (Arkansas), 257 pp. Part 2 (Missouri), 383 pp.

Part 1 (Arkansas). Reminiscences of an ex-slave who played freedom songs in a brass band in the Union Army during the Civil War (211). References to slaves "stealing away" at night for preaching and religious services (232). Reference to 3 ring-games: 1. Honey, honey bee (72). 2. Ball I can't yall (72). 3. Old lady hypocrit' (72).

Texts of 2 songs and of 5 couplets. See Rawick SONG COLLECTIONS (no. 1835).

Part 2 (Missouri). References to the impromptu composition of slave songs (32, 160), to playing the tambourine (159), to slave preaching in cabins (267), slaves stealing away from their cabins to hold prayer-meeting services in arbors on Saturday evenings or on Sundays (288, 305-6), and mannerisms in the preaching style of the antebellum preacher (344).

Description of 1 ring-game: Swing ole Lizy single (267), and reference to 1 dance (ring-game): High buck, low do (299). Texts of 8 songs and of 4 couplets. See Rawick SONG COLLECTIONS (no. 1835).

1797 _____. Vol. 12. GEORGIA NARRATIVES. Part 1, 352 pp. Part 2, 357 pp.

Part 1. Discussion of dancing to the music of quills (46), banjo and fiddle (81, 191, 197). Description of slave orchestras comprised of quills and tin pans (99), banjo and quills (170), fiddles, tin cans, and straws (used to beat on the fiddles) (163), as well as cow-hide drums, cow saw-bones, and broom straws (227). References to "chairback preachers" (=unordained ministers) who preached on the plantations to the slaves in their cabins (77, 114). Discussion of the custom of preaching funeral sermons several months after the burial of the deceased (207-08).

Summaries of 2 parables employed by a slave preacher: 1. I'se seed good corn growin' in de grass (296). 2. If you can't keep up wid de man at de foot, how is you gwine to keep up wid de higher-up folks? (296). Text of 1 Jack o'lantern tale (31). Description of 1 ring-game: Crow game (307).

Texts of 10 songs and of 1 couplet. See Rawick SONG COLLECTIONS (no. 1836).

Part 2. Description of a baptismal ceremony (5, 215-16). References to dancing to the music of banjo and quills (6), bucket drums and gourds (171), banjo and fiddle (284). Description of the singing of songs at a corn-husking festival (6), a buck-dancing festival (151), and a cake-walking festival (348). Comment on the practice of using pots to muffle sounds during prayer-meeting services (27) and on the oral transmission of the slaves' religious songs (186).

Description of 2 buck dances (188, 216). Reference to 1 sermon: Buy de truf and sell it not [funeral oration] (287). Texts of 14 songs and 4 couplets. See Rawick SONG COLLECTIONS (no. 1836)

1798 _____. Vol. 13. GEORGIA NARRATIVES. Part 3, 346 pp. Part 4, 364 pp.

Part 3. References to slaves blowing quills (85) and dancing to the music of a quill band (206). Discussion of one plantation dance where music was provided by a string band of fiddle, banjo, and trumpet (124); sets called for the dance included the 16-hand cotillion, Virginia reel, and quadrille (124). References to a slave preacher and his sermon (168), and to a funeral sermon given several months after the burial (330). Several descriptions of corn-shucking festivals, singing songs (254, 334) and dancing to fiddle and banjo (224). Comment on the custom of blowing a horn to assemble slaves (249, 250) and on a slave singing spirituals while washing clothes, keeping time with her arms (321).

Reference to 1 dance tune: Billy in de low grounds (196). Texts of 2 songs and 1 couplet. See Rawick SONG COLLECTIONS (no. 1837).

Part 4. Discussion of the performance practice of singing songs at corn-husking festivals (6-7, 81, 119-20). Description of how to make quills (40) and a gourd fiddle (200). References to dancing to the music of fiddle and bucket drum (64), fiddle and banjo (145), banjo and quill (337). Description of a dancer who balanced a cup of water on her head while dancing (337). Comment on the blowing of horns to awaken slaves, etc. (195, 356-357). References to slaves preaching in cabins at night (33); to the practice of preaching the funeral sermon one year after the burial (363). Excerpt reprint of an ordinance passed by the city of Augusta, Georgia (7 February 1862), which prohibited Negroes from preaching or exhorting "except at funerals or sitting-up with the dead" (319).

Description of 1 dance: Green dance (40); of 1 ring-game: Peep Squirrel (215, 334). References to 4 ring-games: 1. Mollie Bright (205). 2. William Trembletoe (205). 3. Fox (205). 4. Paddle-the-cat (205).

Summaries of 8 tales: 1. Ghost haunts house where gold is buried (246). 2. Master-John tale (246-47). 3. Woman returns from dead (247). 4. Spirit haunts unfaithful lover (248). 5. Conjure tale (248-49). 6. Woman hears cry of dead child (250-51). 7. Witch caught out of her skin (266-67). 8. Jack-o-Lantern tale (267).

Texts of 5 songs. See Rawick SONG COLLECTIONS (no. 1837).

1799 _____. Vol. 14. NORTH CAROLINA NARRATIVES. Part 1. 460 pp.

Discussion of children participating in a corn-husking festival, helping to shuck corn and patting their feet in time to the music (74). References to slaves singing to the accompaniment of banjo (83) and dancing to music of fiddle (209). Comment on the use of a pot to muffle sounds during prayer-meeting services in the cabin (396).

Texts of 2 songs: 1. Oh, mother, let's go down, down in the valley to pray (143-144). 2. We camp a while in the wilderness (144). Texts of 2 couplets: 1. Some folks says a nigger won't steal (95). 2. Run, nigger, run (95). Texts of 2 tales, one a Master-John tale, one a devil tale: 1. Jack (239-240). 2. Jack and the devil (240).

1800 _____. Vol. 15. NORTH CAROLINA NARRATIVES. Part 2. 435 pp.

Part 2. References to slaves holding prayer-meeting services in their cabins and using pots to muffle the sound (56, 133). Also to the blowing of a horn to call the slaves together (85, 144); to the practice of the slaves pattin' their feet while singing songs (132), and to the singing of spirituals while working (345).

Text and music of 1 song: 1. Remembuh me, remembuh me, oh Lord remember me (249). Text of 1 song: I wonna be ready (395). Text of 1 tale: The witch at the well (141-42).

1801 _____. Vol. 16. KANSAS, KENTUCKY, MARYLAND, OHIO, VIRGINIA, AND TENNESSEE NARRATIVES. 454 pp.

1. Ohio. References to dancing to the music of fiddle (38) and banjo (47), and to a fiddler who played for dances of white society (100). Also References to black preachers who preached during the antebellum era to slaves (67, 89).

References to 3 dance tunes: 1. Soldier's joy (100). 2. Jimmy Long Josey (100). 3. Arkansas traveler (100). Texts of 3 songs. See Rawick SONG COLLECTIONS (no. 1838).

2. Kentucky. Transcribed text of 1 sermon taken from a scrapbook dated 1839, which includes the text of 1 song (36-39). References to slave parties called "Dideoos," where banjos provided the music for dancing (62-63). Discussion of the practice of preaching the funeral sermon several months after burial (65). Description of a Negro Holiness meeting, where music was supplied by an ensemble consisting of piano, banjo, guitar, and several tambourines (98-99). Description of a children's ring dance (113) and comment on the popularity of "singing festivals" among slaves (114).

Text of 1 sermon: Ub dar's wun ting wot de Lord abominerates worser nor anudder, it is a wicked nigger (36-38). Text of 1 tale: Mr. Rabbit and Mr. Coon (117-118). Description of a children's ring dance (113). Texts of 8 songs and of 1 couplet. See Rawick SONG COLLECTIONS (no. 1838).

3. Maryland. Discussion of musical instruments made from the sawed-off horns of dead cows and bulls (33). Comment on the practice of singing to the accompaniment of jew's harp and fiddle or banjo (61-62), and reference to a black preacher who composed spirituals(72).

Texts of 2 songs. See Rawick SONG COLLECTIONS (no. 1838).

4. Tennessee. Comment on the slaves using pots to muffle sounds during prayer meetings (47). Summaries of 3 tales: 1. Master and John (7). 2. Partridge and a fox (7). 3. Parson tale (46).

5. Virginia. Comment on the practice of singing songs to the accompaniment of banjo (29). Texts of 4 songs, including 3 freedom songs. See Rawick SONG COLLECTIONS (no. 1838)

1802 _____. Vol. 17. FLORIDA NARRATIVES. 379 pp.

Discussion of a slave who improvised songs in the Geechee dialect, singing these songs out of her hands (40). References to the practice of blowing a horn to awaken slaves (141, 243) or to signal them in the fields (77); also to slaves dancing to the music of fiddle (97, 330) or fife, fiddle, or banjo (244); and to the slaves singing spirituals as work songs (243). Description of baptismal services where the candidates marched slowly to the river, singing religious songs (209, 245), and comment on the call-and-response dialogue between black minister and his congregation during sermons (353). Also comment on the slaves telling animal tales (136)

Texts of 2 songs, one a children's song: 1. Little boy, little boy, who made your breeches? (136). 2. T'ank ye Marster Jesus, t'ank ye (Cho: Da heben gwinter be my home) (160-161). References to 2 dance tunes: 1. Green corn dance (97). 2. Cut the pigeon wing (97, 330). Refers to 1 tale: 1. Raw head and bloody bones (136).

1803 _____. Westport, CT: Greenwood Press, 1975. 322 pp. Vol. 18. UNWRITTEN HISTORY OF SLAVERY (FISK UNIVERSITY).

Narratives collected in Tennessee and Kentucky by Ophelia Settle Egypt of Fisk University (Nashville, Tennessee) during the years 1929-1930 contain references to slave children gathering secretly in the woods to sing spirituals (16), to the use of pots to muffle sound during cabin prayer-meeting services (24, 35), to slaves being forced to dance to the music of fiddle or banjo in the slave pens where they were waiting to be sold (74-75). Also discussion of the performance practice of singing songs at "corn-husking" festivals (77, 99-100, 106). Comment on plantation dances, where the dancing was accompanied by the music of fiddle (81, 218), banjo (81), bass fiddle, and "big fiddle" [=cello?] (251). References to one ex-slave who learned to play the fiddle by practicing on a long gourd with horse-hair strings (131) and to a fiddler patting his foot as he played (295).

Summary of 1 sermon. References to 2 play-games: 1. Molly Bright (293). 2. Three-score-and-ten (293). Texts of 20 songs and 2 song couplets. See Rawick SONG COLLECTIONS (no. 1839).

1804 _____. Vol. 19. GOD STRUCK ME DEAD (FISK UNIVERSITY). 218 pp.

Narratives gathered from ex-slaves during the years 1927-1929 by A. P. Watson, a graduate student at Fisk University (Nashville, Tennessee), include accounts of slaves called to preach (4-6, 14-15, 18, 153), of a preacher who preferred not to speak from prepared texts (12), and of the preachers who took their texts from the Bible (18, 148-49). Comment on the practice of slaves being awakened on the plantation by blowing horns (104), and on the funeral practice of slaves singing and dancing the shout en route to the burial ground (159). References to a round dance accompanied by the fiddle (61), to dancing the cakewalk (127) and the pigeon-wing (157).

Texts of 2 songs, one a "dance-holler": 1. Your sins are all washed away (Cho: Free, free, my Lord) (53). 2. Oh, brother, I love Jesus, for His name's so sweet (Cho: I'm just now from the fountain) (172). Summary of 1 sermon: Man compared to a broken clock that is discarded (77). Reference to 1 dance: Arkansas traveler (170).

1805 Rawick, George P.(gen. ed.), Jan Hillegas, and Ken Lawrence, eds. THE AMERICAN SLAVE: A COMPOSITE AUTOBIOGRAPHY. [Supplement, Series 1. Westport, CT: Greenwood Press, 1977.] Vol. 1. ALABAMA NARRATIVES. 499 pp.

Comment on slaves singing, dancing the shout, and hollering at funerals (41), and learning to sing religious songs from each other (96). Discussion of performance practice associated with singing corn hollers at corn-shucking festivals (170, 204, 398). Description of a gourd and horse-hair fiddle, and of how to play the hand saw and "case knife" (398). References to the telling of ghost tales (190-91), dancing to fiddle music (167, 235, 358), the blowing of horns to summon or awaken slaves (100, 169), to the practice of serenading slave couples at weddings (425), and to the use of wash pots to muffle sounds at cabin prayer-meeting services (450).

Texts of 6 tales: 1. Why de deer doan lak de tarrypin (102-103). 2. Ghost tale (190-192). 3. Ghost tale (192-194). 4. Ghost tale (215-217). 5. The briar patch (310-312). 6. Capture of possum (408-409). Texts of 14 songs and 5 song couplets. See Rawick SONG COLLECTIONS (no. 1840).

1806 _____. Vol. 2. ARKANSAS, COLORADO, MINNESOTA, MISSOURI, AND OREGON AND WASHINGTON NARRATIVES. 291 pp.

1. Oregon. Narratives include interview with a fiddler who discussed the music that he played for dances (273-75). References to the slaves' use of kettles filled with water to muffle sounds of prayer and their singing during prayer meetings in cabins (280).

2. Missouri. Narratives include description of the funeral of an ex-slave, with comment on the call-and-response chanting of minister and congregation, and on the performance practice of the worshipers patting feet and swaying their bodies in time to the music while singing (137). References to the practice of lining-out hymns (156-57), to the impromptu composition of songs, the singers making up rhyme schemes as they sang (187). Also references to ex-slaves playing tambourines (187), harps, and French harps supplied by the Germans the Civil War (256).

Text of 1 song: Oh, Lord, I'm coming home (137).

3. Minnesota. Narratives include the text of 1 couplet: It must be de Kingdom's comin' (127).

1807 _____. Vol. 3. GEORGIA NARRATIVES. Part 1, 342 pp.

Discussion of the practices of the slaves holding secret prayer-meeting services in their cabins at night and using pots to muffle the sounds of prayer and singing (7, 15, 258). References to the slave preachers called "cheer-backers," who preached in brush arbors and in cabins but were not permitted to baptize converts (83). Also discussion of the use of tin buckets, pans, sticks, and quills as musical instruments (84), and description of the construction of quills (84, 116). Definition of the art of singing by one ex-slave as "the ability to carry a tune"---not simply "knowing the lines and words." The words were improvised during the singing to fit the tune (195).

Texts of 3 tales: 1. The mistis what got bury (133). 2. Same, version 2 (234). 3. Raw head and bloody bones (192-93). Description of 2 dances, 1 ring-game: 1. Ring dance (85). 2. Plantation dance [untitled] (170). 3. Peep Squirrel (197). References to 3 dances: 1. Turkey trot (85). 2. Buzzard lope (85). 3. Mary Jane (85). Texts of 10 songs. See Rawick SONG COLLECTIONS (no. 1841).

1808 _____. Vol. 4. GEORGIA NARRATIVES. Part 2, 332 pp. (paginated 343-675).

Narratives include references to slaves dancing the pigeon-wing and shuffle-toe to the music of the banjo (422), dancing to the music of quills (441), banjo, guitar (630), and violin, banjo, and an improvised fiddle fashioned after a saw (630). Comment on one dance practice where the dancer balanced a glass of water on the head while dancing (442). References to singing, pattin', dancing in cabins (455) and the telling of tales (479).

Texts of 5 songs: 1. I'll be de head, You be de back (p. 398). 2. Steal all down, And don't slight none (468). 3. Jesus built that dwelling house (Cho: Thank God de angel done move, Move, member) (555). 4. Oh, hand me down (Cho: Hand me down de silver trumpet) (598-599). 5. My Lawd is so high, You can't come over Him (599). Text of 1 couplet: Hardes' work ever done was hacking round a pine (486).

Description of 4 ring-games: 1. Fish (398-99). 2. Coonsy (399). 3. Hands up and go round, old Georgia (399). 4. Mary Jane (468). Texts of 9 tales (7 witch tales, 1 conjure tale, 1 ghost tale): 1. Skinny story version 1 (394-95). 2. Witch out of her skin (396-97). 3. Conjure tale (426). 4. Skinny story, version 2 (465-66). 5. Skinny, skinny, version 3 (549-50). 6. Skinny story, version 4 (559-60). 7. Origin of witchcraft (584-86). 8. Skinny, skinny, version 5 (597). 9. The Mistis what got bury (591). Reference to 1 sermon: Marvel not---ye must be born again (555).

1809 _____. Vol. 5. INDIANA AND OHIO NARRATIVES. Indiana: 275 pp. Ohio: 212 pp. (paginated 277-489).

1. Indiana. Discussion of the singing of black boatmen along the Ohio River, with the observation that roustabouts frequently used different tunes for the same text (28). Comment on the popularity of preachers who preached about freedom (48) and exhorted from personal experiences (142); references to the use of a tub to muffle sounds during prayer meetings held in cabins (160). Discussion of the character of the slave songs, the evolvement of the songs out of the experience of slavery, their lack of conformance with fixed rules, and unusual rhythmic features (127). References to the square dance and play party as popular entertainment forms, accompanied by the music of fiddles, banjoes, or guitars (148). Conjectures about the origin of the song "Run, nigger, run" as having originated in Kentucky and taken to Indiana by settlers (226).

Description of 1 ring-game (177). Texts of 3 tales: 1. Ghost story (67-68). 2. The haunted house (90-91). 3. Ghost story (92). Texts of 7 songs. See Rawick SONG COLLECTIONS (no. 1842)

2. Ohio. Comment on the slaves dancing to fiddle music (288), singing work songs (341); on the

singing of songs en route to the graveyard, with the mourners following behind the coffin drawn on a "spring" wagon; on the practice of clapping hands along with singing at prayer meetings and dancing the shout (317).

Texts of 3 songs. See Rawick SONG COLLECTIONS (no. 1842).

1810 _____. Vol. 6. MISSISSIPPI NARRATIVES. Part 1, 331 pp.

Part 1. References to the blowing of a bugle at 4 a.m. to awaken the slaves (57); to religious services in the brush arbor (104, 218), "down under the hill" in the night (249), in a "big ditch" (265), "in de fiel's" (311), and under the trees (315). Discussion of ring games (285, 292); dancing the double-shuffle and the pigeon-wing (229); dancing to fiddles and banjos---"no mandolins and guitars then"---(124) to fiddles and guitars (157), to banjos (292); and comment on a woman who danced with a pail of water on her head (325). Also the observation that no children were allowed to attend corn shuckings (219), and description of how to make a drum with a keg and a coon skin (124). References to singing the hymn "De Day ob Jubilee is Come" (157) and to a ring-game song (285).

Texts of 9 songs and 4 couplets. See Rawick SONG COLLECTIONS (no. 1843)

1811 _____. Vol. 7. MISSISSIPPI NARRATIVES. Part 2, 468 pp. (paginated 332-800).

Part 2. Discussion of burial customs (411) and to the fact that sometimes there were no burial ceremonies (580), of religious services held in brush arbors in the woods (567, 749), of religious services held in the fields (757), in plantation cabins (671), and in the plantation church (645). References to an African preacher (645), to the lining-out of hymns (744), to slaveholders who did not allow their slaves to attend church or to have religious services (405), and to a plantation where there were religious services only once a year--in July for 3 days (418). Also references to dancing to fiddles, banjos, accordions (745), to home-made banjos and mouth harps made of reeds (419), to fiddle and "knocking two bones behind the fiddle" (375). References to a slave quartet entertaining at the master's parties (684). Comment on the use of signals for slave gatherings, beginning of the work day, etc., by the blowing of a horn (490, 755); the horn was over a foot long and kept polished so that it shone (756).

Texts of 8 songs. See Rawick SONG COLLECTIONS (no. 1844)

1812 _____. Vol. 8. MISSISSIPPI NARRATIVES. Part 3, 549 pp. (paginated 801-1349).

Part 3. Discussion of dancing: of masters who played the fiddle for the dances of their slaves dances (930, 1293), of plantations where slave dances were held every Saturday night (826), and on some Saturday nights to the music of fiddle, banjo, and "bones" (942); of dancing to the music of fiddle and accordion (967), of fiddles and drums (1245), of harp [=harmonica], of jugs, and combs [=hair combs covered with paper] (1288). Also references to two slaves who "knock the back-step" (i.e., beat on the stair tread) while the fiddler played for dancing (930), to slaves dancing with only patting for music (1206), and to girl born in Africa who danced African dances (803). References to 3 dance steps: "knock the pigeon wing" and "step the heel and toe" (905), "cut the pigeon wing" (1196). Observation that slave fiddlers played for their masters' dances (1026, 1172).

Also references to the fact that religious services were forbidden by some slaveholders, to services held in the fields (892), to services held in cabins with wash pots turned upside down in front of doors or inside on the floor to cover the sound of singing and praying (804, 1221, 1307). Description of funeral traditions (1273); detailed description of African funeral traditions in a narrative of an African preacher (810). Observation that some slaveholders did not allow their slaves to have funerals (1084, 1298).

References to musical instruments used as signals to awaken slaves, call them to work, call them to the "big house," etc.: the blowing of horns (1025), of bugles (1297, 1305), the ringing of big bells (929, 939), the blowing of a conch horn (1289).

Texts of 5 songs: 1. Raise de heaven as high as de sky (932). 2. De gospel train is a-coming (955). 3. I know, I know dese bones gwine rize agin (Cho: Dese bones gwine rize agen) (1098). 4. Saw my mother, flying by de skies (1129). 5. I'm in dis fiel' of battle (Cho: I'm on my way) (1150). Text of 1 couplet: Am I born to die today Ter lay dis body down (914).

1813 _____. Vol. 9. MISSISSIPPI NARRATIVES. Part 4, 557 pp. (paginated 1350-1907).

Part 4. Discussion of the songs of black boatmen by a stevedore in an interview (1373-75). References to slaves dancing to the music of fiddles (1417, 1457, 1491), to the music of fiddles, tambourines, and bone beaters (1665), and to the fiddle and banjo (1898). References to singing accompanied by fiddles and banjos (1748), and to a work gang singing songs while picking cotton (1748). Comment on a female preacher active in Grenada County, Mississippi, ca. 1890 (1511).

Texts of 2 ghost stories (1405, 1744). Description of 1 dance: the Pigeon-toe (1503); and references to the back-step (1503, 1589). Also references to 4 dance tunes: 1. Arkansas traveler (1399, 1440). 2. Sally Goodin' (1399). 3. De cracklin' hen (1399). 4. Turkey in de straw (1432, 1859). Texts of 7 songs and of 3 couplets. See Rawick SONG COLLECTIONS (no. 1845).

1814 _____. Vol. 10. MISSISSIPPI NARRATIVES.

Part 5, 505 pp. (paginated 1908-2413).

Part 5. References to religious services held in the woods or bush arbors (1921, 2230, 2247), and in log cabins on the plantation (2247). Comment on the slaves dancing to the music of fiddles and banjos (1950, 1959, 2051), to mandolin and fiddle music (2027), to fiddles and guitars (2159, 2234, 2242), and to banjo and pattin' juba (1939). Comment on the popular dance steps, such as clogging and pigeoning (2057), shuffling and heel-and-toe (2409). References to the blowing of a cow horn or a big bell to summon the slaves to work or to assemble them for other purposes (1948, 2149, 2199, 2242). Discussion of the preacher (2241) and baptizing (2221); of slaves singing as they worked in the fields (2360); of slaves hanging a wash pot "bottom upwards" to catch the noise of their singing and praying (2403) or putting their heads in a barrel or wash pot when they prayed (2097).

Description of 1 ring game and text of the ring-game song, "Rabbit and Peavine" (2092). Text of 1 tale: Brer Guinea and Brer Rabbit (2182). Text of 10 songs. See Rawick SONG COLLECTIONS (no. 1846).

1815 _____. Vol. 11. NORTH CAROLINA AND SOUTH CAROLINA NARRATIVES. 326 pp.

1. North Carolina. Narratives include references to slaves slipping away from their cabins at night to hold prayer-meeting services, and to the use of a pot to muffle the sounds of prayer and singing in their cabins at night (5).

Texts of 5 tales: 1. Pateroller tale (cante-fable) (9-10). 2. Br'er Rabbit and the three bears (36). 3. Br'er Fox and Br'er Turkey (38). 4. Ghost story (39). 5. Haunted house (39).

2. South Carolina. Description of slaves making horns (95) and quills (128). References to performance of the "flat-foot dance" (64), the shout at funerals and wakes (77, 317), and dancing to the music of fiddle and quills (128). Description of the conversions of two preachers (117-18, 219-20). Reference to the slaves' dislike of "whispering" preachers (181), to slaves gathering in the quarters on Saturday evenings and singing old songs (135), and to the singing of reels (112). Description of 1 play game, hack-back (127) and references to cutting jigs (128) and the shout (77, 317).

Texts of 2 tales: 1. Fishing on Sunday (118). 2. Witch cat (118-119). Texts of 15 songs and 2 couplet song texts. See Rawick SONG COLLECTIONS (no. 1847)

1816 _____. Vol. 12. OKLAHOMA NARRATIVES. 401 pp.

Discussion of the practices of slaves slipping away from their quarters at night to sing and pray in ditches (47) and of holding prayer-meeting services in their cabins, using pots to muffle sounds in order to avoid detection (47, 267). References to tales about "Ole Raw Head and Bones" and to ring games (193). Comment on June 19th as a popular festival commemorating emancipation in Texas (194). Description of dancers doing the "Georgia minstrel" (219); and references to slaves dancing to the music of fiddle (219, 263, 346), of a pair of bones, horse ribs, banjo, or pattin' (263), of a whistler (263) or bugler (347), and keeping time to music by beating on chair backs (263).

Texts of 5 songs: 1. Know nothing 'bout Abe Lincoln (Cho: Heard of 'im) (2). 2. So many pretty gals, So they say (193). 3. Old man, old man, your hair is getting gray (280). 4. Oh, Jesus is a rock in a weary land (297). 5. I went down to dad's old corn field (Cho: Run, nigger, run, de patteroll'll git you) (325).

1817 _____. THE AMERICAN SLAVE: A COMPOSITE AUTOBIOGRAPHY. [Supplement, Series 2. Westport, CT: Greenwood Press, 1979.] Vol. 1. ALABAMA, ARIZONA, ARKANSAS, DISTRICT OF COLUMBIA, FLORIDA, GEORGIA, INDIANA, KANSAS, MARYLAND, NEBRASKA, NEW YORK, NORTH CAROLINA, SOUTH CAROLINA, OKLAHOMA, RHODE ISLAND, WASHINGTON NARRATIVES. 402 pp.

1. Alabama. Collection includes descriptions of corn-huskings, corn songs, and performance practice (11, 14). References to slaves dancing to the beating of pans, clapping of hands, and music of fiddle, quills, and strings (14).

Text of 1 corn-husking song: Boss man, boss man. Please give me my time (14). Text of 1 couplet: Polk an' Clay went to war (11).

2. Arizona. References to slaves singing and praying around a black kettle to muffle sound (126), and singing and praying over the sick (230). Comment on dancing to the music of fiddle and banjo (167).

Text of 1 dance call (60). Texts of 2 songs: 1. Give me that old time religion (126). 2. Run, nigger, run (139). Text of 1 ghost tale (105).

3. Indiana. Texts of 2 tales: 1. The hoodoo doctor (275-76). 2. The haunted farm (276-77).

4. Nebraska. Comment by one ex-slave on the Foot Washing Baptists "drownin' you, jumpin' in the water, and shoutin' in the pulpit" (332).

Texts of 2 songs: 1. I'm gonna lay down my burden down (Cho: Down by the river side) (313). 2. The wind blows East (Cho: Amaze in Grace) (348). References to 4 sermons: 1. A eagle stirrin' ther's nest (326). 2. Dry bones in the graveyard (352). 3. And they played on the harp of a thousand strings (352). 4. Spirit of men made perfect (352).

5. New York. Narrative of an ex-slave (born in Tennessee) has a John Hardy ballad text (360-61).

1818 _____. Vol. 2. TEXAS NARRATIVES. Part 1, 470 pp.

Texas narratives include original transcripts

which are longer than the edited versions that were deposited at the Library of Congress by workers of the WPA Writers Project, and which contain explicit information about race relations and folklore. Discussion of how there was dancing to the music of banjo and tin drums (99), of the fiddle (262-63, 304, 311, 443), of fiddle, banjo, and piano (342), of banjo and bones (360), of banjo, Jew's harp, accordion, and pieces of steel (468). Also references to the jig dance (169), the improvisation of songs (236), telling of ghost tales (360), to the practices of the slaves stealing away at night to pray and of using wash pots to muffle sounds of prayer (401), and to the shout (129).

Description of a "jigging contest" (468) and 4 play-games: 1. Doll, doll, young lady (154). 2. Winsome lady's garden (154). 3. Hop light, ladies, d'cake all dough (155). 4. Lincoln Board, don't fool me (155). References to 2 dance tunes: 1. Snow-bud on de ash bank (263). 2. Chicken in de bread tray (263). References to 4 dances: 1. Cut de pigeon wing (271, 437). 2. Cut de buck (271). 3. Break down (437). 4. Round dance (457).

Texts of 25 songs and of 4 couplets. See Rawick SONG COLLECTIONS (1848)

1819 _____. Vol. 3. TEXAS NARRATIVES. Part 2, 482 pp. (paginated 471-953).

Part 2. References to slaves dancing to the music of banjos, fiddles, and singing (497-99), of whistles (515), of banjo and tin pan-drum (566, 592), of fiddles, banjos, guitars, and singing (614), of home-made whistles and Jew's harp (913). Discussion of the performance practice of singing spirituals at different tempos, depending upon the nature of the religious service (e.g., funeral or prayer-meeting, 517-18). References to pattin' (912), the singing of work songs (609), to blowing horns to awaken the slaves on the plantation (797). Also to 2 ghost tales (609, 756), the cake walk (913), and the shout (516-17). Description of the the Adam and Eve dance (729) and 2 ring games: 1. Wolf over the river (947). 2. Chase the squirrel (683).

Text of 1 tale: Ridge Graveyard ghost (891-893). Reference to 1 tale: 1. Bloody bones (609). Texts of 18 songs and of 2 couplets. See Rawick SONG COLLECTIONS (no. 1849).

1820 _____. Vol. 4. TEXAS NARRATIVES. Part 3, 485 pp. (paginated 955-1439).

Part 3. Description of a pattin' dance-party (975), the dancing of "four-handed" reels (1255), of square dancing (1375, 1411), the jig dance (1411), the round dance (1411), and of a fiddler's contest (1373-1375). Discussion of the improvisation of work songs (978). Comment on stylistic distinctions between the slaves' religious music and contemporary black religious music (1065). References to dancing to the music of the fiddle (975, 1310, 1373-75), of fiddle and banjo (1064), and of banjo (1189). Also references to singing performance practice (1262), the making of gourd fiddles and quill flutes (1262), and the popularity of reels, waltzes, and gallops among the slaves (1283).

References to 6 fiddle tunes: 1. Wolves a-howlin' (1374). 2. Corn shuckin' (1374). 3. Dyin' cowboy (1374). 4. Daddy's pack o'hounds (1374). 5. Wild horse in de cane brake (1374). 6. Dat big black bear will get you honey (1374). Texts of 5 folk tales: 1. Ghost tale (1136-1137). 2. Master and John: Theft of corn (1197-1198). 3. Bre'r Fox, Bre'r Rabbit, and Bre'r Elephant (1198). 4. Bre'r Fox is Bre'r Rabbit's riding horse (1198-1199). 5. Talking horse (1199). Description of 4 dances: 1. Bald horse [ring-game] (1133). 2. Four-handed reel (1255). 3. Square dance (1375, 1411). 4. Round dance (1411-1412). Reference to 1 ring-game: Chicken crow befo' day (1283).

Excerpts of 2 sermons: 1. De way ob de Lawd am mysterious (1389-1390). 2. Christ nailed to the Cross (1392). Texts of 33 songs; texts of 2 couplets. See Rawick SONG COLLECTIONS (no. 1850).

1821 _____. Vol. 5. TEXAS NARRATIVES. Part 4, 489 pp. (paginated 1441-1925).

Part 4. Discussion of the various forms of dance accompaniment: banjo, beating tin pans (1448, 1764), fiddle (1816, 1897). References to play-games (1449, 1496), the telling of tales about Africa (1453-1454, 1807), and to tales about ghosts and animals (1504, 1624). Also references to the slaves singing religious songs (1464, 1588-1589, 1593, 1829, 1833, 1912), work songs (1535), and corn-husking songs (1843). Comment on the case of slaves singing field hollers to alert workers of the approach of their masters (1732), and on the practice of singing to the accompaniment of Jew's harp and flutes made from tree saplings (1739). Also comment on the distinction between a burial and a funeral---the latter takes place several weeks after the burial (1466). Reference to the preaching of blacks (1817).

Texts of 5 tales, of which 3 are ghost tales (1563-64, 1624, 1624). 4. Br'er Rabbit and Br'er Fox: Invitation to dance (1624-1625). 5. The kidnapping of grandmother from Africa (1807). Description of 1 play game, Molly bright (1827), and reference to 1 play game, See-saw, wolf over the river (1449). References to 2 dances: 1. Quadrilles (1794). 2. Jigs (1794). Texts of 21 songs. Texts of 8 couplets. See Rawick SONG COLLECTIONS (no. 1851).

1822 _____. Vol. 6. TEXAS NARRATIVES. Part 5, 502 pp. (paginated 1927-2429).

Part 5. Discussion of how the slaves danced to the accompaniment of a home-made drum (1931), the fiddle (2001, 2297), accordion and fiddle, (2027, 2204), fiddle, banjo, and guitar (2105), the fife (2243), fiddle and banjo (2111), and fiddle, clevis, and pin [sic] (2414). Comment on the slaves singing songs while seated in a circle (2111) and on performance practice (2388).

References to ghost tales and ghost songs sung on Halloween (2103).

References to 8 dances: 1. Rabbit dance (1936). 2. Round dance (2001). 3. Ground shuffle (2080, 2090). 4. Pigeon wing (2080, 2090, 2120). 5. Back step (2080, 2090). 6. Jig (2111). 7. Cake-walk (2120). 8. Four double-head dance (2205). Description of 1 play game: Oh, Sister Phoebe (2242). References to 6 fiddle tunes: 1. Colorado (2328). 2. Washington (2328). 3. Young girl (2328). 4. Old girl (2328). 5. High heel shoes (2328). 6. Calico stockings (2328).

Texts of 32 songs and 5 couplets. See Rawick SONG COLLECTIONS (1852)

1823 ____. Vol. 7. TEXAS NARRATIVES. Part 6, 485 pp. (paginated 2431-2914).

Part 6. Discussion of dances accompanied by banjo and the beating of tin pans (2451, 2502), fiddle and banjo (2648), accordion and bass fiddle (2812), fiddle and accordion (2905). References to antebellum slave preachers in Texas (2510). Comment on the restrictions imposed upon preachers and slaves to keep them from slipping away at night to hold prayer-meeting services (2614). Discussion of the "Sheep Calling Baptists" (2783), of religious conversion meetings (2528-29, 2781-82), of slave funeral rites, and improvised religious singing (2600). Also discussion of singing to the music of guitar and fiddle (2745) and to the different songs of field hands at work (2759). Reference to a 3-string fiddle player who played and sang songs for slaves while they worked (2531-32).

Texts of 2 Halloween tales: 1. Three witches (2790-2792). 2. The old owl (2792-2793). References to 3 tales: 1. Raw heads an' bloody bones (2719). 2. Free at last (2781). 3. Princely ancestors from Africa (2903). Description of a voodoo dance (2784-85), a circle dance (2707), and of 3 play games: 1. Wolf over the river (2503). 2. Playing Sho', sho' (2527). 3. Puss wants a corner (2527).

Texts of 19 songs; of 3 couplets. See Rawick SONG COLLECTIONS (no. 1853).

1824 _____. Vol. 8. TEXAS NARRATIVES. Part 7, 479 pp. (paginated 2915-3402).

Part 7. Discussion of the various kinds of dance accompaniment used: dancing to the music of fiddle, Jew's harp, and hoe scraped with a knife (2980), blow harps (=tin cups full of holes) and blow quills (3131), banjo (2998), and fiddle (3274). References to dance performance practice (2980) and the improvisation of songs (3175, 3203). Description of a baptism (3043) and of a corn-shucking festival (2981).

Texts of 4 tales: 1. Race of Rabbit and Tortoise (3165, 3183). 2. Possum story (3176-77). 3. and 4. Religious tales (3177, 3177-78). References to 6 dances: 1. Swing de corner (2998). 2. Cuttin' d' chicken wing (2998). 3. Breakdown dance (2998). 4. Ring dance (3094). 5. Corn shucking march (3173). 6. Quadrille (3274). References to 5 play-games: 1. Frog in the middle (3041). 2. Old Molly, Whoop Scooop (3041). 3. Young gal loves candy (3223). 4. Hide and whoop (3223). 5. Ring 'round de center (3238).

Texts of 23 songs; of 2 couplets. See Rawick SONG COLLECTIONS (no. 1854).

1825 ____. Vol. 9. TEXAS NARRATIVES. Part 8, 486 pp. (paginated 3403-3889).

Part 8. Discussion of slaves dancing to the music of fiddle (3547, 3692, 3702, 3758, 3764, 3789, 3851), and to the music of a "reed" (3822-23). References to the slaves humming their religious songs in the fields while working (3653); gathering in their quarters at night to tell tales, play fiddle and accordion (3701); to performance practice associated with the singing of an ax-cutting song (3605). Comment by one informant on the case of a black overseer who was allowed to preach to the slaves, but was not permitted to read books (3809). Observation that slave children played and danced with Indian children (3822). Description of a slave burial, which was accompanied by the singing of spirituals and marching around the grave site (3774).

Texts of 5 folk tales: 1. Man hunts possum (3542). 2. Br'er Rabbit takin' time (3543). 3. The haunted hole (3588-89). 4. Riverboat ghost tale (3744-45). 5. Mermaids ghost story (3745). References to 4 dances: 1. Arkansas traveller (3852). 2. Seven-step schottish (3851). 3. Square dance (3851). 4. Round dance (3851). References to 4 play games: 1. Eleven stars gwine to fall (3655). 2. Gwine up North, new-bound wearing broadcloth (3655). 3. Chickens crowing for midnight, it's almost day (3655). 4. Red morocco shoes and stockings (3802).

Texts of 9 songs and of 3 couplets. See Rawick SONG COLLECTIONS (no. 1855).

1826 ____. Vol. 10. TEXAS NARRATIVES. Part 9, 486 pp. (paginated 3891-4377).

Part 9. Transcripts of interviews with 8 white informants include references to slaves singing work songs (3933, 4113, 4149-50). Slave narratives include description of a corn-husking festival (4148-4149); and references to the slaves dancing to music of the fiddle and Jew's-harp (4049), of pan banjo and harp (4133), of banjo (4014), and of banjo, fiddle, and bones (4302). Description of folk-crafted banjos and fiddles (4302). Explanation of the context in which one group of slaves sang patty-roller songs (4114). Description of a prayer-meeting and text of the sermon preached there (4151-52).

Description of 1 play game, Weevily wheat (4049) and reference to 1, Wind de ball, Suzy (4242). Text of 1 sermon: An' all de Kings and de rulers cum an bowed down befo' de golden image (4151-4152). Texts of 16 songs and of 2 couplets. See Rawick SONG COLLECTIONS (no. 1856).

SONG COLLECTIONS

1827 RAWICK, George P., ed. THE AMERICAN SLAVE: A COMPOSITE AUTOBIOGRAPHY. Westport, CT: Greenwood Press, 1972. Vol. 2. SOUTH CAROLINA NARRATIVES. Part 1, 348 pp. Part 2, 346 pp. Texts of 34 songs; 6 couplets.

Chorus firstlines

Ah, Lord, Great camp meetin', 2-169
Chillun, wha' yuh gwinna do, 1-332
Don' tech my water-fall, 2-155
Down into de river, 2-41
Hol' on, 2-168
I can't stay behind, 2-170
Meet me at de crossroads, 1-286
Now he hatch, 1-115
O, let us go where pleasure is, 1-135
River of Jordan, 2-40
Roll' em and boll 'em!, 2-164
Some day you got to lay down, 1-266
To lay dis body down, 2-89
Wuan' for ole Satan, 2-170

Verse firstlines

All de medicine you may buy, 1-266
The blackest nigger I ever did see, 1-286
Bye-o-baby, go sleepy, 1-116
Climb up de walls of Zion, 2-169
Come along, my dear loving brother, 2-41
Come ye dat love de Lord, 1-196
Down in de water, 2-40
Freedom forever, 2-157
Go round, look at the mornin' star, 2-170
Goin' to carry dis body, 2-89
He gwinna place one foot in de sea, 1-332
I am bound for de Promise land, 1-133
I sees de lighthouse, 1-277
If you want to know my name, 2-164
Is you over, 2-51
Jesus listening all de day long, 1-86
Lord, I know dat my time ain't long, 1-287
Lord, Lord, Heaven, 2-134
Master gone away, 2-197
Motherless chilluns sees hard times, 2-46
O-ou-ou-o-ou, Do-mi-nici-o, 2-146
O, Heaven, when shall I see, 1-180
O, my sister, how you walk on de cross, 1-285
Old Daddy Rodgers and merry wuz she, 2-163
Rock-a-bye!, 2-164
Room anough, 2-170
Run away, sojus of the cross, 2-168
See w'en e rise, 2-170
Send Tom Taggum to drive Bone Baggum, 2-164
Star in de East, 1-195
Stay in the field, 1-111
Tech me all round my waist, 2-155
We got a home ober dere, 1-135
Wish I had a hundred dog, 1-115

Couplet texts:

John Henry was a man, 2-52
Job, Job, farm in a row, 2-40
Juber dis, Juber dat, 1-242
Marse Hampton was a honest man, 2-29
Marse Hampton et de watermelon, 2-29
O Zion, wanta to git home, 2-51

1828 ____. Vol. 3. SOUTH CAROLINA NARRATIVES. Part 3, 286 pp. Part 4, 275 pp. Texts of 18 songs: 6 couplets.

Chorus firstlines

Bow-hoo, oo-hoo, 4-239
But give me Jesus, 4-90
Howl! howl!, 4-109
I'm gwine to get drunk again, 4-108
Way down in de lonesome valley, 4-107

Verse firstlines

Bulldogs a barkin', 4-109
Come on baby, let us go down, 3-279
Dark midnight is my cry, 4-90
Dey ain' had no eyes for to see, 4-246
Do, Lord, remember me, 3-218
Down to de water, 3-173
Go way, ole man, 3-274
Hancock ride de big gray horse, 4-238
I got somethin' to tell you, 4-239
Kitty died O-O, 4-108
Les go down to de water, 3-138
Little boy wouldn't swim, 4-138
Lord, I wonder when de lighthouse, 3-84
Mary bring de news, 4-192
De mockin' birds a singin, 4-107
O, didn't it rain?, 3-85
O, run here, believer, 3-61
Rabbit in de hollow, 4-105
Trouble water today, 3-278

Couplet texts

Hawk and buzzard went to law, 4-21
Juber this, Juber dat, 3-278
Little boy, wouldn't swim, 3-138
Loup de la-loop, deacon coming out, 3-138
My mammy got meat laid away, 3-278
Would have been married, 3-152

1829 ____. Vol. 4. TEXAS NARRATIVES. Part 1, 308 pp. Part 2, 295 pp. Texts of 49 songs; 5 couplets.

Chorus firstlines

A-rockin' on my knee, 2-38
But de grave it wouldn't hold him, 1-140
But us souls go marchin' home, 2-27
Help me to trust him, 2-243
Hush! boys, Don't make a noise, 2-29
Keomo, kimo, darro, wharro, 2-27
O, boys, O, Down in Shiloh town, 2-286
Old massa run away, 2-28
Shoo, members, shoo, 2-221
Sing-song, Kitty, 2-27

Verse firstlines

Adam's fallen race, 2-243
Chickama, craney crow, 1-171
Dere a frog live in a pool, 2-27
Dinah got a meat skin lay away, 2-286
Don't steal my sugar, 2-242
Down in Shiloh town, 2-286
Early in de mornin', 2-29
Gen, can, candio, Old Man Dandio, 1-171
Heavenly land, I's gwinter be Gawd, 2-243

Hop light, li'l lady, 1-286
I goes to church in early morn, 2-89
I goes up on de meatskins, 2-233
I sing because I'm happy, 2-192
I went to the barn, 2-167
I's am climbin' Jacob's ladder, 2-150
If you wants to bake a hoecake, 2-233
It's gettin' mighty late, 2-235
De Jews done kill pore Jesus, 1-140
Juba this and Juba that, 2-167
Keep 'way from me, hooddoo, 2-3
Kitty, in de corner, 2-103
La Boulangere ait ta victoire, 2-153
Milk in de dairy nine days old, 2-27
De moonlight, a shinin' star, 2-38
Mourner, fare you well, 2-62
My knee bones am aching, 2-7
O, de devil drempt a dream, 1-275
O, de Yankee come to put de nigger free, 2-227
De old bee make de honeycomb, 1-150
Old cotton, old corn, 2-99
Old marster eats beef, 2-89
Old possum in the holler log, 2-221
Ole massa's gone to Philiman York, 2-194
Our bodies bound to morter, 2-27
Over yonder is de wild-goose nation, 2-98
De rough, rocky road, 2-26
Run, sinner, run, 1-140
Shoo the devil out the corner, 2- 221
Sinner, blind, Johnnie, 2-62
Sisters, won't you help me, 2-170
Stand your storm, 2-194
Swing low, sweet chariot, 2-26
This ain't Christmas mornin', 2-167
Up de hill and down de holler, 2-52
Walk, you nigger, 2-164
De way to bake a hoecake, 2-233
We'll put for de South, 1-150
Where you goin', buzzard?, 2-43
White folks, have you seed old massa, 2-28

Couplet texts

In de new Jerusalem, 2-238
Master say yo' breath smell of brandy, 2-167
Oh, do what Sam done, 2-238
Oh, I's gwine home, 2-16
Rabbit, rabbit, jump fru' de crack, 2-103

1830 _____. Vol. 5. TEXAS NARRATIVES. Part 3, 274 pp. Part 4, 237 pp. Texts of 32 songs; 3 couplets.

Chorus firstlines

But I ain't free, 4-172
Down by de riverside, 3-21
O, go to sleepy, 3-23
O, row, who laid dat rail, 4-185
Shoo a la a day, 3-126

Verse firstlines

Ain't no more cane on de Neches, 3-27
As I went down in de valley to pray, 4-185
Come along, make no delayin', 4-114
De boll weevil is a li'l bug, 3-28
Dere's a old plow hoss, 3-79
Eighteen-twenty-one, 4-213
Herodias go down to de river, 4-94
Hi, ho, ug, de sharp bit, 4-31
Hits a mighty dry year, 4-185
Hurrah! Mister Bluecoat, 4-226
I ain't gwine study war no more, 3-21
I'm drinkin' of rum, 3-195
I'm in a lady's garden, 4-53
I'm in de well, 4-49
Mammy went 'way, 3-23
Massa sleeps in de feather bed, 4-172
Master of de house, 4-159
My knee bones achin', 3-9
My old missus promise me, 3-126
Nigger mighty happy, 4-65
Put on my long white robe, 4-94
Rabbit in de briar patch, 4-172
Run, nigger, run, 3-126, 3-222, 4-152
Skip frog, answer your mother, 3-7
Sugar in de gourd, 3-127
Times are gittin' hard, 4-185
Up de hill and down de hollow, 3-105
Walkin' in de parlor, 3-224
We'll stick to de hoe, 4-65

Couplet texts

The racoon am de funny thing, 4-53
When de sun go down, 4-184
When I's here you calls me honey, 4-53

1831 _____. Vol. 6. ALABAMA AND INDIANA NARRATIVES. Part 1 (Alabama), 436 pp. Part 2 (Indiana), 217 pp. Texts of 24 songs; 7 couplets. Numbers below refer to Part 1.

Chorus firstlines

Come jine the roust-a-boat band, 93
Go choose yo' east, 256
I wan' you to come, 121
I's goin' home to live with de Lord, 146
Jes' carry me and bury me, 227
Jesus will talk and walk, 250
Methuselah was a witness, 141
Move de member, move Daniel, 93
Oh, Good Shepherd, feed a-'mah sheep, 152
Swing low, chariot, 228
Thank God Almighty I' free at las', 169

Verse firstlines

Boss man, please gimme my time, 243
Dark cloud arising like gwine to rain, 280
Down by the river side, 250
Fool my massa seben years, 168
Goin' home soon in de mornin', 146
Hawk an' de buzzard went down, 388
Here the trumpet stand, 93
I am a sojer of de Cross, 121
I really believe Christ is comin' again, 427
I wonder whar was good ol' Dan'el, 161
I'm goin' away, 161
De John T. Moore, de Lula D., 284
Mammy, is Ol' Massa gwin'er sell us tomorrow, 211
A motherless chile sees a hard time, 73
Read in de Bible, 141
Saturday night an' Sunday, too, 387
Set down, 93
Sheep's in de cotton patch, 107
Slav'-y chain done broke, 169
Trouble here and dey's trouble dere, 228
When I was in my worldly ways, 227

White folks says nigger won't steal, 239
Wonderful Peter, wonderful Paul, 152
You jumped and I jumped, 412

Couplet texts

Angels in de water, 171
Last word he said, 398
Old John Bell is de'd en gone, 223
Polk and Clay went to war, 193
Shoo, gander, th'ow yo' feathers, 2
Up an' down de Mobile Ribber, 350
Whar you gwine buzzard, 388

1832 _____. Vol. 7. OKLAHOMA AND MISSISSIPPI NARRATIVES. Part 1 (Oklahoma), 362 pp. Part 2 (Mississippi), 174 pp. Texts of 18 songs; 4 couplets.

Chorus firstlines

Den I'm a-goin' home, 1-139
Mumbledy, 1-245
Set in de corner, 1-53
'Tis the old ship of Zion, 1-154
Yes, Ma'am, 1-99

Verse firstlines

Clark et the watermelon, 1-274
Come on chariot, 2-7
Don't mind working from sun to sun, 1-296
Drinkin' o' de wine, 2-95
Free at las,' 1832, 1-116
Here come de marster, 2-11
I fooled ole mastah seven years, 1-274
I'll be God O'mighty, 1-361
It has landed my old mammy, 1-154
Kinky head, whar-fore you skeered, 2-35
Let me nigh, by my cry, 2-160
Little pinch o' pepper, 1-245
Miss Ca'line gal, 1-99
My mother prayed in de wilderness, 1-139
Old Gen'l Pope had a shot gun, 2-138
Run tell Coleman, 2-161
What yo' gwine do, 1-53
You steal my pardner, 1-99

Couplet Texts

Run, nigger, run, 2-48, 2-162
I went down in de valley to pray, 1-360
Old Mister Yankee think he is so grand, 2-173

1833 _____. Vol. 8. ARKANSAS NARRATIVES. Part 2, 354 pp. Texts of 8 songs; 2 couplets. Part 1 has no song collection.

Chorus firstlines

Baby, ba, ba, 80
Run, nigger, run, 323
Steal away to Jesus, 1833, 330
Verse firstlines

Hush-a-bye, bye-yo'bye, 241
I belong to the band, 330
Little baby's gone to heaven, 124
O, lousy nigger, O, grandmammy, 110
Old cow died, 80
Saddy night and Sunday too, 195
You may call me Raggedy Pat, 335

Couplet Texts

Gimme this old time religion, 202
Run, nigger, run, 195

1834 _____. Vol. 10. ARKANSAS NARRATIVES. Part 5, 368 pp. Texts of 5 songs; 5 couplets.

Chorus firstlines

All of my sins are taken away, 353
And we'll live forever more, 320
Run, nigger, run, 268

Verse firstlines

Chick-a-ma, craney crow, 321
If I could, I surely would, 353
That nigger run, 268
We'll land over shore, 320
You have to mind, 108

Couplet texts

If you don't beleave, 149
Nigger makes de cotton, 285
Red shirt, nigger got a red shirt, 162
Run, nigger, run, 25, 293
We will camp awhile, 270

1835 _____. Vol. 11. ARKANSAS NARRATIVES (PART 7) AND MISSOURI NARRATIVES. Part 1 (Arkansas), 257 pp. Part 2 (Missouri), 383 pp. Texts of 10 songs and 9 couplets.

Chorus firstlines

Before I'd be a slave, 1-211
Dis is de buryin' ground, 2-160
Rock, the cradle, John, 2-160

Verse firstlines

Ask my Lord for mercy, 2-160
By'n by don't you griebe after me, 2-337
Down in Mobile, 1-208
If it hadn't been for Uncle Abraham, 2-50
Jesus in his chariot rides, 2-46
Oh, de win's in de wes', 2-337
Our little meetin' 'bout to break, 2-306
Rain around, ain't goin' rain no more, 2-47
Rasslin' Jacob, don't weep, 1-211
You, by word, now all we go, 2-160

Couplet texts

Free, free my Lord, 2-317
I'm a goin' away tomorrow, 1-216
My old mistress promised me, 1-211
Old Virginia nigger say, 1-192
Run, nigger, run, 1-82, 1-159
The spectator bought my wife and child, 1-52
Way over in the promised land, 2-119
We walk around and shake hands, 2-360
You ought to have been there, 2-260

1836 _____. Vol. 12. GEORGIA NARRATIVES. Part

1, 352 pp. Part 2, 357 pp. Texts of 25 songs; 4 couplets.

Chorus firstlines

Cause us is gwine home, 1-293
Fire, O, keep the fire burning, 2-24
Jest before day, 2-26
Run, nigger, run, 1-143
Shout, the Heaven-bound King, 2-350
Star risin' in de mornin', 2-266
Too late, sinner, 2-25
Whar would I be, 1-286
Will surely cry that day, 2-349

Verse firstlines

All my sisters gone, 1-286
Bright angel, come change my name, 2-349
Chickimy, craney crow, 1-221
Git on board, 1-290
God A'mighty, when my heart begins to burn, 2-265
Hush little baby, 1-111
I am a Baptist born, 2-355
I'se wukkin' on de buildin', 2-284
If a seeker gets to Heaven, 2-350
In dat day dat you died, 2-266
Jesus will fix it for you, 1-186
Marchin' for de water, 2-216
My sister, I feels 'im, 2-26
Never mind what Satan says, 2-24
Never seen the like, 2-25
O, Jane! Love me lak you useter, 1-166
O, Lord! Us takes 'em to de graveyard, 1-349
O, Miss Liza, Miss Liza Jane!, 2-110
O, living man, come view de ground, 2-5
Shuck up dis corn, 1-293
Walk like ladies, 1-55
The wind blows East, 2-349
Yes, I hollow at the mule, 1-162
You'd better be praying, 2-349

Couplet texts

Pickin' out de cotton, 2-119
Steal 'round dem corners, 2-268
Tarrypin, when you comin' over, 2-111
Who's been here since I been gone, 2-7

1837 _____. Vol. 13. GEORGIA NARRATIVES. Part 3, 346 pp. Part 4, 364 pp. Texts of 8 songs; 1 couplet.

Verse firstlines

A frog went courtin', 4-87
Don't you see the lightning, 4-215, 4-234, 4-348
Oh, I wouldn't have a poor girl, 4-200
Old Granny Mistletoe, 4-8
Run, nigger, run, 3-214
You beat me and you kick me, 4-265

Couplet text

Oh, my haid, my pore haid! 3-254

1838 _____. Vol. 16. KANSAS, KENTUCKY, MARYLAND, OHIO, VIRGINIA, AND TENNESSEE NARRATIVES. Texts of 17 songs; 1 couplet. States are represented below by initials preceding the page numbers.

Chorus firstlines

Can't you carry me o'er, V-5
I'm gwine to lebe you, M-72
Wen I git in de kingdom, K-103
Yo' ar' free, yo' ar' free, V-6

Verse firstlines

A snake head an' er lizard tail, K-121
Ain't no more blowin' of dat fog day horn V-4
Black-Eye Susie, you look so fine, O-100
Heave away! I'd rudder co't a yallar gal, K-102
Kimo, Kimo, dar you are, V-5
Mammy, don't yo' cook no mo', V-5
O! I'se a-gwine to lib always, K-103
Oh, where shall we go when de great day comes, M-35
Ol' Aunt Katy, fine ol' soul, O-38
Ol' hen, she flew ovah de garden gate, O-98
Old Ebe he was de second man, K-38
Ole Brer Rabbit, shake it, K-63
Ole Massa take dat browncoat, K-102
'Twas 1861, the Yankee made de rebels run V-4
We'll walk dem golden streets, K-103
When dat are ole chariot comes, M-72
Who ting-a-long, K-15

1839 _____. Westport, CT: Greenwood Press, 1975. Vol. 18. UNWRITTEN HISTORY OF SLAVERY (FISK UNIVERSITY). Texts of 20 songs; 2 couplets.

Chorus firstlines

Gonna git on to heaven, 280
In that morning, 319
Must be now that the kingdom's come, 252
Steal away, steal away, 281
Washed in the blood of the Lamb, 280

Verse firstlines

Chillen, I'm free, 280
Give me Jesus, and you can have the world, 99
I come to pray, 281
I hope to join the army, 108
I hope to meet you in the promised land, 320
I'll go away to the Sunday School, 319
I'm bound for the promised land, 280
If you want to drink, 100
Lie low, nigger, 78
Moses smote the water, 47
My Lord, He called me, 281
O, my good Lord, go low in the valley, 47
Old master's gone away, 252
Rassal Jacob, rassal as you did, 49
Ring a ring a rineo, 84
Rock me, Julie, Rock me, 295
Shout, He never said a mumbling word, 79
Sister Mary in that day, 319
We will drink out of the well, 281

Couplet texts

Sleepy creature, 118
I'm going down to the river of Jordan, 321

1840 Rawick, George P. (gen. ed.), Jan Hillegas, and Ken Lawrence, eds. THE AMERICAN SLAVE: A COMPOSITE AUTOBIOGRAPHY. [Supplement, Series 1. Westport, CT: Greenwood Press, 1977.] Vol. 1. ALABAMA NARRATIVES. 499 pp. Texts of 14 songs; 5 couplet texts.

Chorus firstlines

Been reelin' en er rockin', 7
I'm rollin' in Zionee, 5
One born, Isalites shoutin', 6
Settin' down side de Lam', 6

Verse firstlines

Captain uv de ship, 7
Down by the river side, 235
Hawk and der buzzard, 410
Hypocrite somepin' God despises, 6
I want mo' religion, 50
I wonder where's my mother, 6
The John T. Moore, the Lula D., 263
Lord, I wonder whut's de matter, 5
Mammy, is Massa gwine sell us tomorrow, 155
My lates' sun is sinkin' fas', 199
Please ol' moster don't whip me, 33
Satu'day night and Sunday too, 409
Wants my friends to go wid me, 165
Yon comes ole Marster Jesus, 453

Couplet texts

Gallaniper horsefly, 358
I'm going home to my loving Jesus, 445
Run, nigger, run, 426
Shoo, shoo, gander, 56
Whoo-dee dee, hey, 286

1841 _____. Vol. 3. GEORGIA NARRATIVES. Texts of 10 songs; 2 couplets. 342 pp.

Chorus firstlines

Run, nigger, run, 96, 185
Soo-oo-oo-k, Janey, 188

Verse firstlines

All I want is Jesus, 10, 17
Goin' home soon in de mornin', 254
I'm bound fer the promise land, 135
I'm gwine ter tell the Lord, 134
Jest befo' day, I feels 'im, 259
My brother, where were you?, 255
Our troubles will soon be over, 9, 17
Short steady, I am running, 66

Couplet texts

I am glad salvation is free, 228
Shake your leg, everybody, 116

1842 _____. Vol. 5. INDIANA AND OHIO NARRATIVES Part 1 (Indiana), 275 pp. Part 2 (Ohio), 212 pp. Paginated 277-489. Texts of 10 songs.

Chorus firstlines
Ah'm gwine to glory, hallelujah, 1-128
Glory be to King Immanuel, 1-128
De massa run, ha, ha, 1-108

Verse firstlines

All around my house, 1-128
Cherry bound and Durham, you, 2-486
Has anybody seen my massa, 1-108
My ole missus promise me, 1-69
Oh, de hardshell ship is er moughty good ship, 2-462
One day, old Satan went abroad, 1-128
A rich man, he sold me, 1-177
Run, nigger, run, 1-69, 1-227
Some folks say that a nigger won't steal, 1-69
We're travelin' to the grave, 2-317

1843 _____. Vol. 6. MISSISSIPPI NARRATIVES. Part 1, 331 pp. Texts of 9 songs; 4 couplets.

Chorus firstlines

De las' round, 47
Rango, rango, 75
Since I bin in de lan', 244

Verse firstlines

Captain, give me your daughter, 75
Come 'long gals an' let's go to Boston, 280
Come on, Chariot, and take her home, 61
Here come de marster, 91
Howdy, my brethern, Howdy yo' do, 244
O, yes, we'll gain de day, 223
See my brudder down de hill, 244
We is gwine er round, 47
Went up ter de river, 229

Couplet texts

Don't you see dem sixteen of chullun, 224
Step light, ladies, de cake is all dough, 47
Run, nigger, run, 47, 279
Watch de sun, see how she run, 243

1844 _____. Vol. 7. MISSISSIPPI NARRATIVES. Part 2, 468 pp. Paginated 332-800. Texts of 8 songs.

Chorus firstline

Run, nigger, run, 743

Verse firstlines

Going to de meeting house, 749
I's gwine ter heaven when I die, 722
O, Lord, cum free dis nigger, 716
O, grave yard, 674
Once I was so lucky, 582
Run Liza Jane and take her home, 705
Who been here since I been gone, 375

1845 _____. Vol. 9. MISSISSIPPI NARRATIVES. Part 4, 557 pp. Paginated 1350-1907. Texts of 7 songs; 2 couplet texts.

Chorus firstlines

De Cap'n am a white man, 1374
Ha, ha, ha, Yo' an' me, 1589
Since I'se bin in de lan', 1554

Verse firstlines

Ah cuss dat Steamboat Rover, 1375
De dandy Womac am a backin' boat, 1374
Free at las', Thank God almighty, 1603
Hopping Mad'son backs out on time, 1374
Howdy my brethern, how d' yer do, 1554
Me and my wife lived all er lone, 1589
De Pearl, she am de fines' boat, 1374

Couplet texts

Run, nigger, run, 1428
Swing low, sweet chariot, 1424

1846 ____. Vol. 10. MISSISSIPPI NARRATIVES. Part 5, 505 pp. Paginated 1908-2413. Texts of 10 songs.

Chorus firstlines

I'm bound to cross Jordan, 2093
No moah, my Lord, 2101

Verse firstlines

I'll never turn back no moah, 2101
My knees is worn, 2046
My mother prayed in de wilderness, 2009
O, lil Liza, lil Liza Jane, 2113
Old Massa say, Pick dat cotton, 2039
Ole Ship o' Zion come here, 2371
One of dese mawnin's, 2093
Sun gwine down, Lord, 2274
Who is dat a-coming, 2370
You're selling me to Georgy, 2107

1847 ____. Vol. 11. NORTH CAROLINA AND SOUTH CAROLINA NARRATIVES. 326 pp. Texts of 15 songs; 2 couplets. All songs listed below are from South Carolina.

Chorus firstlines

Bye and bye, 87
O-ou-ou-o-ou, Dominicio, 145
O, glory hallelujah, 88
Roll, Jordan, roll, 111
Sunday mornin' band, 113

Verse firstlines

Hold out true believer, 283
I got beef in de market, 113
I went over Jordan, 111
I'm a-goin' home, 89
I'm gwine to join de band, 112
Mother, where shall I meet you, 87
O, git on board, 81
O, my sister, how you walk on de cross, 113
One for Paul, en one for Silas, 110
Resurrection drawin' nigh!, 110
Way over in the promised land, 88
We are a-slippin' through the gates, 89
When I go to heaven, 237

Couplet texts

Didn't my Lord deliver Daniel, 283
Didn't my soul feel happy, 1815

1848 ____. THE AMERICAN SLAVE: A COMPOSITE AUTOBIOGRAPHY. [Supplement, Series 2. Westport, CT: Greenwood Press, 1979.] Vol. 2. TEXAS NARRATIVES [Part 1]. 470 pp. Texts of 25 songs; 4 couplet texts.

Chorus firstlines

An' He nebber say a mumblin' word, 130
An' He nevah said a word, 440
But de grave it would not hol' Him, 411
Doll, doll, young lady, 154
Hallelujah, we mus' be bo'n r' God, 282
I'd been marry seben year ago, 162
I'm coming, 236
No man can hindah!, 440
O, gimme er little time ter pray, 132
Run, nigger, run, 304, 312
Run, sinner, run, 411
See, can't you jump fer joy, 131
Sometimes I feel like a motherless child, 130
W'en I git home t'Heben, 282
Well, so I kin die easy, 129
Well, so I kin die in Jesus, 438
Well, tone the bell easy, 438
Went t' d' garden, 162

Verse firstlines

Cold frosty mornin', 304, 312
Dey crucified my Lawd, 130, 440
Hits eighteen-hundred an' forty-nine, 451
I been in de storm so long, 132
I wrastled wid Satan, 130
I'se goin' from de cotton field, 439
Jesus rides a milk-white hoss, 440
De Jews done kill po' Jesus, 411
Lincoln Board, Don't fool me, 155
My Lawd calls me, 131
My ol' gray headed mudder, 158
O, I want two wings, 131
Old Marster, heah we are, 311
De ole bee make de honey-comb, 451
Sister, you better min', 131
Sit down, sister, 129
We'll put fer de Souf', 452
Wen Gen'al Lee surrendahed, 312
When I was boun' and in trouble, 440
When you hear dat I'm dyin', 129
When you see me dying, 438
Whoa-a-a, Come along, 39

Couplet texts

Hallelujah, we mus' be bo'n 'r' God, 282
I'd been marry seben year ago, 162
I'm coming, I'm coming, 236
W'en I git home t'Heben, 282

1849 ____. Vol. 3. TEXAS NARRATIVES [Part 2]. 482 pp.; paginated 471-953. Texts of 18 songs; 2 couplets.

Chorus firstlines

Dat sun's a slantin', 911

For 'ligion is so sweet, 770
Hold up, American spirit, 631
Hush, somebody callin' my name, 890
I'm clim'in' Jacob's ladder, 510
I'm lookin' fer my Jesus, 890
It is the old time religion, 847
O, Lawd, how long, 716
Patty pat, 912
Roll, Jordan, roll, 770
Swing low, sweet chariot, 517

Verse firstlines

Can can, candido, ol' man dandio, 507
Chickama, craney crow, 506
Dere's some for Paul, 510
Hit's good to be dere, 704
I looked over Jordan, 517
I'm goin' away tomorrow, 716
I'm so glad that trouble don't last away, 890
Kum along true believer, 911
Little chil'ren, I am going home, 615
De Lord said Baptism hit must be, 770
Mix de meal, fry de batter, 515
No mo' auction block fer me, 891
O, shout, my sister, 770
O, you mus' be born ag'in, 510
Rabbit foot quick, 912
Shadders, dey er creepin', de 911
Steal away an' pray, 890
Steal away to Jesus, 510

Couplet texts

It is the old time religion, 847
O, Lawd, how long, 716

1850 ____. Vol. 4. TEXAS NARRATIVES. Part 3, 484 pp. Paginated 955-1439. Texts of 33 songs; 2 couplets.

Chorus firstlines

A rockin' on my knee, 1347
Because I don' wanter stay yere, 1320
Couldn't hear nobody pray, 976
Hush, hush, boys, 1325
I's boun' to carry my soul, 1320
I'se in some ladie's garden, 1133
It's almost day, 975
Methuselah wuz a witness, 1015
O, run, nigger run, 1433
Ol' marster run away, 1324
Ole Satan am er liah, 1257
Religion is so sweet, 1302
Shoo-a-la-a-day, 1196
Sing song Kitty, 1322

Verse firstlines

Bald horse buried in de turnip patch, 1133
Chicken crow at midnight, 975
Chicken in de bread pan, 1375
Early in de mawnin', 1325
Go tell Aunt Nancy, 1011
Goin' down ter town, 1189
Hop light, little lady, 1065
I am going to preach my gospel, 977
I'm bound fo' the Promised land, 1282
Keep 'way f'om me hoodoo, 1257
Let's go down to Jordan, 1302
Milk in de dairy nine days ol', 1322
De moonlight, a shinin' star, 1347
Mourner, fare you well, 1424
My knee-bones am aching, 1262
My old mistus promise me, 1196
O, de devil drempt a dream, 1023
Our bodies boun' to morter and decay, 1321
De please Marster, don't ketch me, 1433
Read in de Bible, 1015
De rough, rocky road, 1320
Say brudders, will you meet me, 1321
Sinner blin', Johnnie can't you ride, 1424
Swing low, sweet chariot, 1320
Tune up de fiddle, 1375
Two barrels pickled pork, 976
Up de hill an' down the holler, 1391
W'ite folks, hab you seed ol' marster, 1324
Way down yonder by myself, 976
We'll camp aw'ile in the wilderness, 1320
Whar you goin' buzzard, 1362
William Trimbletoe, 1010
Yo-o-o, swing long my bullies, 978

Couplet texts

O-ho, I'se gwine home, 1280
Up de hill, down de level, 1133

1851 ____. Vol. 5. TEXAS NARRATIVES. Part 4, 489 pp. Paginated 1441-1925. Texts of 27 songs; 8 couplets.

Chorus firstlines

And then we all go home, 1828
Come to the water side, 1912
I am a soldier of the cross, 1912
I want to go there, too, 1828
Juba this and Juba that, 1816
Never ter return no more, 1465
Thank God Almighty, we're free at last, 1647

Verse firstlines

Abe Lincoln freed the nigger, 1691, 1693
Come thee to love de Lord, 1647
Cum along my brother, 1465
Hallelujah! Union forever, 1691, 1693
I goes to church in de early morn, 1583
I's a climbin' Jacob's laddah, 1778
De jaybird died wid de whoopin' cough, 1460
Jesus my all to Heaven is gone, 1828
Kitty, Kitty, in d' corner, 1628
Let us go down ter Jordan, 1465
O, get down, old Riley to me so, 1816
Old cotton, old co'n, 1602
Old master eats beef, 1582
Old master's gone to Philiman York, 1913
Rabbit gittin' up in a holler, 1550
Setch a kickin' up san', 1459
Sisters, won't you help me, 1834
Somebody's knockin' at your door, 1464
Stand your storm, 1912
Sugar in d' gou'de, 1550
This ain't Christmas mornin, 1816
This baptizing shall go on, 1912
W'en de clouds hang heavy, 1794
Walk, walk, you nigger, 1786
Walkin' wid de angels, 1466
You better read the Bible, 1828
You say you love yo' broth'ah, 1465

Couplet texts

Always from Kare, 1495
Free, free as de jay bird, 1844
Go away ole man, 1496
It was good enough for our father, 1764
Old hog 'round de bench, 1732
Pull de husk, break de ear, 1843
Rabbit, rabbit, jump fru' d' crack, 1628
Set knee to knee, 1591

1852 _____. Vol. 6. Texas Narratives. Part 5, 502 pp. Paginated 1927-2429. Texts of 32 songs; 4 couplets.

Chorus firstlines

A-lookin' fer a home, 2429
Bye and bye, 2296
Down by the riverside, 2390
For de work is mos' done, 1969
Grease dat wooden leg, Dinah, 2204
Hard times, cum agin no mo', 2076
Help me to trust Him, 2119
I call myself a chile of God, 2339
O, boys, O, 2205
O, Lord, forgive, 2297
O, reign, Marse Jesus, reign, 2131
Run, nigger, run, 2048
Shoo, members, shoo, 2026
Sing high de loo, 2025
Sinner, don' stay away, 2388

Verse firstlines

Adam's fallen race, 2119
Ain't no mo' cane one de Nechiz, 2422
De boll weevil is a little bug, 2429
Dere's room enuf in Hebben, 2388
Dinah got a meat skin lay away, 2204
Don't steal my sugar, 2118
Down in Shiloh town, 2205
Dram, Old Master David, 2303, 2312
E'en hang up de fiddle, 2357
Early one morning, on my Massa's farm, 1936
Effen religion wuz a ting dat money could buy, 2131
Froggie went a-co'tin, 1979
Heavenly land, I's gwinter beg God, 2119
Hits gettin' mighty late, 2105
How freely will I go, 2131
I ain't gwine study war no more, 2390
If yer wants ter bake a hoe cake, 2101
Lawd, since I laid my burden down, 2388
My knee bones achin', 2339
No more bull whips, 2090
O git up gals in de mawnin', 2414
O, Mrs. Ghost, wid yer rainment so white, 2103
O, Sister Phoebe, how merry were we, 2242
O, rock along, Susie, 2213
Ol' possum in a holler log, 2025
Rooster in de chicken coop, 1937
Shoo de debil out de corner, 2026
Show pity, Lord, 2297
'Tis de song of de weary, 2076
Way down is the good old Daniel, 2296
We are climbin' Jacob's ladder, 1969
You ole rogue Susie, 2133

Couplet texts

Deep river, my home is ovar Jordan, 2075
In de new Jerusalem, 2111
O, do w'at Sam done, 2111
Possum up de gum stump, 2103
Yonder come mommer, Julie, 2341

1853 _____. Vol. 7. TEXAS NARRATIVES. Part 6, 485 pp. Paginated 2431-2914. Texts of 19 songs; 3 couplets.

Chorus firstlines

Heben gwinter be my home, 2812
Let's go down t' Jerd'n, 2722
Pig-o-o-o, come on, 2697
Run, nigger, run, 2812

Verse firstlines

All don't form a row shan't drink, 2533
Chicama-chicama craney-crow, 2527
Cotton-eyed Joe, 2532 , 2546
De blue bonnet flag, 2625
De mawnin' star is risin', 2696
Hat, old hat looks like a crow's nest, 2525
I went down in the valley, 2600
Jerd'n ribber so still 'n' col', 2722
Knock on the anvil, 2532
Little chillens, y' better b'lieve, 2812
O, little Mary, I want my dinner, 2696
O, little Mary, I want some water, 2697
Reglar, reglar, roll over, 2524
Rock, Daniel, w'at yer cumin' here fer, 2781
Sheep shear corn, 2533, 2547
That old bald nigger, 2532 , 2547
William, William, treble toe, 2527

Couplet texts

It was good for our fathers, 2466
I heard from heaven today, 2533
You can have all the world, 2716

1854 _____. Vol. 8. TEXAS NARRATIVES. Part 7, 479 pp. Paginated 2915-3402. Texts of 24 songs; 2 couplets.

Chorus firstlines

Adam in de gyarden, 3175
Come and join de ban', 3328
Come inchin' 'long, 3176
Free me, Lord, 3058
Give me Jesus, 3057, 3366
Ha! I'm bound away fer de wild Miz-zou-rye, 3153
O, hood a laddy, 3173
So happy, 3361
Steal away to Jesus, 3327
We hab some licker on de way, 3175
We hafter linger on de way, 3175

Verse firstlines

Ain't you weary trablin', 3328
At dark of midnight w'en I rise, 3366
The Bible do me here below, 3216
Free at las', 3080
How long us hafter linger, 3175
I killed an old grey goose, 3011
I'm drinkin' of rum, 3153

I'm going away to the city, 3057
I'm in some lady's garden, 3061
In the mornin' when I rise, 3057
It's a crane, de same old crane, 3011
Jesus has been wid us, 3174
O, Ebe, w'er is Adam, 3175
O, get up gals in de mawnin', 2980
O, yes, we hab some licker, 3175
Ol' Satan thought he had me fas', 3176
Old Satan mighty busy, 3058
Run, negro, run, negro, 3214
Shuck man can't let get away, 3173
They nailed Him to the cross, 3290
W'en my Lord calls me, 3327
Walking in the parlor, 3216
We will cross de ribber of Jordan, 3361
What ship is dat sailing so slow, 3328

Couplet texts

My sister, you better min', 3175
Swing low, sweet chariot, 3041

1855 _____. Vol. 9. TEXAS NARRATIVES. Part 8, 486 pp. Paginated 3403-3889. Texts of 9 songs; 3 couplets.

Chorus firstlines

Hi, ho, ug, De sharp bit, 3605
Run, nigger, run, 3758

Verse firstlines

Dat ration day cum once a week, 3742
Herodias went down to de river one day, 3818
Nigger mighty happy w'en he layin' by de corn, 3741
Put on my long white robe, 3818
Read in de Gospel of Math-yew, 3724
Up de hill and down the holler, 3875
We'll stick ter de hoe, 3740

Couplet texts

When I'm here you'll call me honey, 3710
The raccoon is a funny thing, 3710
Rise, shine, give God glory, 3724

1856 _____. Vol. 10. TEXAS NARRATIVES. Part 9, 486 pp. Paginated 3891-4377. Texts of 16 songs; 2 couplets.

Chorus firstlines

O, row, who laid dat rail, 4148
Run, nigger, run, 4023, 4114, 4357

Verse firstlines

As I went down in de valley to pray, 4150
Big yam taters in de Sandy lan', 4047
Come along, true believer, 4150
Eighteen-hundred-twenty-one, 4276
Hits a mighty dry year, 4148
Hop light, lady, de cake all dough, 4049
I sittin' on de riverside, 4045
Let's go down to Jordan, 4264
Masse sleeps in de feathah bed, 4113
Master of de house, 4045
Rabbit in de briar patch, 4113
De time is right now, 4152
De top bolls aint open, 4149
Up the hill and down the holler, 4357
What's de use of repinin', 4045

Couplet texts

Look over yonder, what I see, 4026
Times are gittin' hard, 4150

V

THE EARLY TWENTIETH CENTURY

LITERATURE: 1900–1920

SOCIAL ACTIVITIES

1857 Aimes, Hubert H. S. "African Institutions in America." JOURNAL OF AMERICAN FOLK-LORE 18 (January-March 1905): 15-32.

Connecticut writer's discussion of slave festivals in the United States, Brazil, and the West Indies during the eighteenth and nineteenth centuries includes references to primary sources that report on the election of black "governors" in colonial New England and on the associated 'Lection Day parades and balls.

Description of 2 slave dances: calenda and congo (25).

1858 Anderson, Robert Ball. FROM SLAVERY TO AFFLUENCE: MEMOIRS OF ROBERT ANDERSON, EX-SLAVE. Hemingford, NE: Hemingford Ledger, 1927. 59 pp. Reprint. Edited by Daisy Anderson Leonard. Steamboat Springs, CO: The Steamboat Pilot, 1967. 80 pp.

Ex-slave Robert Anderson (1843-1930), born in Green County, Kentucky, discusses religious services on the plantation, where meetings were held in the open around a bonfire because there was no praise-cabin (21-23). Also comment on musical practices, song types, instruments, improvisation, and other performance practice (24-26); on social affairs and the distinction between secular and religious dancing (30-33).

References to 4 dances: 1. Double shuffle. 2. Juba. 3. Heel and toe. 4. Buck and wing.

1859 Avirett, James Battle. THE OLD PLANTATION: HOW WE LIVED IN GREAT HOUSE AND CABIN BEFORE THE WAR. 3d ed. New York: F. T. Neely, c.1901. 202 pp.

Discussion of the "three great high feasts on the plantation"---Christmas, hog-killing, and corn-shucking (140-53). Also discussion of slave dances: double-shuffle, break-down, chicken-in-de-bread-tray, pigeon-wing, and cakewalk (193).

1860 Bennett, Arnold. [Ragtime]. BOSTON SYMPHONY ORCHESTRA PROGRAMME 32 (4 March 1913): 1186-96. Originally published in the LONDON TIMES, 8 February 1913.

Composer's letter to the editor includes discussion of ragtime, its characteristic features, and its relationship to the slave songs. Observation that "ragtime represents the American nation" and will probably influence the character of American composition in the future.

1861 Boyle, Virginia Frazer. "A Kingdom for Micajah." HARPER'S MONTHLY MAGAZINE 100 (March 1900): 527-35.

A short story about a freed black man named Micajah, written by an novelist of Tennessee, includes discussion of slaves on a southern plantation in antebellum times and the cakewalk, which the slaves performed to celebrate the wedding of their master's daughter. Also reference to the slaves' "bran" dance.

1862 _____. "Ole Marse and Aunt Nancy." HARPER'S WEEKLY 53 (19 June 1909): 22-23.

Short story about slaves on a plantation in the antebellum South includes comment on the fact that the slaves distinguished between religious dancing and secular dancing; the latter was called "debil" dancing.

1863 Brooke, Thomas Preston]. "The Permanence of 'Ragtime' Music." LITERARY DIGEST 24 (29 March 1903): 427.

Discussion in defense of ragtime, which includes comment on black dances---juba, the buck-and-wing---draws on an article previously published in the CHICAGO TRIBUNE. Observation that "no more inspiring ragtime was ever played than that which [the] old plantation darky patted."

1864 Bruce, Philip Alexander. SOCIAL LIFE OF VIRGINIA IN THE SEVENTEENTH CENTURY: An Inquiry into the Origin of the Higher Planting Class, Together with an Account of the Habits, Customs, and Diversions of the People. Richmond, VA: Printed for the Author by Whittet and Shepperson, 1907. 268 pp.

Reference to a slave fiddler of the seventeenth century who gained a reputation among the colonists for his talent, and who played for social events of the planters (181).

1865 Cade, John B. "Out of the Mouths of Ex-Slaves." JOURNAL OF NEGRO HISTORY 20 (1935): 294-337.

Black professor at Southern University (Louisiana) assigned his graduate students (who were mostly in-service teachers) to interview ex-slaves in Louisiana in the 1929-30 academic year. Reports on the religious activities of the slaves (327-331) include references to secret prayer meetings in brush arbors and the use of pots turned upside down or quilts hung around the worshippers to muffle the sounds. Also discussion of dancing, ring plays, musical instruments (333-334).

1866 Chesnutt, Charles W. THE MARROW OF TRADITION. New York: Houghton, Mifflin, and Company, 1901. Reprint. New York: Arno Press and the New York Times, 1969. 329 pp.

Novel of the Afro-American writer, which is based upon the Wilmington (North Carolina) Riot of 1898, includes references to a folk sermon (226), and to blacks dancing the cakewalk and the buck dance (117-19).

1867 Clinkscales, John George. ON THE OLD PLANTATION: REMINISCENCES OF HIS CHILDHOOD. Spartanburg, SC: Band and White, 1916. Reprint. New York: Negro Universities Press, 1969. 142 pp.

Comment by a white southerner on a black fiddler who provided dance music for the plantation slaves' annual cakewalk (12), on the hymn singing of the slaves in their cabins (46), and on the performance of the "shout" after religious services (138-39).

1868 Cole, Bob, and J[ohn] Rosamond Johnson. "Four Negro Songs." LADIES HOME JOURNAL (May 1905): 29; (June 1905): 31; (July 1905): 23; (August 1905): 19.

The black composers intended the songs "to illustrate the growth of the forms of negro music from the old days of minstrelsy to the present...." The second song, "Darkies Delight," quotes the refrain of a well-known folksong, "Carve dat possum"; the third song, "The Spirit of the Banjo," aims to "represent the old-time banjo song of the cotton fields."

1869 Cuney-Hare, Maud. "Folk Music of the Creoles." Parts 1, 2. MUSICAL OBSERVER 19 (September-October 1920): 16-18; (November 1920): 12-14. Reprint in NEGRO ANTHOLOGY MADE BY NANCY CUNARD, 1931-1933. London: Wishart & Company, 1934. See also Nancy Cunard, NEGRO. AN ANTHOLOGY, edited and abridged by Hugh Ford, 242-46. New York: Frederick Ungar Publishing Company, 1970.

The first essay of this Afro-American music historian centers on the creole dance, its rhythms and performance practice. Essay 2 focuses on the creole slave songs and dances in New Orleans, Louisiana, particularly those associated with the Place Congo. Description of the creole folk-crafted musical instruments: drums, banjos, quills, and the marimba.

Descriptions of 3 dances: 1. Guiouba (=Juba). 2. two dances in Place Congo. 3. Vaudaux or Voudoo. References to 4 dances: 1. Babouille. 2. Counjaille or Counjai. 3. Bamboula. 4. Calinda.

Texts and music of 2 songs: 1. Quand patate la cuite na va mange. 2. Quand mo te jeun'. Texts of 5 songs: 1. Noon! Drowsy and sweet, the patois croon. 2. C'est Michie Cayetane, qui sorti la Havane. 3. Aurelia, mo connai toi. 4. To, to, to! 'Ca qui la'. 5. Voyez ce mulet la, Musiueu Bainjo. References to 5 songs: 1. Aie! Aie! Voudou Magnan! 2. Aie, Calinda! Danse! Calinda! 3. Por piti Lolotte. 4. Aurore Pradere, belle 'ti fille. 5. Creole Candjo.

1870 Darby, Loraine. "Ring-Games from Georgia." JOURNAL OF AMERICAN FOLK-LORE 30 (January-March 1917): 218-21.

Discussion of performance practice associated with the dance-songs of black children. Music and texts of 2 ring-game songs: 1. All around the May-pole (the May-pole song). 2. This lady she wears a dark-green shawl. Texts of 5 ring-game songs: 1. Did you go to the hen-house? (Cho: Good old egg-bread). 2. Way down yonder. 3. Old green field. 4. My old mistress promised me (Cho: Take your lover in the ring). 5. In come another one (High, O).

1871 Dickson, Harris. "The Way of the Reformer." SATURDAY EVENING POST 179 (12 January 1907): 6-7, 22.

Survey of social life and mores in Vicksburg,

Mississippi, around the turn of the twentieth century includes description of a typical dance hall, where the black "professor" (=pianist) played and everyone danced "with all formalities waived." Also comment on the Negro work gangs "singing the conju songs of barbaric Africa."

Text of 1 song: My gal lives in de white folk's yard.

1872 _____. "The J'iner: Ole Reliable J'ines the Army, the Jail, and the Cotton Pickers." SATURDAY EVENING POST 183 (10 September 1910): 24-25, 65-67.

Short story about the black community in Vicksburg, Mississippi, after the Civil War includes description of black Union Army veterans (formerly of Company H, 46th U.S. Colored Troops) marching in a parade to the music of fifer and drummer.

1873 Duke, Basil. REMINISCENCES OF GENERAL BASIL W. DUKE, C.S.A. Garden City, NY: Doubleday, Page and Company, 1911.

Memoirs, which were originally published in HOME AND FARM MAGAZINE (Louisville), include reference to the use of a "big conch shell" rather than a horn for calling the slaves together. The houseboy was in charge of beating the shell.

1874 Dunbar, Olivia Howard. "The Greatest of These." HARPER'S MONTHLY MAGAZINE 108 (December 1903-May 1904): 487-90.

Short story written by a black writer includes description of a lawn party and the dance music performed for the party by a banjoist, who played simultaneously his banjo and a mouth harp. Later, the banjoist/harpist was joined by an Italian, who cranked on his hand-organ.

1875 Dunbar, Paul Laurence. "A Supper by Proxy." SATURDAY EVENING POST 173 (10 November 1900): 26-27. Reprint. IN OLD PLANTATION DAYS. New York: Dodd, Mead & Company, 1903. Reprint. New York: Negro Universities Press, 1969.

Afro-American poet-writer, in a short story about antebellum plantation slaves, offers description of the hand patting and feet shuffling that accompanied the singing of the Juba dance-song. Also comment on the juba dance.

Text of 1 juba rhyme: Mas' done gone to Philamundelphy, Juba, Juba (Cho: Oh, Juba dis and Juba dat).

1876 _____. "Ash-Cake Hannah and Her Ben." SATURDAY EVENING POST 173 (8 December 1900): 1900): 16-17. Reprint in OLD PLANTATION DAYS.

Short story written by the black American poet includes description of Christmas festivities of the slaves, with comment on the singing of Christmas songs and dancing to the music of fiddle and banjo.

Text of 1 Christmas song: Oh, moughty day at Bethelem.

1877 Europe, James Reese. "A Negro Explains Jazz." LITERARY DIGEST 61 (26 April 1919): 28-29.

Account of an interview with black bandmaster Europe includes his discussion of a folk-crafted instrument made from wood of the china berry tree. Also comment on how the musicians in his band "embroider their parts in order to produce new, peculiar sounds."

1878 Ferguson, David LeRoy. "With This Black Man's Army." INDEPENDENT 97 (15 March 1919): 368.

The account of a black minister includes comment on a Negro Stevedore Band of the U.S. Army and the kind of music it played in France during World War I.

1879 Graham, Alice. "The Negro Craze for the Reed Organ in the South." ETUDE (November 1916): 826.

Discussion of the plantation workers' love for the reed organ and of the quality of the music they improvised on the instrument: "slow tempo, sad and melancholy in style." Observation that they purchased organs even if they had to deny themselves food, and that they spent hours improvising, "which is called 'pranking'."

1880 Hegan, Alice Caldwell. "The Watermelon Stockings." ST. NICHOLAS: AN ILLUSTRATED MAGAZINE FOR BOYS AND GIRLS 30 (December 1902): 156-61.

Short story about a black girl named "Amazing Grace" includes references to 2 dance steps: 1. Pigeon-wing. 2. Mobile buck.

1881 Inglis, William. "Is Modern Dancing Indecent? A Calm and Unbiased Consideration of a Remarkable Phase of Contemporary Life." HARPER'S WEEKLY 57 (17 May 1913): 11-12.

Essay about social dancing in New York City in the early 1910s includes references to a group of eight black bellhops at a local hotel who played for dancing on their banjos, mandolins, and guitars, and who also sang as they played.

Text of 1 song. 'Way down in Mississippi.

1882 Johnson, James Weldon. THE AUTOBIOGRAPHY OF AN EX-COLORED MAN. Boston: Sherman, French & Company, 1912. 207 pp. Reprint. New York: Alfred A. Knopf, 1927.

Novel of black writer-scholar Johnson includes detailed description of the cakewalk "in its original form" (85-87), of ragtime performed in a nightclub by a black pianist (98-101), and of a "Big Meeting" (=revival meeting) in a rural community of Georgia (?) that includes discussion of the preacher's oratory style and of the singing leader, known as Singing Johnson (173-82).

Texts of 2 songs (179): 1. Swing low, sweet chariot. 2. Steal away to Jesus.

1883 Lee, Florence Whiting. "Christmas in Virginia before the War." SOUTHERN WORKMAN 37 (December 1908): 686-89.

Discussion of Christmas Day celebrations among antebellum plantation blacks in Virginia includes description of a dance and reference to 1 dance song: De lonesome win' he holler.

1884 Mason, George C. "Old Plantation Life in Rhode Island." NEW ENGLAND MAGAZINE n.s. 21 (February 1900): 735-40.

Discussion of plantation life in Rhode Island in the late eighteenth century includes description of 'Lection Day celebrations and a corn-husking festival.

1885 McDonald, James J. LIFE IN OLD VIRGINIA. A Description of Virginia, More Particularly the Tidewater Section, Narrating Many Incidents Relating to the Manners and Customs of Old Virginia So Fast Disappearing as a Result of the War between the States, Together with Many Humorous Stories. Norfolk, VA: The Old Virginia Publishing Company, 1907. 374 pp.

Discussion of plantation life by a former state senator of Virginia includes description of slave dances (pigeon wing, jig) and instruments (fiddle, banjo, jews harp, mouth harp), including pattin' (177). Also description of a corn shucking (231-233) and a slave wedding (96). Detailed analysis of a folk sermon (277-82).

Texts of 4 songs: 1. Dis co'n, it are good (233). 2. The old ship of Zion (277). 3. I'se got on de back uv de Baptis' mule (Cho: An' I'll ride right on to glory) (280). 4. (Cho: This old time religion) It was good for our fathers (282).

1886 Mears, H. H. "Chris'mus." HARPER'S WEEKLY 55 (16 December 1911): 25.

Poem written in Afro-American dialect contains references to pattin', shufflin', and jiggin'.

1887 Moderwell, Hiram Kelly. "Ragtime." NEW REPUBLIC (16 October 1915): 284-86.

Discussion of ragtime as the "one true American music" includes the text of 1 couplet: An' he gave them commishun to fly, Brudder Lass'rus.

1888 Northrup, A. Judd. "Slavery in New York." NEW YORK STATE LIBRARY BULLETIN HISTORY No. 4 (May 1900): 243-310.

A former judge's discussion of the Pinkster Day celebrations of slaves in colonial New York (283) includes references to dancing accompanied by music performed on an eel-pot and log drums. Reference to 1 song: Hi-a bomba bomba.

1889 Palmer, Frederick. "Black Face and White Soul." COSMOPOLITAN 67 (August 1914): 306-19.

Short story about a black man's adventures in Mexico includes description of his playing his mandolin---how he talks to his instrument, calling it Missy; plays many song types, French and Spanish as well as plantation melodies; and "summons a host of memories" for his listeners (312).

1890 Platt, Orville H. "Negro Governors." PAPERS OF THE NEW HAVEN COLONY HISTORICAL SOCIETY 6 (1900): 315-35.

This paper, read before the Society on 21 November 1898, includes discussion of the election of black "governors" in Connecticut and Rhode Island in the eighteenth and early nineteenth centuries, and references to black revelers singing songs in "the various languages of Africa" and playing "musical instruments of their native country" (324).

1891 Porter, Grace Cleveland. NEGRO FOLK SINGING-GAMES AND FOLK GAMES OF THE HABITANTS. London: J. Curwen & Sons, [1914].

Collection includes tales about plantation life in Maryland and Mississippi. Also discussion of ring-game songs and dances from Georgia and Mississippi. Description of a Brer Rabbit dance (ix). Summaries of 2 folk tales (viii): 1. The talking catfish. 2. Ran-tan-tony, Brer Rat and Brer Rabbit.

Texts and music of 11 ring-games: 1. We're marchin' on dis camp groun' (1). 2. Your darlin', my darlin', can't yo' ketch dat Squirrel (4). 3. De Queen ob England (6). 4. I'm walking on the levee (8). 5. I los' mah mistis' dairy key (10). 6. Bounce aroun' to-di-iddy-um (12). 7. Come, mah little darlin' an' take a walk wid me (14). 8. Fly roun', fly roun' (16). 9. The needle's eye (18). 10. Mah heart's gone away to Loosiana (20). 11. Turn, cinnamon, turn (22). Text of 1 ring-game: One-er-mah-ury, dickery-seben (vii).

1892 Pringle, Elizabeth W. Allston. [Patience Pennington, pseud.] A WOMAN RICE PLANTER. New York: Macmillan Company, 1913. 447 pp. Reprint. Microfiche. Chicago: Library Resources, 1970.

Memoirs of a white southern woman who managed a rice plantation in South Carolina, aided only by black workers, many of them ex-slaves. Discussion includes description of a funeral procession (59-60), and comment on the voice quality of the slaves' singing. Also discussion of Christmas festivities (274), which included dancing to the music of fiddle, tambourine, bones, drum, and sticks; and of the singing of "speretuals" at a funeral "settin' up" (361).

1893 "A Real Voodoo Dance." NASHVILLE AMERICAN 7 March 1906. Clipping. Allen Brown Collection (Scrapbook), "Musical Topics," 6: 270. Boston Public Library, Boston, Massachusetts.

Description of voodoo ceremonies witnessed by a journalist in the swamps and forests of Florida and Georgia includes references to the chanting of "doleful hymns" and to the "slow, whirling dance" associated with the "quaint rites," especially at Christmas time.

1894 Rice, Edward LeRoy. MONARCHS OF MINSTRELSY. New York: Kenny Publishing Company, 1911. 366 pp.

History of American minstrelsy includes discussion of several black minstrels who began their careers as street criers or folk dancers and singers: Picayune Butler (30), Horace Weston (46), and Master Juba (48).

1895 Robinson, William H. FROM LOG CABIN TO PULPIT; OR, FIFTEEN YEARS IN SLAVERY. Eau Claire, WI: The Author, 1903. 123 pp. Rev. ed. Eau Clare, WI: James H. Tifft, 1913. 200 pp. Page references below are to the 1903 ed.

Autobiography of the ex-slave preacher (b. 1848) from Wilmington, North Carolina, includes references to a slave ball, where the music was provided by tambourine, banjo, and bones (70). Also discussion of the use of kettles and other cooking utensils by the slaves to muffle the sound of singing and prayers during worship services.

Texts of 3 songs: 1. He delivered Daniel from the lion's den (53). 2. Get you ready, there's a meeting here tonight (71). 3. Free at last (114).

1896 Sherlock, Charles Reginald. "From Breakdown to Ragtime." COSMOPOLITAN 31 (October 1901): 631-39.

Discussion of Ethiopian minstrelsy and the white, stage-Negro delineators at the end of the nineteenth century includes references to genuine slave dances---break-down and cakewalk---and a detailed description of the Essence of Ole Virginny (634-35).

Text of 1 chorus: Wheel about, turn about, do jis so (632).

1897 Sousa, John Philip. "American Music and Ragtime." MUSIC TRADE REVIEW 37/14 (3 October 1903): 8.

Report on Sousa's "views on the permanency of ragtime," expressed during his visit to Chicago, notes that he said, "Ragtime is an established feature of American music." References to the popularity of ragtime among the crowned heads of Europe.

1898 Spenney, Susan Dix. "Riddles and Ring-Games from Raleigh, South Carolina." JOURNAL OF AMERICAN FOLK-LORE 34 (January/March 1921): 110-15.

Description of ring-play activities by a Hampton graduate. Texts and music of 7 ring-game songs performed by black children in Raleigh, North Carolina: 1. King William was King George's son. 2. London Bridge is burning down (Cho: Heist, go, ladies, turn!). 3. It rains, it hails. 4. Grandaddy is dead. 5. Hands all 'round (Cho: Jing jang!). 6. Reg'lar, reg'lar, rolling under. 7. Ol' mist'is calls me. Also included are ring-game descriptions of nos. 1, 2, 3, 4, and 6.

1899 Stanton, Frank L. "The Ghostly Christmas Dance." SATURDAY EVENING POST 173 (8 December 1900): 13.

Poem written in Afro-American dialect identifies 2 dance figures: double-shuffle and pigeon-wing. Also references to the fiddler and the "beating of the bones."

1900 _____. "The Banjo Dancer." SATURDAY EVENING POST 176 (24 August 1903): 9.

Poem written in Afro-American dialect about black folk dancing refers to 5 dances: 1. Way down in Alabama. 2. Tennessee's a-comin'. 3. Rabbit-in-de-briar-path. 4. Ole Kentucky. 5. Ole Ferginny reel.

1901 Stuart, Ruth McEnery. NAPOLEON JACKSON, THE GENTLEMAN OF THE PLUSH ROCKER. New York: Century Company, 1904. 132 pp. Reprint. Microfiche. Lexington, KY: Lost Cause Press, 198-.

Novel about an ex-slave washerwoman and her family, set on a plantation in the post-Civil War era, includes a detailed description of an impromptu dance, accompanied by the singing of on-lookers, that took place outside her cabin (65-77).

1902 Turner, Edward Raymond. THE NEGRO IN PENNSYLVANIA. SLAVERY---SERVITUDE---FREEDOM. 1639-1861. Washington, DC: American Historical Association, 1911. 314 pp. Reprint. New York: Arno Press and the New York Times, 1969.

Comment on slaves playing fiddles and dancing in Potter's Field (42), "wandering Negro exhorters" (45), and the songs of chimney sweeps (124).

1903 Turner, James. "Slavery in Edgecombe County [North Carolina]." HISTORICAL PAPERS, Published by the Trinity College Historical Society, Durham, NC, Ser. 12 (1916): 5-36.

Discussion of slave marriages (28) and the use of a pot turned upside down to deaden the sound of the slaves' dancing (27).

1904 Washington, Booker T. "Christmas Days in Old Virginia." SUBURBAN LIFE 5 (December 1907): 336-37. Reprint in THE BOOKER T. WASHINGTON PAPERS.... Vol. 1. THE AUTOBIOGRAPHICAL WRITINGS. Urbana: University of Illinois Press, 1972. Page references are to the reprint edition.

Account of how the slaves celebrated Christmas includes a detailed description of the corn-shucking festival and of the singing that accompanied the "Yule Log" ceremonies (394-97).

1905 Weeden, Howard [Harriet Weeden]. BANDANNA BALLADS, INCLUDING "SHADOWS ON THE WALL." New York: Doubleday and McClurg Company, 1899. 91 pp. Reprint of selected rhymes. LADIES HOME JOURNAL (April 1900): 9.

Collection of the writer's poems about antebellum plantation life includes many references to black folk traditions---singing, banjo playing, and dancing. One rhyme describes in detail the sound of the banjoist's song.

1906 Williams, Timothy Shaler. "The Sports of Negro Children." ST. NICHOLAS: AN ILLUSTRATED MAGAZINE FOR BOYS AND GIRLS 30 (September 1903): 1004-7.

Discussion of game-songs, ring-games, and dances of black children in the South.

Texts of 5 game-songs: 1. Hop like de rabbit, ho! 2. De willow-tree I nebber saw. 3. Don't you tell dose girls I love it to my heart (Cho: Rice-cake, sweet me so). 4. Ho, Nannie! Hand me the gourd to drink water. 5. Here's Miss Phoebe sits under a June-apple tree (Cho: An' a sweet little one, heigh-ho!).

Descriptions of 7 dances and ring-games: 1. Rap-jacket. 2. Hop like de rabbit, ho!. 3. De willow-tree I nebber saw. 4. Drinking water. 5. Shouting Josephine. 6. Here's Miss Phoebe. 7. Cake walk.

1907 Wise, Jennings Cropper. YE KINGDOME OF ACCOWMACKE; OR, THE EASTERN SHORE OF VIRGINIA IN THE SEVENTEENTH CENTURY. Richmond, VA: The Bell Book & Stationery Company, 1911. 406 pp. Reprint. Baltimore, MD: Regional Publishing Company, 1967.

A chapter devoted to slaves and freedmen, who are identified by name (285-88), includes reference to the slave fiddler belonging to Capt. Richard Bayly of Accomac County (322-23).

1908 Woodberry, George E., ed. "The Poe-Chivers Papers: First Authentic Account of One of Poe's Most Interesting Friendships." CENTURY MAGAZINE 65 (February 1903): 545-58.

Discussion focuses primarily upon the correspondence of Dr. Thomas H. Chivers of Oaky Grove, Georgia, with writer Edgar Allen Poe. Contains a letter addressed to Augustine Duganne, dated 17 Dec. 1850, that describes a Negro jig (555).

Text of 1 dance song: I doane lyke de cown feeale (Cho: Too, Mark, a-Juba) (555).

THE RELIGIOUS EXPERIENCE

1909 Abbott, Ernest Hamlin. "Religious Life in America. IV---Religious Tendencies of the Negro." OUTLOOK 69 (28 December 1901): 1070-78.

Discussion focuses upon the movement of blacks away from "emotionalism" in their worship services, citing as examples of emotionalism the vociferous oratory of local preachers, the "Amen Corner," and the singing performance practice that distorts the original melodies of familiar Protestant tunes.

1910 Aery, William Anthony. "Better Education for Negro Ministers." SOUTHERN WORKMAN 49 (October 1920): 458-67.

Discussion of the program of a Negro ministers' institute conducted at Betlis Academy, near Trenton, South Carolina, for rural preachers.

References to 5 songs sung at public sessions: I want to be ready. 2. Swing low, sweet chariot. 3. Every time I feel the spirit. 4. We are climbing Jacob's ladder. 5. I know the Lord has laid His hands on me.

1911 Aleckson, Samuel William. BEFORE THE WAR, AND AFTER THE UNION: AN AUTOBIOGRAPHY. Boston: Gold Mind Publishing Company, 1929. 171 pp.

Ex-slave Samuel Aleckson (b. 1852) began writing his autobiography during his "middle life," when he was faced by the prospect of going blind. Later he recovered his sight and health. His discussion includes description of a Methodist church service (27-28) and a folk tale about Jack O-Lantern (62).

Texts of 3 songs: 1. De hebben bells er ringing (63). 2. No fearin, no doubtin (131). 3. Gib me dat old time religion (160). References to 2 songs: 1. I run from Pharo, lem me go (63). 2. Roll, Jordan, roll (131).

1912 Alexander, John Brevard. REMINISCENCES OF

THE PAST SIXTY YEARS. Charlotte, NC: Ray Printing Company, 1908. 513 pp. Reprint. Sanford, NC: Microfilming Corporation of America, 1979.

Memoirs of a slaveholder who lived in Mecklenburg County, North Carolina, include references to slave congregation singing (240), description of a slave wedding (242-44), and comment on slaves worshipping in white churches.

1913 Allen, P. L. "Negro Churches." NATION 78 (26 May 1904): 405-6.

Discussion of the Negro church, based on the report of the Atlanta Conference of 1898, includes reference to its antecendents as the "wild gatherings in the African jungles for the Obeah sorcery." Also comment on the slave preacher Uncle Jack of Virginia.

1914 Alston, Jacob Motte. RICE PLANTER AND SPORTSMAN: THE RECOLLECTIONS OF J. MOTTE ALSTON, 1821-1909. 148 pp. Edited by Arney R. Childs. Columbia: University of South Carolina Press, 1953.

Discussion of slave life includes references to the slaves' reversion to African customs after the Civil War (48) and to the religious instruction of the slaves on the plantation (121).

1915 Ames, Mary. FROM A NEW ENGLAND WOMAN'S DIARY IN DIXIE IN 1865. Springfield, MA: The Plimpton Press, 1906. 125 pp. Reprint. Microfilm. New Haven, CT: Yale University Library, 1987.

Native of Boston signed with the Freedmen's Bureau in 1865 and was sent to teach on Edisto Island, South Carolina, where she remained a year. Her diary includes discussion of a Praise Meeting held in a Baptist church and description of the shout (81-82, 115).

References to 6 songs: 1. Heaven's bell ringing for believers. 2. Sister, you come too late. 3. Don't judge me, Lord, O Lord. 4. Thar's rejoicing ober yonder (45). 5. Oh, Lord, don't be offended (82). 6. When Gabriel blow his horn (82).

1916 Bennett, John. "A Revival Sermon at Little St. John's." ATLANTIC MONTHLY 98 (August 1906): 256-68.

Description of a revival meeting at a black church in rural South Carolina includes comment on the chanted prayer of the preacher, which erupted into song and was accompanied by antiphonal refrains from the congregation. Transcription of the sermon with musical transcriptions of the chanted passages of the sermon. Also comment on the Amen Corner and the character of the old-time Negro spirituals.

Texts and music of 2 couplets: 1. O, hit may be de las' time yo'll ebber hyeah me (256). 2. He dat beliebe hat ebber lastin' life (259). Text and music of 4 songs: 1. Yes, Lord, oh muhsiful God (263). 2. Holy, L'd God a'mighty (263). 3. Oh, hell so deep (Cho: Oh, Lord, wut ha'am I done? (264). 4. Dis time a-nuddeh yeah, I may be gawn (267). Text of 1 sermon: An' dey shill hongry no mo'; Revelation 7:16-17 (258-67).

1917 Brawley, Benjamin Griffith. A SHORT HISTORY OF THE AMERICAN NEGRO. New York: Macmillan Company, 1913. 247 pp.

Black historian's chapter on "The Negro Church" includes discussion of the influence of African religions on the black church, on voodoo, the Negro priest (155-56), and on folk-lore and folk music, including references to ragtime (192-94).

1918 Broughton, N. B. "The Negro in Slavery Days." ALEXANDER'S MAGAZINE 6 (15 September 1908): 201-202.

Discussion of the religious life of the slaves in this black magazine by a white writer of Raleigh, North Carolina, includes the observation that meetings conducted by black preachers were "always held in the open air." Also notes that the slaves had very little opportunity to receive religious instruction before the emancipation.

1919 Bruce, Thomas S. "Among the Colored Churches." CHRISTIAN WATCHMAN & REFLECTOR (WATCHMAN-EXAMINER) 81 (12 April 1900): 31.

Comment on the spiritual and financial condition of black churches in Massachusetts, particularly in Boston, includes description of a prayer-meeting service in that city. Also references to preaching, singing, prayers, and exhortations.

1920 Burlin, Natalie Curtis. "Negro Music at Birth." MUSICAL QUARTERLY 5 (January 1919): 86-89. Reprint of excerpts in CURRENT OPINION 66 (March 1919): 165-66.

Folklorist's description of a typical black camp-meeting service in the rural South includes discussion of the singing of old plantation melodies and the accompanying performance practice. Comment on the oratory style of the preacher, on the "Amen Corner," the communal responses of the congregation, and the moan. Description of how a new song "was born" through collective improvisation, beginning with the mutterings, ejaculations, moans, etc. of the group. Also references to performance practice associated with singing at the Calhoun Industrial School, in a rural church in Virginia, and in a tobacco factory.

1921 Carthel, Joseph. "The Present Condition of the Negro." ALEXANDER'S MAGAZINE 6 (15 September 1908): 210-11.

Article published in this black magazine by the General Secretary of the Alabama State Sunday

School observes that many black churches in rural areas had preaching only once or twice a month because they had no "trained" leaders.

1922 Cocke, Sarah Johnson. "The Rooster and the Washpot." SATURDAY EVENING POST 179 (2 June 1917): 77, 81.

Short story contains description of a revival service held in a black community, called Eastwood, and of the conversion experiences of the residents. Comment on the singing and moaning of the congregation during the service.

Text of 1 song: Yer got ter walk in de narrer path.

1923 Coppin, Levi Jenkins. UNWRITTEN HISTORY. Philadelphia: A.M.E. Book Concern, c.1919. 375 pp. Reprint. New York: Negro Universities Press, 1968.

Autobiography of a bishop of the A.M.E. Church refers to congregations singing "make-as-you-go" hymns as well as the standards (25), and to the opposition of Bishop Daniel Payne to corn-field ditties, prayer-meeting bands, the "swaying of the body and stamping of the feet" when singing, and the "old form of sensational worship." Description of the slave funeral, distinguishing between the burial and the funeral ceremony (55-58), and of the "pertracterable (i.e., protracted) meetings" held in the fall of the year, where some got religion "by way of the mourner's bench" (105-06). Also reference to fiddlers playing for "buck dances," huskings, and parties.

References to 3 sermon texts used by black preachers: 1. Tell me, O, Thou whom my soul loveth. 2. I seek my brethern (Genesis 37:16). 3. Blessed is the man that walketh not in the council of the ungodly (118-21).

1924 Daniels, John. IN FREEDOM'S BIRTHPLACE. A STUDY OF THE BOSTON NEGROES. Boston: Houghton Mifflin Company, 1914. Reprint. New York: Arno Press and the New York Times, 1969. 496 pp.

Study includes discussion of a service attended by the author at the Church of God, Saints of Christ, with comment on the performance practice of the singing and on a "violent dance" by a woman who was "testifying" (244-246). Also references to the voice quality of Negro singing (200).

Texts of 2 songs: 1. God was a man (245). 2. Teach all the nations of Thy commands (245).

1925 Davenport, Frederick Morgan. "The Religion of the American Negro." CONTEMPORARY REVIEW 88 (September 1905): 369-75.

Discussion of the religious practice and rites of the black church in the rural South, particularly the prayer-meeting service. Reference to the folk preacher as "a descendent of the medicine-man of the African clan." Extensive comment on the oratory of the folk preacher, the singing of religious songs, and ecstatic seizure.

Reference to 1 religious dance: the flower dance. Description of 2 shouts: 1. the "roper dance." 2. Rocking Daniel. Text of 1 couplet: Rock Daniel till I die.

1926 _____. PRIMITIVE TRAITS IN RELIGIOUS REVIVALS: A STUDY IN MENTAL AND SOCIAL EVOLUTION. New York: Macmillan Company, 1905. 323 pp. Reprint. New York: AMS Press, 1972.

Discussion of African and Afro-American religious traditions (45-59) includes comment on voodoo rites (47) and description of a religious service of the "Sheep-Calling Baptists" in Alabama (48) and of a church service in Tennessee (50-51). Comment on performance practice, congregational responses to sermons, religious dancing, and ecstatic seizure. Description of the shout and other religious dances (54-55): the roper dance, found in Alabama, and "rocking Daniel," performed at the Primitive Orthodox Zion Church in Yamassee, Florida.

Text of 1 chorus: Rock, Daniel, till I die (55).

1927 Davis, Sidney Fant. MISSISSIPPI NEGRO LORE. Jackson, TN: McCowat-Mercer, 1914. 35 pp.

Collection of essays includes description of the worship services of blacks in Mississippi (16-20).

Text of 1 sermon: The beautifulness of heaven. Text of 1 couplet: 1. God showed Noah by the rainbow sign. Text of 1 chorus: It rains and it hails, and it is cold and stormy weather.

1928 Dickson, Harris. "The Grand Organizer: An Episode in the Activities of 'Reverend' Criddle." SATURDAY EVENING POST 185 (4 January 1913): 8-9, 33-34.

Short story about a preacher and a mutual-aid society organized for the purpose of burying its members includes description of a funeral and the marching brass band that escorted the hearse and mourners to the cemetery.

1929 Douglass, E. W. "A Teacher's Reminiscences." AMERICAN MISSIONARY (MAGAZINE) n.s. 65 (February 1911): 725-26.

Discussion of a northern missionary working among blacks in Virginia in 1865 includes comment on the black preacher.

Sermon texts: 1. Moses and the Ten Commandments. 2. Touch one string and all the bells ring.

1930 Dowd, Jerome. "Sermon of an Ante-Bellum

Negro Preacher." SOUTHERN WORKMAN 30 (November 1901): 654-58.

This paper, presented by a professor at the University of Wisconsin to the Historical Society of Trinity College in Durham, North Carolina, focuses on the black folk sermon. Comment on a Christmas sermon delivered by the Rev. Hester ("Uncle Mose").

Text of 1 sermon: Christmas; Luke 2:7.

1931 Drews, William J. "Music and the Negro." MUSICAL RECORD 24 (1 September 1900): 395-96.

Reminiscences of a slaveholder's son about his childhood in southern Virginia includes comment on the outdoor religious services of slaves held in the groves on Sundays. References to singing, the shout, and other practices associated with the worship service. Observation that slaves frequently made up words to fit melodies of Protestant hymns, and also composed their own hymns. Also references to the African Church in Richmond, Virginia; to its pastor, the Rev. John Jasper; and to his famous sermon, "De sun do move."

Texts of 2 songs: 1. We shuck dat corn, and blow dat horn. 2. Oh, Johnny Booker, help dis nigger. References to 3 songs: 1. Run, nigger, run, de patarole el cotch you. 2. We is all agwine to de shuckin'. 3. Dear, dear, Belinda.

1932 Du Bois, William Edward Burghardt. "The Religion of the American Negro." NEW WORLD: A QUARTERLY REVIEW OF RELIGION, ETHICS, AND THEOLOGY 9 (December 1900): 614-25.

Black sociologist's historical survey of the black church includes discussion of the preacher, of sacred song, and religious worship practices, including the shout and ecstatic seizure. Also references to Voodoo worship.

Texts of 2 songs: 1. Children, we all shall be free. 2. Before I'll be a slave.

1933 _____. THE NEGRO. New York: Henry Holt Company, 1915. 254 pp. Reprint. New York: Oxford University Press, 1970.

Comment on the analogy to be drawn between the African tribal priest and the plantation preacher, who attempted to interpret the supernatural; comfort the sorrowful; and express the longings, disappointments, and resentments of a "stolen people." Observation that the early American black church, non-Christian in origin, was based upon an adaptation of obi worship or voodooism (113). Reference to black "governers" in colonial New England (115).

1934 _____, ed. THE NEGRO CHURCH. Atlanta University Publications 8. Atlanta: Atlanta University Press, 1903. Reprint. New York: Arno Press and the New York Times, 1968. 212 pp.

Historical survey of the black church in the United States from its origin through the turn of the twentieth century includes discussion of pioneering black clergyman in the 1700s and 1800s (21-37, 123-25). Description of the shout "Rocking Daniel" (67).

Text of a shout couplet: Rock Daniel, rock Daniel till I die (67).

1935 Dunbar, Paul Laurence. "The Fruitful Sleeping of the Rev. Elisha Edwards." THE STRENGTH OF GIDEON, AND OTHER STORIES. New York: Dodd, Mead & Company, 1900. 362 pp. Reprint. New York: Arno Press and the New York Times, 1969.

Short story about a congregation's problems with its pastor includes descriptions of Sunday services, and of the preaching of both the minister and the exhorter.

1936 _____. "The Walls of Jericho." SATURDAY EVENING POST 173 (6 April 1901): 14-15. Reprint in IN OLD PLANTATION DAYS. New York: Dodd, Mead and Company, 1903. 307 pp.

Short story about a preacher and his rival exhorter, who competed against each other in a prayer meeting, includes description of the service and comment on plantation songs and the shout.

Texts of 2 songs: 1. Someone buried in de graveyard (Cho: Go sound de Jubilee). 2. Den we'll ma'ch, ma'ch down (Cho: In de day o' Jubilee).

1937 _____. "One Christmas at Shiloh." In THE HEART OF HAPPY HOLLOW. New York: Dodd, Mead and Company, 1904. 309 pp. Reprint. Freeport, NY: Books for Libraries Press, [1970].

Story about a folk-oriented church in New York City with a southern-born congregation includes discussion of the character of the folk preacher.

1938 Estes, Phoebe Beckner. "The Reverend Peter Vinegar." SOUTHERN FOLKLORE QUARTERLY 23 (December 1959): 239-52.

Biographical study of Alexander ("Peter") Campbell Vinegar (1842-1905), legendary black preacher of Lexington, Kentucky, and founder of the Campbellite Church there, includes excerpts from sermons he preached and references to sermons of some of his contemporaries. Comment on the context in which the sermons were delivered, based upon interviews with local residents who knew the minister.

Texts of 4 sermons (fragments): 1. And de Lawd brought chaos out-a confusion. 2. A damned hot day. 3. Take dat sin out-a-yo' bosom. 4. When Gabriel blows dat hor'n.

References to 16 sermons: 1. Watch dat snake. 2. Kill old Speck. 3. Hell ain't but a mile from Lexington. 4. Hold dat tiger. 5. The debbie [sic] is a porcupine. 5. The goneness of the past. 7. For de bed am too short, and de river am too narrow. 8. The eagle stirreth her nest. 9. White hoss and de rider. 10. Dry bones in de valley. 11. Sammy Rabbi. 12. Down where de columbine twineth, and de whangdoodle moaneth for its mate. 13. A wheel in der middle of er wheel. 14. Thirteen men coming down a dirt road. 15. Death in de pot. 16. Pearl Bryant is dead, and couldn't find her head.

1939 Faduma, Orishatukeh. "The Defects of the Negro Church." Occasional Paper No. 10. THE AMERICAN NEGRO ACADEMY OCCASIONAL PAPERS, 1-22. Washington, DC: Published by the Academy, 1904. Reprint. New York: Arno Press and the New York Times, 1969. Abstract in SOUTHERN WORKMAN 32 (April 1903): 229-32.

Paper delivered before the American Negro Academy in December, 1902, by a black minister contains detailed discussion of the black preacher and folk practices in the black church. Comment on "apocalyptic sermons," the "mystic preachers known as mourners, shouters, and visioners," and "excessive emotionalism in religion."

1940 Ferris, William H. "A Historical and Psychological Account of the Genesis and Development of the Negro's Religion." A.M.E. CHURCH REVIEW 20 (1904): 343-53.

Black clergyman's historical survey of the black church in the United States includes discussion of the oratory of the black preacher and the sacred music, particularly the jubilees and plantation songs. Comment on the songs as expressions of the slave's aspirations, longings, and sorrows. Observation that the conjure women and voodoo priest are counterparts to the African Shaman and medicine man.

1941 _____. "The Old Time and the New Time Negroes." AMERICAN MISSIONARY (MAGAZINE) n.s. 62 (October 1908): 359-60.

Comparison of the antebellum Negro's lifestyle to that of the contemporary Negro includes discussion of antebellum preachers and cites the names of two: John Jasper of Richmond, Virginia, and John Brown of Jacksonville, Florida.

Fragment text of 1 sermon: De sun do move.

1942 Fisher, Miles Mark. THE MASTER'S SLAVE: ELIJAH JOHN FISHER: A BIOGRAPHY BY HIS SON MILES MARK FISHER. Philadelphia: Judson Press, 1922. 194 pp. Reprint. Microfiche. Chicago: Library Resources, 1971.

Black minister's biographer discusses how congregations responded to the oratory style of the black preacher (87-88). Also comment on worship services held in the "brush arbor" (9).

1943 Fleming, Walter L. "Plantation Life in the Old South and the Plantation Negroes...." SOUTHERN REMINISCENCES OF JEFFERSON DAVIS. JOURNAL OF AMERICAN HISTORY 3 (1909): 233-46.

References to the slave preacher Uncle Bob, owned by Jefferson Davis and his brother Joseph, who lived on the Brierfield plantation in Warren City, Mississippi.

1944 Goldsborough, Edmund K. OLE MARS AN' OLE MISS. Washington, DC: National Publishing Company, 1900. 219 pp. Reprint. Freeport, NY: Books for Libraries Press, 1972.

Sketches about slave life along Maryland's Eastern Shore includes discussion of folk sermons, a Christmas cakewalk festival (60), and singing performance practice (32, 109), including the singing of boat songs (186, 192, 199).

Texts of 4 sermons: 1. Fogitfulness; Acts 7:8 (21-26). 2. King David in Juda; Samuel 63.6 (60-75). 3. Les us meck brick; Exodus 5 (138-146). 4. His bref kin leth coals (164-170).

Texts of 5 songs: 1. When Israel wuz in Egypt's land (Cho: Go down, Moses) (27-28, 185). 2. Zion is de place fuh me (Cho: Oh, I want to git da) (30). 3. Didn't my Lord deliver Daniel? (Cho: And why not a every man?) (32). 4. I ain't no tukkey buzzard (36). 5. Oh, cum' long Moses (Cho: Let meh people go) (187, 192, 196).

1945 Goldstein, Walter. "The Natural Harmonic and Rhythmic Sense of the Negro." MUSIC TEACHER'S NATIONAL ASSOCIATION PROCEEDINGS, Series 12 (1918): 29-30.

Discussion of the innate musicality of the Negro includes description of a religious service at the Gretna Colored Baptist Church (in New Orleans?). Comment on the chanted, "incoherent biblical narrative" of the preacher and the responses of the congregation in "pentatonic wailings in unison and in harmony...." References to 4 songs: 1. Little David, play on your harp. 2. Tone those bells. 3. I couldn't hear nobody pray. 4. Shout all over God's heaven.

1946 Hatcher, William E. JOHN JASPER, THE UNMATCHED NEGRO PHILOSOPHER AND PREACHER. New York: Fleming H. Revell Company, c.1908. 183 pp. Reprint. New York: Negro Universities Press, 1969.

Written by a white Baptist minister of Richmond, Virginia, this study of the celebrated black preacher John Jasper (1812-1901) of Richmond includes biographical details and discussion of Jasper's preaching style and personal philosophy. Also description of Jasper's singing, including the text of his favorite song, and comment on his performance of a "shouting song" (83-84). Discussion of congregational responses to Jasper's sermons (162), of congregational singing after his preaching (172, 182), and of funeral and burial traditions (37-43).

Text of 1 song: Ev'budy got ter rise ter meet King Jesus (83). Texts of 5 sermons: 1. The creation (47-53). 2. Dem sebun wimmin (89-93). 3. The stone cut out of the mountain (108-20). 4. The sun do move, including the Lord God is a man of war (127-49). 5. Funeral sermon (175-81). Summaries of 4 sermons: 1. Joseph and his brethern (66). 2. Enoch (68). 3. Ascension of Elijah (69). 4. The raising of Lazarus (70). References to 6 sermon texts: 1. Revelation 6:2 (38). 2. Daniel 2:45 (108). 3. Isaiah 4:1 (89). 4. Daniel in the lions' den (104). 5. The raising of Lazarus (104). 6. Joseph and his brethern (104).

1947 Heard, William H. FROM SLAVERY TO THE BISHOPRIC IN THE A.M.E. CHURCH: AN AUTOBIOGRAPHY. Philadelphia: A.M.E. Church, 1924. 104 pp.

Narrative of an ex-slave (b. 1850), who later became Bishop of the African Methodist Episcopal Church, includes explanation of the difference between a preacher and an exhorter in the A.M.E. Church (68).

1948 Henry, Howell M. THE POLICE CONTROL OF THE SLAVE IN SOUTH CAROLINA. Emory, VA: The Author, 1914. 216 pp. Reprint. New York: Negro Universities Press, 1968.

Discussion of the slaves gathering "for religious and social purposes" includes references to them being allowed to have their own service after the service for the whites. Observation that their services consisted of songs, testimony, exhortations, and the recounting of religious experiences (135).

1949 Hicks, William. HISTORY OF LOUISIANA NEGRO BAPTISTS FROM 1804 TO 1914....Nashville, TN: National Baptist Publishing Board, [1915]. 251 pp.

Study includes biographical sketches of slave and free-born Baptist preachers active in Louisiana before the Civil War. Also discussion of nineteenth-century black Baptist institutions in the United States. Comment on the conditions under which these pioneers preached the Gospel.

1950 Hodgson, Frances Potter. "Ante-Bellum and War Memories of Mrs. Telfair Hodgson," edited by Sarah Hodgson. GEORGIA HISTORICAL QUARTERLY 27 (December 1943): 350-56.

Recollections written in 1907 by Frances Hodgson include discussion of the singing of boat songs by slaves (351) and comment on burial ceremonies in the African tradition (352).

1951 Holloway, Houston Hartsfield. "Autobiography of Houston Hartsfield Holloway, Put into This Package by His Eldest Son, J. W. Holloway, September 6, 1932. Nashville, Tennessee." Manuscript. 204 pp. Washington, D.C., Library of Congress, Manuscript Division, Miscellaneous Collections.

Autobiography of ex-slave preacher (1845-c.1907) of Upson, Georgia, includes detailed description of the antebellum preacher (78-82, 118-120) and comment on the practice of preaching the memorial sermon one month after burial (79-80). Also discussion of corn-shucking festivals and corn songs (12, 29-39), the fiddler (13), quilting festivals (49), and dancing to music of a banjo (54). Description of 3 ring-games (36-38).

References to 2 sermons: 1. There remaineth, therefore, a feast for the people of God (80). 2. He that heareth these things of mine doeth them (118-20).

Text of 1 couplet: I cum from Tennessee (54). Texts of 6 songs: 1. Heare, ratter, come dog (Cho: Heare, ratter, heare) (12). 2. I wonder whear's the bugle (Cho: O bugle, blow) (13). 3. Oh, Billy Boundle (Cho: Bombe low) (13). 4. Oh, boys, I know you heare me (Cho: Oh, ho, hor-or-eo (31). 5. Leade old Aunt Easter Moland (Cho: Moland, corn, Moland (31). 6. Young lady's don't you pitty me? (Cho: I am in them lady's garden (37-38).

1952 Jamison, Monroe Franklin. AUTOBIOGRAPHY AND WORK OF BISHOP M. F. JAMISON, D.D....A NARRATION ON HIS WHOLE CAREER.... Nashville: Printed for the Author by the Publishing House of the M. E. Church, 1912. 206 pp.

Autobiography of this ex-slave preacher of Georgia includes references to 2 sermon texts (50, 51): 1. Awake, O sword against my shepherd, and against the man that is my fellow (Zach. 13). 2. Jesus wept (John 11:35).

1953 Jernegan, Marcus W. "Slavery and Conversion in the Colonies." AMERICAN HISTORICAL REVIEW 21 (April 1916): 504-27.

Documentation of the religious instruction given to slaves, rate of conversion, etc., by such societies as the Society for the Propagation of the Gospel in Foreign Parts, Associates of Dr. Bray, Society for Promoting Christian Knowledge, and Society for Promoting Christian Learning. Comment on the rarity of converted slaves; most remained heathen because of the neglect or hostility of their masters to conversion.

1954 Johnson, Clifton. HIGHWAYS AND BYWAYS OF THE SOUTH. New York: MacMillan Company, 1904. 362 pp. Reprint. Micro-opaque. Louisville, KY: Lost Cause Press, 1965.

Travel narrative includes comment on poor blacks and whites in the South after the Civil War. Description of the oratory style of a black preacher (57-58), of a black baptism (283-85), and of blacks dancing to the accompaniment of a guitar (73-74).

Text of 1 sermon (excerpt): 1. Vision of a rich man, a poor man, a lame man, and a bond man

(58). Texts of 3 Afro-American animal tales (199-304): 1. Brer Wolf's little tar man (299-302). 2. The frog, the mouse, and the hawk (302-304). 3. How the mud-turtle came to live in the water (304-305).

1955 Johnson, James Weldon. FIFTY YEARS AND OTHER POEMS. Boston: Cornhill Company, 1917. 92 pp. Reprint. New York: AMS Press, 1975.

Anthology of the black writer's poems, which he compiled in commemoration of the fiftieth anniversary of the Emancipation Proclamation, includes numerous references to the black oral traditions: to the spirituals and quoting of spiritual verses (6, 7); to the banjo and its dance music (74); and to folktale characters such as Brer Rabbit and Brudder Possum (79-82). Also description of a "Big Meeting" (85-90).

1956 Johnson, Thomas Lewis. TWENTY-EIGHT YEARS A SLAVE; OR, THE STORY OF MY LIFE ON THREE CONTINENTS.... Twenty-Eight Years a Slave in Virginia, Afterwards, at Forty Years of Age, a Student in Spurgeon's College, Missionary in Africa, Evangelist in England. Bournemouth [England]: W. Mate & Sons, Ltd., 1909. 266 pp. Reprint. Microfilm. London: The British Museum Library, c.1977.

Ex-slave Johnson (born 1836 in Rock-Rayman, Virginia) settled in Richmond, Virginia, in 1852. His autobiography includes references to the fact that the slaves sang songs that later were sung by the Jubilee Singers (10, 13); to a great revival in the United States in 1857, during which thousands of slaves were converted (14); and to the rejoicing of the slaves when the Union Army marched into Richmond on 3 April 1865, bringing freedom. Also comment on the "double-meaning" of the slave songs (19).

Texts of 2 songs: 1. Steal away, steal away, steal away to Jesus (19). 2. Slavery's chain is broke at last (32).

1957 Johnston, Elizabeth Bryant. THE DAYS THAT ARE NO MORE. New York: Abbey Press, c.1901. 224 pp. Reprint. Freeport, NY: Books for Libraries Press, 1972.

Collection of short stories includes a character sketch of a typical antebellum plantation preacher (34-44). Also references to impromptu songs and sermons.

1958 Kealing, H. T. "A Race Rich in Spiritual Content." SOUTHERN WORKMAN 32 (January 1904): 41-44.

Comment on the transition in the black church from folk traditions to more sophisticated forms of worship, citing as an example the ex-slave minister of Arkansas who preached to his congregation "without any long agonizing or shouting."

1959 Kearney, Belle. A SLAVEHOLDER'S DAUGHTER. London: Abbey Press, c.1900. 269 pp. Reprint. New York: Negro Universities Press, 1969.

Chapter 6 of this book by a Mississippian, "A Negro Sermon," is devoted to discussion of worship services, "lining out," the shout, and the vocal quality of the congregational singing (57). Also description of a burial service held in March 1899 and the funeral that came several weeks later (58-61).

1960 Leigh, James Wentworth. OTHER DAYS. London: T. Fisher Unwin, 1921. 255 pp.

English clergyman's discussion of aspects of slave culture, including dancing (109), quality of the singing, and performance practice (157-58). Also description of a Baptist-church baptism in New York City (90); of a religious service held in a church near Savannah, Georgia; and of the shout danced by young people (130). Comment on the differences between the minstrel song and the genuine plantation song (155).

Texts of 4 songs: 1. Preacher glad, preacher glad. 2. What makes the preacher preach so hard 3. My sin is heavy, I can't get along. 4. Graveyard, you ought to know me.

1961 Lowery, Irving E. LIFE ON THE OLD PLANTATION IN ANTE-BELLUM DAYS. Columbia, SC: State Company, 1911. 186 pp.

Ex-slave author (b. 1850) became a Methodist minister after Emancipation. His autobiography includes description of a slave wedding (61-63), Christmas festivities (64), religious services (71-80), voodoo (81-84), "burying" and funeral ceremonies (85-87), a corn-shucking festival (95-98), a camp meeting (113-114), and comment on a slave blowing a horn at four o'clock in the morning to call workers to the fields (126).

Text of 1 sermon: Matthew 12:41. The men of Nineveh shall rise in judgement....(71-80).

1962 MacLean, Annie Marion. "A Town in Florida." THE NEGRO CHURCH. Atlanta University Publications, No. 8, edited by W. E. Burghardt DuBois, 64-68. Atlanta: Atlanta University Press, 1903. Reprint. New York: Arno Press and the New York Times, 1968.

Report on three black churches of Deland, Florida: Missionary Baptist, Bethel A.M.E., and St. Annis' Primitive Baptist. Discussion of the communion service in the Primitive Baptist Church, which ended with a foot-washing ceremony followed by a religious dance called "Rocking Daniel." Description of the dance and other related performance practice.

Text of 1 chorus: Rock Daniel, rock Daniel (67).

1963 Mason, Ethel Osgood. "The Negro and the Union Army in War Time." SOUTHERN WORKMAN

34 (October 1905): 546-47.

Memorabilia and excerpts from the memoirs of General John Eaton, white former commander of the 17th Ohio Volunteers, a black regiment, and later U.S. Commissioner of Education. References to folk preachers and text of a prayer about Jefferson Davis.

1964 Matthews, Essie Collins. AUNT PHEBE, UNCLE TOM AND OTHERS: CHARACTER STUDIES AMONG THE OLD SLAVES OF THE SOUTH, FIFTY YEARS AFTER. Columbus, OH: Champlin Press, 1915. 140 pp. Reprint. Microfiche. Louisville, KY: Lost Cause Press, 1972.

Discussion of the living conditions among ex-slaves in the South after the war includes chapters about their religious life on the plantation and their celebration of Christmas.

Texts of 6 songs: 1. Pray, chilun, pray! Oh, pray to de Lord (30). 2. Long time, sister, sense I saw yo' (30). 3. Lightnin' flash, an' yo' will not come (Cho: Yo' won't come, sinner, an' yo' won't come!) (30). 4. Jesus rides a milk-white horse (Cho: An' no man can hinder) (31). 5. Dark clouds am risin' (31). 6. Early in de mornin' when I rise (Cho: Gib me Jesus) (31).

1965 Murphy, Jeanette Robinson. SOUTHERN THOUGHTS FOR NORTHERN THINKERS AND AFRICAN MUSIC IN AMERICA. New York: Bandanna Publishing Company, 1904. 47 pp.

Collection of essays about black life and culture in the North and South includes discussion of songs (13-16, 23-36), sermons (12-13, 16, 18, 23), the shout (15), and performance practice. Description of a foot-washing ceremony (15). References to 1 dance: the buzzard-lope (15).

Texts of 2 tales: 1. How the hands of the Negro became white (17). 2. Moss Nora and the flood (25). Texts of 5 sermons: 1. I's sorry fo' bits (13). 2. De future ob yo' pas' (116). 3. De prodigal son (18). 4. "Ligion am a light race (18). 5. De tower ob Babel (18). Texts and music of 29 songs; texts of 7 songs. See SONG COLLECTIONS (no. 2307).

1966 Murray, Ellen. "One of the Least: A Bit of Folklore." SOUTHERN WORKMAN 31 (October 1902): 562-63.

Text of a folk prayer offered at a black church service on St. Helena Island, South Carolina.

1967 O'Connell, L. "The Folk Songs of Afro-America." MUSICIAN 11 (October 1906): 503-4.

British writer's discussion includes the observation that Americans lack the expressions of emotional experience known as People's Songs, except for the slaves' songs. Comment on the musical characteristics and performance practice of the slave songs; description of the shout and shout songs, and discussion of the quasi-musical oratory style of the black Methodist preacher. Texts of 14 songs. See SONG COLLECTIONS (no. 2308).

1968 Odum, Howard W. "Religious Folk-Songs of the Southern Negro." AMERICAN JOURNAL OF RELIGIOUS PSYCHOLOGY AND EDUCATION 3 (July 1909): 265-365.

Scholar's discussion of the musical structure of the spirituals, of the textual content of the songs, of performance practice associated with congregational singing, and of the role of the black preacher in improvising songs on the spot for use by his congregation. Also description of the compositional process involved in interpolating the spiritual into the sermon, and of the shout (283-84).

Texts of 147 songs sung by blacks in Tennessee, Mississippi, Florida, and Georgia. See SONG COLLECTIONS (no. 2310). Texts of 6 couplets: 1. A mighty sea of glass mingled wid fier (298). 2. Sometimes I hangs my head an' cries (298). 3. Dere's a tree in paradise (300). 4. I looked toward dat northern pole (300). 5. Oh, sinner, you'd better get ready (313). 6. He gib de bone a mighty shake (331).

1969 Ovington, Mary White. "A Slave's Reminiscences of Slavery." INDEPENDENT 68 (26 May 1910): 1131-36.

Essay by the white social activist and author, based upon her interviews of ex-slaves in Alabama, includes comment on the "foot-washing" ceremony at a Missionary Baptist church.

Text of 1 couplet: Oh, the stars in the elements are falling.

1970 Park, Robert E. "The Money Rally at Sweet Gum." SOUTHERN WORKMAN 42 (October 1913): 537-46.

Discussion of fund-raising drives for schools and churches in Black Belt of the rural South includes the observation that the church invariably served as focal point for such activities in the Afro-American community. Discussion of aspects of the religious services, the "raising of hymns," the "Amen corner," and the "mourner's bench."

1971 Person, Mary Alice. "The Religion of the Negro." SOUTHERN WORKMAN 32 (July 1904): 403-4.

Paper read at Hampton Institute on 21 April 1904 by a Hampton graduate includes comment on the folk imagery employed in Afro-American religious services, such as "the long white robe," "golden slippers," and "golden streets". Observation that these images "possessed a peculiar charm for the slave, for to him they meant the ending of the life of drudgery which he was then leading."

1972 Proctor, Henry Hugh. "The Theology of the Songs of the Southern Slave." SOUTHERN WORKMAN 36 (November 1907): 584-92; (December 1907): 652-56.

Pastor of the First Congregational Church (Colored) in Atlanta, Georgia, proceeds from the premise that the Bible consists of a collection of deliverances, addresses, sermons, discourses, songs, letters, and narratives that provide the basis for a theology, and attempts to formulate a theology of religious concepts based on the songs of the southern slaves. Discussion of such topics as: the slave's belief in God, Christ, and the Holy Spirit; his belief in the Christian life; belief in Satan; and belief in the future life.

Texts of 12 songs. See SONG COLLECTIONS (no. 2314). Texts of 17 couplets: 1. I wonder where Sister Mary's gone (586). 2. He is King of Kings (586). 3. Oh, He sees all you do (586). 4. Oh, Lord, oh my Lord (587). 5. The Jews killed poor Jesus (587). 6. Reign, oh reign, oh reign, my Saviour (587). 7. When Peter was preachin' at Pentecost (588). 8. Those angels' wings are tipped with gold (589). 9. My sister's took her flight (589). 10. Trials and troubles are on the way (590). 11. You say you're aiming for the skies (591). 12. You say the Lord has set you free (591). 13. What do you say, seekers (591). 14. Oh, make a-me holy (592). 15. Old Satan's like a snake in the grass (652). 16. There's a better day a-comin' (653). 17. Oh, Lord, these bones of mine (653).

1973 Russell, Sylvester. "The Original Music of the Slaves." FREEMAN (Indianapolis), 21 October 1905: 5.

Black journalist's discussion of the origin of the slave's religious music includes description of the singing in the tradition of slave-music performance that is found in some "present-day churches."

1974 Sisk, Glenn. "Funeral Customs in the Alabama Black Belt, 1870-1910." SOUTHERN FOLKLORE QUARTERLY 23 (September 1959): 169-71.

Description of the mortuary customs of rural blacks in Alabama includes references to the singing of hymns and other religious songs at burial services. Discussion of one instance in which the funeral sermon was delayed and preached twenty-one days after the entombment of a murdered victim.

1975 Smith, Charles Spencer. A HISTORY OF THE AFRICAN METHODIST EPISCOPAL CHURCH, Being a Volume Supplementary to a History of the African Methodist Episcopal Church, by Daniel Alexander Payne, D.D., LLD., Late One of its Bishops, Chronicling the Principal Events in the Advance of the African Methodist Episcopal Church from 1856 to 1922. Philadelphia: Book Concern of the A.M.E. Church, 1922. 570 pp. Reprint. New York: Johnson Reprint Corporation, 1968.

Black minister's historical account includes a reprint of Payne's description of "Praying and Singing Bands" (126-27). See no. 951.

1976 Smith, Daniel Elliot Huger. A CHARLESTONIAN'S RECOLLECTIONS, 1846-1913. Charleston, SC: Carolina Art Association, c.1950. 162 pp.

Posthumously published memoirs include discussion of social conditions, mores, and religious life of the slaves (29-37). Description of the plantation preacher, his oratory style, and his congregation. Also description of the shout and various secular dances.

Text of 1 song: I look to de eas'--and I look to de wes' (Cho: De udder side o' Jordan) (32). Text of 1 sermon: The great battle (49-52).

1977 Snyder, Howard. "A Plantation Revival Service." YALE REVIEW n.s. 10 (October 1920): 168-80.

Clergyman's discussion of a Mississippi plantation revival service held at a local church includes the observation that the congregation had neither piano nor organ, nor was there a choir. Comment on the singing of spirituals and related performance practice; on religious dancing, the shout; and an outdoor baptismal ceremony witnessed by the author on another occasion.

References to 2 songs: 1. Swing low, sweet chariot. 2. Roll, Jordan, roll. Text of 1 sermon (excerpts): 1. Adam and Eve in Garden of Eden.

1978 _____. "Plantation Pictures II: The Ordination of Charlie." ATLANTIC MONTHLY 127 (March 1921): 338-42.

Discussion of a folk-church ordination service, where twelve ordained ministers questioned the black applicant, includes description of the song-service that preceded the ordination.

1979 Stanford, P. Thomas. "Life and Work of the Rev. John Jasper." COLORED AMERICAN MAGAZINE 3 (July 1901): 207-17.

Obituary for the Rev. John Jasper (1812-1901), ante-bellum preacher and pastor of the Sixth Mt. Zion Baptist (Colored) Church in Richmond, Virginia, includes excerpts from his sermons.

Texts of 3 sermons: 1. The sun do move. 2. A four-cornered earth. 3. The sun went down.

1980 Tarbell, John H. "My Experiences Photographing the Negro in the South." NEW ENGLAND MAGAZINE n.s. 29 (December 1903): 463-78.

These reminiscenses of the noted photographer's

travels in the South during the 1890s include comment on the black preacher, and one in particular, Pastor Rumley, who preached an "extraordinary sermon on 'De Valley ob de Dry Bones'," which brought him considerable reputation in his native town." Also discussion of a black church, of a folk sermon, the shout, and ecstatic seizure.

Reference to 1 song: Roll, Jordan, roll. Reference to 1 sermon: De valley ob de dry bones.

1981 UNWRITTEN HISTORY OF SLAVERY. Fisk University, Social Science Source Document No. 1. Nashville, TN: Fisk University, 1945. 332 pp. Reprints. Washington, DC: Microcard Editions, 1968. Also in THE AMERICAN SLAVE..., edited by George P. Rawick. Vol. 11. Westport, CT: Greenwood Press, 1975. See no. 1803.

More than 100 slaves were interviewed by Ophelia Settle Egypt, a research staff member at Fisk University, during the years 1929-30, most of them residents of Tennessee and Kentucky. The introduction to the collection, written by Egypt, J. Masuoka, and Charles S. Johnson, focuses on the slavery system "as a moral order" and on the merit of the interviews as valuable social documents. The interviews include numerous references to singing, dancing, musical and religious practices; also descriptions of funerals (23), weddings (3), religious services (21, 53, 112, 159), corn shuckings (34, 46, 130); and references to fiddles and banjoes (110), to the bass fiddle and "big fiddle" (126), to a homemade fiddle (64).

Texts of 20 songs. See Rawick SONG COLLECTIONS (no. 1839).

1982 Washington, Booker T. "The Religious Life of the Negro." NORTH AMERICAN REVIEW 181 (July 1905): 20-23.

Black educator, public figure, and founder of Tuskegee Institute offers comment on the characteristic features of the slave's religion and the plantation church, and on African survivals in the religious practices.

1983 _____. THE STORY OF THE NEGRO: THE RISE OF THE RACE FROM SLAVERY. New York: Doubleday, Page & Company, 1909. 2 vols. Reprint. New York: Peter Smith, 1940.

Discussion of slave life includes references to the African-born story-teller Toko and his fables (1: 72-73) and other African survivals in the United States (1: 103); to the black church and several renowned preachers, among them, John Jasper, George Liele, Jack of Virginia, and Ralph Freeman (1: 251-58). Also comment on recreational activities, such as hog-killing and corn-husking festivals (1: 158-61). The discussion of folksong includes comment on performance practice and the double meaning of the slave-song texts (1: 100, 160; 2: 3-4, 258-71).

Text of 1 couplet: Oh, Lord, Oh my Lord (2: 260). Texts of 6 songs: 1. Mother, is Massa goin' to sell us tomorrow? (Cho: Fare you well, mother) (1: 100). 2. Massa's niggers am slick and fat (Cho: Turn out here and shuck dis corn) (1: 160). 3. We'll soon be free (2: 4). 4. Children, we shall all be free (2: 4). 5. I know moon-rise (2: 263). 6. O wrestlin' Jacob, Jacob (2: 263).

1984 Woodson, Carter Goodson. THE HISTORY OF THE NEGRO CHURCH. Washington, DC: Associated Publishers, c.1921. 330 pp. Reprint. 1972.

Black historian devotes Chapter 3, "Pioneer Negro Preachers," to biographical sketches of early black churchmen, most of them ex-slaves who had preached on street corners or in the fields in their early careers. Comment on the relations between black Christians and the Methodist and Baptist churches (143-44).

Text of 1 song: Oh, freedom! freedom over me (187).

1985 Work, John Wesley. "In the Bottom." Typescript. 90 pp. Nashville, Tennessee, Fisk University Library, Special Collections.

Detailed discussion by black folklorist-composer-professor (at Fisk) of the folk church, its sacred folk music, and its secular folk music. Comment on performance practice, on the various types of spirituals, and their function in the liturgy. Also discussion of the various types of secular songs, analysis of the folk sermon, and description of the folk quartet.

1986 Wyeth, John Allan. WITH SABRE AND SCALPEL: THE AUTOBIOGRAPHY OF A SOLDIER AND SURGEON. New York: Harper & Brothers, 1914. 534 pp.

Discussion of conditions in the South by this Confederate Army officer includes references to the "Bresh-Harbor" revivals of the Negroes (33). Comment on slave exhorters, religious singing, and the spirituals (34-35); on the improvisation of songs at a corn-shucking festival in Alabama (57-58); on tale telling (65); and on slaves dancing to music of the banjo, fiddle, patting, or crude orchestras composed of triangles and jawbones of an ox or horse (59-61). Reference to the telling of tales (65).

Text of 1 tale: Uncle Efra'm and the Lord (65-66). Reference to 1 song: I'm gwine away to leave you (58). Texts of 8 songs. See SONG COLLECTIONS (no. 2326).

THE SONG

1987 "American Music---What Is It?" MUSICAL AMERICA (14 July 1906): 7.

Discussion of the various positions held by music critics, composers, and others about whether Negro and Indian music can serve as the basis for an American school of composition concludes that it can not. Also reference to an article published in the ETUDE in which a critic rejects the view that the Negro music is original: "[It] is not negro music at all, but merely white music that has been assimilated and sung by the black man."

1988 "The Armstrong League." SOUTHERN WORKMAN 41 (March 1917): 186.

Report on a historical meeting of the Armstrong League of Hampton Workers at Hampton Institute on 27 January 1911 contains reference to 1 battle song sung by the enlisted black soldiers during the Civil War: They look like men of war.

1989 "At Home and Afield---Hampton Incidents: The Christmas Holidays." SOUTHERN WORKMAN 43 (January 1914): 60.

Review of a Christmas Concert given at Hampton Institute on 18 December 1913, in which R. Nathaniel Dett, composer and musical director at Hampton, explained the structure of the "Negro scale." Reference to 1 Christmas song: Go tell it on the mountain.

1990 _____. "Entertainment." SOUTHERN WORKMAN 42 (October 1913): 573.

Review of a concert given on 19 August 1913 at Hampton Institute by Miss Mary Lane, a Hampton librarian, includes references to 2 songs: 1. The rocks and the mountains. 2. Gwine to ride up in de chariot.

1991 Aylward, William J. "Steamboating through Dixie." HARPER'S NEW MONTHLY MAGAZINE 131 (September 1915): 512-22.

Discussion of the sights to be seen along the Mississippi River from aboard a steamboat sailing from St. Louis, Missouri, to New Orleans, includes comment on black roustabouts (=stevedores), southern planters, and black workers in the levee camps along the river.

Texts of 2 songs: 1. O Lawd, hab mercy on sinful Sam. 2. Oh, awa'--ay yondah is an i-i-land!

1992 Bagley, Julian E. "Rufus Did It." SOUTHERN WORKMAN 46 (October 1917): 546-52.

Graduate of Hampton Institute includes the text of 1 song in a short story he wrote: Let us cheer the weary traveler.

1993 Barrett, Harris. "Negro Folk Songs." SOUTHERN WORKMAN 41 (April 1912): 238-45.

Discussion by the Hampton Institute alumnus and cashier at the institution of the importance of preserving the Negro songs and of Hampton's aim in teaching its students the "beauty and power" of the songs. Classification of the songs into five categories: spirituals and religious songs, cradle songs, work songs, game and dance songs, and songs of freedom. Comment on the context in which these songs were performed and associated performance practices. Descriptions of the cakewalk and the ring-game.

Texts of 7 songs: 1. Oh, Daniel cast in de lion's den (Cho: My Lord delibered Daniel). 2, Mother, is massa gwine to sell us tomorrow? 3. Go to sleep. 4. Come here, nigger. 5. Come, my love, an' go wid me (ring-game). 6. Oh, freedom! 7. It sets my heart quite in a flame (Cho: They look like men of war). References to 5 songs: 1. Steal away to Jesus. 2. If you want to see Jesus, go in the wilder-ness. 3. They crucified my Savior and nailed Him to de cross. 4. O Lord, O my good Lord, keep me from sinking down. 5. No more auction block for me.

1994 Barry, Phillips. "Negro Folk-Songs from Maine." BULLETIN OF THE FOLKSONG SOCIETY OF THE NORTHEAST No. 8 (1934): 13-16; No. 9 (1935): 10-14; No. 10 (1935); 21-22. Reprint in NEGRO FOLK-SONGS FROM MAINE. Philadelphia: American Folklore Society, 1960.

Three articles by Phillips Barry, editor of and chief contributor to the BULLETIN, include discussion of a song repertory that came from a community of ex-slaves (a "cultural island") in Brownville, Maine, during the post-Civil War years. By 1880 the blacks had moved away. The songs were written down by Susan M. Lewis, who learned them from her brothers, who had learned them from black quarrymen of Brownville. Also references to the shout (8: 14; 9: 12).

Texts and music of 5 songs: 1. Hail, brudder, hail (Cho: Oh, Jordan stream, beautiful stream) (8: 15). 2. When de Lawd spreads His guidin' wings (9: 13). 3. O, look up yonder, whut I see (Cho: Oh, de wintah, de wintah) (10: 21). 4. O de good old chariot swing so low (Cho: Swing low, sweet chariot) (10: 21). 5. Dere I shall see my mudder (Cho: So will I go) (10: 22).

1995 Barstow, Marjorie. "Singers in a Weary Land." WORLD OUTLOOK (October 1919): 22.

Discussion of the quality of Negro folksong, of the subjects covered by the song texts, and of the meaning of the texts.

Texts of 7 songs: 1. You say you're aiming for the skies. 2. I may be sick and cannot rise. 3. I got my ticket fer de train. 4. I know moonrise, I know star-rise. 5. I looked over Jordan (Cho: Swing low, sweet chariot). 6. Walk 'em easy 'round de Heaven. 7. Ah got shoes, you got shoes.

1996 Bassford, Homer. "On the Old Mississippi Speedway." SATURDAY EVENING POST 172 (6 January 1900): 596.

Description of a boat race between two steamboat captains sailing down the Mississippi River from St. Louis, Missouri, to New Orleans during the summer of 1870. Observation that one riverboat, the Lee, was manned by twenty black sailors, who sang continuously as they worked.

Text of 1 boat song: Oh, fare you well, Miss July (Cho: Old Stormy was a mighty man).

1997 Bennett, John. "Gullah: A Negro Patois." Parts 1, 2. SOUTH ATLANTIC QUARTERLY 7 (October 1908): 332-47; 8 (January 1909): 39-52.

Discussion of the patois dialect of blacks living along the coastal islands of the United States includes comment on their songs and reference to a tale, "Buh Sun" (7: 345).

Text of 1 Charleston oysterman song: Buh Rabbut, wuh yuh duh do dey? (7: 332). Texts of 2 couplets: 1. An a rally an' er hole een muh han', hebbenlye angel (7: 333). (2) Who da' duh mongkey de mongkey? (8: 40).

1998 Blanton, Joshua E. "Men in the Making." SOUTHERN WORKMAN 48 (January 1919): 17-24.

Black song leader in charge of informal singing at ten United States Army camps for colored soldiers during World War I discusses the training and lifestyles of the soldiers.

Text of 1 song: Come along, children, come along (Cho: Goin' to raise a rukus tonight).

1999 Booth, Vincentine T. "Easter Pictures." SOUTHERN WORKMAN 32 (April 1903): 233-35.

Comment on songs sung by members of a colored settlement in Hampton Roads, Virginia, during their Easter Day celebrations.

Texts of 3 songs: 1. He 'rose, He 'rose. 2. Oh, de land I am bound for. 3. In bright mansions above. Reference to 1 song: Nobody knows the trouble I've seen.

2000 Boyd, Bettie Cabbell. "Letter from Former Student." SOUTHERN WORKMAN 31 (July 1902): 409.

Hampton graduate of the Class of 1880 discusses a song sung about 1880 at the Institute: De foxes hab' holes in de groun'.

2001 Bray, Josephine Compton. "More 'Mammy' Stories." NEW ENGLAND MAGAZINE n.s. 45 (February 1912): 594-606.

This "Mammy" story is one of several published by Bray during the years 1909-1913 about an ex-slave, Mammy, and her young mistress, Miss Caroline, who have moved to the North. Mammy tells tales about plantation life to her new neighbors, including Negro folk tales and songs.

Text of 1 song (596): I heah dat trumpet when it soun' (Cho: A few mo' days). Reference to 1 song (598): Bye, Mammy's little baby.

2002 _____. "Mammy's Ghost Story." NEW ENGLAND MAGAZINE n.s. 47 (August 1912): 276-81.

This ghost story includes the text of 1 song (277): Ole Pharoah's hos' got drowned!

2003 _____. "Mammy's Jack O'Lantern." NEW ENGLAND MAGAZINE n.s. 49 (May 1913): 133-35.

One of several "Mammy" stories, this one includes the text of 1 song: When Mars Jesus call me (133).

2004 Burlin, Natalie Curtis. "Folk-Music in America: Four Types of Folk-Songs in the United States." CRAFTSMAN 21 (January 1912): 414-20.

Folklorist's discussion of the folksongs of the aboriginal Indians, American blacks, the "mountain whites" of Kentucky and Georgia, and American cowboys includes references to 2 Negro songs: 1. Nobody knows de trouble I've had. 2. Oh, Freedom over me.

2005 _____. "The Negro's Contribution to the Music of America: The Larger Opportunity of the Colored Man of Today." CRAFTSMAN 23 (March 1913): 660-69.

Survey of early twentieth-century black musicians and music focuses largely on ragtime, the cake-walk, and syncopated dance band music, but does include references to folk music and folk performance practice.

Text of 1 song: Oh, freedom. Text of 1 couplet: Tell ole Pharaoh, Let my people go.

2006 _____. "Again the Negro." POETRY. A MAGAZINE OF VERSE 11 (October-March 1917-18): 147-50.

Reflection on Vachel Lindsay's poem, "Negro Sermon," in which he uses phrases from plantation songs, calls to the author's mind examples of "genuine folk-songs" that she heard sung by a native of St. Helena's Island, off the coast of South Carolina.

Texts of 2 songs: 1. Ah read about Samson from his birth (Cho: Gawd's a-gwine t' move all de troubles away. 2. Ef yo' see ma mudder (Cho: O, ride on, Jesus).

2007 _____. "Hymn of Freedom." SOUTHERN WORKMAN 47 (October 1918): 475.

Discussion of a new hymn text, "O, march on, Freedom," that is sung to the melody of old Negro spiritual, "O, ride on, Jesus." It was first sung at St. Helena Island, South Carolina (where the spiritual tune originated) in July 1918.

2008 _____. NEGRO FOLK-SONGS (HAMPTON SERIES) [4 books in one collection]. New York: G. Schirmer, c.1918-1919. Reprint. 1984.

Folklorist was asked to collect and record folk-songs sung by the Hampton Students by Robert Moton, at that time Commandant at Hampton Institute (later president of Tuskegee). Detailed discussion of performance practice, song types, dialect and diction, harmonies, improvisation ("extemporaneous singing") in the foreword to each collection. Also discussion of the conditions under which Burlin began collecting and recording songs about 1915, using an Edison cylinder phonograph; of the singers; and of the history of the songs. Comment that [she has] "added nothing....The harmonies are the Negroes' own. Every note in every voice was written down as sung by Negroes."

Texts and music of 19 songs. See SONG COLLECTIONS (no. 2295).

2009 _____. "Black Singers and Players." MUSICAL QUARTERLY 5 (1919): 499-504.

Comment on the fact that the Hampton student choruses of 900 singers sing "in parts" spontaneously--without having been taught, and although not divided and seated according to parts.

2010 Byam, C. Perry. "A Nine-Year Old Warrior: The Personal Recollections of the Youngest Union Soldier in the Civil War, His Battles, His Boyish Pranks, and His Experiences as First 'Man' to Enter Vicksburg after Siege." HARPER'S WEEKLY 53 (12 June 1909): 24-25.

Discussion of the siege of Vicksburg, Mississippi, by a Civil War veteran, formerly a drummer for Company D, Twenty-Fourth United States Regiment of the Iowa Volunteer Infantry, includes references to the black cook of a commanding officer in the Union Army.

Text of 1 song sung by the cook: I hung my jawbone on de fence.

2011 [Carter, William, arr.] PLANTATION LULLABIES. Hamilton, Ontario (Canada): Duncan Lithograph Company, [1909]. 56 pp.

Although this collection has no commentary, its titlepage and front and back covers provide some information. The collection represents "Songs sung by the Celebrated Colored Concert Company under the management of Wm. Carter, for 25 years Manager and Proprietor of the Famous Canadian Jubilee Singers." Since this troupe was organized in 1884, the publication date of the booklet probably is 1909. Other titlepage facts include the note that the choir made a "Five Years' Tour of Great Britain. Three Years' Tour of United States." On the front and back covers appears the motto: "What We Have We'll Hold."

Music and texts of 13 songs. Texts of 54 songs. See SONG COLLECTIONS (no. 2296).

2012 Cobb, Irvin S. "Quality Folks." SATURDAY EVENING POST 190 (24 November 1917): 7-10.

American journalist and humorist, in a short story about the relations of two southern belles with their black nannie, includes the text of 1 camp-meeting song: Hab a lovin' mother, been climbin' up de hill so long (Cho: Den chain dat lion down, good Lawd!).

2013 Coleridge-Taylor, Samuel. TWENTY-FOUR NEGRO MELODIES TRANSCRIBED FOR THE PIANO. Op. 59. 127 pp. Bryn Mawr, PA: Oliver Ditson Company, 1905. Reprint. New York: Da Capo Press, 1980.

In the Foreword, the Afro-British composer discusses the quality and features of the African and Afro-American folksongs he has chosen to arrange for the piano, stating his purpose to be: "What Brahms has done for the Hungarian folk-music, Dvorak for the Bohemian, and Grieg for the Norwegian, I have tried to do for these Negro melodies....The actual melody has in every case been inserted at the head of each piece as a motto." The sources for the composer's songs were Frederick J. Loudin, manager of the Jubilee Singers, and three collections of the Fisk Jubilee songs that were available to him in London.

Texts and music of 15 songs, mostly choruses. See SONG COLLECTIONS (no. 2297).

2014 Conrad, Georgia B. "Reminiscences of a Southern Woman." SOUTHERN WORKMAN 30 (February 1901): 77-80; (March 1901): 167-71; (May 1901): 252-59; (June 1901): 357-59; (July 1901): 407-11.

Memoirs of the daughter of a rice planter of the Georgia Sea Islands include discussion of her recollections of plantation life on Broughton Island, in Macintosh County, c1859-1866. Comment on the songs of the slaves, on an African princess who sang African songs to the plantation children, and a black family of Sapelo Island, near Darien, Georgia, who worshipped Mohammed.

2015 Cook, Will Marion. "The Dawn of New Music---Negro Aspirations." DAILY NEWS (London) (16 May 1903): 6.

Black composer and conductor describes in detail the "peculiarities of Negro music" in an interview with a London journalist during the period the Walker and Williams show, IN DAHOMEY, was playing in London (1903). Cook was the musical director of the show.

2016 _____. "Famous Orchestra Hopes to Visit West Africa." WEST AFRICA (August 1919):

739. See also "The New Minstrelsy. Making a School of Negro Music." AFRICAN WORLD (August 1919) and "Will Preserve and Cultivate the Music of the Colored Race." MUSICAL AMERICA (February 1920).

Black composer and conductor discusses some features of Negro music, and the importance of that part of his mission which "is to perpetuate and develop the spirituals," in an interview with a London correspondent during the period his Southern Syncopated Orchestra was performing in London (1919).

2017 Cuney-Hare, Maud. "Afro-American Folk-Song Contribution." MUSICAL OBSERVER 15 (February 1917): 13, 21, 51.

Discussion by the Afro-American author and musician of the origin and significance of Negro folk songs, with focus on music of the antebellum South. Suggestion that many songs had African ancestry; also that there was similarity of themes between African and Afro-American songs. Discussion of the secret West African societies, which were founded to teach song and dance. Classification of Afro-American folk songs into five categories: work songs, spirituals, shout songs, love songs, and burial songs.

References to 3 songs: 1. Wrestling Jacob. 2. Weeping Mary. 3. Ain't I glad I got out of the wilderness.

2018 _____. "The Sailor and His Songs. Romance of the Sea Chantey and Folk-Song." MUSICAL OBSERVER 18 (January 1919): 9-10, (March 1919): 14-15.

Discussion of the probability of an African or Afro-American origin for many sea chanties. Comment on the custom of Anglo-American trading vessels carrying "checquered crews"---that is, one watch was composed of white men and another of colored men. References to primary informants of the nineteenth century who describe the chanteys of black seamen. Also references to the rhythmic cries of the black stevedores who sang as they worked and to the Negro versions of white sea chanties.

Music and texts of 3 songs: 1. I'm gwine to Alabamy. 2. O, graveyard. 3. O General Florido.

2019 Daingerfield, Henrietta G. "Uncle Billy's Mo'ners." SOUTHERN WORKMAN 30 (February 1901): 95-103.

Short story about a young Confederate officer, set in Virginia during the Civil War, includes the text of 1 improvised song: O, our brother's gone and lef' us (100).

2020 Daingerfield, Nettie G. "Aunt Lucy." SOUTHERN WORKMAN 34 (May 1905): 279-84.

Short story about black folk life includes the text of 1 couplet: We mus' not wu'k (284).

2021 Damrosch, Walter. "A Musician's Tribute." SOUTHERN WORKMAN 41 (April 1912): 202-04.

Address by the German-born symphonic conductor given at a Hampton Institute Meeting held in the home of Mrs. James Townsend in West Park, New York, includes comment on Afro-American songs.

2022 Dett, R. Nathaniel. "The Emancipation of Negro Music." SOUTHERN WORKMAN 47 (April 1918): 172-76.

The black composer and music professor at Hampton Institute prepared this article as one of the chapters on black music for the pamphlet "American Pageants, Festivals, and Plays," used by U. S. Department of Education. Comment on the pioneering work of John W. Work, George White, the Fisk Jubilee Singers, and other collectors who sought to rescue black song from the stereotyped parodies of black-face minstrels and their imitators and to elevate black folksong to a position of dignity in world music.

2023 _____. [Touisant L'Ouverture, pseud.]. "Negro Music." Typescript. 28 pp. Cambridge, Massachusetts, Harvard University, Houghton Library.

In 1920 this four-part essay won Harvard University's Bowdoin Literary Prize for Dett. Discussion of the origin and development of Negro religious and secular music, and of "Negro Music of the Present." Comment on composers who have collected and arranged Negro folksong, and who have used folk idioms in their composed music (21-24). References to the large festivals of Negro folksong staged in several large cities in recent years (21).

2024 Dromgoole, Will Allen. "Old Swing-a-low." SOUTHERN WORKMAN 33 (August 1904): 450-55.

The text of the song "Swing low, sweet chariot" is interwoven throughout this short story.

2025 DuBois, W. E. B. THE SOULS OF BLACK FOLK. Chicago: A. C. McClurg & Company, 1903. 264 pp. Reprints. New York: Fawcett Publications, 1961. Millwood, NY: Kraus-Thomson Organization, 1973. Also in THREE NEGRO CLASSICS. New York: Avon Books, 1965. Page references below are to the Fawcett edition.

Discussion of "the spiritual world" in which black Americans were living at the beginning of the twentieth century contains a chapter entitled "Of the Sorrow Songs" (Chapter 14), which includes discussion of the history and the meaning of the slave songs. Quotation of melodic incipits of the slave songs at the head of each chapter throughout the book, and quotation of text incipits in Chapter 14. Detailed attention given to songs Du Bois identifies as "master songs" (184-86), which include: 1. Swing low, sweet chariot, 2. Roll, Jordan, roll, 3. You may bury me in the East, 4. Nobody knows the trouble

I've seen, 5. Been a'listenin', 6. My Lord, what a mourning, 7. My way's cloudy, 8. Wrestlin' Jacob, and 9. Steal away. Detailed discussion of religious matters and the folk preacher in Chapter 10, "Of the Faith of the Fathers."

Texts of 3 songs: 1. Oh, Freedom (148). 2. I walk through the churchyard (181). 3. Michael, haul the boat ashore (189). Music and texts of 3 songs: 1. Poor Rosy (187). 2. Let us cheer the weary traveler (191). 3. Do bana coba, gene me (184).

2026 Elson, Louis Charles. "American Folk-Song." MUSICIAN 17 (December 1912): 816-17.

Survey of American folk music includes discussion of the southern plantation music. Argument advanced that this music is of American origin, a direct outcome of American life and surroundings, and is not African folk song transplanted to America. References to 3 songs: 1. Jews, screws, defidum. 2. Jews crucified Him. 3. Oh, death.

2027 _____. THE HISTORY OF AMERICAN MUSIC. New York: Macmillan Company, 1904. 380 pp. Rev eds. 1915. 1925. Reprint of 2d rev. ed. New York: Franklin Burt, 1971.

Historical survey includes discussion of the slave music, its quality and characteristic features (133-34). Also comment on the banjo and the "pseudo-plantation music called ragtime or ragged time."

2028 "Emancipation Day." AMERICAN MISSIONARY (MAGAZINE) n.s. 56 (January 1902): 84.

Editorial describing an Emancipation Day service at Fisk University contains the chorus text of an old plantation song sung on that occasion: March on and you shall gain the victory.

2029 "Enigmatic Folksongs of the Southern Underworld." CURRENT OPINION 67 (September 1919): 165-66.

Discussion of the "blues" includes quotations from interviews with Gilda Gray (a Broadway, white singer of blues), which appeared in the NEW YORK HERALD, and quotations from articles published in the NEW YORK SUN by its dramatic editor and by Walter Kingsley. Detailed discussion of the general character of the blues, its distinguishing features, and how it differs from the spiritual.

Text of 1 blues: Oh, the old dirty dozen. Reference to 1 Negro dance: the shimmy.

2030 F., C. M. "Negro Folk Songs: Hampton Series. Recorded by Natalie Curtis Burlin." Unsigned review. SOUTHERN WORKMAN 47 (July 1918): 359-60.

Reviewer discusses the four songs published in vol. 1 of Burlin's collection: 1. O ride on, Jesus. 2. Go down, Moses. 3. Couldn't hear nobody pray. 4. Good news, the chariot's coming.

2031 _____. "Negro Folk-Songs, Hampton Series, Recorded by Natalie Curtis Burlin." Unsigned review. SOUTHERN WORKMAN 47 (October 1918): 505.

Reviewer discusses the sources for songs in Burlin's second volume: 1. God's a-gwine ter move all de troubles away. 2. 'Tis me, O Lord. 2. Listen to de lambs. 4. O, ev'ry time I feel de spirit.

2032 _____. "Negro Folk-Songs, Hampton Series, Recorded by Natalie Curtis Burlin." Unsigned review. SOUTHERN WORKMAN 49 (February 1920): 94.

Discussion of sources for songs in the fourth volume of the series: 1. Peanut picking song. 2. Hammering song. 3. Go ter sleep, mammy's baby. 4. Come, ma love, an' go wid me. 5. A rattler went down dat holler lawg. 6. Captain, go side-track yo' train.

2033 Fenner, Thomas, comp. CABIN AND PLANTATION SONGS, AS SUNG BY THE HAMPTON STUDENTS, Arranged by Thomas P. Fenner, Frederic G. Rathbun, and Miss Bessie Cleaveland. 3rd Edition Enlarged by the Addition of Forty-Four Songs.... 166 pp. New York: G. P. Putnam's Sons, 1901. Reprint. New York: AMS Press, 1977.

This edition represents the contributions of three white music directors at Hampton Institute: Fenner compiled the first collection in 1874; Rathbun added to the collection during his tenure and produced the second edition in 1891; and Cleaveland, who took charge of the music program at Hampton in 1892, added songs to the basic core to produce the 1901 enlargement. The introduction of previous editions reappears here, with its discussion of the character and origin of the plantation songs and comment on the Hampton Student Singers.

Texts and music of 116 plantation songs. See SONG COLLECTIONS (no. 2298).

2034 _____. RELIGIOUS FOLK SONGS OF THE NEGRO. Arranged by the Musical Directors of the Hampton Normal and Agricultural Institute from the Original Edition by Thomas P. Fenner. Hampton, VA: The Institute Press, 1909. 166 pp. Reprint. 1924.

The contributors of new songs to this edition include black teacher-collectors, among them, Fisk professor Frederick J. Work, Mrs. Jennie C. Lee of Tuskegee, and music instructors of the Calhoun and Penn schools. In addition to a reprint of the Preface and Introduction published in previous editions, there is a "Note to New Edition" by Robert Moton, dated May 11, 1909, which offers comment on the "priceless legacy" of the plantation songs. Moton, a Hampton graduate and onetime Commandant at Hampton (later president of Tuskegee), led the singing of plantation songs at Hampton for "nearly a score of years."

Texts and music of 139 songs. See SONG COLLECTIONS (no. 2299).

2035 _____. RELIGIOUS FOLK SONGS OF THE NEGRO, AS SUNG ON THE PLANTATIONS. New edition. Arranged by the Musical Directors of the Hampton Normal and Agricultural Institute. From the original edition by Thomas P. Fenner. Hampton, VA: The Institute Press, 1916. 175 pp.

The Preface includes discussion of performance practice associated with Negro camp-meeting songs and comment on some editorial changes. Some of the songs are accompanied by notes about performance by the original singers.

Texts and music of 142 plantation songs. See SONG COLLECTIONS (no. 2299).

2036 "Folk-Song Festival Given by Harlem Chorus...." MUSICAL AMERICA (8 December 1917): 13.

Review of this folksong concert includes references to the singing of both arranged spirituals and spirituals in their original forms. Comment on the festival's organizer and director, Azalia Hackley.

2037 "Folk-Song Concert." SOUTHERN WORKMAN 43 (May 1914): 273-74.

Review of a concert given at the Hotel Chamberlin in Old Point Comfort, Virginia, on Easter Day, 1914.

References to 8 songs sung on this occasion: 1. I'm a-rollin' through an unfriendly world. 2. I want to be ready. 3. O, Freedom. 4. Walk together children. 5. He is King of Kings. 6. Couldn't hear nobody pray. 7. Roll Jordan, roll. 8. Dust and ashes.

2038 Forbes, George W. "Afro-American Folk-Songs Only Basis for a National Music." A.M.E. CHURCH REVIEW 31 (July 1914): 85-87.

Librarian of the Boston Public Library, in a review of Edward Krehbiel's book, AFRO-AMERICAN FOLK SONGS (see no. 2075), offers comment on the arguments of Krehbiel and Antonin Dvorak regarding the use of black folk-songs as a foundation for an American school of national music.

2039 Foster, Jeanne Robert. "Songs of the War Days." PHOTOGRAPHIC HISTORY OF THE CIVIL WAR IN TEN VOLUMES, edited by Francis T. Miller, 9: 342-53. New York: Review of Reviews Company, 1911.

Discussion of the origin of some of the Negro spirituals. Texts of 4 songs: 1. My father, how long. 2. Many thousand go. 3. Pray on. 4. Meet, O Lord.

2040 Foster, Mary E. "Graduates and Ex-Students." SOUTHERN WORKMAN 43 (March 1914): 190.

Letter written by a graduate of Hampton Institute about the Armstrong Day celebrations held at the school where she teaches, in Pocomoke City, Maryland, contains references to songs her pupils sang which were favorites of General Samuel Armstrong, founder-director of Hampton Institute.

References to 4 songs: 1. He is King of Kings. 2. O, Freedom. 3. Battle hymn of the Republic. 4. They look like men of war.

2041 Frissell, Sydney Dodd. "Hampton in Thirty Years." SOUTHERN WORKMAN 44 (September 1915): 523-26.

Comment by the Executive Secretary of the National Hampton Association on performances given in 1915 by the Hampton Singers, now known as the "Gold Medal Quartet," in California, Montana, the Dakotas, and Washington includes references to spirituals and "Juba" patting songs.

References to 6 songs: 1. There's a meeting here tonight. 2. Ezekiel saw the wheel. 3. Lord, I don't feel noways tired. 4. Roll de ol' chariot along. 5. Swing low, sweet chariot. 6. Roll, Jordan, roll.

2042 Gaul, Harvey B. "Samuel Coleridge-Taylor: An Afro-British Composer." MUSICIAN 22 (August 1917): 577.

White composer's biographical sketch of the Afro-British composer includes quotations from his discussion of the distinctive characteristics of Afro-American folksongs and their kinship with traditional African melodies.

Reference to 1 song: Didn't my Lord deliver Daniel?

2043 _____. "Negro Spirituals." NEW MUSIC REVIEW AND CHURCH MUSIC REVIEW 17 (April 1918): 147-51.

Composer's discussion of the several types of plantation songs---spirituals, worksongs, revival songs, shouts---of the themes of the texts, and of the musical elements of the songs. Also extensive comment on performance practice, particularly as associated with work songs, and the observation: "wherever longshoremen are colored, you will hear the men singing. The leader carries the burden, the men take up the chorus, sailor chanty fashion."

2044 Gibson, John William and William Henry Crogman. PROGRESS OF A RACE; Or, the Remarkable Advancement of the American Negro from the Bondage of Slavery, Ignorance and Poverty to the Freedom of Citizenship, Intelligence, Affluence, Honor and Trust. Atlanta: J. L. Nichols & Company, 1902. 732 pp.

Chapter 17, entitled "Plantation Melodies," includes texts of 9 slave songs (641-54). Most of the texts were taken from the Hampton Students collections.

Texts and music of 11 songs. See SONG COLLECTIONS (no. 2300).

2045 Grant, Frances R. "Negro Patriotism and Negro Music. How the Old 'Spirituals' Have been Used at Penn School, Hampton, and Tuskegee to Promote Americanization." OUTLOOK 121 (26 February 1919): 343-47.

An account of Natalie Curtis Burlin's work in the South in studying and collecting the folk music of the Negro.

Music of 1 spiritual: Ride on, Jesus (with specially written text). Reference to 1 song: God's a-gwine ter move all de troubles away.

2046 Hallowell, Emily, ed. CALHOUN PLANTATION SONGS. Boston: C. W. Thompson & Company, 1901. 61 pp. 2d ed. 1907. 74 pp.

Brief history and description of the Calhoun Colored School in Lowndes County, Alabama, by one of its white teachers. Discussion of how the songs were transcribed from the singing of the students and of the "peculiarities of rhythm, melody, harmony and text" in the songs. Preface to the second edition includes the observation that the songs originated among the cotton-field workers in Alabama, who were "untouched by civilization."

Texts and music of 54 songs in the 1st ed.; 69 songs in the 2d ed. See SONG COLLECTIONS (nos. 2301, 2302).

2047 Hamilton, Jeff. MY MASTER: THE INSIDE STORY OF SAM HOUSTON AND HIS TIMES BY HIS FORMER SLAVE, JEFF HAMILTON, as Told to Lenoir Hunt. Dallas, TX: Manfred Van Nord & Company, 1940. 141 pp.

Slave narrative includes references to singing in its description of slave life in Texas.

2048 "Hampton Incidents." SOUTHERN WORKMAN 36 (April 1907): 247-48.

Obituary notice for Eunice Congdon Dixon, New England missionary who worked among the ex-slaves, contains references to singing and to a song sung at her funeral at Hampton Institute.

Text of 1 song: My mother's gone to glory. References to 2 songs: 1. Jacob's ladder. 2. Yes, Jesus loves me.

2049 _____. "November 15---December 15." SOUTHERN WORKMAN 32 (January 1904): 58.

Discussion of the songs sung by Hampton students at the dedication services for the new Army YMCA Building at Fort Monroe, Virginia, which was donated by Helen Gould.

References to 3 songs: 1. My Lord, what a morning. 2. Wasn't dat a wide ribber. 3. Ezekiel saw a wheel.

2050 "Hampton's Anniversary." SOUTHERN WORKMAN 44 (June 1915): 360-61.

Review of a concert includes discussion of the origin of spirituals sung on the occasion of Hampton's Anniversary celebration in 1915.

References to 3 songs: 1. Don't be weary traveler. 2. Let us cheer the weary traveler. 3. Run to Jesus.

2051 Hardee, Charles S. H. "Notes and Documents: Reminiscences of Charles Seton Henry Hardee." Edited by Martha Gallaudet Waring. Parts 1-3. GEORGIA HISTORICAL QUARTERLY 12 (June, September, December 1928): 158-76; 255-88; 353-89.

Memoirs of a southern planter, edited by his granddaughter, include references to an African-born slavewoman who told him African stories when he was a child, and sang African songs.

Text of 1 song: Dare's a ting dey call him de 'Gater.

2052 Harris, Corra. "The Recording Angel." SATURDAY EVENING POST 184 (9 March 1912): 15-18.

Short story about life in a southern community, Ruckersville, after the Civil War includes description of black field hands working with their picks and singing as they worked: "every stroke of every pick being accompanied by a humorous grunt...."

Text of 1 song: Dig my grave wid er silver spoon, lemme down wid er golden chain.

2053 Harrison, Ruth M. "Jerry." PUTNAM'S MONTHLY 7 (December 1909): 312-20.

Jerry sings and plays his banjo in a short story about a man's resourcefulness in concealing a military secret during the Civil War.

Text and music of 1 song: An' I'se got but one sweetheart in town.

2054 Hensel, William Uhler. "The Treason Trials

of 1851: An Historical Sketch." HISTORICAL PAPERS AND ADDRESSES OF THE LANCASTER COUNTY HISTORICAL SOCIETY 15 (1911). 134 pp. Reprint as THE CHRISTIAN RIOT AND THE TREASON TRIALS OF 1851: A HISTORICAL SKETCH. New York: Negro Universities Press, 1969.

Account includes description of black merry-makers at an "apple boiling," where the apples were boiled in a huge kettle, while the slaves danced around the fire and sang.

Text of 1 song: Leader, what do you say (107). Text of 1 chorus: Take me back to Canada (28).

2055 Hobson, Anne. IN OLD ALABAMA: BEING THE CHRONICLES OF MISS MOUSE, THE LITTLE BLACK MERCHANT. New York: Doubleday, Page and Company, 1903. Reprint. Freeport, NY: Books for Libraries Press, c.1976.

There is no introduction to this collection of tales and plantation songs, and it is not clear which tales and songs are folk composed as distinguished from those written by the author. References to a cane-grinding festival (103-13) and to plantation dances, such as the pigeon-wing (111, 161), dog-short and pulled-de-root (232), beat-de-mule and snake dance (111-12).

Texts of 47 songs. See SONG COLLECTIONS (no. 2303). Texts of 10 tales. See TALE COLLECTIONS (no. 2289).

2056 Hopkins, Pauline E. "Famous Women of the Negro Race: Harriet Tubman ('Moses')." COLORED AMERICAN MAGAZINE 4 (January-February 1902): 210-23.

Black writer's biographical sketch of Harriet Tubman---freedom fighter and conductor of the "underground railroad"---includes texts of spirituals Tubman used as "alerting songs" for helping slaves to escape on the underground railroad.

Texts of 2 songs: 1. When dat ole chariot comes. 2. Moses, go down in Egypt (Cho: Let my people go).

2057 _____. CONTENDING FORCES: A ROMANCE ILLUSTRATIVE OF NEGRO LIFE NORTH AND SOUTH. Boston: Colored Co-Operative Publishing Company, 1900. 402 pp. Reprint. New York: Oxford University Press, 1988.

Collection of 22 short stories about Afro-American life in the North and the South. The second story, "The Days Before the War," includes description of plantation life in the South and performance practice associated with singing.

Texts of 2 worksongs: 1. Turn dat han' spike roun' and roun' (32). 2. Hark, dat mery, purty bell go jing-a-ling (33).

2058 _____. "A Dash for Liberty." COLORED AMERICAN MAGAZINE 3 (August 1901): 243-47.

Fictional account of a fugitive slave living in Canada who returns to Virginia in 1840 to rescue his wife includes description of a corn-shucking.

Text of 1 song: All dem purty gals will be dar (Cho: Shuck dat corn before you eat). (244)

2059 House, Grace Bigelow. "The Little Foe of All the World." SOUTHERN WORKMAN 35 (November 1906): 598-614.

Short story contains texts of 2 songs: 1. I wants to climb up Jacob's ladder (Cho: I'se gwine to praise ye de Lord) (600). 2. O, He gave me a ticket (Cho: Jes go on! I'll go wid yo') (608).

2060 _____. "The Promise of A Better Day." SOUTHERN WORKMAN 37 (October 1908): 547-57.

Short story written by a teacher at the Penn School on St. Helena Island (South Carolina) about a native of the island includes the texts of 2 songs: 1. March de angels march (Cho: Roll Jordan). 2. O, none in all the world before were ever glad as we.

2061 _____. "Stormy." SOUTHERN WORKMAN 39 (April 1910): 221-33.

Short story about Stormy, a black child of the South Carolina Sea Islands, includes the text of 1 song: Oh, de wind it blows so loud (230).

2062 _____. "Origin of the Hymn [of Freedom]." SOUTHERN WORKMAN 47 (October 1918): 474-75.

Comment on the new hymn "O, March On Freedom," which was first sung in 1918 to the tune of the spiritual "O, Ride On Jesus."

2063 Howard, John Tasker, Jr. "Capturing the Spirit of the Real Negro Music." Book Review. MUSICIAN 24 (March 1919): 13.

Music historian's review of Burlin's collection entitled NEGRO FOLK SONGS (see no. 2008) includes discussion of her tour through the South and the recordings she made. Comment on the performance practice associated with singing of these songs and on their musical characteristics.

Texts and music of 4 songs (excerpts): 1. Oh, every time I feel the spirit. 2. Oh, way down yonder by myself (Cho: Couldn't hear nobody pray). 3. Good news, chariot coming, An' I don't want her to leave me behin'. 4. O, listen to the lambs, all a-crying. References to 3 songs: 1. God's a-gwine ter move all de troubles away. 2. Go down, Moses. 3. O, ride on, Jesus.

2064 _____. "Our Folk Music and Its Probable

Impressions on American Music of the Future---Casual Remarks by Way of Survey." MUSICAL QUARTERLY 7 (April 1921): 167-71.

Discussion of black folk music includes comment on the controversy over whether it has African origins or "was acquired from the itinerant [white] revivalists who travelled through the South." Also the observation that popular music has been influenced by Negro folksong and dance.

2065 Howell, W. D. "Savannah Twice Visited." HARPER'S MONTHLY MAGAZINE 138 (February 1919): 319-32.

Discussion of a visit to Savannah, Georgia, contains reference to the street cry of a black peddler: A crab, buyer! A crab.

2066 Hubbard, William Lines. "Negro Music and Negro Minstrelsy" in HISTORY OF AMERICAN MUSIC. AMERICAN HISTORY AND ENCYCLOPEDIA OF MUSIC, edited by W. L. Hubbard, vol. 8, 49-70. Toledo, OH: Irving Squire, 1908.

Discussion of the slave songs, their character and performance practice (52-54), and of musical instruments used by the slaves (50-51).

Texts of 4 choruses (54): 1. Nobody knows who I am. 2. O, Satan comes like a busy ole man. 3. I'm gwine to tell you 'bout de comin' ob de Saviour. 4. Poor Rosy, poor gal.

2067 "The Hymn in the Camps." SOUTHERN WORKMAN 47 (October 1918): 476-78.

Discussion of how black soldiers were taught to sing spirituals and other Negro folksongs during World War I by Joshua E. Blanton and other black song leaders.

References to 4 songs: 1. Children, Hail, Hail, Hail. 2. We are climbing Jacob's ladder. 3. Where shall I be when the first trumpet sounds? 4. O, march on, Freedom (to the tune of O, ride on Jesus).

2068 Johnston, Harry H. THE NEGRO IN THE NEW WORLD. London: Methuen & Company, 1910. 499 pp.

Englishman's discussion of black culture includes comment on the singing of plantation songs at Tuskegee and Hampton (391-92).

Text of 1 song: March de angels, march (Cho: Roll, Jordan, roll Jordan, roll Jordan roll) (392).

2069 Jones, J. Ralph, interviewer. "Portraits of Georgia Slaves." Edited by Tom Landess. GEORGIA REVIEW v. 21 (Spring 1967): 126-132; (Summer 1967): 268-73; (Fall 1967): 407-11; (Winter 1967): 521-25; v. 22 (Spring 1968): 125-27; (Summer 1968): 254-57.

Interviews of former Georgia slaves, conducted in the 1930s by J. Ralph Jones (later, president of Grambling College), were undertaken at Mr. Jones' own initiative and are not part of the W.P.A. project (see nos. 1786-1826) or the collection of the United Daughters of the Confederacy. Discussion of prayer meetings held in the slaves' cabins (21: 128).

Texts of 3 songs (21: 128, 271): 1. Jest befo' day, I feels 'im (Cho: The spirit, I feels 'im). 2. Our troubles will soon be over (Cho: I'm going to live with Jesus---after while). 3. All I want is Jesus (Cho: You may have all the world, just give me Jesus).

2070 "The Jubilee Singers." FISK UNIVERSITY NEWS 2/5 (October 1911). 59 pp.

This number contains articles written by persons who were associated with the original Fisk Jubilee Singers, among them: Mary E. Spence (white), the first chaperon, and Ella Sheppard Moore, the first pianist-accompanist. Discussion of the blending of voices (56) and references to the effect that the troupe's singing of "Steal away" had on audiences.

2071 [Judge, Jane.] "Savannah Hears Folk Song Festival." NEW YORK AGE. 18 January 1918. Originally published in the SAVANNAH MORNING NEWS.

Concert review includes discussion of the Negro folksong festival with a chorus of 250 trained and directed by Azalia Hackley. Comment on the quality of the singing---"its unusual intervals, its minors, its weird harmonies"---and the types of songs performed.

2072 Keyser, Frances Reynolds. "One Woman's Work for the Race, in Florida." A. M. E. CHURCH REVIEW 31 (July 1914): 107-11.

Discussion of the work of black educator Mary McLeod Bethune in rural Florida includes the text of a favorite "jubilee song" she sang as a child while working in the rice fields of South Carolina.

Text of 1 song: 1. Before I'd be a slave I'd be buried in my grave.

2073 Kidson, Frank. "Negro Music of the U. S." GROVE'S DICTIONARY OF MUSIC AND MUSICIANS, edited by J. A. Fuller Maitland, 3: 359-62. London: Macmillan Company, 1907.

Discussion of the origin, quality, and performance practice of Negro folk music includes examples of songs and two melodies identified as "of Negro origin" in eighteenth-century sources.

Music and texts of 3 songs: Nobody knows de trouble I've had. 2. O, graveyard, O, graveyard. 3. Belle Layotte. Music and texts of 2 couplets: 1. In de mornin' when I rise. 2. Turn, sinner, turn today. Two melodies without texts: 1.

Pompey ran away (=Negro jig, Virginia). 2. Negro Dance.

2074 Krehbiel, Henry Edward. "Lafcadio Hearn and Congo Music." MUSICIAN 11 (November 1906: 544-46.

Music critic of the NEW YORK TRIBUNE discusses an editorial published in the NEW YORK SUN that claims Lafcadio Hearn concluded the slave songs heard in the Place Congo Square in New Orleans, Louisiana, were not African in origin but rude adaptations of French and Spanish songs. Critic offers proof that Hearn stated the Creole music to be largely Negro. Also discussion of the characteristics of the creole slave songs and performance practice.

Text of 1 song with African refrain: Ouende, ouende, macaya!.

2075 _____. AFRO-AMERICAN FOLKSONGS: A STUDY IN RACIAL AND NATIONAL MUSIC. New York: G. Schirmer, 1914. 176 pp. Reprint. Portland, ME: Longwood Press, 1974.

Detailed discussion and analysis of the slave songs, including comment on African music and its relationship to the Afro-American. Author examined 527 songs to determine modal characteristics of the slave song repertory, rhythmic features, prevalent song types, poetic forms, and related matters. Also discussion of creole songs and Afro-American dances.

Music and texts of 29 songs. Text only of 1 song. See SONG COLLECTIONS (no. 2304).

2076 "Legitimizing the Music of the Negro." CURRENT OPINION 54 (May 1913): 384-85.

Discussion of the danger of "spiritual corruption" in harmonizing spirituals for concert performance. Reference to the use of the flatted seventh in some spirituals. Also quotations from articles of Henry E. Krehbiel and Natalie Curtis Burlin. Black singers advised to "learn and perpetuate these songs as they were created and sung."

2077 Leiding, Harriette Kershaw. STREET CRIES OF AN OLD SOUTHERN CITY. Charleston, SC: Dragget Printing Company, 1910. 12 pp. Reprint. 1927.

Monograph contains examples of street cries, description of the black peddlers, and comment on performance practice. Two street cries in this collection served as thematic material for George Gershwin's opera, PORGY AND BESS.

Texts of 2 cries: 1. Old Joe Cole---good old soul. 2. Load my gun wid sweet sugar plum. Texts and music of 9 cries: 1. Raw! Raw! Raw swimp [=shrimp]. 2. She craib! She craib! 3. Red rose tommaytoes. 4. Monkey meat. 5. Charcoal. 6. Whiting. 7. Strawberry. An e fresh an e fine. 8. Green peas! Sugar peas! 8. An a dawtry daw. Text of 1 boat song: Rosy am a handsome gal.

2078 Lemmerman, Karl. "Correspondence---Improvised Negro Songs." NEW REPUBLIC 13 (22 December 1917): 214-15.

Discussion of songs heard about 1907 at a black camp-meeting service along the Ohio River near the Kentucky-West Virginia border.

Texts of 6 songs: 1. Hold your light, Brudder Robert (Cho: Hold your light on Canaan's Shore). 2. Brudder, Keep your lamps trimmin' and a-burnin'. 3. Dere's no rain to wet you. 4. O, walk 'em easy round de heaven. 5. De gospel ship is sailin' (Cho: Hosann-sann). 6. O, de ole nigger-driver (Cho: O, gwine away!).

2079 Lewis, Joseph Vance. OUT OF THE DITCH. A TRUE STORY OF AN EX-SLAVE. Houston, TX: Rein & Sons Company, 1910. 54 pp.

Description of plantation life after Emancipation by ex-slave Lewis, who later became a lawyer, includes references to the songs sung by the slaves when they learned they were free (10-11) and to other plantation songs (14-15).

References to 4 songs: 1. Before I'd be a slave (parody, 10). 2. My good Lord done been here (14). 3. O, rise, shine, the light is coming (15). 4. Give me that old time religion (20).

2080 Lomax, John Avery. "Some Ballads of North Carolina." NORTH CAROLINA BOOKLET 11 (July 1911): 26-42.

Folklorist's assorted collection contains fragments of fifteen, Negro song texts from North Carolina. Informants are identified. See SONG COLLECTIONS (no. 2305)

2081 _____. "Some Types of American Folk-Songs." JOURNAL OF AMERICAN FOLK-LORE 28 (January-March 1915): 1-17.

Miscellaneous collection of folksong texts includes one identified as a black folk ballad.

Text of 1 song: (Ballet of the Boll-Weevil) If anybody axes you who wuz it writ dis song (15).

2082 _____. "Self-Pity in Negro Folk-Songs." NATION 105 (9 August 1917): 141-45.

Folksong collector's discussion of improvisation, the subjects covered in the song texts, and performance practice, with comment on the singers' propensity for "changing words...to suit their purposes." Identification of the songs as "living growing organisms mirroring [the Negro's] mind as it is today," and of the blues as, "an endless type...sung by all Negroes who will sing 'worl'ly songs' at all."

Texts of 15 songs. See SONG COLLECTIONS (no. 2306).

2083 Lorenz, Edmund S. PRACTICAL CHURCH MUSIC. New York: Fleming H. Revell Company, c.1909. 423 pp.

Hymn composer's discussion of spirituals and gospel songs (91-112) advances the thesis that the slave songs did not originate among the slaves but were the "direct off-spring of the white man's spirituals" (92).

2084 Marteau, Henri. "Marteau Looks to South for America's Future in Music." MUSICAL AMERICA (28 April 1906): 11.

French violinist's discussion of America's musical development includes comment on the style and quality of the old southern Negro melodies, especially the "rhythm, which is unmistakably new in music."

2085 Mason, Daniel Gregory. "Folk-Song and American Music." MUSICAL QUARTERLY 4 (July 1918): 323-32.

Composer's discussion of the characteristic features of Negro folksong, and of its quality, includes musical analysis with selected examples to illustrate the points made.

Music and texts of 5 choruses: 1. I went to the hillside. 2. You may bury me in the East. 3. Didn't my Lord deliver Daniel. 4. Oh, yes, I'm going up. 5. Deep River.

2086 McBryde, John McLaren, Jr. "A Modern Miracle Play." ATLANTIC MONTHLY 110 (August 1912): 266-69.

Comment on the experience of witnessing "a dramatic representation of the visit of the Queen of Sheba to King Solomon," performed in a small church in the mountains of southwest Virginia. Given twice in one evening, performance was arranged by the pastor to raise money for the church.

Text and music of 1 song: Dere wuz ten, ten wirgins w'en de bride-groom come. References to 2 songs: 1. Come w'ere de lilies blow. 2. Jesus de light uv de worl'.

2087 McCullagh, Herbert. "The Possibilities of Negro Music." Music Review. MUSICIAN 10 (December 1905): 529.

Discussion of the possibilities of using authentic African and Afro-American folk melodies for extended classical music compositions, as demonstrated by composer Samuel Coleridge-Taylor in TWENTY-FOUR NEGRO MELODIES...(1905).

2088 Miles, Emma Bell. "Some Real American Music." HARPER'S NEW MONTHLY MAGAZINE 109 (June 1904): 118-123.

Discussion focuses on the argument that genuine American folk music is represented by songs of white mountaineers from the Carolinas, Kentucky, and Tennessee, that black folk songs and Indian music are not representative of the "true" American character.

Texts and music of 2 songs: 1. Hit's the old Ship of Zion. 2. Some have fathers up in glory (Cho: On the other bright shore).

2089 Miller, George A. "Canning Negro Melodies." LITERARY DIGEST 52 (27 May 1916): 1556-58.

Discussion of phonograph recordings of Negro melodies includes the observation that "the character of the words and music of most of them [are] determined by the trade or occupation of the Negro who sings them."

Texts of 5 songs, as sung by a washerwoman, cotton pickers, a ditch digger, a young tenor, and a dancer: 1. Trouble gwine ter war'y me down. 2. Somebody buried in de graveyard (Cho: If you git dare befo' I do). 3. Goalman, goalman, goalman day. 4. Old Massa bought a yallow gal (Cho: Den ha', ha', my darlin' chile). 5. Walkin' on de green grass.

2090 Miller, Kelly. "An Effectual Prayer." SOUTHERN WORKMAN 30 (September 1901): 504-9.

Short story written by the black writer and Howard University professor about a slave boy and the slaveholder's son includes references to slave singing.

Text of 1 chorus: O Judgement, Judgement, Judgement Day is rolling around (507).

2091 _____. RACE ADJUSTMENT. New York: The Neale Publishing Company, 1909. 307 pp. Reprint. New York: Arno Press and the New York Times, 1968.

Collection of essays written by black professor at Howard University includes some that were previously published. A chapter entitled "The Artistic Gifts of the Negro" includes comment on plantation melody, its sources, its qualities, and its meaning (236-39). Also a brief discussion of ragtime (240).

2092 Moderwell, Hiram Kelly. "The Epic of the Black Man." NEW REPUBLIC 12 (8 September 1917): 154-55.

Focus upon the spiritual as the "stirring record of a race," and discussion of imagery and symbolism in the spirituals, which served as a "religious veil which permitted the slave to live his own varied emotional life without interference from his master."

Texts of 3 choruses: 1. Bendin' knees a-achin'. 2. You may bury me in the East. 3. Walk together, children.

2093 Moore, Ella Sheppard. "Prince Henry and the Fisk University Jubilee Singers." AMERICAN MISSIONARY (MAGAZINE) n.s. 56 (April 1902): 194-96.

Organist-pianist of the original Fisk Jubilee Singers describes the audience given to the Singers by Prince Henry of Germany during his visit to Nashville, Tennessee, on 27 February (1902?).

Text of 1 chorus: Oh, bye-and-bye, bye-and-bye, I'm going to lay down my heavy load. References to 2 songs: 1. Oh, walk together, children. 2. Swing low, sweet chariot.

2094 Moton, Robert Russa. FINDING A WAY OUT. AN AUTOBIOGRAPHY. College Park, MD: McGrath Publishing Company, 1920. 296 pp.

Black educator's discussion of the singing of plantation songs at Hampton Institute in Virginia includes comment on the negative attitude of the "coloured" students towards the songs (57-61, 93). Also, discussion of how, as a plantation child, he and a friend were "frequently called into the 'big house' to perform" (18-19).

2095 Murphy, Jeannette Robinson. "Black Mammy, Creditor." CENTURY 64 (October 1902): 966-67.

A singer-writer's discussion of the role of the black mammy in raising white children of South: "She enters into the children's inner secrets, sees life from the little ones' standpoint, as we white mothers seldom can."

Text and music of 1 song: Who's gwine nuss de baby? (Cho: Roll 'im an' er roll 'im baby).

2096 _____. "The True Negro Music and Its Decline." INDEPENDENT 55 (23 July 1903): 1723-30.

Discussion of the musical characteristics of the plantation songs includes comment on the geographical origin of several songs and instructions regarding their performance. Quotations from interviews with former slaves, who stated that they improvised these songs after "wrestling with the spirit."

Text and music of 7 songs: 1. Oh, de prodigal son he left home by himself. 2. Ole ship o' Zion. 3. Sinnah! Yer walkin' on er slender stran'. 4. Daniel, ahong! [sic] In de lion's den! 5. Ready fo' de water? (Cho: Oh, yes! Bright shines de day). 6. I don't want er be buried in de storm (Cho: Sometimes my troubles make me tremble). 7. Mary, what yer gwine er name dat purty leetle baby? (Cho: Glory be to yer new-bawn King!).

2097 "Negro Folk Songs Acclaimed as America's Musical Treasure." MUSICAL AMERICA (3 August 1918): 20.

The programming of a Negro spiritual, "God's a-gwine ter move all de troubles away," on a concert given at the Metropolitan Opera House by the Schola Cantorum, directed by Kurt Schindler, led to discussion of the spiritual, its quality, significance, and characteristic features.

2098 "Negro Folk Songs." Unsigned review. SOUTHERN WORKMAN 38 (August 1909): 422-23.

Review of the new edition of RELIGIOUS FOLK SONGS OF THE NEGRO, AS SUNG ON THE PLANTATIONS (see no. 2035) contains discussion of folksong performance practice.

2099 "Negro Music in the Land of Freedom." OUTLOOK 106 (21 March 1914): 611-12.

Review of a concert given in Carnegie Hall by black musicians includes comment on the "real untutored singing of Negroes in the heart of the South." Observation that Will Marion Cook was successful in using Negro themes in his composition and in instructing his Afro-American Folk-Singers how to sing spirituals.

2100 "Negro Music." SOUTHERN WORKMAN 47 (July 1918): 323-24.

Editorial discussion of the fact that Negro spirituals were sung on a concert given by the Schola Cantorum in New York (Kurt Schindler, conductor, Harry T. Burleigh, soloist) includes the citing of other instances in which white composers and organizations employed Afro-American folk songs.

Reference to 1 song: God's a gwine ter move all de troubles away.

2101 "Negro Spirituals in France." SOUTHERN WORKMAN 47 (November 1918): 523.

Discussion by a YMCA worker of black servicemen singing their folksongs in France during World War I, and comment on the songs.

Text of 1 song: It is good for a world of trouble (Cho: Give me that old-time religion).

2102 Oberholtzer, Ellis Paxson. PHILADELPHIA. A HISTORY OF THE CITY AND ITS PEOPLE.... Philadelphia: S. J. Clarke Publishing Company, 1912. 4 vols.

History of Philadelphia includes several pages given over to discussion of street vendors (2: 91-95), most of whom were black in the antebellum years. Texts of several street cries given, including that of "the hominy man," whose cry was "most musical of all cries."

Texts of 3 cries: 1. De hominy man. 2. Yere's the white whitey wash. 3. Pepper-pot, all hot.

2103 Odum, Anna Kranz, compiler. "Some Negro

Folk-Songs from Tennessee." JOURNAL OF AMERICAN FOLK-LORE 27 (July-September 1914): 225-65.

Anthology compiled by a native of Athens, Georgia, consists of a miscellaneous collection of Afro-American folklore, obtained from children in Sumner County, Tennessee. Description of the performance practice associated with the singing of the folksongs, and references to the use of unlimited variation, the combining of texts of different songs, and the freedom of the "part" singing.

Texts of 25 songs. See SONG COLLECTIONS (no. 2309).

2104 Odum, Howard W. "Folk-Song and Folk-Poetry as Found in the Secular Songs of the Southern Negroes." Parts 1, 2. JOURNAL OF AMERICAN FOLK-LORE 24 (July/September, October/December 1911): 255-94; 351-96. Reprint. NEGRO WORKADAY SONGS, by Howard Odum and Guy Johnson. Chapel Hill: University of North Carolina Press, 1925.

Scholar's collection includes blues, gambling songs, work songs, knife-songs, train songs, love songs, dance-songs, and ballads. Observes that the songs originated with the Negroes, or were "so completely adapted as to become folk songs." Discussion of performance practice and "the facility of the negroes in producing their own songs from material of any sort."

Texts of 127 songs. See SONG COLLECTIONS (no. 2311).

2105 ____. "Negro Hymn." JOURNAL OF AMERICAN FOLK-LORE 26 (October-December 1913): 374-76.

Sociologist's discussion of the content of a song collected in Grovetown, Georgia, by Emma Backus.

Text of 1 song: Hypocrite, hypocrite, God despise (Cho: Ain't gwine grieve my God no more).

2106 Owen, May West. "Negro Spirituals: Their Origin, Development and Place in American Folk-Song." MUSICAL OBSERVER 19 (December 1920): 12-13.

Contrary to the title of this article, its focus is on the use of black spirituals as thematic sources for trained composers.

References to 4 songs: 1. Standin' in de need of prayer. 2. Wait till ah put on my crown. 3. Things up yonder white as snow. 4. Leanin' on de Lawd.

2107 Park, Robert E. "The Conflict and Fusion of Cultures with Special Reference to the Negro." JOURNAL OF NEGRO HISTORY 4 (April 1919): 111-133.

The sociologist read this paper at the annual meeting of the American Sociological Society at Richmond, Virginia, in 1918. Discussion focuses on the question of whether Afro-American culture is distinctive, with comment on its religion (118-23), including voodoo and the African practices of the Sea Islands blacks, and on the spirituals (123-27).

Text of 1 song: An' I couldn't hear nobody pray.

2108 Payne, Lewis. "The Negro in the World of Music." ETUDE (June 1916): 759.

Comment on the quality of the "original" Negro songs.

2109 Peabody, Charles. "Notes on Negro Music." JOURNAL OF AMERICAN FOLK-LORE 16 (July 1903): 148-52. Reprints. SOUTHERN WORKMAN 32 (May 1904): 305-09. BLACK PERSPECTIVE IN MUSIC 4 (July 1976): 133-37.

Archaeologist's discussion of Afro-American folk music and performing practice that he observed during an excavation in Coahoma County, Mississippi, in 1901-1902 includes comment on song types, voice quality, and rhythmic matters.

Text and music of 1 song: Went down town 'bout a quarter to eight. Melody (without text) of 1 song. Texts of 10 couplets: 1. They had me arrested for murder. 2. Some folks say a preacher won't steal. 3. Old Brudder Jones setten on de log. 4. Old Dan Tucker he got drunk. 5. I don't gamble but I don't see. 6. When I look up over my head. 7. The reason I love my baby so. 8. Say, Sal, don't you powder so. 9. O, we'll live on pork and kisses. 10. I'm so tired I'm most dead.

2110 Peabody, Francis Greenwood. EDUCATION FOR LIFE. THE STORY OF HAMPTON INSTITUTE. Told in Connection with the Fiftieth Anniversary of the Foundation of the School. New York: Doubleday, Page and Company, 1918. 393 pp.

Discussion of the history of Hampton includes comment on the Negro spirituals, their quality, "weird melodies," "strange harmonies, and "cadences that swerve and droop to minor keys" (76, 129-34). References to first lines of several spirituals. Also review of the tours of the Hampton singers and the money they raised to build Virginia Hall (erected 1875).

2111 "Percy Grainger's Tribute to the Music of the American Negro." CURRENT OPINION 59 (August 1915): 100-101.

Discussion of the similarity between Negro plantation melodies and the folk music of the British Isles includes excerpts from interviews of Grainger that were published in the NEW YORK EVENING POST and the MUSICAL QUARTERLY. Also comment on improvisation: "it is not so much the melody in these songs which attracts one as it is the method of singing---especially the part-singing."

2112 Perrow, Eber Carle. "Songs and Rhymes from the South." Parts 1-3. JOURNAL OF AMERICAN FOLK-LORE 25 (April-June 1912): 137-55; 26 (April-June 1913): 123-73; 28 (April-June 1915): 129-90.

Scholar's immense collection of about 235 folk-songs, collected primarily in the "region of the southern Appalachian Mountains," consists of a wide variety of work songs, dance songs, love songs, and other secular types, of which approximately half are traced to Negro origin. Also included are a few spirituals. Many songs are represented in variant versions, and sources are given (both manuscript and informants).

Text and music of 5 songs. Texts of 134 songs. See SONG COLLECTIONS (no. 2312).

2113 Peterson, Clara Gottschalk. CREOLE SONGS FROM NEW ORLEANS IN THE NEGRO DIALECT. New Orleans: L. Grunewald Company, 1902. 20 pp. Reprint. Microfiche. Chicago: Library Resources, 1970.

Collection compiled by the sister of the pianist-composer Louis Moreau Gottschalk represents slave songs of "historical interest" that she learned as a child. Except for a few used by her brother in his early compositions, the songs were "unknown to the public" before her publication.

Texts and music of 12 songs. See SONG COLLECTIONS (no. 2313).

2114 Portor, Laura Spencer. "Those Days in Old Virginia. A Picture of the South before the War." 5-part serial. LADIES HOME JOURNAL 19 (February-June 1902).

Discussion of life on the plantation during the antebellum period includes description of a corn shucking festival with comment on the quality of the singing of the workers---"a weird kind of recitative...the others coming in on impromptu choruses as they worked" (February, 4). Also description of a slave wedding, which took place in the "big dining room"; of a slave christening (April, 12); and of a slave funeral (June, 10).

2115 Pound, Louise. "The Ancestry of a 'Negro Spiritual'." MODERN LANGUAGE NOTES 33 (November 1918): 442-44.

Comment on the relationship between the Negro song "Weeping Mary" and a white song that begins with the same first line, concludes that the Negro song was borrowed from a white repertory.

Text and music of 1 song: If there's anybody here like Weeping Mary.

2116 Pratt, Lucy Agnes. "The Evolution of Slim." SOUTHERN WORKMAN 32 (November 1903): 558-64.

Instructor's discussion of the black children who attend her classes at the Whittier School in Hampton Roads, Virginia, includes the text of 1 song: I'm a rollin' through an unfrien'ly worl' (559).

2117 Pringle, Elizabeth W. Allston (Patience Pennington, pseud.] "Rab and Dab. A Woman Rice-Planter's Story." ATLANTIC MONTHLY 114 (November 1914): 577-89.

Story of how the author came to know and eventually take care of two mischievous young boys, Jonadab and Rechab.

Text and music of 1 song: Oh-ye! No-e Oh-ye Noa', H'ist de winda le' de duv' cum een.

2118 _____. CHRONICLES OF CHICORA WOOD. New York: Charles Scribner's Sons, 1922. 363 pp.

Autobiographical novel of a former slaveholder's daughter centers on plantation life in South Carolina. Discussion of boatmen's songs (69), songs slaves sang after learning they had been freed (272), and their dancing (272-73).

References to 4 songs (69): 1. Roll, Jordan, roll. 2. Run, Mary, run. 3. Drinkin' wine. 4. Oh, Zion. Text of 1 song: In case I neber see you any mo'.

2119 Ranson, A. R. H. "Reminiscences of the Civil War by a Confederate Staff Officer." SEWANEE REVIEW 21 (October 1913): 428-47.

Discussion of plantation life in the South before the Civil War by a native of Cantonville, Maryland, includes description of the singing of a black driver.

Text of 1 song: See de bull go to school (Cho: An dat is de las' of old blind John).

2120 Read, Angelo. "Negro Melodies, Not American Music." MUSICAL AMERICA (11 August 1906): 2.

Advancement of the thesis that the black man did not create his own music but took over white music and assimilated it according to his capacity, especially the music of Scotch settlers in the South. Rejection of Dvorak's and MacDowell's claims to have drawn upon Negro and Indian themes, respectively, in their composition, thus making their music "National" or American.

2121 "The Real Negro Music." NEW YORK SUN, 16 May 1900. Clipping. See A. A. Brown Scrapbooks, "Musical Topics," 2: 39. Boston Public Library. Boston, MA.

Sub-title of article is, "Don't Seek for It in

Artificially Made 'Coon Songs'." The writer, a native of Alexandria, Louisiana, traces the origin of such popular songs as "De New Bully" and "Mistah Johnson, Tu'n Me Loose" back to folk roots. Discussion of worksongs and description of a camp meeting.

Texts of 3 songs: 1. Ol' Saytin come-a down a-readin'. 2. Jesus sont 'is wo'ld ter me. 3. Ah stepped acrost de Pargound (Cho: Who's on de way). References to 4 songs: 1. Swing-a dat shinin' s'ode [=sword]. 2. Rock-a-mah soul in de buzzum o' mah Jesus. 3. Ah's giving atter mah bugle. 4. Trouble in de law-groun's.

2122 "Recognition of Negro Music." SOUTHERN WORKMAN (January 1920): 6-7.

Discussion of a concert given by the Musical Arts Society under the direction of Frank Damrosch, on which two spirituals were performed, includes quotations from a review published by Henry Krehbiel in the NEW YORK TIMES, in which he noted that the spirituals, arranged by Natalie Curtis Burlin, were given "the proper treatment...[were not] spoiled by too much sophistication. Also quotations from Burlin in regard to "the artistic utterance of the Negro [as] a lasting offering to our national culture."

References to 2 songs: 1. Dar's a star in de Eas'. 2. Mary had a Baby.

2123 Reddick, K. D., and Phil V. S. Lindsley, comps. NATIONAL JUBILEE MELODIES. 23rd ed. Nashville, TN: National Baptist Publishing Board, c1916.

Miscellaneous collection of plantation songs compiled and published in order to "save the old slave songs for posterity." Gathered by black collectors Reddick of Americus, Georgia, and Lindsley of Nashville, from the "various rice, cane, and cotton plantations of the South."

Texts and music of 139 songs. See SONG COLLECTIONS (no. 2315).

2124 Richardson, Clement. "Rural School Improvement in Alabama: Part II, Community Cooperation." SOUTHERN WORKMAN 42 (November 1913): 604-09.

Discussion by a college professor at Tuskegee Institute of the importance of religion and song in fund-raising activities for black elementary schools in the rural South.

Reference to 1 song: Bye and bye when the morning comes.

2125 Robinson, Frances. "Folk-Music." CURRENT LITERATURE 30 (March 1901): 350-51.

Discussion of folksong includes comment on the four general types of "negro songs...[which] have never been created by way of artistic composition, but have sprung into life ready-made": 1. imitations of ballads, jigs, etc. 2. imitations of Methodist and Baptist hymns. 3. "recitative-style songs, or airs more closely adhering to the original African types." 4. French creole tunes of New Orleans.

2126 Rodeheaver, Homer A. RODEHEAVER'S PLANTATION MELODIES. Chicago: The Rodeheaver Company, 1918. 34 pp. 2d ed. 1918. 48 pp.

The first edition of the hymn composer's collection of "Modern, Popular and Old-Time Negro Songs of the Southland" has no introductory text. The preface of the second edition includes reference to Negroes singing spirituals for the compiler's mother "in the mountains of East Tennessee."

Texts and music of 47 songs. See SONG COLLECTIONS (nos. 2316, 2317).

2127 [Roosevelt, Theodore]. "President Extols Music of Negroes." MUSICAL AMERICA (24 February 1906): 10.

Brief article includes a quotation from the President of the United States, who visited the Industrial Institute at Manassas, Virginia, and spoke to the black students about the "importance and dignity" of Negro spirituals.

2128 Rowland, Kate. "Street Cries of Philadelphia." PAPERS OF THE CITY HISTORICAL SOCIETY OF PHILADELPHIA (1922): 91-110.

Local historian read this paper before the Society in January 1920. Discussion of black and white street criers of the past includes description of the following black criers and their songs: 1. chimney sweep (92-93), 2. crab man (98), 3. white-wash man (99), 4. the original hominy man in 1828 (100), 5. rags man (102-103), 6. stevedores (105), 7. pepper-pot ladies (107).

Texts and music of 9 street cries (98, 100, 101, 103, 109).

2129 Scarborough, Dorothy. FROM A SOUTHERN PORCH. New York: G. P. Putnam's Sons, 1919. 318 pp.

Narrative by the southern writer contains a potpourri of reminiscences about life in the South, with focus on the social life, customs, and music of blacks in Virginia and Texas. Discussion of the music and textual characteristics of black folk song, and observation of the singers' predilection for repetition and borrowing phrases, which are carried from one song to another (56-57). Author states that she did not edit the songs she published, but transcribed them as she heard them. Also discussion of the various kinds of folk dances (315-16).

Texts of 33 songs. See SONG COLLECTIONS (no. 2317)

2130 Scott, Emmett J. SCOTT'S OFFICIAL HISTORY OF THE AMERICAN NEGRO IN THE WORLD WAR. Chicago: Homewood Press, 1919. 511 pp.

Chapter 22 of this historical survey, written by Booker T. Washington's former private secretary (later Howard University administrator) and entitled "Negro Music that Stirred France," devotes several pages to discussion of Negro traditional music in army camp life. Comment on the musical "stunts" of the soldiers, the singing of spirituals and parodying the texts, the improvisation of songs about army life, the use of guitars, banjos, and mandolins, and the jazz and dance "stunts" of the servicemen (300-304).

2131 Smith, Frances. "The Glory of the Glow Worm." NEW ENGLAND MAGAZINE n.s. 44 (March 1911): 120-25.

Short story about a black woman's aspirations for her son includes the text of 1 song: Ebber sence de 'Mancipation Proclamation.

2132 Smith, N. Clark, arr. NEW JUBILEE SONGS FOR QUARTETTE, CHOIR, OR CHORUS: Concert, Church, & Home. Chicago: Jubilee Music Company, c. 1906. 13 pp.

The preface of this collection, compiled by the black composer-music educator, includes discussion of performance practice associated with the singing of early revival songs.

Texts and music of 8 songs. See SONG COLLECTIONS (no. 2318).

2133 _____. NEW PLANTATION MELODIES AS SUNG BY THE TUSKEGEE INSTITUTE QUARTETTE. Chicago: N. C. Smith, 1909. 4 pp.

Pamphlet includes songs arranged for male ensemble and a list of other Negro folksongs sung at Tuskegee Institute.

Texts and music of 2 songs: 1. Rolling in Zion's Jubilee. 2. You call me a hypocrite, member, do.

2134 Sneed, Leonora. "Types of Rice Plantation Negroes." SOUTHERN WORKMAN 32 (February 1903): 107-11.

Discussion of a song collected from Mr. Bombazine, a former slave residing in town of St. Mary's, near the Okeefeenokee Swamp between Georgia and Florida.

Text of 1 song: O, I long for to reach dat heavenly sho' (111).

2135 "Sources of Congo Songs." MUSICIAN (Boston) 11 (November 1906): 546.

Reprint of an editorial originally published in the NEW YORK SUN, which refutes the idea that the slave songs heard in the Place Congo at New Orleans, were of African origin. Observation that Lafcadio Hearn, early collector of creole songs, reached the conclusion that these songs were "rude adaptations of Spanish and French songs that slaves had heard in Santo Domingo."

2136 Speers, Mary Walker Finley, collector. "Maryland and Virginia Folk-Lore, Camp-Meeting Hymn" JOURNAL OF AMERICAN FOLK-LORE 26 (April-June 1913): 190.

Text and music of 1 camp-meeting song: I uz dere win he walk'd in Galilee.

2137 Stanley, May. "R. N. Dett, of Hampton Institute, Helping to Lay Foundation for Negro Music of Future." MUSICAL AMERICA (6 July 1918): 17.

Interview with black composer Dett includes long quotations from his statements about the use of Negro themes in composition, and about the meaning and significance of the plantation melodies.

2138 Steward, T. G. "Correspondence---Negro Imagery." NEW REPUBLIC 12 (29 September 1917): 248.

Discussing of singing heard at a religious meeting of blacks in Georgia. Text of 1 song: Dark clouds a-risin' (Cho: Ah, sinner, ain't you tired of sinnin'?).

2139 Stuart, Ruth McEnery. PLANTATION SONGS AND OTHER VERSES. New York: D. Appleton and Company, 1916. 135 pp.

Collection of thirty rhymes written by the author in Afro-American style and dialect contains references to singing, dancing, religion, and performance practice.

2140 Taylor, Susie King. REMINISCENCES OF MY LIFE IN CAMP WITH THE 33RD UNITED STATES COLORED TROOPS LATE 1ST SOUTH CAROLINA VOLUNTEERS. Boston: Printed for the Author, 1902. 82 pp. Reprint. New York: Arno Press and the New York Times, 1968.

The black nurse (b. 1848), writing about her work among soldiers of the First South Carolina (Colored) Volunteers during the Civil War, offers comment on her life as a former slave in Savannah, Georgia. Discussion of the arrest of slaves, including her grandmother, for singing a freedom song at a church meeting in a suburb of Savannah about 1861.

Text of 1 song: Yes, we all shall be free (8).

2141 Thomas, William Holcombe. "Some Current Folk-Songs of the Negro and Their Economic Interpretation." Austin, TX: Published by the Folk-Lore Society of Texas, 1912. 13 pp.

This paper was read before a meeting of the

Folk-Lore Society of Texas in 1912. Discussion of the contemporary songs of the black man and the societal context in which they developed, with focus on the blues and other secular music.

Texts of 11 songs. See SONG COLLECTIONS (no. 2319)

2142 Tiersot, Jean-Baptiste Elisee Julien. "Musical Ethnology in America---Negro Melodies." MUSICIAN 12 (March 1907): 118-19.

Comment by the French musicologist on the thesis that Afro-American songs bear no trace of African ancestry. Also discussion of performance practice.

Text and music of 3 songs: 1. Oh, walk together children, don't you get weary. 2. Papa dit non, maman dit non. 3. Quand patat' la cuit...no mange li.

2143 Upton, George Putnam. THE SONG: ITS BIRTH, EVOLUTION, AND FUNCTION. Chicago: A. C. McClurg & Company, 1915: 111-19.

Discussion of Ethiopian minstrelsy by the former music journalist of the CHICAGO TRIBUNE includes comment on the relations between minstrelsy and Negro folksong. Observation that Dan Rice's songs and dances were parodies of authentic slave songs.

Text of 1 couplet: Wheel about and turn about and jump just so (116). Texts of 13 songs. See SONG COLLECTIONS (no. 2310).

2144 Washington, Booker T. THE STORY OF MY LIFE AND WORK. Naperville, IL: J. L. Nichols & Company, c.1900. 423 pp. Reprint. New York: New American Library, 1970.

President and founder of Tuskegee Institute refers to the singing of slave music on the campus: "Tuskegee students are famous for their fine singing of plantation melodies, and it is the object of the Institute to make these old, sweet, slave songs a source of pride and pleasure to the students" (417). Also comment on "the wail in plantation melodies" (108).

2145 _____. UP FROM SLAVERY. New York: Doubleday, Page & Company, 1901. 330 pp. Reprint. Williamstown, MA: Corner House Publishing Company, 1971.

Autobiography includes discussion of the significance of the references to freedom found in the texts of the slave songs (19-20). Also references to a house organ found in the cabin of poor ex-slaves (179) and to a Christmas season "frolic" (135).

2146 _____. Preface to TWENTY-FOUR NEGRO MELODIES TRANSCRIBED FOR THE PIANO BY S[amuel] COLERIDGE-TAYLOR, vii-ix. Bryn Mawr, PA: Oliver Ditson Company, 1904. Reprint. New York: Da Capo Press, 1980.

Preface offers a biographical sketch of the Afro-British composer and discussion of Negro spirituals, with references to the relationship between the spirituals and African folksong, to the origin of the spirituals, and to performance by contemporary groups.

2147 _____. "The Old Plantation Songs of the Negroes." ETUDE 34 (September 1916): 673.

Posthumous publication of an article about the meaning of the slave songs includes the text of a couplet: Keep me from sinking down.

2148 Washington, Margaret Murray [Mrs. Booker T. Washington]. "Songs of Our Fathers." COLORED AMERICAN MAGAZINE 8 (1905): 245-53.

Discussion by Mrs. Washington, also a member of the Tuskegee faculty, includes discussion of the importance of the spiritual for the slave during the long years of oppression.

Texts of 5 songs: 1. Run to Jesus, He will be your dearest friend. 2. Isaac a ransom while he lay upon the altar bound (Cho: Didn't old Pharaoh get lost?). 3. Didn't my Lord deliver Daniel. 4. Keep a-inching along (Cho: Jesus will come by'n bye). 5. Oh, brethern, rise and shine and give God the glory. Texts of 3 choruses: 1. I'm troubled in mind. 2. Nobody knows the trouble I see, Lord. 3. Fight on and you shall gain the victory. References to 4 songs: 1. Children, we all shall be free. 2. Wait a little while, then we'll sing a new song. 3. Walk together, children, don't you get weary. 4. Steal away to Jesus.

2149 _____. "Are We Making Good?" INDEPENDENT 84 (4 October 1915): 22.

Discussion of the role of black women in the South in helping to improve the education of black women on the plantations. Text of 1 song that the author heard sung on the plantation by women: Don't call the roll till I get there.

2150 Webb, W. Prescott. "Notes on Folk-Lore of Texas." JOURNAL OF AMERICAN FOLK-LORE 28 (July-September 1915): 290-99.

Discussion of the differences between the folksongs of the "modern Negro" and those of the slave, with comment on the subject matter of the two types of song and its relevance to the lifestyles of the singers. Analysis of the song "Railroad Blues," one of the longest Negro ballads in existence with its eighty-seven stanzas, and comparison of it to antebellum songs.

Texts of 5 songs: 1. As I walked out by de light ob de moon. 2. Lightnin' is a yaller gal. 3. I went to the bar-room 'bout nine o'clock. 4. I drove my cart to de mill. 5. Every time you hear me sing this song.

2151 White, Clarence Cameron. "Negro Music: A Contribution to the National Music of America." Articles 1-4. MUSICAL OBSERVER 18 (November-December 1919): 18-19; 19 (January 1920): 16-17; (February 1920): 50-51; (March 1920): 13.

Discussion by the Afro-American composer and concert violinist of black folk music in the United States includes comment on the origin of the slave songs and primary sources of information about this music; performance practice associated with the singing of spirituals; and musical characteristics of the folk song. Observation that most of the surviving slave songs are spirituals and work songs, which became a source for the blues, and that spirituals often were an outgrowth of sermons delivered at camp-meeting services or nightly prayer meetings. References to the shout as a "relic" of the African past. Also references to Brer Rabbit tales. In the final article is discussion of the dissemination of the spirituals by Fisk student groups and the American Folk Song Singers of Washington, D. C.

Text and music of 2 couplets. Texts of 3 songs. Texts and music of 18 songs. See SONG COLLECTIONS (no. 2320).

2152 White, Newman I. "Racial Traits in the Negro Song." SEWANEE REVIEW 28 (July 1920): 396-404).

Comment on the character of the black man as reflected through his songs. Discussion of texts obtained from informants of Mississippi, Alabama, and Louisiana.

Texts of 4 songs: 1. I been 'buked an' I been 'bused. 2. I got a brudder 'way in de glory. 3. Captain, Captain, you must be cross. 4. Take my hammer.

Texts of 21 couplets: 1. Gon'a put on my shoes. 2. Ah'm gon'a have a little walk. 3. Two white horses, side by side. 4. Dem golden slippers I'm gwine to wear. 5. Sinner-man sittin' on de gates of Hell. 6. I lub dat woman. 7. Now look-a-here, woman. 7. It ain't no use a-pleading now. 8. Ashes to ashes, dust to dust. 9. Through de winder, through de blin'. 10. You gwine kill yo' fool self workin'. 11. Me and my pardner, pardner Jack. 12. Pick, I'll drive you so low down. 13. Captain, Captain, gimme my time. 14. Woke up dis mornin' with a knife in my han'. 15. Hello, Captain, how do you do. 16. My ole 'oman keep on a-grumblin'. 17. Nigger and white man playin' seven-up. 18. When you smell yo' cabbage burnin'. 19. A long-tailed rat and a bowl of souse. 20. It's gwine to be twelve o'clock in Hell. 21. Lord, you work me so hard.

2153 _____. "The Collection of Folk-Lore." ALABAMA EDUCATIONAL ASSOCIATION BULLETIN 35 (June 1915): 119-26.

Miscellaneous collection contains references to 12 songs and texts of 15 songs. See SONG COLLECTIONS (no. 2323).

2154 _____. "Negro Songs and Folk-Lore." Typescript. Cambridge, Massachusetts. Harvard University, Houghton Library. 3 vols. Reprint in AMERICAN NEGRO FOLK-SONGS. Hatboro, PA: Folklore Associates, 1928.

Discussion of the characteristic features of Negro songs in volume 2, including comment on the two classes of song, on the relationships between the songs and vaudeville songs and minstrel songs, and on the songs as a reflection of the black man's world-view. The collection contains approximately 875 texts, including couplets and variant versions for many of the songs. Volumes 1 and 2 were presented to the Harvard Library in 1918; Volume 3 was donated several years later. There is an index of first lines and of titles.

2155 Williams, Charles P., arr. THE WORLD-FAMOUS WILLIAMS' COLORED SINGERS. American Folk Songs As Sung by Williams' Jubilee Singers. Chicago: Press of the Rosenow Company, [c.1920]

Collection includes information about the founding of the Williams' Jubilee Singers in 1904, about its early history, its tours abroad, and other relevant facts. Also includes names of the singers over two decades.

Text and music of 18 songs. See SONG COLLECTIONS (no. 2324).

2156 Williams, Emily Harper. "The Emancipation of Negro Music." MUSICAL AMERICA (5 January 1918): 48.

Discussion of Negro folksongs and ragtime by the Chairman of the Committee on Music for the National Association of Colored Women, includes comment on the style and quality of the music and on performance practice. Also comment on black composers who have used Negro themes in their composition and the observation that Dvorak's "From the New World" Symphony "caught accurately the true spirit of Negro Music."

References to 3 songs: 1. Dis time anodder year I may be gone. 2. In bright mansions above. 3. Go, Mary, and toll de bell.

2157 Wilson, H. J. "The Negro and Music." OUTLOOK, December 1906: 823-26.

Discussion of the importance of music to the black man and description of Negro folk music style. Music and text of 1 song: Let my people go (824).

2158 Work, Frederick Jerome, arr. NEW JUBILEE SONGS AS SUNG BY THE FISK JUBILEE SINGERS OF FISK UNIVERSITY. Nashville, TN: Fisk University, c1902. 47 pp.

Collection gathered by the black folklorist and music educator includes comment in the Preface on the fact that it has been eighteen years since the last collection of Fisk Jubilee Songs was published, and that many of the old songs have been subjected to variations in the texts and music over the years. Also new songs have been identified.

Texts and music of 47 songs. See SONG COLLECTIONS (no. 2325).

2159 _____. FOLK SONGS OF THE AMERICAN NEGRO. Introduction by John Wesley Work. Nashville, TN: Fisk University Press, 1907. 48 pp.

Discussion of the character of black folksong with focus on its "syncopated, rhythmic, sacred melody" and on performance practice, particularly in the black church.

Texts and music of 91 songs. See SONG COLLECTIONS (no. 2326).

2160 Work, John Wesley. FOLK SONG OF THE AMERICAN NEGRO. Nashville, TN: Fisk University Press, 1915.

Detailed discussion and analysis of Negro folksong by the black folklorist and professor at Fisk, including comment on its origin, its relationship to the folklore of other ethnic groups, which are "agencies of preservation and development" (90-99), and its importance for the black man. Classification of the songs by type. Also discussion of the tours of the Fisk Jubilee Singers.

Music and texts of 9 songs. Texts of 55 songs. See SONG COLLECTIONS (2327).

2161 Work, Monroe N. "The Spirit of Negro Poetry." SOUTHERN WORKMAN 37 (February 1908): 73-77.

Exploration of the thesis that the antebellum folk songs of the slaves masked the black man's true feelings by this black professor at Georgia State Industrial College (Savannah, Georgia).

Texts of 5 songs: 1. Ole Massa take dat new brown coat. 2. No mo' peck of corn foh me. 3. (Cho: We'll walk dem golden streets). 4. (Cho: I'se a-gwine to hol' out to de en'). 5. (Cho: Heave away, heave away).

2162 Young, Martha. [Eli Shepperd, pseud.]. PLANTATION SONGS FOR MY LADY'S BANJO, AND OTHER NEGRO LYRICS AND MONOLOGUES. New York: Robert Howard Russell, 1901. 150 pp.

About one-half of this large collection is given over to rhymes written in dialect, which include extensive comment on oral traditions, particularly banjo playing, pattin' Juba, dancing, and plantation festivals, such as "Hog-Killin' Times" (70). The other half consists of "Hymns of the Black Belt"---25 texts of spirituals and worksongs that appear to have been altered in various ways.

THE TALE

2163 Allen, Junius Mord[ecai]. RHYMES, TALES, AND RHYMED TALES. Topeka, KS: Crane and Company, 1906. 155 pp.

Black poet's collection of twenty-three pieces, written mostly in dialect, includes numerous references to black oral traditions. The rhyme "Squeak of the Fiddle" (25-28) offers detailed description of folk dancing and of the quality of the fiddle music.

Text of 1 song: "Fo dis time ernuther year (119).

2164 B., J. E. "NEGRO FOLK RHYMES, by Thomas W. Talley of Fisk University." Book review. SOUTHERN WORKMAN 51 (May 1922): 247-48.

The reviewer feels that to the Southerner, black or white, "this book is a faithful record of the songs and rhymes of a folk of bygone days."

Texts of 2 songs: 1. She hug me, an' she kiss me. 2. Look down dat lonesome road.

2165 Backus, Emma M. "Folk-Tales from Georgia." JOURNAL OF AMERICAN FOLK-LORE 13 (January-March 1900): 19-32.

Texts of 10 folk tales, of which 7 are about Brer Rabbit and his friends. See TALE COLLECTIONS (no. 2284).

2166 Backus, Emma M. and Leitner, Ethel Hatton. "Negro Tales from Georgia." JOURNAL OF AMERICAN FOLK-LORE 25 (April-June 1912): 125-36.

Texts of 9 tales collected in Columbia County, Georgia. See TALE COLLECTIONS (no. 2285)

2167 Boyle, Virginia Frazer. DEVIL TALES. New York: Harper & Brothers, 1900. 210 pp. Reprint. Freeport, NY: Books for Libraries Press, 1972.

The skimpy plot that ties together the collection of tales is based on the plantation nanny, who responds to the pleas of her white charges, "Mammy, tell us a tale." Numerous references to hoodoo, magic, ghosts, and the devil in the tales. Also references to 3 dances (96): 1. Pea-patch ladies. 2. Chicken-in-the-bread-tray. 3. Buzzard lope.

Texts of 10 tales. See TALE COLLECTIONS (2286).

2168 Chesnutt, Charles Waddel. "Lonesome Ben." SOUTHERN WORKMAN 29 (March 1900): 139.

Black novelist's short story, set in Beaver Creek, North Carolina, offers information about story-telling traditions among blacks in the rural South about the turn of the twentieth century.

2169 Cooke, Grace MacGowan. "A Plantation Story: Being Aunt Jinsey's Tale of the Bird that Brought Bargins." ALEXANDER'S MAGAZINE 1 (March 1906): 55-56.

Folk tale in dialect about a sparrow who brought destruction upon herself and her family.

2170 Cotter, Joseph Seamon. NEGRO TALES. New York: Cosmopolitan Press, 1912. 148 pp. Reprint. Miami, FL: Mnemosyne Publishing Company, 1969.

Most of the tales in this collection were probably written by the black Kentucky-born poet. While all draw upon the traditions of Negro folk tales, some appear to be genuine folk expression. Most are fables.

Texts of 5 tales: 1. Kotchin' de Nines ("a Negro tale current in Louisville"). 2. The Jackal and the Lion ("an African folk-lore tale"). 3. How Mr. Rabbit secures a pretty wife and rich father-in-law. 4. The little boy and Mr. Dark. 5. The boy and the Ideal.

2171 Cross, Tom Peete. "Folk-Lore from the Southern States." JOURNAL OF AMERICAN FOLK-LORE 22 (April-June 1909): 251-55.

Miscellaneous collection of black folk-lore obtained by the Massachusetts author during the summer of 1907 in southeastern Virginia and Alabama centers primarily on witches and conjurers.

Text of 1 tale (summary): The witch-cat.

2172 Culbertson, Annie Virginia. AT THE BIG HOUSE. Indianapolis, IN: Bobbs-Merrill Company, 1904. 348 pp. Reprint. Photocopy. Ann Arbor, MI: University Microfilms, Inc., 1976.

Miscellaneous collection of Indian and Afro-American tales collected in southeastern Virginia and North Carolina.

Text of 1 Negro song (284-85): Whar's all dem chillen dress' in white (Cho: Oh, we'll end dis war, down by de river side). Texts of 23 tales. See TALE COLLECTIONS (no. 2287).

2173 Davis, Henry C. "Negro Folk-Lore in South Carolina." JOURNAL OF AMERICAN FOLK-LORE 27 (July-September 1914): 241-54.

The compiler of the miscellaneous collection of Afro-American folklore includes discussion of the black singer's practice of combining stanzas of several songs together to improvise a new one, retaining only the tune and chorus of the original song. References to 28 songs, to 5 dance and ring-game songs. Also description of 4 plantation dances: 1. Pairing off (252-253). 2. Mr. Cooler (253). 4. Roxanna, go gal, go (254).

Texts of 3 tales: 1. The fox and the goose (243-244). 2. Why the Negro works (244). 3. Why the cat eats first (244-245).

2174 Davis, Mary Evelyn Moore. "The Cottonwood-Tree" and "De Witch-'ooman an' de Spinnin'-Wheel." JOURNAL OF AMERICAN FOLK-LORE 18 (July-September 1905): 251-55.

Texts of 2 tales collected in Louisiana.

2175 Faulkner, William J. THE DAYS WHEN ANIMALS TALKED. BLACK AMERICAN FOLK TALES AND HOW THEY CAME TO BE. Chicago: Follett Publishing Company, 1977. 190 pp.

Collection was compiled by Fisk University Minister Faulkner, who also served as pastor of several local churches in Nashville, Tennessee, over the years of his long career. The sources of his tales were ex-slave Simon Brown and other elderly ex-slaves who lived in and around Darlington County, South Carolina, in Faulkner's childhood during the years 1900-1907. Discussion includes comment on the importance of Negro folk tales for the history of black culture.

Texts of 33 tales. See TALE COLLECTIONS (no. 2288)

2176 Fortier, Alcee. "Four Louisiana Folk-Tales." JOURNAL OF AMERICAN FOLK-LORE 19 (April-June 1906): 123-26.

Tales collected by the Tulane University professor from black folk in St. Mary Parish, Louisiana. Texts of 4 tales: 1. The little boy of the government. 2. The king and the three women. 3. The ferocious beasts. 4. How the ash-tree grew.

2177 "A Georgia Tale." CURRENT LITERATURE (=CURRENT OPINION) 30 (March 1901): 302.

Text of a Brer Rabbit tale: Brer Rabbit and the corn husking.

2178 Hampton Folk-Lore Society. "Alabama Folk-Lore." SOUTHERN WORKMAN 32 (January 1904): 49-52.

Text of 1 song: Bungle-toe, bungle-toe cleavin' on to yo' life (Cho: Go 'way, Brother Big Eye). Texts of 3 tales: 1. Why the buzzard has a red head. 2. How the guinea-hen got ahead of the rabbit. 3. Brer Rabbit and Brer Fox.

2179 Harris, Joel Chandler. THE TAR-BABY AND OTHER RHYMES OF UNCLE REMUS. New York: D. Appleton & Company, 1904. 190 pp. Reprints. Atlanta: Cherokee Publishing Company, 1984. THE COMPLETE TALES OF UNCLE REMUS, edited by Richard Chase. Boston:

Houghton Mifflin and Company, 1955.

Miscellaneous collection of tales, songs, and sayings in Afro-American dialect includes 15 animal tales based upon such stock plantation characters as Brer Rabbit, Fox, Bear, and Terrapin. Song types represented include camp-meeting hymns, play-party, corn-shucking, and work songs.

2180 Harvey, Emily N. "A Brer Rabbit Story." JOURNAL OF AMERICAN FOLK-LORE 32 (July-September 1919): 443-44.

Cante-fable collected at Fort Mitchell, Alabama, from ex-slaves includes the text of 1 tale: Brer Rabbit in the briar patch. Also the text of the related song: Lee cum Lee cum Gen-i-ke-buk-o-buk-Lee ki.

2181 House, Grace Bigelow, collector. "I sho be lub dat buckra." SOUTHERN WORKMAN 37 (April 1908): 242-46.

Master-John folk tale using the dialect of the South Carolina Sea Islands.

2182 Jamison, Cecilia Viets. "A Louisiana Legend concerning Will 'O Wisp." JOURNAL OF AMERICAN FOLK-LORE 18 (July-September 1905): 250-51.

Ghost tale collected from an elderly black woman in New Orleans, Louisiana, about 1890: The Will-o-the wisp.

2183 McBryde, John M., Jr. BRER RABBIT IN THE FOLK-TALES OF THE NEGRO AND OTHER RACES. Reprinted from SEWANEE REVIEW (April 1911). Sewanee, TN: University Press at the University of the South, 1911. 24 pp.

Discussion includes summary of a Brer Rabbit tale that essentially is the same as a Hottentot tale about the hare (19-20).

2184 Murray, Daniel. "Three New Folk-Lore Stories (Current in Maryland during Colonial Times)." COLORED AMERICAN MAGAZINE 14 (1908): 104-9.

Animal tales that the black writer learned as a child during the period 1859-60 in Baltimore, Maryland, from Basil Banks, a local black story teller.

Texts of 3 tales: 1. Mr. Fox's unfortunate purchase. 2. Mr. Fox and Mr. Harry in partnership. 3. Mr. Fox and Mr. Harry meet at the fishing shore.

2185 Newell, William Wells. "The Ignis Fatuus, Its Character and Legendary Origin." JOURNAL OF AMERICAN FOLK-LORE 17 (January-March 1904): 39-60.

Tale obtained by the educator and founder of the American Folk-Lore Society from a black woman in Baltimore, Maryland. Text of 1 tale: The Jack-o-lantern.

2186 Ovington, Mary White. "Vacation Days on San Juan Hill---A New York Colony." SOUTHERN WORKMAN 38 (November 1909): 627-34.

Discussion by the social worker, later treasurer of the NAACP, of the lifestyles of residents of the San Juan Hill, a black neighborhood on the west side of New York City. Comment on the Peter Rabbit tales she heard, the children's play- and ring-game songs, a street preacher and his gospel band, and the singing of plantation songs.

Text of 1 song: Heben! Heben! All der people talkin' about heben aint goin' dar (633).

2187 Owen, Mary Alicia. "Pig-Tail Charley." JOURNAL OF AMERICAN FOLK-LORE 16 (January-March 1903): 58-60.

Tale obtained by the president of the Missouri Folklore Society from a black informant of Kentucky.

2188 Parsons, Elsie Clews. "Folk-Tales Collected at Miami, Florida." JOURNAL OF AMERICAN FOLKLORE 30 (April-June 1917): 222-27.

Discussion includes short biographical sketches of informants from whom the folk tales were collected. Texts of 16 tales. See TALE COLLECTIONS (2291).

2189 _____. "Tales from Guilford County, North Carolina." JOURNAL OF AMERICAN FOLK-LORE 30 (April-June 1917): 168-200.

Miscellaneous collection includes many Brer Rabbit types. Informants are identified.

Text and music of 1 song: Anyhow, anyhow (200). Texts of 4 songs: 1. Rabbit good fry (175). 2. You can't git me now (178). 3. Oh, my! By de hair of my chin, chin, chin (187). 4. To-day I was buried (198). Texts of 62 tales. See TALE COLLECTIONS (no. 2290).

2190 Richardson, Clement, and Monroe Work. "Folk-Tales from Students in Tuskegee Institute, Alabama." JOURNAL OF AMERICAN FOLK-LORE 32 (July-September 1919): 397-401.

Miscellaneous collection of tales obtained by Tuskegee faculty members from students includes one ballad: Mr. Froggie went to ride.

Texts of 5 tales: 1. Old man on a hunt. 2. Escape up the tree. 3. The tree closes. 4. Take my place. 5. Fatal imitation.

2191 Showers, Susan Hathaway. "Alabama Folk-Lore." Parts 1, 2. SOUTHERN WORKMAN 29

(March 1900): 179-180; (July 1900): 441-44.

Discussion of Alabama folklore by a black former instructor at Hampton Institute and the Calhoun School includes description of children's ring-games and dance-songs.

Descriptions of 2 ring games (444): 1. Come home, Lily. 2. O walk down in Louisiana. Texts of 6 ring-game songs (444): 1. Lost my glove yesterday. 2. Come home, Lily, sometime, sometime. 3. Draw a bucket of water. 4. Chicken, chicken, my cranie crow. 5. Plant my cotton in the middle of May. 6. O walk down in Louisiana. References to 2 tales (179): 1. Tar baby. 2. How Brer Rabbit made Brer Fox his riding horse.

2192 Smiley, Portia. "Folk-Lore from Virginia, South Carolina, Georgia, Alabama, and Florida." JOURNAL OF AMERICAN FOLK-LORE 32 (July-September 1919): 357-83.

Miscellaneous collection of folklore obtained by a black teacher---who taught at Hampton Institute, the Calhoun Colored School (Alabama), the Haines Institute (Georgia), and the Industrial Training School (Daytona, Florida)---includes a wide variety of tale and song types. Also description of an African shout (378), shouts in Florida and South Carolina, funeral services, and ring-games.

Texts and music of 2 songs: 1. Ariddle um, ariddle um, ariddle um aree (Cho: Peep squirrel). 2. Higha! Magalujasay! Texts of 38 tales. See TALE COLLECTIONS (no. 2292).

2193 Speers, Mary Walker Finley. "Negro Songs and Folk-Lore." JOURNAL OF AMERICAN FOLK-LORE 23 (October-December 1910): 435-39.

Discussion by a folklorist of Maryland includes comment on the characteristics of the folklore.

Texts of 2 songs: 1. Who built de ahk? 2. Dere is no hidin' place down yhar. Text of 1 tale: How Mistah Mayship cum ter bahk.

2194 _____. "Maryland and Virginia Folk-Lore." JOURNAL OF AMERICAN FOLK-LORE 26 (July-September 1912): 284-86.

Texts of 5 tales: 1. How the colored folk came into existence. 2. How the colored man obtained his well-known sobriquet of "coon." 3. A Negro's explanation of the currents one sometimes feels when passing along a country road at night. 4. How Mistah Yhar's probed dat Mistah Fox uz 'is riden hoss. 5. Why February hasn't 30 days.

2195 Stafford, O. Alphonso. "Folk Literature of the Negro." CRISIS (October 1915): 296-99.

Discussion of the different types of black folktales with identification of the heroes of the fable types as the tortoise, spider, and rabbit. Observation that the African brought his tales with him to the New World. A distinguishing theme is the triumph of wit and cleverness over brute force. Comment on the musical instruments used to accompany the tales, songs, and dance.

2196 Steiner, Roland. "Notes and Queries--Sol Lockhart's call." JOURNAL OF AMERICAN FOLKLORE 13 (January-March 1900): 67-70.

Story about a local preacher beginning his ministry. Text of 1 preacher tale: Sol Lockhart's call.

2197 Stewart, Sadie E. "Seven Folk-Tales from the Sea Islands, South Carolina." JOURNAL OF AMERICAN FOLK-LORE 32 (July-September 1919): 394-96.

Tales collected by a black graduate of Hampton Institute and teacher at the Penn School on St. Helena Island, South Carolina, are mostly animal tales about Brers Rabbit, Fox, and Terrapin.

Texts of 5 folk tales: 1. The relay race. 2. Fire test: Mock plea. 3. In the well. 4. Who dives the longest: Carload of fish. 5. The rich old man.

2198 Talley, Thomas Washington. "Negro Folk Tales." Typescript. Private collection of Thomasina Talley Greene. Jefferson City, Missouri. 557 pp.

Tales collected by the black scientist, musician, and college professor at Fisk University were obtained from ex-slaves in the South. Many cantefables included. Reprint of some tales in Talley's NEGRO FOLK RHYMES...(see no. 2200).

Texts of 15 folk tales. See TALE COLLECTIONS (no. 2293).

2199 _____. "The Origin of Traditions; Or the Interpretations of Traditions through Negro Traditions." Typescript. Private collection of Dr. Thomasina Talley Greene. Jefferson City, Missouri. 277 pp. Reprint (abridged). PHYLON, fourth quarter (1942): 371-76.

Origins traced from the beginnings of man's cultural development to the present. Discussion of the thesis that the traditions handed down are only partially tried and true.

Texts of 2 songs: 1. Oh, saints and sinners will you go? (1). 2. I'll tell you what I love the best (11). Texts of 2 couplets: 1. Old Satan is a liar and a conj'er too (11). 2. The Bible is our engineer (11).

2200 _____. NEGRO FOLK RHYMES, WISE AND OTHERWISE. New York: Macmillan, 1922. 347 pp. Reprints. Port Washington, NY: Kennikat Press, c.1968. Folcroft, PA: Folcroft Library Editions, 1980.

Detailed analysis of the Negro folk rhyme, with comment on its basic elements and discussion of the various types. Collection of 349 rhymes includes twelve collected from black societies outside the United States. Included are a general index and a Comparative Study Index.

Texts and music of 3 songs: 1. De jaybird jump from lim' to lim' (14). 2. Possum meat is good and sweet (23). 3. De frog went a courtin' (190). Texts and music of 4 field cries (279-80). Music of 2 quill tunes (306-07).

2201 Wiley, George E. SOUTHERN PLANTATION STORIES AND SKETCHES. New York: J. J. Little Press, 1905. 127 pp. Reprint. Freeport, NY: Books for Libraries Press, 1971.

Collection of twelve short stories about the plantation life of ex-slaves in the South includes description of a corn shucking (41-51) and comment on a black fiddler who composed a piece, entitled "Prayer Meeting," in which he imitated the sounds of a religious service---the exhortation, prayer, and singing (86).

Summary of 1 tale: The owl...wat could talk (62-64).

2202 Wise, John S. "An Extinct Race: Master and Man--Owner and Friend." SATURDAY EVENING POST 178 (27 January 1906): 4-6.

Discussion by a southerner of slavery in antebellum Virginia includes references to the cook, Old Charlotte, who told tales to the white children about Uncle Remus and ghosts. Summary of 1 folk tale: The September gust.

2203 Work, Monroe. "Folk-Tales from Students in the Georgia State College." JOURNAL OF AMERICAN FOLK-LORE 32 (July-September 1919): 402-5.

Collection of Brer Rabbit tales by the black sociologist, educator, and director of records and research at Tuskegee Institute from 1908 on.

Texts of 6 tales: 1. In the pea-patch: take my place. 2. Challenged to butt. 3. Challenged to butt: Buried tail: playing poisoned. 4. Mock fire: playing poisoned. 5. Three legs. 6. Rabbit seeks a tail: gives himself away (2 versions).

2204 Wylly, Charles Spalding. THE SEED THAT WAS SOWN IN THE COLONY OF GEORGIA--THE HARVEST AND THE AFTERMATH, 1740-1870. New York: Neale Publishing Company, 1910. 163 pp. Reprint. Microfilm. Chapel Hill: University of North Carolina, 1987.

Memoirs include discussion of the founders and residents of the coastal islands of Sapelo, Saint Simon, and Jekyl, South Carolina, and of the field slaves and house servants.

Texts of 2 tales: 1. How Buh was 'got his leetle wais' (146-50). 2. Mary Bell (150-56).

ARTWORKS: 1900-1920

SOCIAL ACTIVITIES

2205 Adams, John Wolcott. "Some kin' er debil dance, whar you stan's on your toes an' spreads yours skirts." [1909]. Mixed media. Published in "Ole Marse and Aunt Nancy," by Virginia Frazer Boyle. HARPER'S WEEKLY 53 (June 1909).

Scene shows the interior of a rude cabin where 4 women are gathered, 3 of them watching the dancing of the fourth one. The dancer, a mature woman, appears to be singing as she executes the dance steps vigorously, holding her voluminous skirts in curtsey fashion and lifting the left leg high. Two of the spectators clap with gusto, and all 3 appear to be singing along with the dancer. Occasion: indoor entertainment.

2206 Banjo, folk-crafted. Early 20th century. Photograph. Published in DRUMS AND SHADOWS: SURVIVAL STUDIES AMONG GEORGIA COASTAL NEGROES, pl. 3. Works Projects Administration, Savannah Unit, Georgia Writer's Project. Athens: University of Georgia Press, 1941. Reprint. 1986.

Handmade banjo, with five strings, made by an ex-slave. Musical artifact.

2207 Banjoist [untitled]. Early 20th century. Photograph. Richmond, Virginia. Valentine Museum, Cook Collection. Published in LIFE UNDER THE PECULIAR INSTITUTION..., by Norman R. Yetman, Appendix [n.p.]. New York: Holt, Reinhardt, and Winston, 1970.

Portrait of a portly banjoist, dressed in tattered clothes, who appears to be singing loudly with mouth open wide as he strums on a large banjo held in the conventional way. The banjo's short fifth string is clearly visible. Occasion: indoor domestic music.

2208 Bartsch, Carl. Boy Playing a Banjo [untitled]. [1902]. Mixed media. Published in "Joggin' Erlong," by Paul Laurence Dunbar. COSMOPOLITAN: A MONTHLY ILLUSTRATED MAGAZINE 33 (June 1902).

One of four illustrations [untitled] used to accompany a poem written by black poet Dunbar. Depiction of an adolescent boy, sitting on the ground with legs crossed, playing the banjo. He holds his instrument in the conventional manner, and seems to be singing as he plays. Occasion: indoor domestic music.

2209 Demuth, Charles. "Marshall's." 1915. Watercolor and pencil on paper. Reproduced in CHARLES DEMUTH, by Alvord Eiseman, 39, pl. 6. New York: Watson-Guptill Publications, 1982. Also known as "Negro Girl Dancer."

Scene shows the interior of the Marshall's Hotel cafe, located on West 53rd Street in New York City. In the early twentieth century the hotel was a gathering place for the black elite of the artistic world---the artists, writers, musicians ---also for white artists and intellectuals. Four entertainers, 3 jazzmen and 1 female dancer, are in the foreground; an indeterminate number of patrons, black and white, sit at cafe tables in the right background. Paper festoons hang from the low ceiling.

The central figure, the dancer, holds her head sharply to the left, almost resting it on her left shoulder, and waves her arms about while kicking high with the left leg, balancing herself on her right toe. Her expression is serious, almost brooding. Immediately to her right is the portly banjoist, who, with head thrown back, smiles broadly as he picks his instrument, his left hand working low on the fingerboard. On the floor by his side is a second banjo. To the left of the dancer is the drummer, except that he is cut out of the picture with only his right arm and hand visible, along with his snare drum. He strums lightly on the drum with the back of his fingers. Considerably behind the dancer, the pianist, his back to the viewer, is hunched over the keyboard. One eye is drawn in such manner that it stares eerily at the viewer. There is music on the piano stand, but he appears not to be reading it. The banjoist also performs without music. Occasion: indoor professional entertainment.

2210 _____. "Negro Jazz Band." 1916. Watercolor and pen on paper. Philadelphia, Pennsylvania. Private Collection.

This is another depiction of a jazz combo in the Marshall's Hotel setting, but with different models than those in the painting of 1915. The singer stands in front of the jazzmen with mouth open (as if singing), her head resting on her right shoulder, arms outstretched on either side, and legs widespread with her feet planted firmly on the floor. Behind her the drummer strums on a snare drum with two sticks; at his feet is a larger drum to which cymbals are affixed. The pianist, to the rear left of the drummer, sits on the edge of his piano stool, but leans backwards, eyes turned towards the banjoist, ignoring the sheet music before him. In the background, the banjoist sits high above the others on an elevated stand, which positions him at the peak of a kind of pyramid formed by the entertainers. The drummer's face is lifted towards the banjoist, as if he were the group's leader. Occasion: professional entertainment.

2211 _____. "Negro Jazz Band." 1916. Watercolor and pen on paper. New York City. Irwin Goldstein Collection. Reproduced: DEMUTH: THE MECHANICAL ENCRUSTED ON THE LIVING, by David Gedhard and Phyllis Plous, 33. Santa Barbara: University of California, 1971.

CHARLES DEMUTH, by Barbara Haskell, pl. 19. New York: Whitney Museum of American Art in association with Harry N. Abrams, 1987. Also known as "Negro Girl Singer."

Another version of the jazz group depicted in no. 2210, which appears to be more carefully conceived and differs in several details. In the background paper festoons, streamers, and bells hang from the low ceiling. In the foreground a woman in rather elaborate attire sings with great intensity, with one arm outstretched, the other hanging at her side with clenched fist, and with feet spread far apart and planted firmly on the floor. Behind her, to the right, the drummer beats his snare with sticks. To the left rear is the pianist, who sits hunched over the keyboard. Although his back is to the viewer, his right hand is visible, being lifted high over the keyboard as if he were about to strike the keys with considerable force. At the top of the picture is the banjoist. As in the earlier study, the drummer's head is turned upwards, as if he is following the lead of the banjoist. Although there is sheet music on the piano stand, none of the musicians uses music. Occasion: indoor professional entertainment.

2212 _____. "At Marshall's." 1917. Watercolor and pen on paper. Collection of the Barnes Foundation. Merion Station, Pennsylvania. Reproduced in CHARLES DEMUTH, by William Murrell, 49. New York City: Whitney Museum of American Art, 1931. Also in THE ART OF PAINTING, by Albert C. Barnes, 342. 3d ed. New York: Harcourt, Brace & Company, 1937.

Scene set in Marshall's cafe shows in the foreground the huge figure of a rather thin, male dancer, which fills the picture. Dressed in skin-tight pants and jacket, he dances on his toes, with head thrust forward, arms lifted high but bent at the elbows so that the forearms and wrists dangle, and legs extended to the side, but bending at the knees and crossed at the ankles. He wears what seems to be a black mask of feline character, which covers his head and extends down over his nose, and black gloves with the thumb cut out. In the background an indeterminate number of patrons, black and white, sit at the cafe tables. Paper festoons and bells hang from the low ceiling. Occasion: indoor professional entertainment.

2213 Drum, folk-crafted. Photograph. Early 20th century. Published in DRUMS AND SHADOWS: SURVIVAL STUDIES AMONG GEORGIA COASTAL NEGROES, pl. 4d. Works Projects Administration.... Athens: University of Georgia Press, 1941. Reprint. 1986.

Log drum, covered with goatskin, was made by ex-slave James Collier. Musical artifact.

2214 Dunton, W. Herbert. "Those big blunt fingers were able to make the strings come alive." [1914]. Mixed media. Published in "Black Face and White Soul," by Frederick Palmer. COSMOPOLITAN: A MONTHLY ILLUSTRATED MAGAZINE 57 (August 1914).

Scene shows a group of 4 persons (2 white males, 1 white woman, 1 black woman) gathered on a porch, listening intently to the music of a black man, seated on the steps, who plays the mandolin. Occasion: outdoor entertainment.

2215 Emancipation Day Parade [untitled]. [1902]. Photograph. Published in "The Penn School on St. Helena Island," by Henry Wilder Foote. SOUTHERN WORKMAN 31 (May 1902).

Scene shows an Emancipation Day parade in progress on St. Helena Island, South Carolina. Led by a drum major, the marching unit consists of 10 men playing brass instruments. An indefinite number of children prance alongside the marchers as "second liners." Occasion: outdoor procession.

2216 Fiddler [untitled]. Early 20th century. Photograph. Washington, D. C. Library of Congress. Prints and Photographs Division. Published in LIFE UNDER THE PECULIAR INSTITUTION..., by Norman R. Yetman, Appendix [n.p.]. New York: Holt, Reinhardt, and Winston, 1970.

Portrait of a elderly, smiling fiddler, seated on a rude bench, who is dressed somewhat formally in a wrinkled frockcoat. He holds his fiddle in position as if preparing to play, but he looks into the eyes of the viewer rather than at his fiddle. Occasion: portraiture.

2217 Fischer, Anton Otto. "Dis yer flu, moaned Johnson." [1919]. Mixed media. Published in "African Golf," by Peter Clark MacFarlane. SATURDAY EVENING POST 191 (February 1919).

Full caption is: "Dis yer flu," moaned Johnson. "I done got de flu somepin powerful. Better keep away from me." Scene shows a barracks, where 5 soldiers are at ease: One soldier is reading to his comrade in a bed, who has pulled the covers up to his chin. Around a table are seated 3 men; a guitarist sings and plays for the enjoyment of the other two. Occasion: indoor domestic music.

2218 Frost, Arthur Burdett. "The Corn-Shucking." [1904] Wash. Published in TAR-BABY AND OTHER RHYMES OF UNCLE REMUS, by Joel Chandler Harris, 146. New York: D. Appleton & Company, 1904.

Illustration for the poem, "Corn-Shucking Song," depicts a plantation corn-shucking festival in progress outdoors in the evening. Men and women, 8 or more, sit in a circle around a huge pile of corn, husking the corn and singing as they work. A spectator, who stands near the workers, is also singing, and the "general" (song leader) stands atop the pile of corn, waving his hands energetically as if conducting the singing, while he too sings. In the foreground a young boy hauls a bucket of water towards the site of the festival. Occasion: outdoor work-festival activity involving song.

2219 _____. "Plantation Play-Song (Putnam County, 1856)." [1908]. Pen and ink. Published in UNCLE REMUS, HIS SONGS AND SAYINGS, by Joel Chandler Harris, 193. Rev. ed. New York: Appleton-Century Company, 1908. Reprint. PLANTATION SONGS..., by Ruth McEnery Stuart, frontispiece. New York: D. Appleton Company, 1916.

Portrait of a banjoist used to accompany the poem "Plantation Play-Song...." Seated on a crate, the banjoist bends over his instrument as he plays, resting it on his right thigh, and his feet are planted far apart. Occasion: indoor domestic music.

2220 Gleizes, Albert. "Composition (for 'Jazz') (pour 'Jazz')." 1915. Oil on board. Reproduced in ALBERT GLEIZES, 1881-1953, by Daniel Robbins, 68, pl. 78. Exhibition Catalogue. New York: Published by the Solomon R. Guggenheim Museum, 1964.

The French cubist artist came in contact with black jazzmen when he came to New York in 1913 to exhibit for the Armory Show and was inspired to produce this painting. Despite its abstraction, the painting can be readily perceived as representing a seated banjoist plucking his instrument. Its juxtaposed planes of various shapes and sizes seem to throw particular focus on circular movements, which echo the circle made by the body of the banjo. In some details, it is more realistic than the painting (no. 2221) for which it served as a study. Occasion: portraiture.

2221 _____. "Jazz." 1915. Oil on board. Lyons, France; Rene Deroudille Collection. Also exhibited under the title "Banjo." Reproduced in ALBERT GLEIZES. A RETROSPECTIVE EXHIBITION, by Daniel Robbins, 69, pl. 79. Exhibition Catalogue. New York: Published by the Solomon R. Guggenheim Foundation, 1964.

Although rooted in the cubist tradition, this painting obviously represents its basic theme, showing two banjoists, who hold their distorted instruments at sharply vertical angles to the trunks of their bodies. In the foreground, the shifting planes and circular gestures suggest a black jazzman: a black hand with white fingernails grasps a banjo fingerboard, and there are motifs that suggest knotty hair and thick lips. The second jazzman, positioned behind the other one, probably is a mulatto, or may be white. Occasion: portraiture.

2222 "Gourd-Bodied Fiddle." Folk-crafted instrument. Early 20th century. Ferrum, Virginia. Private Collection. Reproduced in THE AFRO-AMERICAN TRADITION IN DECORATIVE ARTS, by John Michael Vlach, 25. Exhibition Catalogue. Cleveland: Cleveland Museum of Art, 1978.

A short neck is attached to the fiddle's elongated body (made of maple wood ?). It is believed to have come from the Upper Shenandoah Valley in Virginia. Occasion: musical artifact.

2223 Hampton Institute Camera Club. Banjo Player [untitled]. [1901]. Photograph. Published in CANDLE LIGHTIN' TIME, by Paul Laurence Dunbar, 126. New York: Dodd, Mead, and Company, 1901.

Scene shows the interior of a rude cabin, with a bed in the far corner of the room. In the foreground, a man plays a banjo, which rests on his lap; his legs are crossed at the knees, and he tilts backwards in his chair. Although the banjoist, who faces the camera, appears to be playing for his own enjoyment, his eyes are directed towards a half-opened door in the rear of the room, where 3 children of various sizes stand quietly, listening to the music. Occasion: indoor domestic music.

2224 _____. "Step wid de banjo an' glide wid de fiddle." [1904]. Photograph. Published in SPEAKIN' O' CHRISTMAS, by Paul Laurence Dunbar, 62. New York: Dodd, Mead, & Company, 1904.

Full-length portrait of an elderly banjoist depicts him singing as he plays on a home-crafted banjo. The instrument is made of a cigar box and wooden slat; eight pegs are visible, but the fret-board is not clearly seen. Occasion: indoor domestic music.

2225 Johnson, Clifton H. "The Jew's-Harp." [1904]. Photograph. Published in HIGHWAYS AND BYWAYS OF THE SOUTH, by Clifton Johnson, 49. New York: MacMillan Company, 1904.

In a woodland setting, 2 adolescent boys listen to the music of a third boy, sitting on the ground, who is playing a jew's-harp. He holds the tongue (lamella) end of the home-crafted instrument in his left hand, using the thumb or index finger (it is not clear which) of the right hand to activate it. Occasion: outdoor entertainment.

2226 Johnston, Harry H. (?) "A Real Negro Minstrel, Louisiana." [1910]. Photograph. Published in THE NEGRO IN THE NEW WORLD, by Harry H. Johnston, 392. London: Methuen & Company, 1910.

Scene shows a young man playing a guitar; in the background is a house enclosed by a picket fence. He concentrates on his playing, with tightly closed mouth, and holds his instrument, which is supported by a strap around his neck, in the conventional manner. Occasion: outdoor domestic music.

2227 Kemble, Edward W. "The Cake Walk." Pen and ink. Published in "The Sports of Negro Children," by Timothy Shaler Williams, 1006. ST. NICHOLAS: AN ILLUSTRATED MAGAZINE FOR BOYS AND GIRLS 30 (September 1903).

Scene shows the interior of a cabin, with an open door to the left and a table, on which there is a large cake, set up in front of the door. An indeterminate number of couples, small boys and girls paired, march rather primly around the table, obviously dressed in their Sunday best. The boy in the head couple waves a small flag, and several of the children are smiling. A portly woman, arms akimbo, stands behind the table, judging the contestants for the prize, the large cake. Occasion: indoor recreation.

2228 _____. "The Game of 'Rap-Jacket'." [1903]. Pen and ink. Published in "The Sports of Negro Children," by Timothy Shaler Williams. ST. NICHOLAS: AN ILLUSTRATED MAGAZINE FOR BOYS AND GIRLS 30 (September 1903).

Scene shows a group of children playing a combative game in front of a cabin. Arranged in two facing rows, the participants, 3 girls and 7 boys, brandish long switches in their hands as they advance towards each other, all the while singing a chorus, "Rice-cake, rice-cake, rice-cake/Sweet me so." Occasion: outdoor recreation.

2229 _____. "The Plough-Hand's Song...." Pen and ink. Published in THE TAR-BABY AND OTHER RHYMES OF UNCLE REMUS, by Joel Chandler Harris, 149. New York: D. Appleton & Company, 1904.

Miniature portrait used by the author to accompany a poem entitled "The Plough-Hand's Song (Jasper County---1860)," depicts a young girl blowing a straight trumpet (without valves or pistons), approximately 3 feet long. Occasion: outdoor work activity.

2230 Mandolin and guitar players [untitled]. Photograph/Stereograph. 1902. Copyright by the Detroit Photographic Company. Washington, D. C. Library of Congress Collection, Prints and Photographs Division.

Scene shows two young men leaning against the outside wall of a frame house. The younger man, who is half-seated on the window sill, plays on a guitar; his companion plays the mandolin. Both are plucking their instruments, as distinguished from strumming, and neither uses plectrums. The broad smiles on both faces suggest they are posing for the photographer rather than actually playing. Occasion: outdoor recreation.

2231 Matthews, Essie Collins. "The Amen was hardly spoken." [1915]. Photograph. Published in AUNT PHEBE, UNCLE TOM AND OTHER CHARACTER STUDIES AMONG THE OLD SLAVES OF THE SOUTH, FIFTY YEARS AFTER, by Essie Collins Matthews, 112. Columbus, OH: Champlin Press, 1915.

Full-length portrait of a male fiddler used by the author to illustrate her discussion of the Irwin Russell poem, "Christmas Night in the Quarters" (see no. 1469): "The 'Amen' was hardly spoken when the fiddler is heard tuning up his instrument and the call comes, 'Git yo' pardners, fust kwatillion!'." Seated in a low chair in the corner of a room, the fiddler holds his instrument in a sharp right-angle position to his body, steadying it against his chest, with his knees tucked up in its support, and holds the bow parallel to his body. It is not clear whether the fiddler posed for the photo or whether he was actually playing as the photo was taken. Occasion: indoor portraiture.

2232 McConnell, Emlen. "Touching Elbows with the Fifer Strode Ole Reliable." [1910]. Mixed media. Published in "The J'iner," by Harris Dickson. SATURDAY EVENING POST POST 183 (September 1910).

Depiction of a section of a military parade in Vicksburg, Mississippi, shows a fifer and drummer, dressed partially in regimental attire, marching at the head of a procession. Spectators include 3 men, a woman, and 10 or more children, several of whom march alongside the unit as "second liners," their mouths open as if they were singing. Occasion: outdoor procession.

2233 _____. "Their Antic Follies on the Guitar." [1904]. Crayon (?). Published in "The Negro of Today: His Prospects and His Discouragement," by Joel Chandler Harris. SATURDAY EVENING POST 176 (January 1904). Reprint. "The Vardaman Idea: How the Governor of Mississippi Would Solve the Race Question," by Harris Dickson. SATURDAY EVENING POST 179 (April 1907).

Outdoor scene depicts a man, seated on a wooden bench, who is singing forcefully and accompanying himself on a guitar. He holds the instrument in a slanting position, braced against his chest and supported by his left leg, which crosses the right at knee level. The position of his right hand, lifted in the air, indicates he is strumming the guitar, as distinguished from plucking it. Occasion: outdoor domestic music.

2234 McPherson, Carol. "So I kept on jes a steppin' it off...." [1903]. Photograph. Published in IN OLD ALABAMA. BEING THE CHRONICLES OF MISS MOUSE, THE LITTLE BLACK MERCHANT, by Anne Hobson, frontispiece. New York: Doubleday, Page and Company, 1903.

Full caption: "So I kept on jes a steppin' it off, en fo' I knowed what I wuz doin', I wuz gibbin' 'em de snake dance." Depiction of an elderly woman, wearing a turban, dancing energetically, with her right leg lifted high and toe pointed, and both hands holding her skirts in curtsey fashion. She dances without musical accompaniment. Occasion: outdoor recreation.

2235 Mears, W. E. "Celebrating Christmas." [1911]. Mixed media. Published in "Chris'-mus," by H. H. Mears. HARPER'S WEEKLY 55 (December 1911).

Scene shows the interior of a cabin in the evening, where a party is in progress. An indeterminate number of spectators watch a couple dance before a huge, blazing fire to the music of fiddle and banjo. The couple steps forward vigorously, joining hands with one arm lifted in the air and the other hanging to the side, the woman lifting her skirt in curtsey fashion. The fiddler holds his instrument in the conventional folk manner; the banjoist, whose legs are crossed at knee level, steadies his instrument on the lower thigh. Most of those present appear to be singing, including the dancers. Occasion: indoor entertainment.

2236 _____. "When had such music ever been heard?" [1904]. Mixed media. Published in "The Greatest of These," by Olivia Howard Dunbar. HARPER'S NEW MONTHLY MAGAZINE 108 (February 1904).

Scene shows an evening lawn party in progress. A young couple dances energetically, the young man with his arm around the woman's shoulder and his right hand clasping her left hand. They take large leaping steps with bended knees. The black banjoist, seated, rests his instrument on his thigh as he plucks it, and the Italian, standing, plays a hurdy-gurdy. Occasion: outdoor entertainment.

2237 Men Dancing (untitled). [1903]. Mixed media. Published in "The Banjo Dancer," by Frank L. Stanton. SATURDAY EVENING POST 176 (August 1903).

Three illustrations, grouped as a triptych, depict 3 entertainers: a banjoist is in the center with dancers on either side. The dancers, dressed in shirtsleeves and vests, lean backwards as they move in shuffle steps with bended knees, and with arms lifted but with limp wrists hanging down. Both watch their feet closely. The smiling banjoist, who is dressed rather formally with tie and jacket, plunks away on his instrument, which he holds in conventional manner, resting its head against his crossed knees. Occasion: outdoor entertainment.

2238 Miner, Leigh Richmond. "A Frolic." [1906]. Photograph. Published in JOGGIN' ERLONG, by Paul Laurence Dunbar, 85. New York: Dodd, Mead & Company, 1906.

In an outdoor scene taken by the black photographer, a couple is shown dancing near a rather dilapidated frame house, with their backs to the camera. They hold their arms high in a rounded position, and their feet are planted widely apart. Occasion: outdoor recreation.

2239 "Miss Hairston Teaching Folk Games." [1919]. Photograph. Published in "Hampton at Penn School," by Jackson E. Davis, 83. SOUTHERN WORKMAN 46 (February 1919).

Outdoor scene shows a group of 25 or more children and their instructor playing a ring-game on the green at the Penn School on St. Helena Island, South Carolina. The children move rapidly counter-clockwise in a circle, singing as they move. Occasion: outdoor recreation.

2240 Otto, J. W. "Good hand on dat ole banjo!." [1901]. Photograph. Published in PLANTATION SONGS FOR MY LADY'S BANJO, AND OTHER NEGRO LYRICS AND MONOLOGUES, by Eli Shepherd, 30-31. New York: R. H. Russell, 1901.

Depiction of a young woman dancing in an open field to the music of a banjo. She lifts her skirts slightly on either side and, smiling broadly, turns her head sharply towards the musician as if flirting with him. He, standing to her rear, returns her smile, strumming all the while. Ocassion: outdoor recreation.

2241 _____. "Den I reckon de wise folk...." [1901]. Photograph. Published in PLANTATION SONGS FOR MY LADY'S BANJO, AND OTHER NEGRO LYRICS AND MONOLOGUES, by Eli Sheppherd, 60-61. New York: R. H. Russell, 1901.

Full caption: "Den I reckon de wise folks might and may never find nothin' t'all to say But we'd des all laugh together!". Depiction of 2 adolescent boys in an indoor setting: one plays the guitar, the other accompanies him with vigorous hand-clapping and foot-tapping. The guitarist hold his instrument in a sharply slanting position, its body secured against his chest and the neck lifted high over his shoulder. Both boys appear to be singing. Occasion: indoor domestic music.

2242 _____. "Make a pretty motion...." [1901]. Photograph. Published in PLANTATION SONGS FOR MY LADY'S BANJO, AND OTHER NEGRO LYRICS AND MONOLOGUES, by Eli Sheppherd, 16. New York: R. H. Russell, 1901.

Full caption: "Make a pretty motion--tu-re-lu-re--/I got a mighty motion--tu-re-lu-re--/Who gwine take de cake!" Scene shows a young woman, smiling broadly, who is dancing in an open field. She lifts her skirts daintily with the right hand, and at the same time lifts her right leg, pointing her toe, while balancing on the sole of her left foot. There are no spectators. Occasion: outdoor recreation.

2243 _____. "Set Jo Bob playin'...." [1901]. Photograph. Published in PLANTATION SONGS FOR MY LADY'S BANJO..., by Eli Sheppherd, 64-65. New York: R. H. Russell, 1901.

Full caption: "Set Jo Bob playin' wid his fiddle

in his hands, And slyly grease his bow---." In an outdoor setting 2 women and a girl converse with a fiddler in front of the door of a rude cabin. The fiddler, seated on a barrel, holds his instrument under his chin in readiness to play, but his bow is held vertically in a resting position on his thigh. Occasion: outdoor domestic music.

2244 Pemberton, John P. "Jerry's melodious bass broke into the old song." [1909]. Crayon. Published in "Jerry," by Ruth M. Harrison. PUTNAM'S MONTHLY 7 (December 1909).

Scene shows a nicely furnished bedroom. Tilted back in his chair, a middle-aged man is singing and accompanying himself on a banjo, held in the conventional manner. He appears to be plucking the strings, as distinguished from strumming; the fifth short string is clearly visible. Occasion: domestic music.

2245 Picabia, Francis. "Chanson negre I." 1913. Watercolor. New York City, Metropolitan Museum of Art, Alfred Stieglitz Collection. Reproduced in FRANCIS PICABIA, by William Camfield, no. 27. Exhibition Catalogue. New York: Solomon R. Guggenheim Foundation, 1970. Also in FRANCIS PICABIA, Stadtischen Kunsthalle Dusseldorf and Kunsthaus Zurich, no. 984. Exhibition Catalogue. Cologne: Du Mont Buchverlag, 1983.

The avant-garde painter of Paris came to New York for the Armory Show of 1913 and was taken to a cafe, where, for the first time, he heard a black singer. Inspired by the "coon song" of the singer, he produced two paintings, giving both the title "Chanson negre." Despite its abstract style, the painting includes motifs that can be discerned as representing a singer: brown hips at the center interlock with swirling planes and occasional abrupt bars and spikes. Occasion: indoor professional entertainment.

2246 _____. "Chanson negre II." 1913. Watercolor on paper. Reproduced in PICABIA, by Maria Lluisa Borras, 142. New York: Rizzoli International Publications, 1985.

Encompassing more compartmentalized units than "Chanson negre I," the painting nevertheless includes motifs that suggest the black singer: the disembodied profile of a head in the lower left center, flowing lines (hair?) that intersect with rectangular and triangular shapes, which suggest waving arms and a swaying body. Occasion: indoor professional entertainment.

2247 "Playing Games at Recess in the Pole Road School, Henrico." [1913]. Photograph. Published in "Practical Training in Negro Rural Schools," by Jackson Davis. SOUTHERN WORKMAN 42 (December 1913).

Scene shows a group of 16 children and their teacher playing a ring-game in a clearing in the woods at Henrico, Virginia. The children move rapidly counter-clockwise in a circle, singing as they walk. One child stands in the center of the circle. Occasion: outdoor recreation.

2248 Potthast, Edward. "With a whirl, she advanced to her husband." [1901]. Mixed media. Published in NAPOLEON JACKSON, THE GENTLEMAN OF THE PLUSH ROCKER, by Ruth McEnery Stuart, 70. New York: Century Company, 1901.

Depiction of a middle-aged woman dancing with her husband in an open space in front of their cabin. The woman's left arm is lifted high, her left leg kicks high under her billowing skirts, and with her right hand she lifts her apron daintily in curtsey fashion. The man, approaching her from about two feet away, lifts his left hand high, positioning his right hand on his hip and dancing on his toes, the right foot crossing the left one. Of the 4 spectators, three children and the grandmother, two are also dancing. The grandmother whirls about at a distance of about five feet with both arms lifted over her head; a little girl, dancing in front of the cabin door, lifts both arms high in the air and kicks with her right leg, balancing on the toe of the left one. There is no musical accompaniment. Occasion: outdoor recreation.

2249 Tarbell, John H. "The Nursing-Place of Minstrelsy." [1910]. Photograph. Published in "Southern Silhouettes," by Pauline Carrington Bouvre, 183. NEW ENGLAND MAGAZINE n.s. 43 (October 1910).

Outdoor scene shows an adolescent boy, seated on a crate, plucking the strings of a mandolin. With legs crossed, he steadies the instrument on his lap. His 3 admiring friends, two sitting on the ground and the other on a small crate, listen intently to his music. Occasion: outdoor entertainment.

2250 Weeden, Howard [Harriet]. "Dancing in the Sun." [1900]. Wash (?). Published in SONGS OF THE OLD SOUTH, by Howard Weeden, 31. New York: Doubleday, Page, & Company, 1900.

Illustration to accompany a poem, "Dancing in the Sun," depicts a tattered, adolescent boy dancing out of doors. With right arm lifted high over his head and left hand stretched out before him, he balances on his left toe as he executes a kicking step, crossing the right leg over the left one. There is no musical accompaniment. Occasion: recreational activity.

THE RELIGIOUS EXPERIENCE

2251 Frost, Arthur. "Under the trees in the wood-lot." [1900]. Mixed media. Published in "Asmodeus in the Quarters." DEVIL

TALES, by Virginia Frazer Boyle, 80. New York: Harper Brothers, 1900.

Illustration depicts an elderly man dancing around a smoldering fire at night, and chanting an incantation (?) as he dances. Occasion: outdoor religious scene.

2252 "I Would Like to Read a Sweet Story of Old." [1907]. Photograph. Published in SOUTHERN WORKMAN 36 (December 1907).

Scene shows the interior of a cabin: an elderly couple and a young man (son?) are seated around a small table, on which an oil lamp burns. The son is reading the Bible; the elderly people listen intently. Occasion: indoor religious instruction.

2253 "Jes gib huh an-nubba dip, Pawson Demby...." [1900]. Pen and ink. Published in OLE MARS AN' OLE MISS, by Edmund K. Goldsborough, 50-51. Washington, DC: National Publishing Company, 1900.

Caricatural depiction of an outdoor baptismal service shows the parson and a woman partially immersed in frigid water in the foreground. The congregation, gathered on the shore and clothed in winter attire, sings as it gives close attention to the ceremony. Occasion: outdoor religious service.

2254 Justice, B. Martin. The Preacher [untitled]. [1900]. Mixed media. Published in "How Brother Parker Fell from Grace," by Paul Laurence Dunbar. SATURDAY EVENING POST 173 (July 1900).

Portrait of an elderly preacher, who leans heavily on his pulpit, making strong gestures with his hands stretched out before him, as he earnestly addresses the (unseen) congregation. Occasion: religious portraiture.

2255 _____. "Marching around and around..." [1901]. Mixed media. Published in "The Walls of Jericho," by Paul Laurence Dunbar. SATURDAY EVENING POST 173 (April 1901).

Full caption: "Marching around and around the inclosure, chewing vigorously in the breathing spaces of the hymn." Scene shows an indeterminate number of men and women dancing the shout in a clearing of a wooded area. Some in the clockwise-moving circle dance with bodies bent forward from the waist, some bend backwards; arms are extended to the side with palms outstretched or waving in the air; some women wave kerchiefs as they dance. Many appear to be singing. In the foreground a woman dances alone, her left arm uplifted, the right arm hanging at her side, her mouth open as if singing, and eyes closed. Occasion: outdoor religious ceremony.

2256 _____. "Stan' still, stan still, I say, an' see de salvation." [1901]. Pen and ink. Published in "The Walls of Jericho," by Paul Laurence Dunbar. SATURDAY EVENING POST 173 (April 1901). Reprint. IN OLD PLANTATION DAYS, by Paul Laurence Dunbar, 36. New York: Dodd, Mead & Company, 1903.

Caricatural portrayal of a plantation exhorter in a woodland setting. He stands on a log, leaning forward, with both hands lifted high and mouth open, as if reaching the climactic point of his exhortation. Occasion: outdoor religious portraiture.

2257 _____. "I tell you, de gospel is a p'inted swo'd to de sinnah." [1903]. Wash. Published in IN OLD PLANTATION DAYS, by Paul Laurence Dunbar, 56. New York: Dodd, Mead & Company, 1903.

Scene shows the interior of a small church, where a religious service in is progress. The preacher, addressing his congregation, has moved from behind the pulpit, is standing to the left of it, leaning forward with both arms outstretched, the left arm lifted higher than the right, and his mouth open wide as if he has reached a climactic point in his sermon. His attention obviously is focused on a man sitting on the first bench. The other members of the mostly male congregation listen intently, some of them with smiles on their faces. Occasion: indoor religious service.

2258 Kemble, Edward Windsor. "He preached a powerful sermon...." [1904]. Pen and ink. Published in THE HEART OF HAPPY HOLLOW, by Paul Laurence Dunbar, 150. New York: Dodd, Mead & Company, 1904.

Half-length portrait of a preacher, who stands in the pulpit of his church with flashing eyes and wide open mouth, as if he were delivering fiery sermon. One spectator (deacon?) sits behind the pulpit. Occasion: indoor religious service.

2259 _____. "Revival Hymn." [1904]. Pen and ink. Published in THE TAR-BABY AND OTHER RHYMES OF UNCLE REMUS, by Joel Chandler Harris, 129. New York: D. Appleton & Company, 1904.

Miniature caricatural portrait (bust) used to accompany a poem, "Revival Hymn," depicts an elderly deacon, or preacher, singing with mouth open as widely as possible. Occasion: indoor religious portraiture.

2260 _____. "Camp-Meeting Song." [1904]. Pen and ink. Published in THE TAR-BABY AND OTHER RHYMES OF UNCLE REMUS, by Joel Chandler Harris, 135. New York: D. Appleton & Company, 1904.

Miniature portrait (bust) used to illustrate a poem entitled "Camp-Meeting Song," depicts a woman singing with eyes lifted upwards, mouth open wide, arms outstretched, and hands clinched together. Occasion: outdoor religious portraiture.

2261 _____. "He'd call dem Scriptures out." [1916]. Pen and ink. Published in PLANTATION SONGS..., by Ruth McEnery Stuart, 46. New York: D. Appleton & Company, 1916. etc

Half-length portrait of a preacher, used to accompany a poem, "Reverend Mingo Millenyum's Ordination," depicts him standing in his pulpit with an open Bible before him. With frowning visage, mouth open wide, left hand lifted high over his head, and fist clenched, he seems to be delivering a fiery sermon. Occasion: religious portraiture.

2262 _____. "Oh, Shoutin's Mighty Sweet." [1916]. Pen and ink. Published in PLANTATION SONGS AND OTHER VERSES, by Ruth M. Stuart, frontispiece. New York: D. Appleton & Company, 1916.

Half-length portrait of a woman dancing the shout. With eyes lifted upwards, mouth open wide, arms held to the side but with palms extended, she appears to be moving along rapidly, singing all the while. Occasion: indoor religious portraiture.

2263 Matthews, Essie Collins. "Brudder Brown." [1915]. Photograph. Published in AUNT PHEBE, UNCLE TOM AND OTHER CHARACTER STUDIES AMONG THE OLD SLAVES OF THE SOUTH ..., by Essie Collins Matthews, 111. Columbus, OH: Champlin Press, 1915.

Portrait of an elderly preacher used to illustrate the author's discussion of a passage in the Irwin Russell poem, "Christmas Night in the Quarters" (see no. 1469): "See Brudder Brown---whose saving grace/Would sanctify a quarter race...." The preacher stands with bowed head and left arm lifted high as if giving a benediction. Occasion: indoor religious portraiture.

2264 Miner, Leigh Richmond. "An Ante-Bellum Sermon." [1906]. Photograph. Published in JOGGIN' ERLONG, by Paul Laurence Dunbar, 74-78. New York: Dodd, Mead, & Company, 1906.

The sequence of five portraits (full and half-length) depicts a middle-aged minister delivering a sermon in five different positions, thus forming a kind of photo-journalistic series. He stands before a simple wooden table, on which are placed an open Bible and his top hat. The photographs show the minister in the following poses: (1) He stands very straight with both hands on hips, fixing the congregation (not included in the photograph) with a challenging look. (2) He bends forward, resting his left hand on the table and lifting the right arm, with clenched fist, into the air. (3) He bends forward even more, resting both hands on the table. (4) Raising both hands in the air, with fists clenched, and still bent forward, he lowers his head to read from the Bible. (5) Still bent forward, he lifts his head to look directly at the congregation, holding down the pages of the Bible with his left hand, while pointing at the congregation as if to give special emphasis to what he is saying. None of the photographs includes the congregation. Occasion: religious portraiture.

2265 Otto, J. W. "He sat right side of de 'Lasses Pool." [1901]. Photograph. Published in PLANTATION SONGS FOR MY LADY'S BANJO..., by Eli Sheppherd, 104-05. New York: R. H. Russell, 1901.

Full-length portrait of an elderly preacher standing in an open field. With mouth open wide, left arm outstretched to the side and index finger pointing, he seems to be delivering a sermon. Occasion: religious portraiture.

2266 "The Sabbath Sun Shone Down upon Their Proudly Marching Ranks." [1913]. Mixed media. Published in "The Grand Organizer: An Episode in the Activities of 'Reverend' Criddle," by Harris Dickson. SATURDAY EVENING POST 185 (January 1913).

Scene shows a funeral parade in progress (in Vicksburg, Mississippi, according to the text of the article). A strutting drum major leads a marching band of 25 or more brasses and a drum. Indeterminate number of spectators includes 8 or 10 children, boys and girls, who prance alongside the band as "second liners." Occasion: outdoor procession.

2267 Wicker, Harry. "From the mourner's bench came loud wails...." [1917]. Mixed media. Published in "The Rooster and the Washpot," by Sarah Johnson Cooke. SATURDAY EVENING POST 179 (June 1917).

Scene depicts a humble church where a religious service is in progress, the preacher leading his congregation in a hymn from the pulpit, with one hand lifted in the air. An indeterminate number of worshippers fill the scene: those in the foreground present their backs to the viewer except for one girl; in the background, 7 or 8 men and women stand around the pulpit sit on the mourner's bench. Many worshippers appear to be singing. Occasion: indoor religious service.

THE SONG

2268 Catharat, M. "Chimney Sweep." [1910]. Crayon (?). Published in STREET CRIES OF AN OLD SOUTHERN CITY, by Harriette Kershaw Leiding, 10. Charleston, SC: Press of the Dagget Printing Company, 1910.

A boy street crier advertises his services with song as a chimney sweep on a street corner in Charleston. Occasion: outdoor work activity involving song.

2269 _____. "Come on, chilluns, get yu' monkey meat." [1910]. Crayon (?). Published in STREET CRIES OF AN OLD SOUTHERN CITY, by Harriette Kershaw Leiding, 7. Charleston, SC: Press of the Dagget Printing Company, 1910.

Portrayal of a female street peddler, who is selling monkey meat (that is, coconut and molasses candy) on a street in Charleston, South Carolina. She sits on the curb, her wares in a basket beside her. Occasion: outdoor work activity involving song.

2270 _____. "Swimp [sic] Peddler." [1910]. Crayon (?). Published in STREET CRIES OF AN OLD SOUTHERN CITY, by Harriette Kershaw Leiding, 10. Charleston, SC: Press of the Dagget Printing Company, 1910.

Torso-portrait of a adolescent shrimp peddler, shown with a basket of his wares atop his head and singing lustily. Occasion: outdoor work activity involving song.

2271 Desch, F. H. "Spots! Git yuh fresh spots!" [1904]. Crayon. Published in "In and About Old Hampton." BOOKLOVERS MAGAZINE 4 (November 1904).

Full-length portrait of a boy peddling fish, who is singing his street cry: "Spots! Git huh fresh spots." Occasion: outdoor work activity involving music.

2272 Kemble, Edward W. "So wid my hoe I go...." [1916]. Pen and ink. Published in PLANTATION SONGS AND OTHER VERSES, by Ruth McEnery Stuart, 20. New York: D. Appleton & Company, 1916.

Full caption: "So wid my hoe I go---row on row." Half-length portrait of a field hand, used to accompany a poem, "Plantation Hoe Song," depicts a male worker in the (cotton?) fields, singing as he moves down the rows. Occasion: outdoor work activity involving song.

2273 Kirk, Manual L. "Rockaby Song." [1901]. Mixed media. Published in "A Rockaby Song," by Frank L. Stanton. SATURDAY EVENING POST 174 (August 1901).

Used to accompany a composed poem, the scene shows a humble kitchen in which a woman, seated in a rocking chair near the kitchen table, sings a lullaby to her baby, who is cradled in her arms. Occasion: indoor domestic music.

2274 Otto, J. W. "Dey are at de ax swing...." Photograph. Published in PLANTATION SONGS FOR MY LADY'S BANJO, AND OTHER NEGRO LYRICS AND MONOLOGUES, by Eli Sheppherd, 82-83. New York: R. H. Russell, 1901.

Full caption: "Dey are at de ax swing and de song sing now---." Scene shows men at work in the clearing of a woods, 3 of them splitting a huge log with axes. One worker strikes the log; the others stand in readiness for their turns. Some appear to be singing. Occasion: outdoor work activity involving song.

2275 Regimental Quartet [untitled]. [1919]. Photograph. Published in "Men in the Making," by Joshua E. Blanton. SOUTHERN WORKMAN 48 (January 1919).

Photograph, copyrighted by the Committee on Public Information, shows the men's quartet of the 301st Stevedore Regiment singing outdoors. Standing in a semicircle before a building, they entertain 6 soldiers (four seated), one of whom plays a banjo. Occasion: outdoor entertainment.

2276 Smith, Alice. "Vegetubble Mauma." [1910]. Print. Published in STREET CRIES OF AN OLD SOUTHERN CITY, by Harriette Kershaw Leiding, 4. Charleston, SC: Press of the Dagget Printing Company, 1910.

Depiction of a female street peddler singing about her wares on a street in Charleston, South Carolina. She carries a huge basket of vegetables on her head as she walks along, holds one arm akimbo with hand on her hip and carries a blanket on the other arm. Occasion: outdoor work activity involving song.

2277 Work, John Wesley (?). "Daddy's Comin' Home." [1915]. Photograph. Published in FOLK SONG OF THE AMERICAN NEGRO, by John Wesley Work, 13. Nashville, TN: Fisk University Press, 1915.

Portrait of a mother singing a lullaby to the infant cuddled in her arms used by the author to illustrate a song text, "Daddy's comin' home, my baby/Heah him a-whistlin' low...." Occasion: indoor domestic music.

THE TALE

2278 Frost, Arthur Burdett. "You wanter hear a tale?..." [1904]. Mixed media. Published in THE TAR-BABY AND OTHER RHYMES OF UNCLE REMUS, by Joel Chandler Harris, 58. New York: D. Appleton & Company, 1904. Reprint (as "Brer Rabbit ain't see no peace w'atsumever"). UNCLE REMUS, HIS SONGS AND SAYINGS, by Joel Chandler Harris, 64. New York: Appleton-Century Company, 1908.

Full caption: "You wanter hear a tale? Well, you

sho' do skeer me! Kaze how kin you sit right still?" Scene shows the interior of a rude cabin, with a bed in one corner and clothes hanging on pegs on the wall. Uncle Remus sits hunched over on a wooden bench, his arms resting on his knees and pointing with his index finger, as he tells a tale to a small white boy, who listens attentively. Occasion: indoor tale telling.

2279 Hampton Institute Camera Club. Male Story Teller [untitled]. [1901]. Photograph. Published in CANDLE LIGHTIN' TIME, by Paul Laurence Dunbar, 122. New York: Dodd, Mead, & Company, 1901.

Scene shows the interior of a rude cabin: a man is telling a tale to 3 children in front of a roughly contructed brick fireplace. Sitting on the edge of his chair, with outstretched hands tightly clasped, the tale teller presents a serious mien. One child lies on the floor at the man's feet; the second, a small girl, leans on his lap; and the third tilts backwards in his small chair opposite the man's chair. All are deeply engrossed in the story. Occasion: indoor tale telling.

2280 _____. Male Story Teller [untitled]. [1901]. Photograph. Published in CANDLE LIGHTIN' TIME, by Paul Laurence Dunbar, 124. New York: Dodd, Mead & Company, 1901.

The scene and the participants are the same as in no. 2279, but the action is different. The [ghost?] story has reached its climax, and the man's face reflects its horror. The children are frightened: The boy in the chair covers his face with his hands, the second boy has risen from the floor to his knees, and the little girl has moved to a protected place between her father's legs, hiding her face on his chest. Occasion: indoor tale telling.

2281 Miner, Leigh Richmond. "A Cabin Tale." [1906]. Photograph. Published in JOGGIN' ERLONG, by Paul Laurence Dunbar, 96. New York: Dodd, Mead & Company, 1906. The photographer was a member of the Hampton Institute Camera Club.

Scene depicts an elderly man, seated in a chair outside the door of a frame house, telling a story to a young white boy. The man seems to be in an early part of his story: he presents a quiet, serious mien, resting his hands on his thighs as he looks down at the boy. The boy, sitting on the door sill facing the story teller with his face in his hands, is totally engrossed in the story. Occasion: outdoor tale telling.

2282 _____. "A Cabin Tale." [1906]. Photograph. Published in JOGGIN' ERLONG, by Paul Laurence Dunbar, 98. New York: Dodd, Mead & Company, 1906.

This scene is a sequel to the one in no. 2281, but the positions of the participants have changed: The elderly man, now sitting with his back to the door, looks off into space as if recounting something unusual. The white boy, now seated on a keg facing the story teller, with his hand resting on the man's knee, seems perturbed. Occasion: outdoor tale telling.

2283 Taylor, William Ladd. "The Story of the Tar-Baby." [1913]. Mixed media. Reproduced in "The Fourth of a New Series of American Literature Pictures Painted by W. L. Taylor." LADIES HOME JOURNAL 30 (November 1913): 15.

Caption: " 'Ef you don't lemme loose I'll knock you agin,' sez Brer Rabbit...." Scene shows the interior of a humble cabin, where an elderly Uncle Remus is telling a tale to 2 white children, a girl and a boy. Uncle Remus leans forward a smile on his face, with one elbow resting on his knee and the other arm resting on his lap. The children, listening attentively, smile as Uncle Remus recounts the adventures of Brer Rabbit. Occasion: indoor tale telling.

COLLECTIONS OF TALES AND SONGS: 1900–1920

THE TALE

2284 Backus, Emma M. "Folk-Tales from Georgia." JOURNAL OF AMERICAN FOLK-LORE 13 (January-March 1900): 19-32. Texts of 10 tales.

Brer Rabbit's cool air swing, 22
How come the Mooly Cow don't have no horns, 28
How the little boy went to heaven, 30
When Brer Fox don't fool Brer Rabbit, 24
When Brer Frog give a big dinner, 25
When Brer Rabbit get Brer Bear churched, 19
When Brer Rabbit was Presidin' Elder, 20
When Brer Wolf have his corn shucking, 21
When Mr. Pine-Tree and Mr. Oak-Tree..., 29
When Sis Coon put down Brer Bear, 26

2285 Backus, Emma M. and Ethel Hatton Leitner. "Negro Tales from Georgia." JOURNAL OF AMERICAN FOLK-LORE 25 (April-June 1912:) 125-36. Texts of 9 tales.

Bro' Rabbit an' de water-millions, 126
Bro' Fox an' de follish jaybird, 127
The graveyard snake and rabbit, 133
How Brer Fox dream he eat Brer 'Possum, 131
The Spanish moss, 135
When Brer Rabbit help Brer Terapin, 128
When Brer Rabbit saw Brer Dog's mouth, 125
When Brer 'Possum attend Miss Fox's house-party, 130
Why Mr. Owl can't sing, 134

2286 Boyle, Virginia Frazer. DEVIL TALES. New York: Harper and Brothers, 1900. Texts of 10 tales.

Asmodeus in the quarters, 77
The black cat, 167
Dark er de moon, 105
The Devil's little fly, 53
A Kingdom for Micajah, 23
Liza, 193
Old cinder cat, 1
The other maumer, 133
Stolen fire, 157
The taming of Jezrul, 91

2287 Culbertson, Annie Virginia. AT THE BIG HOUSE. Indianapolis, Indiana: The Bobbs-Merrill Company, 1904. 23 tale texts.

Brother Squirrel and Molly Hare, 135
The fox and the duck, 279
The fox and the hot potatoes,, 327
The funeral of Mr. Dog, 333
The lazy fox,, 253
Mis' Cat and Mr. Frisky Mouse, 86
Mis' Goose deceives Mr. Bear, 186
The mocking-bird and the dry-fly,, 308
Molly Cotton-tail steals Mr. Fox's butter, 245
Mr. Bear and Mr. Terrapin go courting, 237
Mr. Bear tends store for Mr. Fox, 194
Mr. Fox and Molly Hare go fishing, 16
Mr. Fox turns farmer, 155
Mr. Fox's funeral, 6
Mr. Hare and Mr. Elephant, 297
Mr. Terrapin gets the nose-bleed, 49
Origin of the cat, 215
The saucy young frog, 314
The toad and the terrapin, 302
The toad, the grasshopper and the rooster, 41
Why crabs walk backward, 207
Why moles have hands, 273
Why the flounder is flat, 129

2288 Faulkner, William J. THE DAYS WHEN ANIMALS TALKED. BLACK AMERICAN FOLKTALES AND HOW THEY CAME TO BE. Chicago: Follett Publishing Company, 1977. Texts of 33 tales.

Brer Bear gets a taste of man, 85
Brer Fox meets Mister Trouble, 137
Brer Fox tries farming, 110
Brer Possum and Brer Snake, 99
Brer Rabbit and Brer Cooter race, 132
Brer Rabbit and his riding horse, 146
Brer Rabbit dances for a wife, 141
Brer Rabbit goes a-courting, 75
Brer Rabbit keeps his word, 95
Brer Rabbit rescues his children, 168
Brer Rabbit's protest meeting, 115
Brer Tiger and the big wind, 89
Brer Wolf and Brer Fox get a big surprise, 164
Brer Wolf plants pinders, 102
Brer Wolf wants the honey, 139
Brer Wolf's magic gate, 80
Brer Wolf's second pinder patch, 106
Fishing with bare hands, 26
How the cow went under the ground, 152
How the slaves helped each other, 34
Riddle for freedom, A, 66
Run, Brer Gator, run, 128
Simon and the pater-rollers, 29

2289 Hobson, Anne. IN OLD ALABAMA. BEING THE CHRONICLES OF MISS MOUSE, THE LITTLE BLACK MERCHANT. New York: Doubleday, Page and Company, 1903. Texts of 10 tales.

2290 Parsons, Elsie Clews. "Tales from Guilford County, North Carolina." JOURNAL OF AMERICAN FOLK-LORE 30 (April-June 1917): 168-200. Texts of 62 tales.

2291 Parsons, Elsie Clews. "Folk-Tales Collected at Miami, Florida." JOURNAL OF AMERICAN FOLK-LORE 30 (April-June 1917): 222-227. Texts of 16 tales.

2292 Smiley, Portia. "Folk-Lore from Virginia, South Carolina, Georgia, Alabama, and Florida." JOURNAL OF AMERICAN FOLK-LORE 32 (July-September 1919): 357-83. Texts of 30 tales.

How Duck saw day, 362
The imitative choir, 369
Incriminating the other fellow, 366
Jonah, 371
The Lord and Toby, 361
Lover warned, 363
The master disguised, 362
The murderous mother, 364
Out of her skin, 363
Racing a ghost, 367
Running hand, 365
Seeking the Lord, 369
The single ball, The, 370
Takes no risk, 360
Three sweethearts, 372
Two daddies, 372
Us, 364
Where did Adam hide, 371
Who darkens that hole, 371
Witch-cat, 364
Wolf's tail to the hungry orphan, 361
Zip! Zip!, 365

2293 Talley, Thomas Washington. "Negro Folk Tales." Manuscript. Jefferson City, Missouri. Collection of Dr. Thomasina Talley Greene. Texts of 15 tales.

Cotton-eyed Joe, 44
Courting old woman, 338
Devil's daughters, 419
The headless man, 116
How the bear lost his judgeship, 201
Origin of the dog's habits, 394
Overseers of Negro slaves, 477
Parrot overseer, 304
Riddle them right, 505
Why the Jaybird goes...on Friday, 86
Why the buzzard is black, 174
Why the cat and the dog are enemies, 367
Why the preacher dresses in black, 273
De wull-er-de-wust, 2

THE SONG

2294 Bennett, John. "A Revival Sermon at Little St. John's." ATLANTIC MONTHLY 98 (August 1906): 256-68. Texts and music of 9 songs.

An' dey shill hongry no mo', 260
Dis time anuddeh yeah I may be gawn, 267
He dat beliebe hat ebberlastin' life, 259
Holy, holy, holy, Lo'd God A'mighty, 263
John, O, John, come up hytheh, 260
O, hit may be de las' time, 256
Oh, Hell so deep, an' Hell so wide, 264
Woe ter all dem dat bin wukkers er inequitty, 265
Ye-e-es, Lo'd, O-o-oh, muhsiful God, 263

2295 Burlin, Natalie Curtis. NEGRO FOLK-SONGS (HAMPTON SERIES). Recorded by Natalie Curtis-Burlin in Four Books. New York: G. Schirmer, 1918-19. Texts and music of 19 songs. Texts only of 2 songs.

Chorus firstlines

Chicka-hanka, chicka-hanka, 4-37
Come out hyah and shuck dis co'n, 3-35
Couldn't hear nobody pray, 1-29
Dis cotton want a-pickin' so bad, 3-14
Go down, Moses, 1-21
Go ter sleep, mammy's baby, 4-33
God's a-gwine ter move all de troubles away, 2-36
Good news, chariot's coming, 1-38
I want to go t' Hebb'n in de mo'nin', 1-11
O, Eliza, lil' Liza Jane, 4-43
O, listen to de Lambs, 2-15
Screw dis cott'n, heh, 3-31
'Tis me, 'tis me, O, Lord, 2-15
'Way down in de cott'n fiel', 3-23
You kin do jes'-a what you please, 4-13

Verse firstlines

Bigges' pile seen sence I was bo'n, 3-35
Boss is callin'-huh!, 4-28
Cap'n, go side-track yo' train, 4-37
Come on sister wid yo' ups and downs, 2-24
Come, ma love, an' go wid' me, 4-43
Dar's a long white robe in de Hebben, I know, 1-38
Genesis you understan', 2-36
Go ter sleep, go ter sleep, 4-33
I kin fill dis basket, 4-13
I's got a mudder in de Hebb'n (T), 1-9
In the valley on my knees, 1-29
Ma head got wet wid de midnight dew (T), 1-6
O, ev'ry time I feel de spirit, 2-29
O, massa said from firs' to las', 3-23
O, ride on, Jesus, 1-11
One twenties of May mo'nin', 3-14
A rattler went daown dat holler lawg, 4-40
'Tis not ma Mudder, but it's me, O Lord, 2-15
When Israel was in Egypt's land, 1-21

2296 Carter, William. PLANTATION MELODIES. Hamilton, Ontario, Canada: Duncan Lith Company, c.1909. Texts and music of 13 songs; texts only of 54 songs. Music is indicated by use of the letter M.

Chorus firstlines

Been listening all the night long, 5
Children, hail, hail, hail, 10
Crying amen, thank God, 49
Daniel saw a stone, 5
Go chain the lion down, 13
Good news, chariot's coming, 11
Hail, hail, I'll tell you when I get over, 18
He's the Lily of the valley, 43
I'm a-rolling, I'm a-rolling, i (M)
I'm rolling, I'm rolling, 17
If ye love God, serve him, 8
In my Father's house, 7
Jerusalem morning, Jerusalem morning by the light, 9
Mary and Martha just gone along, 16
May the Lord, He will be glad of me, 44
My brethern, don't get weary, vi (M), 20
My Lord delivered Daniel, v (M), 30
My Lord, what a mourning, 47

Verse firstlines

2297 Coleridge-Taylor, Samuel. TWENTY-FOUR NEGRO MELODIES TRANSCRIBED FOR THE PIANO. Op. 59. Bryn Mawr, PA: Oliver Ditson Company, 1905. Texts and music of 15 songs (choruses).

2298 Fenner, Thomas P. CABIN AND PLANTATION SONGS, AS SUNG BY THE HAMPTON STUDENTS, Arranged by Thomas P. Fenner, Frederic Rathbun, and Bessie Cleaveland. 3rd Edition Enlarged by the Addition of Forty-Four Songs. New York: G. P. Putnam's Sons, 1901. Reprint. New York: AMS Press, 1977. Music and texts of 116 songs. Same repertory as in the 1891 edition (see no. 1752) with the addition of 44 songs as listed below.

Chorus firstlines

Verse firstlines

2299 Fenner, Thomas P., comp. RELIGIOUS FOLK SONGS OF THE NEGRO, AS SUNG ON THE PLANTATIONS. Arranged by the Musical Directors of the Hampton Normal and Agricultural Institute from the Original Edition by Thomas P. Fenner. Hampton, VA: Institute Press, 1909, 1916. Music and texts of 116 songs. Same repertory as in the 1901 edition with the addition of 24 songs, as listed below (except for 1 non-spiritual).

Chorus firstlines

Verse firstlines

2300 Gibson, John William, and William Henry Crogman. PROGRESS OF A RACE: OR, THE REMARKABLE ADVANCEMENT OF THE AMERICAN NEGRO .... Atlanta: J. L. Nichols & Company, 1902. 732 pp. Texts of 11 songs.

Chorus firstlines

Children, hail, hail, hail, 640
My Lord delivered Daniel, 639
Oh, nobody knows de trouble I've seen, 640
Oh, swing low, sweet chariot, 635, 636
Oh, 'way over Jordan, 637

Verse firstlines

The angels done changed my name, 634
Ef eber I land on de oder sho', 638
I done been to heaven, 635
I met a pilgrim on de way, 639
I went to the hillside to pray, 634
I'm born of God, I know I am, 637
Jus' stan' right still and steady yo'self, 634
Oh, de good ole chariot swing so low, 635
Oh, look up yander, what I see, 640
Shine shine, I'll meet you in that morning, 635
Sometimes I'm up, sometimes I'm down, 640

2301 Hallowell, Emily, comp. CALHOUN PLANTATION SONGS. Boston: C. W. Thompson & Company, 1901. 61 pp. Texts and music of 54 songs; text of 1 song.

Chorus firstlines

Am I born to die, 31
Amazing grace how sweet de soun', 50
An', O Lord, de angel done change my name, 9
Calvary, Calvary, 35
Carrie' my Lord away, 16
Chillen, I done been home, 43
Come an' listed in de field, 32
Di'n' yo know, pilgrim, 45
Done foun' my los' sheep, 10
End o' dat morning, Good Lord, 25
Fo' de Lord, fo' de Lord, 42
Good Lord, shall I be de one, 48
Heaven, heaven, eb'rybody talking 'bout heaven ain't goin' there, 58
Hold out yo' light, 27
Holy, holy, holy is my God, 44
I'll meet you up yonder, 18
In de army, in de army, 54
Is jus' de same today, 30
Jesus lock de lion'...jaw, 19
Keep a-inching along, 7
O, Lord, write my name, 49
O, poor sinner, O now is yo' time, 28
O, redeem, redeem, been washed in de blood, 52
O, sister don't ye wan' to go to Heaven, 17
O, what a band ob music, 56
O, wheel, wheel in de middle ob de wheel, 23
O, yes, yonder come my Lord, 38
Roll de ol' chariot along, yes, 22
Rolling an' a rocking them in His arms, 13
Rolling in Zion, Jubalee, 36
Somebody knocking at yo' do', 12
Until I reach-a my home, 39
Weeping Mary, tall angel at the bar, 46
Who dat yonder under de sun, 14
Wrastling Jacob, Day is a breaking, 41

Verse firstlines

Baptist, Baptist, unbeliever, 19
Better min' sister how you walk, 49
Dark was de night, an' col' de groun', 31
Don't you hear God talking, hammering, 60
Eb'ry time I think about Jesus, 35
Ef my sister want to go, 59
Ef yo' mother want to go, 22
Father Abraham sitting down, 26
Go Mary an' toll de bell, 14
God knows 'tis a better day, 54
Got to go to judgment by myself, 57
Heaven so high an' I so low, 18
I been fo' thousand years serving my God, 40
I died one time, gwine to die no mo', 7
I know my Jesus loves me, 36
I love to hear my basso, 56
I see my mother coming, 48
I was way down a-yonder a-by myself, 9
I've got a robe, you got a robe, 58
Jacob's ladder long an' tall, 16
John de Bunyan, O Lord, 61
Keep yo' foot up on de treadle, 46
Knocks like Jesus, 12
Lord I neber knowed de battle was so hard, 15
Matthew cried out, Lord, is it I, 52
My Lord had one hundred sheep, 10
My soul wants something that's new, 47
O, dat sun gwine down, 38
O, de blin' man stood on de way an' cried, 29
O, deacon, can' you hold out yo' light, 27
O, gambler, get up off o' yo' knees, 25
O, he wrastled all night, 41
O, I done been home, 43
O, Lamb! Sitting down side ob my Jesus, 59
O, Lord, I wonder, by and by, 60 (T)
O, way down yonder 'bout some graveyard, 45
O, some say gi' me silber, 39
O, who dat coming ober yonder, 20
One day as I was a-walking along, 42
Paul an' Silas boun' in gaol, 44
Pray on my brudder, 32
Praying in de lan', 17
So glad I done done, 21
Sorry to tell you, Lord, Lord, 61
Takes a little bit ob man to rock Dan, 24
Tell me sinner an' tell me true, 13
Way up on de mountain, 34
Way up on de mountain top, 23
We are climbing Jacob's ladder, 33
We're singing, singing tonight, 19
What yo' gwine to do, 28
When I was seeking Jesus, 50
When Moses an' his so'diers, 30
Where shall I be when de firs' trumpet soun', 8
You got a right, I got a right, 40

2302 _____. CALHOUN PLANTATION SONGS. 2d ed. Boston: C. W. Thompson & Company, 1907. Texts and music of 69 songs. 74 pp. Same repertory as in the 1st edition with the addition of 15 songs, as listed below. A supplement published in 1905 included 9 of the songs listed below.

Chorus firstlines

All the way to Calvary, 64
Drive Satan away, 70
Gwine to quit all my worldly ways, 69

Verse firstlines

2303 Hobson, Anne. IN OLD ALABAMA; BEING THE CHRONICLES OF MISS MOUSE, THE LITTLE BLACK MERCHANT. New York: Doubleday & Page Company, 1903. Texts of 47 songs.

Chorus firstlines

Verse firstlines

2304 Krehbiel, Henry Edward. AFRO-AMERICAN FOLK-SONGS: A STUDY IN RACIAL AND NATIONAL MUSIC. New York: G. Schirmer, 1914. Music and texts of 28 songs. Texts of 7 songs.

Chorus firstlines

Verse firstlines

2305 Lomax, John Avery. "Some Ballads of North Carolina," NORTH CAROLINA BOOKLET 11 (July 1911): 26-42. Texts of 13 songs.

Chorus firstlines

Verse firstlines

2306 Lomax, John Avery. "Self-Pity in Negro Folk-Songs." NATION 105 (9 August 1917): 141-47. Texts of 15 songs.

Chorus firstlines

Verse firstlines

2307 Murphy, Jeanette Robinson, comp. SOUTHERN THOUGHTS FOR NORTHERN THINKERS AND AFRICAN MUSIC IN AMERICA. New York: The Bandanna Publishing Company, 1904. 47 pp. Texts and music of 29 songs; texts of 5 songs.

Chorus firstlines

Verse firstlines

Oh, de stars in de elements am shinin', 35
Oh, de Prodigal Son he left home, 32
Oh, God commanded old Norah one day, 34
Ole ship o' Zion, 32
One mornin' I was a walkin long, 35
Possum up de gum stump, 16 (T)
Purtiest ting dat ebber I done, 35
Ready fo' de water, 32
Rise, shine, git along ter glory, 16 (T)
Sinnah! yer walkin' on a slender stran', 32
Talk about de wheel ob time, 34
Who dat yonder dressed in white, 31
Who's gwine nuss de baby, 31
Yer see heah ma sistah, 33
Yoop, tiddy yoop, tiddy yoop, 14

2308 O'Connell, L. "The Folk Songs of Afro-America." MUSICIAN (Boston) 11 (October 1906): 503-4. Texts of 14 songs.

Chorus firstlines

O, come down, come down, John, 503
Oh, what you say, John, 504
Oho, oho, ho, ah, yah! Ya-ah-ah, 504
Way down in de valley, 504

Verse firstlines

Hold your light, Brudder Robert, 503
I know moon-rise, 504
In de days ob de deep tribulashun, 503
In de mornin', 504
De lightnin' an' de flashin', 503
My army, cross over, 503
No mo' peck o' corn foh me, 504
O, de ole nigger driver, 503
Oh, Susannah! Fare you well, 503
Oh, what you reckon de Debbil say, 504
Oh, who all dem come dress' in white, 504
Rise up in due time, 503
We'll soon be free, 504
What boat is dat, my darlin' honey, 504

2309 Odum, Anna Kranz, comp. "Some Negro Folk-Songs from Tennessee." JOURNAL OF AMERICAN FOLK-LORE 27 (July-September 1914): 225-65. Texts of 28 songs.

Chorus firstlines

All my sins been taken away, 259
Behold the city, she move along, 258
Do Lord, remember me, 256
Don't you hear dat water rollin', 263
Have Monday, Tuesday, Wednesday..., 262
I love my Jesus, yes I do, 259
Jesus is waitin' all de time, 256
Keep er-inchin' erlong, 262
Little David, play on your harp, 263
No, Naaman, go down an' wash, 264
Wasn't that a mighty day, 264

Verse firstlines

Been fightin' in the city, 258
Blessed be the Name of the Lord, 263
By an' by when de mornin' come, 258
David was a baby lyin' at Mary's arm, 264
David was a shepherd-boy, 263
Don't call the roll, John, till I get there 261
Down by the river side Jordan, 263
Drinkin' bottle an' bawn, 265
Go 'long to sleep, my little baby, 265
Goin' to wake up de dead, 257
How you know the blood done sign my name, 258
I am hungry, want to eat, 256
I was down in the valley, 262
I'm goin' home on the mornin' train, 259
I've got a mother in the Rock of Ages, 256
Just plenty good room, 259
Leave your house-rent here, 265
Listen at the lambs all cryin', 261
My Lord told me not to work on Sunday, 262
O, auntie, won't you taste, 260
O, brother, don't stay away, 260 (T)
O, Lord, I'm sick, 256
O, Naaman the leper, the honorable man, 264
Oh, that blind man stood on the way, 264
Sweepin' through the gate, hallelujah, 259
Way by an' by, brother hammer, ring, 265
Whar shall I be when the first trumpet sound, 257
When I am hungry, do feed me, Lord, 256

2310 Odum, Howard W. "Religious Folk-Songs of the Southern Negroes." AMERICAN JOURNAL OF RELIGIOUS PSYCHOLOGY AND EDUCATION 3/3 (July 1909): 265-365. 127 song texts.

Chorus firstlines

Bear yo' burden, sinner, 317
Come over, den, 334
Do my Lord remember me, 324
Down on my knees, 358
Drinkin' of the wine, 355
En, ho, ho, didn't it rain, 349
For the Bible it tell me so, 335
Free, free, my Lord, 308
Get in the Union, 319
Giv' me Jesus, 325
Goin' down to Jordan, 347
Goin' to wake up the dead, 312
Hallaluyer, good Lord, 304
Hark, the downward road is crowded, 312
He is waitin', Lord, 318
Heal me, Jesus, heal me, Jesus, 358
Heaven, heaven, 328
I am goin' to trust in the Lord, 285
I thought I had religion, 304
I'm er pore little orphan chile, 340
I'm going there to see my classmates, 357
I'm workin' on the building, 310
In hell ole Cy did cry, 286
In the wheel, 316
Jesus rose on Sunday mornin', 333
Keep er-inchin' erlong, 322
Lord, I jus' got over-er, 306
My trouble is hard, O yes, 351
O de blood...done sign my name, 345
O my Lord's comin' again, 311
O my Lord, shall I be the one, 342
O, didn't it rain, 350
O, steal away, steal away, 357
Ole Jonah cried, 360
One mornin' soon, 335
Paul and Silas bound in jail, 348
Sinner die...in de midnight dew, 313
Stan' still, walk sturdy, 325
Tell all dis worl', 346

Verse firstlines

2311 Odum, Howard W. "Folk-Song and Folk-Poetry in the Secular Songs of the Southern Negroes." Parts 1, 2. JOURNAL OF AMERICAN

FOLK-LORE 24 (July-September 1911): 255-94; (October-December 1911): 351-96. Texts of 129 songs.

A yellow girl I do despise, 375
Ain't it dinner--ho, ho, 385
Ain't you sorry, 366
Baby's in Memphis layin' 'round, 383
Baby, baby, didn't you say, 274
Baby, you ought-a tole me, 275
Baby, you sho' lookin' warm, 274
Brady went to hell, 353
Brother Rabbit, Brother Bear, 386
The burly coon, you know, 281
Carried my woman to the world's fair, 373
Casey Jones was an engineer, 351
Come 'way to Georgia to git on a hog, 270
Come an' go to sweet Tennessee, 276
Comin' down State Street, comin' down Main, 285
The day I lef'--huh--my mother's hous', 380
Dem skeeters day callin' me cousin, 268
Dey tell me Joe Turner he done come, 351
Diamon' Joe, you better come, 280
Do lak' I use ter, 357
Don't hit that woman, 286
Don't you hear them bells a-ringin', 375
Don't you remember one mornin', 383
Dony got a hole in de wall, 263
Early in de mornin', Honey, I'm goin' rise, 381
Ev'y since I lef' dat county farm, 357
'Fo' long, honey, 363
Give me a little buttermilk, ma'am, 364
Goin' to Atlanta, goin' to ride de rod, 279
Goin' to my shack, 357
Got up in the mornin', 271
H-i-g-h-t, red bird flyin' round here, 392
Had ole gal one time, name was Cross-eyed Sally, 376
Hey--slip--slide him, 391
Hop right, goin' to see my baby Lou, 284
I gamble all over Kentucky, 368
I got a woman an' sweetheart, too, 277
I got mine, boys, 369
I got up one mornin' jes' 'bout four o'clock, 289
I love my babe, an' wouldn't put her out, 278
I love that man, O God! I do, 286
I pawn my watch an' I pawn my chain, 384
I thought I had a friend was true, 388
I want to see do my baby know right from wrong, 273
I was bohn in a mighty bad lan', 355
I went down on Number One, 290
I went down to New Orleans, 354
I went up Zion Hill this mornin', 264
I went up to Odd-Fellows Hall, 369
I wouldn't have a yellow gal, 284
I wus goin' down the railroad, 353
I'm dat fortune-teller man, 358
I'm goin' 'way, comin' back some day, 175
I'm goin' 'way, goin' 'way, 283
I'm po' boy 'long way from home, 270
If I die in Arkansa', 273
If I had it, you could git it, 385
If you don't find me here, 272
If you don't like the way I work, 389
If you want to go a courtin', 285
If you want to see dat mule kick, 372
If you want to marry, 285
It breaks my heart to see my baby part, 389
It's ninety-six miles from Birmingham, 280
It's no use you sendin' no word, 277
Ja-gooze said a befo' he died, 384
Joseph Mica was good engineer, 352
Just as sho' as train, 362
Late every evenin', 276
Late las' night an' night befo', 280
Lawd, I went to my woman's do', 283
Lilly was a good girl, 366
Look'd down de road jes' far as I could see, 272
Lost John, help me to look, 365
Make me a palat on de flo', 278
Mamma goin' to cook some, 365
Me'n my pahdner an' two'r three mo', 383
Monday I was 'rested, Tuesday I was fined, 293
My love for you is all I knew, 287
My name is Uncle Sam, 358
Nex' day when show wus gone, 374
Nigger be a nigger whatever he do, 370
Nigger up-stairs got hundred dollars, 368
No more good time, woman, 279
O, Brer Rabbit! you look mighty good, 356
O, girl, O girl, what have I done, 287
O, Julia Waters! do you remember the day, 360
O, mother! I'm dreaming, 387
Ole aunt Dinah has a garden, 392
One was a boy, an' one was a girl, 277
Quit, stop, I say! Don't you hear, 370
Railroad Bill mighty bad man, 290
Railroad Bill was mighty sport, 292
Rich folks worries 'bout trouble, 387
Rollin'-mill done shut down, 359
Rubber-tired buggy, double-seated hack, 354
Run here, Mama! Run here, Mama, 386
Satisfied, tickled to death, 355
Say, look here, Jane!, 265
See dat mule a-comin', ain't got half a load, 371
Settin' in de wily woods, 371
Shake hands an' tell yo' babe good-bye, 270
Sister Mary, Aunt Jane, 387
Slow train run thru' Arkansas, 293
Some one went home an' tole my wife, 289
Stagolee, what's dat in yo' grip, 288
Things ain't the same, babe, since I went away, 281
Thought I heard that K.C. whistle blow, 287, 361
Under the rail, under the tie, 384
Well, I started to leave, 283
Well, I thought I heard that K. C. whistle blow, 361
Well, I tole my captain my feet wus cold, 381
Well, I'm goin' to buy me a little railroad, 282
Well, if that's yo' man, 282
Well, it make no difference, 267
Well, possum meat's so nice an' sweet, 376
Well, she ask me--whuk--in de parlor, 380
Well, the cocaine habit is might' bad, 358
Went up town Friday 'bout four o'clock, 284
Went up town wid my hat in my han', 356
Willie, Willie, Willie, bully, 390
Yes, he caught poor John, 265
Yes, there's going to be a ball, 266

2312 Perrow, Eber Carle. "Songs and Rhymes from the South." Parts 1-3. JOURNAL OF AMERICAN FOLK-LORE 25-28 [1] (April-June 1912): 137-55; [2] (April-June 1913): 123-73; [3] (April-June 1915): 129-90. Texts and music of 4 songs. Texts of 86 songs.

Chorus firstlines

And I wuz fo' hundud miles away fum home, 2-170
Baby! Baby!, 2-127
'Baccer sellin' high, 3-139
Come on, Mr. Tree, yer almost down, 3-138
Dahuh's no hidin' place daown dah-uh, 2-162
David play on your harp, hallelu', hallelu', 2-161
Diamond Joe...Run get me Diamond Joe, 3-132
Dis mornin', er dis evenin', so soon, 3-137
Done writ down yo' name, 2-155
Ef it hadn't been fer dat Cottoneye Joe, 3-189
En he'll lay yo po body daown, 1-155
For this work is 'most done, 2-156
Glory halleluger, 3-190
Help me to holler rabbit now, 3-132
Hoe yer corn, hoe yer corn, 2-154
I'm a rowdy old soul, 2-126
I'm goin' home on the mornin' train, 2-162
I'se gwine Sunday mornin', 2-154
If I can, if I can, 2-170
Keep yo' seat, Miss Liza Jane, 3-180
Love it am a killing thing, 3-190
Moanish lady, an' you shall be free, 2-157
My good Lawd been here, bless my soul, 2-155
My Lord, he died on de cross, 2-156
O, Lord, it's hard to be a nigger, 3-140
O, mary, don't you weep, don't you moan, 2-156
O-o death! How kin I go wid you, 2-154
Oh, come 'long, boys, an' shuck dat corn, 2-131
Oh, ho! my honey! take one on me, 3-133
Oh, Moana, you shall be free, 3-135
Oh, wasn't I lucky not to lose, 3-134
Rise an' shine, mourner, 2-147
Run, nigger, run, de paterrol ketch yuh, 3-138
Starry light and starry crown, 2-160
Sunshine...in my face dis mornin', 3-154
Uncle Eph's got de coon, 2-158
Walk...John Booker, with yo' new boots on, 3-138
We will wait on de Lawd, 2-162 (M)
Who's been a-foolin', who's been a-tryin', 3-187
Workin' in de pea-vines, oh, ho, 2-127
You're goin'-a miss me by my walk, 2-161

Verse firstlines

A die, a die, a die, 3-138
Adam was the first man, 2-159
Allie Bell, don't you weep, 3-188
As I was coming through my field, 2-2-158
Aught for aught an' figger fuh figger, 3-140
Away down yonder on Sixteenth Street, 2-171
Boatman, boatman, blow yuh ho'n, 3-140
Captain, Captain my feet are cold, 2-172
Casey Jones left Jackson Yards, 2-166
Chickens on my back, and bloodhounds on my track, 2-170
Col' frosty mo'nin, nigger mighty good, 3-139
Dat negro come to my house, 3-141
Dere's one, dere's two, dere's three little angels, 2-154
Done all I can do trying to get along wid you, 3-189
Ef you want yo buckwheat cakes, 3-141
Es I was runnin' through de fiel', 3-138
Every time the sun goes down, 3-190
Get ready, chillun, less go home, 2-162
Goin' down tuh Lynchburg town, 3-139
Here's old Norah, 2-158
Honey, when I had you, you wouldn't do right, 3-187
I got a crown, you got a crown, 2-161
I got a gal in de white folk's ya'd, 3-135
I hitched my horse to the poplar trough, 2-125
I laid in jail, back to the wall, 3-190
I uster drive a long-horn steer, 2-126
I went down to the depot, 2-172
I went into the wilderness, 2-161
I wish I was in Texas, 2-131
I'm er livin' easy, 3-137
I'm going in de house and close my door, 3-189
I've got a girl in Baltimore, 2-156
If I come out on two, 3-132
If I should marry a scoldin' wife, 3-188
Jes' look yonder what I see, 2-147
Love it am a killing thing, 3-190
Keep your eye on the captain, 2-172
My Lord called me and I mus' go, 2-148
My ole mistis promised me, 3-138
Oh de bullfrog tried for to court de alligator, 2-136
Oh, ain't dat a mighty wonder, 2-155
Oh, big Bayou wuz a good ole town, 3-141
Oh, de men for de women, 3-133
Oh, freedom, freedom, freedom, 3-143
Oh, my soul, my soul, 2-160
Oh, whar shall I be when de great trumpet soun', 2-155
Oh, where was you when de steamer went down, 3-189
Ol' black bar live down on Quibber, 3-142
Old cornfield rabbit got a mighty habit, 2-132
Old Judge Watson a mighty fine man, 3-141
The ole bluejay on the swingin' lim', 2-133
De ole caow crossed de road, 2-129 (M)
De ole hen she cackled, 2-129
Ole Marster, an' old Mistis, 3-134
One day ez I wuz walkin', 2-162 (M)
A possum up the 'simmon-tree, 2-131
Purty yaller gal had er hole in her stockin', 3-188
Rabbit in the log, and I got no dog, 2-127
Railroad Bill cut a mighty big dash, 1-155
The rain it rained, the wind it blew, 2-170
Rise, mourner, rise, and don't be ashame', 2-155
Satan's mad and I am glad, 2-154
See dem ole farmers goin' on to town, 3-137
Shuck corn, shell corn, carry corn to mill, 3-139
Sinner, I come to you by Hebbin's decree, 2-154
Some folks say that Cain killed Abel, 2-160
Some folks say that a nigro won't steal, 3-135
Some of these days I'm going to go crazy, 3-189
Sometimes I lib in de country, 3-141
Talk about me, talk about you, 2-161
Tell me Jo Turner's come to town, 1-155
There was a moanish lady, 2-157
The time is coming and it won't be long, 3-189
Turkey in de bread-tray, 2-127
Uh'm gon' tell yuh 'bout my pardner, 2-172 (M)
We are climbin' Jacob's ladder, 2-156
When I was young and in my prime, 3-138
White man goes tuh college, 3-140
Who's dat comin', all dressed in red, 2-156 (M)
Whoa, mule, whoa, mule, I say, 3-180
With them bloodhounds on my track, 2-170
Working on the railroad, 2-171
Wukking all day in de cotton fiel', 2-153
Yonder come chillun dressed in white, 2-156
You go out and you don't come back, 3-190

2313 Peterson, Clara Gottschalk. CREOLE SONGS

FROM NEW ORLEANS IN THE NEGRO DIALECT. New Orleans: L. Grunewald Company, 1902. Texts and music of 12 songs.

En avan' Grenadie, 9
Garde piti milat' la, 17
Mouche Mazireau, 4
Neg' Pa' Capab Marene, 19
Ou som Sourou cou, 11
Papa va a la Riviere, 20
Po' pitie Mamze Zizi, 6
Quan patata la cuite, 15
Quan' mo te dan' aran chimain, 3
Salangadou, 12
Une deusse troisse, 16
Zelim to quitte la plaine, 7

2314 Proctor, Henry Hugh. "The Theology of the Songs of the Southern Slave." Parts 1, 2. SOUTHERN WORKMAN 36 (November 1907): 584-92, (December 1907): 652-56. Texts of 12 songs.

Chorus firstlines

In bright mansions above, 655
In dat great gettin' mornin', 654
Keep a-inching along, 591
My Lord, what a mornin', 655
You may bury me in the East, 653

Verse firstlines

As I went down in the valley to pray, 652
Green trees are bending, 586
I looked over Jordan, an' what did I see, 589
I went to the hillside, I went to pray, 589
If you want to catch that heavenly breeze, 588
De Lord spoke to Gabriel, 589, 654
No more auction block for me, 592
'Twas inch by inch I sought the Lord, 591
We want no cowards in our band, 591
Were you there when they crucified my Lord, 587

2315 Reddick, K. D., and Phil V. S. Lindsley, eds. NATIONAL JUBILEE MELODIES. Nashville: National Baptist Publishing House, c1916. 55 pp. Collection of 160 items includes music and texts of 139 plantation songs.

Chorus firstlines

Ain't that a pity, Lord, 146
All over this world, 8
Am I born to die, 101
And I couldn't hear nobody pray, 90
As I went down in the valley to pray, 66
Before I'd be a slave, 118
Before I'd be a slave, 95
Before this time another year I may be gone, 135
Better get you ready, 75
Brother, when that train comes along, 80
By and by I'll go and see her, 58
By the grace of God I'll meet you, 59
Come a-leaning on the Lord, 137
Come down, come down, my Lord, 133
Come here, Lord, 42
Daniel saw the stone, rolling, rolling, 140
Don't let it be said, too late, 93
Don't let nobody turn you roun', 50
For my Lord says there's room enough, 44, 150
For the Lord, for the Lord, 149
Free at last, free at last, 9
Get right, stay right, 122
Give me that old-time religion, 5
Going home in the chariot in the morning, 132
Going to mourn and never tire, 78
Good Lord, shall I be the one, 64
Good Lord, when I die, 24
Great day, great day, 52
Hail, hail, I belong to the blood washed army, 76
Hallelululu, hallelu, O my Lord, 26
He rose...from the dead, 54
He sees all you do, hears all you say, 104
Heav'n, heav'n, Ev'rybody talking 'bout heav'n, ain't going there, 130
Hold the wind, hold the wind, 106
I aint goin' t' study war no more, 12
I feel like...my time ain't long, 144
I heard the preaching of the Elder, 57
I'll be lying in my grave when the first trumpet sounds, 68
I'll be there in the morning, 126
I'm a walking in the light, 94
I'm a-rolling...thro' an unfriendly world, 74
I'm going to land on-a that shore, 125
I'm leaning on the Lord, 51
I'm working on the building for my Lord, 110
If you just hold out, 123
In a my heart, In a my heart, 38
In-a this-a band we have sweet union, 15
Is there anybody here who loves my Jesus, 7
It's me, O Lord, standing in the need of prayer, 120
Jesus rose...and gone to heaven on the cloud, 67
Jubilee, jubilee, O Lordy, 111
Keep a-inching along, 92
King Jesus is a-listening, 79
Lead me, Lead me, my Lord, 141
Like Jesus, like Jesus, 139
Listen to the lambs, all a-crying, 145
Little David, play on your harp, 100
Look away in the heaven, 102-103
Lord, I can't turn back, 32
Lord, I just got over, 148
Lord, I know I've been changed, 34
Lord, I'm almost home, 6
Lord, oh, hear me praying, 105
Most done toiling here, O bretheren, 73
My Lord, what a morning, 35
My good Lord done been here,, 99
Nobody knows the trouble I see, Lord, 153
O he that believeth...hath an everlasting life, 11
O Lamb, beautiful Lamb, 142
O Mary, don't you weep, don't you mourn, 97
O my good Lord, show me the way, 138
O poor sinner, O now is your time, 81
O reign, O reign, O reign, my Saviour, 124
O rocks, don't fall on me, 134
O the sunshine...in a my soul this morning, 16
O this is the healing water, 53
O, by and by, by and by, 136
O, by and by, by and by, 41
O, give me your hand, 143
O, I can't stay away, 115
O, I know the Lord...laid His hands on me, 60
O, steal away and pray, 36
O, the old ark's a-movering, 39
O, wheel, O wheel, 46

Verse firstlines

Sister, you better mind how you talk, 29
Sister, you ought to been down to the spring, 108
Some of these mornings bright and fair, 97
Some say that John the Baptist, 79
Soon one morning death come, 28
Talk about me just as much as you please, 106
Tell John not to call the roll, 55
Tell me how did you feel, 51
That heavenly land all lined with gold, 148
There are angels hov'ring round, 113
There will be no sorrow there, 116
There's a starry crown, 123
They crucified my Saviour, 54, 67
This world's a wilderness of woe, 7
Train is a-coming, 75
Trials dark on ev'ry hand, 112
Virgin Mary had one son, 27
Want to go to Heaven when I die, 24
We need more lab'rers in the harvest field, 147
Went to the graveyard the other day, 144
What is the matter with the mourners, 111
What kind o' shoes are those you wear, 20
What kind of shoes you going to wear, 22
What you goin' t' do when my Lord calls you, 89
When I was living at hell's dark door, 104
When you see my coffin come, 146
You got to stand a test in judgment, 31
You may hinder me here, 32
You may search from sea to sea, 139
You say you're aiming for the skies, 143
You'll hear a sinner mourn, 35
Zekiel saw the wheel of time, 46

2316 Rodeheaver, Homer. RODEHEAVER'S PLANTATION MELODIES. Chicago: The Rodeheaver Company, 1918. Texts and music of 32 songs.

Chorus firstlines

Ain't goin' t' study war no more, 6
Den, chil'ren, keep in de middle ob de road, 30
Free grace and dying love, 19
Git on board, little children, 11
Go down, Moses, 17
Great day...the righteous marching, 7
I'm a-rolling, I'm a-rolling, 23
I'm troubled, I'm troubled, 31
In-a my heart, in-a my heart, 2
It may be tomorrow, 21
It's me, it's me, O Lord, 1
Judgment, Judgment, Judgment day, 32
O, I know the Lord, 16
O, the old ark's a-movering, 18
Oh, 'way over Jordan, 5
Oh, Peter, go ring dem bells, 26
Oh, we'll wait till Jesus comes, 24
Rise, shine, give God the glory, 8
Somebody's knocking at your door, 3
Steal away, steal away, 9
Swing low, sweet chariot, 13
There's one wide river, 20
Tis the old ship of Zion, 24
To turn back Pharoah's army, 25
Yes, I want God's heaven to be mine, 15
Yes, yes, my Lord, 29

Verse firstlines

Chariot rode on the mountain top, 7
Come along, come along, 24
Gospel train's a-comin', 11
Did you ever see the like before, 16
Do you think I'll make a soldier, 8
Goin' t' lay down my burden, 6
Gwine to write to Massa Jesus, 25
I got-a shoes, you got-a shoes, 10
I hailed to my sister, 15
I hear dem angels a-calling loud, 30
I looked over Jordan, and what did I see, 13
I wonder where my mother is gone, 26
I'm a-gona walk on the streets of glory, 4
I'm born of God, I know I am, 5
I've a good old mother in the heaven, 32
I've got a mother in de heaven, 27
Knocks like Jesus, 3
Lord, I want to be a Christian, 2
Mary and a-Martha's just gone 'long, 19
My Lord calls me, 9
Not my brother, not my sister, but it's me, O Lord, 1
O, brothers, won't you help me, 23
O, Jesus, my Saviour, 31
O, you might as well live in union, 21
Oh, hallelujah to the Lamb, 24
Old Noah he built himself an ark, 20
See that sister dressed so fine, 18
Were you there when they crucified my Lord, 22
What kind of shoes you going to wear, 29
When Israel was in Egypt's land, 17

2317 _____. RODEHEAVER'S PLANTATION MELODIES. 2d ed. Chicago: The Rodeheaver Company, 1918. Texts and music of 46 songs. Same repertory as in the first edition (see no. 2316) with the addition of 14 songs as listed below.

Chorus firstlines

All my sins are taken away, 43
And I couldn't hear nobody pray, 34
He 'rose, He 'rose, 40
Hold the wind, hold the wind, 33
In-a that morning, O my Lord, 39
Listen to the lambs all a-crying, 38
Little David, play on your harp, 35
Lord, oh, hear me praying, 44
Most done toiling here, 42
My Lord, what a morning, 36
My soul is a witness for my Lord, 46
O, Mary, don't you weep, 45
O, my good Lord, show me the way, 41
Then my little soul's goin' t' shine, 37

Verse firstlines

Come on, sister, with your ups and downs, 38
I love to shout, I love to sing, 42
I'm goin' t' join that big 'soc'ation, 37
In the valley on my knees, 34
Like Peter when you said to him, 44
Little David was a shepherd boy, 35
My Lord's done just what he said, 43
Noah sent out a mourning dove, 41
O, Lord, I've done what you told me to do, 39
Some of these mornings bright and fair, 45
Talk about me just as much as you please, 33
They crucified my Saviour, 40
You read in the Bible and you understand, 46
You'll hear a sinner mourn, 36

2318 Scarborough, Dorothy. FROM A SOUTHERN PORCH. New York: G. P. Putnam's Sons, 1919. Texts of 33 songs.

Chorus firstlines

Do you call dat religion, 294
God moved on de waters, 305
In de mawnin' you shall be free, 209
Oh, run, nigger, run, or de paterroler'll git you, 53
Oh, shout de glory, 204
Pickin' on de bottle, 97
Pretty Betty Martin, tiptoe, tiptoe, 98
Reel, Dinah, po' gal, 52
Rise, shine an' gib God de glory, 264
Swing low, sweet chariot, 189
Well, who stole de lock, 99
When I swim de golden ribber, 296

Verse firstlines

A hawss an' a flea an' a little mice, 315
Angel come down an' trouble de waters, 264
As I come 'long de new-cut road, 98
As I walked out to my corn-fiel', 53
Come, all you people, 307
De grass-mo-whopper settin' on de sweet potato vine, 54
De ham-bone am sweet, 248
De ol' bee makes de honeycomb, 58
De tree toad, he ain' got but one song, 96
Delijah was a woman fine and fair, 298
Frankie was a good girl, 301
I found a little weevil, 55
I looked over Jordan, and what did I see, 189
I was walkin' 'long de new-cut road, 97
It was in the year nineteen hundred an' twelve, 305
Jakey went a-huntin' one moonshiny night, 244
Marse mocking bird, you sho' am prissy, 119
My little dog begin to bark, 243-244
My ol' friend was as cute as a mouse, 99
Oh, de bumberlybee am a pretty little thing, 52
Oh, Mary, don't you weep no more, 262
Once dere was a moanin' lady, 224
Possum up de gum stump, 58
Raccoon up de 'simmon tree, 209
Some preachers, dey is preachin', 294
Wake, oh, mistis, peas in de pot, 246
Way down yander on de bank-ter-wank, 56
Well, I heard a mighty rumbling, 204
When I swim de golden ribber, 296
When boys fust go a-courtin', 165

2319 Smith, N. Clark, comp. NEW JUBILEE SONGS FOR QUARTETTE, CHOIR, OR CHORUS: CONCERT, CHURCH, & HOME. Chicago: Jubilee Music Company, c1906. 13 pp. Texts and music of 8 songs.

Chorus firstlines

Free at las', free at las, 11
Git on board, children, 7
I couldn't hear nobody pray, 5
Joshua fought de battle of Jerico, 17
Swing low, sweet chariot, 15
We'll stan' on the rock of Zion, 9
When the rocks an' the mountains shall all fade away, 3
Yes, I will die in the field, 13

Verse firstlines

Good mornin', brother pilgrim, 17-18
I looked over Jordan an' what did I see, 15
O, brothers don't you think it best, 11
O, what do you say, preacher, 13
Sinner, sinner give up yo' heart to God, 3
Sister, you better git ready, 9
The gospel train is comin', 7
When I went down in the valley, 5

2320 Thomas, William H. "Some Current Folk-Songs of the Negro and Their Economic Interpretation." A Paper Read before the Folk-Lore Society of Texas, 1912. Austin, TX: Published by the Folk-Lore Society, c1912. 10 pp. Texts of 17 songs.

Chorus firstlines

O, my Lord, save me from sinking down, 8
Oh, Daniel, hallelujah, 7
Oh, Lord, Baby, take a look at me, 12
Tell all the members I'm a new-born, 7

Verse firstlines

A brown-skinned woman...chocolate to the bone, 10
Daniel in that lion's den, 7
Don't you leave me here, 12
I dreamt last night I was walking around, 10
I got the blues, but I haven't got the fare, 9
I lookt at the sun and the sun lookt high, 8
I went to the jail house, 12
I went to the valley, 6
If you don't quit monkeying with my Lulu, 10
Jack o'Diamonds...is a hard card to roll, 11
The jurymen found me guilty, 11
O, Lord, sinner, you got to die, 8
The reason why I don't work so hard, 8
Say, when I die, bury me in black, 10
Seven stars in his right hand, 8
White folks are all time bragging, 9
Working on the section, 12

2321 Upton, George Putnam. THE SONG: ITS BIRTH, EVOLUTION, AND FUNCTION. Chicago: A. C. McClurg & Company, 1915. Texts of 14 songs.

Chorus firstlines

General Jackson, mighty man, 114
I am a trubble in de mind, 112
In de mornin' when I rise, 112
De ladies in de parlor, 111
Little David, play on your harp, 113
Nobody knows the trubble I've had, 112
O, de mugwump roosts in de hollow log, 115
O, graveyard, O, graveyard, 113
Old Satan told me to my face, 112
Swing low, sweet chariot, 113

Verse firstlines

Cowboy on de middle o' island, 114
I looked over Jordan and what did I see, 113
Ole Maus William he gone to legislator, 115

They took him down to the gallows, 115

2322 White, Clarence Cameron. "Negro Music: A Contribution to the National Music of America---Articles 1-4." MUSICAL OBSERVER 18 (November-December 1919): 18-19; 19 (January 1920): 16-17; 19 (February 1920): 50-51; 19 (March 1920): 13. Texts and music of 11 songs; text of 1 song.

Chorus firstlines

Go down, Moses, 50
O, didn't it rain, 50
O, hail, Mary, hail, 19
O, the old ark's a-movering, 50
Oh, femme Romulus, oh belle femme, 19
Sometimes I feel like a motherless child, 17
Steal away, steal away, 16
You may bury me in de East, 51

Verse firstlines

All dem Mount-Zion member, 12
As I walked down de new cut road, 19
I want some valiant soldier here, 19
I'm gwine to Alabamy, oh--, 18
I'm troubled, I'm troubled, 16
Michael row de boat ashore, 18
Mo parle, Remon!, 19
We will march through the valley, 16
Were you there when they crucified my Lord, 17 (T)
When Israel was in Egypt's land, 50

2323 White, Newman I. "The Collection of Folk-Lore." PROCEEDINGS OF THE ALABAMA EDUCATIONAL ASSOCIATION 35 (June 1916): 119-26. Texts of 15 songs.

Hey, Bull and Ben tally-wham, 3
Hypocrity...dress so fine, 14
I had a good lookin' woman, 9
I had a mule and he wouldn't gee, 10
I had a mule one time, 4
Oh well, it's rainin' here, 8
Rabbit on de lawg, 5
Sistah Mary wove three links of chain, 15
Take mah hammer, carry it to mah cap'n, 2
Well, Mr. Peckerwood, what yo' head doin' red, 7
Well, it keeps on rainin', 6
Well, the farmer tol' the merchant, 13
When I leave here jumpin', 11
When you smell yo' cabbage burnin', 12
Yonder comes Noah stumblin' in the dark, 1

2324 Williams, Charles, compiler. AMERICAN FOLK SONGS AS SUNG BY WILLIAMS' JUBILEE SINGERS. Chicago: Williams Lyceum Bureau, n.d. Collection of 25 songs includes texts and music of 19 plantation songs.

Chorus firstlines

Dar's a jubilee, 1
Den children keep in de middle of de road, 10
Get on board, children, 22
Hallelu, hallelu, Hallelujah to de Lamb, 14
I want to be ready, 17
In bright mansions above, 21
Joshua fought de battle of Jericho, 16
Now ain't them hard trials, 8
Oh, brethren, rise and shine, 17
Oh, He sees all you do, 9
Oh, stand the storn, 21
Oh, way over Jordan, 21
Prepare me, prepare me, Lord, 11
Roll, Jordan, roll, 15
You'll hear the trumpet sound, 21

Verse firstlines

As I go down the stream of time, 11
Bright sparkles in the churchyard, 18
Come down, come down, my Lord, come down, 17
Come my sisters and breathren too, 14
De devil tho't he had me fast, 1
Don't you want to be a soldier, 17
The foxes have holes in the ground, 8
Good morning, brother pilgrim, 16
The gospel train is coming, 22
I hear dem angels a calling loud, 10
I want to go to heaven when I die, 21
John said the city was just four-square, 17
My Lord calls me, 9
My Lord what a morning, 21
My father's gone to glory, 21
My ship is on the ocean, 21
O, brothers, you ought t'have been there, 15
Well, I heard a mighty rumbling, 4
Wrestling Jacob, Jacob, day is a breaking, 22

2325 Work, Frederick Jerome, compiler. NEW JUBILEE SONGS AS SUNG BY THE FISK JUBILEE SINGERS OF FISK UNIVERSITY. Nashville, TN: Fisk University, c.1902. Music and texts of 47 songs.

Chorus firstlines

And I won't stop praying, 42
Before I'd be a slave, 6
Before this time another year, 31
Can't you live humble?, 25
Come a-leaning on the Lord, 18
For my Lord, for my Lord, 37
Give me Jesus, 40
Going to hold out to the end, 27
Good Lord, when I die, 15
Hail, hail, I belong to the bloodwashed army, 13
Hallelujah! and a hallelujah!, 47
I am so glad, I am so glad, 28
I heard the preaching of the Elder, 33
I know I have another building, 26
I know the Lord's laid his hands on me, 7
I'm a-going to join the band, 12
In a my heart, 17
In-a this-a band we have sweet music, 35
Let us cheer the weary traveller, 37
Like Jesus, like Jesus, 23
Little David, play on your harp, 41
Live a-humble, live a-humble, 4
O rocks, don't fall on me, 30
O, a little talk with Jesus, 24
O, by and by, 45
O, I can't stay away, 32
O, my good Lord, show me the way, 22
O, my soul's been anchored in the Lord, 43
O, nobody knows a who I am, 39
O, the old ark's a-movering, 19

Verse firstlines

2326 _____. FOLK SONGS OF THE AMERICAN NEGRO. Nashville, TN: Work Brothers and Hart Company, 1907. Music and texts of 91 songs. Same repertory as in Work's NEW JUBILEE SONGS (no. 2325) with the addition of 44 songs as listed below.

Chorus firstlines

Verse firstlines

2327 Work, John Wesley. FOLK SONG OF THE AMERICAN NEGRO. Nashville, TN: Fisk University, 1915. Texts and music of 9 songs; texts of 55 songs.

Chorus firstlines

Verse firstlines

2328 Wyeth, John Allan. WITH SABRE AND SCALPEL: THE AUTOBIOGRAPHY OF A SOLDIER AND SURGEON. New York: Harper & Brothers, 1914. Texts of 6 songs; texts of 3 choruses.

Chorus firstlines

Verse firstlines

BIBLIOGRAPHY

The titles listed below represent the most useful of the many sources that we consulted in compiling this work. Although the chief value of the books was to serve as bibliographies, thus providing guidance to the literature, they also helped us to identify important contributors to the history of African-American culture. Titles that came to our attention too late to be used in our research are indicated by asterisks.

THE AMERICAN PERSONALITY. THE ARTIST-ILLUSTRATOR OF LIFE IN THE UNITED STATES, 1860-1930. Grunwald Center of the Graphic Arts. Los Angeles: University of California, 1976.

Abrahams, Roger David. AFRO-AMERICAN FOLKTALES. STORIES FROM BLACK TRADITIONS IN THE NEW WORLD. New York: Pantheon Books, 1985.

Alho, Olli. THE RELIGION OF THE SLAVES: A STUDY OF THE RELIGIOUS TRADITIONS AND BEHAVIOR OF PLANTATION SLAVES IN THE UNITED STATES, 1830-1865. Helsinski: Academia Scientiarum Fennica, 1976.

Andrews, William L. TO TELL A FREE STORY. THE FIRST CENTURY OF AFRO-AMERICAN AUTOBIOGRAPHY, 1760-1865. Urbana: University of Illinois Press, 1986.

Barker, Virgil. AMERICAN PAINTING: HISTORY AND INTERPRETATION. New York: Macmillan, 1950.

Berger, Max. THE BRITISH TRAVELLER IN AMERICA, 1836-1860. New York: Columbia University Press, 1943.

Blassingame, John W. THE SLAVE COMMUNITY. PLANTATION LIFE IN THE ANTEBELLUM SOUTH. New York: Oxford University Press, 1972.

_____. SLAVE TESTIMONY. TWO CENTURIES OF LETTERS, SPEECHES, INTERVIEWS, AND AUTOBIOGRAPHIES. Baton Rouge: Louisiana State University, 1977.

Brignano, Russell C. BLACK AMERICANS IN AUTOBIOGRAPHY. Durham, NC: Duke University Press, 1984.

Brown, Howard Mayer. "Iconography of Music." THE NEW GROVE DICTIONARY OF MUSIC AND MUSICIANS, s.v. "iconography." Edited by Stanley Sadie. London: Macmillan Company, 1980.

Brown, Howard Mayer, and Joan Lascelle. MUSICAL ICONOGRAPHY: A MANUAL FOR CATALOGUING MUSICAL SUBJECTS IN WESTERN ART BEFORE 1800. Cambridge: Harvard University Press, 1972.

Brown, Sterling Allen. THE NEGRO IN AMERICAN FICTION. Washington, DC: Associates in Negro Folk Education, 1937. Reprint. New York: Arno Press and the New York Times, 1969.

Bullock, Penelope L. THE AFRO-AMERICAN PERIODICAL PRESS, 1838-1909. Baton Rouge: Louisiana State University Press, 1981.

Carter, George C., Peter Ripley, and Jeffrey Rossbach, eds. BLACK ABOLITIONIST PAPERS, 1830-1865: A GUIDE TO THE MICROFILM EDITION. Sanford, NC: Microfilming Corporation of America, 1981.

Clark, Thomas. TRAVELS IN THE OLD SOUTH: A BIBLIOGRAPHY. Norman: University of Oklahoma Press, 1956.

Clarke, Erskine. WRESTLIN' JACOB. A PORTRAIT OF RELIGION IN THE OLD SOUTH. Atlanta, GA: John Knox Press, 1979.

Corn, Wanda M. "Coming of Age: Historical Scholarship in American Art." ART BULLETIN 70 (1988): 188-207

Cresswell, Donald, ed. THE AMERICAN REVOLUTION

IN DRAWINGS AND PRINTS. Washington, DC: Library of Congress, 1975.

*Davis, Gerald Lewis. "The Performed African-American Sermon." Ph.D. diss. University of Pennsylvania, 1978.

Davis, Charles, and Henry L. Gates. THE SLAVE'S NARRATIVE. New York: Oxford University Press, 1985.

De Lerma, Dominique-Rene. BIBLIOGRAPHY OF BLACK MUSIC. Vols. 1-4. THE GREENWOOD ENCYCLOPEDIA OF BLACK MUSIC. Westport, CT: Greenwood Press, 1981-84.

Donaldson, Mary Katherine. "Paintings and Illustrations of Nineteenth-Century Black Folk Culture in the United States." 1986. Typescript.

Dorson, Richard M. AMERICAN FOLKLORE. Chicago: University of Chicago Press, 1959.

Driskell, David Clyde. TWO CENTURIES OF BLACK AMERICAN ART. New York: Alfred P. Knopf, 1976.

DuBois, W. E. Burghardt, ed. A SELECT BIBLIOGRAPHY OF THE NEGRO.... Atlanta: Atlanta University Press, 1905. Reprint. ATLANTA UNIVERSITY PUBLICATIONS, no. 10. New York: Arno Press and the New York Times, 1969.

Emery, Lynne Fauley. BLACK DANCE IN THE UNITED STATES FROM 1619 TO 1970. Palo Alto, CA: National Press Books, 1972.

Epstein, Dena J. SINFUL TUNES AND SPIRITUALS: BLACK FOLK MUSIC TO THE CIVIL WAR. Urbana: University of Illinois Press, 1977.

_____. "Slave Music in the United States before 1860: A Survey of Sources, Parts 1, 2." MUSIC LIBRARY ASSOCIATION NOTES 20 (Spring, Summer 1963): 195-212; 377-90.

Fielding, Mantle. MANTLE FIELDING'S DICTIONARY OF AMERICAN PAINTERS, SCULPTORS AND ENGRAVERS. 1926. With an Addendum...by James F. Carr. New York: James F. Carr, 1965.

Fisher, Miles Mark. NEGRO SLAVE SONGS IN THE UNITED STATES. New York: American Historical Association, 1953.

Floyd, Samuel A., and Marsha J. Reisser. BLACK MUSIC IN THE UNITED STATES: AN ANNOTATED BIBLIOGRAPHY OF SELECTED REFERENCE AND RESEARCH MATERIALS. Millwood, NY: Kraus International Publications, 1983.

Foner, Philip S. HISTORY OF BLACK AMERICANS. 3 vols. Westport, CT: Greenwood Press, 1975-83.

Foster, Frances Smith. WITNESSING SLAVERY. THE DEVELOPMENT OF ANTE-BELLUM SLAVE NARRATIVES. Westport, CT: Greenwood Press, 1979.

Fox, James Edward. "Iconography of the Black Man in American Art, 1710-1900." Ph.D. diss. University of North Carolina at Chapel Hill, 1979.

Franklin, John H. A SOUTHERN ODYSSEY: TRAVELERS IN THE ANTEBELLUM NORTH. Baton Rouge: Louisiana State University Press, 1976.

Gambee, Budd Leslie. FRANK LESLIE AND HIS ILLUSTRATED NEWSPAPER, 1855-1860. Publications of the Department of Library Science, Studies 8. Ann Arbor: University of Michigan Press, 1964.

Gephart, Ronald M. REVOLUTIONARY AMERICA, 1763-1789: A BIBLIOGRAPHY. Washington, DC: Library of Congress, 1984.

Greene, Lorenzo Johnston. THE NEGRO IN COLONIAL NEW ENGLAND, 1620-1776. New York: Columbia University Press, 1942.

Groce, George C. and Wallace, David H. THE NEW-YORK HISTORICAL SOCIETY'S DICTIONARY OF ARTISTS IN AMERICA, 1564-1860. New Haven: Yale University Press, 1957.

Gubert, Betty Kaplan, ed. EARLY BLACK BIBLIOGRAPHIES, 1863-1918. New York: Garland Publishing Company, 1982.

Hamilton, Sinclair. EARLY AMERICAN BOOK ILLUSTRATORS AND WOOD ENGRAVERS, 1670-1870. 2 vols. Princeton, NJ: Princeton University Press, [1958].

Haywood, Charles. A BIBLIOGRAPHY OF NORTH AMERICAN FOLKLORE AND FOLKSONG. 2 vols. New York: Greenberg Publications, 1951.

Hills, Patricia. THE PAINTERS' AMERICA. RURAL AND URBAN LIFE, 1810-1910. New York: Praeger and Whitney Museum of American Art, 1974.

Hoornstra, Jean, and Trudy Heath, eds. AMERICAN PERIODICALS, 1741-1900: AN INDEX TO THE MICROFILM COLLECTIONS. Ann Arbor: University Microfilms International, 1979.

Horn, David. THE LITERATURE OF AMERICAN MUSIC IN BOOKS AND FOLK MUSIC COLLECTIONS: A FULLY ANNOTATED BIBLIOGRAPHY. Metuchen, NJ: Scarecrow Press, 1977.

*Horn, David, with Richard Jackson. THE LITERATURE OF AMERICAN MUSIC IN BOOKS AND FOLK MUSIC COLLECTIONS: A FULLY ANNOTATED BIBLIOGRAPHY. SUPPLEMENT 1. Metuchen, NJ: Scarecrow Press, 1988.

Hubbard, Geraldine Hopkins, ed. ANTI-SLAVERY PROPAGANDA IN THE OBERLIN COLLEGE LIBRARY. Microcard Collection. Louisville, KY: Lost Cause Press, 1968.

Hunter, Sam. AMERICAN ART OF THE TWENTIETH CENTURY. New York: Harry N. Abrams, c.1972.

Igoe, Lynn Moody, with James Igoe. 250 YEARS OF AFRO-AMERICAN ART: AN ANNOTATED BIBLIOGRAPHY. New York: R. R. Bowker Company, 1981.

Jackson, Bruce. THE NEGRO AND HIS FOLKLORE IN NINETEENTH-CENTURY PERIODICALS. Austin: Published for the American Folklore Society by the University of Texas Press, 1967.

*Jones, Alice Marie. "The Negro Sermon: A Study

in the Sociology of Folk Culture." Master's Thesis. Fisk University, 1942.

Jones, Robert, et al, eds. ATLANTA UNIVERSITY AND BELL & HOWELL: BLACK CULTURE COLLECTION CATALOGUE. 3 vols. Wooster, OH: Bell & Howell, 1974.

Jordan, Casper LeRoy, comp. "The Levi Jenkins Coppin Collection at Carnegie Library, Wilberforce University." Wilberforce, OH: Wilberforce University, 1957.

Kaplan, Sidney. THE PORTRAYAL OF THE NEGRO IN AMERICAN PAINTING. Brunswick, ME: Bowdoin College Museum of Art, 1964.

Lesser, Alexander, compiler. "Bibliography of American Folklore, 1915-1928." JOURNAL OF AMERICAN FOLKLORE 41 (January-March 1928): 1-60.

Levine, Lawrence. BLACK CULTURE AND BLACK CONSCIOUSNESS: AFRO-AMERICAN FOLK THOUGHT FROM SLAVERY TO FREEDOM. New York: Oxford University Press, 1977.

Loggins, Vernon. THE NEGRO AUTHOR: HIS DEVELOPMENT IN AMERICA. New York: Columbia University Press, 1931.

Lord, Albert Bates. THE SINGER OF TALES. Harvard Studies in Comparative Literature, 24. Cambridge: Harvard University Press, 1960.

Lovell, John. BLACK SONG: THE FORGE AND THE FLAME. New York: Macmillan Company, 1972.

Mallett, Daniel Trowbridge. MALLETT'S INDEX OF ARTISTS, INTERNATIONAL-BIOGRAPHICAL.... 1935. SUPPLEMENT. New York: R. R. Bowker, [1940]. Reprint. New York: Peter Smith, 1948.

*Martin, Francis John. "The Image of Black People in American Illustration from 1825 to 1925." Ph.D. diss. University of California at Los Angeles. 1986.

Matthews, Geraldine, compiler. BLACK AMERICAN WRITERS, 1773-1949: A BIBLIOGRAPHY AND UNION LIST. Compiled by Geraldine O. Matthews and the African-American Materials Project Staff. North Carolina Central University at Durham, School of Library Science. Boston: G. K. Hall, 1975.

Matthews, William, comp. AMERICAN DIARIES: AN ANNOTATED BIBLIOGRAPHY OF AMERICAN DIARIES WRITTEN PRIOR TO THE YEAR 1861. Berkeley: University of California Press, 1945.

Mesick, Jane Louise. THE ENGLISH TRAVELER IN AMERICA, 1785-1835. New York: Columbia University Press, 1922.

THE MICROBOOK LIBRARY OF AMERICAN CIVILIZATION. 4 vols. Chicago: Library Resources, 1971.

Mitchell, Henry V. BLACK PREACHING. San Francisco: Harper & Row, 1970.

Monghan, Frank. FRENCH TRAVELLERS IN THE UNITED STATES, 1765-1932. New York: New York Public Library, 1933.

Mott, Frank Luther. A HISTORY OF AMERICAN MAGAZINES, 1741-1930. 5 vols. Cambridge: Harvard University Press, 1930-1968.

Mullin, Michael, ed. AMERICAN NEGRO SLAVERY. A DOCUMENTARY HISTORY. Columbia: University of South Carolina Press, 1976.

Novak, Barbara. AMERICAN PAINTING OF THE NINETEENTH CENTURY; REALISM, IDEALISM, AND THE AMERICAN EXPERIENCE. New York: Praeger, 1969.

Oliver, Paul. SONGSTERS AND SAINTS: VOCAL TRADITIONS ON RACE RECORDS. Cambridge (England): Cambridge University Press, 1984.

Parry, Ellwood C. THE IMAGE OF THE INDIAN AND THE BLACK MAN IN AMERICAN ART, 1590-1900. New York: G. Braziller, 1974.

Pitz, Henry Clarence. TWO HUNDRED YEARS OF AMERICAN ILLUSTRATION. New York: Random House, c1977.

Porter, Dorothy. B. THE NEGRO IN THE UNITED STATES: A SELECTED BIBLIOGRAPHY. Washington, DC: Library of Congress, 1970.

Raboteau, Albert. SLAVE RELIGION: THE "INVISIBLE INSTITUTION" IN THE ANTEBELLUM SOUTH. New York: Oxford University Press, 1978.

Richardson, Edgar Preston. PAINTING IN AMERICA: THE STORY OF 450 YEARS. New York: Crowell, 1956.

Richardson, Harry V. DARK GLORY: A PICTURE OF THE CHURCH AMONG NEGROES IN THE RURAL SOUTH. New York: Friendship Press, 1947.

Ricks, George Robinson. SOME ASPECTS OF THE RELIGIOUS MUSIC OF THE UNITED STATES NEGRO: AN ETHNOMUSICOLOGICAL STUDY WITH SPECIAL EMPHASIS ON THE GOSPEL TRADITION. New York: Arno Press and the New York Times, 1977.

Rogers, William Allen. A WORLD WORTH WHILE; A RECORD OF "AULD ACQUAINTANCE." New York: Harper & Brothers, 1922.

Rosenberg, Bruce A. THE ART OF THE AMERICAN FOLK PREACHER. New York: Oxford University Press, 1970.

Sabin, Joseph, and Wilberforce Eames. BIBLIOTHECA AMERICANA. A DICTIONARY OF BOOKS RELATING TO AMERICA...FOR THE BIBLIOGRAPHICAL SOCIETY OF AMERICA. New York: Publishing House of William Edwin Rudge, 1892-1928.

Sernett, Milton C. BLACK RELIGION AND AMERICAN EVANGELICALISM. Metuchen, NJ: Scarecrow Press and the American Theological Association, 1975.

Sherman, Joan R. INVISIBLE POETS. AFRO-AMERICANS OF THE NINETEENTH CENTURY. Urbana: University of Illinois Press, 1974.

Skowronski, JoAnn. BLACK MUSIC IN AMERICA: A BIBLIOGRAPHY. Metuchen, NJ: Scarecrow Press, 1981.

Smith, Page. A NEW AGE NOW BEGINS: A PEOPLE'S HISTORY OF THE AMERICAN REVOLUTION. 2 vols. New York: McGraw-Hill Book Company, 1980.

-----. THE NATION COMES OF AGE: A PEOPLE'S HISTORY OF THE ANTEBELLUM YEARS. New York: McGraw-Hill Book Company, 1981.

-----. TRIAL BY FIRE: A PEOPLE'S HISTORY OF THE CIVIL WAR AND RECONSTRUCTION. 2 vols. New York: McGraw-Hill Book Company, 1982.

Southern, Eileen. THE MUSIC OF BLACK AMERICANS: A HISTORY. 1971. 2d ed. New York: W. W. Norton Company, 1983.

Starling, Marion Wilson. THE SLAVE NARRATIVE: ITS PLACE IN AMERICAN HISTORY. Boston: G. K. Hall, 1981.

*Stuckey, Sterling. SLAVE CULTURE. NATIONALIST THEORY AND THE FOUNDATIONS OF BLACK AMERICA. New York: Oxford University Press, 1987.

Szwed, John F., and Roger D. Abrahams. AFRO-AMERICAN FOLK CULTURE: AN ANNOTATED BIBLIOGRAPHY OF MATERIALS FROM NORTH, CENTRAL, AND SOUTH AMERICA, AND THE WEST INDIES. Publications of the American Folklore Society. Philadelphia: Institute for the Study of Human Issues, 1978.

*Thompson, Lawrence S., comp. THE SOUTHERN BLACK: SLAVE AND FREE. A Bibliography of Works in Microform Edition Issued by the Lost Cause Press, Lexington, Kentucky. Troy, NY: Whitson Publishing Company, 1970.

Tuckerman, Henry T. AMERICA AND HER COMMENTATORS. New York: Charles Scribner, 1864.

Wagner, Jean. BLACK POETS OF THE UNITED STATES: FROM PAUL LAURENCE DUNBAR TO LANGSTON HUGHES. Translated by Kenneth Douglas. Urbana: University of Illinois Press, 1973.

*Warner, Thomas E. PERIODICAL LITERATURE ON AMERICAN MUSIC, 1620-1920: A CLASSIFIED BIBLIOGRAPHY WITH ANNOTATIONS. Published for the College Music Society. Warren, MI: Harmonie Park Press, 1988.

Washington, Joseph R. BLACK RELIGION. Boston: Beacon Press, 1964.

Weitenkampf, Frank. AMERICAN GRAPHIC ART. Rev. ed. New York: Macmillan Company, 1924.

_____. "The Negro in Art." THE INDEPENDENT (New York) 49 (August 1897): 1105.

White, Dana F., and Victor A. Kramer, eds. OLMSTED SOUTH. OLD SOUTH CRITIC/NEW SOUTH PLANNER. Westport, CT: Greenwood Press, 1979.

Work, Monroe N. A BIBLIOGRAPHY OF THE NEGRO IN AFRICA AND AMERICA. New York: H. W. Wilson Company, 1928.

NAME INDEX

Index numbers refer to entry numbers, not to pages.

AUTHORS AND COLLECTORS

[Slave narratives are indicated by an asterisk.]

A

B

C

D

ARTISTS, ILLUSTRATORS, AND PHOTOGRAPHERS

SUBJECT INDEX

LITERATURE

C

E

F

ARTWORKS

SONG INDEX

FIRST LINES OF CHORUSES

D

E

J

P

R

U

V

W

Y

FIRST LINES OF VERSES

D

E

H

I

J

P

Q

R

T

U

Y

Z

About the Compilers

EILEEN SOUTHERN is Professor Emerita of Music and Afro-American Studies at Harvard University and Editor/Co-publisher of *The Black Perspective in Music.* She has contributed articles to *Journal of American Musicology, Acta Musicologica, American Music,* and other scholarly journals. She also served as an area editor of and contributor to *The New Grove Dictionary of Music and Musicians.* Her book publications include *The Buxheim Organ Book, The Music of Black Americans: A History,* and *Biographical Dictionary of Afro-American and African Musicians.*

JOSEPHINE WRIGHT is Professor of Music at the College of Wooster. She has published articles in *The Musical Quarterly, The Black Perspective in Music, Women's Studies Quarterly,* and *The New Grove Dictionary of Music and Musicians.* She is the author of *Ignatius Sancho; An Early African Composer.* Southern and Wright are preparing a companion volume to the present work offering a pictorial record of Afro-American traditions (Greenwood Press, forthcoming).